The NEW Trader's Tax Solution

Wiley Trading

Beyond Candlesticks / Steve Nison
Beyond Technical Analysis, Second Edition / Tushar Chande
Contrary Opinion / R. Earl Hadady
Day Trader's Course / Lewis Borsellino with Patricia Crisafulli
Day Trader's Course Workbook / Lewis Borsellino with Patricia Crisafulli
Day Trader's Manual / William F. Eng
Encyclopedia of Chart Patterns / Thomas Bulkowski
Exchange Traded Funds and E-Mini Stock Index Futures / David Lerman
Expert Trading Systems / John R. Wolberg
Four Steps to Trading Success / Clayburg
Fundamental Analysis / Jack Schwager
Hedge Fund Edge / Mark Boucher
Intermarket Technical Analysis / John J. Murphy
Intuitive Trader / Robert Koppel
Investor's Quotient / Jake Bernstein
Long-Term Secrets to Short-Term Trading / Larry Williams
Managed Trading / Jack Schwager
Mathematics of Money Management / Ralph Vince
McMillan on Options / Lawrence G. McMillan
Neural Network Time Series Forecasting of Financial Markets / E. Michael Azoff
New Fibonacci Trader / Robert Fischer, Jens Fischer
New Market Timing Techniques / Thomas R. DeMark
New Market Wizards / Jack Schwager
New Money Management / Ralph Vince
New Options Market, Fourth Edition / Max Ansbacher
New Science of Technical Analysis / Thomas R. DeMark
New Technical Trader / Tushar Chande and Stanley S. Kroll
New Trader's Tax Solution: Money-Saving Strategies for the Serious Investor / Ted Tesser
New Trading Dimensions / Bill Williams
Nonlinear Pricing / Christopher T. May
Option Advisor / Bernie G. Schaeffer
Option Market Making / Alan J. Baird
Option Pricing: Black-Scholes Made Easy / Jerry Marlow
Option Strategies, 2nd Edition / Courtney Smith
Options Course/ George A. Fontanills
Options Course Workbook / George A. Fontanills
Outperform the Dow / Gunter Meissner, Randall Folsom
Point and Figure Charting, Second Edition / Thomas J. Dorsey
Schwager on Futures/ Jack Schwager
Seasonality / Jake Bernstein
Sniper Trading and *Sniper Trading Workbook* / George Angell
Stock Index Futures & Options / Susan Abbott Gidel
Stock Market Course and *Stock Market Course Workbook* / George A. Fontanills and Tom Gentile
Study Guide for Trading for a Living / Dr. Alexander Elder
Study Guide to Accompany Fundamental Analysis / Jack Schwager
Study Guide to Accompany Technical Analysis/ Jack Schwager
Technical Analysis / Jack Schwager
Technical Analysis of the Options Markets / Richard Hexton
Technical Market Indicators / Richard J. Bauer Jr., and Julie R. Dahlquist
Trader Vic II / Victor Sperandeo
The Trading Athlete: Winning the Mental Game of Online Trading / Shane Murphy and Doug Hirschhorn
Trading Chaos / Bill Williams
Trading for a Living / Dr. Alexander Elder
Trading Game/ Ryan Jones
Trading in the Zone / Ari Kiev, M.D.
Trading Systems & Methods, Third Edition / Perry Kaufman
Trading to Win / Ari Kiev, M.D.
Trading with Crowd Psychology / Carl Gyllenram
Trading with Oscillators / Carl Gyllenram
Trading without Fear / Richard W. Arms, Jr.
Ultimate Trading Guide / John Hill, George Pruitt, and Lundy Hill
Value Investing in Commodity Futures / Hal Masover
Visual Investor / John J. Murphy

The NEW Trader's Tax Solution

Money-Saving Strategies for the Serious Investor

TED TESSER, CPA

A Marketplace Book

John Wiley & Sons, Inc.

This book is printed on acid-free paper. ♾

Published by John Wiley & Sons, Inc., New York.
Published simultaneously in Canada.

Library of Congress Cataloging-in-Publication Data:

ISBN 0-471-20999-6

Printed in the United States of America.

10 9 8 7 6 5 4 3 2 1

For
my mother,
Dorothy Tesser,
with love

Contents

Preface

THE ECONOMIC GROWTH AND TAX RELIEF RECONCILIATION ACT OF 2001

On June 7, 2001, President Bush signed into law the largest tax reduction bill in 20 years. This bill significantly affects the following areas of the tax code:

- Current tax rates
- Retirement planning
- Estate tax provisions

What else is there? I don't believe that it is a matter of sheer coincidence that these three areas are the exact same areas that the Triple Crown Strategy addresses (later in this book). These areas of the tax law are, in fact, the three major sources of taxation for both traders and nontraders alike, and by dividing the law up into these three sections, it makes what was already a complex and nebulous law somewhat clearer.

This tax act makes over 400 changes to the law, but it is the timetable for full enactment, the many phase-outs, and multiple effective dates that makes this bill so much fun. The true test for any tax law is ultimately how it is interpreted, and we must await a future Blue Book (congressional interpretation) and further refinement of the grey areas, by the IRS (through future IRS Revenue Procedures) to clarify and interpret the law. This law will be no exception to how the process unfolds. Because of this, much of what follows is my best educated interpretation of the law. That will have to do until further clarification is given to us from both Congress and the Courts.

Tax Rate Cuts

10% tax bracket. A section of this tax bill reinstates a 10% tax bracket, which replaces the 15% minimum tax rate of the previous law. This provision is grandfathered back to January 1, 2001. Because of the way it is structured, most people's taxes will be reduced by 5% of the first $6,000 of taxable income ($300 single; $600 married). The bottom line is that this cut becomes maximized at the following levels:

- $600—Married filing jointly ($12,000×5%)
- $300—Single tax payers ($6,000×5%)
- $500—Single parent–Head of household ($10,000×5%)

Upper brackets reduced. More significant (although less publicized), there is a general reduction of tax rates which is granted in installments, with the first reduction effective on July 1, 2001. Eventually the top rate will effectively drop from 39.6% to 35%. The rates will decrease in *percentage* points with the schedule looking something like this:

Year:	28% Rate to:	31% Rate to:	36% Rate to:	39.6% Rate to:
2001	27.5%	30.5%	35.5%	39.1%
2002–3	27%	30%	35%	38.5%
2004–5	26%	29%	34%	37.6%
2006 on	25%	28%	33%	35%

Capital gain rates. With few exceptions, the capital gain rates stay the same, for now, at a 20% maximum rate for any capital asset held for a year or more. The two most common exceptions to this are for collectibles (28% maximum) and depreciation recapture (25%). Any capital asset held for less than a year will be taxed at the short-term rate (same as ordinary income), and consequently will now benefit from the overall decrease in tax rates.

Illustration

This is a comparison of what typical tax savings could look like for three tax payers based on the combination of decreases just discussed:

Taxable Income	Filing Status	Saved in 2001	Saved in 2002	Saved in 2010
$ 100,000	Single	$ 669	$ 1,038	$ 2,513
	Married	881	1,162	2,730
$ 500,000	Single	2,669	5,038	17,889
	Married	2,881	5,162	18,116
$2,000,000	Single	10,169	20,038	86,899
	Married	10,381	20,162	90,987

As you can see, the true savings kick in during the last phase of this bill, and this is especially true if you have taxable income of over $1,000,000. Please note that this chart does not consider the Alternative Minimum Tax (AMT). More on the AMT in subsequent sections of the book. It is estimated, however, that the number of taxpayers impacted by the AMT will increase significantly under the new tax act.

You can use this chart to project a close approximation to what you will save with this new tax law by taking the amount closest to your taxable income and multiplying the difference by ½ of 1% in 2001, 1% in 2002, and 3% in 2010 (if taxable income is over $290,000 in 2006 or subsequent years the percentage you use is 4.6%).

For example if you are single and have taxable income projected at $1,700,000 for the next nine years, you would start with $2,000,000, and back out the $1.7 million. This leaves you with $300,000 as a differential. You multiply and extend it out as follows:

2001: $300,000 × .005 = $1,500

$10,169 tax savings on $2,000,000
−1,500 reduction in tax
$ 8,669 adjusted tax savings

2002: $300,000 × .01 = $3,000

$20,038 tax savings on $2,000,000
−3,000 reduction in tax
$17,038 adjusted tax savings

2010: $300,000 × .046 = $13,800

$86,889 tax savings on $2,000,000
−13,800 reduction in tax
$73,089 adjusted tax savings

Marriage tax penalty. Since income tax rates increase geometrically, married taxpayers typically have suffered over the years. An example of this can be seen in the following illustration.

Illustration

If Dick earns $25,000 and is taxed at the 15% level; and Jane earns $25,000 and is taxed at the 15% level, why should Dick and Jane get married and earn $50,000 jointly, only to be taxed at the 28% level? The answer to this is that in previous years, they were paying a premium for being married. At one point, there was a marriage credit, which somewhat offset this penalty, but that was eliminated in Reagan's 1986 Tax Bill.

Starting in 2008 the law will be changed so that two people earning the same amounts after they are married, but now filing jointly, will be taxed at roughly the same rate as they were previously, as single people. This essentially does away with the antiquated system of penalizing married people, by accelerating the tax brackets at a geometric rate, rather than arithmetically. This fundamental has been at the core of our tax system, since its inception in the early twentieth century. I think it is unfair and, in fact, counterproductive.

So, you may ask, what's the problem—this is all changing, isn't it? My gripe here is: *Why wait so long?* Is the government afraid that if they implement this prior to 2008 there will be such an onslaught of marriages that the clergy will not be prepared for it? I cannot think of any other valid reason they should wait seven years to put it into effect—can you?

Furthermore, in 2009 married people will get twice the standard deduction that single people get, (as opposed to the smaller percentage that they currently get today). Another antiquated section of the Code whose time has come. But again, why wait for 2009? Does it really take eight years to change the law on such a simple, straightforward, concept.

Phase-out of itemized deductions and personal exemptions. Indirectly related to this, is the repeal of itemized and personal exemption phase-outs. In the previous law, itemized deductions and personal exemptions were phased out and limited, so that taxpayers in the upper tax brackets realized a very limited benefit from these two areas of the tax code. In fact, over certain income levels, the personal exemption deduction was entirely eliminated. The new tax law has changed this section, so that upper income taxpayers are no longer penalized for doing well.

The phase-in starts in 2006, when it reverts to one-third of what it would have been without the phase-out; in 2008, it is returned to a level of two-thirds of what it would have been; and in 2010 it is changed back to where the deductions and exemptions are equal for taxpayers of all income brackets.

Again, the only problem I have with this section of the new law is that I hope we all live long enough to see it enacted. Two presidencies and a whole host of potential tax law changes away seems like an eternity. Furthermore, I have a problem with the fact that it reverts back to tax levels of the old law, immediately following the year it comes into effect. This law eliminates most changes, and brings tax levels right back to where they were before the law was passed—a full phase-out again of deductions and exemptions.

A Word on January 1, 2011

The huge problem I have with this tax act is that this bill will virtually disappear on the above date. That's right—disappear! This bill could have just as well been called "The 2001 Vanishing Tax Act." Provisions such as this personal exemption penalty and standard deduction penalty are all repealed in 2010. What they don't tell you is what happens on January 1, 2011 . . . you guessed it: Everything that was put into effect in 2010 (which may have taken nine years to fully enact) is fully repealed on January 1, 2011! What a deal—huh?

ESTATE TAX PLANNING IN THREE WORDS OR LESS—CALLING DR. KEVORKIAN!

There are very few unambiguous, crystal-clear sections of the new tax bill, but this is one of them: If you die between January 1 and December 31, 2010, you will pay no estate tax on your estate. If you die January 1, 2011, or anytime subsequent to that, you get stuck with the whole 55% tax on your taxable estate—again.

From what I hear, Kevorkian's 2010 schedule is "waiting list only," but surely if you put it off any longer, he will not even have room for you. So to really do some shrewd estate tax planning, call to schedule your appointment today.

This repeal of the estate tax is one of the centerpiece's of the new tax act. However, as previously mentioned, this repeal is not effective until January 1, 2010. The uncertainty of all the events that will take place between now and then, and the potential political climate at that time, make reliance on this repeal a poor approach to planning your estate. More appropriate is the use of the Triple Crown, as addressed later in this book. Nonetheless, the understanding of what will transpire now and prior to 2010 are important, so here we go:

Provisions Effective in 2002

The following provisions of the Act are effective in 2002:

1. Increase in the gift and estate tax unified exemption—increased to *$1,000,000 from $675,000.*
2. Reduction of the top rate from *55% to 50%.*

Provisions after 2002

Reduction of the gift and estate tax as illustrated on the following chart is effective after 2002:

Year	Maximum Tax Bracket	Applicable Level
2001	55% + 5% Surtax	$ 675,000
2002	50	1,000,000* (Gift = $1,060,000)
2003	49	1,000,000* (Gift = $1,060,000)
2004	48	1,500,000
2005	47	1,500,000
2006	46	2,000,000
2007–8	45	2,000,000
2009	45	3,500,000
2010	Estates are not taxed—Gifts taxed at individual rates	0

*Currently, this exemption amount is the same for gift and estate tax, except for the year 2001–2003 when it is $1,000,000 for estate taxes, but $1,060,000 for gift tax.

1. Raising of the threshold at which the top bracket begins, so that the maximum rate kicks in at a higher level, thereby reducing the overall gift and estate tax payable by any individual, see chart above.
2. Full *repeal* of the estate (but not gift) tax in the *year 2010*. Under current law, the repeal only lasts one year; to qualify you must die during this period of time—January 1, 2010, after 12 A.M., through December 31, 2001, prior to 12 A.M., Midnight.
3. A change in the manner in which carryover basis of a capital asset is calculated, making it more consistent with other sections of the Tax Code.
4. After December 9, 2009, transfers of wealth to *nonresident aliens,* will be treated as sale of the property. The transferor will recognize income to the extent that the fair market value of the property received by the transferor exceeds the cost basis of the property. All calculations should be clearly indicated on the tax return.
5. The law now directly states that the taxpayer is required to put all detailed information on the tax return that applies to this transaction in the year it is required to be reported. This information includes, but is not necessarily limited to:
   - Name and address of the recipient.
   - Identification number (Social Security or EIN) of the recipient.
   - Transferor's adjusted basis (cost plus capital improvements).

There is a whole host of items that have not yet been examined in detail. I am certain that this tax bill will reopen a box of questions that have been raised previously, but not addressed. I do not want to make this book so technically detailed that readers will be lost, but it is important to understand the basics of these principles. One of these areas is that of cost basis and the calculation of a prior gift or inheritance. When this asset is sold by the recipient, how does that get reported? Has any tax been paid on this asset that can be used as a credit now? These are questions that should be looked at to ascertain the correct amount of tax due on this sale.

Basis Consideration

Even if the estate tax is forever repealed, estate tax planning will continue to be a complex issue. This is because assets will, hopefully, continue to appreciate and bring in income. The issue then becomes a quantitative one—one in which a determination must be made of the cost (basis), sales price (amount realized), and ultimately gain or loss (the amount recognized).

The issues seem to be the same ones under consideration prior to this law—how much did you receive as a gift or inheritance, how much did you sell it for, and what is the difference between these two numbers? I always believed as much input as you can get in on that valuation process, the better off you will be. You must also keep in mind that any tax paid during this process should be considered because it is not required of you to pay tax twice on the same transaction.

What to Do until 2010

Whatever your ultimate goals are, it is strongly recommended here that you take advantage of the increased gift and estate tax exemption which goes up to $1,000,000 in 2001; $1,500,000 in 2004; $2,000,000 in 2006; and $3,500,000 in 2009. In 2009, the top estate tax rate will drop to 45% and is then repealed to 0% in 2010. You must plan to utilize this amount, no matter if your assets' net worth is greater or lesser than the threshold amounts in the chart. You should consider using the complete exemption as soon as possible, but you should get counsel on how to properly set this up—the difference will be well worth any additional cost to you to do so.

You should also review your will and make sure the amounts stated do not lock you into small specific amounts that will be useless after this law comes into effect. If the will needs to be changed, I advise doing so, as soon as possible.

RETIREMENT PLAN PROVISIONS

The Tax Act increased the *maximum amount* of *deductible contributions* that can be made to Individual Retirement Accounts (IRAs), Employer Sponsored Salary Deferral Plans (401ks), Defined Contribution

Keogh Plans, Simplified Employee Plans (SEP IRAs), and SIMPLE Plans (Specific Types of IRA). In addition, a *catch-up provision* has been passed that allows individuals who have reached the age of 50 to catch up on their retirement contributions.

Because of the new Tax Act, younger taxpayers have been given the benefit of being able to make larger contributions to their retirement plans for a longer period than taxpayers who are closer to retirement age. The new Tax Act attempts to reduce this imbalance by allowing individuals who are over the age of 50 to make catch-up contributions to their plans. These catch-up contributions are in addition to the annual maximum contributions that can be made. The following chart shows the annual dollar amount of these contributions, based on the type of plan. As you can see, by 2006 these catch-up contributions will be very significant to individuals in employer sponsored plans.

		Maximum Contribution in		
Type of Plan	**Initial Year**	**2002**	**2003**	**When Fully Effective**
401k/SEP	2002	$ 11,000	$ 12,000	$15,000–2006
Keogh:				
Defined contribution	2002	40,000	40,000	Same as 2002
Defined benefit	2002	160,000*	160,000*	Same as 2002
IRA	2002	3,000	3,000	5,000 in 2008
SIMPLE	2002	7,000	8,000	10,000 in 2005
Catch-up contributions**				
Self-sponsored plans	2002	500	500	1,000 in 2006
Employer sponsored	2002	1,000	2,000	5,000 in 2006
SIMPLE plans	2002	500	2,500	2,500 in 2006
Deemed IRAs under employer plans	2003	3,000	3,000	5,000 in 2008

*Funded for this amount of benefit.
**For individuals over 49 years of age.

Beyond these increases, the Act permits qualified employer plans to allow employees to elect to treat a portion of their voluntary contributions as contributions to a separately maintained traditional or Roth IRA.

A married couple could gift an additional $650,000 to their beneficiaries free of gift taxes in 2002 (in additional to the annual exclusion that is normally present). By making a gift in 2002, all future appreciation will be out of their estate. They and their heirs gain an edge because:

1. The transferred assets and all future appreciation will go to their beneficiaries free of gift and estate tax, regardless of any future law changes, including the possibility that the estate tax is not repealed either beyond the year it is intended (2010), or even if it never comes to be repealed at all.
2. By using certain entities, such as the Family Limited Partnership (FLP), they have the opportunity to save even more on estate and gift taxes. This will be addressed in full in later sections of this book (see "The Triple Crown"). You can retain control of the assets for management purposes and control as to when the distributions are made from the partnership. However, this tax benefit illustrates the huge difference between control and ownership. The objective in this game of tax reduction is to control everything, but own nothing. *Ownership equates to taxation.* Additionally, valuation discounts are available that will allow you to increase the amount of tax-free gifts that you can make.

There is a provision of this new law that gives individuals a tax credit for retirement plan contributions made to qualified plans during the period 2002–2006. This amount is nonrefundable and you must qualify by not having income above a certain level in any year. These levels are as follow:

- $50,000 if Married Filing Jointly
- $25,000 if Single
- $37,500 if you qualify as Unmarried, Head of Household

If you qualify, this credit will offset both your regular and your AMT tax, if applicable. Dependents and full-time students are not eligible for this credit.

Other provisions include:

- The maximum annual contribution limit for qualified plan purposes increases from $170,000 to $200,000 after 2001.
- The rules permitting rollovers between various plans have been liberalized.
- Plan loans to sole proprietors, partners, or S corporation owners are permitted starting in 2002. The loans must be made available to participants who are not owners as well.

EDUCATION INCENTIVES

No tax bill would be complete without some tinkering with programs that affect social policy toward education. This tax bill is no different, clearly demonstrating our elected officials' stance on promoting education through various tax incentives.

Educational IRAs

Education IRAs have been expanded significantly to increase both the amount that can be contributed to the plans and the number of individuals who will qualify for the program. Additionally, tax-free distributions will be allowed for a wider range of qualified education expenses. Here are the key provisions:

1. The maximum contribution for each plan is increased to $2,000 from $500 under prior law.
2. Partial contributions can be made until income exceeds $220,000.
3. You can use the IRA funds to pay for all levels of education, not just college, as was under prior law, and can now be used for grades as low as kindergarten all the way up through grade 12. There is no need any longer to wait to use the funds until college.
4. Furthermore, it does not matter if the school is private, public, or religious. It can qualify for use of the funds.
5. Qualified education expenses include:
   —Tuition
   —Books and supplies
   —Room and board (including extended day programs)
   —Transportation
   —Computer equipment, software, and Internet access (*Note:* Software designed for sports, hobbies, and games are excluded unless predominantly used in education.)
   —Tutoring
6. Age limitations are waived for children with special needs.

Contributions to Educational IRAs continue to be nondeductible, but the account grows tax free, and distributions are tax free as well. This savings can be significant in future years.

Employer Provided Educational Assistance

Distributions from employer-provided educational plans are excluded from income to the tune of $5,250 annually, if used to pay for qualified education expenses. This is one of the few provisions passed that is intended to be permanent. This ends the annual extension of this provision and the annual concerns of those in the middle of college as to whether or not the provision would be around for the remainder of their time in school. Starting in 2002, the provision will cover higher education courses such as medical and/or dental school, MBAs, law degrees, and other similar professional courses which were previously precluded from being allowable.

CONCLUSION

The 2001 Tax Bill was packed with some gimmicks, but it did grant some relief to many people. Once again, though, the government has further complicated the law, and, committed to *phase-outs* and *tax reductions* for the next *10* years!

I have been doing this a long time and, in tax terminology, "a couple of years" commitment is long term. Over the past few decades, the government has a track record of changing the tax law an average of once every four years. The huge problem with this piece of tax legislation is that the biggest tax reduction comes . . . you guessed it—in year 10.

It will cost the government many billions of dollars to just bring the economy back to where it was before the September 11, 2001, tragedy. And, the economy was not in great shape before then. And, as I watch Nasdaq—down another 3 percent intraday, I can't help but wonder where the money will come from. It makes me wonder: *Do you really think the estate tax will disappear in 2010?*

Don't get me wrong. Whatever the cost, I feel we need to provide President Bush and the armed forces the resources to reduce the terrorist threat in America and free countries around the world. This is not only to protect the citizens of the free world, but also because he has inherited his father's legacy of dealing with the Middle East terrorists.

It is my contention that Pork Projects, such as the ones discussed later in this book, are a good part of the reason why a flat tax has never passed. It is also why, in my opinion, the likelihood of the passage of a flat tax in the future is minimal. Some system of linking direct percentage taxes to either earnings or consumption would be a much more efficient way to bring in money and far less costly for the government to maintain and supervise. Bringing in money is only part of the objective.

Most politicians are not stupid, though, and the successful ones have uncanny survival instincts. The vanishing estate tax provision should cost the American public approximately $1.6 trillion if fully enacted; but it is not due to be fully enacted until the year 2010—at least two presidencies (and probably two tax bill changes) from now. The government has once again accomplished what they do best—putting something on the table with one hand and, when we are not looking, taking it off with the other!

All of these areas affect Traders, but the immediate impact of this bill will not affect whether or not one qualifies, nor where to reap the benefits which were granted in the 1997 tax act—that bill was one chockful of Trader Tax benefits. Nonetheless, the law has changed many areas, and it is important to be aware of how and to what extent.

The long and short of it is, do not do your tax planning based on promised phase-outs and reductions slated to begins sometime in the future. Read and implement the strategies in this book and take your tax and economic destiny into your own hands!

Acknowledgments

With loving thanks for their support to Carole Tesser, Dr. Lawrence and Diane Tesser, Meredith and Joshua Tesser, Cristopher and Jim Novick, Lauren and Kevin Dyer, Rachel and Elliott Gordon, Ed Peck, Jennifer Schuchman, and Nichole Hagner.

Introduction

We Are All Traders!

This is not a book about *traders*—it is a book about *solutions.*

This is also not a book just for *traders.* Although one of the strategies in this book applies specifically to those who actively manage their own investment accounts to the level at which that activity becomes a business to them, this book is for anyone living in the United States today—or for that matter for anyone with any U.S. income at all.

Inherent in the premise that there is a *solution* is the fact there must be a *problem*—which there is.

In fact, there are several problems, not the least of which is that investors in this country are paying too much tax to the federal and various local governments on their investments and other income. That is the first part of the problem.

The second part is that Americans today are not prepared for retirement, in terms of either their savings or their investments. And they are not at all prepared for the tax consequences of the decisions they make today that will ultimately affect that retirement.

The final component of this multilevel problem can best be described by a plaque I once saw posted in a colleague's office. It read:

> When you are alive, the government will try to tax whatever they can.
> When you retire, they will tax whatever they let you save while you worked.
> And, when you die, they will take whatever they missed while you were alive.

This is unfortunate but true.

For those of you who are lucky enough to have built up any wealth and who now think you will be able to pass it on to your heirs, the U.S.

government has a nasty little surprise for you. The relative who will inherit the bulk of what you spent your whole life accumulating will be your greedy Uncle Sam.

As I said, this is not a book about Problems; it is a book about Solutions. And, as you can now surmise, the problems for which I will be providing solutions are: most people pay too much tax while they are alive and working; most are not saving enough for retirement; many of those who do save will give most of that income back to the government when they retire; some will have it litigated away by lawsuits. The money that is left after you die will most likely go not to the people you would prefer, but rather to a relative you would probably rather disinherit.

Among other things, this book will show you how to disinherit the federal government. It will show you how to provide for an abundant retirement—a goal that most people have no idea how to achieve—and it will also show you how to protect the wealth you've worked so hard to accumulate. These solutions can be implemented by virtually anyone willing to spend the time to learn them. *This book will ultimately show you how to keep the profits you work so hard to earn—investing, trading, or just simply working.*

1

The Basics of Accumulating Wealth and Keeping It

THE FOUNDATION—THINGS YOU NEED TO KNOW

In this book, I provide a framework that provides you with a better opportunity to master the technicalities of income tax, retirement plans, and estate tax planning for anyone who owns or has ever owned an investment.

I'll mention some tax code sections; however, retention of the specific sections is unimportant. I leave them there only as a reference point. I'm going to lay the groundwork for you and provide you with a set of concepts on how to understand these things in planning your own financial destiny.

An understanding of these concepts and the establishment and implementation of these techniques and strategies are crucial in your determination of how much wealth you would like to have in your lifetime and how much you would like your family to have in the future. The choice is yours as to whether you and your family are getting wealthier over the years or just getting by.

THE BASICS OF TAX PLANNING

In my 20-plus years in this field, one thing with which I've always struggled is how to minimize the effect of taxes for my clients. For the most part, the better they did, the worse my clients' tax positions became. This was because of the ruinous effect of capital gains taxes, income taxes, estate taxes, gift tax, and all the other state and local taxes. In order for them to maintain the same return in any given tax environment, it always seemed that my clients were forced to take many more risks with their capital to offset the impact of taxation.

Most people eventually give back 91 percent of their wealth to the government over their lifetime. (This concept will be explained in detail in subsequent chapters.) This and some of the other things I discuss in these next few sections will be hard to believe. They're going to sound far-fetched and too good to be true. Let me assure you that everything I recommend is clearly defined in the tax code.

RED, GRAY, OR BLACK-AND-WHITE? CHOOSE YOUR TAX STRATEGY

There are several types of strategies that you can implement to avoid taxes and to increase wealth.

1. The first type is strategies that are considered to be in the *red*—strategies that will clearly flag audits and, in fact, may subject the preparer and the filer to tax-motivated transaction (TMT) penalties. None of my strategies will even approach this area.
2. The next type is strategies that fall into the *grey* area of the law—very aggressive strategies that may at some point be challenged because of subjective interpretations of the law. Again, none of my strategies fall into the grey area of the law *unless I specifically qualify* them by stating so. It is then up to you to decide your level of risk.
3. The third type is strategies that are clearly *black-and-white* interpretations of the law, and these are the types of strategies I love to deal with. It is not worth the risk of subjecting my clients or myself, for that matter, to the possibility of penalties, interest, and additional tax. I would much rather sleep well at night than implement a strategy that at some point may be challenged and disallowed by the Internal Revenue Service (IRS) or any other government body.

The strategies that I discuss in this book are strategies that fall into the black-and-white category unless otherwise clearly stated. They are well defined, and they abide with the very letter of the law.

Furthermore, these are *not* hypothetical strategies that were thought up by someone in some back room and never tried and tested. These are strategies that I have used on my own tax returns, in my estate plan, and in those of my clients for many years. They are strategies that you can take home with you today and implement in developing your own tax reduction, retirement plan enhancement, and estate tax elimination plan.

A *Forbes*[1] article dealt with devious tax shelters. In "Tax Shelter Hustlers," Janet Novack and Laura Saunders discussed how the large accounting firms are peddling highly aggressive tax strategies to their clients for a percentage of the tax savings. They stated:

> Recently, *Forbes* obtained copies of two different letters whose first paragraphs contained what you see at left. ["Dear______ , As discussed, set forth below are the details of our proposal to recommend and implement our tax strategy to eliminate Federal and state Income taxes associated with (the company's) income for up to five (5) years ("the Strategy").]
>
> Each was sent by the accounting firm Deloitte & Touche this fall to a medium-size corporation.
>
> We agreed not to identify the recipients, but we can say that neither is a Deloitte audit client. We can also say that each letter demands a bounty for zeroing out the company's taxes: a contingency fee of 30% of the tax savings, plus out-of-pocket expenses. Deloitte promises to defend its "strategy" in an IRS audit—but not in court—and to refund a piece of the fee if back taxes come due.
>
> Pay attention. These letters are prime evidence of a thriving industry . . . that has received scant public notice: the hustling of corporate tax shelters. These shelters are being peddled, sometimes in cold-call pitches, to thousands of companies.
>
> Will the shelters hold up in court? Maybe yes, maybe no, but many schemes capitalize on the fact that neither the tax code nor the IRS can keep up with the exotica of modern corporate finance. Hesitant at first to participate, respectable accounting firms, law offices, and public corporations have lately succumbed to competitive pressures and joined the loophole frenzy.
>
> This new industry is quite apart from the so-called corporate-welfare tax breaks knowingly granted by legislators, such as for exports or R&D.
>
> The new corporate tax shelters have nothing to do with public policy and everything to do with arcane quirks in the tax code. Congress often knows nothing about these breaks and isn't happy when it does hear of them. These unintended tax breaks are saving corporate buyers up to $10 billion in tax a year, estimates Stanford law professor Joseph Bankman. That's still a small part of the $190 billion in corporate tax collections, but business is booming and there's nothing to slow it down: "I'd be astounded if it doesn't grow dramatically next year," says Bankman.
>
> Deloitte & Touche and the other Big Five accounting firms have grabbed the lead in this hugely profitable new business. But they aren't alone: Investment banks and tax-product boutiques are also peddling shelters. Law firms such as King & Spaulding and Skadden, Arps are raking in huge fees writing opinions to justify them.
>
> Haven't corporations always hired advisers to help minimize their taxes? Yes, but not like this. "This is a totally new phenomenon," says John Chapoton, a former Treasury official now with Vinson & Elkins. Why is it happening now? In part it's related to the growth of derivatives.

> The same minds that figured out how to split a security into a multitude of different cash flows and contingent returns are now engineering products in which the tax benefits are split off from the underlying economics of a deal. It's no coincidence that many of the new crop of shelters use swaps, collars, straddles, and newfangled preferred stock as building blocks.
>
> It has taken a while for inhibitions to be shed and the most outlandish gimmicks to propagate.
>
> In addition, tax advisers are no longer just devising specific strategies to deal with a client's tax needs as they arise, as in the past. Today's shelter hustlers parse the numerous weaknesses in the tax code and devise schemes . . . that can be pitched as "products" to corporate prospects. Then they sell them methodically and aggressively, using a powerful distribution network not unlike the armies of pitchmen who sold cattle and railcar tax shelters to individuals in the 1970s and 1980s.
>
> For tax professionals, the temptation to grab a piece of this profitable business is also intense. Recently the IRS got an anonymous letter blowing the lid off a particularly smelly scheme, and it was signed simply "A Pressured Practitioner." Former IRS Commissioner Lawrence Gibbs likens today's corporate shelters to the abusive individual shelters of 20 years ago: "It's virtually the same thing, with a bit more sophisticated product. Once something like this gears up, it's hard to stop, and the government is far behind the curve." To combat some of these schemes, the IRS can invoke a Supreme Court case from 1935, *Gregory v. Helvering*. It says that if a transaction superficially follows all rules but is devoid of economic substance and produces tax savings Congress didn't intend, it can be considered a sham and disallowed. Unfortunately for the tax cops, this sham doctrine is extremely fuzzy, whereas the rules that define the various components of a transaction are often well defined. This difference is ripe for exploitation, because the IRS is not equipped to find most shelters and even those which are discovered are unlikely to incur penalties.
>
> Says one lawyer: "The IRS misses nine out of ten shelters. On the tenth, the company settles and pays back taxes and the government agrees to no penalties. That's a small roll of the dice for the company."

Good news for you, the reader?

None of the strategies I discuss in forthcoming chapters have even come close to being in that article. None of the strategies presented in the pages that follow even border on the aggressiveness that the "Big Four Firms" are actively promoting. These firms are known for their conservatism!

That should give you some degree of confidence in what I will present to you in this book. You should have even more confidence in the fact that I have gone to audit at least once, and in most cases many times, on each and every strategy I discuss—I have won!

THERE IS NO MYSTERY TO SAVING TAXES

There are only two types of income tax strategies: (1) those that involve *income,* and (2) those that involve *deductions.*

The first type we will look at are those strategies that involve doing something with your *income.* You can really only do four things with your income:

1. Transform it—for example, into a lower tax bracket.
2. Avoid it—for example turn taxable income into nontaxable.
3. Decrease it.
4. Defer it—into another year or tax period.

On the other hand, you can really only do four things with your *expenses:*

1. Create them—through the creation of paper losses (expenses you would normally have and now turn into deductions).
2. Accelerate them—into the current year.
3. Transform them—into more favorable deductions (i.e., Schedule C deductions rather than itemized; we will talk more about this concept).
4. Increase them—make expenses that were nondeductible into deductible expenses.

Most people feel that taxes are mandatory, but they are not. My strategy consists of using these eight components to *ELIMINATE* or to significantly reduce your federal and state income tax, tax on your retirement plan, and the burdensome estate tax.

By now you're probably saying to yourself, "That's insane." Well, I'm going to make an even crazier statement:

The federal income tax, the retirement tax, and the estate tax are *voluntary* taxes. You can pay them if you want to, but if you wish to avoid them, you do not have to pay.

I am not talking about tax protestors—those who say the income tax is illegal, that the tax system was never ratified in the law. Take my word for it, income tax is legal, and might makes right. If the government wants to tax you, they will. Fighting them is going to result in some unsavory consequences for you.

Rather than fighting them, I liken my strategies to *tax judo.* In other words, I use the government's own tax laws to help me to limit or eliminate tax.

THE PARADIGM SHIFT TO TAX FREEDOM

In the sixteenth century, people believed the earth was the center of the universe. They thought that all the planets revolved around the earth. To think otherwise would have been heresy. In the late 1500s an Italian scientist named Galileo invented the telescope and with it discovered that the earth was simply one of several planets revolving around the sun.

Up until 1491, everybody knew the earth was surely flat. If you sailed far enough to the world's outer reaches, you would reach the end and fall off into space—until an Italian sailor named Christopher Columbus sailed from Europe to the West Indies and proved that the earth was in fact round.

Up until the middle of the twentieth century, science was convinced that energy and matter were two distinct quantities. Along came a scientist named Albert Einstein who proved, along with his theory of relativity, that energy and matter were, in fact, the same.

What I have just illustrated is a concept called the *paradigm shift.* A *paradigm* is a set of rules or precepts through which the universe is viewed. It is a framework through which people make sense of everything around them. A *paradigm shift,* on the other hand, is what occurs when something comes along to alter that set of rules or framework, and hence an *epiphany,* or major change in consciousness, is attained.

As Dorothy Parker once said, "There are two sure things in life—death and taxes." I say, "There is only one sure thing, and that is death—everything else is negotiable."

And "everything" includes the payment of taxes. The remainder of this book presents many strategies that can help you to achieve this *paradigm shift.*

2

The Trader's Tax Solution

THERE'S TOO MUCH TAX . . . HERE'S WHAT YOU CAN DO ABOUT IT

Whenever I give a seminar, I start by asking my audience what their reasonable expectation of annual return on investment capital is. Depending on the audience, I usually get answers of between 15 percent and 35 percent a year.

This high expectation is probably due to the fact that the stock market has done exceptionally well over the past decade, even considering the recent bear market. Most people have grown accustomed to double-digit returns. In fact, in a recent *New York Times* survey, most of the people questioned expected to make at least 35 percent on their money per year over the next five years!

In actuality over the past 60 or so years, the stock market has yielded about 12 percent annually. It doesn't matter what number you use, my illustration will make the same point. But for the sake of this illustration, let's assume that you could make 25 percent per year in the stock market (the average rate of return over the past few years). Let's also assume that you get out of college with no money; you get a job, get married, and start putting away money for retirement. In fact, you and your spouse each put away $2,000 per year into a mutual fund that earns 25 percent per year. That's all you ever do.

If you start at age 21, in a couple of years you and your wife are making $100,000 jointly, with a 5 percent increase in salary per year. You both work until you are age 65, but you save nothing but the $2,000 per year each until you retire. You may be surprised to find that by the time you retire, you and your spouse will have accumulated over $9 million—a tidy sum on which to retire! *This is the power of compound interest and starting early in life.*

That return is predicated on two essential assumptions: (1) that your interest accrues annually and (2) that you pay your taxes annually.

Now suppose that the fantasy couple had made one small adjustment to their financial plan: All the preceding conditions remained the same, but somehow they were able to avoid or to defer paying tax on this investment income during the period they saved the money, and they reinvested that income.

The next question I usually ask my seminar audience is what they think the end result would be then. I usually get a wide array of answers—twice that amount, four times that amount, and sometimes, in a rare instance, ten times that amount—but none is ever close to the true increase in wealth that would take place.

The true answer to this question is that if you were able to do the exact same thing and avoid paying tax on the income, you would end up with approximately *$367 million* after the same period of time. This is an increase of *almost 41 times* the amount you would have if you paid tax on the money!

Then, I really hit them with the kicker. This result does not even consider the possibility of deducting the annual amount contributed—such as into an individual retirement account (IRA).

If the fantasy couple were able to contribute the $2,000 each to an IRA or some other deductible retirement plan, the end result would be even more startling. The sum of money available for retirement at age 65, if the $2,000 per person, per year savings, were deductible, would skyrocket to *over $510 million* (see Exhibit 2.1). This is an increase of almost 57 times the amount without tax planning!

Remember nothing has changed here except the way the money was handled from a tax perspective. It was the same amount, the same rate of return, the same frequency of investment.

EXHIBIT 2.1 Total Net Wealth

Age	Taxable*	Tax Deferred	Tax Deductible*
21	$ 0	$ 0	$ 0
35	181,313	438,747	608,452
50	1,354,160	12,908,697	17,936,459
65	9,037,741	367,325,985	510,428,024

* Assumes today's federal tax rates for a married couple, with similar income, taking the standard deduction, and living in a state with the average income tax rate of 7 percent.

"THANKS A MILLION, UNCLE SAM." (OR SHOULD I SAY $89,500.49 AFTER TAXES!)

"I have a full-time job . . .
I work for the government."

A. Taxpayer

According to Dave Dreman, investment columnist for *Forbes* magazine and author of *The New Contrarian Investment Strategy,* the odds of getting on the Forbes 400 list are about 650,000 to 1. The odds of staying on the Forbes 400 list for four generations are approximately 5 million to 1. In short, the odds against *staying* rich are many times greater than the odds of *getting* rich.

Most people in my audiences are happy to hear that the lowest tax bracket in the United States was decreased to 15 percent in a prior tax act. They are also thrilled to hear that the tax rate on long-term capital gains was decreased from a maximum 28 percent to a maximum 20 percent on investments held more than a year. What most people don't realize, however, is that this fact does not make much of a difference to them over the course of a working career. In my studies, I have found that the average American taxpayer will eventually forfeit approximately 91 percent of every penny he or she earns to the government—that's right, 91 percent.

What I'm saying here is that the average American, over the course of his or her lifetime, is in the 91 percent tax bracket. Exhibit 2.2 illustrates my calculations:

What this means is that most people over the length of a 50-year working career are actually working 45½ years for the government! Looking at this another way, for every 80-hour, 2-week period you

EXHIBIT 2.2 The 91% Tax Bracket

Average tax rate	28.00%
Social Security and Medicare	7.65
Average state income tax	5.00
Sales tax (Average U.S. city sales tax rate = 6%, and 90% of all income earned is spent.)	5.40
Average federal estate tax rate	42.00
Average state inheritance tax	3.00
	91.05%

work, your heirs will receive less than *one day's* earned income. That's a pretty nasty tax bite. We will address the estate tax in a minute.

DOES ANYONE FEEL MORALLY OBLIGATED TO PAY THE MAXIMUM INCOME TAX?

I sometimes ask my seminar attendees if any of them think it is their civic duty or moral obligation to pay taxes. Although few admit it, I have found that many people have this deep-seated belief.

I don't know where it came from—public school, the church, toilet training at too young an age. It doesn't matter. It stands in the way of progress. You will never learn to implement these tax-saving strategies if subconsciously you feel there is something wrong with what you are doing. For those of you that might still be harboring this belief, let me try to educate you.

In case you haven't noticed, government is now big business—in fact, it is our country's biggest business. The United States used to be an agricultural country. In the eighteenth and early nineteenth centuries, more people were employed in agriculture than in any other sector of the economy. That changed with the Industrial Revolution. Throughout the late nineteenth and early twentieth centuries, manufacturing was this country's biggest industry.

In the mid-1960s with the advent of The Great Society, President Lyndon Johnson expanded the payrolls of the government to where the government itself became this nation's leading industry and leading employer.

The government owes you $4 trillion. For those of you not familiar with the term "pork barreling," let me introduce you. The government routinely spend billions every year to fuel their machine.

Before reelection each year, congressmen and congresswomen routinely try to spend money on their district to help get votes. This way, they can go home and say, "Look at all I've done for you—reelect me, please!"

Congress is somewhat of a good old boys' club, and each member is sensitive to this scheme and knows he or she may have to get someone else's help to pass their special interest bill in the next few years. So it is somewhat of a "you wash my back, I'll wash yours" situation.

Pork barreling is the way in which one congressperson will vote for another's (sometimes dumb) project with the understanding that the favor will be returned. There have been some pretty stupid pieces of legislation passed as a result of this practice.

HOW TO DIRECT THE GOVERNMENT IN YOUR BEST INTERESTS

For those of you who are not convinced of the questionable moral obligation of paying taxes, I have a suggestion for you. If you don't take the necessary steps to plan for your tax bill each year, why don't you do the alternative to strategic tax planning? Because your money's going on a one-way trip to Washington anyway, why not send it in with a road map—that's right, a *set of directions* for how the government should spend your money!

Make a list of the government agencies to which you would like to give up to 50 percent of the benefit of your labor for the past year. Let me give you a prototype map that you could use: Let's say, hypothetically, that you had a really great year trading. You made several million dollars—as did several of my young whiz kid clients last year. Exhibit 2.3 is a suggested list of grants you might like to subsidize for the federal government this year. Perhaps you would like to indicate right on your tax return (you can use a supplementary schedule if necessary) where you would like the money to go. That way the government can continue to fund some of the fine programs such as these that were established in the past few years.

Unfortunately, I did not have enough money left over to provide for two other projects still underway. In a recent budget allocation, the government spent $94.6 million to purchase 173 fax machines for the Air Force. That came to a little over half a million dollars per machine. From what I understand, they are still not happy with the purchase and are taking bids for the next batch.

Also underway in my home state of Florida is the Jacksonville Expressway Project. They allocated another $9.7 million to that—with plenty more to go. The best estimates project a completed expressway at some undetermined time in the future at a cost to the taxpayers of approximately $34 million PER MILE!

So it won't take you long to determine how much of your earnings you would like these agencies to have. I'm sure your money will be greatly appreciated, much more so than if it was saved or spent by you or your family.

Another alternative to this strategy, if you do not wish to send a specific allocation with your tax return each year, is to at least send instructions on each separate quarterly tax payment you make each year. That way, the government will know immediately where to put your money as it receives it. For example, in 1998, I wanted to be sure that my first-quarter estimated tax payment was used in the program I

EXHIBIT 2.3 Suggested Government Grants

Bequest	Purpose
$229,460	This was the amount spent by the government in studying the mating habits of house flies. Gary Blomquist, a biochemist at the University of Nevada, admitted that Uncle Sam may not get anything of practical value from the amount of money that they gave him to research the mating habits of house flies. The National Science Foundation (NSF) awarded this first amount.
$70,000	This was an additional amount that the Department of Agriculture provided to Mr. Blomquist to continue his study and to focus on the phermones, or chemical compounds, secreted by insects, that affect the behavior of others. With this additional $70,000, he has done extensive lab work trying to understand how these phermones affect house flies, bark beetles, and German cockroaches. Because of this amount of money, he has been able to create a new *transsexual house fly*, or basically a male that acts like a female. Mr. Blomquist admits that any meaningful results of his research would require many years and many hundreds of thousands of dollars more. *Perhaps when you pay your tax, you would like to provide him with the additional money for his research.*
$107,000+	Robert Wyer, a professor of psychology at the University of Illinois, received more than $107,000 from the NSF to study why some jokes are funny and others are not. "We are interested in what goes on in the head when people hear these communications."
$122,851	Professor Wyer also received an additional amount from the National Institute of Mental Health to study "the theory of humor elicitation."
$170,000	A further amount was granted by the NSF to Professor Wyer for a new project called *cognitive consequences of emotion.* "It is important for people to understand why other people laugh. We are not really interested in any particular joke, but we are interested in why one might have this effect and another may not."
$71,562	This amount was granted to Dr. Jonathan Coopersmith, a professor of technology at Texas A&M University, and he is in the middle of his six-year study on the history of fax machines. Coopersmith told the *New York Post* that he traced the origins of the fax machine to patent applications made in the 1840s—even though the telephone wasn't invented until 1876. He said he's investigating why it took nearly a century for this idea to become a reality. Coopersmith traveled to Switzerland on the government's behalf to visit the Library of International Telecommunications. *Perhaps we should ask him why he didn't have the information faxed to him!*

EXHIBIT 2.3 ***(Continued)***

Bequest	Purpose
$194,000	Walter Stone, a professor of political science at the University of Colorado, found out why some people run for Congress and others don't. This question was answered at the cost of a mere $194,000 awarded to him by the NSF.
$239,986	Boston University was granted this amount to study "the olfactory guided orientation of the American lobster."
$172,000	Was granted to Cornell University to investigate why people feel remorse over what they do and over what they don't do.
$275,000	This amount was granted to the University of Miami to analyze values and norms among Zambian adolescents.
$1,651,859	**Total Suggested Bequest**

most supported. So I sent them a check that looked something like Exhibit 2.4. As you can see in the memo section, I clearly indicated that I was particularly interested in seeing the continuation of that "Transsexual House-Fly" program.

In all seriousness, good tax planning is essential. If it is not properly done, the government has a plan for you. Your plan is much more involved than simply avoiding taxes. It is also the process of determining how you want your property to grow for retirement and how this can be done with the maximum growth for your future.

EXHIBIT 2.4 A Typical Quarterly Estimated Government Bequest Check

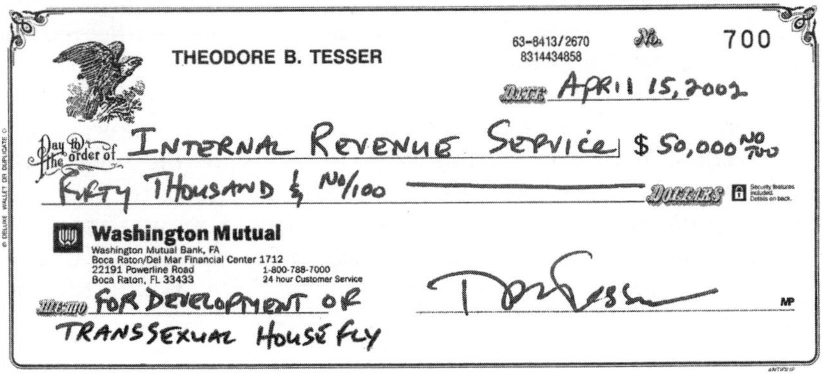

INVESTORS ARE HIT PARTICULARLY HARD

N. Vestor Becomes A. Trader—What a Difference a Trade Makes!

A prospective client was referred to me last year with a tax problem. He had heard that I was an expert in the field of investment taxation, and he wanted to confirm the fact that he had to pay the government almost $88,000 in taxes on what he considered to be a modest profit.

The facts of Mr. N. Vestor's circumstances were as follows:

- He had recently started managing his own investment account.
- In his first year of doing so, full time, he did quite well—a profit of over $300,000.
- Unfortunately, he also had some expenses, which consumed a great part of his profits.
- He spent over $150,000 on data feed, computers, trading systems, office furniture, and so forth.
- His investment interest expense that year was over $50,000 because he did not have the capital necessary to do what he wanted with his own money.
- He attended many investment seminars and had considerable expense in doing so.
- Although he felt he had enough deductions to cover most of the income he made, for tax purposes, his prior accountant told me that many if not most of these deductions would be lost.
- He had never heard of the Alternative Minimum Tax, a situation in which I have found many investors to be lately.

A quick illustration of N. Vestor's original 1998 federal tax return—still unfiled at that point—appear in Exhibits 2.5 through 2.11 on pages 30–38.

As you can see, the tax consequences of being an investor were dire!

He owed approximately $66,500 in federal tax, and another $22,500 in New York State and New York City income taxes.

After reexamination of the facts and circumstances and my review of his Trader Questionnaire, I discovered that N. Vestor, was, in fact, A. Trader in disguise. I found that he had really met most of the criteria for being considered a business and, consequently, was entitled to a great many tax benefits he had bypassed as an investor. On completion of the revised tax return, the difference in total tax liability, for federal and state, was significant. See Exhibits 2.12 through 2.15 on pages 40–46.

THE GOVERNMENT'S FREE LUNCH—YOUR TAX RETURN!

Tax planning is a difficult thing to do. No one likes to think about it! Most people confuse good tax planning with tax return preparation and make the sad mistake of thinking that their accountant will take care of the planning for them. This is akin to thinking that the dentist will brush your teeth for you or that the cardiologist will clear your arteries after you eat poorly all year. The fact of the matter is that most accountants are so busy filling out forms that they fail to formulate deductions, when in reality that should be their major task.

Tax planning is a year-round job. And it is ultimately *your* job. But it is also one that will be worth its weight in gold for you if done properly. You have a choice, and not doing your job is making a choice—it is giving the government the opportunity to feast on your earnings.

STARVING THE GOVERNMENT—TRADER STATUS

For those who qualify, one of the best tax-reduction strategies is filing as a trader. The major advantage of this strategy is that you are able to deduct, dollar-for-dollar, the expenses incurred in your trading business. If you do not establish yourself as a "Schedule C—Trader," you will be forced to deduct your investment expenses as miscellaneous itemized deductions on Schedule A—assuming that you have enough deductions to itemize.

As mentioned earlier, the major downside to being an "investor" is that before any expenses can be deducted against your income, you must exceed a base amount commonly referred to as the "2 percent floor." This amount is equal to 2 percent of your adjusted gross income before itemized deductions.

Furthermore, starting in 1991, another amount was deductible from all your itemized deductions before they could be subtracted from income. This amount is currently equal to 3 percent of your adjusted gross income above the $100,000 level (indexed in the future to increase). It has been my experience that once a floor is set, the government quickly builds on it.

The overall result of recent tax acts is that the trader has lost a good part of his or her deductions for expenses associated with the production of investment income. But in 1997 Trader Status was given new life finally, and true validity in the IRS Code!

INVESTOR, TRADER, OR BROKER-DEALER/MARKET MAKER—WHAT'S THE DIFFERENCE?

One of the areas of the tax law discussed for several years among tax practitioners involved in investment taxation is the *classification* of "investor." Up until the Tax Reform Act of 1986, the only significance this distinction had for the taxpayer was on the question of how much investment interest expense was deductible as an itemized deduction. The rule, prior to tax reform, was that investors could deduct all of their investment interest expense, or margin interest, up to their investment income. Beyond this amount, they were allowed to deduct an additional $10,000 in margin interest. For example, if an investor had $30,000 in interest, dividends, and net capital gains and had margin interest of $60,000, he or she would be able to deduct only $40,000 in that year as investment interest expense. The remainder, $20,000, would have to be carried over to future years in order to be deductible.

With the Tax Reform Act of 1986, as you will recall, this was changed so that the $10,000 deduction beyond investment income has been eliminated. Under the current law, only $30,000 of investment interest can be deducted against $30,000 of investment income. The $30,000 balance will have to be carried to future years when it can be deducted against future investment income.

If, on the other hand, an investor were to be classified as more than just a *passive investor,* indeed, if he or she could be classified as an *active trader,* then investment interest expense would no longer be considered investment interest expense. It would more accurately be classified as a *business-related* interest expense. Thus, it would be *fully* deductible as an expense of doing business as a trader.

There is a distinction between three types of individuals: (1) the investor, (2) the trader, and (3) the dealer. Never before has this distinction been so important.

A Broker-Dealer/Market Maker

The law is quite clear on the distinction of dealer, or market maker.

> A "dealer" in securities—that is, one who is a merchant of securities with an established place of business who regularly engages in the purchase of securities and their resale to customers with the intent of making a profit—may treat the securities held as inventory (Reg. Section 1.471-5). A dealer may be an individual, a partnership, or a corporation. Unlike securities held by investors, securities held for sale to customers in the ordinary course of business are not capital assets. See paragraph 1760.[1]

What this section of the IRS Code addresses is a very specific type of activity. It is describing a *market maker,* or one who does business with the intent of facilitating trade for one or more of the major exchanges. A market maker is a legal distinction, a designation that must be bestowed on an individual who fulfills certain criteria established by the various stock exchanges. This designation grants certain privileges that go beyond the ones we have been considering. Not only can market makers deduct dollar for dollar any amount of any types of expense they incur in conducting the business of their profession, they also get another break for which neither traders nor investors are eligible—a market maker gets to consider any stock, option, or other investment vehicle that he or she buys or sells as a "noncapital asset," or an inventory item. *This means that such a dealer in securities would not be limited to the $3,000 per year capital loss limitation to which other taxpayers are subject (including non–Section 475 traders).* Section 475 will be discussed shortly.

The law states specifically that these investment vehicles, because they are being purchased and sold as business items and are not being traded for a dealer's own account, should be treated as business inventory. If a dealer lost $100,000 in the market as a market maker, he or she would be able to take the entire loss, plus any expenses incurred in generating this loss, as a business loss on his or her tax return. Reporting this loss as a business loss, not a capital loss, is quite different from the way all other taxpayers would be required to report capital transactions (limited to a net $3,000 loss per year).

An Investor

In contrast, an investor is defined by the tax law as:

> a person who buys and sells securities for his own account . . . however, a person can be a dealer in securities and still trade for his own account. Thus, if the business of being a dealer is simply a branch of the trading activities carried on by such person, the securities inventoried may include only those held for the purpose of resale and not for investment (Code Section 263A).[2]

Basically, *investors* are clearly defined as those who invest in securities for their own accounts. Dealers in securities may also be investors; and, if they were, each activity must be treated differently for tax purposes.

Furthermore, all expenses incurred in the activity of investing are considered to be *investment expenses,* which would be deducted as miscellaneous itemized deductions on Schedule A of an investor's tax return.

A Trader

There is no election on your tax return to become a trader. However, the case law as decided in various district courts, as well as in the Supreme Court, does make a third distinction as follows:

> Because a trader, as distinguished from a dealer, in securities is subject to the capital gain and loss limitations, it is important to distinguish between a securities "dealer" and a securities "trader." A securities dealer is comparable to a merchant in that he purchases stock in trade (securities) with the expectation of reselling at a profit. Such profit is based on hopes of merely finding a market of buyers who will purchase the securities from him at a price in excess of their cost. **On the other hand, a securities trader buys and sells securities for his own account.** A trader's expectation of making a profit depends upon such circumstances as a rise in value or an advantageous purchase to enable him to sell at a price in excess of cost.[3]

YOU MAY BE A TRADER AND NOT KNOW IT!

One of the earlier references to trader status came in the August 1992 issue of *The Tax Advisor.* It contained an article by Scott P. Murphy, a CPA from Akron, Ohio. The article addressed the question of how one distinguishes between the three classifications just discussed. In this article Mr. Murphy stated that ever since the Revenue Act of 1934, it has been well known that there are three types of individuals or entities who have transactions with respect to stocks or securities: dealers, investors, and traders.

He went on to advise that, by far, the largest number of taxpayers are considered to be investors. For these taxpayers, gains and losses on transactions in stocks and securities are treated as capital gains or losses. Individual taxpayers who are investors may deduct portfolio and investment management expenses as only 2 percent floor itemized deductions. Thus, many of these expenses become nondeductible. In addition, the deductibility of investment interest expense by an investor may be limited, particularly in years of low investment income.

Dealers such as Wall Street brokerage houses or market makers on the floors of the various exchanges are those who hold stocks or securities primarily for sale to customers in the ordinary course of business. These taxpayers recognize ordinary gains and losses on transactions in securities, and they are able to deduct, in full, all costs relative to these investments as ordinary business expenses.

Murphy goes on to discuss the third designation, that of a trader:

> A **trader** is an investor who speculates and trades securities on his own account. He does not hold securities for resale to customers. **However, the trader's stock activity is of the nature that rises to a level of being a trade or business.** If a taxpayer is classified as a trader, gains or losses on securities transactions give rise to capital gains or losses under Section 1221. However, portfolio and investment management expenses and investment interest expenses become deductible without limitation under Section 162 in arriving at adjusted gross income. This can be a significant benefit to many taxpayers who have lost deductions as a result of severe limitations imposed by recent tax law changes.[4]

This is quite a significant distinction, and one that has become even more important with the passage of the Tax Reform Act of 1986. To qualify as a trader, there are no fixed requirements in the tax Code. It is agreed that the taxpayer must trade in stocks, securities, futures contracts, or options on a relatively short-term basis. If there is a preponderance of frequent trades, short-term in nature, relative to long-term positions, this would be an indication of the taxpayer's status as a trader.

In addition, the taxpayer must be involved in tracking daily market movements to be in position to profit on a short-term basis. Therefore, technical analysts—those who analyze the market on a predominantly short-term basis using chart and volume formations—are more likely to be considered traders than fundamental analysts.

Because fundamental analysts look beyond short-term chart formations to decide which direction a security or the market in general will most likely go, they are more inclined to take longer-term positions and are less likely to be viewed as traders. Also, traders must be able to show that they spend a great deal of time managing the buying and selling of securities or other trading vehicles.

Although the number of trades is not the exclusive factor, certainly a taxpayer with a large number of short-term transactions will be in a better position to demonstrate that he or she qualifies as a trader. However, the length of the trades and the nature of the type of trading are generally the determining factors, rather than purely the number of trades.

As dealer status would be beneficial when losses are realized on stock transactions, very few individuals or entities would be able to qualify for such status. However, there are probably a great many taxpayers who qualify for trader status. In some cases this may be as beneficial as or even more beneficial than being a dealer, because in most cases no self-employment tax would be due on the profits.

The case of the *Estate of Louis Yaeger* and the court decision on it is an excellent example of this situation. If you are interested in other case law that elaborates on how these factors are viewed, see: *Kemon*, 16 TC 1026 (1951); *Huebschman*, TC Memo 1980–537; *King*, 89 TC 445 (1987); *Reinarch*, USTC par. 9274 (1967); *Fuld*, USTC par. 9123 (1943); and *Whipple*, USTC par. 9466 (1963).

CASE IN POINT—WAS LOUIS YAEGER A TRADER?

A most significant case relevant to this discussion is that of the *Estate of Louis Yaeger v. the Commissioner.*[5] The issue in question was whether margin interest expense (investment interest) should be subject to the limitations provided in the law. At the time the case went to court, the annual deduction for investment interest expense was limited to $10,000 in excess of investment income. Anything more than that amount would have to be carried over to another year.

Louis Yaeger was a full-time investor/trader. But which of the two designations more accurately fit the type of activity in which he participated? If he were to be considered a trader, then all interest generated from his trading activities could be deducted as a general business expense. If, on the other hand, he were to be considered an investor, he would be subject to the investment interest expense limitation.

The importance of this issue increased tenfold because Yaeger was no longer either one of those two designations. He was, in fact, dead. This meant that on his final tax return, the amount of investment interest expense allowed to be deducted would be final. Because there would be no more investment income, there would be no way to carry forward any disallowed investment interest expense for use in future years.

When the estate filed the posthumous personal tax return for Mr. Yaeger, they took the position that he was a trader and consequently deducted all investment interest expense as a cost of doing business. This was disallowed by the IRS under audit examination and was contested in the Tax Court by the estate.

The decision was made *against* the estate and *declined* the late Mr. Yaeger the status of trader:

> Interest expense: Trade or business expense: investment interest expense. Interest expense incurred by the taxpayer when buying and selling securities was determined to be investment interest expense since the taxpayer was found to be an investor rather than a trader. The two fundamental criteria that distinguish traders from investors in securities are the length of their holding period and the source of their profit. Most of the taxpayer's sales were of securities held for over a year and most of

his profit came from holding stock until its market improved. His emphasis on capital growth and profit from resale indicated that his activity was investment motivated. Back references: Paragraphs 1332.1475 and 1425.50.[6]

Before exploring the court decision in detail, let's examine the background of Mr. Yaeger and the nature of his investing/trading activities. Louis Yaeger graduated from Columbia University School of Business and Finance, went to work as an accountant, and subsequently became employed as an audit agent for the IRS. After several years, he left the IRS to become a bond salesman and investment counselor.

He then began actively trading stocks and bonds for his own account, in addition to his investment consulting business. Twenty years later, Mr. Yaeger gave up his investment consulting business because the management of his own account had grown so demanding and time consuming. Thereafter he devoted himself exclusively to trading his own account, which he did as his sole occupation until the day he died.

Mr. Yaeger maintained a handful of accounts with several brokerage firms, including his largest at H. Hentz and Co. At that time, it was the largest account the firm had ever maintained for a U.S. citizen. Yaeger maintained an office at H. Hentz and Co., where he spent most of his working day and conducted most of his trading activity. The firm provided Yaeger with a private office, an assistant, a telephone, use of the secretarial pool, and access to the research staff and facilities of the firm.

Mr. Yaeger spent a full day at his office researching investment opportunities and placing orders. He would then go home to read more financial reports late into the night. He worked every day of the week; and when he was out of town, he maintained continual telephone contact with the brokers who handled his account. Yaeger was actively trading his own account in the stock market the day he died.

The tax returns in question were for two years, 1979 and 1980. During these years, the activities of his account, which were viewed as evidence for the classification of activity, were as follows:

	1979	1980
Purchase transactions	1,176	1,088
Sales transactions	86	39
Number of shares bought	1,453,555	1,658,841
Number of shares sold	822,955	173,165

As you can see, Louis Yaeger did quite a bit of investing/trading. He subscribed to a distinct investment strategy. His strategy was to buy the stock of undervalued companies and then hold the stock until it reached a price that reflected the underlying value of the company. He hardly ever purchased blue chip stocks, and most of the stocks he held paid no dividends. Instead, Mr. Yaeger looked for companies that were experiencing financial trouble but whose underlying value was not reflected in the stock price.

The strategy he employed was extremely successful and required extensive research that went beyond the study of popular publications. He would spend much time reviewing annual reports and brokerage house reports. Once Yaeger determined his target, he would begin buying the stock of the company in small quantities to avoid attracting attention from other investors. When he obtained a sizable amount of stock, he would let his position be known and would take whatever steps he felt were necessary to improve the position of the company. He often supplied managers with unsolicited business advice and even went so far as to attempt to arrange mergers or acquisitions for them.

In addition to selecting these types of companies, Yaeger increased the gain on his investments by extensively using margin debt. He financed his purchases using the maximum allowable margin, generally 50 percent. If the value of his holdings increased, he would use that increase in value as equity to support more debt.

From time to time, Yaeger shifted accounts from one brokerage house to another to maximize the amount of margin debt he could carry. Several times during his career, Yaeger was overleveraged and suffered substantial losses when he was forced to sell enough stock to cover his margin debt.

During 1979 and 1980, the amounts reported on Yaeger's tax returns were as follows:

Character of Income	**1979**	**1980**
Long-term capital gain	$13,839,658	$1,099,921
Short-term capital gain	184,354	728,404
Dividends	2,339,080	3,648,441
Interest	57,958	91,717
Director's fees	0	10,600
	$16,421,050	$5,579,083

Clearly, Louis Yaeger made a great deal of money from these activities. Furthermore, it is apparent that interest and dividends comprised a relatively small part of his overall income. However, the percentage of total sales of securities he held for 12 months or more was 88 percent and 91 percent in 1979 and 1980, respectively. The purchase dates of the securities sold in 1980 ranged from March 1970 to December 1979.

In 1979, Yaeger did not sell any security that he had held for less than three months, and in 1980, he did not sell any security that he had held for less than six months. On Schedule C on his tax returns, Yaeger deducted interest expense in 1979 and 1980 of $5,865,833 and $7,995,010, respectively.

The sole issue considered by the Tax Court was whether the claimed deductions for interest that Yaeger incurred in purchasing securities on margin were subject to the limitation of deductibility of investment interest as described in Section 163(d) of the IRS Code.

This issue boiled down to whether or not Yaeger's stock market activities constituted investment activity or trading in securities as a trade or business. According to the Tax Court, the main question was whether Yaeger was interested in deriving income from capital appreciation or from short-term trading. The Tax Court determined that Yaeger was an investor, not a trader, because he held stocks and bonds for lengthy periods of time anticipating that they would appreciate in value. In other words, he was basically investing for fundamental reasons, rather than technical. Thus, the interest expense he had incurred was investment *interest* within the scope of Section 163(d) and subject to the restrictions of that section.

WHAT THIS ALL MEANS

The IRS Code does not define *trade* or *business* as it applies to trading activities. In another case, *Higgins v. Commissioner,* the following determination was made: "The Internal Revenue Code does not define 'trade or business.' Determining whether a taxpayer's trading activities rise to the level of carrying on a trade or business turns on the facts and circumstances of each case."[7]

A 1984 decision in the case of *Moller v. Commissioner* put forth: "In determining whether taxpayers who manage their own investments are traders, relevant considerations are the taxpayer's investment intent, the nature of the income to be derived from the activity, and the frequency, extent, and regularity of the taxpayer's securities transactions."[8]

Furthermore, the "Federal Tax Report" states that traders' profits are derived from the direct management of purchasing and selling. They buy and sell securities with reasonable frequency in an endeavor to catch the swings in the daily market movement and thereby to profit on a short-term basis. Investors, though, derive profit from interest, dividends, and capital appreciation of securities. They are primarily interested in the long-term growth potential of their stocks.

Thus, the two fundamental criteria that distinguish traders from investors are the *length of the holding period* and the *source of the profit.* The activity of holding securities for a length of time to produce interest, dividends, and capital gains fits the definition of an investor.

It is true that Louis Yaeger initiated more than 2,000 securities transactions in 1979 and 1980 and pursued his security activities vigorously on a full-time basis. And, there is no doubt, as the Tax Court stated, that Yaeger: "Maintained a margin of debt which would have caused a more fainthearted investor to quail. However, no matter how large the estate or how continuous or extended the work required may be, the management of securities investments is *not* the trade or business of a trader."[9]

More important, most of Yaeger's sales were of securities held for more than a year. He did not sell any security held for less than three months, and he realized a profit on the securities through both dividends and interest as well as capital gain. Most of this profit came from the holding of undervalued stock until its market improved. This emphasis on capital growth and the profit from resale indicates an investment-motivated activity. So Louis Yaeger was an investor and was *not* eligible for a trader's deductions, that is, all trading expenses, including interest, as well as other trading expenses as part of the cost of doing business.

SCHEDULE C—BORN TO BE FILED

If you have determined that you qualify as a trader, you are in a whole new ball game. Expenses such as computer programs and equipment, online data retrieval services, investment advisory fees, and other such related expenses now are directly deductible from your trading income.

The question, however, becomes, "How do I set this whole thing up?" The way to do it is similar to the way in which any sole proprietor in business would do—on Schedule C. It is obvious that expenses should be reported on Schedule C; however, the question has been raised, "Since the income for a trader still consists of capital transactions, shouldn't it be reported on Schedule D?" The answer is yes. The transactions are basically transactions as defined in Section 1221 of the Code. In fact, Form 1099B is often generated showing total year-end gross proceeds from securities transactions.

Other questions usually asked are: "Because the income generated is *not* really investment income but rather is considered as active business income, shouldn't it be subject to self-employment tax? In this case, wouldn't it then be reported on Schedule C, as well as Schedule SE, the form for calculating self-employment tax?"

The answer is no (not unless a Section 475 election is made in which case the income is still not subject to self-employment tax). The income is still considered to be capital gain income or loss and it is not subject to self-employment tax. *A loss would thereby still be limited to a net $3,000 (without Section 475).*

In addition, because the income is not earned, no retirement plan contribution should be made against it. If that is your intent, your trading should be done through a Sub S corporation, which pays you a salary. Then you can set up a retirement plan based on your earned income (salary).

Because the income is of one type (capital) and the expenses are ordinary, you must use two forms to report it. The income should go through Schedule D and the expenses through Schedule C. If there are Section 1256 transactions (futures and certain kinds of options), you must use Form 6781 first, and then go to Schedule D. It is as simple as that.

Keep these points in mind when comparing the tax treatment of the three classifications discussed in this chapter: market makers, traders, and investors.

More about Market Makers

Market makers should treat all income (or loss) as ordinary. The stocks they hold are like inventory to them. Therefore, they can recognize an unlimited loss on trading (beyond the $3,000 capital loss limitation). *They are the only classification who can do this (without making a Section 475 election).*

They must also pay self-employment tax on their trading income, to which traders are not subject. They treat all expenses as ordinary business expenses on their Schedule C.

More about Investors

For investors, all income (or loss) on trades is capital (not ordinary). Therefore, losses are limited to a net $3,000 in any one year. There is no self-employment tax due on this income. All related expenses are considered to be investment expenses and deductible only as itemized deductions. They are subject to the limitation of 2 percent to 3 percent on miscellaneous itemized deductions.

More about Traders

Traders are a cross between market makers and investors. They trade their own portfolios but to such a high level of activity that it is considered a business.

The expenses, therefore, are treated as ordinary business expenses and are 100 percent deductible on Schedule C. The income (or loss), however, is still considered capital and must be reported on Schedule D (without Section 475). No self-employment tax is calculated on it (even with Section 475). A trading loss is still limited to a net $3,000 each year on Schedule D. It can, however, be carried forward indefinitely until it is used up.

To summarize let me repeat: Although your expenses, as a trader, are fully deductible on the Schedule C, your net trading loss is still limited to $3,000 per year on the Schedule D, unless you elect Section 475.

OTHER BENEFITS OF CLAIMING TRADER STATUS

Robert Frost once said: "By working hard eight hours a day, you may eventually get to be boss and be able to work hard twelve hours a day."

The most important component of a successful business plan is just that, the plan. As a trader, you must consider every contingency in formulating that plan. That means that you want to make absolutely certain that you fit the criteria of a trader as outlined previously and that you keep a set of books and records to document the business nature of your trading in case you are questioned by the IRS.

Furthermore, all of your deductible trading expenses should be well supported and documented, including the following:

- Accounting fees.
- Automobile expenses.
- Books and audio/videotape courses on investing.
- Brokerage account management fees.
- Calculators, adding machines, cassette tape recorders, and typewriters.
- Costs of collecting interest and dividends.
- Costs of managing investments for a minor.
- Financial advice on audio/videotapes.
- Oral or printed tax advice (such as the cost of *The NEW Trader's Tax Solution,* by Ted Tesser).
- Home computer and software.
- Data retrieval service.
- Trading advice.

- Interest expense.
- Legal fees.
- Entertainment and meals during which business is conducted.
- Safe deposit box rental for storage of investment documents.
- Salary of bookkeepers, accountants, or others who keep your investment records.
- Subscriptions to investment publications.
- Trips to look after investments (such as real estate) or to visit with investment advisers or money managers.
- Cost of attending trading seminars.
- Videotape recorder used for education.
- The portion of your home expenses that qualifies as home-office deductions.

Any item such as a VCR, home computer, or cassette tape recorder that is used for both business and pleasure can be assigned a percentage of business use. For any of these, that percentage of its cost can be deducted as a business expense.

IT'S YOUR BUSINESS—WHY NOT DEDUCT IT?

When you have a business, almost every related business activity becomes legally tax deductible. If the business generates income, it may still generate thousands of dollars of tax deductions that can be used to shelter other income from tax.

In fact, a small business—particularly, for readers of this book, a small trading business—is one of the few true tax shelters left. After the Tax Reform Act, there aren't many activities left that allow the use of tax deductions from one source, your business, to offset taxable income from other sources, such as your job. The business becomes a tax shelter when it shows a "paper loss." Taxable income is actually reduced by the amount of deductions legitimately associated with the business that are in excess of business income. These deductions can be used to offset income from other sources.

In a business, many of the personal things you own become fully or partially tax deductible when you can show that the items or activities are connected to your small business. In fact, it's almost like a half-price sale on every expense you can deduct. *Everything is cheaper when you deduct it!*

EXHIBIT 2.5 U.S. Individual Income Tax Return

FORM 1040 Department of the Treasury – Internal Revenue Service
U.S. Individual Income Tax Return 2000 (99) IRS Use Only – Do not write or staple in this space.

For the year Jan. 1 – Dec. 31, 2000, or other tax year beginning , 2000, ending , 20 OMB No. 1545-0074

Label (See instructions on page 19.) Use the IRS label. Otherwise, please print or type. LABEL HERE

Your first name and initial: N. VESTOR	Last name	Your social security number: 123-45-6789
If a joint return, spouse's first name and initial	Last name	Spouse's social security number
Home address (number and street). If you have a P.O. box, see page 19.: C/O TED TESSER-6274 LINTON BLVD. #102	Apt. no.	▲ **IMPORTANT!** ▲ You **must** enter your SSN(s) above.
City, town or post office, state, and ZIP code. If you have a foreign address, see page 19.: DELRAY BEACH, FL 33484		

Presidential Election Campaign (See page 19.) **Note.** Checking "Yes" will not change your tax or reduce your refund. Do you, or your spouse if filing a joint return, want $3 to go to this fund? You: ☐ Yes ☒ No Spouse: ☐ Yes ☐ No

Filing Status (Check only one box.)

1 [X] Single
2 [ ] Married filing joint return (even if only one had income)
3 [ ] Married filing separate return. Enter spouse's soc. sec. no. above & full name here ▶
4 [ ] Head of household (with qualifying person). (See page 19.) If the qualifying person is a child but not your dependent, enter this child's name here ▶
5 [ ] Qualifying widow(er) with dependent child (year spouse died ▶). (See page 19.)

Exemptions

6a ☒ **Yourself.** If your parent (or someone else) can claim you as a dependent on his or her tax return, **do not** check box 6a. No. of boxes checked on 6a and 6b: 1
b ☐ **Spouse**
c **Dependents:**

(1) First Name Last name	(2) Dependent's social security number	(3) Dependent's relationship to you	(4) Chk if qualifying child for child tax credit (see page 20)

If more than six dependents, see page 20.

No. of your children on 6c who: ● lived with you ● did not live with you due to divorce or separation (see page 20). Dependents on 6c not entered above. Add numbers entered on lines above ▶ 1

d Total number of exemptions claimed

Income

Attach Forms W-2 and W-2G here. Also attach Form 1099-R if tax was withheld. If you did not get a W-2, see page 21. Enclose, but do not attach any payment. Also, please use Form 1040-V.

Line	Description		Amount
7	Wages, salaries, tips, etc. Attach Form(s) W-2	7	
8a	**Taxable** interest. Attach Schedule B if required	8a	
b	**Tax-exempt** interest. **Do not** include on line 8a ... 8b		
9	Ordinary dividends. Attach Schedule B if required	9	
10	Taxable refunds, credits, or offsets of state and local income taxes (see page 22)	10	
11	Alimony received	11	
12	Business income or (loss). Attach Schedule C or C-EZ (#1) NONE	12	
13	Capital gain or (loss). Attach Schedule D if required. If not required, check here ▶ ☐	13	301,519
14	Other gains or (losses). Attach Form 4797	14	
15a	Total IRA distributions ... 15a ... b Taxable amount (see pg. 23)	15b	
16a	Total pensions and annuities ... 16a ... b Taxable amount (see pg. 23)	16b	
17	Rental real estate, royalties, partnerships, S corporations, trusts, etc. Attach Schedule E	17	
18	Farm income or (loss). Attach Schedule F	18	
19	Unemployment compensation	19	
20a	Social security benefits ... 20a ... b Taxable amount (see pg. 25)	20b	
21	Other income.	21	
22	Add the amounts in the far right column for lines 7 through 21. This is your **total income** ▶	22	301,519

Adjusted Gross Income

Line	Description		Amount
23	IRA deduction (see page 27)	23	
24	Student loan interest deduction (see page 27)	24	
25	Medical savings account deduction. Attach Form 8853	25	
26	Moving expenses. Attach Form 3903	26	
27	One-half of self-employment tax. Attach Schedule SE	27	
28	Self-employed health insurance deduction (see page 29)	28	
29	Self-employed SEP, SIMPLE, and qualified plans	29	
30	Penalty on early withdrawal of savings	30	
31a	Alimony paid. b Recipient's SSN ▶	31a	
32	Add lines 23 through 31a	32	0
33	Subtract line 32 from line 22. This is your **adjusted gross income** ▶	33	301,519

KFA **For Disclosure, Privacy Act, and Paperwork Reduction Act Notice, see page 56.** IF0US1 11/07/00 Form **1040** (2000)

Form 1040 (2000) N. VESTOR | 123-45-6789 Page 2

Section	Line	Description	Box	Amount
Tax and Credits	34	Amount from line 33 (adjusted gross income)	34	301,519
	35a	Check if: ☐ **You** were 65 or older, ☐ Blind; ☐ **Spouse** was 65 or older, ☐ Blind. Add the number of boxes checked above and enter the total here ▶ 35a		
	b	If you are married filing separately and your spouse itemizes deductions, or you were a dual-status alien, see page 31 and check here ▶ 35b ☐		
	36	Enter your **itemized deductions** from Schedule A, line 28, **or standard deduction** shown on the left. **But** see page 31 to find your standard deduction if you checked any box on line 35a or 35b **or** if someone can claim you as a dependent	36	#6 135,092
	37	Subtract line 36 from line 34	37	166,427
	38	If line 34 is $96,700 or less, multiply $2,800 by the total number of exemptions claimed on line 6d. If line 34 is over $96,700, see the worksheet on page 32 for the amount to enter #7	38	0
	39	**Taxable income.** Subtract line 38 from line 37. If line 38 is more than line 37, enter -0-	39	166,427
	40	**Tax** (see page 32). Check if any tax is from **a** ☐ Form(s) 8814 **b** ☐ Form 4972	40	47,965
	41	Alternative minimum tax. Attach Form 6251 #8	41	18,580
	42	Add lines 40 and 41 ▶	42	66,545
	43	Foreign tax credit. Attach Form 1116 if required	43	
	44	Credit for child and dependent care expenses. Att. Form 2441	44	
	45	Credit for the elderly or the disabled. Attach Schedule R	45	
	46	Education credits. Attach Form 8863	46	
	47	Child tax credit (see page 36)	47	
	48	Adoption credit. Attach Form 8839	48	
	49	Other. Check if from **a** ☐ Form 3800 **b** ☐ Form 8396 **c** ☐ Form 8801 **d** ☐ Form (specify)	49	
	50	Add lines 43 through 49. These are your **total credits**	50	
	51	Subtract line 50 from line 42. If line 50 is more than line 42, enter -0- ▶	51	66,545
Other Taxes	52	Self-employment tax. Att. Sch. SE	52	
	53	Social security and Medicare tax on tip income not reported to employer. Attach Form 4137	53	
	54	Tax on IRAs, other retirement plans, and MSAs. Attach Form 5329 if required	54	
	55	Advance earned income credit payments from Form(s) W-2	55	
	56	Household employment taxes. Attach Schedule H	56	
	57	Add lines 51 through 56. This is your **total tax** #9 ▶	57	66,545
Payments	58	Federal income tax withheld from Forms W-2 and 1099	58	
	59	2000 estimated tax payments and amount applied from 1999 return	59	
	60a	**Earned income credit (EIC)**	60a	
	b	**Nontaxable earned income: amt.** ▶ **and type** ▶ No		
	61	Excess social security and RRTA tax withheld (see page 50)	61	
	62	**Additional child tax credit. Attach Form 8812**	62	
	63	**Amount paid with request for extension to file** (see page 50)	63	
	64	Other payments. Check if from **a** ☐ Form 2439 **b** ☐ Form 4136	64	
	65	Add lines 58, 59, 60a, and 61 through 64. These are your **total payments** ▶	65	0
Refund	66	If line 65 is more than line 57, subtract line 57 from line 65. This is the amount you **overpaid**	66	
	67a	Amount of line 66 you want **refunded to you** ▶	67a	
	b	Routing number ▶ **c** Type: ☐ Checking ☐ Savings		
	d	Account number		
	68	Amount of line 66 you want **applied to your 2001 estimated tax** ▶	68	
Amount You Owe	69	If line 57 is more than line 65, subtract line 65 from line 57. This is the **amount you owe.** For details on how to pay, see page 51 ▶	69	66,545
	70	Estimated tax penalty. Also include on line 69	70	

Standard Deduction for Most People — Single: $4,400; Head of household: $6,450; Married filing jointly or Qualifying widow(er): $7,350; Married filing separately $3,675.

If you have a qualifying child, attach Schedule EIC.

Refund: Have it directly deposited! See page 50 and fill in 67b, 67c, and 67d.

Sign Here — Under penalties of perjury, I declare that I have examined this return and accompanying schedules and statements, and to the best of my knowledge and belief, they are true, correct, and complete. Declaration of preparer (other than taxpayer) is based on all information of which preparer has any knowledge.

Joint return? See page 19. Keep a copy for your records.

Your signature	Date	Your occupation	Daytime phone number
Spouse's signature. If a joint return, **both** must sign.	Date	Spouse's occupation	May the IRS discuss this return with the preparer shown below? (see page 52)? ☒ Yes ☐ No

Paid Preparer's Use Only

Preparer's signature	Date	Check if self-employed ☐	Preparer's SSN or PTIN
Firm's name (or yours if self-employed), address, and ZIP code	Waterside Financial Services 6274 Linton Blvd., Suite #102 Delray Beach, FL 33484	EIN	Phone no. (561) 865-0071

IFOUS1A 11/22/00 — Form **1040** (2000)

EXHIBIT 2.6 Schedule A—Itemized Deductions

SCHEDULES A&B (Form 1040) — **Schedule A – Itemized Deductions** — OMB No. 1545-0074 — **2000**

Department of the Treasury Internal Revenue Service (99) — ▶ Attach to Form 1040. ▶ See Instructions for Schedules A and B (Form 1040). — Attachment Sequence No. 07

Name(s) shown on Form 1040: N. VESTOR — Your social security number: 123-45-6789

Section	Line	Description	Line no.	Amount	Line no.	Amount
Medical and Dental Expenses		**Caution.** Do not include expenses reimbursed or paid by others.				
	1	Medical and dental expenses (see page A-2)	1			
	2	Enter amount from Form 1040, line 34 ... 2				
	3	Multiply line 2 above by 7.5% (.075)	3			
	4	Subtract line 3 from line 1. If line 3 is more than line 1, enter -0-			4	0
Taxes You Paid (See page A-2.)	5	State and local income taxes	5			
	6	Real estate taxes (see page A-2)	6			
	7	Personal property taxes	7			
	8	Other taxes. List type and amount ▶	8			
	9	Add lines 5 through 8			9	0
Interest You Paid (See page A-3.)	10	Home mortgage interest and points reported on Form 1098	10			
	11	Home mortgage interest not reported to you on Form 1098. If paid to the person from whom you bought the home, see page A-3 & show that person's name, ID no. & address ▶	11			
Note. Personal interest is not deductible.	12	Points not reported to you on Form 1098. See pg. A-3	12			
	13	Investment interest. Attach Form 4952, if required. (See page A-3.)	13	51,357		
	14	Add lines 10 through 13			14	51,357
Gifts to Charity (If you made a gift and got a benefit for it, see page A-4.)	15	Gifts by cash or check. If any gift of $250 or more, see pg. A-4	15			
	16	Other than by cash or check. If any gift of $250 or more, see page A-4. You **must** attach Form 8283 if over $500	16			
	17	Carryover from prior year	17			
	18	Add lines 15 through 17			18	0
Casualty and Theft Losses	19	Casualty or theft loss(es). Attach Form 4684. (See page A-5.)			19	0
Job Expenses and Most Other Miscellaneous Deductions	20	Unreimbursed employee expenses – job travel, union dues, job education, etc. You **must** attach Form 2106 or 2106-EZ if required. (See page A-5.) ▶	20			
	21	Tax preparation fees	21			
(See page A-5 for expenses to deduct here.)	22	Other expenses – investment, safe deposit box, etc. List type and amount ▶ Depreciation #2 — 5,000; Investment Expenses #3 — 89,942	22	94,942		
	23	Add lines 20 through 22	23	94,942		
	24	Enter amount from Form 1040, line 34 ... 24 — 301,519				
	25	Multiply line 24 above by 2% (.02) #4	25	6,030		
	26	Subtract line 25 from line 23. If line 25 is more than line 23, enter -0-			26	88,912
Other Miscellaneous Deductions	27	Other – from list on page A-6. List type and amount ▶			27	0
Total Itemized Deductions	28	Is Form 1040, line 34, over $128,950 (over $64,475 if married filing separately)? ☐ **No.** Your deduction is not limited. Add the amounts in the far right column for lines 4 through 27. Also, enter this amount on Form 1040, line 36. ☒ **Yes.** Your deduction may be limited. See page A-6 for the amount to enter. Reduction -5,177 #5			28	135,092

KFA **For Paperwork Reduction Act Notice, see Form 1040 Instructions.** IF0US2 11/03/00 **Schedule A (Form 1040) 2000**

Form **4562**

Department of the Treasury
Internal Revenue Service (99)

Depreciation and Amortization
(Including Information on Listed Property)

▶ See separate instructions. ▶ Attach this form to your return.

OMB No. 1545-0172
2000
Attachment Sequence No. 67

Name(s) shown on return: N. VESTOR
Identifying number: 123-45-6789
Business or activity to which this form relates

Part I Election To Expense Certain Tangible Property (Section 179) Note: If you have any "listed property," complete Part V before you complete Part I.

1	Maximum dollar limitation. If an enterprise zone business, see page 2 of the instructions	1	$20,000
2	Total cost of section 179 property placed in service. See page 2 of the instructions	2	
3	Threshold cost of section 179 property before reduction in limitation	3	$200,000
4	Reduction in limitation. Subtract line 3 from line 2. If zero or less, enter -0-	4	
5	Dollar limitation for tax year. Subtract line 4 from line 1. If zero or less, enter -0-. If married filing separately, see page 2 of the instructions	5	

6 (a) Description of property	(b) Cost (business use only)	(c) Elected cost

7	Listed property. Enter amount from line 27	7	
8	Total elected cost of section 179 property. Add amounts in column (c), lines 6 and 7	8	
9	Tentative deduction. Enter the smaller of line 5 or line 8	9	
10	Carryover of disallowed deduction from 1999. See page 3 of the instructions	10	
11	Business income limitation. Enter the smaller of business income (not less than zero) or line 5 (see instructions)	11	
12	Section 179 expense deduction. Add lines 9 and 10, but do not enter more than line 11	12	
13	Carryover of disallowed deduction to 2001. Add lines 9 and 10, less line 12 ▶	13	

Note: Do not use Part II or Part III below for listed property (automobiles, certain other vehicles, cellular telephones, certain computers, or property used for entertainment, recreation, or amusement). Instead, use Part V for listed property.

Part II MACRS Depreciation for Assets Placed in Service Only During Your 2000 Tax Year (**Do not** include listed property.)

Section A - General Asset Account Election

14 If you are making the election under section 168(i)(4) to group any assets placed in service during the tax year into one or more general asset accounts, check this box. See page 3 of the instructions ▶ ☐

Section B - General Depreciation System (GDS) (See page 3 of the instructions.)

(a) Classification of property	(b) Month and year placed in service	(c) Basis for depreciation (business/investment use only - see instructions)	(d) Recovery period	(e) Convention	(f) Method	(g) Depreciation deduction
15a 3-year property						
b 5-year property						
c 7-year property						
d 10-year property						
e 15-year property						
f 20-year property						
g 25-year property			25 yrs		S/L	
h Residential rental property			27.5 yrs	MM	S/L	
			27.5 yrs	MM	S/L	
i Nonresidential real property			39 yrs	MM	S/L	
				MM	S/L	

Section C - Alternative Depreciation System (ADS): (See page 5 of the instructions.)

(a) Classification of property	(b) Month and year placed in service	(c) Basis for depreciation	(d) Recovery period	(e) Convention	(f) Method	(g) Depreciation deduction
16a Class life					S/L	
b 12-year			12 yrs		S/L	
c 40-year			40 yrs	MM	S/L	

Part III Other Depreciation (**Do not** include listed property.) (See page 5 of the instructions.)

17	GDS and ADS deductions for assets placed in service in tax years beginning before 2000	17	
18	Property subject to section 168(f)(1) election	18	
19	ACRS and other depreciation	19	

Part IV Summary (See page 6 of the instructions.)

20	Listed property. Enter amount from line 26	20	
21	**Total.** Add deductions from line 12, lines 15 and 16 in column (g), and lines 17 through 20. Enter here and on the appropriate lines of your return. Partnerships and S corporations - see instructions (42)	21	5000
22	For assets shown above and placed in service during the current year, enter the portion of the basis attributable to section 263A costs	22	

KFA **For Paperwork Reduction Act Notice, see page 9 of the instructions.** GF0US7 10/26/00 Form **4562** (2000)

EXHIBIT 2.8 Investment Interest Expense Deduction

Form **4952** — **Investment Interest Expense Deduction** — OMB No. 1545-0191 — **2000**

Department of the Treasury
Internal Revenue Service (99)

▶ Attach to your tax return.

Attachment Sequence No. **72**

Name(s) shown on return: N. VESTOR — Identifying number: 123-45-6789

Part I Total Investment Interest Expense

1	Investment interest expense paid or accrued in 2000. See instructions	1	51,357
2	Disallowed investment interest expense from 1999 Form 4952, line 7	2	
3	**Total investment interest expense.** Add lines 1 and 2	3	51,357

Part II Net Investment Income

4a	Gross income from property held for investment (excluding any net gain from the disposition of property held for investment)			4a	
b	Net gain from the disposition of property held for investment	4b	301,519		
c	Net capital gain from the disposition of property held for investment	4c			
d	Subtract line 4c from line 4b. If zero or less, enter -0-			4d	301,519
e	Enter all or part of the amount on line 4c, if any, that you elect to include in investment income. Do not enter more than the amount on line 4b. See instructions ▶			4e	
f	Investment income. Add lines 4a, 4d, and 4e. See instructions			4f	301,519
5	Investment expenses. See instructions			5	
6	**Net investment income.** Subtract line 5 from line 4f. If zero or less, enter -0-			6	301,519

Part III Investment Interest Expense Deduction

7	Disallowed investment interest expense to be carried forward to 2001. Subtract line 6 from line 3. If zero or less, enter -0-	7	0
8	**Investment interest expense deduction.** Enter the **smaller** of line 3 or 6. See instructions	8	51,357

For Paperwork Reduction Act Notice, see back. Form **4952** (2000)

KFA IFOUS29 10/24/00

EXHIBIT 2.9 Alternative Minimum Tax—Individuals

Form **6251** — Department of the Treasury, Internal Revenue Service

Alternative Minimum Tax - Individuals

▶ See separate instructions.
▶ Attach to Form 1040 or Form 1040NR.

OMB No. 1545-0227 — **2000** — Attachment Sequence No. **32**

Name(s) shown on Form 1040: N. VESTOR — Your social security number: 123-45-6789

Part I — Adjustments and Preferences

1 If you itemized deductions on Schedule A (Form 1040), go to line 2. Otherwise, enter your standard deduction from Form 1040, line 36, here and go to line 6	1	
2 Medical and dental. Enter the smaller of Schedule A (Form 1040), line 4 **or** 2 1/2% of Form 1040, line 34	2	
3 Taxes. Enter the amount from Schedule A (Form 1040), line 9	3	
4 Certain interest on a home mortgage **not** used to buy, build, or improve your home	4	
5 Miscellaneous itemized deductions. Enter the amount from Schedule A (Form 1040), line 26	5	88,912
6 Refund of taxes. Enter any tax refund from Form 1040, line 10 or line 21	6	( )
7 Investment interest. Enter difference between regular tax and AMT deduction	7	
8 Post-1986 depreciation. Enter difference between regular tax and AMT depreciation	8	
9 Adjusted gain or loss. Enter difference between AMT and regular tax gain or loss	9	
10 Incentive stock options. Enter excess of AMT income over regular tax income	10	
11 Passive activities. Enter difference between AMT and regular tax income or loss	11	
12 Beneficiaries of estates and trusts. Enter the amount from Schedule K-1 (Form 1041), line 9	12	
13 Tax-exempt interest from private activity bonds issued after 8/7/86	13	
14 Other. Enter the amount, if any, for each item below and enter the total on line 14.		

a Circulation expenditures		h Loss limitations	
b Depletion		i Mining costs	
c Depreciation (pre-1987)		j Patron's adjustment	
d Installment sales		k Pollution control facilities	
e Intangible drilling costs		l Research & experimental	
f Large partnerships		m Section 1202 exclusion	
g Long-term contracts		n Tax shelter farm activities	
		o Related adjustments	

14	14	
15 **Total Adjustments and Preferences.** Combine lines 1 through 14 ▶	15	88,912

Part II — Alternative Minimum Taxable Income

16 Enter the amount from **Form 1040, line 37.** If less than zero, enter as a (loss) ▶	16	166,427
17 Net operating loss deduction, if any, from Form 1040, line 21. Enter as a positive amount	17	
18 If Form 1040, line 34, is over $128,950 (over $64,475 if married filing separately), and you itemized deductions, enter the amount, if any, from line 9 of the worksheet for Schedule A (Form 1040), line 28	18	(5,177)
19 Combine lines 15 through 18 ▶	19	250,162
20 Alternative tax net operating loss deduction. See page 6 of the instructions	20	
21 **Alternative Minimum Taxable Income.** Subtract line 20 from line 19. (If married filing separately and line 21 is more than $165,000, see page 7 of the instructions.) ▶	21	250,162

Part III — Exemption Amount and Alternative Minimum Tax

22 **Exemption Amount.** (If this form is for a child under age 14, see page 7 of the instructions.)

IF your filing status is:	AND line 21 is not over . . .	THEN enter on line 22 . . .
Single or head of household	$112,500	$33,750
Married filing jointly or qualifying widow(er)	150,000	45,000
Married filing separately	75,000	22,500

If line 21 is **over** the amount shown above for your filing status, see page 7 of the instructions. — 22

23 Subtract line 22 from line 21. If zero or less, enter -0- here and on lines 26 and 28 and stop here ▶	23	250,162
24 If you reported capital gain distributions directly on Form 1040, line 13, **or** you completed Schedule D (Form 1040) and have an amount on line 25 or line 27 (or would have had an amount on either line if you had completed Part IV) (as refigured for the AMT, if necessary), go to Part IV of Form 6251 to figure line 24. **All others:** If line 23 is $175,000 or less ($87,500 or less if married filing separately), multiply line 23 by 26% (.26). Otherwise, multiply line 23 by 28% (.28) and subtract $3,500 ($1,750 if married filing separately) from the result ▶	24	66,545
25 Alternative minimum tax foreign tax credit. See page 7 of the instructions	25	
26 Tentative minimum tax. Subtract line 25 from line 24 ▶	26	66,545
27 Enter your tax from Form 1040, line 40 (minus any tax from Form 4972 and any foreign tax credit from Form 1040, line 43)	27	47,965
28 **Alternative Minimum Tax.** Subtract line 27 from line 26. If zero or less, enter -0-. Enter here and on Form 1040, line 41 #8 ▶	28	18,580

For Paperwork Reduction Act Notice, see page 8 of the instructions. Form **6251** (2000)

KFA IFOUS33 10/23/00

EXHIBIT 2.10 N. Vestor Investment Expenses Line 22–Schedule A 12/31/98

Car expense	$ 3,115
Accounting fees	2,250
Office expense	4,561
Equipment lease	5,050
Repairs to machinery	3,166
Supplies	5,069
Utilities—Phone lines	2,611
Computer expenses	2,955
Historical data services	3,061
Internet services	2,050
Online trading data	7,010
Other trading expenses	4,116
Professional publications	3,116
Trading advisory services	35,179
Trading periodicals	6,633
Total investment expenses to line 22–Schedule A	$89,942

EXHIBIT 2.11 Resident Income Tax Return

New York State Department of Taxation and Finance

IT-201

Resident Income Tax Return 2000

For office use only

New York State • City of New York • City of Yonkers

For the full year January 1, 2000, through December 31, 2000, or fiscal year beginning 00 and ending

ATTACH LABEL OR PRINT OR TYPE

Important: You **must** enter your social security number(s) in the boxes to the right.

Your First Name and Middle Initial	Your Last Name (for joint rtn, enter spouse's name below)	Your Social Security Number
N.	VESTOR	123-45-6789
Spouse's First Name and Middle Initial	Spouse's Last Name	Spouse's Social Security Number

Mailing Address (number and street or rural route)	Apartment Number	New York State County of Residence
C/O TED TESSER-6274 LINTON BLVD.		•

City, Village or Post Office	State	ZIP Code	School District Name
DELRAY BEACH	FL	33484	•

Permanent Home Address (see instructions) (number and street or rural route) — Apartment Number — School District Code Number . . . .

City, Village or Post Office — State NY — ZIP Code — If Taxpayer is Deceased, Enter First Name and Date of Death

Staple check or money order here.

(A) Filing status – mark an 'X' in one box:

1 X Single
2 ___ Married filing joint return (enter spouse's social security number above)
3 ___ Married filing separate return (enter spouse's social security number above)
4 ___ Head of household (with qualifying person)
5 ___ Qualifying widow(er) with dependent child

(B) Did you itemize your deductions on your 2000 **federal** income tax return? . . . . . Yes X No ___

(C) Can you be claimed as a dependent on another taxpayer's federal return? . . . . . Yes ___ No X

(D) If you do not need forms mailed to you next year, mark an 'X' in the box (see instructions) X

(E) City of New York residents only: (see instructions)
(1) Were **you** 65 or older on 1/1/2001? . . . Yes ___ No X
(2) Was your **spouse** 65 or older on 1/1/2001? . . . Yes ___ No ___

Federal income and adjustments

Only full-year New York State residents may file this form. For lines 1 through 18 below, enter your income items and total adjustments as they appear on your federal return (see instructions). Also, see instructions for showing a loss.

1	Wages, salaries, tips, etc	1	
2	Taxable interest income	2	
3	Ordinary dividends	3	
4	Taxable refunds, credits, or offsets of state and local income taxes (also enter on line 23 below)	4	
5	Alimony received	5	
6	Business income or loss (attach a copy of federal Schedule C or C-EZ, Form 1040)	6	
7	Capital gain or loss (if required, attach copy of federal Schedule D, Form 1040)	7	301,519.
8	Other gains or losses (attach copy of federal Form 4797)	8	
9	Taxable amount of IRA distributions	9	
10	Taxable amount of pensions and annuities	10	
11	Rental real estate, royalties, partnerships, S corporations, trusts, etc (attach copy of federal Schedule E, Form 1040)	11	
12	Farm income or loss (attach copy of federal Schedule F, Form 1040)	12	
13	Unemployment compensation	13	
14	Taxable amount of social security benefits (also enter on line 25 below)	14	
15	Other income (see instructions) Identify:	15	
16	Add lines **1** through **15**	16	301,519.
17	Total federal adjustments to income (see instructions) Identify:	17	
18	**Subtract line 17 from line 16. This is your federal adjusted gross income**	18	301,519.

New York additions (see instructions)

19	Interest income on state and local bonds and obligations (but not those of New York State or its local governments)	19	
20	Public employee 414(h) retirement contributions from your wage and tax statements (see instructions)	20	
21	Other (see instructions) Identify:	21	
22	Add lines **18** through **21**	22	301,519.

New York subtractions (see instructions)

23	Taxable refunds, credits, or offsets of state and local income taxes (from line 4 above)	23	
24	Pensions of NYS and local governments and the federal government (see instructions)	24	
25	Taxable amount of social security benefits (from line 14 above)	25	
26	Interest income on U.S. government bonds	26	
27	Pension and annuity income exclusion	27	
28	Other (see instrs) Identify:	28	

2000

29	Add lines **23** through **28**	29	
30	**Subtract line 29 from line 22. This is your New York adjusted gross income** (enter the line 30 amount on line 31 on page 2)	30	301,519.

021007 NYIA1312L 12/19/00 Form **IT-201** (2000)

Form IT-201 (2000) **Page 2**

Tax computation (see instructions) N. VESTOR 123-45-6789

31	Enter the amount from **line 30** on page 1 (this is your New York adjusted gross income)	31	301,519.
32	Enter the **larger** of your standard deduction (from instructions) or your itemized deduction (from Form IT-201-ATT, Part I, line 14; attach form). Mark an 'X' in the appropriate box ■ •__ Standard ■ • X Itemized ...	32	101,319.
33	Subtract line 32 from line 31	33	200,200.
34	Exemptions **for dependents only** (not the same as total federal exemptions; see instructions)	34	,000.
35	**Subtract line 34 from line 33. This is your taxable income.**	35	200,200.
36	New York State tax on line 35 amount (use red **NYS Tax Table**; if line 31 is more than $100,000, see instructions)	36	13,714.

New York State credits and other taxes (see instructions)

37	New York State Household Credit (from table I, II, or III in the instructions)	37	
38	Subtract line 37 from line 36 (if line 37 is more than line 36, leave blank)	38	13,714.
39	New York State nonrefundable credits (from Form IT-201-ATT, Part IV, line 55)	39	
40	Subtract line 39 from line 38 (if line 39 is more than line 38, leave blank)	40	13,714.
41	Net other New York State taxes (from Form IT-201-ATT, Part II, line 33; attach form)	41	
42	**Add lines 40 and 41. This is the total of your New York State taxes**	42	13,714.

City of New York and City of Yonkers taxes and credits

43	City of NY resident tax (use the **City of NY Tax Table**)	43	7,446.		
44	City of New York Household Credit (from table IV, V, or VI in instructions)	44			
45	Subtract in 44 from in 43 (if in 44 is more than in 43, leave blank)	45	7,446.	See instructions for figuring city of New York and city of Yonkers taxes, credits, and tax surcharges.	
46	Other city of New York taxes (from Form IT-201-ATT, Part III, line 38; attach form)	46			
47	Add lines 45 and 46	47	7,446.		
48	City of New York nonrefundable credits (from Form IT-201-ATT, Part IV, line 58)	48			
49	Subtract line 48 from line 47 (if line 48 is more than line 47, leave blank)	49	7,446.		
50	City of Yonkers resident income tax surcharge (see instructions)	50			
51	City of Yonkers **nonresident** earnings tax (attach Form Y-203)	51			
52	Part-year city of Yonkers resident income tax surcharge (attach Form IT-360.1)	52			
53	**Add lines 49 through 52. This is the total of your city of New York and city of Yonkers taxes**	53	7,446.		

Voluntary gifts/contributions (whole dollar amounts only; see instructions)

54	Return a Gift to Wildlife ■ w Missing/Exploited Children Fund ■ c		
	Breast Cancer Research Fund ■ b Olympic Fund ■ o		
	Alzheimer's Fund ■ a **Total of your line 54 gifts and contributions .**	54	
55	Add lines 42, 53, and 54. This is your total New York State, New York City and Yonkers taxes, and gifts/contributions	55	21,160.

Payments and refundable credits (see instructions)

56	NY State Child and Dependent Care Credit (from Form IT-216; attach form)	56	
57	NY State Earned Income Credit (from Form IT-215, attach form)	57	
58	Real Property Tax Credit (from Form IT-214, line 17; attach form)	58	
59	City of NY School Tax Credit **(also complete (E) on page 1; see instrs.)**	59	45.
60	Other refundable credits (from Form IT-201-ATT, Part IV, line 72)	60	
61	Total **New York State** tax withheld	61	
62	Total **city of New York** tax withheld	62	
63	Total **city of Yonkers** tax withheld	63	
64	Total of estimated tax payments, and amount paid with extension Form IT-370	64	
65	**Add lines 56 through 64.** This is the total of your payments	65	45.

Mail your completed return to:

State Processing Center
P.O. Box 61000
Albany NY 12261-0001

Staple your wage and tax statements at the bottom of page 1 of this return.

Refund – If line 65 is more than line 55, figure your refund. (see instructions)

66	Subtract line 55 from line 65. This is the amount you **overpaid**	66	
67	Amount of line 66 that you want **refunded to you** ■ Refund	67	
	a Routing number ●		
	b Type: ● Checking • Savings		
	c Account number ●		
68	Estimated tax only Amount of line 66 that you want applied to your 2001 estimated tax. ■ 68		

You can choose to have your refund sent directly to your bank account. See instructions and fill in lines 67a, b, and c.

(Do not include any amount that you claimed as a refund on line 67.)

Amount you owe – If line 65 is less than line 55, figure the amount you owe (see instructions)

See instructions for the proper assembly of your return and attachments.

69	Subtract line 65 from line 55. This is the **amount you owe**. (Make check or money order payable to **NY State Income Tax;** write your social security number and 2000 Income Tax on it.) Owe	69	22,124.
70	Estimated tax penalty (include this amount in line 69 or reduce the overpayment on line 66. See instructions.) ■ 70	1,009.	

Sign your return below.

71 I authorize the Tax Department to discuss this return with the paid preparer listed below. (Mark the Yes or No box; see instructions.) X Yes ___ No

Sign your return here	Your Signature	Date	Spouse's Signature (if joint return)	Daytime Phone Number (optional)
Paid preparer's use only	Preparer's Signature	Date	Firm's Name (or yours, if self-employed) and Address Waterside Financial Serv., Inc 6274 Linton Blvd., Suite #102 Boca Raton, FL 33484	
	Check if self-employed ☐ Preparer's SSN or PTIN EIN 65-0664126			

022007 NYIA1312L 12/01/00 Form IT-201 (2000)

A. Trader versus N. Vestor—Side by Side

Let's compare the two returns line by line:

Line/Section	T/R Ref.	N. Vestor	A. Trader (Non § 475 Elector)
12-Form 1040	#1	Not applicable No Schedule C	Full dollar-for-dollar deduction. On Schedule C.
22-Schedule A vs. Form 4562	#2	Limited depreciation	Section 179–more taken on Sched. C.
	#3	Some investment expenses nondeductible	Fully deductible on Sched. C.
25-Schedule A	#4	2%–3% Floor	Not applicable
28-Schedule A	#5	Reduction in itemized deductions due to income	Not applicable
36-Form 1040	#6	Only itemized deduction	Standard deduction in addition to trading expenses
38-Form 1040	#7	Exemption phase out due to income	No exemption phase out
41-Form 1040	#8	Alternative Minimum Tax	No Alternative Minimum Tax
57-Form 1040	#9	Tax = $66,545	Tax =$23,705
70-Schedule IT201	#10	Tax = $22,124	Tax =$9,367
Total Tax		**$88,669**	**$33,072**

Presto change-o—a 63 percent tax reduction!

EXHIBIT 2.12 1040 U.S. Individual Income Tax Return

FORM **1040** Department of the Treasury – Internal Revenue Service
U.S. Individual Income Tax Return **2000** (99) IRS Use Only – Do not write or staple in this space.

For the year Jan. 1 – Dec. 31, 2000, or other tax year beginning , 2000, ending , 20 OMB No. 1545-0074

Label (See instructions on page 19.) Use the IRS label. Otherwise, please print or type. LABEL HERE

Your first name and initial	Last name	Your social security number
A. TRADER PROFIT-NO 475		123-45-6789
If a joint return, spouse's first name and initial	Last name	Spouse's social security number
Home address (number and street). If you have a P.O. box, see page 19.	Apt. no.	▲ **IMPORTANT!** ▲ You **must** enter your SSN(s) above.
C/O TED TESSER-6274 LINTON BLVD. #102		
City, town or post office, state, and ZIP code. If you have a foreign address, see page 19.		
DELRAY BEACH, FL 33484		

Presidential Election Campaign (See page 19.) **Note.** Checking "Yes" will not change your tax or reduce your refund.
Do you, or your spouse if filing a joint return, want $3 to go to this fund? ▶ You: ☐ Yes ☒ No Spouse: ☐ Yes ☐ No

Filing Status Check only one box.

1 [X] Single
2 [ ] Married filing joint return (even if only one had income)
3 [ ] Married filing separate return. Enter spouse's soc. sec. no. above & full name here ▶
4 [ ] Head of household (with qualifying person). (See page 19.) If the qualifying person is a child but not your dependent, enter this child's name here ▶
5 [ ] Qualifying widow(er) with dependent child (year spouse died ▶). (See page 19.)

Exemptions

6a ☒ **Yourself.** If your parent (or someone else) can claim you as a dependent on his or her tax return, **do not** check box 6a.
b ☐ **Spouse**
No. of boxes checked on 6a and 6b: 1

c **Dependents:**

(1) First Name Last name	(2) Dependent's social security number	(3) Dependent's relationship to you	(4) Chk if qualifying child for child tax credit (see page 20)

If more than six dependents, see page 20.

No. of your children on 6c who:
● lived with you
● did not live with you due to divorce or separation (see page 20)
Dependents on 6c not entered above
Add numbers entered on lines above ▶ 1

d Total number of exemptions claimed

Income

Attach Forms W-2 and W-2G here. Also attach Form 1099-R if tax was withheld.

If you did not get a W-2, see page 21.

Enclose, but do not attach any payment. Also, please use Form 1040-V.

Line	Description		Amount
7	Wages, salaries, tips, etc. Attach Form(s) W-2	7	
8a	**Taxable** interest. Attach Schedule B if required	8a	
b	**Tax-exempt** interest. **Do not** include on line 8a — 8b		
9	Ordinary dividends. Attach Schedule B if required	9	
10	Taxable refunds, credits, or offsets of state and local income taxes (see page 22)	10	
11	Alimony received	11	#1
12	Business income or (loss). Attach Schedule C or C-EZ	12	-200,678
13	Capital gain or (loss). Attach Schedule D if required. If not required, check here ▶ ☐	13	301,519
14	Other gains or (losses). Attach Form 4797	14	
15a	Total IRA distributions — 15a; b Taxable amount (see pg. 23)	15b	
16a	Total pensions and annuities — 16a; b Taxable amount (see pg. 23)	16b	
17	Rental real estate, royalties, partnerships, S corporations, trusts, etc. Attach Schedule E	17	
18	Farm income or (loss). Attach Schedule F	18	
19	Unemployment compensation	19	
20a	Social security benefits — 20a; b Taxable amount (see pg. 25)	20b	
21	Other income.	21	
22	Add the amounts in the far right column for lines 7 through 21. This is your **total income** ▶	22	100,841

Adjusted Gross Income

Line	Description		Amount
23	IRA deduction (see page 27)	23	
24	Student loan interest deduction (see page 27)	24	
25	Medical savings account deduction. Attach Form 8853	25	
26	Moving expenses. Attach Form 3903	26	
27	One-half of self-employment tax. Attach Schedule SE	27	
28	Self-employed health insurance deduction (see page 29)	28	
29	Self-employed SEP, SIMPLE, and qualified plans	29	
30	Penalty on early withdrawal of savings	30	
31a	Alimony paid. b Recipient's SSN ▶	31a	
32	Add lines 23 through 31a	32	0
33	Subtract line 32 from line 22. This is your **adjusted gross income** ▶	33	100,841

KFA **For Disclosure, Privacy Act, and Paperwork Reduction Act Notice, see page 56.** IFOUS1 11/07/00 Form **1040** (2000)

EXHIBIT 2.12 *(Continued)*

Form 1040 (2000) A. TRADER PROFIT-NO 475 — 123-45-6789 Page **2**

Tax and Credits

Standard Deduction for Most People
Single: $4,400
Head of household: $6,450
Married filing jointly or Qualifying widow(er): $7,350
Married filing separately $3,675.

Line	Description	Box	Amount
34	Amount from line 33 (adjusted gross income)	34	100,841
35a	Check if: ☐ **You** were 65 or older, ☐ Blind; ☐ **Spouse** was 65 or older, ☐ Blind. Add the number of boxes checked above and enter the total here ▶ 35a		
b	If you are married filing separately and your spouse itemizes deductions, or you were a dual-status alien, see page 31 and check here ▶ 35b ☐		
36	Enter your **itemized deductions** from Schedule A, line 28, **or standard deduction** shown on the left. **But** see page 31 to find your standard deduction if you checked any box on line 35a or 35b **or** if someone can claim you as a dependent	36	(#6) 4,400
37	Subtract line 36 from line 34	37	96,441
38	If line 34 is $96,700 or less, multiply $2,800 by the total number of exemptions claimed on line 6d. If line 34 is over $96,700, see the worksheet on page 32 for the amount to enter	38	(#7) 2,800
39	**Taxable income.** Subtract line 38 from line 37. If line 38 is more than line 37, enter -0-	39	93,641
40	**Tax** (see page 32). Check if any tax is from a ☐ Form(s) 8814 b ☐ Form 4972	40	23,705
41	Alternative minimum tax. Attach Form 6251	41	(#8) NONE
42	Add lines 40 and 41 ▶	42	23,705
43	Foreign tax credit. Attach Form 1116 if required	43	
44	Credit for child and dependent care expenses. Att. Form 2441	44	
45	Credit for the elderly or the disabled. Attach Schedule R	45	
46	Education credits. Attach Form 8863	46	
47	Child tax credit (see page 36)	47	
48	Adoption credit. Attach Form 8839	48	
49	Other. Check if from a ☐ Form 3800 b ☐ Form 8396 c ☐ Form 8801 d ☐ Form (specify)	49	
50	Add lines 43 through 49. These are your **total credits**	50	
51	Subtract line 50 from line 42. If line 50 is more than line 42, enter -0- ▶	51	23,705

Other Taxes

Line	Description	Box	Amount
52	Self-employment tax. Att. Sch. SE	52	
53	Social security and Medicare tax on tip income not reported to employer. Attach Form 4137	53	
54	Tax on IRAs, other retirement plans, and MSAs. Attach Form 5329 if required	54	
55	Advance earned income credit payments from Form(s) W-2	55	
56	Household employment taxes. Attach Schedule H	56	
57	Add lines 51 through 56. This is your **total tax** ▶	57	(#9) 23,705

Payments

If you have a qualifying child, attach Schedule EIC.

Line	Description	Box	Amount
58	Federal income tax withheld from Forms W-2 and 1099	58	
59	2000 estimated tax payments and amount applied from 1999 return	59	
60a	**Earned income credit (EIC)**	60a	
b	**Nontaxable earned income: amt.** ▶ and type ▶ No		
61	Excess social security and RRTA tax withheld (see page 50)	61	
62	**Additional child tax credit. Attach Form 8812**	62	
63	**Amount paid with request for extension to file** (see page 50)	63	
64	Other payments. Check if from a ☐ Form 2439 b ☐ Form 4136	64	
65	Add lines 58, 59, 60a, and 61 through 64. These are your **total payments** ▶	65	0

Refund

Have it directly deposited! See page 50 and fill in 67b, 67c, and 67d.

Line	Description	Box	Amount
66	If line 65 is more than line 57, subtract line 57 from line 65. This is the amount you **overpaid**	66	
67a	Amount of line 66 you want **refunded to you** ▶	67a	
b	Routing number ▶ c Type: ☐ Checking ☐ Savings		
d	Account number		
68	Amount of line 66 you want **applied to your 2001 estimated tax** ▶	68	

Amount You Owe

Line	Description	Box	Amount
69	If line 57 is more than line 65, subtract line 65 from line 57. This is the **amount you owe.** For details on how to pay, see page 51 ▶	69	23,705
70	Estimated tax penalty. Also include on line 69	70	

Sign Here

Joint return? See page 19. Keep a copy for your records.

Under penalties of perjury, I declare that I have examined this return and accompanying schedules and statements, and to the best of my knowledge and belief, they are true, correct, and complete. Declaration of preparer (other than taxpayer) is based on all information of which preparer has any knowledge.

Your signature	Date	Your occupation	Daytime phone number: 561-865-0071
Spouse's signature. If a joint return, **both** must sign.	Date	Spouse's occupation	May the IRS discuss this return with the preparer shown below? (see page 52)? ☒ Yes ☐ No

Paid Preparer's Use Only

Preparer's signature	Date / Check if self-employed ☐	Preparer's SSN or PTIN
Firm's name (or yours if self-employed), address, and ZIP code: Waterside Financial Services, 6274 Linton Blvd., Suite #102, Delray Beach, FL 33484	EIN	Phone no. (561) 865-0071

IFOUS1A 11/22/00 — Form **1040** (2000)

EXHIBIT 2.13 Profit or Loss from Business

SCHEDULE C (Form 1040)
Department of the Treasury Internal Revenue Service (99)

Profit or Loss From Business
(Sole Proprietorship)
▶ Partnerships, joint ventures, etc., must file Form 1065 or Form 1065-B.
▶ Attach to Form 1040 or Form 1041. ▶ See Instructions for Schedule C (Form 1040).

OMB No. 1545-007
2000
Attachment Sequence No. 0

Name of proprietor: A. TRADER PROFIT-NO 475
Social security number (SSN): 123-45-6789

A Principal business or profession, including product or service (see page C-1 of the instructions): TRADER
B Enter code from pages C-7 & 8: ▶ 523900
C Business name. If no separate business name, leave blank.
D Employer ID number (EIN), if any

E Business address (including suite or room no.) ▶
City, town or post office, state, and ZIP code

F Accounting method: (1) ☒ Cash (2) ☐ Accrual (3) ☐ Other (specify) ▶
G Did you "materially participate" in the operation of this business during 2000? If "No," see page C-2 for limit on losses ☒ Yes ☐
H If you started or acquired this business during 2000, check here ▶ ☐

Part I Income

1 Gross receipts or sales. **Caution:** If this income was reported to you on Form W-2 and the "Statutory employee" box on that form was checked, see page C-2 and check here ▶ ☐	1	
2 Returns and allowances	2	
3 Subtract line 2 from line 1	3	
4 Cost of goods sold (from line 42 on page 2)	4	
5 **Gross profit.** Subtract line 4 from line 3	5	
6 Other income, including Federal and state gasoline or fuel tax credit or refund (see page C-2)	6	
7 **Gross income.** Add lines 5 and 6 ▶	7	

Part II Expenses. Enter expenses for business use of your home **only** on line 30.

8 Advertising	8		19 Pension and profit-sharing plans		19	
9 Bad debts from sales or services (see page C-3)	9		20 Rent or lease (see page C-4): a Vehicles, machinery & equipment		20a	5,05C
10 Car and truck expenses (see page C-3)	10	3,115	b Other business property		20b	
11 Commissions and fees	11		21 Repairs and maintenance		21	3,166
12 Depletion	12		22 Supplies (not included in Part III)		22	5,069
13 Depreciation and section 179 expense deduction (not included in Part III) (see page C-3)	13	23,150	23 Taxes and licenses		23	
			24 Travel, meals, and entertainment: a Travel		24a	6,511
			b Meals and entertainment	8,711		
14 Employee benefit programs (other than on line 19)	14		c Enter nondeductible amount included on line 24b (see page C-5)	4,356		
15 Insurance (other than health)	15					
16 Interest: a Mortgage (paid to banks, etc.)	16a		d Subtract line 24c from line 24b		24d	4,355
			25 Utilities		25	2,611
b Other	16b	51,357	26 Wages (less employment credits)		26	
17 Legal and professional services	17	2,250	27 Other expenses			
18 Office expense	18	4,561	(from line 48 on page 2)		27	83,233

28 **Total expenses** before expenses for business use of home. Add lines 8 through 27 in columns ▶	28	194,428
29 Tentative profit (loss). Subtract line 28 from line 7	29	-194,428
30 Expenses for business use of your home. Attach **Form 8829**	30	6,250
31 **Net profit or (loss).** Subtract line 30 from line 29. • If a profit, enter on **Form 1040, line 12,** and **also** on **Schedule SE, line 2** (statutory employees, see page C-5). Estates and trusts, enter on Form 1041, line 3. • If a loss, you **must** go to line 32.	31	-200,678

32 If you have a loss, check the box that describes your investment in this activity (see page C-5).
- If you checked 32a, enter the loss on **Form 1040, line 12,** and **also** on **Schedule SE, line 2** (statutory employees, see page C-5). Estates and trusts, enter on Form 1041, line 3.
- If you checked 32b, you **must** attach **Form 6198.**

32a ☒ All investment is at risk.
32b ☐ Some investment is not at risk.

For Paperwork Reduction Act Notice, see Form 1040 instructions. **Schedule C (Form 1040) 20**

KFA IF0US4 11/08/00

EXHIBIT 2.13 *(Continued)*

Schedule C (Form 1040) 2000 A. TRADER PROFIT-NO 475 123-45-6789 Page **2**

Part III Cost of Goods Sold (see page C-6)

33 Method(s) used to value closing inventory: a ☐ Cost b ☐ Lower of cost or market c ☐ Other (attach explanation)

34 Was there any change in determining quantities, costs, or valuations between opening and closing inventory? If "Yes," attach explanation ☐ Yes ☐ No

35 Inventory at beginning of year. If different from last year's closing inventory, attach explanation	35	
36 Purchases less cost of items withdrawn for personal use	36	
37 Cost of labor. Do not include any amounts paid to yourself	37	
38 Materials and supplies	38	
39 Other costs	39	
40 Add lines 35 through 39	40	
41 Inventory at end of year	41	
42 **Cost of goods sold.** Subtract line 41 from line 40. Enter the result here and on page 1, line 4	42	

Part IV Information on Your Vehicle. Complete this part **only** if you are claiming car or truck expenses on line 10 and are not required to file Form 4562 for this business. See the instructions for line 13 on page C-3 to find out if you must file.

43 When did you place your vehicle in service for business purposes? (month, day, year) ▶ ________________

44 Of the total number of miles you drove your vehicle during 2000, enter the number of miles you used your vehicle for:

a Business ________________ b Commuting ________________ c Other ________________

45 Do you (or your spouse) have another vehicle available for personal use? ☐ Yes ☐ No

46 Was your vehicle available for use during off-duty hours? ☐ Yes ☐ No

47a Do you have evidence to support your deduction? ☐ Yes ☐ No

b If "Yes," is the evidence written? ☐ Yes ☐ No

Part V Other Expenses. List below business expenses not included on lines 8-26 or line 30.

COMPUTER EXPENSE		2,955
HISTORICAL DATA SERVICES		3,061
INTERNET SERVICES		2,050
ONLINE TRADING DATA		7,010
OTHER TRADING EXPENSES		4,116
PROFESSIONAL PUBLICATIONS		3,116
TRADING ADVISORY SERVICES		35,179
TRADING PERIODICALS		6,633
TRADING SEMINARS		19,113
48 **Total other expenses.** Enter here and on page 1, line 27	48	83,233

IFOUS4A 11/09/00 Schedule C (Form 1040) 2000

SCHEDULE D (Form 1040)

Department of the Treasury Internal Revenue Service (99)

Capital Gains and Losses

▶ Attach to Form 1040. ▶ See Instructions for Schedule D (Form 1040).
▶ Use Schedule D-1 for more space to list transactions for lines 1 and 8.

OMB No. 1545-0074

2000

Attachment Sequence No. 12

Name(s) shown on Form 1040: A. TRADER PROFIT-NO 475

Your social security number: 123-45-6789

Part I Short-Term Capital Gains and Losses – Assets Held One Year or Less

1 (a) Description of property (Example, 100 sh. XYZ Co.)	(b) Date acquired (Mo., day, yr.)	(c) Date sold (Mo., day, yr.)	(d) Sales price (see page D-6)	(e) Cost or other basis (see page D-6)	(f) Gain or (loss) Subtract (e) from (d)
1	Various	Various	301,519	0	301,519

2 Enter your short-term totals, if any, from Schedule D-1, line 2	2		
3 **Total short-term sales price amounts.** Add column (d) of lines 1 and 2	3	301,519	
4 Short-term gain from Form 6252 and short-term gain or (loss) from Forms 4684, 6781, and 8824	4		
5 Net short-term gain or (loss) from partnerships, S corporations, estates, and trusts from Schedule(s) K-1	5		
6 Short-term capital loss carryover. Enter the amount, if any, from line 8 of your 1999 Capital Loss Carryover Worksheet	6	( )	
7 **Net short-term capital gain or (loss).** Combine column (f) of lines 1 through 6 ▶	7	301,519	

Part II Long-Term Capital Gains and Losses – Assets Held More Than One Year

8 (a) Description of property (Example, 100 sh. XYZ Co.)	(b) Date acquired (Mo., day, yr.)	(c) Date sold (Mo., day, yr.)	(d) Sales price (see page D-6)	(e) Cost or other basis (see page D-6)	(f) Gain or (loss) Subtract (e) from (d)	(g) 28% rate gain or (loss) *(see instr. below)

9 Enter your long-term totals, if any, from Schedule D-1, line 9	9		
10 **Total long-term sales price amounts.** Add column (d) of lines 8 and 9	10		
11 Gain from Form 4797, Part I; long-term gain from Forms 2439 and 6252; and long-term gain or (loss) from Forms 4684, 6781, and 8824	11		
12 Net long-term gain or (loss) from partnerships, S corporations, estates, and trusts from Schedule(s) K-1	12		
13 Capital gain distributions. See page D-1	13		
14 Long-term capital loss carryover. Enter in both columns (f) and (g) the amount, if any, from line 13 of your 1999 Capital Loss Carryover Worksheet	14	( )	( )
15 Combine column (g) of lines 8 through 14	15		
16 **Net long-term capital gain or (loss).** Combine column (f) of lines 8 through 14 ▶	16		

Next: Go to Part III on the back.

* **28% rate gain or loss** includes all "collectibles gains and losses" (as defined on page D-6) and up to 50% of the eligible gain on qualified small business stock (see page D-4).

For Paperwork Reduction Act Notice, see Form 1040 Instructions. **Schedule D (Form 1040) 2000**

KFA IFOUS5 12/07/00

EXHIBIT 2.15 Resident Income Tax Return

New York State Department of Taxation and Finance

Resident Income Tax Return 2000 **IT–201**

For office use only

New York State • City of New York • City of Yonkers

For the full year January 1, 2000, through December 31, 2000, or fiscal year beginning 00 and ending

Important: You **must** enter your social security number(s) in the boxes to the right.

ATTACH LABEL OR PRINT OR TYPE

Your First Name and Middle Initial	Your Last Name (for joint rtn, enter spouse's name below)	Your Social Security Number
A. TRADER	PROFIT-NO 475	123-45-6789
Spouse's First Name and Middle Initial	Spouse's Last Name	Spouse's Social Security Number

Mailing Address (number and street or rural route)		Apartment Number	New York State County of Residence
C/O TED TESSER-6274 LINTON BLVD.			•
City, Village or Post Office	State	ZIP Code	School District Name
DELRAY BEACH	FL	33484	•

Permanent Home Address (see instructions) (number and street or rural route)	Apartment Number	School District Code Number
City, Village or Post Office	State ZIP Code NY	If Taxpayer is Deceased, Enter First Name and Date of Death

(A) Filing status – mark an 'X' in one box:

1 X Single
2 ___ Married filing joint return (enter spouse's social security number above)
3 ___ Married filing separate return (enter spouse's social security number above)
4 ___ Head of household (with qualifying person)
5 ___ Qualifying widow(er) with dependent child

Staple check or money order here.

(B) **Did you itemize your deductions** on your 2000 **federal** income tax return? ..... Yes ___ No X

(C) **Can you be claimed** as a dependent on another taxpayer's federal return? ..... Yes ___ No X

(D) **If you do not need forms mailed** to you next year, mark an 'X' in the box (see instructions) X

(E) **City of New York residents only:** (see instructions)
(1) Were **you** 65 or older on 1/1/2001? ... Yes ___ No X
(2) Was your **spouse** 65 or older on 1/1/2001? ... Yes ___ No ___

Federal income and adjustments

Only full-year New York State residents may file this form. For lines 1 through 18 below, enter your income items and total adjustments as they appear on your federal return (see instructions). Also, see instructions for showing a loss.

1	Wages, salaries, tips, etc	1	
2	Taxable interest income	2	
3	Ordinary dividends	3	
4	Taxable refunds, credits, or offsets of state and local income taxes (also enter on line 23 below)	4	
5	Alimony received	5	
6	Business income or loss (attach a copy of federal Schedule C or C-EZ, Form 1040)	6	-200,678.
7	Capital gain or loss (if required, attach copy of federal Schedule D, Form 1040)	7	301,519.
8	Other gains or losses (attach copy of federal Form 4797)	8	
9	Taxable amount of IRA distributions	9	
10	Taxable amount of pensions and annuities	10	
11	Rental real estate, royalties, partnerships, S corporations, trusts, etc (attach copy of federal Schedule E, Form 1040)	11	
12	Farm income or loss (attach copy of federal Schedule F, Form 1040)	12	
13	Unemployment compensation	13	
14	Taxable amount of social security benefits (also enter on line 25 below)	14	
15	Other income (see instructions) Identify:	15	
16	Add lines 1 through 15	16	100,841.
17	Total federal adjustments to income (see instructions) Identify:	17	
18	**Subtract line 17 from line 16. This is your federal adjusted gross income**	18	100,841.

New York additions (see instructions)

19	Interest income on state and local bonds and obligations (but not those of New York State or its local governments)	19	
20	Public employee 414(h) retirement contributions from your wage and tax statements (see instructions)	20	
21	Other (see instructions) Identify:	21	
22	Add lines 18 through 21	22	100,841.

New York subtractions (see instructions)

23	Taxable refunds, credits, or offsets of state and local income taxes (from line 4 above)	23	
24	Pensions of NYS and local governments and the federal government (see instructions)	24	
25	Taxable amount of social security benefits (from line 14 above)	25	
26	Interest income on U.S. government bonds	26	
27	Pension and annuity income exclusion	27	
28	Other (see instrs) Identify:	28	
29	Add lines 23 through 28	29	
30	**Subtract line 29 from line 22. This is your New York adjusted gross income** (enter the line 30 amount on line 31 on page 2)	30	100,841.

2000

021007 NYIA1312L 12/19/00 Form **IT-201** (2000)

Form **IT-201** (2000) Page **2**

Tax computation (see instructions) A. TRADER PROFIT-NO 475 123-45-6789

Line	Description		Amount
31	Enter the amount from **line 30** on page 1 (this is your New York adjusted gross income)	31	100,841.
32	Enter the **larger** of your standard deduction (from instructions) or your itemized deduction (from Form IT-201-ATT, **Part I, line 14**; attach form). Mark an 'X' in the appropriate box ● X **Standard** ● __ **Itemized**	32	7,500.
33	Subtract line 32 from line 31	33	93,341.
34	Exemptions **for dependents only** (not the same as total federal exemptions; see instructions)	34	,000.
35	**Subtract line 34 from line 33. This is your taxable income**	35	93,341.
36	New York State tax on line 35 amount (use red **NYS Tax Table**; if line 31 is more than $100,000, see instructions)	36	6,004.

New York State credits and other taxes (see instructions)

Line	Description		Amount
37	New York State Household Credit (from table I, II, or III in the instructions)	37	
38	Subtract line 37 from line 36 (if line 37 is more than line 36, leave blank)	38	6,004.
39	New York State nonrefundable credits (from Form IT-201-ATT, Part IV, line 55)	39	
40	Subtract line 39 from line 38 (if line 39 is more than line 38, leave blank)	40	6,004.
41	Net other New York State taxes (from Form IT-201-ATT, Part II, line 33; attach form)	41	
42	**Add lines 40 and 41.** This is the total of your New York State taxes	42	6,004.

City of New York and City of Yonkers taxes and credits

Line	Description		Amount
43	City of NY resident tax (use the **City of NY Tax Table**)	43	3,408.
44	City of New York Household Credit (from table IV, V, or VI in instructions)	44	
45	Subtract ln 44 from ln 43 (if ln 44 is more than ln 43, leave blank)	45	3,408.
46	Other city of New York taxes (from Form IT-201-ATT, Part III, line 38; attach form)	46	
47	Add lines 45 and 46	47	3,408.
48	City of New York nonrefundable credits (from Form IT-201-ATT, Part IV, line 58)	48	
49	Subtract line 48 from line 47 (if line 48 is more than line 47, leave blank)	49	3,408.
50	City of Yonkers resident income tax surcharge (see instructions)	50	
51	City of Yonkers **nonresident** earnings tax (attach Form Y-203)	51	
52	Part-year city of Yonkers resident income tax surcharge (attach Form IT-360.1)	52	
53	**Add lines 49 through 52.** This is the total of your city of New York and city of Yonkers taxes	53	3,408.

See instructions for figuring city of New York and city of Yonkers taxes, credits, and tax surcharges.

Voluntary gifts/contributions (whole dollar amounts only; see instructions)

54 Return a Gift to Wildlife w ___ Missing/Exploited Children Fund c ___
Breast Cancer Research Fund b ___ Olympic Fund o ___
Alzheimer's Fund a ___ **Total of your line 54 gifts and contributions** 54 ___

55 **Add lines 42, 53, and 54.** This is your total New York State, New York City and Yonkers taxes, and gifts/contributions 55 9,412.

Payments and refundable credits (see instructions)

Line	Description		Amount
56	NY State Child and Dependent Care Credit (from Form IT-216; attach form)	56	
57	NY State Earned Income Credit (from Form IT-215, attach form)	57	
58	Real Property Tax Credit (from Form IT-214, line 17; attach form)	58	
59	City of NY School Tax Credit **(also complete (E) on page 1; see instrs)**	59	45.
60	Other refundable credits (from Form IT-201-ATT, Part IV, line 72)	60	
61	Total **New York State** tax withheld	61	
62	Total **city of New York** tax withheld	62	
63	Total **city of Yonkers** tax withheld	63	
64	Total of estimated tax payments, and amount paid with extension Form IT-370	64	
65	**Add lines 56 through 64.** This is the total of your payments	65	45.

Mail your completed return to:
State Processing Center
P.O. Box 61000
Albany NY 12261-0001

Staple your wage and tax statements at the bottom of page 1 of this return.

Refund – If line 65 is **more than** line 55, figure **your refund.** (see instructions)

66 Subtract line 55 from line 65. This is the amount you **overpaid** 66 ___

67 Amount of line 66 that you want **refunded to you** **Refund** 67 ___

a Routing number ___ b Type: ● Checking ● Savings
c Account number ___

You can choose to have your refund sent directly to your bank account. See instructions and fill in lines 67a, b, and c.

68 Estimated tax only — Amount of line 66 that you want applied to your 2001 estimated tax. (Do not include any amount that you claimed as a refund on line 67) 68 ___

Amount you owe – If line 65 is **less than** line 55, figure the **amount you owe** (see instructions)

See instructions for the proper assembly of your return and attachments.

69 Subtract line 65 from line 55. This is the **amount you owe.** (Make check or money order payable to **NY State Income Tax**; write your social security number and 2000 Income Tax on it.) **Owe** 69 9367

70 Estimated tax penalty (include this amount in line 69 or reduce the overpayment on line 66. See instructions.) 70 ___

Sign your return below.

71 I authorize the Tax Department to discuss this return with the paid preparer listed below. (Mark the Yes or No box; see instructions.) X **Yes** **No**

Sign your return here	Your Signature	Date	Spouse's Signature (if joint return)	Daytime Phone Number (optional) 561-865-0071
Paid preparer's use only	Preparer's Signature / Check if self-employed	Date / Preparer's SSN or PTIN / EIN	Firm's Name (or yours, if self-employed) and Address: Waterside Financial Services, 6274 Linton Blvd., Suite #102, Delray Beach, FL 33484	

022007 NYIA1312L 12/01/00 Form **IT-201** (2000)

3

Recent Trader Cases

THE CASE OF FREDRICK R. MAYER

May 11, 1994—T.C. Memo 1994-209 (for the years ended 1986, 1987, 1988).

The question considered for this decision was whether substantial stock market investing meant Trader Status.

In its ongoing consideration of the requirements for claiming Trader Status, the Tax Court has recently shed further light on what it is looking for. Although the qualifications for this most favored tax treatment are still somewhat subjective, each Tax Court decision makes the issue just a bit clearer.

In the case *Fredrick R. Mayer* (T.C. Memo 1994-209), the Tax Court was asked to consider the proper classification of an individual who actively managed his own assets. The taxpayer took the position that he was a "trader in securities." As the court reiterated in this decision, with regard to "Trader Status" in particular, the term "Trade or Business" is not defined in the Internal Revenue Code. Whether trading securities constitutes a trade or a business in any year is a *question of fact,* and the Tax Court reserves the right to determine such designations on a case-by-case basis, in each particular year.

Perhaps the biggest impact of claiming "Trader Status," rather than "investor," is that itemized deductions for investment advisory fees, money management fees, custody and administrative fees, subscriptions to investment advisory publications, data fees, computer hardware and software, and similar type expenses become miscellaneous itemized deductions.

The tax implications here are huge. A trader gets a dollar-per-dollar write-off of these expenses on Schedule C (for businesses), whereas the investor must deduct them on Schedule A (for itemized deductions). Miscellaneous itemized deductions are deductible *only* to the extent that they exceed 2 percent (and at some higher income levels 5 percent) of a taxpayer's adjusted gross income. On the other hand, if costs qualify to be listed as business expenses on Schedule C, they are subtracted directly from the adjusted gross income—they are 100 percent deductible at any level. For a trader, they are considered to be *ordinary and necessary* trade or business expenses.

There are strict limitations on the deductibility of "margin interest" for investors. It is subject to a limitation of the amount of investment income earned in any one year. As a trader, all margin interest becomes "business interest"—once again 100 percent deductible.

The trader may also qualify for the home office deduction and a Section 179 write-off for new assets, whereas an investor may not. (Under Section 179, equipment is written off in one year, rather than being depreciated over a period of time.)

Now for the *Fred Mayer* case: Fredrick Mayer sold an oil drilling company in June 1980 for $134 million (60 percent of this money was his). He formed a corporation called "Captiva" for the sole purpose of managing his money. In forming Captiva, his concept was that he would be a "manager of money managers." Mr. Mayer, whose primary focus was on the preservation of capital, felt it would be easier and safer to do business in the corporate form—his liability would be limited. He hired several people to run the administrative side of the company and to help him monitor the money managers he used.

Those people hired eight money managers for the diversification of his portfolio. Each had a different style of trading; each was a specialist in a different field, as follows:

1. *Relative value* of the investment—primarily focused on buying any type of stock that was currently undervalued in the market.
2. *Investing* in emerging industries.
3. *Contrarian* investments—those were out of favor at that time.
4. *High-tech companies* only.
5. *New trends* in industry stocks.
6. *Foreign stocks.*
7. *Large foreign stocks*—those that were doing extremely well (trends).
8. *Small capitalized stocks.*

Mayer monitored these advisers, each of whom had *sole discretion* of a trading account, and he retained the right to dismiss them at any point (although he rarely did). Managers could be dismissed if they did not trade in the style for which they were hired or if they did not keep pace with the goal set for them—10 percent profit per year.

Mayer gave the money managers *three* years to prove themselves. Each manager would inform Mayer in writing of the results of his or her portion of trading the funds on a *quarterly* basis. And Mayer monitored them on a monthly basis by reviewing monthly statements.

Mr. Mayer had *no formal training* in securities or in trading, and he never held a seat on any exchange. He read investment publications, traded with the information he gained from talking to knowledgeable people, and attended investment seminars on a regular basis. His full-time job was working for Captiva, and he paid himself a salary of approximately $90,000 annually.

There were over one thousand trades a year, and over the three-year period in question—1986, 1987, and 1988—the trading activity averaged about $16 million a year. As you can see, he was quite good at picking profitable money managers and making money.

More specifically his picture looked like this:

Year	Trades	Gross Receipts	Gains
1986	1,140	$16,636,674	$7,501,905
1987	1,569	18,506,218	4,308,066
1988	1,136	14,547,758	535,917

The expenses he wrote off against this income were substantial, but nowhere near the magnitude of his income. The expenses included investment management fees, bank service charges, legal and professional fees, office rent, interest, postage and office, custodial fees, and other miscellaneous trading expenses. The sum totals of expenses for the three years were as follows:

Year	Total Schedule C Expenses
1986	$1,276,124
1987	1,433,385
1988	1,364,917

Even after expenses, he still had a nice profit, on which he paid tax!

In addition to having capital "traded" by money managers, a substantial portion of Mr. Mayer's equity was tied up in other *venture capital activities*. The following schedule reflects this activity:

Date	Amount in Venture Capital
12/31/86	45.61% of funds
12/31/87	49.21% of funds
12/31/88	44.91% of funds

This was viewed by the Tax Court as a significant factor in the decision.

For this and several other reasons I will now discuss, the Tax Court determined that *Fredrick Mayer was an investor, not a trader.* They reconfirmed several requirements that they had already determined as factors in establishing Trader Status. In other words, they broke no new ground broken here, but rather reinforced what they have been and are still looking for. But there were some other interesting issues raised by the IRS and this case, some of which are still not resolved. I will deal with those in a minute.

In determining whether a taxpayer who manages his own investments is either a trader or an investor, the courts will look to three *predominant but nonexclusive* factors:

1. The taxpayer's investment intent.
2. The nature of the income to be derived from the activity.
3. The frequency, extent, and regularity of the transactions.

Thus what the courts are saying is that the taxpayer's activity constitutes trading if, and only if, these conditions are true: First, that the trading is substantial—he trades a lot. Second, that the trader seeks to catch short-term swings in daily market movements and to profit from these changes. He must trade in this manner, rather than profiting from a longer-term holding of investments. Third, trading income must be a substantial part of his investment income (interest, dividends, and capital gains).

Mr. Mayer, it was determined, met the first of these criteria—in each year in question, his trading was substantial, both in dollar amount and in number of trades.

Thus, whether he was a trader hinged on whether he sought to capitalize on short-term swings in the market, to produce substantial trading income. Mr. Mayer admitted that he was in the market for longer-term capital appreciation, and, in fact, he put this stated objective into the contracts he established with his money managers.

The court stated that it took two fundamental criteria into consideration—the length of the holdings and the source of the profit. They looked at his investments and determined the following facts. For the years in question, the securities sold had weighted holding periods of:

Year	Weighted Average Holding Period
1986	317 days
1987	439 days
1988	415 days

For these three years, the percentage of stocks with holding periods of 30 days or less ranged from 0.01 percent to 5.41 percent. By contrast the percentage of stocks with holding periods of *a year or more* ranged from 32.47 percent to 44.17 percent. Approximately two-thirds or more of Mayer's stocks sold during any year were held *longer than six months.* Additionally, Mayer did not allocate *any of his expenses* to reflect these investment activities! He took them all as *trading expenses.*

Recall that the amount of money invested in venture capital activities was significant. These were longer-term investments, often taking years to bring income. These investments tied up the funds so that they could not be used for short-term trading and provided further evidence that Mayer's objective was *not* short-term trading.

The nature of the income was also a problem. The majority of the annual income came from interest, dividends, and long-term (L-T) capital gains—not from short-term (S-T) trading. These figures reflect the comparatively low percentage of trading income:

Year	L-T Gains	Dividends	Interest	S-T Gains—% Income
1986	$6,483,428	$ 548,299	$853,579	$1,018,477—11.44%
1987	3,666,105	590,761	919,381	641,961—11.03
1988	177,060	1,049,087	787,783	358,857—15.12

As you can see, the courts had good reason to consider Mr. Mayer an investor, not a trader.

As I mentioned, there were several *other issues* raised and addressed in this case. I will mention them briefly and give you their significance, but a complete discussion of these issues would each take another full report. These other issues were raised:

- Mayer stated that if the court ruled he was not a trader, he wanted *to capitalize* the expenses and make them part of the cost of acquiring the asset—to deduct the expenses in that manner. There is some precedent in the courts for this, and under certain circumstances it has been permitted. However, the courts refused his request and determined that it was not appropriate in this instance.
- Mayer stated that if he could not take the course of action just mentioned, then he wanted to take the income as *passive income*—so that he could write off his passive activity losses against it. The courts ruled that it was, in fact, portfolio income, not passive income, and that under no circumstances could it be taken as passive.

Furthermore, I believe, this position taken by Mayer was contradictory to the position he first took of being an *active* trader. It did not make sense. One cannot be both active and passive with respect to the same activity—for tax purposes at least.

- There was another potentially significant issue raised by the Internal Revenue Service. They took the stance in their brief that *if a trader gives up full discretion* of his trading accounts to a money manager, even if he actively monitors that manager, *he is an investor by doing so.* In other words, they argued that the mere fact that a taxpayer cedes full discretion over trading activity to money managers precludes classification as a trader—even if all other criteria are met.

  This issue could be serious because, although the *courts did not rule on this,* it indicates the first time the IRS has taken this position. (The court did not get to this issue because they had already determined from the other factors that Mayer did not meet the criteria for Trader Status.) Clearly, for the IRS to introduce this issue and apparently want to litigate it is significant.

  One of my contacts at the IRS recently informed me that although there is no *official stance* on the matter (i.e., no position paper has been written), the IRS does have an *unofficial position* on it.

  There are times when it may allow Trader Status, and other times when it will probably not. It depends largely on how the money manager–trader relationship is established between the manager and the client.

In my practice, I am now working closely with those clients who use money managers. We are striving to put safeguards in place to make the situation more favorable to them. The use of money managers raises serious questions, such as how much of the portfolios can be managed by money managers, what language should be put into agreements between traders and money managers, how the trader can keep some discretion on the account, how other types of trading vehicles are treated (i.e., partnerships), and many more relevant issues.

All in all, *the case for declaring Trader Status has been strengthened by the Mayer decision.* The courts once again have laid out the factors that are necessary for a person to qualify—and this is the second time in two years that this has been done. This is no less than a judicial attempt to let traders/investors know more definitively what they are looking for. Additional questions were raised, however, and in time more of the answers will be determined. But for now, *if you meet the basic criteria for Trader Status, it is one of the most effective tax saving techniques available today under current law.*

Note: Because no definitive ruling on using money managers was established, you are advised to make an agreement with your manager that reflects the IRS desire for you to retain final control in this matter. Have it put in writing that you still maintain the final say in all trades—not giving up full discretion to the manager.

THE CASE OF RUDOLPH STEFFLER

1995 (for the years ending 1985, 1986, 1987).

The question resolved in this case was if there was substantial trading to constitute Trader Status.

Rudolph Steffler involved the years 1985, 1986, and 1987 and was settled in June 1995. This is a case that upset a lot of people. In fact, Joe Gelband wrote about this case in *Barron's* in September 1995 along with the *Paoli* decision, the next case we're going to talk about. What Gelband decided, by looking at both of these cases, was that Trader Status is becoming a lot more difficult to claim. That may, in fact, be the case, but I don't think the *Steffler* decision is anything to be upset about. Let me tell you why.

In *Steffler,* the court questioned whether or not the pattern of trading was frequent, regular, and continuous enough to constitute a business. Was there substantial trading? The court ruled that the number of commodity trades and the number of days in which Steffler traded were not substantial enough to have him qualify as a trader. Let's look at what he did: Steffler made just 5 trades in 1985, 8 trades in 1986, and 14 trades in 1987. He traded 27 times over a three-year period on 27 different days, and he claimed Trader Status. Was he a trader? Does this level of activity constitute substantial trading? The courts said that it didn't.

Now, if he had documented the fact that even though he traded on 27 days in three years and if he had documented the fact that he studied the markets and chose not to trade on those other days, would that have been enough to justify him as a trader? I don't know if 27 trades in three years on 27 different days is enough to constitute substantial activity.

I'll tell you something significant though—the courts did not penalize him. Although they charged him with tax and with interest, they didn't put what's known as a "tax-motivated transaction" label on it. They didn't charge him penalties—and they could have. They can charge up to 50 percent in penalties and more if they feel it was tax motivated. They didn't do that on Steffler's trading income. What that action shows me is that if you can substantiate your position, if you have records for being a trader, you should go ahead and take the chance. This was good news!

THE CASE OF STEPHEN A. PAOLI

1991 (for the year ended 1982).

The issue to be resolved in this case was whether or not the trading was frequent, regular, and continuous enough to constitute Trader Status.

Let's look at the case that is the most disturbing one for me, that of *Stephen A. Paoli,* which came out in 1991.

Paoli claimed Trader Status in 1982. Again, the question was whether trading was frequent, regular, continuous, and substantial enough to be considered a business. The courts made the distinction between an activity *that is entered into for profit* as opposed to one *that is a business.* And they went further—let's look at some of the details.

The courts said the burden of proof that a person has a business is on the taxpayer, especially in the case of an investor claiming Trader Status. In other words, the burden of proof is on *you* to prove that what you're doing is frequent, regular, continuous enough, and substantial enough to be considered a business, *especially* when you're investing your own account.

You have to prove that you're trading instead of investing. Let's look at the case, and I'll tell you why I find this case so disturbing. In 1982, Paoli had *326 transactions.*

- 205 of these transactions, or almost 63 percent, were held less than 30 days.
- 40 percent of all his trades were made during a one-month period.
- 71 percent of the trades were made over four months.
- He only made one trade in October and no trades in November and December.

What the court said was that this was *substantial* trading, but that it was not done on a frequent, regular, and continuous basis, which is necessary for Trader Status.

Quite frankly, I think this decision is a mockery of the law, made because the courts did not fully understand what is involved in trading. My opinion is that to be a profitable trader, it is just as important *not* to trade as it is to trade.

Many times you've got to look at the market and say, *"Today I choose not to trade."* But remember, there was a three-month period in which he only had one trade, and he said that he put in between four and five hours a day, every single day of the year. There was a *credibility* problem with Paoli. I'll go into the details in a second.

The courts also said that the *linkage of his expenses, particularly interest,* was not definitively established between his trading business and his deductions. Paoli deducted $64,000 of interest, $32,000 of that interest was from accounts that only had 4 percent of the trades. One of his accounts, Dean Witter, had no trades; it was an investment account. He deducted $8,000 of interest from Dean Witter and $24,000 of interest from E.F. Hutton, which was only 4 percent of the trades (the rest was investments).

He didn't allocate any part of his investment interest expense to investments. He took the entire $64,000 as trading interest. He should have allocated half of that interest—$32,000—to investments, but he *deducted it all.* This was the first chink in his credibility. It looked like a scam to the courts.

Paoli also received $100,000 in management fees from his manufacturing company. This led the courts to rule that his was not a valid business. The burden of proof is on the taxpayer to establish that trading is a valid business other than an activity entered into for profit.

The business of trading is different from every other business. You own a shoe store, you only make profit in one month, that's still a business, even if you closed down after a month. The business of trading is different. It has slightly different standards. These cases are coming out now, and the courts are looking at them a little more closely.

Paoli took the hard-and-fast position that he devoted four to five hours every day to trading, even though there were eight months in which he had very little activity. He said he devoted that time even in the months that he did not trade. He didn't establish it, although he said he did it. The court didn't believe him. The opinion reads: "The petitioner testified that he spent four to five hours every day engaged in his stock purchase and sale activity. While his testimony would tend to support his claim that the activity constituted a trade or business, we find it unconvincing."

The court is saying that if Paoli had supported that claim, even though he didn't trade, it would have ruled in his favor. But the court found it unconvincing. "We find it especially hard to believe, for example, that the petitioner spent four to five hours every day in October, November, and December making only one sale and no purchase of stock during this three-month period. We do not accept Mr. Paoli's testimony on this claim."

Clearly, he had a substantial source of income unrelated to his stock activity. Remember? He earned $100,000 managing his company and thus was not required to rely on trading activity as his needs of livelihood. "We do not accept the petitioner's brief testimony that he spent four hours a day throughout the year engaged in this activity. We cannot fairly conclude that the petitioner has satisfied this burden of proof."

It is important to note that the courts are stricter, will hold a Trader to higher standards, if he or she has another substantial source of income and is *not trading as a full-time job.* The court implied that if it had believed that Paoli spent this time trading every day, then it would have accepted his position.

If you have substantial income from somewhere else, for example, investments, it may be harder to prove that you're in the trading business as a business, which is what the courts are looking for. They're looking for someone who trades frequently, regularly, and continuously. So how can you make your case more credible if you don't trade every day—if you take time off, or if you only trade part of the time? Allocate some of your expenses to investments. And keep a *trading log*. If you spend substantial time studying and analyzing the markets, keep a log—a trading diary—of your activity. Have it notarized on a monthly basis. If you spend 20 days a month (the normal number of trading days during the month) studying the markets and you trade on only two or three days, having decided on the other 17 days that it's not good for you to trade, write it in your diary. Show that you put the time into your activity. Make your credibility your number-one concern because it is that important.

Although these cases were decided against the taxpayers, it is my overall opinion that they strengthened the concept of Trader Status and the taxpayer's ability to use it. The decisions added validity to the existence of the Trader Status and gave taxpayers more specific guidelines for taking the Trader Status position.

If you use the logs provided in this book in Appendix H, you will ensure the maximum position for Trader Status.

TRADER STATUS—OTHER CASES

Cases in Which Trader Status *Was* Allowed

1. *Snyder v. Commissioner* (1935): The Supreme Court stated that a taxpayer can be involved in the "business" of trading securities.
2. *Higgins v. Commissioner* (1941): The Supreme Court ruled that whether or not the trading activities of a taxpayer constitute carrying on a business, an examination of the facts is required in each case.
3. *Fuld v. Commissioner* (1943): Taxpayers were held to be Traders because of a large number of trades, none of which were held for as long as *two years*.
4. *Commissioner v. Nubar* (1951): It was held that the extensive trading of stocks and futures constituted engaging in a trade or a business.

5. *Kemon v. Commissioner* (1953): The court determined that Traders are sellers who take advantage of short-term price fluctuations to sell at a gain over cost.
6. *Liang v. Commissioner* (1955): Relevant considerations to Trader Status is the intent of the Trader to derive profits from frequent trading.
7. *Reinach v. Commissioner* (1967): Option writer did not have to prove that this activity was a trade or a business due to the nature of the instrument (options).
8. *Marlowe King v. Commissioner* (1978): Futures Trader was allowed to deduct all expenses incurred with business of trading futures, even though some gains were long term. Trader's business of trading futures was upheld because of the nature of futures contracts.
9. *Levin v. United States* (1979): A Trader is an active investor because he or she does not passively accumulate earnings but rather manipulates his or her holdings. A Trader's profits are derived through trading.
10. *Ropfogel v. United States* (1992): U.S. District Court (Kansas) determined that criteria for Trader Status is comprised of six factors.

Cases in Which Trader Status Was Disallowed but Guidelines Were Established

Note that the issue of Trader Status, and the category, was not denied; but rather its existence was reinforced, even though these specific cases were denied. The courts just provided more guidelines for taxpayers to follow:

1. *Purvis v. Commissioner* (1976): Attorney denied status for failure to file Schedule C.
2. *Moeller v. United States* (1983): Despite full-time management of securities and large investments, taxpayers were not Traders because their investments were long term.
3. *Stephen A. Paoli* (1991): Trading deemed not to be frequent, regular, and continuous. Credibility was the issue.
4. *Frederick R. Mayer* (1994): Trading advisers were objected to by the IRS in determination of Trader Status—courts never ruled on this issue. Trader Status was denied because advisers were *investors*.
5. *Rudolph Steffler* (1995): Distinction was made between "business" and "activity entered into for profit." Substantial number of trades was the key issue.

4

The 1997 Trader's Tax Act—The Most Significant Changes for the Trader and the Investor since 1986

The Tax Reform Act of 1986 was sold to the American public as being "a tax simplification package." In reality it turned out to be the most far-reaching, significant, and complicated piece of tax legislation ever passed, especially for the American investor. There were two pieces of tax legislation and one major tax act passed between 1986 and 2001, the 1997 Tax Act being the most significant for the trader. The Omnibus Budget Reconciliation Act (OBRA) of 1990 and the Revenue Reconciliation Act of 1993 were minor in comparison to the Taxpayers' Relief Act of 1997.

In this section, I will go into the major areas of change, for investors and traders of stock and commodity futures and futures options, which were affected by the 1997 Taxpayers' Relief Act.

THE TOP 10 LIST OF THINGS TO KNOW

In many ways, the Taxpayers' Relief Act of 1997 should be called the "*Traders'* Tax Relief Act of 1997," or better yet the "Traders' Tax Survival Act of 1997." Here is a list of the top 10 reasons why the name should be changed:

10. *Long-Term Capital Gains Tax Is Reduced.* An investor's maximum rate on net capital gains has been reduced from 28 percent to 20 percent. Gains currently taxed at 15 percent will be taxed at 10 percent.

More specific details on this provision to follow in the section entitled "Capital Gains or Loss Rules."

9. *Commodities Are Still Taxed as 60 Percent Long-Term Capital Gains.* And even more amazingly, the 60 percent part will be taxed at the *lowest rate*—no matter how long you have held the commodity! That means a 20 percent and in some cases a 10 percent tax rate on most of the gain. This applies to all Section 1256 transactions, including options on commodities and certain index options (OEX and certain others) as addressed in my book *The Traders' Tax Survival Guide.*

Trading commodities such as Standard & Poor's (S&P) futures instead of mutual funds or stocks can save you up to 50 percent tax on most of the gain!

8. *Both Deductible and Nonretirement Plans Are Now More Accessible to a Majority of Traders.* The observation of many lawmakers and other people is that Americans are not saving enough money to retire and to provide for long-term financial goals. (This is a subject I address in this book in Chapter 6.) Many observers believe also that they must address the concerns that they have with regard to these issues. In order to do so, and in order to boost people's savings for retirement, they put the following provisions into effect in the 1997 tax law. As I mentioned in the Preface, the 2001 Tax Act added its own twist.

- *Deductions for IRA Contributions.* For a number of years, tax-law restrictions have made it impossible for many people to fund individual retirement accounts (IRAs) on a fully tax deductible basis. The individuals who have been affected are those who are considered to have been "active participants" in employer-sponsored retirement plans and who have an adjusted gross income (AGI) over specific levels.

  For married couples, the active participation of one spouse in an employer-sponsored plan has been enough to trigger possible limitations on IRA deductions for both spouses if the AGI limits are exceeded.

  The new tax law restores the IRA deduction for certain taxpayers (subject to income limitations) by raising the AGI limits applicable to active participants and by liberalizing the "tainted spouse provision."
- *Roth IRAs–a New Nondeductible IRA.* An improved version of a nondeductible IRA is now called the Roth IRA, and it is available to many taxpayers today (subject to some income restrictions). Contributions to the Roth IRA will not be deductible. It is considered to be a "backloaded IRA."

But account holders will have the ability to withdraw funds completely tax free under certain conditions. Previously, investments built up tax deferred in nondeductible IRAs, but the earnings were subject to taxes at the time of withdrawal. This is changed in the Roth IRA. Taxpayers may also roll over amounts from existing deductible and nondeductible IRAs to a Roth IRA (subject to some AGI restrictions). However, any taxable amounts that are rolled over from a current IRA must be included in income. If the rollover is made before 1999, the income is includable and prorated over the next four tax years. This still makes sense for many profitable traders.

- *Penalty-Free Early Withdrawals.* Some people are hesitant to place their savings in an IRA because they don't want to incur a 10 percent penalty should they need to withdraw the funds before age 59½. Although the tax code does permit pre-age 59½ withdrawals without penalty in some circumstances (disability, for example), these situations are limited. The new tax law increases the number. In addition to education-related withdrawals, the new tax law allows distributions for qualifying first-time home-buying expenses for up to $10,000 without penalty effective for 1998 and subsequent years.
- *Excess Retirement Accumulations.* An additional 15 percent excess accumulation tax used to be charged on certain retirement plan distributions that exceeded $160,000 or more, adjusted for the cost-of-living adjustment (COLA) amounts. This 15 percent "success tax" has been repealed. There had been a window of opportunity up through the year 2000 for people to withdraw this amount without incurring excess accumulation tax; however, this has now been repealed permanently.

7. *Education Tax Incentives Are Another Gift to Taxpayers.* Many students and their families will have new opportunities to save taxes as a result of the "Traders' Tax Survival Act of 1997."

- *Hope and Lifetime Learning Credits.* Starting in 1998 a new Hope scholarship credit became available against federal income taxes for qualified tuition and related expenses paid for a student's first two years of postsecondary education at eligible educational institutions. The qualified expenses must be incurred on behalf of the taxpayer, the taxpayer's spouse, or a dependent.

- *Education Loan Interest.* In repealing the tax deduction for personal interest, the Tax Reform Act of 1986 rendered most interest paid on student loans nondeductible. Now the situation is going to change for some taxpayers.

  The new tax law allows some taxpayers who pay interest on qualified higher education loans taken for themselves, their spouses, or any dependent (as of the time the debt was incurred) to deduct interest paid during the first 60 months (whether or not they are consecutive months) in which interest payments are required on the loan. Again, these breaks disappear when AGI exceeds certain levels.
- *Educational IRAs.* The new law creates a new type of tax-favored IRA that is designed to be used by those saving for a child's future education expenses. Beginning in 1998 annual, nondeductible contributions of up to $500 per beneficiary may be made until the time the beneficiary turns age 18. Withdrawals to pay qualified higher education expenses of the child (the designated account beneficiary) are tax free.

  The $500 permissible contribution is phased out once again for taxpayers with modified AGI above certain levels—$95,000 for a single person, ($150,000 on a joint return). No contribution to an educational IRA is allowed once modified AGI is higher than $110,000, ($160,000 on a joint return).
- *Other Tax Breaks for Education.* Additional provisions in the new tax law are designed to help students and their families. They include:

  —*Increased employer-paid educational assistance.*
  —*Penalty-free IRA withdrawals, as discussed previously.*
  —*Qualified tuition programs.* If otherwise eligible, public or private schools of higher education may establish tax-exempted, prepaid tuition programs effective as of 1998. Previously, such programs had to be state sponsored.

6. *Changes in Estate and Gift Taxes Benefit the Successful Trader and Investor.* When many people think of taxes, income taxes are the ones that come to mind. Few people realize, however, that the gift and the estate taxes—the so-called transfer taxes—can also put an extremely heavy burden on the taxpayer with rates that range as high as 55 percent on cumulative taxable transfers made during one's lifetime and at one's death.

The 1997 tax law reduced estate taxes for many individuals, but the 2001 Tax Act changed this further as discussed in the Preface.

5. *The Tax on the Gain from the Sale of Principal Residence Is Greatly Reduced.* For years, two breaks have been available on capital gains earned on the sale of a principal residence: First, homeowners of any age have been able to defer all or part of their gain by buying a qualifying replacement residence within two years before or after the sale. Second, homeowners aged 55 or older could permanently exclude up to $125,000 of gain from gross income by making a one-time special election.

The new tax, for sales made after May 6, 1997, does away with these two breaks, replacing them with a new, universal exclusion that should benefit most homeowners. Under the new provision, an exclusion for gain of up to $250,000 is available to individuals other than married couples filing a joint return. For joint returns filed for the year of the sale, the exclusion applies to as much as $500,000 of the gain.

There are certain phaseouts if your property has been depreciated for business use, and it may be worthwhile consulting a qualified tax accountant to determine if this break applies fully for you or is phased out.

4. *Child Tax Credit Relief Is Expanded for Many Taxpayers.* Early in the budget deal-making process, families with children were targeted as a group deserving relief. But eligibility for child care credit and the size of the credit were big questions. These questions were resolved only after very, very tough negotiations between lawmakers and the Clinton administration. The results pleased many taxpayers.

In general, starting in 1998, taxpayers could claim a tax credit for each "qualifying child." The credit was for $400 per child in 1998 and $500 per child in 1999 and later years. A "qualifying child" is one who:

- Is the taxpayer's dependent.
- Has not attained the age of 17 as of the close of the calendar year in which the taxpayer's taxable year begins.
- Is a taxpayer's son or daughter (by blood or legally adopted) or descendent of either, a stepson or stepdaughter, or an eligible foster child.
- Is a U.S. citizen, a national, or a legal resident.

Again, there are certain income phaseouts under the new law.

3. *The Alternative Minimum Tax Does Not Apply to the Preferences on Long-Term Capital Savings. Question:* How many readers think that the alternative minimum tax is a separate tax calculation that the

government makes and comes up with and then allows you to pick the *lower* of these two tax rates?

For those of you who answered yes, I have a bridge somewhere out in Brooklyn that I think you'd be interested in.

Answer: The *alternative minimum tax (AMT)* is a separate tax calculation that adds back certain deductions and then recalculates your tax including the deductions you took. At that point, the government makes you pick the higher of the two tax rates as being the tax that you owe. At certain income levels, you lose *all* deductions. So you must consider the AMT in doing tax planning strategies.

The alternative minimum tax system is specifically designed to ensure that individuals who benefit from regular deductions and tax preferences in computing their normal taxes will still pay what the law considers to be their fair share of taxes. For some time, analysts have been predicting that many more individuals would have to pay alternative minimum tax in the future unless the alternative minimum tax exemption amounts were raised.

But, guess what? This law actually had some breaks with regard to the AMT for traders: First, trading expenses included on Schedule C are still not subject to the alternative minimum tax. Second, the capital gains preference exclusion as discussed in #10 and #9 is not subject to the AMT.

2. *The Home Office Now Becomes Available for Many More Traders.* In 1993, the U.S. Supreme Court handed down a decision that effectively eliminated the ability of many individuals to claim tax deductions for home office expenses such as depreciation, utilities, and repairs.

The basic effect of that decision, however, was to deny a home office deduction to many individuals who use their homes regularly and exclusively for some functions related to their trades or business (for example, administrative work) but whose *principal place of business* is deemed to be elsewhere. In this situation, a home office deduction may not be claimed unless the home office is either (1) in a separate structure not attached to the dwelling unit or (2) used as a place of business to meet with patients, clients or customers in a normal course of business.

However, traders have had the ability to deduct home offices in many more cases. In recognition of the fact that a growing number of individuals are managing their business activities and, in fact, trading from their homes, Congress modified the law, effective for taxable years beginning after 1998, to provide that a home office qualifies as a "principal place of business" (1) if the home office is used by the taxpayer to conduct administrative or management activities of a trade or business and (2) if there is no other fixed location of the trade or business where the taxpayer conducts substantial, administrative, or management activities of the trade or business.

This is a big break for traders, liberalizing the home office deduction for those traders who also trade from other places outside of the home. Thus, even if an individual carries out administrative or management activities while traveling (for example, from a hotel room or car), the home office deduction will still be available. Similarly, if an individual does occasional paperwork or other administrative tasks at a fixed location of the business outside of the home, it will still be possible to claim a home office deduction if the other requirements are met. Taking the home office deductions may actually add credibility to your claiming Trader Status.

Trader Status Was Finally Acknowledged in the Tax Law.

Did they approve Trader Status? No.

Did they deny it? No.

Do they even know that we're out there? You bet they do!

For the first time in Tax Reform History, Congress acknowledged our existence. They addressed the Trader Status issue; however, they let the definition of who qualifies stay purposely vague.

Because of this, however, we can still defer to the cases coming down from the tax court, the Supreme Court, and the various district courts as to our interpretation of who qualifies for Trader Status and the various other issues that we must address with regard to what the criteria are. (There will be more on this in following chapters.)

SECTION 475 FOR TRADERS OF THEIR OWN ACCOUNTS

Mark-to-Market Provisions—Section 475 Transactions

Prior tax law. Under the tax changes in the 1993 legislation, specifically Section 475, a dealer *must* value his inventory at market value and mark it to market at year-end if the security is considered to be inventory to him. Thus, any securities dealer is now being taxed on *unrealized appreciation* in his or her inventory account at year-end.

The securities that are identified by the dealer as being investments, however, are not subject to the tax on unrealized gains or losses, and they need not be marked to market at year-end. When a securities dealer initiates a position as a dealer, he or she must decide whether to put the security into his or her inventory account or investment account. Securities that are held for investments by dealers must be identified in the dealer's records by the close of business on the day of acquisition to qualify for capital gains treatment. Losses from the sale of investment securities are capital losses where the security was identified as being held for investment purposes.

The 1997 tax law. There have been several major revisions to Section 475 and related sections. The 1997 tax act allows security traders, commodity traders, and commodity dealers to *elect* mark-to-market accounting similar to the *requirement* that currently exists for securities dealers. The election applies to tax years ending after August 5, 1997.

Commodity dealers and traders of securities or commodities were not previously covered under IRS Code Section 475. Traders of securities were not covered because they did not buy or sell to customers as required by Section 475. Commodity *dealers* and traders of commodities were not covered by Section 475 because commodity derivatives were not considered securities for the purpose of Section 475.

Under the new law, the category of taxpayer being considered is *extremely* important because securities dealers are still *required* to use mark to market. However, securities traders, commodities dealers, and traders of commodities may *elect* to use mark-to-market methods. Therefore, the trader-versus-dealer distinction is extremely important in this sense.

Similarly, investors are not permitted to mark to market their positions, and traders are. Hence, the distinction between an investor and a trader becomes even more important under the new tax law. (See the introduction where I make the distinction between the three categories of taxpayer.)

Commodities dealers who elect to mark to market will be required to value their inventory of commodities at fair market value. Generally, any noninventory commodity or commodity-based derivative held at year-end will be treated as if it were sold for its fair market value. The definition of a *commodity* has been expanded to include options, forwards, futures, short positions, notional principal contracts, or other derivatives for which a commodity is the underlying property for the purpose of Section 475. The difference now is that by marking the position to market, *any gain or loss will be considered ordinary and will not qualify for Section 1256 treatment. Any loss would also be considered ordinary and not subject to the $3,000-per-year net limitation.*

The election does not require the consent of the IRS if it is made for the first tax year ending after August 5, 1997. However, once an election is made, it cannot be revoked without permission of the IRS. Adjustments are made to the actual gain or loss when property is ultimately sold after having been marked to market under this election.

Securities or commodities held for investment are excluded. Only securities or commodities used in the business of traders and commodities dealers can be marked to market. Investment securities must be identified as not subject to the election. This identification must be made in the books and records. Taxpayers must be able to demonstrate by clear and convincing evidence to the satisfaction of the IRS that the identified property has no connection to the business activities of the trader or dealer. In addition, any security that hedges another security cannot be classified as investment property. Investment securities and commodities held on the date of enactment must be identified within 30 days of the enactment.

Separate elections must be made for each specific business of taxpayers. No clear method for making the election is indicated as of yet. An election under these rules is considered a change in accounting. Code Section 481 adjustments due to the change are taken into account over four years. Revenue Procedure (Rev. Proc.) 99-17 was put out in March 1999 to clarify some of these issues. This is still a very convoluted subject.

If the mark-to-market election is made, the character of income or loss will be considered ordinary. Therefore, making this election should not be done without careful planning and decision making. Under the Technical Corrections Act (HR 2645), it was decided that the income, although ordinary, will not be considered self-employment income. *This could be a big bonus for traders,* but the election should be made only after consulting a competent tax professional.

Historically, traders have always recognized capital gains and losses as not ordinary. Because the election will result in ordinary gain or loss, the capital loss limitation rules as well as Sections 263(g), 263A, 1256(a) and the short-sale rules (IRC 1233) and wash sale rules (IRC 1091) will *not* apply to mark-to-market properties.

Wash Sale Rules

The *wash sale rule* defers recognition of losses arising from the sale of securities if substantially identical property is acquired within a period of 30 days prior to or 30 days subsequent to the sale. This prevents a taxpayer from recognizing a sale in one year and instituting the exact same position immediately. Regulations that were adopted by the IRS extend the modified wash sale rules to straddles.

If a taxpayer disposes of part of a straddle, any loss is disallowed to the extent of any unrecognized gain at year-end. The disallowed loss is carried over to subsequent years. These provisions differ from wash sale rules with regard to securities in that the regulation disallows losses only to the extent of unrealized gains. The wash sale rule for securities disallows the entire loss.

The new tax law has essentially left this provision unchanged except as addressed in changes to Section 475. (See Appendix I for more detail on the wash sale rule.)

Short Sale Rules

A *short stock sale* occurs when an individual contracts to sell stock that he or she does not own or does not wish to deliver at the time of the sale. A short sale seller usually borrows the stock for delivery to the buyer.

At a later date, the short seller will repay the borrowed shares by either purchasing those shares or by relinquishing the shares that he or she already held but did not want to give up at the time the short sale was made. The seller will usually pay interest for the privilege of having borrowed the stock to sell short. This will be treated as investment interest expense for tax purposes.

If a short seller "shorts against the box," he or she already owns the stock at the date it is shorted but chooses to short shares other than the ones he or she owns. A shorting-against-the-box transaction had been treated as identical to that of simply shorting the stock under the old law.

The act of delivering the stock to the lender (repaying) is called "closing the short sale." This is also true in the case of shorting against the box. In both cases, this is the point that the taxable event occurs.

When a stock is sold short and the transaction is closed, a seller will realize a gain on the transaction if the price paid for the borrowed shares is lower than the price for which the shares were sold. If the seller covers at a higher price, he or she will realize a capital loss.

In other words, it was possible for an investor to short a stock, even though he or she owned it at the time. This used to allow for the locking in of gains on a stock, without actually selling that stock. And, in doing so, an investor used to be able to postpone the realization of capital gains that would then be incurred and reported by the outright sale of the stock.

The straddle regulations adopt a modified short sale rule for offsetting positions to prevent an investor from using non-1256 straddles to convert short-term capital gains into long-term capital gains or vice versa. The holding period from the part of the position that is the straddle does not begin until the date the straddle terminates, unless the entire position was long-term before the straddle was established. Positions that fall into this category as being a straddle have no holding period to consider while the straddle is in place; for existing positions held short-term that then become part of the straddle, the holding period is eliminated and begins again when the straddle is ended. Where positions were held long-term prior to establishing the straddle, loss on any position in the straddle will be treated as long-term capital loss.

These provisions have been drastically changed as a result of the Taxpayers' Relief Act of 1997. Shorting against the box has essentially been eliminated.

SUMMARY AND CONCLUSION

The Taxpayers' Relief Act of 1997 was the most sweeping tax legislation for traders since the *Tax Reform Act of 1986.* Little of that has been changed since it was passed. The 2001 Tax Act put its own spin on the 1997 changes, but the major benefits remain.

5

The Triple Crown

THE MOST EFFECTIVE TAX-SAVING STRATEGY I HAVE EVER KNOWN

In baseball as well as horse racing, there is a special significance to the "Triple Crown." I have named my first strategy the Triple Crown because it is a three-step plan that accomplishes three very important goals. This section will show you how to cut your current taxes by up to 50 percent, how to build up substantial wealth for retirement, and ultimately how to create a multimillion dollar estate for your heirs—tax free.

STEP 1—THE BUSINESS

The Basics

Most people don't realize that having a business is truly the last great tax reduction opportunity left in America today. There are really two tax systems in existence for U.S. citizens. One is for employees; the second is for employers—the owners of businesses.

If you're an employee, you can deduct itemized deductions *below the line,* such as mortgage interest, real estate taxes, charitable contributions, IRA contributions, and other miscellaneous itemized deductions. However, if you are a business owner, you get all sorts of deductions in addition to the ones that employees get. And these deductions are not only more numerous but are also deducted in a *more advantageous manner—above the line,* rather than below it.

Establish a Business

This is step one of my three-step plan.

People already in business have the structure through which they can enact the second and third parts of my strategy. But for those of you not in business, let me say that a business is like money in the bank—it is something everyone should have.

And for those of you who have no business, let me offer you one—*the business of trading.*

Establish a Trading Business

Background. If you read my original work, *The Serious Investor's Tax Survival Guide,* and my follow-up, *The Trader's Tax Survival Guide,* you know that there is a new breed of investor—the trader. In order to understand the exact nature of what a trader does and his or her advantages, you must understand the other types of participants in the market.

The first is the *broker-dealer/market maker.* The function of this participant is defined within the law and is actually quite clear. Under Reg Section 1.471-5, the IRS Code defines "a dealer in securities" as someone who engages in the purchase of securities for resale to customers with the intent of making a profit.

Keep in mind the distinction "resale to customers." The broker-dealer/market maker is a merchant with an established place of business who regularly engages in this practice. He or she therefore treats for-sale securities or commodities as inventory, and these items are treated as *ordinary,* not capital, assets. *This results in the generation of ordinary income or loss, not capital income or loss.*

The Code Section is very specific as to the type of activity required. It states that someone who does business with the intent of facilitating trade for one or more of the major exchanges is a broker-dealer/market maker. It is a legal definition, and, in fact, certain criteria must be fulfilled in order to meet this. This designation also grants certain privileges that go beyond those of an investor. Dealers can deduct, dollar for dollar, any amount of expense they incur in transacting their business.

There is another difference and that is that the broker-dealer/market maker is not limited to the $3,000 per year capital loss to which other taxpayers are (including most traders). *This is a major distinction.* Also, any income generated from these assets will also be considered ordinary *with regard to self-employment tax, retirement plan contributions, self-employed health deduction, and, as of the OBRA tax act of 1993, mark-to-market considerations (Section 475).* Broker-dealer/market makers *must pay self-employment tax* on their trading income.

The factors that indicate that one is a broker-dealer/market maker include selling to outside customers, being licensed by regulatory bodies, maintaining a regular place of business, and owning or leasing a seat on a recognized exchange. The burden of proof of being a broker-dealer/market maker is always on the taxpayer, as is the burden of proof of being a trader. This distinction applies to a dealer in stocks, commodities, options, and all related futures contracts.

An *investor*, on the other hand, is defined in the tax code under Section 263(a) as a person who buys or sells securities *for his or her own account*. Investors are clearly defined as investing for *their own accounts* as opposed to dealers who buy and sell for *resale to customers*.

All expenses of the investing activity are considered to be investment expenses. They are treated as miscellaneous itemized deductions on Schedule A of an investor's tax return and are also subject to significant limitations and phaseouts.

All income is considered to be capital gains income and not subject to self-employment tax (under most circumstances), not eligible for retirement plan contributions, and hence reported on Schedule D. Furthermore, an investor is *always* limited to a $3,000 per year net capital loss deduction, which can be carried forward (or even back, in the case of Section 1256 transactions).

A *trader* is a hybrid category. There is no election on the tax return that one would make to indicate that he or she is a trader. There have been cases decided over the past 65 years in the Supreme Court and in various district Tax Courts that have recognized this hybrid category. The decisions in these cases have recognized that traders are investors who engage in the purchase and sale of securities for their own accounts. However, they do so at such a *high level of activity* that it becomes a business to them.

There are no objective requirements in the tax code to qualify a person as a trader; and until the Taxpayers' Relief Act of 1997, the distinction was barely acknowledged in the IRS Code. It was agreed that the taxpayer must trade in stocks, securities, futures contracts, or options on a relatively short-term basis; however, this classification was purely subjective. But now, in paragraph 341 of the new tax act, Congress has defined *traders* as "taxpayers who are in the business of actively buying, selling or exchanging securities or commodities in the market. On the other hand, dealers deal directly with customers when they regularly buy or sell securities in the course of their business. . . ." *It is significant that Congress acknowledged this classification in the text of the new law.*

Furthermore, on December 17, 1997, the Joint Committee on Taxation issued its report (aka, the Blue Book), to explain the new tax law. On page 180 of this report, Title X, Section A (financial products), subsection 1001(b), the Joint Committee stated: "Traders in securities generally are taxpayers who engage in a trade or business involving active sales or exchanges of securities on the market *rather than to customers."* What the Joint Committee basically has done is allude to, but not strictly defined, a trader.

In Chapter 3 of this book, in the section "Trader Status—Other Cases," I gave a list of what I consider to be the court cases that have been most influential in determining Trader Status. In these cases, the courts looked for someone who:

- Traded on a frequent, regular, and continuous basis.
- Had a substantial number of trades.
- Did short-term trading.
- Spent a substantial amount of time trading.
- Had a small percentage of income derived from dividends.
- Took trading expenses on IRS Schedule C.
- Had an office—whether at home or elsewhere.

What the courts *never tell* you is how *frequent, regular,* and *continuous* the trading must be (although they *do* shed new light on what they consider it to be). They *never tell* you *how many* trades it takes to be considered substantial. They *never tell* you what short-term trading must be in order to qualify you as a trader. They *never tell* you what constitutes a substantial amount of time spent trading. They *never tell* you what amount of dividends they will allow you to earn before they disqualify you from being a trader.

They do tell you that it must be on Schedule C. Although they do not discount a home office, they do require that an office be present. In fact, part of the provisions of the new tax act has liberalized the deduction of a home office.

What these cases do explain is that they have established further criteria for who fits this definition. The details of these three new landmark cases were addressed in Chapter 3.

Implementation. Filing as a trader truly is the best tax shelter available for investors who meet the requirements. With the higher phaseouts, you need as many deductions as possible. For those of you who don't meet the criteria to be a trader, do not despair. I have worked with many investors and helped them to achieve Trader Status.

The results. Here is a brief summary of the major advantages that a trader has over an investor:

- Trading expenses are not subject to a 2 percent to 3 percent floor on Schedule A; investment expenses are. Trading expenses are deducted on Schedule C, dollar for dollar.

- Itemized deductions are not even necessary in order to deduct trading expenses. A trader can take a standard deduction and, in addition to this, still deduct trading expenses on Schedule C.
- Investment seminars, which were determined as nondeductible to investors in the 1986 tax act, are now considered trading seminars and are still deductible.
- Investment interest expense, which was severely limited under the 1986 tax act, is now considered to be trading interest (a normal business expense) and is 100 percent deductible.
- Section 179 depreciation, which was not allowed to investors, is now available to traders.
- The home office expense, which cannot be deducted by investors, now becomes deductible and, in fact, becomes one of the criteria in establishing Trader Status.

To sum up, traders still receive capital gain or loss treatment on the purchase or sale of their transactions; however, the related expenses may be deducted from ordinary income as a necessary business expense. This is a big benefit.

Although the trader is still subject to a $3,000 per year net capital loss deduction for any trading loss, he or she may deduct 100 percent of business expenses as ordinary. With the passage of the Taxpayers' Relief Act of 1997, *this $3,000 limitation can be avoided if the trader elects to mark-to-market under Code Section 475.* If you are a trader, making a Section 475 election allows you to capitalize on some of the perks from this new bill. You can now purchase up to $18,000 in equipment and get a one-time write-off annually. As long as you have income to cover it, you can deduct up to $18,000 of new purchases on your current tax return. Any computer, business machine, fax, phone, or auto used in business can qualify.

If you are real shrewd, you can time your purchase at year-end and buy some of the items on December 31 and the rest on January 1 of the next year to maximize the write-off for your situation. Remember, you can charge these items on a credit card or a store charge account and, thus, have a record of the purchase on the day the transaction takes place. They do not have to be paid for at that time.

If you qualify for Trader Status and have children, it is a good idea to hire your son or your daughter to work for you and deduct his or her allowance as salary or commission (as long as the reasonableness of compensation test is met). The government has now given us several more options, along with some interesting food for thought—especially with the liberalization of retirement plan and VEBA contributions.

Another Important Component

A trader can elect Section 475 mark-to-market. By doing so, he or she can deduct more than a $3,000 net loss (if he or she had a losing year).

Background. With the passage of the 1993 tax act, broker-dealer/market makers were required through Section 475 to mark their positions to market, thereby forcing them to put all their trading income or losses on Schedule C and not allowing them to carry over any unrealized gains into the next year. This really didn't do much to affect their tax situation, other than preventing them from carrying over gains into the following year. Their income or losses were already reportable on Schedule C.

With the passage of the 1997 tax act, traders were given the option of electing Section 475, thereby granting them the same privilege as dealers. *The major difference here is that if a trader elects Section 475, although the income becomes ordinary income reportable on the 4797, it is not self-employment income.* This was further clarified in the Technical Corrections Act that followed the tax bill. For further clarification of this, see the Congressional Blue Book report that interprets the tax act. On page 181 of this Blue Book report, under an explanation of this mark-to-market provision, the Blue Book states:

> The Act allows security Traders and commodity Traders and dealers to elect application of the mark-to-market accounting rules which apply only the security dealers under prior law . . . Congress intended that gain or loss that is treated as ordinary solely by reason of the election would *not* be treated as other than gain or loss from a capital asset, for purposes of determining an individual's net earnings from self-employment under the Self-employment Contributions Act (Section 1402) . . .

What this is essentially doing is giving the trader a tremendous benefit—the best of both worlds. Traders now have the option of deciding whether to treat their losses as ordinary and still maintain the integrity of keeping the income from being subject to self-employment tax.

Implementation. There is no box to check for one to elect Section 475—as there is no box to check to elect Trader Status. The way to elect Section 475 is to report the income on a 4797.

Important considerations. *Make sure you check with a competent tax adviser before electing Section 475.*

Please do not make this election without consulting with a competent tax professional—the implications of doing it are significant, and the manner in which you make the election is important!

The IRS issued Revenue Procedure 99-17, which changed the timing in which the Section 475 election must be made. It said that for 1998 the election must be made with the filing of the 1998 tax return or the extension for it, whichever comes first. For the 1999 tax return, it must be done at the same time as the 1998 election—with the filing of the 1998 extension.

They also said that for now you can just attach a written statement with the return, but that they would issue a new form to file to make the election in the near future.

One caveat: If you trade commodities or commodity options, you give up some preferred tax treatment. Consult with your tax adviser before making this election to determine if it is appropriate for you. This is serious business—*do not do it yourself!*

To sum up. For the first time in tax-reform history, Congress validated the existence of traders in the 1997 IRS Code. The Technical Corrections Act was then passed and like all tax bills, certain issues that were skipped in the original Tax Act or that needed clarification were addressed.

They addressed the Trader Status issue but let the definition of who qualifies stay purposely vague. Because of this, however, we can still defer to the cases coming down from the Tax Court, the Supreme Court, and the various district courts as to our interpretation of who qualifies for Trader Status and the various other issues that we must address with regard to that criteria.

In the final analysis, a trader is judged by the frequency of trades, the number of trades, the holding period of the trades, the amount of time spent trading, whether substantial dividends are accrued on the trading account, the existence of a Schedule C, and the existence of an office.

In Chapter 3, I included a list of key trader cases over the past 65 years—both favorable and unfavorable. For those of you who don't already have a business, I suggest you qualify for Trader Status—now more than ever, it is important to do so!

STEP 2—THE ENTITY

How to Choose the Proper Entity

The second step to my three-step approach is to put your business in an entity that is most advantageous to you. The preferred structure of choice, as far as I am concerned, is the establishment of a corporation as general partner within a limited partnership. For those of you who have family members, a family-limited partnership is the ultimate vehicle.

The corporation, which is owned 100 percent by you, becomes a 2 percent owner in the family-limited partnership. The rest of your family can then be given low-percentage shares in this new entity. This is not a requirement, as you can then become a 98 percent limited partner instead. By doing this, you can allow the corporation to earn a management fee for managing the family-limited partnership (your business—more specifically, in this case, a trading business).

It is through this structure that you can draw fees and determine to some extent how much of the income your entities earn by managing the trading business. Earned income can be used for setting up the third component of my three-step approach, a retirement plan and ultimately the VEBA.

This must be done within the parameters of *reasonable compensation* for services rendered.

Background. A trader who trades as a business can do so in one of several ways. He or she can initially set up on a Schedule C and file this as part of the individual income tax return (Form 1040). This is fine to start; however, as one becomes more involved in the business of trading, it is clear that the formation of a separate business entity is the preferred way to go.

The creation of a corporation and a family-limited partnership is ultimately the best way to add flexibility to your trading business as well as to insulate the assets from potential liability. A Schedule C trader, unless he or she elects Section 475 (mark-to-market), reports all income on Schedule D and all expenses as ordinary on Schedule C. Although the expenses are ordinary, the income maintains the character of capital gain income. Because of this, it is not subject to self-employment tax, does not qualify for pension plan contributions, and *does not allow the trader the opportunity to deduct self-employed health deductions.*

The real problem occurs with retirement plan contributions because there is no *self-employment* income. The only way to establish a retirement plan and to allow for the deductions associated with defined benefit and defined contribution plans is by drawing salary against the trading income. A self-employed individual *cannot* accomplish this on a Schedule C. To do this, a trader must establish an entity.

A *C corp* is a corporation that remains a taxable entity within itself. It pays corporate income tax rates, and the profit or loss does not pass through to the individual's tax return. A C corp may, in fact, also be subject to a personal holding company surtax on the income. It is my opinion now that if the trader elects mark to market, Section 475, and the income becomes ordinary within the corporation, then the personal holding company problem may be eliminated.

Another consideration is the fact that C corps are subject to double taxation (see the section on dividends in my original *Trader's Tax Survival Guide).* You would have to provide for a way to get the money out of the corporation without being taxed twice. We have been successful in attaining this, and you should consider the C corp for many reasons. For this reason, we make them 2 percent partners in the FCP and regulate the flow of income to them to fund various programs.

Limited liability companies are far too complex for serious discussion in this limited work; and for the most part, S corps and family-limited partnerships can accomplish the same desired results. The family-limited partnership is discussed in a following section.

An *S corp* is essentially a corporation that acts and looks like a corporation but is taxed on the individual's tax return. A reason for establishing an S corp is that of asset protection. An S corp is a stand-alone entity, although it is taxed on an individual's tax return. Because of this, anybody suing the individual trader would not generally be able to get to the assets of the S corp. On the other hand, anyone suing the S corp would not be able to get at the assets of the trader outside of the corporate entity, if the corporate entity is properly maintained.

A trader should consider forming a separate corporation because it will make him a "small fish in a large pool" for audit purposes. I truly believe that corporations are less subject to audit than are individuals. This is especially true in light of the fact that a trader will generally trade a large number of transactions throughout the year and generate a large amount of gross proceeds. This huge gross proceeds figure, often times in the millions, will be more susceptible to audit on an individual's tax return than on that of a corporation. A corporation, on the other hand, is in a pool with corporations such as Exxon, IBM, and Coca-Cola. For this reason, tax returns with gross proceeds in the millions will not even raise an IRS eyebrow. Million dollar numbers on corporate tax returns are commonplace.

If you have read my books *The Serious Investor's Tax Survival Guide* or *The Trader's Tax Survival Guide,* you will recall that there is also a certain degree of comparison from year to year for audit selection. If somebody decides to be a trader one year and starts generating millions of dollars of gross sales from trades, his or her tax return may be kicked out in a computer comparison between this year and last year.

However, if one switches entities to a corporation, there will not be the discrepancy in the year-to-year figures on the individual's tax return (generated by multi–million dollar gross proceeds). *If your accountants tell you this is not so, fire them—it is!*

Furthermore, in electing Section 475, a trader has effectively made a one-time election for the entity in which he or she is trading. If the trader decides next year or in subsequent years to go back to a non-475 election, he or she cannot do so in the same entity without first asking the IRS for permission. As an individual electing 475, this reversal is a very difficult thing to do. However, as a corporate entity (or LLC) electing 475, it is much easier for a trader to terminate the corporation or LLC, along with the 475 election, and in subsequent years to decide whether he or she wants to elect 475 in a new entity.

Implementation. As a corporation, it is easy to deduct ordinary, normal, and reasonable expenses associated with doing business in the corporation. There should be little question as to the business nature of the entity if it is a corporation. Expenses such as the following become dollar-for-dollar deductions.

- VEBA or other Section 419 expenses.
- Accounting fees.
- Automobile expenses.
- Books and audio/videotape courses on investing.
- Trading seminars.
- Brokerage account management fees.
- Calculators, adding machines, cassette tape recorders, and typewriters.
- Cost of managing investments for a minor.
- Financial advice on audio/videotapes.
- Oral or printed tax advice (such as the cost of *The NEW Trader's Tax Solution* by Ted Tesser or any of his video courses).
- Home computers and software.
- Data-retrieval service.
- Trading advice.
- Business interest expense.
- Legal fees.
- Entertainment and meals during which business is conducted.
- Safe deposit box rental and storage space for trading documents.
- The salary of bookkeepers, accountants, or others who keep your trading records.
- Subscriptions to trading publications.

- Trips to look after your trading account and conferences with trading advisers.
- An audiotape recording used for education.
- The portion of your home expenses that qualifies as home-office deductions.

You will need to incorporate and to choose a state of origin to be your home corporate headquarters.

An Additional Tax-Saving Strategy

Incorporate in a tax-free state. The strategy is to transfer wealth out of your own state to a tax-free state by loaning money to the taxable entity from the tax-free entity. The interest charged is earned tax free and is deductible in the taxable state.

Background. Most states charge an income tax all their own. There are several states, however, that do not have a state income tax for residents. These states are: Florida, Texas, Nevada, Washington, Tennessee, Alaska, and New Hampshire.

Be careful, however, to note that if you are still a resident of a taxable state, you may be subject to resident state income tax on the flow-through part of the income from your S corp.

Implementation. You may contact the Secretary of State yourself and go through the paperwork to set up a corporation. However, it is preferred that you retain a professional to do this properly. It will be well worth the cost of doing so in avoiding the hassle of incorporating incorrectly. You will want to work with professionals who have experience specifically with traders, so they can incorporate specific benefits into the entity. CPAs with experience in this area can be much less costly than attorneys and do a better job because of their specialty.

The Family-Limited Partnership

Use the family-limited partnership to further reduce or avoid taxation, legally.

If you have ever been to a magic show, you have probably seen this staple of any good magic act: The magician takes a hat, puts something into the hat, waves his magic wand over the hat, and reaches in and pulls out something like a rabbit.

This next section teaches you how to do a similar magic trick. It will allow you to take whatever assets you have in your possession and throw them into this magic hat called the *limited partnership.*

When you put your property into this magic hat, you will be making a contribution to the partnership and in return you will be getting back units of whatever is in the magic hat. You or others, at some later date, can then put additional assets into the hat, for example, more cash or insurance on your life, the deed to your real estate used by your business, or even the business itself. The hat will work just the way the magician's did on stage because it will enable its owners (let's call them partners) to invest or safeguard and to manage the assets placed into the hat. It's a *magic* hat because if things go as planned, more assets will come out than were placed in. And wealth will mysteriously change hands from one party to the next, to end up in the hands of whoever you'd like.

Imagine that the hat's assets are managed according to terms of a special document. That document will be called a *partnership agreement,* and it will spell out how the assets in the hat are to be managed and invested or how the business in the hat is to be run. The partnership agreement will also spell out who will receive the income and the assets from the hat and under what conditions they will do so. The key is that you own the hat and administer and manage all of the assets in it. You also control the magic wand that you will wave over the hat. You can tap three times and determine which owners will have what assets and who will share what with each other.

If you look at a partnership as a magic hat, you will see that it can come in many different shapes and sizes to meet different needs and objectives. Once you determine the hat you will be using, you can hold ownership to the hat but yet have the assets in the hat *not be taxed to you.* This is the first piece of magic.

You can also, over time, change the shape and the size of the hat that is holding more or fewer assets in it. You can shape the hat to meet the needs and the objectives and circumstances of the owners or prospective owners of the assets in the hat. This is the second part of the magic act.

If knowledge is power, knowing about partnerships—general and family-limited partnerships, in particular—will make you a very powerful and wise magician in tailoring your financial, income, and estate plan.

Why is this? Because partnerships are truly magic. They are one of the cutting-edge estate- and income-tax-planning tools of the twenty-first century. Understanding the pros and cons of the partnership is essential for those who would like to have some or all of their wealth preserved and passed to their heirs.

There are a number of reasons why you need to have more than a cursory understanding of partnerships. First, they are the centerpiece of estate planning for some of the wealthiest people in our country at this time. Why is this? Family-limited partnerships allow *participation* without *taxation*. Family-limited partnerships can also be used to significantly reduce federal and state death taxes and to create special gift and estate tax *valuation discounts*, yet at the same time allow an impressive degree of control over assets.

Second, partnerships *avoid estate death tax inclusion of life insurance* contracts, just as they could in an irrevocable insurance trust but without some of the Crummey power issues.

And third, a properly structured partnership can add a significant layer of *creditor protection* to your assets.

These three reasons should be enough, but I'd like to add one more. Your knowledge of partnerships will *distinguish you from most other people* in tax and estate planning.

Now, I'm *not* going to teach you how to be a master magician. I just want to show you one or two tricks. I will focus only on those things you *must know* rather than those things that are *nice to know*. When I'm finished, you will certainly understand how to pull a rabbit from the hat with this powerful magic called the family partnership.

I must warn you in advance that partnerships are somewhat complicated and that you must be prepared to go beyond the surface. It is extremely important that you understand the basics and that the entity that you set up be qualified and well structured under state and federal law. I will show you the many benefits of using a partnership as well as the costs and the downsides of using one. After the pros and cons, I will explain the tax implications.

What is a family partnership? A *family partnership* is the entity created when two or more related parties act together in enterprise for their *common, economic benefit*. Also, at least one of the partners must *transfer title* of some property to the partnership. Also, please note that the term *partners* is broadly defined. A corporation, a trust, or even another partnership can be a partner.

Now, I'd like you to circle the word *enterprise*. Enterprise implies *activity*, and this is important in our discussion of forming partnerships. The formal definition of a partnership provides that there must be an association of two or more persons to carry on as co-owners of a business for profit. The parties to the agreement typically contribute money or other assets, labor, or skills and in turn receive the right to share the profits of the enterprise.

A Double Winner—Using the LLC, Sub S Corp, or C Corp as a General Partner

There are two types of partnerships—*general* and *limited.*

1. In a *general partnership,* all partners have *unlimited liability* for partnership recourse debts and all partners are *legally entitled to participate in the management* of the partnership.

Each general partner is *personally liable* for the neglect or the wrongful acts committed by the other persons in the partnership as they pertain to conducting partnership business operations. That means that if a creditor sues the partnership and there aren't enough partnership assets to satisfy the claim, each and every general partner's personal assets can be attached to satisfy the debt. Also, because each general partner can act on behalf of the partnership, each partner's commitments bind all of the other partners.

General partners are often allowed to transfer all or a portion of his or her right to partnership profits. Most partnership agreements *prohibit* the transfer of the right to *participate* in management or other major activities of the general partnership.

2. In a *limited partnership,* as the name implies, at least one partner has *limited liability.* On the other hand, there must be *at least one general partner in a limited partnership.* Only the general partner assumes full liability for the partnership's recourse of debts. *Note that the same person can be both the general partner and the limited partner.* With a corporation or LLC as general partner, it is given more credibility, because although you are not both GP and LP, essentially the effect is the same—control is yours.

Recourse debts are those that allow the creditor to pursue beyond the asset itself, beyond the partnership itself, for collection. The creditor has recourse to the personal assets of the general partner. Additionally, only the general partner may manage the business and act on behalf of the partnership. Limited partners are only liable for the debts assumed by the partnership up to the assets they have contributed to the partnership. Limited partners are not allowed to act on behalf of the general partner or to participate in the partnership's management in any way.

Think of limited partners as passive investors who receive a return on their investment from the partnership rather than from its underlining assets. Limited partners do have certain rights, and they are significant: In a limited partnership, the death of a limited partner will not terminate the partnership—only the death and withdrawal of all of the general partners does that.

As in the case of a general partner, typically a limited partner can assign his or her share of the partnership profits to third parties. This is very important. A limited partner *cannot* sell or give away other rights, such as the right to vote on investments or operations of the enterprise. The general partner in a limited partnership cannot assign his or her interest to another person without the consent of all other partners.

Partners put in and take out assets in a number of different ways. This adds to the flexibility that a partnership provides and gives the participants cash flow control over the partnership.

Some of the ways that partners get income and assets out of a partnership are:

- The general partner is entitled to receive management fees for services rendered.
- The partnership can pay out money or other property from the partnership in the form of *distributions*. Distributions can be made to all partners, including limited partners, and should typically be made to partners in proportion to the value of their interest.
- Partners can choose to revoke their partnership interest.

Because a partnership is a contract between parties, the parties can choose to revoke the partnership at any time and divide up the net assets as long as all the partners consent. The partnership can make loans to its partners, if the partnership agreement provides for bona fide, secured, interest-bearing loans to all partners or third parties. All property transferred to the partnership and all property purchased by the partnership is held in the partnership's name. The partners own partnership assets only as participants in the partnership. In other words, each partner co-owns all partnership assets with all the other partners. Likewise, each partner has an intangible interest in the firm's net profits.

Advantages of Limited Partnerships

- Excellent wealth-shifting tool.
- Easy division of difficult assets.
- Means to avoid probate administration.
- Pass-through net operating loss.
- No double taxation of income.
- Special allocations of income and deductions.
- Structural flexibility.
- No restrictions on who may be partners.

- Ease of placing property in and taking property out.
- Shift of responsibility for investment and operating decisions.
- Means to vary levels of compensation to partners.
- Flexibility for investing.
- Avoidance of publicity in disputes.
- Ability to use an arbitrator instead of a judge in disputes.
- Provisions whereby losers of arbitration must pay for costs.
- High level of certainty in partnership treatment.
- Simplicity.
- Ease of maintenance.
- High level of control without jeopardizing income-tax and estate-tax advantages.
- Excellent creditor protection.
- Ease of inclusion throughout different states.
- Unifying the investment and administration decisions.
- Ability to diversify the assets.
- Discounts afforded for estate-tax and gift-tax purposes.

Four cases illustrate some of the advantages of partnerships.

Case 1. Excellent wealth-shifting tool. Suppose my daughter and I enter into a trading business together. We'd like to operate using an entity to shift both income and wealth to my daughter. Let's also say that I transfer a building that I own worth $2 million with a basis of $200,000 into the partnership.

Initially, I receive the entire general and limited partnership interest. Then I retain, for example, a 40 percent interest and give my daughter an amount of units worth 60 percent. So I've made a gift to her of about 60 percent of $2 million or $1.2 million. I have also retained an interest worth approximately $800,000.

Note that I've said "about" and "roughly." This is because the valuation may be discounted, and I will speak more about that in a minute. In this partnership arrangement, I will be the general partner and my daughter will be the limited partner.

Let's look at the pros and cons of this vehicle. As far as benefits go, first of all, a partnership is an excellent *wealth-shifting tool.* Shifting wealth and spreading income among the members of the family unit is one of the most important principles of income and estate-tax planning. A family partnership is a practical way of doing that. By merely amending the partnership agreement with a stroke of a pen, you can increase or decrease the relative interest of any participant.

In this example, let's assume I wanted to make a gift to my daughter of $600,000—30 percent of the $2 million value of the partnership. I've retained a 70 percent interest, and she now has a 30 percent interest.

Now, if we're both general partners, both of us are equally entitled to manage the partnership. If, at some later date, I want to make additional gifts to my daughter, I merely amend the partnership agreement. I give her a greater percentage and retain a smaller one for myself.

For example, assume that while the partnership is still worth $2 million, I give her an additional 2 percent by amending the partnership agreement. The 2 percent interest I would be giving her would be worth $40,000 (2 percent of $2 million). I could split the gift with my wife and pay no gift tax on the transfer of ownership. By keeping the gift within our annual exclusion limits, I could continue to give my daughter gifts until the entire value of the property was shifted to her.

Caveat: There is, of course, a catch. If the underlying property owned by the partnership grows in value over time, I will not only have to give away the original principal but also the appreciation as well. The faster the appreciation, the longer it would take to shift 100 percent of the partnership, unless of course I was going to pay some gift tax on the transfer or use all of my unified credit.

Partnerships are great wealth-shifting tools for one other reason. Assets that are *difficult to divide,* such as a farm, a house, or an incorporated business, can more easily be gifted if the property is placed into the partnership (the magic hat) and partnership units are assigned to our children and other participants.

One more advantage is the *avoidance of probate administration.* Because an interest in the partnership is *personal property,* even if the partnership holds *real estate,* the partnership provides a way to convert real property to personal property. What that means is that the real estate avoids probate in your estate. This avoidance of probate can save significant expense and aggravation in settling an estate.

Another advantage is the ability to *pass through a net operating loss.* In the early years of a business's existence, typically there are net operating losses (NOLs). These losses generally cannot be taken against the owner's other income if the business operates as a C corp. However, if a general partnership is properly designed, these losses can be deducted personally against the participants' other income.

Items of income, deduction, gain, and loss at the partnership level pass through with the same character they had previously. So income deductions and losses are reported by the partner as if they were earned or lost directly by him or her. This can *avoid the all-encompassing double taxation* of C corps: the income is taxed first to the corporation and second as a nondeductible dividend when it is paid out to its shareholder. In partnerships, the income is taxed only once to the partners when it is earned.

There are *special allocations* available as well. Within limits, it is often possible to allocate income and even income tax deductions and other credits among the partners in ways that optimize their personal income-tax planning.

Structural flexibility of the partnership is another advantage. The rights and interests of family partnership owners can be structured in almost any way you can imagine.

Suppose you own a building. It is possible to give away a very small percentage of that building by placing it into a partnership and amending the agreement year after year to give each or any member a larger percentage.

Returning to the example in Case 1, if the total value of my partnership grew to $4 million, I can only give my daughter a ½ percent interest each year ($20,000) to keep my gift within the annual gift-tax exclusion limits.

Note that there's no restriction on the identity or number of partners. Corporations, trusts, estates, or even other partnerships may be partners in a limited partnership. There could be an unlimited number of partners, which allows for some very creative planning techniques. Keep in mind, however, that if the partnership gets too big, different tax rules apply.

It is much easier to place property into and to take property out of a partnership than it is with a corporation. The tax problems associated with withdrawal of capital are minimal in a partnership but significant if the business was formed as a corporation. Different family members have different needs and circumstances, and hence structural flexibility is important. By allocating different interests in the family-limited partnership, each with different characteristics, you can simultaneously retain adequate income for retirement and hold on to control of the underlying assets of a business. You can also *shift responsibility for investing or operating the partnership to others.* This way you can ensure that many generations of your family share in the profits.

At the same time, you can provide a *higher level of compensation* to your children who work in the partnership rather than you do to nonworkers. You can also shift a higher level of income to those who are needy in the family, and you can restrict the flow of income or assets to those children who are financially secure or who are acting in an irresponsible manner. By utilizing this technique, you can maximize the shifting of wealth as well as the splitting of income to all the generations involved. Shifting wealth and splitting income is the name of the game in income and estate-tax planning for everybody.

Another advantage to family-limited partnerships is the *flexibility* it provides for investing. As you are aware, state and federal laws govern to a great extent how businesses operate and how investment decisions are made. Typically, a general partner in a partnership is judged by business judgment rules, which are much more flexible and reasonable than other standards. So the family partnership is much more flexible than a general partnership.

Furthermore, family-limited partnerships help *avoid publicity.* If there is litigation going on with respect to a trust, the odds are that the lawsuit will be both bitter and, in the case of celebrities and well-known parties, a matter of public knowledge. It is difficult to bind the parties to silence in a trust. However, a skillful CPA can draft a partnership agreement to restrict future potential trouble so that the parties are bound, in spite of a dispute, to submit the disagreement to binding arbitration and to remain silent on the matter. This is useful because an arbitrator is a business person, rather than a jury or a judge. This person will usually be sophisticated and familiar with your business or investments. So arbitration is far preferred than judicial settlement. Trial publicity generally works against the wealthy and for the less wealthy children. A confidentiality provision in the partnership agreement can not only help avoid publicity but can also reduce the seriousness and fallout of a disagreement.

It is also possible to provide in the partnership agreement that the *loser of an arbitration must pay all costs.* That will help cut down on frivolous legal actions. It will also discourage lawsuits brought about merely to harass another partner.

In my opinion, one of the biggest advantages of a family-limited partnership is that we know how the law will treat almost any partnership event with a high level of certainty. In a limited liability company, for example, which is a fairly new entity, we are not so certain.

Also, *simplicity* is one more advantage. It is very easy to form a partnership. Aside from an agreement between the parties, you only need to transfer property into the entity. In the case of a family-limited partnership, all you need is a certificate. With a partnership only one transfer is mandated. Once the property is placed into the entity, a simple agreement or amendment to the partnership agreement shifts wealth. Corporations, on the other hand, require a state-issued charter and may have to consider issues such as personal holding company tax, accumulated earnings tax, and collapsible corporation rules.

Maintenance of a partnership and the *ease* with which this is done are other advantages. It is possible for you to maintain a very high level of control over the gifted assets, even while you shift wealth to another family member. By naming yourself as managing partner, you can keep most, if not all, of the managerial control of the property until you choose to shift it to any of the other partners.

You have the flexibility of deciding to be, or not to be, the sole general partner. What's amazing about this is that a high level of control can be maintained *without jeopardizing the income-tax or estate-tax advantages.* You can decide if and when cash or property distributions will be paid out to the limited partners. By choosing to reinvest all or a great portion of the partnership's earnings back into the business, you can structure low payouts to the partners. This is particularly useful if your children do not need or shouldn't have much income. On the other hand, when you feel your children deserve or need more, you can then pass it out to them. A trustee of a trust that had this much power would probably cause the assets in the trust to be reverted back to the person who retains the power and to be includable in his or her estate.

Control goes beyond merely cash flow or managerial decisions. For example, assets can be kept in your control by placing them into the partnership hat and binding that hat with a *buy-sell agreement*. The buy-sell agreement could require that any limited or general partner who is divorced, who becomes bankrupt, or who tries to sell or give away his or her interest to somebody other than the partnership itself be precluded from doing that. The partnership agreement can mandate that that person must sell his or her interest back to the partnership and/or its current partners at fair market value.

Case 2. Excellent creditor protection. Now let's look at another critical advantage—*creditor protection*. To a certain extent the partnership magic hat provides a shield against creditors of both you and the limited partners. There are limits to this creditor protection; however, there is a tremendous amount of protection afforded by the partnership hat.

Suppose you set up a partnership and place assets and business interests into that limited partnership. At some later date, let's assume that you were sued and unable to pay the amount in excess of your insurance coverage. Because a partner has no interest in any specific partnership asset, a creditor has no right to the debtor partner's share of the partnership asset. What this means is that once you contribute assets to a partnership in exchange for an interest in that partnership, that interest is nowhere as attractive to others as are the assets contributed. This concept is especially true when you consider the fact that ownership and control have been separated with the family-limited partnership.

Remember, control typically remains in your hands even if a partner's creditors can obtain some ownership in the family-limited partnership.

The main remedy that a creditor has against the partnership is to obtain what's called a *charging order*, that is, a court order against the partnership interest that you own. Essentially, a charging order puts a creditor in the debtor partner's place; but, with proper structuring, that does not have to be a very high position. A creditor would receive only what the debtor partner would have received. Typically, what that means is that debtors cannot reach partnership assets. Creditors cannot vote on partnership decisions. Creditors cannot control the cash flow. In other words, creditors *cannot force a distribution of either income or principal to themselves.*

Now, here is the best part! Generally speaking, a creditor can only receive those distributions that the general partner chooses to make. So even though the creditor may not receive any income in any given year, if the partnership has profits, the tax liability is passed through. *A creditor may have to pay your taxes but not get any of your income if he or she attaches a partnership interest!* You might say that a creditor holds a hot piece of coal. The creditor's hands will be burned if he or she tries to hold onto it.

The creditor has tax liability but no cash to pay the tax. Oftentimes this results in a settlement between the debtor and the creditor under much more favorable terms than otherwise would be possible. The aggravation and the cost of the potential litigation is overwhelming, and most attorneys would probably advise a settlement rather than a long, drawn-out court battle. This is especially true because litigators are generally paid a percentage of what is obtained through litigation. In this case, that amount would probably not be worth the litigation, certainly not worth the cost of litigation to any good attorney.

Case 3. A means to avoid estate or gift tax. Suppose you contribute $500,000 into a limited partnership and get back a partnership interest worth $500,000. And let's assume that for this money you own 25 percent of the enterprise—the total worth is $2 million. Assume that in a few years, the business does well and the value of the entire partnership is now worth $4 million. Your interest would then be worth $1 million (25 percent of $4 million). But, to your heirs, it's really worth a lot less, because if you die and you're in a 55 percent tax bracket, they don't get very much. The question now becomes how can you give it away for estate-tax purposes without giving away control? Also, how can you do this at a discount?

1. Contribute this 25 percent business interest worth $1 million into a *new* family-limited partnership.

2. Become the general partner of the new enterprise. That means that you decide if and when distributions will be made to the partners.

3. Keep 1 percent of the new venture, giving away the remaining 99 percent in equal shares to, say, your daughter, your niece, and your grandson.

4. Take a 25 percent valuation discount when transferring $1 million interest to the new family-limited partnership. The rationale for this discount is that, remember, you only had 25 percent interest in the first partnership. That won't be able to force distributions out of it, and it almost has no market value. So for the purpose of gift tax that drops the value from $1 million to $750,000.

Now, as far as the other partners that you've appointed, they received a lot less than one-third of $750,000. The reason for that is that when you funded this new partnership you placed restrictions on transferability, and your new partners are limited partners—they don't have any say regarding the management, and none of them has the ability to force partnership distributions or liquidity. Also, they can never get at the underlying assets. So an independent appraisal might further discount each interest by, say, another 20 percent. So now you have three individual interests, each worth $200,000.

To recap, you transferred $1 million of wealth at a gift-tax valuation of $600,000. Also, you've only kept a 1 percent interest for yourself and transferred 99 percent of the partnership to your daughter, your niece, and your grandson. Consequently, *all you will be taxed on for estate-tax purposes is 1 percent.*

This is a prime example of how separation of control, beneficial interest, and ownership can be done properly. And remember, *control does not equal taxability.* Taxability equals ownership. You have retained full control over the entity while giving up 99 percent of the ownership.

TANSTAAFL: No Free Lunch

I wouldn't be painting a total picture for you if I didn't at least go over some of the downside points of setting up this entity. Partnerships are no different than any other techniques you will use. They have downsides as well as upsides.

One issue that must be addressed is the issue of strategy considerations. There is no one best strategy for everybody. Each strategy has its own distinct advantages and disadvantages. No strategy is perfect. If it were, I would be in trouble because my job would become obsolete.

The challenge here is to find the right strategy or combination of strategies that fits your own set of circumstances. No estate-planning tool or technique gives you something for nothing. But you have seen some examples of how a good estate-planning strategy can eliminate the tax on wealth entirely if not at least cut it down to manageable proportions.

The concept I'd like to introduce to you now is one that I call TANSTAAFL, which stands for "There Ain't No Such Thing As A Free Lunch." What this means is that each and every strategy does come with some disadvantages. In mapping out a financial plan, you must take into consideration many issues. You must always examine the benefits and the risks attributable to the specific strategy discussed. None of these strategies even border on the area of being highly aggressive.

Here are four of the disadvantages of partnerships:

1. *Stringent rules.* Family partnerships are subject to rules that must be met for favorable income-tax and estate-tax results.

If the rules are met, income will be passed through in the manner in which it was set up. If it is not set up properly, the IRS will claim that ownership should cause inclusion of partnership assets in the general partner's estate.

2. *Complex rules regarding taxation.* In theory, taxation of partnerships is conceptually simple, but in practice these rules can be incredibly convoluted. *You should use a highly qualified CPA to handle all your tax-related matters for the partnership.*

3. *Liability.* This is the single most important potential problem of a partnership. Each *general partner* is potentially liable for the acts of any or all *general partners.* However, limited partners do not have to worry about this problem. If you use a *corporation* as a *general partner* and you own the corporation, you can avoid this problem.

4. *Calendar year.* Partnerships are restricted in that they must use a calendar year, not a fiscal year.

Tax Implications of Partnerships

Having covered some of the key points of partnerships as well as the advantages and disadvantages, I'd like to discuss the crucial *tax implications.* As far as estate-tax purposes go, the valuation discount for estate- as well as for gift-tax purposes is a big advantage. If you can show that the value of the partnership interest that is being transferred has less marketability than liquidation of the underlying assets, then a discount is generally given upon transfer. Retention of significant management control over the assets should *not* trigger estate tax by inclusion of an asset in the estate. You need to comply with family-partnership rules, which substantiate the fact that you have parted with significant control so as to move the underlying assets from the estate.

Even a general partner's rights should not attract estate-tax inclusion of assets, other than the value of his or her specific interest. This means that the only value that should be includible in your estate should be the value of the units of partnership that you have retained as an owner. If limited partnership interests are gifted to other family members, the mere fact that you have retained certain powers as a general partner should not cause inclusion in your estate.

Now, naturally the IRS will treat abuse differently. For example, let's say that you set up a family-limited partnership trading business and name yourself as general partner. You then give your son a hefty salary for managing the enterprise, but he never walks into the office. Let's further assume that he does very little or no work in return for that salary. There's no question in my mind that in this case the IRS will say, "No interest was ever given away. Therefore, the entire partnership should be included in your estate."

Because the limited partnership interest is always included in the donee's partner's estate, his or her executors will need cash to settle the estate if this interest is significant. This is one caveat.

Some caveats. Let's now look at some caveats:

- *Caveat 1—Service-Oriented Businesses:* In many cases, there may be a problem if you are transferring an interest in a service-oriented business but not participating in that business and taking a salary for doing so. If you own, for example, a law firm or an accounting firm and if you participate in this after you transfer it into the family-limited partnership, you should take compensation commensurate with your participation. Otherwise the IRS may be able to disallow this as a tax scam.
- *Caveat 2—Minors:* For a minor to be recognized as a partner in a family-limited partnership, a fiduciary should be appointed on his or her behalf. So you should use a custodian if the partnership interest is relatively small or a trustee in the case of a larger partnership interest. It is also essential that the custodian or the trustee act aggressively to represent and to protect that beneficiary's interest.
- *Caveat 3—Buy-Sell Agreements:* Most partnerships, especially family-limited partnerships, should have a buy-sell agreement. The buy-sell agreement will ensure that the IRS does not take the position that the donor kept essential rights over the family-limited partnership and that the donee never had a real interest. This, of course, can have adverse income-tax as well as estate-tax implications.

Flow-through mechanisms. Let's look at some of the basic, flow-through tax mechanisms of a family-limited partnership.

Income A family-limited partnership is a *flow-through entity.* What that means is that income of the partnership is generally not taxed at the partnership level. Instead, the income is passed directly to the partners. So, in other words, losses and deductions are passed directly through the partnership to the partners.

Also, there is no partnership level alternative minimum tax. Unlike a corporation, a partnership holding large amounts of life insurance, for example, will not incur alternative minimum tax treatment on either the cash value buildup or on death proceeds. This is a major consideration when setting up a buy-sell agreement for the partnership.

As I mentioned before, each partner is taxed on his or her distributed share of partnership income whether or not the managing partner decides to actually distribute it.

Losses Partnership losses may be passed through to the income tax returns of the individual partners, and that often makes it possible to offset personal income against *general* partnership losses. There is, however, a restriction on the pass-through of losses to *limited* partners. This is very restrictive. In other words, if you are not a general partner participating in the management of the partnership, any losses passed through to you as a limited partner may be restricted to passive losses.

When a partner contributes cash or other property, typically that transaction is not considered a disposal or sale of the property. Simply dropping the property into the partnership hat transforms ownership; but for tax purposes, it still remains the same. So you will not typically have to report a gain even if you contributed appreciated assets to the partnership. On the other hand, if you contribute services in return for partnership interest, you will have to report ordinary income.

Withdrawals In most cases, the withdrawal of assets from a partnership can be accomplished without the triggering of a taxable event. This is unlike when you take assets out of a corporation.

In some cases, however, taxable income will be triggered. For instance, accounts receivable, which have not been taken into income by the partnership, or highly appreciated inventory can both cause recognition of income if withdrawn from the partnership.

Gift Tax and Estate Tax Now that we have looked at some of the major *income* tax implications, let's examine some of the significant implications for *gift tax* and *estate tax.* If you contribute money or other assets to a partnership but you did not want to adjust the interest relative to partnership membership, what you will be doing is indirectly making a taxable gift to other partners. This is really the same result as if you put cash or other capital into a corporation and didn't take back stock.

In both cases you would be making a gift to the other shareholders or to the partners of the limited partnership. Gifts, no matter what form they take, can usually qualify for gift-tax exclusions unless, of course, they have future interest in something.

For example, if you gift an interest in a partnership to a family member, either at the beginning of the partnership or at some later date by amending the partnership agreement, the moment you transfer the interest, the additional transfer should qualify for the annual gift-tax exclusion.

An annual exclusion is allowed for the transfer of immediate, unrestricted gifts. As was discussed before, these gifts can often qualify for significant gift-tax valuation discount when made. You must, however, make sure that all the family partnership rules have been met. Failure to meet any one of them could provide evidence that the gift was not complete and might result in estate-tax inclusion.

It is important to keep in mind that the mere fact that you are a managing partner or even the sole general partner would not cause the transfer or the gift to be incomplete. The reason is that state law restricts the power of a general partner over limited partnerships. The general partner cannot abuse the partnership for his or her own benefit to the detriment of the other partners, especially limited partners.

Basis Cash or other property that a partner transfers to the partnership increases his or her basis. The issue of *basis,* the cost you must use upon disposition to calculate a gain or loss, is very important because the more basis a partner has, the less of any distribution that he or she receives from the partnership is subject to tax. A partner is allowed to recover his basis fully before being taxed.

Another reason that basis is important is that the higher a partner's basis, the lower the tax the partner will pay on the sale of his or her partnership interest. Basis of the partners is increased proportionately to their interest when the entity earns a profit. So a partner's share of any profit not withdrawn from the partnership serves to increase his or her basis. That is good because it reduces the gain upon sale of the partnership interest or upon liquidation of the partnership.

On the other hand, basis is reduced proportionately when an entity suffers a loss. A partner's basis is also reduced when the partnership makes a distribution to him or her.

As far as the donee's basis, it is carried over from the donor with an adjustment for any gift tax paid.

Generation-Skipping Transfer Tax A key issue that we must consider is the generation-skipping transfer tax. If you give an interest in a family-limited partnership to one of your grandchildren or to someone in that generation, the generation-skipping transfer tax rules may apply. However, there is a $1 million exemption that can be used to offset all or a large portion of the tax on this direct transfer of a family-limited partnership interest to a grandchild or other skipped relative. Even better is that the direct skipped gift, if it doesn't exceed $10,000, can be excludable under what is known as a quasi-annual exclusion-type rule. In fact, even if the partnership interest for a minor grandchild is transferred into a trust for his or her benefit, it would qualify as a direct skip and be eligible for the $10,000 annual exclusion from the generation-skipping transfer tax, assuming certain requirements were met.

Putting It All Together with Integrated Tax Planning—the CHAMOEBA

A question that is often asked of me is, "Ted, how is the partnership vehicle integrated into a solid tax plan?" As we discussed earlier in this book, it is essential that all of your tax planning needs be met through a coordination of strategies—you must use an integrated approach that utilizes as many tools and techniques as are appropriate for your own needs. I have set up many limited partnerships that placed clients' investment assets into that partnership and allowed them to make gifts of a limited partnership interest while retaining a general partnership interest for themselves.

Oftentimes I illustrate the nature of a family-limited partnership as being *somewhere between an amoeba and a chameleon.* That is because you can change entities as they suit your needs. Amoebas and chameleons change their faces to deal with hostile environments. Let's therefore think of limited partnerships as "changeable CHAMOEBAS." For instance, an S corp or a C corp could be a partner in a general or family-limited partnership. A partnership, either general or limited, could itself be a limited partner or a shareholder of a C corp. A trust could be a partner in a general or limited partnership. The possibilities are only limited by your creativity and by certain state and federal laws to which you must adhere.

Let's examine one example of how the CHAMOEBA could work. Let's assume you transfer almost all of your assets into a family-limited partnership. You retain assets outside of the partnership, such as your Cartier watch or your new Bentley automobile. The partnership agreement gives managing control to the general partner. This general partner now will become a corporation owned by you and your wife. A corporate shareholder's agreement requires that as long as you and your wife are alive, you will be directors of the corporation. So your corporation now indirectly but very efficiently also controls the partnership through ownership in the partnership.

Questions often arise over the types of assets that should be placed in a family partnership. I usually suggest that investment-type vehicles, assets that will probably grow and produce significant income, be placed in a partnership. Also, a family business, which is in its start-up stage, would be a good candidate for being placed in a family-limited partnership. This is because you are able to shift significant wealth at a very early stage, often before the assets have reached their growth peak. We will use our magic hat to produce a rabbit, and we will give that rabbit to whoever needs it and can afford to take the tax hit. But prior to pulling the rabbit out, we throw into the hat all sorts of assets that may or may not have value.

- *Caveat 1*—The assets that should not be placed into a family-limited partnership are items such as your home, your retirement accounts, and any qualified retirement plan assets. You probably don't want to put the stock of S corporations in family-limited partnerships. You should not put stock in a professional corporation into a family-limited partnership. I would also discourage transferring personal-use assets into a family-limited partnership.
- *Caveat 2*—It is not a good idea to put art, jewelry, antiques, or other collectibles into the family-limited partnership. And never put life insurance with a high loan against it into a family-limited partnership because if this policy has a loan in excess of the transfer cost basis, you may be stuck with an unexpected reportable ordinary income gain.

Conclusion—The Rabbit Appears

We've looked at partnerships as being a very important estate-planning tool. As I have demonstrated, they have both advantages and disadvantages. The more I've learned, the more I understand and appreciate family-limited partnerships as one of the most important and viable tools I have to help my clients. Please reread this chapter and make sure you understand how to throw magic dust into the hat and indeed pull out a rabbit. Remember that with a carefully crafted and designed family-limited partnership, you can reduce income tax and federal estate tax, increase planning flexibility, protect your assets from creditors, and retain significant control. *This is truly participation without taxation.*

Implementation of a Partnership

The same person can be both the general and the limited partner. Again, you should use a highly qualified professional to handle all your tax-related matters for the partnership, as it is important to set it up right.

You can use an S corporation as a general partner, and, while owning the S corporation, you have become a double winner.

Just to summarize, the strategy here is to set up a family-limited partnership or a Sub S Corp as your trading vehicle. You then use this entity to establish your next step—the benefit program.

STEP 3—THE VOLUNTARY EMPLOYEE BENEFIT ASSOCIATION

Introduction

Having been in the financial services industry for the past 25 years and having practiced as a CPA for the past dozen or so, I have frequently been asked: "Ted, how can I put away money for retirement, use it as a tax deduction, allow it to grow on a tax-deferred basis, and eventually pass it down to my heirs, tax free?"

My answer to all parts of this question is a solution that has been on the books since 1928—the Voluntary Employee Benefit Association (VEBA).

Section 501(c)(9) of the Internal Revenue Code describes the VEBA as a tax-exempt, ten-or-more multiple-employer welfare benefit trust. It is further defined by Section 419(a)(f)(6), which was passed in 1984. Section 419(a)(f)(6) of the 419 and 419(a) rules were put in originally to curb abuses to VEBAs. If a program qualifies under this section, then it is exempted from the restrictions and prohibitions of Sections 419 and 419(a). In this manner, the greatest tax deferral and asset accumulation program allowed by federal law came into existence.

The complaints that I hear from most people are: "Tax rates are too high; retirement plans are too expensive; they don't benefit the employer as much as they do the employee; and most assets are going to be handed over to the government when they die anyway."

The Wish List

The solution to all of these complaints is the *welfare benefit trust.* If I could have a wish list of advantages that could be attained in any investment vehicle, it would look something like this:

- To grow assets on a *tax-deferred* basis.
- To save money on a *tax-deductible* basis.
- To be *available* to any individual.
- To be completely *approved* by the IRS and U.S. Congress.
- To be fully *protected.*
- To be able to pass the investment to one's heirs, *estate-tax free.*
- To be *flexible* in the amount you contribute.
- To have the principal *guaranteed.*
- To be *versatile.*
- To be *affordable.*

Some list of benefits!

Now let us discuss each of the wishes/benefits.

To grow assets on a tax-deferred basis. If properly structured, a VEBA program will allow you to invest your assets in a 100 percent tax-deferred manner.

To save money on a tax-deductible basis. VEBA programs, if set up properly, are 100 percent tax deductible by the employer.

To be available to any individual. This program is available to virtually any type of business. And if you have no business, don't despair. You can set up a business for the use of such welfare benefit programs.

To be completely approved by the IRS and the U.S. Congress. The VEBA is one of the few programs available today that has already received a favorable letter of determination, that is, the program has received prior approval by the IRS and Congress. There are many advantages to a favorable letter of determination, and this is the basis of the VEBA program. One of the first things that an IRS auditor will ask for when auditing a return is whether or not the plan has an approval letter. A favorable letter of determination is such an approval letter.

To be fully protected. The capital that goes into a VEBA program is protected *unlike any other strategy.* No one can touch the funds in a VEBA—not the IRS, not a bankruptcy court, not a divorce court.

I have an attorney with whom I work who sends all of his people to me prior to letting them file for divorce so that they can put money away in their VEBA. It is not assailable by any source or through any business or personal debt. It is 100 percent protected from creditors.

Wouldn't it be a heartbreak to put away a substantial sum of money and then lose it overnight, not having enough time to rebuild the nest egg? When assets are held in the VEBA, they are protected from all creditors. Not only are the assets in the VEBA, tax deductible and tax deferred, but they are considered to be an *unallocated reserve*—the assets are *not in any participant's name.*

In addition, legislation mandates that the funds will never revert to the business for the exclusive benefit of the participants and their beneficiaries. That means that the VEBA owns the VEBA; the VEBA is the beneficiary of the VEBA; and nobody can ever touch those funds because *there is no incident of ownership* on the part of the owner. The only right the owner has is the right to terminate that VEBA at any time.

To be able to pass the investment to one's heirs, estate tax free. One of the most attractive features of the VEBA is that it is designed so that none of the benefits paid from the VEBA will ever be subject to estate tax. This is because the owners have no incidents of ownership in the assets, including life insurance contracts held by the VEBA.

The VEBA exists under Title 1, Section B, of the Employment Retirement Income Security Act (ERISA), which says that a welfare benefit trust *must have a guaranteed base and it must be self-completing.* That means the assets must be guaranteed. There is only one financial instrument that accomplishes both of these goals, and that instrument is life insurance.

The VEBA is the owner and beneficiary of all insurance contracts. The participants have no vesting in any of the insurance contracts, which means that the employees have only one benefit under this program—they're going to get a huge death benefit, and they have the right to name the irrevocable beneficiary. They also have the right to purchase an individual conversion policy upon termination of employment if they leave. No part of the VEBA can revert to the sponsor at any time.

People ask, "Well, what about the owner of the business?" The owner is actually an employee, so the benefit he gets at termination does not go to the sponsor. It goes to him, as an employee. It is a welfare benefit program for employees. So the sponsor has no ownership right in the trust. Each participant makes the irrevocable designation of a beneficiary, usually in trust for the benefit of the spouse and/or the children. And trust benefits can be extremely useful for solving estate liquidity problems.

There is a limited vesting for employees. As you may or may not know, the average length of service of an employee is about eight years. If an employee leaves after eight years and you have set up a 15-year VEBA program, the employee loses his or her vesting. All the employee goes away with is the right to use a conversion policy. The only people who have a right to share in the benefits of a VEBA are long-term employees who stay with the company forever, a most unlikely situation.

To be flexible in the amount you can contribute. You can put in as much or as little as you want in any year to a VEBA. You are not limited to the rigid qualified plan amounts that go along with that type of retirement program.

To have the principal guaranteed. Safety of investment can be another feature of the VEBA program because it uses life insurance. And no life insurance company, in the history of the United States, has ever defaulted on a life insurance contract. Depending on the type of policy you choose, you can have high, long-term growth of your asset plus a potential 100 percent safety net.

To be versatile. A VEBA plan is one of the most versatile vehicles every enacted. This is because the VEBA is not subject to any rules of a qualified plan. It is not subject to any of the restraints of the Employee Retirement Income Security Act of 1974 (ERISA), either. Under Title 1, Section B of ERISA, all of the contributions to a welfare benefit trust must come from the employer rather than from the employee, and thus the restraints of ERISA are eliminated. This has become one of the finest tools ever for deferring investment dollars and for protecting against estate tax. It is also a tool that gives you an up-front, immediate tax deduction. It is the tool that I like the most because it cuts through all disciplines of financial planning, covering all of the issues: tax planning, estate planning, preservation of funds, asset protection, and solid financial planning. It is truly like having your cake and eating it, too!

To be affordable. What good is a strategy if you can't afford it? VEBAs can be instituted for a relatively small cash outlay.

Hey, VEBA! Where Have You Been All My Life?

Fellow practitioners in the tax field and other people who *should* know about VEBAs often ask me why it is that nobody knows about these things. My reply to that is that VEBAs are the best-kept secret in the IRS Code today, and the reason nobody knows about them is that *up until recently no one needed them.*

In 1974 Congress instituted what could be looked back on now as one of the greatest mass murder schemes in corporate America. What did they murder? The *qualified plan.*

In 1974, through ERISA, Congress sounded the death knell for the small business qualified plan. Congress knew that the IRS had qualified plans in their sights and that if the abuses in them were not curtailed, the IRS was going to kill them altogether.

Congress responded by trying to limit qualified-plan abuse. However, in doing so, they limited the ability of corporate America to get the big tax deductions that they had in the early 1970s.

What Congress did later on, in 1982 and 1984, through the TEFRA Act and the DEFRA Act was to come closer to killing the qualified plan.

- They vested employees.
- They made nondiscriminatory rules.
- They killed the defined-contribution pension plan.

So what does corporate America do when they know they're going to lose something? They immediately put their team of attorneys and accountants to work to begin to research the Tax Code to find something to replace it. And what they discovered in the early 1980s was that these VEBAs had been around, on the books, for well over 50 years and that the unions, in fact, had been utilizing these plans since their inception.

History of the VEBA

In my opinion, *"It took corporate America fifty years to discover the VEBA and about fifteen minutes to abuse it."*

In 1928, the VEBA became law, and there was no regulation of it at that time. Through the 1930s and up until the present, most labor unions adopted welfare benefit plans. There are billions of dollars in VEBAs, and most VEBAs lie with big businesses and unions.

Most Fortune 500 companies have VEBAs. There used to be tremendous abuses within the VEBA system—yachts in the Mediterranean, villas in Switzerland—all of which were being deducted from corporate income. In this way, VEBAs became vehicles of extreme abuse when the deductions were virtually unlimited.

A large company would go out and buy a corporate jet, a chalet in Switzerland, a yacht, and throw them all in a VEBA plan. They would then post a little notice on the bulletin board in the staff dining room saying that the company now owned these great assets for the benefit of the employees *and* that each employee had the right to use these perks whenever they wished.

That's right! Each employee had one weekend a year when he or she could take the corporate jet, go out and hire a pilot, fuel the jet up with expensive fuel, and fly over to Switzerland for a week of skiing fun. Or an employee could charter the company boat—just hire a captain and crew to staff it and take it out for one week a year!

Now, how many salaried employees working in a large company, would generally have access to the type of resources that they would need to utilize these "employee benefits"? But that's what happened—and then the IRS got wind of it. The story that I have heard goes something like this. The IRS commissioner was vacationing at a rather well-to-do coastal resort. He was in his suite looking out over the boats. All of a sudden, into the harbor pulled a huge yacht, and the name of the yacht was, "My VEBA."

The then IRS commissioner wrote the name down, and all day it bothered him. He had heard the term before, but he wasn't certain exactly what it was. On returning to his office at the Service, he looked it up in the Code and discovered that VEBAs had been in the IRS Code since 1928. He also quickly realized that, in fact, they were a good way for companies to abuse IRS breaks that were not meant to fund the purchase of yachts.

The story continues that the commissioner went to Congress, to the Chairman of the House Ways and Means Committee, and said, "Kill it." Congress normally obliges such high-ranking IRS officials (for fear that not doing so would often lead to retaliatory actions against *them*), so the Chairman brought his committee together and tried to do just that—to kill the VEBA.

The Chairman also found out that VEBAs had been in the IRS Code since 1928 and, in fact, that most of the large unions have billions of dollars invested in VEBAs for employee benefit welfare programs. His congressional committee looked at him like he was crazy and said, "There's no way in hell we're going to kill the VEBA. That would be akin to committing political suicide." And he agreed.

To kill the VEBA program would, in fact, had been political suicide for any politician. Could you imagine going back to your district as a politician in, say, Oshkosh, Wisconsin, and telling the daily union officials there that you have just eliminated the employee benefit program that assisted the constituents of that district? There's no way that they could ever do that. So, in the 1980s, Congress and the IRS began limiting the abuses within the VEBA plans and added Sections 419 and 419(A) to the IRS Tax Code, plus the discrimination rules (by adding Section 505). They hoped this would cut down on the abuse.

In 1984 Congress revised these laws and the VEBA restrictions. By the exceptions granted in Section 419(A)(f)(6), a tremendous potential has been unlocked for the welfare benefit programs. People like you and me can now take advantage of them, when prior to this only big businesses and unions could do so.

If a program qualifies under Section 419(A)(f)(6), it is not subject to the restrictions and the prohibitions of 419 and 419(A). What has happened is that Congress has created a very versatile tool for accomplishing all of the objectives listed in the prior list.

The Magic Words—*Tax Deductible*

Under this program, contributions to the VEBA become *100 percent tax deductible.* But more than that, the cash buildup inside a VEBA is 100 percent tax deferred, thus providing both a *great investment* vehicle and a tax-free death benefit. This may also be funded in addition to your current pension plan.

This is the greatest thing in the world for a company with an overfunded pension or a retain-earnings problem. The IRS states explicitly that you can have them both. You are not limited to one or the other. You can have a qualified plan as well as a nonqualified VEBA. This will also allow you to transfer retirement plans, income-tax and estate-tax free, to your heirs.

You can even use variable, whole life, or even universal life insurance. This will allow you to participate in the stock market, and, to have safety of principal, and to build up a huge nest egg for your future.

Skeptics Relax

Some of you skeptics are bound to believe that once again we have something that is "too good to be true." I will, however, try to put your fears at ease. The VEBA is squarely in the black-and-white area of the Code. It has been taken to court and tested time and time again.

The welfare benefit trust, when structured properly, has the approval of Congress, the IRS, *and* Tax Court. In addition, the trust is administered in a manner that fully complies with all regulations. There have been many court cases that have dealt with the welfare benefit trust, specifically as it applies to closely held businesses. (See Appendix C for some of the more technical aspects of the applicable Code provisions and Appendix D, for the court cases that I deem to be significant.)

To Give Is But to Receive—the True Magic of a VEBA

Now, the best part of the VEBA program may indeed be that although it is not meant to be set up as a retirement plan, it is, in fact, a wonderful vehicle for accumulating tax-deferred wealth. In addition to being a tax-deductible vehicle, if set up properly, it will allow the business owner to accumulate and to compound wealth for many years and ultimately to distribute it in his or her retirement.

The way this works is that the law provides that any business owner may, "for reasonable cause," choose to terminate a VEBA program. This could mean that the business owner is going out of business, has an economic need not to continue the VEBA program, or simply has another reasonable cause (i.e., cannot afford to continue or maintain it). If and when this happens, the wealth built up inside the VEBA program will then revert back to the employees—including the owner/employee.

In Exhibit 5.1, you see what could be the contribution to a VEBA program that has been in place several years. The main benefit of this program goes to the owners.

The key to this is that different levels of insurance are being used to cover different employees. KEY #1 and KEY #2 are being covered

EXHIBIT 5.1 A Typical Annual VEBA Contribution

Employee Name	Age	Annual Salary	Survivor Benefit	Plan Contribution	Taxable Income (P.S. 58)
KEY #1	M45	$400,000	$1,600,000*	$37,050	$817
KEY #2	F35	200,000	1,600,000*	37,050	701
EE #1	M41	30,000	300,000	401	371
EE #2	F31	25,000	250,000	352	320
EE #3	F30	15,000	150,000	147	127
Totals:			$3,900,000	$75,000	

Planned Annual Contribution:	$ 75,000
Percentage of benefits to key participants:	98.8%
Anticipated pretax payments—10 yrs.	$ 750,000
Tax savings (50% tax bracket)—10 yrs.	$ 375,000
Net after tax cost (50% bracket)—10 yrs.	$ 375,000
Projected Unallocated Reserve	
—10 Years:	$1,140,000
—20 Years:	$3,015,000

*Compensation subject to Section 505(b) limitations.

with a cash buildup insurance. The cost of this insurance is significantly more than the cheap term insurance chosen to cover nonkey employees EE #1, EE #2, and EE #3. Furthermore, the cash buildup in these two insurance policies provides the basis for future distributable wealth.

One of the things that bothered me initially about the VEBA program when I first heard about it was the fact that there are two types of insurance being used—one a permanent insurance for the owner/key employee, and the other a cheaper term insurance for the non-owner/non-key employee. It bothered me because I felt it was not consistent with Code Section 505, which provides that these VEBA programs be nondiscriminatory. It was only after further research and due diligence on the subject that I realized, in fact, that the difference in levels of insurance is a benefit in which any non-key employee will also participate if he or she remains with the company through the distribution and termination of the VEBA plan.

Neither one of the two key employees in this case owns the VEBA policy. It is the VEBA trust that owns the life insurance policy on the lives of the five employees in this case. The only benefit to which each of the employees is entitled at this point while the VEBA is in existence is the death benefit. This benefit is, indeed, *nondiscriminatory* because the amounts are decided in proportion to the various salary levels of all the employees, and they are decided in a nondiscriminatory manner.

Getting back to Exhibit 5.1, if this contribution were made religiously for 10 years, it would be an anticipated pretax payment of a million dollars. The net tax savings would be $375,000 over the 10-year period, and hence the cost to the key employees (owners of the company) would be $375,000.

Based on current assumptions, at the end of a 10-year period, there would be approximately $1,140,000 remaining in the VEBA plan for allocation. After a period of 20 years, based on current assumptions, there would be $3,015,000, which could then be allocated among the remaining participants in the plan, if the plan were terminated. This is based on current assumptions of a universal policy at current interest rate levels. It would most likely be much greater using a variable policy.

It Works if You Work It! Getting Your Money Out

Let us now look at the hypothetical termination of this plan in Exhibit 5.2 after year 10 and, once again, after year 20. As you will see, the benefits are in the way it accumulates tax-deferred wealth for it participants—especially the key participant—YOU.

Looking at the termination of this VEBA program after a hypothetical contribution for 10 and 20 years, we project that the same employees would be with the company after year 10 in order to be conservative (a rare case). We allocate the total distributable amount based on this percentage. As you will see, 89.38 percent of this amount, or $1,018,932, goes to the key employees, and only 10.62 percent, or $121,068, goes to the non-highly compensated employees.

Again, this is based on the assumption that all three non-key employees will have remained with the company over the 10-year period. This is not likely to be the case, and, in fact, most of them—if not all of them—will have left over the 10-year period. If, in fact, this occurs, the owners/key employees will receive a much greater amount.

We also see this same plan projected to have lasted 20 years. Once again, in this case, we distribute based on the percentage of cumulative salaries. You will then see that most of the employees did not stay even 15 of the 20 years, and because of that, the distribution was much lower to them. In this case, 92.75 percent, or $2,796,413, went to the key employees, 7.25 percent, or $218,587, went to the nonhighly compensated employees.

This is the *true benefit* of a VEBA program. As you can see, inside even a universal policy, which is based on a static interest rate

EXHIBIT 5.2 Termination of VEBA Plan

Year 10
(Projected Plan Assets: $1,140,000)

Name	Years of Participation	Average Annual Salary	Cumulative Salary	Percent Total	Taxable Distribution
KEY #1	10	$500,000	$5,000,000	55.86%	$ 636,804
KEY #2	10	300,000	3,000,000	33.52	382,128
EE #1	10	40,000	400,000	4.47	50,958
EE #2	10	35,000	350,000	3.91	44,574
EE #3	10	20,000	200,000	2.24	25,536
Totals:			$8,950,000	100.00%	$1,140,000

89.38%, or $1,295,409, went to the key employees.
10.62%, or $274,593, went to the non-highly compensated employees.

Year 20
(Project Plan Assets: $3,015,000)

KEY #1	20	$500,000	$10,000,000	57.97%	$1,747,796
KEY #2	20	300,000	6,000,000	34.78	1,048,617
EE #1	20	40,000	800,000	4.64	139,896
EE #2	10	35,000	350,000	2.03	61,205
EE #3	5	20,000	100,000	.58	17,486
Totals:			$17,250,000	100.00%	$3,015,000

92.75%, or $2,796,413, went to the key employees.
7.25%, or $218,587, went to the non-highly compensated employees.

assumption, a great amount of wealth can be built up and accrued for retirement. And although the VEBA program is not meant to be a retirement plan, it can, indeed, be a very valuable tool in planning your future wealth.

Let us now compare the difference between what would be a qualified profit-sharing plan for the same five employees illustrated previously (Exhibit 5.3) and a VEBA program (Exhibit 5.4). The initial survivor benefit in year one would be $58,500 in the qualified plan. In the VEBA, survivor benefits would be far greater—$3,900,000.

The owners in a qualified plan would only be able to contribute $58,500 in deductible contributions, whereas in the VEBA program the contribution, as we noted in Exhibit 5.1, would be $75,000. In the qualified profit-sharing plan, the three nonkey employees would receive a total benefit of $10,500, or 17.95 percent of total contributions. The two key employees, on the other hand, would receive $48,000, or 82.05 percent of the total.

EXHIBIT 5.3 Qualified Profit-Sharing Plan

Name	Age	Annual Salary	Initial Survivor Benefits	15% Profit-Sharing Deposit
KEY #1	M45	$400,000	$24,000	$24,000
KEY #2	F35	200,000	24,000	24,000
EE #1	M41	30,000	4,500	4,500
EE #2	F31	25,000	3,750	3,750
EE #3	F30	15,000	2,250	2,250
Totals		$670,000	$58,500	$58,500

3 Employees = $10,500, or 17.95%, of total contribution
2 Key Employees = $48,000, or 82.05%, of total contribution

ANY TYPE OF BUSINESS ENTITY	PAYS	$1,500 administrative fee
QUALIFIED PROFIT-SHARING PLAN All eligible employees. Tax-deferred growth. Trustee chooses investments.	INTO	$58,500 tax-deductible contribution
INVESTMENTS Stocks, Bonds, Cash, Annuities	YIELDS	BENEFITS Life, Death, Disability: Account balances are subject to vesting and taxation upon withdrawal.

Compare this, however, with the VEBA program—the two key employees would receive $74,100, or 99 percent of total benefit contributions; and the three nonkey employees would receive a mere $900, or only 1 percent of total contributions.

The other fees we will compare are those that typically are associated with qualified plans and VEBA programs. Under a qualified plan, the normal business entity would pay somewhere in the neighborhood of $1,500 as an administration fee.

The qualified profit-sharing plan would vest all eligible employees at the proper time as part of the $58,500 contribution, and the investment would be made in stocks, bonds, cash annuities, and the like, yielding benefits such as investments, life, death, disability insurance, and whatever else the plan chose to invest in.

Keep in mind that in a qualified plan all employees are sooner or later vested. In a VEBA, on the other hand, employees never become vested.

With a VEBA, the business entity must have at least two employees. The charge for setting up a VEBA program is typically a bit more costly than the qualified plan because a VEBA is run by a trustee and

EXHIBIT 5.4 VEBA

Name	Age	Annual Salary	Initial Survivor Benefits	Contribution
KEY #1	M45	$400,000	$1,600,000	$37,050
KEY #2	F35	200,000	1,600,000	37,050
EE #1	M41	30,000	300,000	401
EE #2	F31	25,000	250,000	352
EE #3	F30	15,000	150,000	$147
Totals		$670,000	$3,900,000	$75,000

3 Employees = $900, or 1%, of total contribution
2 Key Employees = $74,100, or 99%, of total contribution

ANY TYPE OF BUSINESS ENTITY Must have at least two employees	PAYS	$1,500 administrative fee $1,000 trustee fee
VEBA 591(c)(9) tax-exempt trust. Tax-deferred growth. Fully insured investment. Trustee invests in insurance policies.	INTO	$75,000 tax-deductible contribution
Life insurance company issues policies.	YIELDS	BENEFITS Death: Beneficiary gets 10 times death benefit, income, and estate-tax free. Life: Distributions are not subject to vesting.

there is a trustee fee involved. Also note the big difference in percentage of retained wealth to the owners.

One of the most attractive features of the VEBA is that it can be designed so that benefits paid from the trust *will never be exposed to estate taxes.* This is because the participants have no "incidents of ownership" in the assets, including the life insurance contracts held by the welfare benefit trust. The VEBA is the owner and beneficiary of all insurance contracts. The participants have no vesting in any insurance contract, other than the right to purchase an individual conversion policy upon termination of their employment.

Advantages of the VEBA

In sum, let us review some of the advantages of a VEBA program:

- Contributions are tax deductible.
- Assets are protected from all creditors.

- A much larger percentage of contributions, often as much as 90 to 95 percent, is used to benefit the owners. Distributions can be taken from the plan before age 59½ and contributions made after age 70½ with no penalties. This is a big difference from the qualified plan.
- Assets accumulate and compound on a tax-deferred basis.
- There is no set annual limit on contributions, and survivor benefits are income-tax free and can be free of estate and gift taxes.
- Employees who terminate prematurely are never vested with respect to benefits.
- This program can be installed to complement qualified plans, such as 401(k)s or profit-sharing plans, and they can be used to offset the tax on qualified plans upon distribution.
- The benefits of the VEBA will be exempt from creditors of both the employer and the participants because they do not possess title or ownership interest in the funds.
- The employer can provide for life insurance needs of the participant.
- The allocation of the distribution of these benefits can be structured to *favor the business owners* by providing larger death benefits and ultimately larger distributions upon termination.
- The investments of the VEBA are safe and held only by major insurance companies that are highly rated.
- VEBAs are managed by third-party independent trustees, usually banks and trust companies, for greater safety.

Conclusion

Recent case law has given us direction on how to structure one of the greatest tax-reduction vehicles available today. With the VEBA, you can now accomplish all of these objectives at once:

- Avoid *current tax* through huge tax deductions.
- Save an *unlimited* amount for *retirement.*
- *Grow it tax free* in addition to getting an up-front tax deduction.
- *Pass the wealth down* to your heirs, estate-tax free.
- Allow assets to accumulate on a *tax-deferred* basis forever.
- Have the *full blessing of the IRS* and Congress with a favorable letter of determination—in other words, this strategy is preapproved.
- Have *no vesting for employees* who terminate prematurely.
- Make *contributions as flexible* as you like in any amount.
- Allow *large contributions* in peak years.

- Allow *early or late distributions without penalties* for distributing prior to age 59½ or for contributing beyond age 70½.
- Provide favorable tax relief for *business owners* (traders).
- Provide full *safety* of investment.
- Provide the ability to *grow funds* in conjunction with *market growth.*
- Acquire *tax-deductible life insurance.*
- Provide funds to *pay estate taxes.*
- *Protect* funds from creditors.
- Have a plan that is *inexpensive* to set up and administer.
- Access the funds within *five years* of contribution!

Being able to vary contributions from one year to the next is one of the more favorable provisions of setting up a VEBA. Although a VEBA is intended to be a permanent welfare benefit plan, there is no fixed obligation to make certain payments each year. This is a big plus.

This also sets up one of the best characteristics of the VEBA, which is that permanent cash buildup may be provided for the owners, whereas cheap term insurance is provided for the employees without violating the nondiscriminatory characteristics of the VEBA. This is particularly significant because when a VEBA is terminated and the amounts are distributed to all of the eligible participants, the owner/employee will be able to reap a greater amount of the seeds that they have sown.

Although the VEBA is *not* meant to be set up as a retirement plan, it is, in fact, a wonderful vehicle for accumulating tax-deferred wealth. In addition to being a tax-deductible vehicle, if set up properly, it will allow the business owner to accumulate and to compound wealth for many years and ultimately to distribute it for his retirement. The way this works is that the law provides that any business owner may, "for reasonable cause," choose to terminate a VEBA program. This could mean that the business owner is going out of business, has an economic need not to continue a VEBA program, or simply for any other reasonable cause (e.g., cannot afford to continue or maintain it). If and when this happens, the wealth built up inside the VEBA program will then revert back to the employees—including the owner/employee. Anything within the VEBA trust will then be distributed in proportion to cumulative salary earned by any employees still with the firm.

The VEBA program, as properly structured, is one of the most versatile and advantageous vehicles available for tax and financial planning today. The VEBA program should be an integral part of anyone's total estate, retirement, and overall financial plan.

THE TRIPLE CROWN

The Triple Crown can make you into a Triple Winner! Here is a summary of the three steps:

1. Establish a Trading business or any other type of business.
2. Establish a family-limited partnership with a corporation as the general partner—you own 100 percent of the stock in the corporation.
3. Fund a VEBA within the corporation by drawing enough management fee to cover the cost, which then becomes a flow through deduction to you.

6

Providing for a Wealthy Retirement

"Baby boomers beware—you can run but you better not hide. Retirement's coming, and it's coming quickly."

THE BIG BOOM OF 50-YEAR-OLDS!

For the 76 million people born between the end of World War II and the election of President Johnson in 1964, there is a crisis in the works. Most are not even aware of the severity of the problem, but more and more people are getting the notion that something is definitely wrong.

In a series of articles, *USA TODAY* examined some of the factors that confront this group of people. Their findings were somewhat startling.

The perceived wealth of today's baby boomers may be fleeting at best and marginal at worst. The series begins with the argument that America's most "privileged generation won't ever have enough money to retire." It continues, "The oldest boomers turn 50 next year, and for many the looming question is not *when* they'll retire, but *if* they can. Millions will have to work eight, 10 or more years beyond the traditional retirement age. Social Security benefits are almost certain to be cut. Pensions are at risk."

Yet they still aren't saving.

Four in ten set aside less than $1,000 in a recent year, according to a *USA TODAY*/CNN Gallup Poll. At the same time, two-thirds expect to live as well—or better—in retirement as they do today.

"I don't think the nation as a whole understands the immensity of the situation that's going to unfold at the beginning of the twenty-first century," says Don Sauvigne, former head of IBM's retirement programs.

Consider this: When baby boomers begin to retire in 2011, *they will need about $1 million in savings to ensure an annual income equivalent to about $50,000 throughout retirement.* And that assumes Social Security benefits and pensions aren't cut.

"People underestimate how long they'll live. They underestimate how much of that time they might be ill. They overestimate how much money they'll have," says Barbara Casey, president of Dreyfus Retirement Services.

Adds Steven Vernon, author of *Don't Work Forever* and Retirement practice director at Watson Wyatt Worldwide, a benefits consulting firm, "If you're saving less than $1,000 and you ask the question at what age will you be able to retire, the answer will probably be well beyond death."

One article in the *New York Times* was entitled *Another Day Older and Running Out of Time.* It discussed a March 1995 survey the *Times* conducted that arrived at a similar conclusion to that of *USA TODAY.* But, this survey found that although most people are not doing anything about it, at least a portion of this generation is *aware* of the situation. The article stated that Americans are indeed frightened and that they are looking toward retirement not with the optimism of their parents, but rather with trepidation. The *New York Times* went on:

> Three out of four working Americans expect people their age to face a financial crisis when they retire, according to a *New York Times*/CBS poll. Over half say they have not begun to save for retirement. And many see themselves reaching old age without the company-paid pensions and Social Security that allowed their parents to live so comfortably.
>
> The new economics of retirement are forcing Americans who want to build a retirement nest egg to wade into the confusing world of stocks, bonds, and mutual funds. They know they must somehow become smart investors to pay for old age. But the poll, and interviews later with those surveyed, show they are largely unprepared, psychologically and financially, to do what they know they should do.[1]

The reality is that Americans are not prepared for retirement, but they are starting to get the message. Unfortunately, however, most Americans are not sure what to do about it.

The purpose of this chapter is to provide some insight into the severity of the situation and, more important, to provide a variety of solutions to this very significant problem. It will be a very practical blueprint for achieving *financial freedom in retirement,* a key element in the winning estate plan.

The strategies I will discuss are the same ones I use in my own economic plans as well as in those of my clients. I will examine specific techniques that you can start using today to create your own road map to a more comfortable retirement.

LIFE'S TOUGH AND THEN YOU RETIRE—HOW TO MAKE IT EASY

Most Americans are so busy trying to increase their day-to-day income that they neglect to concentrate on building future wealth. Daily living and its focus on short-term income and expenses has become so overwhelming that many people lose sight of what should be their greatest concern.

Anytime you make a decision about what to do with one single dollar of your hard-earned money, you are making a serious investment decision—one that will have a profound effect on your future financial life. This is especially true when you consider the enormous rate of compounding of income (or loss of compounded income) that that decision may bring to you by the time you retire (more on the effects of compounding later).

Bypassing one purchase for another is a *serious* decision. Putting your money into the bank, a mutual fund, a nondeductible IRA (individual retirement account), or an annuity, instead of somewhere else, is a *serious investment* decision. What you do with every dollar is so important that it can contribute to a more secure retirement and to the financial fortunes of your heirs. I will show you in this chapter how to make the appropriate choices for your current lifestyle and how these choices can make a significant impact on the money you have for retirement as well as on your estate and the future wealth of your heirs.

There is no time like the right time, and the right time to take action is today. Regardless of whether you're 15 years old or 50, you should start to think of your financial future in very serious terms *now,* or you may not have a financial future to consider at a *later* date.

For any of you who have thought about taking on a second job to help your finances, you should consider this fact: For a fraction of the time and effort, you can make good retirement planning your second job. It is far more profitable, much more fun, and far less exhausting. For approximately one hour per month, you could work at structuring your finances from within a sound retirement-planning context and, in reality, make a small fortune doing it.

In this book I will show you how to wisely use every dollar and how that can be a significant factor in your future financial situation. It is certainly worth your effort to learn more about this and, more important, to implement these strategies into your life. *A simple switch in focus from daily to future accumulation of wealth can make the difference between getting rich or simply getting by.*

DENIAL IS NOT A RIVER IN EGYPT

In assessing the American retirement scene, I am reminded of a film I saw a few years ago, *The New Leaf.* In this film, Walter Matthau plays a man who has lived off a trust fund all his life, but finally the fund has been exhausted.

In a very funny but poignant scene, after the bank has started bouncing checks on him, he approaches a teller at the bank. The teller says to him, "I'm sorry there are no funds to draw this check against."

And Matthau replies, "I know that, but you have to cash this check."

The teller states, "I'm sorry, I can't do that. There's no money in the account."

Matthau replies, "I know that, but can you please cash this check."

And this goes on and on.

Matthau, like the American public, cannot fathom the idea that he has not put away enough and has finally run out of money.

Although many people are starting to realize that a crisis is in the making, few of them are taking immediate action to resolve this. America is in an acute state of denial.

In the *New York Times*/CBS news poll in March of 1995 to which I referred earlier in this chapter, it was reported that although there are significant doubts about the availability of Social Security and pension coverage to be able to provide adequate retirement funds for most Americans, only half have put aside money specifically for retirement.

SEE NO EVIL, HEAR NO EVIL . . . OPENING YOUR EYES

In the *Times* survey, the question was asked, "Have you begun to save money or establish any savings program specifically for your retirement?" Of the people who were not already retired, 47 percent said yes. This group of people had money put away in the following investment vehicles:

401(k) plan	13%
Employer-sponsored pension plan	8
Savings account	7
Individual retirement account	6
Mutual funds	5
Individual stocks	2
Life insurance	1
Other	5

Another question put to the people in this survey was, "Do you think the Social Security system will have the money available to provide benefits you expect for your retirement?" The responses were only 35 percent positive.

When asked if they had an employer-sponsored pension plan, only 49 percent responded that they did. Of this group, only 39 percent expected that it would provide for a comfortable level of retirement.

But the most startling conclusion that this survey reached was that even though Americans have such poor retirement resources and feel so negatively about the pension they have or the Social Security system in general, *over half of them are still counting on Social Security and pensions.*

The question was asked, "Looking ahead to retirement, what do you expect to be your major source of income—Social Security, an employer-sponsored pension plan, or your own retirement savings?" The specific responses to this question were:

Employer-sponsored pension plan	30%
Social Security	22
Savings	39
Other	5[2]

What has become very clear to me is the significant level of denial that future retirees still have about the situation.

The survey asked, "Do you think that most people your age will face a financial crisis when they retire or not?" Although 76 percent of those asked this question responded that they did in fact feel that most people will face a crisis in retirement, only 31 percent felt that they personally will face one.

The question was asked, "Do you think that you personally will face a financial crisis when you retire?" Sixty-one percent of those queried responded that they do not believe that they are personally in danger of facing this crisis.

The *USA TODAY* article quoted Craig Karpel, author of *The Retirement Myth* as saying, "I wouldn't be surprised if a significant number of the baby boom generation falls right out of the middle class." The poll in this article showed people's attitudes toward retirement as putting them in one of four groups. Where do you fit in?

1. *Contented Realists*—26 percent. These people are the best prepared for their retirement—they earn and save the most of any group. Of this group of people, 70 percent earned more than $50,000 per year in 1994, and only 1 percent earned less than $20,000. Overall, 19 percent of all people surveyed earned less than $20,000 last year.

Over 57 percent saved more than $5,000 last year. This was nearly twice the national average. Most of these people have an employer-sponsored retirement plan. The survey found that 84 percent—more than any other group—has this type of plan.

This group of people is generally not worried about having enough money in retirement and are highly knowledgeable about financial planning. More than half stated that they had a *written financial plan* drawn up for their retirement.[3]

Most Contented Realists expect to live off their savings, investments, and job-sponsored retirement plans in retirement. They are also the smallest group of people to expect Social Security to support them.

2. *Worriers*—32 percent. These people earn only slightly less than the Contented Realists, however they have significantly less saved. They are the most pessimistic, and 55 percent of them expect their standard of living to decline in the future.

This group of people worries a great deal about their retirement, but uses much less income to save for it. Even though 40 percent make over $50,000 per year, more than half feel that they do not make enough money to save. Over two-thirds of this group of people agreed with the statement that "There always seems to be something else to spend your money on, rather than save it for the future." One-third of the Worriers stated that they were totally ignorant about retirement planning. This is about the same percentage as the Woefully Unprepared and much greater than the other two groups. More than one-third of this group expects to rely on Social Security as the major source of retirement income. This is also about the same as the Woefully Unprepared. More than 25 percent of Worriers feel that they will have to work at least part time in retirement.

3. *Cautious Optimists*—18 percent. These people are the 180-degree opposites from the Worriers. They are the most realistic of all people surveyed and are doing the most for their retirement planning. Although only approximately one-fifth earn more than $50,000 per year, they have taken steps to prepare for their retirement. In many ways, although this group has lower income, they are very similar to the Contented Realists.

Over one-quarter of these people feel that they are very knowledgeable about investments and retirement plans. This is three times more than the Worriers. Almost one-third of these people have a retirement plan and saved more than $5,000 last year. Only one-third saved nothing last year, compared to almost 40 percent of the Worriers, who earned significantly more.

Similar to the Contented Realists, this group of people feels that savings and investments will be the major source of retirement income and not Social Security.

4. *Woefully Unprepared*—24 percent. This group of people is the poorest of any group surveyed. They are least likely to have a retirement plan, and most of them believe that they will never have enough money to retire.

Only 7 percent earn more than $50,000 per year, and half earn less than $20,000. These people need virtually everything that they earn for their day-to-day expenses. Of these people, 60 percent saved nothing last year, and 40 percent say that Social Security will be their main income in retirement. Over 25 percent of these people plan on working part time during retirement to make ends meet.

AND THE WALLS COME TUMBLING DOWN—THE PILLARS OF RETIREMENT PLANNING

Company retirement plans, personal savings and *IRAs, Social Security,* and *VEBAs* are generally considered to be the four cornerstones of a comfortable retirement. Let's examine several reasons why each of these institutions is in big trouble and then look at my strategies that will serve as alternatives.

A good part of the blame probably rests with the U.S. government and Congress and the tax changes that have taken place. Since the Great Depression, Congress has tried to spark the economy by allowing individuals and companies to avoid or to defer income tax on any money put away for retirement.

But recently, and even more significantly, in their efforts to cut the federal budget deficit, Congress has started taking away some of the tax breaks that promote retirement savings. Furthermore, the Social Security system, which was once believed to be the foundation of retirement income for most Americans, is projected to run out of money in the same year that the youngest group of baby boomers begins collecting Social Security benefits.

Let's briefly examine each of these three components. Later in this chapter, we will look at some of the significant legislation that has been passed, the key dates to be aware of, and other significant factors that may affect each of these pillars. The fourth component has already been introduced—the VEBA should become a dominant force in the twenty-first century.

1. *Company Retirement Plans.* Over the past few years, the government has introduced a series of stringent tax law changes that limit the

amount of money that companies can put away for their employees. The amount of money that individuals can contribute and withdraw has also been restricted.

2. *Personal Savings and IRAs.* In this area, the story is two-fold: (1) There has been a decrease in personal savings over the past decade. (2) The government taxes most savings account interest when it is earned. This occurs regardless of whether the interest is withdrawn or left in the account. There also has been a series of tax law changes that restrict the contribution to and the deductibility of IRAs.

3. *Social Security.* There is another two-pronged situation developing with the Social Security system. The government now taxes 185 percent of Social Security income for many taxpayers. Your Social Security contribution is money that was already taxed before it was taken from you. It is now taxed again at rates of up to 85 percent when you receive it. Consequently, Social Security is ultimately taxed at 185 percent! Additionally, much of the Social Security fund, which was supposed to be growing for the baby boomers to collect, has been used to fund other government projects. It is worth investigating the factor that has contributed to underfunded retirement plans.

THE TAX FACTOR

I did a projection for a conference I gave in Burbank, California, to a group of professional commodity traders. I compared the results over a 35-year period of a trader who traded a $100,000 account that was taxed every year at 50 percent of profits (federal, state, local, and sundry other taxes) with the results of a second trader who traded a $100,000 account tax free. The results amazed me and may, in fact, be quite startling to you.

Assuming a compounded annual rate of return of 25 percent, which for commodity trading is a conservative minimum, the following figures apply. After 35 years of trading an account of $100,000, being taxed at 50 percent of profits, with an annual average compounded rate of return of 25 percent, trader #1 will end up with $6,070,755.

Trader #2, however, who had the exact same return and who started off with the exact same account, but somehow managed to escape taxes for 35 years, ended up with $246,417,033!

That's an increased rate of return of over 4,000 percent, and an additional $240,000,000 over 35 years. If you can somehow escape the onerous tax burden, you will multiply your wealth many, many times

EXHIBIT 6.1 $100,000 to Start

	Taxed	Tax Deferred	Increase
5 years	$ 180,203	$ 305,176	+ 170%
10 years	324,732	931,323	+ 287
15 years	585,178	2,842,171	+ 486
20 years	1,054,509	8,673,617	+ 823
25 years	1,900,260	26,469,780	+1,393
30 years	3,424,330	80,779,357	+2,359
35 years	6,070,755	246,417,033	+4,059

over. Exhibit 6.1 shows $100,000 grown over a 35-year period, both taxed and tax deferred.

PAYING MY FAIR SHARE DOES NOT MEAN THE MAXIMUM TAX I CAN PAY

Let me tell you right off that I pay my fair share of taxes. I believe that everybody should pay their fair share of taxes. I do not necessarily believe that one's fair share of taxes is equal to the maximum tax that can possibly be paid under current law.

I feel that it is each person's responsibility to try to save as much as is legally possible to do under the tax law. In fact, there was a ruling several years ago in which a U.S. Circuit Court Judge Learned Hand stated: "Anyone may so arrange his affairs that his taxes shall be as low as possible. He his not bound to choose a pattern that will best pay the Treasury. No one owes any public duty to pay more than the law demands."

Arthur Godfrey, a prominent radio and television personality of the 1950s, put forth the same sentiment but stated it this way: "I am proud to be an American and to be paying taxes in the U.S. The only thing is, I could be just as proud for half the money."

So, I'd like you to keep in mind that it is everyone's right, if not duty, to avoid taxes; and, in fact, this is a very key component of my retirement strategy. As you can see in my example of the commodity trader, taxes take quite a chunk out of what could be a substantial retirement plan if managed correctly.

A good part of this chapter will be meant to educate you on the tax-deferral or avoidance strategies that pertain to your retirement plan. I'm not going to be writing about those laws that are too complex to understand. What I will be describing are simple investment and tax strategies that will help you to put away and to compound more money for your retirement.

WHAT LIES AHEAD—AND HOW WILL IT AFFECT YOUR RETIREMENT?

Over the past few years, the trend has been toward increasing taxes to fund the wheels of government. So be aware that tax on your retirement funds is likely to increase in the future.

One of the most distressing characteristics of a recent budget submitted to Congress by the Clinton administration, in spite of the fact that it was balanced, was a little noticed side note. In this side note it was projected that the next generation of taxpayers would have to pay somewhere in the neighborhood of *85 percent of their income in taxes.* This was put into a budget that was submitted after passage of a tax bill that decreased the federal deficit. I have previously shown you how this situation already exists (85 percent of income is given away to the tax man).

THE CRUMBLING PILLARS

As I stated earlier, the three conventional pillars of the American retirement system are in big trouble. I explained briefly how taxes contribute to that, and now, I would like to go into further detail about this situation.

Pillar 1—Company Retirement Plans: The Fading Pension

For some time now, the U.S. government has been tinkering with the pension system and the benefits that they will allow. In an article in the *New York Times,* May 4, 1995,[4] "From Washington, the Fading Pension," it is reported that in addition to trying to pay off the deficit, the U.S. government is also committed to "making retirement benefits more equitable."

The *New York Times* article reported that the cumulative result of all the tinkering has been anything *but* more equitable. The consensus of a growing group of experts and economists is that these changes will have a detrimental impact on many of the 41 million workers covered by traditional company-financed pension plans. They also report that because some of the changes are just coming into play and will continue to become effective as the years go on, the impact may not be realized for many years to come. They are in agreement, however, that the baby boomers will be the most affected by these changes.

Some of the impact is already being felt by high-salaried executives who are about to retire or already retired. But at some point, the experts agree, even moderately salaried workers will feel a significant degree of pain.

The *New York Times* isolated four factors at work:

1. The legal changes restrict the amount of money that businesses can put aside each year to finance pension benefits. The government has reduced the tax deductions that businesses can claim for this purpose.

2. A set of changes completed in 1993 has lowered the maximum salary used to calculate *future* pensions.

3. A change was initiated almost a decade ago that limits benefits available for wealthy retirees by putting a limit on the total amount of money that can be paid out in any one year without a surtax.

4. An exploding number of complex regulations are needed to carry out these and other changes. A 1990 study entitled "The Hay/Higgins Study" concluded that these regulations, which cover more than 600 pages, require "an army of lawyers, actuaries, and accountants, who often seem to be the major beneficiaries of the legislation."

The cost of this compliance can be extremely high for a small company, and, in fact, most small companies now must spend about $500 per year, per worker. This gives many of them the excuse to drop traditional pension plans.

The *Times* article concluded that one unintended consequence of all of the exchanges is that the retirement safety net on which American workers have always counted is now unraveling. It stated,

> Something will have to change, nearly all the experts say. They argue that Washington needs to find a way to cut the deficit other than nibbling away at pension benefits.
>
> "On the one hand we want to collect all the taxes we can today," said Olivia S. Mitchell, a professor at the Wharton School of Business at the University of Pennsylvania and executive director of its Pension Research Council.
>
> "On the other, we want to increase retirement savings."
>
> When it comes to pensions, the experts say, the hard reality is that you can't do both.

Some key dates to be aware of regarding pensions are as follows:

1982: Congress cut the maximum pension that can be paid to retirees each year to $90,000 (currently $120,000 with increases for inflation). The old maximum amount prior to this cap was $136,425.

The maximum amount employers and employees can put into 401(k) savings plans per year is also reduced to $30,000 or 25 percent of pay, whichever is less. The prior cap on this was $45,475.

1986: Congress limited 401(k) contributions to $7,000 per year for individuals (currently $9,240 after increases for inflation). It further capped contributions for people earning more than $66,000 per year.

1987: Congress limited employers' calculations of contributions into pension plans for future retirees and excluded any consideration of projected pay raises in this calculation. The intent was to prevent companies from building surpluses and then terminating the plans to reap any excess money.

This was significant because this change forced companies to delay the funding of baby boomers' pensions until later in their careers. Some experts fear that companies will terminate these pension plans rather than make the huge contributions needed for the baby boomers.

1992: Congress devised a scheme to raise money to pay for extended unemployment benefits. The source of this money is withholding-tax payments on pension distributions. The scheme works this way. From now on if you take a direct distribution from your pension plan, the distribution is subject to a 20 percent withholding tax. This is true even if you roll it over within 60 days into a new plan. The only way around this is by doing a trustee-to-trustee transfer of your plan. Prior to this you could roll over the plan and have full use of the entire amount of the money for 60 days.

1993: Congress cut the maximum pay to $150,000 that can be counted when funding pensions or making 401(k) contributions. The prior limit was $235,840. Although this appears only to affect people earning more than $150,000, that is not true. Because of the complexity of this calculation, middle-income-wage earners are, as usual, hit the hardest.

1994: Congress slowed the growth of 401(k) contributions. Prior to this the maximum employee contribution and salary level at which people could contribute had been liberally adjusted for inflation. These amounts of adjustments are now reduced considerably.

2001: Congress allows for catch up provisions in retirement benefits for some taxpayers.

Pillar 2—Savings: The Shrinking American Bank Account

The *USA TODAY*/Gallup poll that I referenced in Chapter 1 projected that 40 percent of all Americans saved less than $1,000 last year. It was also proposed that they would need $1,000,000 by the time they retired to be able to maintain a $50,000 per year annual income in retirement. This was assuming the same level of pension and Social Security as is currently available. This assumption is most likely incorrect because current levels will probably diminish from where they are today.

The poll examined target rates of savings for various groups of Americans and estimated what percentage of take-home pay these people should be saving to maintain their current lifestyle in retirement (as shown in Exhibit 6.2). These figures, too, presume that the current levels of Social Security benefits will not be cut and furthermore that taxes will not be raised—although most experts believe that both will happen.

The experts who projected these levels of savings made several assumptions that give you some idea of the targets for savings. First, these savings targets presume that all the interest earned will be taxed

EXHIBIT 6.2 Target Savings Percentages

	Target Savings Rate for Ages			
Married Couples	**25–34**	**35–44**	**45–54**	**55–64**
Earnings = $30,000				
With pension	0.3%	4.6%	12.0%	11.5%
Without pension	2.3	11.4	18.2	17.7
Earnings = $50,000				
With pension	0.7	6.3	16.6	15.9
Without pension	3.0	11.8	21.5	20.8
Earnings = $75,000				
With pension	1.2	8.3	20.1	19.1
Without pension	4.0	14.1	25.1	24.2
Earnings = $100,000				
With pension	3.9	8.8	17.6	24.7
Without pension	7.8	15.4	23.5	30.1
Earnings = $150,000				
With pension	5.6	11.8	20.6	28.9
Without pension	10.2	19.4	27.4	34.9

on an annual basis. I will investigate several methods to defer taxation on the money you put away for retirement—a concept that is an integral component of my retirement plan strategy.

Second, the savings targets presume that savings will be a major portion of your retirement assets. My strategy refutes that notion, and I will show you how to attain a much higher yield on your retirement money than would be possible through conventional savings accounts. This can be achieved through the use of mutual funds and related products.

The following are some important dates relating to savings and IRAs:

1981: Congress allowed all workers to take a $2,000 tax deduction for contributions to an IRA.

1985: IRA tax deductions peaked at $38.2 billion.

1986: Congress limited deductions for IRA contributions to people without pensions, couples who earn less than $50,000, and singles who earn less than $35,000.

1993: After years of decline, IRA deductions hit $8 billion.

1995: House passed an IRA proposal that would eliminate taxes and penalties for people who use the money before retirement to pay for a first home or for college or medical expenses. Senate action is imminent.

1997: The Roth IRA and Educational IRA are created.

2001: Levels of contribution expanded, and catch-up provisions for those over 49 years of age are added.

Pillar 3—Social Security: The Great Pyramid of Washington, DC

Whenever I address a group of people at the investment seminars I give, I am amazed to find that many of them still believe that the Social Security money taken out of their pay checks each week is being put into an account with their name on it. They actually believe that there is an FICA (Federal Insurance Contributions Act) account for them, collecting interest and being invested, and that it will be there when it's time for them to retire. This is, in fact, the way the Social Security system had been intended to work.

The intent of the Social Security Act of 1935 was that each person would be required to contribute a portion of his or her paycheck to an account that would be held for him or her, earning interest and growing—one that would be ready to be used when retirement came. What has happened over the years, however, is that Congress has tapped into the Social Security system to the point where it has become just another general tax.

In actuality, the use of this money for other projects has been another Congressional scheme to continue their program of pork-barreling—funding each other's special interest programs. *Consequently, there is no Social Security account with your name on it on which you can retire.*

Congress passed a bill several years ago, generally known as "the government reapportionment of assets bill," that entitles it to use any money left, after paying out current Social Security benefits, for virtually anything else they like.

I'm going to make a statement that may startle you: *The Social Security system is the greatest pyramid scheme in the history of the world.* Over the past generation, the workforce has been growing, and this base of cash flow has been used to fund the benefits of a smaller group at the top—those collecting.

What is about to happen, however, is that due to the increase in life expectancy and the increase in projected baby boomer Social Security recipients, the top is about to explode. Furthermore, due to the advent of affordable birth control and changes in social consciousness, the labor force has been shrinking relative to those collecting.

So, the pyramid is about to become inverted. This is where significant trouble lies ahead for the Social Security system. The reserve that was supposed to be built up has virtually been depleted, and the system is projected to run out of money in the near future.

Some key dates to keep in mind are as follows:

> *1983:* Congress raised Social Security taxes to build a surplus to cover baby boomers' retirement benefits. Social Security actuaries predicted that the surplus would last until 2063, when the youngest baby boomers turn 99.
>
> *1994:* Social Security becomes *185 percent* taxable to the individual. This tax hike applies to any taxpayer with income over certain levels. The income calculation is complicated and includes income that is otherwise nontaxable (such as municipal bonds). Prior to this tax-law change, Social Security was only *150 percent* taxable.

I refer to these rates as being 185 percent taxable rather than 85 percent taxable for the following reason: The money that you contributed to the Social Security fund was *taxed already* when it was earned. The money, which was taken from your paycheck, was not a deduction from taxable income—although you never saw it.

What Congress has now done is to pass a law to allow them to *retax* this money. It previously was *retaxed* at 50 percent but now it is retaxed at 85 percent.

2005: The age for collecting full Social Security benefits will increase from 65 to 66. However, many experts feel that at some point prior to this date more restrictions will have to be passed.

2013: Social Security will pay more retirement benefits than it collects in payroll taxes. This is a projection put forth by the trustees of the Social Security system, and at that point, the system will have to depend on income from some other source to fund its payments.

2019: Social Security payments will exhaust interest earnings and go into the trust fund.

2022: The age for collecting full Social Security benefits will increase from 66 to 67. However, many experts feel that at some point prior to this date more restrictions will have to be passed.

2030: The trustees of the Social Security system project that Social Security will run out of money. Baby boomers, aged 67 through 84, are now collecting Social Security.

CONCLUSION: THE 10 DEADLY SINS OF RETIREMENT PLANNING

Why are 95 percent of all Americans living on the edge during their retirement?

Government statistics show that only 5 percent of the people in the United States have enough money for a comfortable retirement. This is not only because of the magnitude of change in society as outlined in this chapter, but also because of ten basic faults—*Ten Sins*—in people's retirement plans:

1. Inadequate savings.
2. Dependence on Social Security for retirement income.
3. A spendthrift lifestyle.
4. Poor understanding of the effect of taxation.
5. Poor understanding of inflation.
6. Poor understanding of true risk—the risk of losing money by not keeping up with inflation.
7. Poor understanding of investments and lack of a sound investment plan.
8. Retirement planning advice from the wrong sources, such as *Money* magazine or the *Wall Street Journal.*
9. Inadequate insurance coverage.
10. Procrastination—*failing to plan is akin to planning to fail.*

Let's compare two people: Each starts working at age 23 and works until he is 53—30 years. (1) Mr. Smartplanner put away a $2,000 IRA contribution for the first eight years of his career and then did nothing more for the next 22 years. (2) Mr. Dumbplanner didn't start to contribute to an IRA until his ninth year of work and put away the same amount until he retired. Let's assume that each put his money in the Standard & Poor's (S&P) index, which has averaged about 11 percent over the past 60 or 70 years.

At the end of 30 years, Smartplanner had $204,000. He only made contributions of $2,000 for eight years—only $16,000—but he started doing it immediately.

On the other hand, Dumbplanner saved $2,000 for each of years 9 to 30. He actually saved almost three times the money that Smartplanner did, but at the end of 30 years, Dumbplanner had only $154,000.

Compound interest is what I call *the eighth wonder of the world.*

7

They Don't Make Hearses with Luggage Racks

"The Lord Giveth, and the IRS Taketh Away."
—Quote posted on the wall of an ex-IRS official.

THE LAST LAUGH

What do Jackie Kennedy Onassis, Groucho Marxs, Elvis Presley, and Senator Robert S. Kerr all have in common? (Aside from the fact that they are all dead.)

Whenever I ask this question in my seminars, I get a mixture of answers. Most of the time people will say, "They're all wealthy," to which I will respond, "No, they all *were* wealthy."

The true answer is that although each of these prominent people had a substantial amount of wealth, and the resources to adequately plan for their own demise, not one of them took the time or the effort to properly prepare for the burdensome estate tax. Although each of these prominent people had a host of professionals at his or her service and the capability of setting up a tax-free estate, each one of these people paid a substantial amount of tax to the government. Additionally, a great deal of their assets went toward paying probate and other legal fees.

Why do you think they auctioned off Jackie Kennedy Onassis's jewelry at Christies? Do you think it was because her heirs got tired of having these heirlooms around? The answer is that although Jackie Kennedy Onassis had a great deal of wealth, much of her assets were put into illiquid types of investments and other property. Therefore, when the estate tax became due, her heirs had to raise the cash necessary to pay the tremendous tax on her estate. Much of her assets was in jewelry and real estate—assets not easily convertible into cash. Therefore, many of them had to be liquidated at fire-sale prices.

Upon their demise, Groucho Marxs and Elvis Presley each forfeited approximately 83 percent and 72 percent of their estates, respectively, in taxes, probate costs, and other legal fees.

And even Robert S. Kerr, the senator from Kansas who in the mid-1970s was the chief proponent of the estate-tax legislation in Congress, was not adequately prepared for his own death. Although, he was a spearhead in the movement to heavily tax people's estate upon death, he did not properly prepare for his own. Because of this, his heirs had to auction approximately $9 million of real estate, realizing only $3 million, in order to raise the cash necessary to pay Kerr's estate-tax bill.

Whenever people think about tax, they usually think about income tax. But, the estate tax is one of the least understood of all the taxes in the current U.S. tax system. It is also one of the most heinous and, in my opinion, one of the taxes that is extremely unfair in its nature and in the sneaky way it comes about.

I say it is one of the most heinous taxes because the estate-tax rates start at a level of approximately 37 percent, and escalate very quickly to a level of 55 percent and then 60 percent (with an additional 5 percent surtax). Compared to the income tax, a tax on which everybody focuses and quite adamantly protests, this is quite extreme. Individual income tax rates start at a comparatively low 15 percent and go to a maximum of 39.6 percent. If you compare the two taxes, the lowest rate for the estate tax picks up where the income tax leaves off!

I feel this is unfair because most of the assets on which you are taxed—or rather on which your estate is taxed—are assets that were built up with *posttax* income. The assets that were built up in an individual's portfolio (and ultimately in an individual's estate) have been taxed already (or in the case of retirement funds, *will* be taxed again). They have been taxed when the income was *earned* by the individual, and they will be *taxed again* when the individual dies. This is one more example—an *extreme* example—of the *double taxation* system.

Another example of double taxation would be the income tax on dividends that individuals must pay after receiving them from corporate investments. In the double taxation system of corporate dividends, taxes are levied on an individual for receiving dividend distributions from a corporation. These dividends are paid by the corporation on income that it had earned and on which it had already paid tax *as a corporation*. The dividend that you receive as *an individual* (and on which you pay tax as an individual) is *not deductible* to the corporation in calculating taxable income on corporate profits. For that reason a dividend is taxed twice: (1) it is taxed on the corporate level as part of corporate income and (2) it is taxed once again by the individual as dividend income.

ESTATE-TAX PLANNING 101: THE BASICS

When you think about a tax return, what do you think about? You think about Form 1040 from the IRS. It arrives in the mail every year around the first week in January. Most people don't even think about the other type of tax return that has to be filed, and this tax return is filed only once. The reason most people don't think about it is because they never see it—when they file it, they're dead. It is filed on their behalf by the executor of their estate.

The estate-tax return is made on Form 706, and let me tell you something: *If you weren't dead already, this tax return would kill you!*

If you look at Exhibit 7.1, you will see a copy of the first three pages of Form 706—a 35-page form! On page one, it basically takes the value of every single asset and summarizes the total value. The assets are then itemized on subsequent pages. The 706 actually marks your positions to market at the end of your life, and the government says, *"Put down everything you own on this tax return."*

Exhibit 7.2 is a table of the estate-tax rates. You can see that the government taxes your estate at rates that start at 37 percent and go up to 60 percent. This does not include another separate tax that is levied by states on estates. This subject will not be addressed here because the states vary so much and the rates differ; but it is also part of the high cost of dying in the United States.

Now, getting back to Form 706 (Exhibit 7.1). On page one of the estate-tax return, after you, or, rather, your executor summarizes all of your assets, and totals their value, you are granted (on line 11) what's known as the *unified credit,* that is, if you haven't already used up your unified credit during your lifetime. The unified credit is an amount that is equal to $625,000 per person (in 1998) and that will escalate gradually to $1 million in the year 2006 (see Exhibit 7.3). (Note that line 11 of page 1 of Form 706 will be $211,300 in 1999.)

Note that: (1) The annual gift-tax exemption is still $10,000 per recipient but now is tied to the C.P.I.; (2) the annual gift-tax exemption will only increase in $1,000 increments, so probably no increase will occur until the year 2002 at a 3 to 3½ percent inflation rate; (3) the Generation-Skipping Transfer Tax exemption of $1 million will increase starting in 1999, rounded to $10,000 increments.

THE UNIFIED GIFT AND ESTATE TAX

There is a single tax rate that applies to both gifts and estates. It is called the unified gift and estate tax. With some exceptions, everything you own or give away, whether during your life or upon your death, is added together to figure out your total tax liability. There is a

EXHIBIT 7.1 United States Estate (and Generation-Skipping Transfer) Tax Return

Form **706** (Rev. August 1993) Department of the Treasury Internal Revenue Service

United States Estate (and Generation-Skipping Transfer) Tax Return

Estate of a citizen or resident of the United States (see separate instructions). To be filed for decedents dying after October 8, 1990. For Paperwork Reduction Act Notice, see instructions.

OMB No. 1545-0015 Expires 12-31-95

Part 1. Decedent & Executor

1a Decedent's first name and middle initial (and maiden name, if any)	1b Decedent's last name		2 Decedent's soc. sec. no.
3a Domicile at time of death (county and state, or foreign country)	3b Year domicile established	4 Date of birth	5 Date of death
6a Name of executor (see instructions)	6b Executor's address (number and street including apt. or suite no. or rural route; city, town, or post office; state; and ZIP code)		
6c Executor's social security number (see instructions)			
7a Name and location of court where will was probated or estate administered			7b Case number
8 If decedent died testate, check here ▶ ☐ and attach a certified copy of the will.	9 If Form 4768 is attached, check here ▶ ☐		
10 If Schedule R - 1 is attached, check here ▶ ☐			

Part 2. Tax Computation

Line	Description			Line	Amount
1	Total gross estate (from Part 5, Recapitulation, page 3, item 10)			1	
2	Total allowable deductions (from Part 5, Recapitulation, page 3, item 20)			2	
3	Taxable estate (subtract line 2 from line 1)			3	
4	Adjusted taxable gifts (total taxable gifts (within the meaning of section 2503) made by the decedent after December 31, 1976, other than gifts that are includible in decedent's gross estate (section 2001(b))			4	
5	Add lines 3 and 4			5	
6	Tentative tax on the amount on line 5 from Table A in the instructions			6	
7a	If line 5 exceeds $10,000,000, enter the lesser of line 5 or $21,040,000. If line 5 is $10,000,000 or less, skip lines 7a and 7b and enter -0- on line 7c	7a			
b	Subtract $10,000,000 from line 7a	7b			
c	Enter 5% (.05) of line 7b			7c	
8	Total tentative tax (add lines 6 and 7c)			8	
9	Total gift tax payable with respect to gifts made by the decedent after December 31, 1976. Include gift taxes by the decedent's spouse for such spouse's share of split gifts (section 2513) only if the decedent was the donor of these gifts and they are includible in the decedent's gross estate (see instructions)			9	
10	Gross estate tax (subtract line 9 from line 8)			10	
11	Maximum unified credit against estate tax	11	192,800.00		
12	Adjustment to unified credit. (This adjustment may not exceed $6,000. See instr.)	12			
13	Allowable unified credit (subtract line 12 from line 11)			13	
14	Subtract line 13 from line 10 (but do not enter less than zero)			14	
15	Credit for state death taxes. Do not enter more than line 14. Compute the credit by using the amount on line 3 less $60,000. See Table B in the instructions and **attach credit evidence** (see instructions)			15	
16	Subtract line 15 from line 14			16	
17	Credit for Federal gift taxes on pre-1977 gifts (section 2012) (attach computation)	17			
18	Credit for foreign death taxes (from Schedule(s) P). (Attach Form(s) 706CE)	18			
19	Credit for tax on prior transfers (from Schedule Q)	19			
20	Total (add lines 17, 18, and 19)			20	
21	Net estate tax (subtract line 20 from line 16)			21	
22	Generation-skipping transfer taxes (from Schedule R, Part 2, line 10)			22	
23	Section 4980A increased estate tax (from Schedule S, Part I, line 17) (see instructions)			23	
24	Total transfer taxes (add lines 21, 22, and 23)			24	
25	Prior payments. Explain in an attached statement	25			
26	United States Treasury bonds redeemed in payment of estate tax	26			
27	Total (add lines 25 and 26)			27	
28	Balance due (or overpayment) (subtract line 27 from line 24)			28	

Under penalties of perjury, I declare that I have examined this return, including accompanying schedules and statements, and to the best of my knowledge and belief, it is true, correct, and complete. Declaration of preparer other than the executor is based on all information of which preparer has any knowledge.

Signature(s) of executor(s) ______________________ Date ________

Form 706 (Rev. 8-93)

Estate of:

Part 3. – Elections by the Executor

Please check the "Yes" or "No" box for each question.	Yes	No
1 Do you elect alternate valuation?		
2 Do you elect special use valuation? If "Yes," you must complete and attach Schedule A-1		
3 Do you elect to pay the taxes in installments as described in section 6166? If "Yes," you must attach the additional information described in the instructions.		
4 Do you elect to postpone the part of the taxes attributable to a reversionary or remainder interest as described in section 6163?		

Part 4. – General Information (Note: Please attach the necessary supplemental documents. **You must attach the death certificate.**)

Authorization to receive confidential tax information under Regulations section 601.504(b)(2)(i), to act as the estate's representative before the Internal Revenue Service, and to make written or oral presentations on behalf of the estate if return prepared by an attorney, accountant, or enrolled agent for the executor:

Name of representative (print or type)	State	Address (number, street, and room or suite no., city, state, and ZIP code)

I declare that I am the ☐ attorney/ ☐ certified public accountant/ ☐ enrolled agent (you must check the applicable box) for the executor and prepared this return for the executor. I am not under suspension or disbarment from practice before the Internal Revenue Service and am qualified to practice in the state shown above.

Signature	CAF number	Date	Telephone number

1 Death certificate number and issuing authority (attach a copy of the death certificate to this return).

2 Decedent's business or occupation. If retired, check here ▶ ☐ and state decedent's former business or occupation.

3 Marital status of the decedent at time of death:

☐ Married

☐ Widow or widower - Name, SSN, and date of death of deceased spouse ▶ ....

☐ Single

☐ Legally separated

☐ Divorced - Date divorce decree became final ▶

4a Surviving spouse's name	4b Social security number	4c Amount received (see instructions)

5 Individuals (other than the surviving spouse), trusts, or other estates who receive benefits from the estate (do not include charitable beneficiaries shown in Schedule O)(see instructions). For Privacy Act Notice (applicable to individual beneficiaries only), see the Instructions for Form 1040.

Name of individual, trust, or estate receiving $5,000 or more	Identifying number	Relationship to decedent	Amount (see instructions)
All unascertainable beneficiaries and those who receive less than $5,000 ▶			
Total			

(Continued on next page)

Form 706 (Rev. 8-93)

Part 4. – General Information (continued)

Please check the "Yes" or "No" box for each question.		Yes	No
6	Does the gross estate contain any section 2044 property (qualified terminable interest property (QTIP) from a prior gift or estate) (see instructions)?		
7a	Have Federal gift tax returns ever been filed? If "Yes," please attach copies of the returns, if available, and furnish the following information:		
7b	Period(s) covered — 7c Internal Revenue office(s) where filed		
	If you answer "Yes" to any of questions 8–16, you must attach additional information as described in the instructions.		
8a	Was there any insurance on the decedent's life that is not included on the return as part of the gross estate?		
b	Did the decedent own any insurance on the life of another that is not included in the gross estate?		
9	Did the decedent at the time of death own any property as a joint tenant with right of survivorship in which (a) one or more of the other joint tenants was someone other than the decedent's spouse, and (b) less than the full value of the property is included on the return as part of the gross estate? If "Yes," you must complete and attach Schedule E		
10	Did the decedent, at the time of death, own any interest in a partnership or unincorporated business or any stock in an inactive or closely held corporation?		
11	Did the decedent make any transfer described in section 2035, 2036, 2037, or 2038 (see the instructions for Schedule G)? If "Yes," you must complete and attach Schedule G.		
12	Were there in existence at the time of the decedent's death:		
a	Any trusts created by the decedent during his or her lifetime?		
b	Any trusts not created by the decedent under which the decedent possessed any power, beneficial interest, or trusteeship?		
13	Did the decedent ever possess, exercise, or release any general power of appointment? If "Yes," you must complete and attach Schedule H.		
14	Was the marital deduction computed under the transitional rule of Public Law 97-34, section 403(e)(3) (Economic Recovery Tax Act of 1981)? If "Yes," attach a separate computation of the marital deduction, enter the amt. on item 18 of the Recapitulation, & note on item 18 "computation attached."		
15	Was the decedent, immediately before death, receiving an annuity described in the "General" paragraph of the instructions for Schedule I? If "Yes," you must complete and attach Schedule I		
16	Did the decedent have a total "excess retirement accumulation" (as defined in section 4980A(d)) in qualified employer plans and individual retirement plans? If "Yes," you must complete and attach Schedule S		

Part 5. – Recapitulation

Item number	Gross estate	Alternate value	Value at date of death
1	Schedule A – Real Estate		
2	Schedule B – Stocks and Bonds		
3	Schedule C – Mortgages, Notes, and Cash		
4	Schedule D – Insurance on the Decedent's Life (attach Form(s) 712)		
5	Schedule E – Jointly Owned Property (attach Form(s) 712 for life insurance)		
6	Schedule F – Other Miscellaneous Property (attach Form(s) 712 for life insurance)		
7	Schedule G – Transfers During Decedent's Life (attach Form(s) 712 for life insurance)		
8	Schedule H – Powers of Appointment		
9	Schedule I – Annuities		
10	Total gross estate (add items 1 through 9). Enter here and on line 1 of the Tax Computation		

Item number	Deductions	Amount
11	Schedule J – Funeral Expenses and Expenses Incurred in Administering Property Subject to Claims	
12	Schedule K – Debts of the Decedent	
13	Schedule K – Mortgages and Liens	
14	Total of items 11 through 13	
15	Allowable amount of deductions from item 14 (see the instructions for item 15 of the Recapitulation)	
16	Schedule L – Net Losses During Administration	
17	Schedule L – Expenses Incurred in Administering Property Not Subject to Claims	
18	Schedule M – Bequests, etc., to Surviving Spouse	
19	Schedule O – Charitable, Public, and Similar Gifts and Bequests	
20	Total allowable deductions (add items 15 through 19). Enter here and on line 2 of the Tax Computation	

CS1

Page 3
Form 706 (Rev. 8-93)

EXHIBIT 7.2 The Uniform Gift- and Estate-Tax Rate Schedules

Property Taxed			Tax	Plus
$ 500,000	to	$ 750,000	$ 155,800	37% of amount over $500,000
750,000	to	1,000,000	248,300	39% of amount over $750,000
1,000,000	to	1,250,000	345,800	41% of amount over $1,000,000
1,500,000	to	2,000,000	555,800	45% of amount over $1,500,000
2,000,000	to	2,500,000	780,800	49% of amount over $2,000,000
2,500,000	to	3,000,000	1,025,800	53% of amount over $2,500,000
3,000,000	to	5,000,000	1,290,800	55% of amount over $3,000,000
5,000,000	to	10,000,000	2,390,800	55% of amount over $5,000,000
10,000,000	to	21,040,000	5,140,800	60% of amount over $10,000,000
21,040,000	and	above	11,764,800	55% of amount over $21,040,000

one-time $675,000 unified credit (in 2001) that can be applied to either gift or estate taxes. The unified credit can be used to offset your tax on either your lifetime gifts or on your taxable estate. Each person gets one unified credit, and it doesn't matter if he or she uses it up during his or her lifetime or to offset estate taxes at the date of death. All the taxable gifts that were made are added to the assets you own at death to figure out your taxable estate. The tax already paid on the gifts is deducted from your taxable estate bill.

There are two exceptions to this rule: (1) an individual can make gifts of up to $10,000 per recipient per year completely tax free; these gifts do not even figure into the taxable estate and are not reported on any tax form; (2) assets freely transferred between spouses.

If you are married, both you and your spouse get one unified credit each. This means that each spouse has an equivalent exemption of $675,000. For couples who have combined estates under $675,000, it doesn't matter who dies first or how much they leave to each other or

EXHIBIT 7.3 The Unified Credit Schedule

	Estate- and Gift-Tax Relief
Year	**Amount Excluded**
2001	$ 675,000
2002 and 2003	1,000,000 (Estate)
	1,060,000 (Gift)
2004 and 2005	1,500,000
2006–2008	2,000,000
2009	3,500,000

their children. No special action is needed to avoid federal estate tax. Each person's unified credit alone will pass the total combined estate-tax free. For couples with larger estates—those exceeding $650,000—the challenge is to avoid tax in the estate of the second spouse to die. All property that is transferred to the surviving spouse escapes tax free (estate-tax free) because of the *unlimited marital deduction,* which is really a deferral.

MULTIPLE CHOICES—A CAREER IN GOVERNMENT OR A CAREER IN GOVERNMENT?

Here's a multiple-choice question for extra credit:

I don't have to worry about taxes. It's all going to my ______?

a. Wife/husband/children
b. Accountant
c. Attorneys
d. The government

To find the answer, read on.

Most people will be the first to tell you, "I don't have enough to worry about estate taxes. And my wife [husband] is going to get everything anyway."

What they really should be saying is, "I don't have to worry about estate taxes. The government, attorneys, and accountants will get everything."

A TYPICAL ESTATE

The typical amount of wealth a person builds over a lifetime can be significant. Whether or not they realize it, most people have accumulated a pretty substantial estate. Let's look at the figures on an actual estate tax return which I prepared for an unmarried client of mine a short time ago. (See Exhibit 7.4.)

If you look at this exhibit, you will see the assets of an exclient of mine (rounded off for this exhibit). This taxpayer had a home that he purchased in 1957 for $35,000. At the time of his death, this home was valued at approximately 14 times that amount, or $500,000. His retirement plan had $750,000 approximately of securities, bonds, and other cash types of investments. He also had an investment account that had approximately $250,000 of small-cap, no-load mutual funds. He

EXHIBIT 7.4 A Typical Estate

Average Wealth Accumulated over a Lifetime

Asset	**Value**
Home	$ 500,000
Retirement plan(s)	750,000
Investments	250,000
Insurance	500,000
Personal possessions	150,000
Total assets	$2,100,000
Federal transfer costs	(901,000)
Left to the next generation	$1,199,000

thought he had taken care of his heirs appropriately by buying an insurance policy that had a face value of approximately $500,000. Additionally, his personal possessions were worth approximately $150,000, which included jewelry, a car, and cash on hand, as well as paintings and other miscellaneous, antique heirlooms. As you can see, the total market value of this portfolio was somewhere around $2.1 million.

All of his life, my client had indicated to me that he felt he didn't have to worry about the estate tax, and, in fact, he believed that he had it well taken care of. What I found out afterward was that he figured he would leave this $2.1 million to his heirs. He hadn't anticipated federal and state estate taxes; probate, attorneys', and executors' fees; and other miscellaneous costs. The total transfer cost of this wealth was 42 percent. He ended up passing on to his heirs only a fraction (about 58 percent) of the wealth that he had accumulated over a lifetime.

YOUR RETIREMENT PLAN GETS HIT WORSE

In Exhibit 7.5 you will see that what you think is retirement-plan wealth that you can pass on to you heirs is actually taxed at a much

EXHIBIT 7.5 The Retirement Plan

Pension	$2,000,000
Income tax	(800,000)
Net assets	$1,200,000
Estate tax	(660,000)
Net from $2,000,000	$ 540,000

higher rate. That is because your wealth is not just subject to estate tax on your death but also to income tax on any tax-deferred wealth you have accumulated. Notice, I say *tax deferred,* not tax free. The slogan around our office is, "You pay now or you pay later, but everyone's gonna pay."

Let's look at how the retirement plan of one of my clients got hit upon his death (the figures are rounded).

Exhibit 7.5 was part of an estate-tax return, in which the gentleman accumulated approximately $2 million for his retirement but ended up passing only a small portion of it on to his heirs. As you can see, he started out with a $2 million pension. When he died, however, income tax became payable and due on the pension that had been tax-deferred over the course of his lifetime. This income-tax rate, including state and federal taxes, was approximately 40 percent, or $800,000. This left a net asset value in his estate of $1.2 million. The transfer cost of this estate was another $660,000 including federal and state estate taxes and other administrative costs as we have discussed. The net result of this was that from a $2 million estate, my client was left with approximately $540,000. The heirs of this estate only received 27 percent of what my client thought he had put away for them.

"The More You Ernst, the More They Takes"

Alvin C. Ernst, CPA, was a founding partner of what was then one of the eight largest accounting firms in the country, Ernst and Ernst, CPAs. This founding partner died at age 56; and although he had the knowledge to have been able to take care of his estate-tax planning, he did not have the forethought to do so. When he died, Alvin Ernst was worth approximately $12.5 million. The amount of wealth that was transferred to his heirs out of this estate ended up being approximately $5.5 million. The figures are shown in Exhibit 7.6.

The problem with Alvin Ernst's estate plan, was that he had none. In other words, *he died intestate. Dying intestate* means dying without any will or estate plan. Because of this, *his heirs received a mere 44 percent* of what they could have had if he had done his homework properly.

The Case of Sewell Avery

Sewell Avery was the president of Montgomery Ward. He died at age 86 with an estate that was valued at a little over $19 million. He had no surviving spouse, and, once again, his heirs received a mere fraction of what they should have. Out of the full estate of $19 million, Mr. Avery transferred only $5,016,041 to his heirs, *a mere 26 percent* of what he

EXHIBIT 7.6 Estate of Alvin C. Ernst, CPA

Estate Value:	$12,642,431
Estate Settlement Costs:	
Debts	6,232
Administration expense	58,862
Attorney's fees	10,000
Executor's fees	10,000
Ohio estate tax	1,226,737
Federal estate tax	5,812,281
Total Costs:	$ 7,124,112
Total Wealth Transfer Cost:	$ 7,124,112
Remaining Estate:	$ 5,518,319

could have had if he had done his homework properly. The figures are shown in Exhibit 7.7.

Tom Carvel—the Ice Cream Magnet

In a June 15, 1998, *Forbes* article entitled "Meltdown of an Ice Cream Fortune," Thomas Easton reported that Tom Carvel made every mistake there was to make in an estate plan. The article warned the reader not to make those same mistakes. As the article related, the scene was a small courtroom in White Plains, New York, where Judge Albert Emanuelli had just concluded two months of all-day depositions in the

EXHIBIT 7.7 Estate of Sewell Avery

Estate Value:	$19,100,000
Estate Settlement Costs:	
Debts	89,000
Administration expense	158,000
Attorney's fee	367,500
Executor's fee	240,000
Estate tax—State*	2,337,970
Estate tax—Federal**	10,891,489
Total Costs:	$14,083,959
Total Wealth Transfer Cost:	$14,083,959
Remaining Estate:	$ 5,016,041

*Illinois, $1,878,552; Oregon, $457,117; Michigan, $2,301.
**No surviving spouse.

latest case that could have come straight from the pages of a Dickens novel. "I came here in 1991, and this case is still being litigated," the judge told the assembled jurors. "Seven years of litigation. I think it's tragic."

The article reported that what could have been a $200 million estate had dwindled down to approximately $60 million. Carvel wanted his money to go to his widow and to local charities, but the biggest recipients of the money, so far, had been his lawyers. The article went on to estimate that had it not been for these legal expenses and other costs of probate, his estate would have been close to $250 million. But the Thomas and Agnes Carvel Foundation has but $12 million and has managed to distribute less than $6 million of that to charitable causes that Carvel had stipulated. His widow is not doing well either. Although, she was supposed to receive the income from her husband's fortune, she has not seen one penny from this part of the estate. The *Forbes* article indicated that what Tom Carvel did wrong was to violate the five basic rules of estate planning:

1. Find a good and trustworthy executor.
2. Anticipate conflicts.
3. Keep it simple.
4. Get your papers in order prior to death.
5. Do not be a control freak.

Because Tom Carvel did not properly take care of each of these five basic rules, he has lost most of his money to court battles, administrative expenses, legal fees, and other costs involved with the probative in estate.

The Case of Howard Hughes

In *Nation's Business* magazine dated April 1997, Randy Myers reported in a story called "Where There's a Will . . . ," that Howard Hughes left an estate worth an estimated $2 billion when he died in 1976. What he did not leave was a will.

It took nearly 15 years and $30 million in legal fees to prove that the various wills that surfaced after his death were forgeries. And it took more than that amount of time and money to settle his affairs. His heirs had to pay millions more in death taxes than would have been necessary had Howard Hughes taken the proper steps to avoid them.

The fact that Howard Hughes wound up giving large sums of money to tax authorities and lawyers was extremely ironic. All of his life, he reported to have hated both. But this also illustrates one of the universal truths of estate planning: *No matter how poorly you plan for the disposition of your estate, the outcome will most likely be worse if you don't plan at all.* In other words, if you fail to plan, you have really planned to fail.

Government officials or perhaps your squabbling heirs will decide what happens to your assets—assets that you have built up over a lifetime. The result, as demonstrated by the Howard Hughes case as well as by many others, oftentimes ends up becoming ugly.

The Case of Reginald Lewis

Reginald Lewis was the richest black man in America, that is, until his untimely death at age 50 on January 21, 1993. Reginald Lewis took $5 million and built it up to $20 million. He bought Beatrice Food products in the last three years of his life. Beatrice Food products was listed, ultimately, as being $450 million worth of assets. Reginald Lewis was not prepared for this untimely death and, consequently, a large part of his estate went to settlement costs and the government.

There's an ironic part to his obituary—there always is. Mr. Lewis's friends and associates said, "He was in perfect health until three months ago when he developed a brain tumor."

The moral of this story is that everybody is in perfect health—until they're not. Don't procrastinate. You will never be younger than you are today. If you understand that you are some day going to die, then you should take the time today to formulate your estate plan.

The Case of Joe Robbie's Dolphins

In a March 1994 article of *Financial Planning Magazine,* Daniel Dunaief, in an article entitled "Don't Get Blind-Sided," reported that estate taxes forced the sale of an NFL franchise. This article reported that despite losing the Super Bowl in 1994 for the fourth straight year, the Buffalo Bills were not the year's biggest losers in the NFL. That distinction belonged to the Robbie family, the former owners of the Miami Dolphins. Torn apart by family dissension, general management, and estate-tax problems (reportedly in excess of $45 million), this family was forced to sell the Dolphins, one of the most valuable franchises in professional sports, at a bargain basement price. The problem with Joe Robbie's estate plan was similar to the problem that all of these other examples have illustrated. There was none!

Exhibit 7.8 shows a list of seventeen other estates of fairly well known people, both high-dollar value and low-dollar value, that have been ravaged over time by the heinous estate tax.

Arranged from highest rate of shrinkage to lowest, this list is full of informative examples. Nat "King" Cole was far from wealthy by

EXHIBIT 7.8 The Impact of Estate-Settlement Costs

	Gross Estate	Total Settlement Costs	Net Estate	Percent Shrinkage
Nat "King" Cole	$ 1,876,648	$ 1,577,740	$ 298,908	84%
Elvis Presley	10,165,434	7,374,635	2,790,799	72
J.P. Morgan	17,121,482	11,893,691	5,227,791	69
William Holden	6,064,731	4,083,853	1,980,878	67
John D. Rockefeller, Sr.	26,905,182	17,124,988	9,780,194	64
Charles Woolworth	16,788,702	10,391,303	6,397,399	62
Karen Carpenter	6,110,476	3,536,987	2,573,489	58
Marilyn Monroe	819,176	448,750	370,426	55
Conrad Hilton	199,070,700	105,782,217	93,288,483	53
William Boeing	22,386,158	10,589,748	11,796,410	47
Natalie Wood	9,779,605	3,784,888	5,994,717	39
Harry S. Truman	747,648	281,280	466,368	38
W.C. Fields	884,680	329,793	554,887	37
Bing Crosby	14,999,678	5,004,403	9,995,275	33
Gary Cooper	4,984,985	1,530,454	3,454,531	31
Franklin D. Roosevelt	1,940,999	574,867	1,366,132	30
Walt Disney	23,004,851	6,811,943	16,192,908	30

today's standards, yet he lost 84 percent of his estate to the government and settlement costs. And Marilyn Monroe, who had a modest estate, lost more than half to the same costs.

CONCLUSION

The moral here is you don't have to be rich or famous to have an estate-tax problem. If you die, you probably will have one—and you *will* die!

As Dorothy Parker purportedly once said at the infamous Algonquin Round Table: "There are only two sure things in life—death and taxes."

But as I have always said: "There is only *one* sure thing in life, and that is death—everything else is negotiable!"

Good estate planning is essential. If it is not properly done, the government has a plan for you. It is much more involved than simply avoiding taxes. It is also the process of determining the manner in which you want your property distributed and how this can be done with the minimum of administrative expense, legal expense, and, most of all, tax expense. Along with taxes, a solid estate plan must consider probate, insurance, investments, charitable contributions, and family wealth distributions. Good estate planning is directly related to a policy of strategic income-tax planning on an annual basis. I will address all of these issues in the next several chapters.

Don't take my word for it. Do your own research. But the truth of the matter is that unless you provide for your own demise, a great deal of the wealth that has managed to escape income tax will disappear with the transfer of your estate.

Remember, the estate tax is to be waived in 2010—for one year. As far as I am concerned, that is not the way to plan your estate strategy. Furthermore, as I stated in the Preface, seeing is believing. There are two more presidential elections prior to 2010, and two more opportunities to change the estate tax law. Even if the repeal comes to pass, January 2011 the estate tax reverts back to levels of pre-reform—a 55 percent estate tax plus 5 percent surtax.

8

Income and Expenses: A Review

INCOME DEFINED

I don't want to get too involved with advanced tax concepts in this book that is geared to the average investor or trader who most likely has a fairly basic knowledge of taxation. However, it is necessary to introduce a few important tax concepts. I do this to build a structure within which we can work on planning your investment-oriented tax strategy to reduce your tax liability. With this in mind, let's begin to look at a few tax definitions so that we understand the rules before we play the game. All the discussions from here on in will address the *cash-basis, calendar-year taxpayer,* a category within which 99 percent of all individual taxpayers fall.[1]

For federal income tax purposes, any acquisition of wealth, except gifts and inheritances, is considered to be income unless it is specifically excluded by Section 61 of the IRS Code. Fourteen specific types of income listed in this section of the IRS Code are the following:

1. Compensation for services, including fees, commissions, fringe benefits, and similar items.
2. Gross income from business.
3. Gains from dealings in property.
4. Interest.
5. Rents.
6. Royalties.
7. Dividends.
8. Alimony and separate maintenance payments.
9. Annuities.
10. Income from life insurance policies.
11. Pensions.

12. Income from discharge of debt.
13. Partner's share of partnership income.
14. Income from an interest in an estate or trust.

> The Tax Court has, through its decisions, developed a concept of income which is quite different from the layman's concept. The Supreme Court has approved this definition: "Income may be defined as the gain derived from capital, labor, or from both combined, provided it be understood to include profit gained through a sale or conversion of capital assets." In addition, the Supreme Court has repeatedly held that Congress' broad definition of what constitutes gross income was intended to tax all gain unless specifically exempted.[2]

In addition to some specific exclusions that were mentioned by the Code, such as damage settlements in personal injury cases, the following three items are particularly relevant to investors and are construed to *not* be income:

1. *Return of capital*—return of your original investment, such as the cost you have paid for shares of stock.
2. *Gifts and inheritances*—nontaxable to the recipient.
3. *Unrealized appreciation*—the value of property that has increased but has not been sold by the investor.

Another relevant investment/tax principle and ruling is that for a cash-basis taxpayer, interest is taxed when it is *received.* For example, the interest on a two-year *certificate of deposit (CD)* that is credited to the account every quarter is taxable in the year in which the interest is credited. The interest on a two-year CD that gets the interest credited at the end of the two-year period is not taxable in the first year, but rather when the interest is received in the account.

Another good example of the different tax treatments would be those involving different forms of U.S. government obligations: the one-year Treasury bill, the three-year Treasury note, and the ten-year Series EE Treasury bond. The U.S. Treasury issuances are an important subject because they are the standard to which most other investments are compared. In terms of rate of return, they are considered no-risk investments. For that reason, I use treasuries as illustrations quite frequently.

The Treasury bill, for example, that would be purchased in June of one year and redeemable in May of the following year would have the interest tacked on when the bill is redeemed. Therefore, the interest would be taxable only in the year of redemption, the following tax year.

Typically, how this works is that the investor would pay, say, $9,700 for a bill that would be redeemed for $10,000. At redemption,

$9,700 would be the nontaxable return of capital, and the $300 would be the interest earned and taxable in the year of redemption. A good tax strategy for an investor wanting to defer income from one year to the next would be to put some money into Treasury bills that would become payable on or after January 2 of the following year.

Compare the prior tax treatment with that of the three-year *Treasury note,* which pays interest every six months. In this case, the interest is taxable as it is received. So, if the same taxpayer purchases a $10,000, three-year Treasury note paying the same $300 per year, but paying $150 semiannually on June 30 and December 31, the interest would be taxable in the year it was paid. An investor who wanted to accelerate income into the current year would opt for this type of government investment vehicle as opposed to the Treasury bill.

Contrast this, again, with the ten-year Series EE treasury bond, which does not pay interest until the bond is redeemed at the end of the ten-year period. In this case, no interest income would have to be declared until the bond matured. This type of investment might be appropriate as a gift to a four-year-old child whom you would not want to have any income received and taxable until he or she turned 14 years old. (Review my section on the kiddie tax in the "Trader's Tax Survival Guide.")

As long as we are on the subject of U.S. Treasuries, several more areas are worth discussing briefly. The first is that *all* interest from U.S. bonds, notes, or bills issued after February 28, 1941, is taxable for *federal* purposes but is exempt from *state* taxation in most states.

The second issue is in the handling of income as interest as opposed to capital gains. Although the method of treatment was much more significant prior to the Tax Reform Act due to the greater difference in tax rates for capital gains, it is still important now. One reason for this importance is the tax-exempt status of the interest, but not the capital gains, from the sale of Treasuries on most state tax returns. It is also important due to the limitations placed on capital losses and in the offset of losses against only capital gains income beyond the $3,000 amount per couple per year.

Capital gains income is defined as the gain associated with the sale or disposition of a capital asset. A *capital asset* as defined by Section 1221 of the IRS Code is any property that is held either as business or nonbusiness property, *except:*

- Inventories.
- Other property held for sale in the normal course of a trade or business.
- An account receivable held in the ordinary course of a trade or business.

- Depreciable business property.
- Real property held in the taxpayer's business.
- A copyright (but not a patent).
- A U.S. government publication held by the taxpayer who received it.

A taxpayer's household furnishings and personal property are capital assets to the extent that any gain realized on the sale of these items is a capital gain and taxed accordingly. However, any loss on such items could not be taken as a deduction on the taxpayer's tax return. (For another case of the "Unlimited Gain/Limited Loss," see the section to follow.)

Obviously, as investors, if you have a gain on the sale of a U.S. Treasury bill, note, or bond, you have a capital gain. But what if the obligation is sold midway through its life? Isn't part of the gain attributable to the interest earned up until that point? The question is a rhetorical one, and the answer is yes. To illustrate this further, let's look at one of the scenarios we examined before. In this example, however, there is a capital gain, as well as interest, involved in the transaction.

In the case of the one-year, $10,000 Treasury bill (T-bill), purchased June 1, for $9,700, let us examine a sale of this item on November 30 of the same year for $9,900. Is the $200 difference between the cost and the sale price of the T-bill interest or is it capital gain? Those of you who think the answer is interest are partially correct, as are those of you who think it is capital gain. In truth, the proper way to handle this transaction is to split the $200 between interest and capital gain.

To do this, we look at the amount that was to be paid as interest on the original T-bill and see that it was $300 for the year on a $9,700 investment, or that it paid 3.09 percent ($300/$9,700). We are only looking at the percentage paid on the investment, and not at the *true yield.* For this calculation, it is appropriate because we are calculating interest paid. We then take the same percentage, multiply it by the investment, and prorate it over the period of time it was held (six months). The calculation would be as follows:

$$\frac{\$9{,}700 \times 0.0309 \times 6 \text{ months}}{12 \text{ months}} = \$150$$

In this example, it is easy because the holding time is exactly a half year. This amount, $150, becomes the *accrued interest* received for holding this T-bill for the six-month period. We would pick this amount up on Schedule B, Part I, line 1, as interest income. However, we know that we also received an additional amount for the T-bill, $50. This extra amount now becomes the capital gain associated with the sale of the T-bill and will be reported on Schedule D, Part I, line 1, as a short-term transaction.

To summarize our T-bill example:

Cost (return of capital):	$9,700
Interest (6/1–11/30):	150 to Schedule B
Short-term capital gain:	50 to Schedule D
Gross proceeds received:	$9,900

Let us look for a minute at what conditions would have to be present for the holder of such a T-bill to receive more money than he or she paid for the bill, excluding the accrued interest portion. Only one scenario could take place in terms of interest rates, that being a decline in the short-term rates. In this case, a T-bill that paid 3.09 percent for another six months would have been worth more now than at issue if T-bills at the time of the sale paid only 3.0 percent.

The same split between interest and capital gain would take place at sale during the holding period of any of the three Treasury items we have discussed. If, in fact, the converse took place and we received less than $9,850 ($9,700 + $150 interest), we would be able to recognize the loss to the extent of the limitation on capital losses (to be discussed later in this chapter). This situation probably would occur if the interest rates went up during the holding period; that is, the T-bill would be worth less at a 3.09 percent rate than a new T-bill paying 3.20 percent.

The last issue involving Treasuries is that of the *exclusion* for U.S. savings bonds used for higher education. Anyone who redeems a qualified U.S. savings bond in a year during which he or she pays qualified higher education expenses may exclude from taxable income any amounts received, providing that certain requirements are met. A qualified U.S. savings bond is one issued after 1989 to an individual who had reached age 24 before the purchase of this bond. Qualified higher education expenses include tuition and fees required for attendance or enrollment at an eligible educational institution of either a taxpayer, his or her spouse, or his or her dependent. This amount, if excludable, is reported on Form 8815 and is carried forward to Schedule B, Part I, line 3, as a subtraction from interest.

EARNED AND PASSIVE INCOME VERSUS INVESTMENT INCOME

Prior to the Tax Reform Act of 1986, the classifications of income were as follows: *earned income,* on which Social Security tax was calculated and paid; and *unearned income,* on which it was not. *Investment income,* a specific type of unearned income generated by capital gains and losses, was taxed at a preferred rate; and *interest and dividends* were taxed at ordinary rates. As we previously noted, the maximum rate of taxation on long-term capital gains was 20 percent.

The Tax Reform Act of 1986 regrouped income into three specific tax classifications: (1) ordinary; (2) portfolio; and (3) passive. There is still earned income and still investment income. The maximum tax rate for long-term capital gains in 1999, however, was once again limited to 20 percent (for assets held longer than 12 months), as opposed to 39.6 percent for other types of income. Yet investment income is now subdivided more specifically into two further classifications: portfolio income and passive activity income.

Portfolio income includes interest, dividends, royalties, and annuities, as well as gains or losses from the disposition of income-producing investment property not derived in the ordinary course of a trade or a business (IRS Code Section 469[e][1]). Portfolio income is distinct and different from passive income.

Passive income, which was defined as a new category under the Tax Reform Act of 1986, is income derived from a "passive activity." A passive activity is one that involves the conduct of any trade or business in which the taxpayer does not materially participate (IRS Code Section 469[c][1]). Activities that are passive generally include partnerships in which the partner does not actively participate. All rental activities are considered passive regardless of whether the investor materially participates.

Distinguishing between the tax classifications of income is not done for the purpose of the taxability of this income. It is basically all taxed at the same rate now, except with regard to the 28 percent maximum tax rate on long-term gains. We separate the two because the type of activity determines the type of loss this activity may potentially generate. This determines how much of the loss can be deducted on your tax return.

UNLIMITED GAINS/LIMITED LOSSES

In the purchase and sale of stocks, for instance, a schism in government policy exists between the treatment of gains and losses. Although the long-term capital gain rate is only 20 percent, the entire capital gain in any year has always been taxed. If, however, the taxpayer/investor has a losing year in the stock market, the story is quite different. That person is only allowed to deduct losses up to the point of her or her gains for that year, plus an additional $3,000 in losses per annum, with the remainder to be carried forward to future years (unless you are a trader electing Section 475).

Let me refer you once again to the current Schedule D tax form for the reporting of capital gains and losses. If you look at this form, you will note that it states: "If line 18 is a (loss), enter here and as a (loss) on Form 1040, line 13, the smaller of these losses: (a) The loss on line 18; or (b) ($3,000) or, if married filing separately, $1,500)." The amount beyond this ($3,000) figure is to be carried forward to future years. This unlimited gain/limited loss business always seemed a bit unfair to me because it appeared as if the government was saying, "If you win, we win; if you lose, we lose, but only up to $3,000."

UNLIMITED INCOME/LIMITED EXPENSES: THE *PIG* AND HIS *PAL*

In the good old pre–tax reform days, you used to get a dollar-per-dollar write-off for all business expenses—assuming, of course, that they met the IRS minimum standards for being ordinary, reasonable, legal, and necessary. In other words, the IRS looked at the *expense* and its necessity to the process of earning income. Back then, all income, other than capital gains, was treated similarly, and so were expenses.

Pre–tax reform, if you bought a piece of rental property that had more expenses than income one year, you got to subtract the loss from your taxable income. Not so anymore. Now that we have passive activity income, we also must contend with passive activity loss.

Passive activity loss (PAL) can be deducted only against passive activity income in any one year except for the year of disposition of the activity: If you have expenses associated with a passive activity, you can deduct them only to the extent that you have income; and if you have more expenses than income in any one year, you must carry them forward to the next year with passive income, and if none, until disposition of the property. Thus was born the PIG (passive income generator)—any passive activity that can generate income in any one year for the main purpose of using up the otherwise wasted passive activity expenses.

In the area of real estate, there is a minor exception to this passive activity rule, which began in 1994. If you, as owner, actively manage the property and participate in such areas as the rental of units and other managerial duties, you must be allowed more of a deduction for expenses beyond income.

WHAT IS AN EXPENSE? THE "FOUR CRITERIA DEDUCTION TEST"

Let's take a look at expenses within the context of the Four Criteria Deduction Test. The IRS Code and related Tax Court decisions have determined that there are four requirements in order for an expense to be deductible. The expense must be:

1. Necessary—to produce income.
2. Ordinary—in the normal course of doing business.
3. Reasonable—with regard to the income being produced.
4. Legal—one allowed under federal or state statute.

The *U.S. Master Tax Guide,* paragraph 902, states:

> Whether an expense is ordinary and necessary is based upon the facts surrounding each particular expense. An expense can be considered necessary if it was appropriate and helpful to the taxpayer's business or if it was clearly and reasonably related to the business. An expense can be considered ordinary if it was one that would normally be expected in the situation, even if the situation would seldom arise.[3]

I learned this in school and have been reminded of it many times during IRS audit: an expense must meet *all* of the *four* criteria to be allowed as a *deduction* on a tax return.

TOTAL RETURN INVESTMENT PLAN (TRIP)

As you keep track of your income and your deductions, you will be surprised how quickly tax planning becomes an integral part of your life. And it needs to be, because if you don't keep track of what is yours, no one else will. In fact, if you try to deal with the tax system in this country without a strategy and some degree of tax knowledge, you will probably lose money.

A client of mine was lucky enough to have shorted crude oil a few years ago. Unfortunately, however, he was not aware of the tax consequences of Section 1256 contracts—contracts that were marked to market on the close of December 31 for tax purposes. For this reason, he had a considerable gain on his 1998 tax return. This wouldn't have been so bad if when he walked into my office on March 15, 1999, for me to prepare the 1998 tax return, he had still had that gain. Unfortunately, he was still holding his short position in crude oil, which, in the first quarter of 1999, rebounded tremendously. For that reason, the $10,000 position that he had originally placed in crude and that had doubled by December 31, 1998, was now worth about half of what it was when he originally started. My client was not aware of the fact that he had to pay tax on a gain that he never saw. This is similar to many stories I hear about people taking on investments and having no idea of the tax consequences.

EXHIBIT 8.1 Calculation of Loss

Value of puts at year end:	$19,500
Purchase price of puts:	−10,000
Gain recognized for taxes:	9,500
28% federal tax + 12% state and city taxes:	× 40%
Tax liability for 1998:	3,800
Puts sold in April 1999 for:	$4,500
Tax paid on phantom gain:	−3,800
Remainder of original investment:	700
New tax basis of investment:	$19,500
Puts sold in April 1999 for:	−4,500
Amount of loss for tax purposes (subject to annual limitation):	$15,000

The figures in Exhibit 8.1 show how the oil investor ultimately took a loss on the position but had to pay tax on a phantom gain.

The moral of this story is that good tax planning can never be separated from good investment planning: they are one and the same, especially in light of recent tax-law changes and some of the hybrid investments that are now offered. It is important that you find a tax adviser who is knowledgeable in investment planning and investment-related taxation and that you use him or her as a final filter for screening all of your investments.

In this next section I will give you a brief and effective way to evaluate your investments from a total return perspective—one that integrates good tax planning with good investment planning. I call this interdisciplinary approach to tax and financial planning *Total Return Investment Planning (TRIP).* It should be an integral part of your investment approach. It is a synthesis that introduces the concept of total return on your money after taxation as the major factor in evaluating your overall investment yield.

As Will Rogers used to say, "I'm not as concerned about the return on my money as I am about the return of my money." Preinvestment tax analysis can be a major factor in effecting a positive outcome in this regard. With this in mind, now let's proceed with my formula for calculating total return on investment (TRIP).

CALCULATION OF TRUE YIELD

Because illustrations always make concepts much clearer, let's start right off by comparing two investments, a fully taxable bond versus a

100 percent nontaxable bond. These bonds are both 10-year bonds and pay interest of 10 percent and 8 percent per annum, taxable and nontaxable, respectively. For the purpose of this illustration, let us further assume that they are purchased by two investors in the same federal tax bracket, a blended 31 percent rate, who live in the same state with a 15 percent state and city tax rate.

Investor One purchased the taxable bond for par value, $10,000, paying 10 percent per year. Using conventional terms, the yield on this investment would be $1,000. Using TRIP, however, we also consider the taxability of this income to determine the after-tax, *true yield* on this investment. The added steps deduct the net taxes on the interest earned each year (Exhibit 8.2).

The result of the calculations demonstrates that the true after-tax yield on the investment is really 5.87 percent, not 10 percent, as Investor One believed it was:

$$\frac{\text{Total return after taxation (\$587)}}{\text{Amount of investment (\$10,000)}} = \text{True yield (5.87\%)}$$

Investor Two purchased a tax-free bond. This is an 8 percent *tax-free,* $10,000 municipal that, because of its 100 percent tax-free status, actually has a *true yield* of 8 percent. We calculate the yield as follows:

$$\frac{\text{Total return after taxation (\$800)}}{\text{Amount of investment (\$10,000)}} = \text{True yield (8\%)}$$

EXHIBIT 8.2

Interest per year	$1,000
Federal tax rate	× .31
Federal tax on interest	$ 310
Interest per year	$1,000
State tax rate	× .15
State tax on interest	$ 150
State tax on interest	$ 150
Federal tax rate	× .31
Credit to federal tax	$ 47
Interest per year	$1,000
Minus federal tax	(310)
Minus state tax	(150)
Credit for deduction	47
Net total return	$ 587

The numerator, Total Return after Taxation, is the huge variable. Its calculation not only depends on the type of investment and its taxability, but also on the investor's federal tax bracket and the state income tax rate in the state where he or she lives. In other words, the true yield will differ from investor to investor, as will the tax status.

Of course, there are all sorts of permutations and variations on this theme, such as the partially tax-free bond, the state tax-free bond (U.S. Treasuries), and the private activity (AMT—alternative minimum tax—addback) bond. But the method is the same. You basically need only six pieces of information to calculate *true yield:*

1. Amount of investment.
2. Annual return.
3. Federal taxability of return.
4. State taxability of return.
5. Marginal federal tax bracket (Exhibits 8.8 and 8.9).
6. Estimated state tax bracket (use 6 percent, if unknown).

I will now give you a format and a sample worksheet (Exhibit 8.3) on which all of the above calculations can be done.

EXHIBIT 8.3 Worksheet for Calculating Your TRIP

1.	Amount invested.	______
2.	Annual projected income from investment.	______
3.	Federal taxable percent of income.[1]	______
4.	Amount of income taxed on federal tax return (line 2 × line 3)	______
5.	State taxable percent of income.[2]	______
6.	Amount of income taxed on state tax return (line 3 × line 5)	______
7.	Federal tax rate (from Section C, line 1).	______
8.	Projected federal tax on return of investment (line 4 × line 7)	______
9.	Estimated state tax on return of investment (line 6 × state rate or .06 if unknown).	______
10.	Federal credit for state tax paid (line 9 × line 7).	______
11.	Annual return net of tax (line 2 – line 8 – line 9 + line 10).	______
12.	True yield (line 11/line 1).	______

[1] As a rule, public activity municipals are 100 percent tax free, private activity municipals are tax free to some degree (percentage can be obtained from a broker), and U.S. treasuries are *100 percent taxable for federal* tax purposes.

[2] As a guide, most states do *not* tax income from U.S. Treasuries and do *not* tax income from *in-state* municipals; but they *do* tax income from *out-of-state* municipals.

EXHIBIT 8.4 Comparison of "True" Yield versus Conventional Yield

	Investor One	Investor Two
1. Amount invested	$10,000	$10,000
2. Annual projected income from investment	1,000	800
3. Federal taxable percent of income	100%	0%
4. Amount of income taxed on federal tax return (line 2 × line 3)	1,000	0
5. State taxable percent of income	100%	0%
6. Amount of income taxed on state tax return (line 2 x line 5)	1,000	0
7. Federal tax rate (from Section C, line 1)	31%	31%
8. Projected federal tax on return of investment (line 4 × line 7)	310	0
9. Estimated state tax on return of investment (line 6 × .15)	150	0
10. Federal credit for state tax paid (line 9 × line 7)	47	0
11. Annual return net of tax (line 2 – line 8 – line 9 + line 10)	587	800
12. True yield (line 11/line 1)	5.87%	8%

Let's now look at the same two examples (Exhibit 8.4), Investor One and Investor Two, and calculate the true yield of their investments using the format just described.

Before we did this calculation, it looked like Investor One had made the better investment choice. Whom do you think is better off now? Clearly, it is Investor Two with a greater true yield on his investment of 8 percent compared with the 5.87 percent of Investor One.

Let's look at one more example. In this case, Investor Three is considering a 10-year, $10,000, partially tax-exempted bond, (75 percent taxable by the federal government, 50 percent taxable by the state), paying 9 percent per year, which she can purchase at par value, or $10,000. This investor is in a 15 percent federal tax bracket and lives in a lower tax state (3 percent). What would the true yield of this investment be for her?

Let's look at the facts as we have them: the six items needed for the TRIP calculation are as follows:

1. Amount of investment	$10,000
2. Annual return	900*
3. Federal taxability	75%
4. State taxability	50%
5. Marginal federal tax bracket	15%
6. State tax bracket	3%

* Bond *pays* 9 percent per year: 9 percent multiplied by $10,000 equals $900.

That's all we need! Using the TRIP, we easily arrive at the investment's true yield (Exhibit 8.5).

This variation demonstrates the simplicity of the calculation even with a seemingly involved tax situation. An investment that apparently had a 9 percent return only had a true yield of 7.87 percent.

THE RISK/REWARD RATIO REVISITED

We have now explored a standard and more accurate method of evaluating investment return. The concept of "true" yield provides a more precise number than simply "yield" and one which is infinitely more useful. At the very least, this should help you tremendously in making more accurate investment choices. It should also assist you in making *wiser* choices because when you evaluate the risk/reward potential of any investment, you now can use a more precise figure for "total return."

EXHIBIT 8.5

	Investor Three
1. Amount invested	$10,000
2. Annual projected income from investment	900
3. Federal taxable percent of income	75%
4. Amount of income taxed on federal tax return (line 2 × line 3)	675
5. State taxable percent of income	50%
6. Amount of income taxed on state tax return (line 2 × line 5)	450
7. Federal tax rate	15%
8. Projected federal tax on return of investment (line 4 × line 7)	101
9. Estimated state tax on return of investment (line 6 × .03)	14
10. Federal credit for state tax paid (line 9 × line 7)	2
11. Annual return net of tax (line 2 – line 8 – line 9 + line 10)	787
12. True yield (line 11/line 1)	7.87%

Space here does not allow me to go into great detail on the concept of risk/reward. This is a book strictly on the taxation of investments and not on their comparative analysis. I do feel it is necessary, however, that you understand the basic concepts involved in this area and how they relate to investment selection as filtered through tax considerations.

When you examine the yield of any investment, you see the need to consider its true yield, as opposed to "pretax yield." In doing so for all your potential investments, you reduce them to their lowest common denominator. Therefore, in speaking of the financial speed of an investment or the rate at which it grows, you have a more realistic figure with which to work.

The question "If a 7 percent yield is good, is a 10 percent yield better?" can be restated in terms of posttax yield. You no longer have to compare apples and oranges, such as in the case of a 10 percent *taxable* investment versus a 7 percent *nontaxable* investment. This has always been confusing and misleading. Now you can translate these percentages into meaningful comparisons and, hence, consider the associated risk in a more consistent manner.

To give you some idea of the significance of this calculation of "return on investment" over a period of time, I'd like to continue with the example of the two investors. Investor One purchased a 10 percent fully taxable bond, whereas Investor Two purchased the 8 percent tax-free bond. The tax considerations are the same as in the first illustration so that the true yield comes out to be only 5.87 percent for the investor with the 10 percent investment.

Let us further assume, for the purpose of this illustration, that the investments are in a *bond fund* as opposed to in a single bond so that the interest will be hypothetically reinvested annually at the same rate of return. We will now look at an entire 10-year period instead of at just one year. You may be surprised at the significance that the method of calculation makes in the potential return on investment over the 10-year period (see Exhibit 8.6).

The figures we would use in estimating the comparative 10-year return on these two investments, without tax consideration, are $15,939 on the 10 percent versus $11,588 on the 8 percent investment.[4] These amounts would also be used in evaluating the risk/reward ratio for each. A total return of $15,939 on an investment of $10,000 is a 159 percent return on capital. This looks much better than the $11,588, or 116 percent, return on capital received by Investor Two. One would probably take a greater risk to achieve this return than he would if he knew the real story.

In the illustration on page 171 (Exhibit 8.7), we see how radically the picture changes with the introduction of true yield.

EXHIBIT 8.6 Calculation Comparison of Return on Two Investments using Old Terminology for "Yield on Investment"

Year		Investor One (10% Taxable)	Investor Two (8% Nontaxable)
1.	Principal:	$10,000	$10,000
	Interest:	1,000	800
2.	Principal:	11,000	10,800
	Interest:	1,100	864
3.	Principal:	12,100	11,664
	Interest:	1,210	933
4.	Principal:	13,310	12,597
	Interest:	1,331	1,008
5.	Principal:	14,641	13,605
	Interest:	1,464	1,088
6.	Principal:	16,105	14,693
	Interest:	1,611	1,175
7.	Principal:	17,716	15,868
	Interest:	1,772	1,269
8.	Principal:	19,488	17,137
	Interest:	1,949	1,371
9.	Principal:	21,437	18,508
	Interest:	2,144	1,481
10.	Principal:	23,581	19,989
	Interest:	2,358	1,599
	End Principal:	$25,939	$21,588

In other words, the 10-year total return on the investment for Investor One has just gone down by $8,249[5] when you include the effect of taxes.

RISK/REWARD RATIO MEETS THE "TAX FACTOR"

Investor One experienced a 46 percent reduction in income; or, to put it another way, total return was overstated by 107 percent.[6] How good does the 76.9 percent[7] 10-year return on investment for Investor One look now as compared to the 116 percent return for Investor Two? Would you be willing to risk as much for an investment that returned 159 percent? I know I wouldn't!

In evaluating a risk/reward ratio, it is apparent that we'd better use accurate figures to evaluate whether an investment is worth the associated risk. Generally, we would require the yield to increase in direct proportion to risk.

EXHIBIT 8.7 Using True Yield to Determine Risk/Reward

Year		Investor One (5.87% Taxable)	Investor Two (8% Nontaxable)
1.	Principal:	$10,000	$10,000
	Interest:	587	800
2.	Principal:	10,587	10,800
	Interest:	621	864
3.	Principal:	11,208	11,664
	Interest:	658	933
4.	Principal:	11,866	12,597
	Interest:	697	1,008
5.	Principal:	12,563	13,605
	Interest:	737	1,088
6.	Principal:	13,300	14,693
	Interest:	781	1,175
7.	Principal:	14,081	15,868
	Interest:	827	1,269
8.	Principal:	14,908	17,137
	Interest:	875	1,371
9.	Principal:	15,783	18,508
	Interest:	981	1,599
	End Principal:	$17,690	$21,588

Modern portfolio theory states that there are historical rates of return for all investments that can be quantified. To accomplish this, models have been developed that evaluate the risk/reward ratios of most investments. It is generally believed that the investor can customize his or her own portfolio to reflect specific needs and tolerance to risk. Up until now, the tax factor has not been included in this calculation.

Under the old definitions of *yield* and *total rate of return*, a financial planner would look at a portfolio and determine that, for example, an investment had a 10 percent rate of return with a standard deviation of 4 percent. What this means, in layperson's terminology, is that there is a 68.25 percent chance that the rate of return will be between 6 percent and 14 percent, depending on future market fluctuations. What this also means, however, is that there is a 31.75 percent chance that the investment will return less than 6 percent and a further chance, however remote, that it may not return anything at all.

The point I'm trying to make here is that when we evaluate investments, we want to know whether the return is really 8 percent or 5.87 percent. Will we earn $15,939 during 10 years or really just $7,690, net of taxes? We need to know this to properly determine whether it is

EXHIBIT 8.8 Marginal Tax Bracket Calculation—Table C

1. Federal marginal tax rate (from Table D)	______
2. State marginal tax rate (6% or 10% if high tax rate)	______
3. Sum of 1 and 2 = Combined marginal tax rate	______

worth the investment risk! Use Exhibits 8.8, 8.9, and 8.10 to complete your calculation.

Note 1: Every taxpayer is entitled to a personal exemption (unless he or she is claimed as a dependent on another's tax return) and a standard deduction. An additional exemption can be claimed for each dependent. Elderly and blind taxpayers are entitled to an additional standard deduction amount. The standard deduction is used by those taxpayers who do not itemize.

Note 2: Of the 50 states and the District of Columbia, all but seven have income tax. The rates go from as low as 1.5 percent to as high as 13 percent (including the local city tax). The average state tax rate is approximately 6 percent. You can use this number in the calculation in Exhibit 8.10; or if you know your state rate, you can use the exact amount. In any event, unless you are a resident of one of the high tax states, such as New York, California, or the District of Columbia, 6 percent is a reasonably accurate estimate.

EXHIBIT 8.9 Federal Tax Rate Schedules for 2001—Table D

Taxable Income				
		Single		
Over	**But Not Over**	**Pay**	**+ % on Excess**	**Of the Amount Over**
$ 0	$ 27,050	$ 0	15 %	$ 0
27,050	65,550	4,075.50	28	27,050
65,550	136,750	14,823.50	31	65,550
136,750	297,300	36,895.50	36	136,750
297,300	—	94,657.50	39.6	297,300
		Married, Filing Jointly		
$ 0	$ 45,200	$ 0	15 %	$ 0
45,200	109,250	6,780	28	45,200
109,250	166,450	24,714	31	109,250
166,450	297,300	42,446	36	166,450
297,300	—	89,552	39.6	297,300

Note: Capital gains are taxed at maximum 20 percent rate.

EXHIBIT 8.10 The Taxable Income Summary Worksheet

1. **Salary and Wages**	______
Employee Business Expenses:	
a. Job-related travel	______
b. Commuting expense to second job	______
c. Professional dues	______
d. Professional journals	______
e. Continuing professional education	______
f. Other job related	______
Total 2106 Expenses (Lines 1(a)–1(f) less 2% of AGI)	(______)
2. **Business and Other Fees or Commissions**	______
Expenses Related to Self-Employment:	
a. Automobile expense to promote business	______
b. Books, subscriptions, journals	______
c. Commissions and professional fees	______
d. Insurance and business interest	______
e. Rent, office expense, and maintenance	______
f. Equipment expense (or depreciation)	______
g. 50% of business meals	______
h. Other business related	______
Total Schedule C Expenses (Lines 2(a)–2(h)	(______)
3. **Interest, Dividends, and Capital Gains**	______
Expenses Related to Investment Income:	
a. Investment adviser fees	______
b. Dues, subscriptions, books	______
c. Computer expense, data, analysis	______
d. Other investment related	______
Total Schedule A Misc. (Lines 3(a)–3(d) less 2% AGI)	(______)
4. **Income from Rentals, Partnerships, Trusts, Sub S Corps, Royalties, Net of Expenses on Schedule E**	______
5. **Other Taxable Income**	______
6. **Less Adjustment for Alimony Paid, Retirement Plans, etc.**	(______)
7. **Less Other Itemized Deductions:**	
a. Medical less 7.5% AGI	______
b. Taxes—State, real estate, other	______
c. Mortgage interest, investment interest (Less limitation to interest)	______
d. Contributions	______
e. Other	______
Total Other Schedule A Expenses (Lines 7(a)–7(e))	(______)
8. **Less Personal Exemptions** ($2,850 each in 2000)	(______)
Taxable Income	______

Exemptions and Deductions:

	Personal	Standard Deduction	
	(Claim 1 for Each Dependent)	Basic	Additional (65 or Older or Blind)
Single:	$2,850	$4,400	$1,100
Married/Jointly:	2,850	7,350	850

9

New World Retirement Planning

The basic strategy here is to fully maximize your deductible retirement plan and afterward to put into nondeductible plans all disposable income that you do not need to support your current lifestyle. There are some qualifications to this statement, as we will explore in this following section.

INDIVIDUAL RETIREMENT ACCOUNTS

Individual retirement accounts (IRAs) are the most widely known type of retirement plan. Contrary to what some people believe, IRAs were not eliminated with the Tax Reform Act of 1986 and, in fact, have been expanded in the Taxpayers' Relief Act of 1997 and the Economic Growth and Tax Relief Reconciliation Act of 2001.

In the Tax Reform Act of 1986, restrictions were put on the amount of money allowable as *deductible* contributions to an IRA each year. Again, in 1997 these restrictions were liberalized. Exhibit 9.1 shows the growth of annual investments of $2,000, $4,000, and $10,000 at 15 percent over a 30-year period with and without taxes being taken out. As you will see, even a nondeductible IRA contribution of $2,000 per year will be worth considerably more in 30 years than if it had been taxed.

This calculation does *not* take into account the tax savings that would be attained by making the same $2,000 a year contribution as tax deductible. In this case, the amount you would have for retirement would be significantly more.

The assumptions made here are as follows: 30-year investment paying 15 percent, compounded annually at a tax rate of 40 percent, federal and state. This is a typical scenario of somebody who could put away

EXHIBIT 9.1 Taxable versus Tax-Free Investing

End of Year	With Tax Protection	Without Tax Protection
$2,000 per Year Available to Invest before Taxes		
5	$ 15,500	$ 13,047
10	46,699	33,121
15	109,435	64,007
20	235,620	111,529
25	489,424	184,648
30	999,914	297,150
$4,000 per Year Available to Invest before Taxes		
5	31,015	26,093
10	93,397	66,241
15	218,870	128,014
20	471,240	223,058
25	978,848	369,296
30	1,999,828	594,301
$10,000 per Year Available to Invest before Taxes		
5	77,537	65,233
10	233,492	165,603
15	547,175	320,034
20	1,178,101	557,645
25	2,447,120	923,240
30	4,999,569	1,485,752

either $2,000 per year, $4,000 per year, or $10,000 per year for their retirement in 30 years.

As you can see, the difference between a taxable investment and nontaxable investment, such as an IRA, is significant. This study is particularly suited in looking at what would happen if you use a Roth IRA (new nondeductible, tax-deferred IRA as granted in the 1997 Taxpayers' Relief Act).

Over a 30-year period, the difference in a return on an investment is as follows:

- For $2,000 a year—an additional $702,764.
- For $4,000 per year—an additional $1,405,527.
- For $10,000 per year—an additional $3,513,817.

These numbers represent total earnings, which, in each case, represent a 337 percent increase in return on investment! That is the difference between letting your retirement money grow in a tax-deferred plan versus one which is taxable.

What are some specific characteristics of an IRA? IRAs were established as part of the Employment Retirement Income Security Act of 1974 (ERISA) as a way for workers to supplement their Social Security retirement income. The provisions of this act allow for a deductible contribution to be made up to 100 percent of salary or $2,000 per wage earner, whichever is lower, with certain restrictions. In addition, a nonworking spouse used to be able to contribute $250 to such a plan—this amount has been raised to $2,000 with the 1997 Taxpayers' Relief Act, and further expanded in the 2001 Tax Act. The deductibility of IRAs depends on several variables. If you are not covered by a retirement plan, there are no income limitations on your ability to contribute other than earned income as just mentioned. If, however, you have another retirement plan, such as a SEP or a KEOGH, you must have income under a certain level.

SIMPLIFIED EMPLOYEE PENSION PLANS

The Simplified Employee Pension Plan (SEP) was developed in the late 1970s as a way for an employee to have a retirement plan without having to deal with all the administrative issues. A SEP is an IRA that must meet special requirements for participants. An employer can establish a SEP, and the maximum amount that can be contributed is 15 percent of each employee's compensation or $32,000, and higher levels in some cases. A participant in a SEP is considered to be an active participant in a retirement plan when evaluating eligibility for IRA deductions. Unlike qualified retirement plans, which will be discussed in the next section, an employer does not have to file the complicated Form 5500 with a SEP or an IRA.

Disclosure of the plan must be made to all employees, outlining such areas as eligibility, contribution formula, limits, plan administrator, terms and rules of the IRA, participants' rights and withdrawal provisions, tax treatment and rollover provisions, and financial disclosures.

Both incorporated and unincorporated businesses can establish SEPs, but employers who establish defined-benefit retirement plans cannot establish a SEP. These plans are frequently used by self-employed people who are considered employees of their own businesses. This effectively raises the maximum limitation on an IRA-deductible contribution from $2,000 to the maximum for a SEP, which may, in some cases, be up to $32,000.

Also, unlike an IRA, the deadline for contributing to a SEP can extend beyond the April 15 due date. You are allowed to contribute to a SEP up until the final extension date of your return, October 15 if properly extended. In addition, you can even *start* a new SEP account through that date and contribute to it to the *prior* period. This is a tremendous advantage for people who need to do some retroactive retirement planning.

For example, let us assume that I am a person with my own business with $100,000 net income on my Schedule C and no retirement plan set up for 1999. In April of the year 2000, I realize that I need to come up with a good way to shelter some income from the prior year to avoid excess tax liability. One way to do this would be to extend my 1999 tax return prior to its due date, April 15, 2000, paying the amount that would be due in taxes net of a 15 percent contribution to my SEP plan (up to the maximum $32,000). Additionally, I would not have to contribute to this plan until the date I file my return, up through October 15, 2000. I could use the tax savings from this future contribution to earn money throughout that year and add to the funds I would have available to contribute to the plan by October 15.

QUALIFIED RETIREMENT PLANS (KEOGHs)

Qualified retirement plans are simply retirement plans that have been sanctioned by the IRS and are commonly referred to as KEOGH plans. When approved, these plans may be used by an employer, and contributions to them will qualify as deductions from income. Self-employed people may also establish these types of plans for themselves because they are considered to be employees of their own businesses.

There are two major types of qualified plans: (1) defined-benefit plan, in which the amounts of *benefits* are regulated; and (2) defined-contribution plan, in which the amount of *contribution* is regulated.

A *defined-benefit plan* will provide for a set return in retirement as a percentage of salary or for a flat, monthly amount. Actuary is determined on an annual of basis, the amount of contribution that is necessary each year for employees covered by this plan. The determining factors are:

- The amount that will be distributed during retirement.
- Ages of the employees covered by the plan.
- Growth of the plan over the preceding year.

This amount of contribution is adjusted annually. The actuary used is certain assumptions for mortality, interest, turnover, and so forth, to establish how much the employer must put into the plan to ensure that there are sufficient funds to provide for the promised benefit.

These plans are most beneficial to self-employed people or to employers with very few or very young employees, with the employer being over age 50. This will allow for maximum contributions to be made for the employer and minimum contributions to be made for other employees. The objectives of an employer setting up this plan are to fund as much of the plan as possible in current and future years to generate as large a tax deduction for the employer as possible. I will demonstrate the effectiveness of such a plan shortly with an example of some recent retirement planning that I have done for one of my clients.

A *defined-contribution plan* is the opposite of a defined-benefit plan in that it does not have a fixed-benefit formula; the contributions are the variables. Defined-contribution plans may take one of the following two major forms:

1. A *money-purchase plan* has a fixed-contribution formula, such as 10 or 15 percent of income. The percentage, however, must be fixed from year to year although the amount of the contribution will vary, depending on the income earned. It is limited to the lower of 25 percent or $32,000 of deductible contributions per year.

2. A *profit-sharing plan* is established and provides participation in the profits of a company by the employees. The overall percentage of contribution is based on profit and can vary from year to year. However, it must have a definite formula for allocating contributions among employees.

General rules governing qualified plans are as follows:

- They must not discriminate among employees.
- They must be in writing.
- They must be of a long and indeterminate term.
- There must be specific rules and regulations that govern eligibility, funding, and benefits.
- To maintain qualification, a plan must meet and maintain certain requirements.
- Individuals can be excluded for only the following two reasons: (1) age—individuals under age 21 may be excluded; and (2) service—plans may require up to three years of service for participation.

Vesting refers to a particular employee's rights to the contributions being fully owned by the employee. The law permits the following two types of vesting in qualified plans:

1. *Five-year cliff:* This requires that the employee be 100 percent vested after five years of service.

2. *Seven-year graded:* Under this type of vesting, an employee must be partially vested after three years of service and fully vested after seven years. The schedule for vesting is 20 percent in the third year and an additional 20 percent in each year up through the seventh year, when the employee is 100 percent vested.

Defined-contribution profit-sharing plans allow a maximum contribution of 15 percent for one plan and 25 percent for two plans, based on compensation up to a maximum of $32,000. Like a SEP, contributions may be made to the plan up to the deadline for the tax return of the business or the personal return in the case of a sole proprietor including extensions. Unlike a SEP, the plan must be established by the *end* of the employer's fiscal year or by December 31 in the case of a personal tax return.

Distributions from a qualified plan can be made for the following reasons:

- *Separation from service:* Prior to age 59½, however, there is a 10 percent premature-distribution penalty plus tax on the amount unless the payout is at age 55 of the participant or due to disability or death. In addition, a penalty can be avoided with a rollover into another plan.
- *Disability or physical impairment:* A qualifying impairment is one that prevents the individual from performing his or her job indefinitely.
- *Death:* Payout to the beneficiary as in the case of an IRA.
- *Age:* Normal distributions may begin at age 59½ without the 10 percent premature distribution penalty.

I'd like to take a look at a real-life situation—that of a client who came to me last year needing to know what to do with $150,000. He thought it might be best to put the money into a tax-free investment and was leaning toward a tax-free municipal bond.

After some discussion, it became clear that this taxpayer had his own business, had virtually no retirement plan, was making good income in his business, had no employees, and was 55 years old.

The first thing that I pointed out to him was that a tax-free municipal bond might not be the best investment vehicle for a person in his situation. The primary tip-off was that he had no retirement plan in place and was relatively close to retirement. The type of retirement plan would then be determined by the more specific circumstances.

I first advised him of the potential disadvantages of purchasing a municipal bond in such a large amount for a retirement investment. *In terms of the investment itself:*

- He would have been locked into a fixed rate of return for a period of time significantly greater than would be available to him through other investments.
- This fixed rate of return would drastically affect the value of the investment over time, although he would be able to redeem the municipal bond at the due date for its face value (assuming liquidity of the issuer). An investor very well might be locked into this investment until that time. If interest rates were to increase from current, historically low levels, as they are apt to do, the investment with a fixed rate of return would be worth considerably less in the open market than he paid for it.
- Given the current level of extremely low interest rates and the prospect of an increase in rates in the future, I did not advise the purchase of anything but very short term, fixed-rate investments (one to five years at the most). Chances are that a longer term, fixed-rate investment would decline in value significantly at some future point.
- Municipalities had been prone to trouble in the past several years, and the future might hold more of the same. Cities and states have been given less financial assistance from the federal government. Before investing in a municipal bond, consider the security of the investment in the event of a potential default by the municipality.

There were other disadvantages of purchasing a municipal bond with such a large investment *in terms of the tax-related issues:*

- Not all municipal bonds are 100 percent free of federal taxes. Due to the expansion of the alternative minimum tax, private-activity bonds are taxable for these purposes.
- Municipal bonds *are* fully taxable to estate if the municipality issuing them is outside of the investor's resident state. In other words, a Connecticut municipal bond, although tax-free on the federal tax return, would be 100 percent taxable on a New York State and New York City tax return. If the investor lived in New Jersey and purchased a New York State municipal bond, the same situation would be true on the New Jersey return.
- Most important, municipal bonds are for tax relief only on the income they produce. There are much better ways to invest for greater tax benefit. This is especially true for a taxpayer who is in business for himself, who is not working for a salary, and who does not already have an existing retirement plan.

When people consider retirement planning, they are often intimidated by the prospect of tying up money for a long period of time. This does not have to be the case. In addition, many people are under the misconception that they are severely limited in their choice of investments in a retirement plan. This is also not the case.

This was a concern of my client, and I showed him that his concerns were not valid. There is a huge array of retirement plan options available. If an investor cannot find one that suits his or her specific needs, he or she can have a retirement plan drafted for a relatively small amount of money by an attorney. The plan would make virtually any investment vehicle available to the investor, any amount of contribution, and a very flexible distribution schedule that would meet his cash flow needs in the future. This was particularly true of a taxpayer over age 55 who could make withdrawals from the plan without penalty at any age after 59½.

10

New World Estate Planning

You can't take it with you, so you had better decide what to do with all the wealth you've accumulated before the government does that for you. As Charles J. Givens put it: "While you are alive, the IRS will attempt to take what you've made. When you are not, the IRS will attempt to take what it missed."[1]

There are two phases to transferring wealth: (1) transferring as much as possible of your assets to future generations while you are still alive, and (2) keeping as much of your wealth as possible out of your taxable estate upon your death. The first phase is commonly referred to as *gifting* and has several benefits. In addition to contributing to the second phase of bypassing estate taxes in the future, gifting can be used in and of itself to transfer income to relatives in lower tax brackets than yours. In this way, less overall tax will get paid on the income that the investment generates.

Many people put off the second phase, *estate-tax planning,* because thinking about dying, especially thinking about your own death, is not very pleasant. In addition, it is a very complicated area and one that is too often misunderstood. Many people are misinformed and assume that estate-tax planning is no longer necessary. They are under the false impression that the estate tax has been repealed, that there is no longer a need to plan an estate, and that under current laws everything will automatically go to the spouse and/or heirs without any problem anyway.

Good estate planning is directly related to a policy of annual gifting to your family. A good estate plan must also consider taxes, probate, insurance, investing, charitable contributions, and family wealth distribution. It is much more involved than simply avoiding taxes; it also involves determining how you want your property distributed and how this can be done with a minimum of administrative and legal expenses.

In his book *Tax Liberty,* Robert C. Carlson stated the following:

> [This discussion of estate tax planning will] point you toward the biggest tax saving opportunities of your life. Why the biggest? Because estate taxes are your final tax bill, and can be the largest taxes your family will have to face. You still have to plan to ensure that the assets will go to your heirs, not the tax collector or lawyer. What's more, good estate planning can help cut taxes *during* your lifetime.[2]

USING THE ANNUAL GIFT-TAX EXEMPTION

The easiest way to reduce your gross estate is to set up a program of gifting your assets annually to your heirs while you are still alive. The law provides for up to $10,000 of property per year to be given from any one person to any other person without gift tax being incurred except with regard to the generation-skipping transfer tax (I will explain the generation-skipping transfer tax further in the next section). If a married couple is making the gift together, regardless of whose property or cash is being gifted, the annual exclusion from gift taxes is $20,000 to any other person. There is no limit on the number of people to whom you can give gifts each year using the $20,000 per couple exclusion. There is also no limit on the amount of cash or property that can be given to your spouse.

No federal gift tax is ever due from the person receiving the gift. It is only the person making the gift who may be subject to gift taxes. There are two further exemptions from gift tax: (1) funds used for education and (2) funds used for medical expenses. In addition to the $10,000 per person, per recipient, per year limit, you can give away or receive any amount of money for education paid directly to an educational institution and/or for medical expenses paid to a health care provider.

Money given to minor children under a gifting program should not be used for necessities such as food, clothing, shelter, or medical care. Because a parent is legally obligated to provide these items, they do not qualify for the annual gift exclusion.

When your gifts to any one beneficiary exceed the $20,000 per couple exclusion, you can start to utilize your unified credit, which is $675,000 (in 2001) per person per lifetime. Any amount of this credit used up while making gifts during a person's lifetime cannot be used to offset the estate tax upon his or her death.

If your policy of gifting is well planned, you can entirely avoid using up any unified credit. It then will be fully available to offset the estate tax on the first $675,000 (in 2001) of taxable estate upon your death. Meanwhile, throughout your lifetime, you will be transferring your wealth to your heirs tax free.

If in any year you generate a taxable gift (above the limits just discussed), you must file a Form 709, Federal Gift-Tax Return. On this tax return, you report the amount of the gift and the beneficiary of the gift, and you calculate the amount of unified credit used in making the gift. Once you exceed this lifetime exclusion, you calculate the tax on the gift as if it were a taxable estate item. All gifts are valued at fair market value at the date the gift is made. If it is a publicly traded stock or similar type item, you determine *mean valuation* by taking an average of the high price and low price for the day.

Consideration: Generation-Skipping Transfer Tax

If a transfer is made between generations out of sequence, there is an additional surtax on the transfer regardless of whether or not the transfer exceeds the annual gift-tax exclusion. In other words, if as a grandparent you transfer an asset to your grandchild without first gifting it to your child and then having your child gift it to his or her child—your grandchild—you will be subject to this surtax. There is a $1,000,000 lifetime exemption per person making the gift (giftor).

Essentially, the government does not want to bypass one level of taxation on the transfer of wealth between generations.

Consideration: Basis When Making Gifts

Don't give away property that shows an unrealized loss. When a recipient receives property as a gift, his or her basis will be the lower of the property's fair market value or the giftor's basis at the time of the gift.

If you give away property that has an unrealized loss or, in other words, the fair market value is lower than the price you paid for the property, no one gets to take the unrealized loss as a deduction. The loss is gone forever as a tax deduction.

But, if you sell the property first, you get to deduct the loss. Then you can give away the cash you receive from the sale of the property and there will still be money left over because of the tax savings for deducting the loss.

Consideration: Property Size When Making Gifts

You can give away any type of property, in any size you wish, to remain within the limits of your $20,000 per couple, per person, gift-tax exemption. If you own a large portfolio of stocks, your spouse and you, jointly, can give away $20,000 worth of shares each year.

Any real estate you have can be divided into $10,000 pieces each year, although deed and title expenses involved could be prohibitive. With real estate, one technique used is to sell the property to the person to whom you will be gifting it and then take back a 100 percent mortgage from the giftee. Then your spouse and you can forgive $20,000 worth of the principal each year as is covered by the annual exclusion.

USING ESTATE-TAX PLANNING STRATEGIES

Good estate-tax planning is a very sophisticated area and should not be attempted alone. This section is meant to familiarize you with the basic concepts, not to make you an expert. You should still consult with a competent estate-tax planner to finalize your blueprint.

Here are four basic ways to approach estate-tax planning:

1. A strategy that focuses on *keeping property out of your gross estate.* One way to achieve this would be, again, to gift as much as possible of your property to your heirs while you are alive. The point here is to try to move your wealth to your heirs without using up the unified credit. Basically, the unified credit is a $675,000 (in 2001) tax credit on assets transferred either through your estate or through gifting above and beyond the amount allowed to be gifted tax free each year. Transfers to a spouse, however, can be unlimited because they are not subject to gift and estate taxation and do not use up the unified credit.

2. A strategy that focuses on *maximizing estate-tax deductions.* For example, you could set up a provision to pay your son a salary as executor of your estate upon your death. The salary would be an administrative deduction from the estate that would be deductible against taxable estate income at, perhaps, the maximum rate of 55 percent. The amount that he received would have to be reported as taxable income on his personal tax return at whatever tax rate he was in, which in 1999 would be a maximum of 39.6 percent. This is still considerably less than the 55 percent maximum estate-tax rate.

On the other hand, you could have your son be the executor without any salary. In that case, he could still receive the money, but it would now be taxed at the estate-tax rate, maximum 55 percent.

3. A strategy that focuses on *maximizing tax credits,* such as for donations to charity or credit for state taxes paid.

4. A strategy that focuses on *carrying adequate estate insurance* to meet all of the tax liabilities. Under this strategy you do not focus on the amount of the estate taxes as long as there is enough insurance outside your estate to cover the tax bill.

Other specific strategies for reducing estate taxes using these four strategies will be included in Chapter 16, 101 Tax-Reduction Strategies.

The estate tax is levied on the entire estate before the assets are passed down to the heirs. The estate tax is generally not an inheritance tax to be paid by the beneficiary when he or she received an inheritance. The estate is liable for the entire tax before anything is distributed. Beneficiaries of a will do not have to pay federal estate taxes on property received, unless it is so specified in the will.

The gross estate is all of the property you owned, valued at its fair market value at the time of your death. There is another way to value a gross estate. Called the *alternate valuation,* it is the value of all the assets six months after the date of death. From the gross estate, deductions are subtracted such as marital, administrative, charitable, and the unified credit. This leaves your taxable estate, against which the estate-tax rate is applied to produce the estate tax due.

OTHER CONSIDERATIONS IN ADDRESSING ESTATE-TAX PLANNING

Be Certain Your Property Is Fairly Valued

Because the estate tax is based on the value of your property, it is critical that you determine an accurate estimate of how much your property is worth before doing any estate-tax planning. Most people either underestimate or overestimate the value of their estates. Some people don't realize that inflation has increased the value of their assets. An estate worth more than $675,000 in 2001 is not that unusual when you consider items such as a home, a pension, investments, insurance, and possibly a business, in addition to the usual personal assets. In estates greater than $675,000, you will need to plan your estate rigorously to avoid paying most of it to the government and attorneys.

On the other hand, your assets, such as real estate, might have lost a substantial amount of their value during the 1980s, in which case you need only a simple estate plan. You should use the services of a reputable appraiser in determining your estate valuation. The benefit of estate planning is directly related to the accuracy of your estimate of the estate's value.

Property You Control Is Considered to Be Property You Own

The government did not want you to be able to avoid paying estate tax by keeping control of property while putting the title in someone else's name. Thus, you cannot reduce estate taxes by putting property into a *living trust* that pays you income for life but gives the remainder to a beneficiary after your death. You will still be considered the owner of the property that you put into a trust if you retain the right to amend or to revoke the trust.

Check Your Estate for Any Hidden Assets

If you have given away property in the past but retained the power or some other interest in the property, it could be included in your estate. Sometimes you may have received a seemingly small, contingent interest in an estate from either a parent or a spouse. This might cause this entire property to be valued in your estate at your time of death.

Sometimes, in someone else's will, you are given the power to determine who gets a particular piece of property after his or her death. This power could cause the property to be included in your estate, even if you do not exercise the power.

Be on the Lookout for Situations in Which a Person Does Not Have Enough Property

In some cases a person may not have enough property to take full advantage of the $675,000 in 2001 estate-tax exemption. If this is the case, you should consider making what is known as a *reverse gift* to this person, even if he or she is elderly or ill and possibly on the verge of dying. A reverse gift is one which is made from a younger generation to an older one.

Property that passes through a descendant's estate gets what is known as a *stepped-up basis;* that is, the person who inherits it is treated for income-tax purposes as if he or she had bought it and paid what it was worth on the date of death (or six months subsequent, if alternate valuation is used).

For example, Mrs. Z, a cancer patient, has $50,000 worth of assets. Her husband has a large estate including $500,000 worth of stock with a basis of $100,000. That means he has $400,000 worth of taxable gain built into the stock. Mr. Z gives the stock to his wife. There is no tax on gifts between spouses. Mrs. Z sets up a revocable living trust and leaves the stock to the children. The children inherit the stock with the basis stepped up to $500,000. Thus, if they turn around and sell it for $500,000, there is no taxable gain.

With these shares, Mrs. Z's estate is still $550,000 and under the exempt amount of $675,000 (in 2001). The stepped-up basis is achieved without paying estate tax, and the property is taken out of Mr. Z's estate where it might be taxed due to additional property he might have over the $675,000 exclusion.

Married Individuals Can Leave All of Their Assets to Their Spouse Free of Any Estate Tax

This sounds like a real bonanza; however, unless a careful plan is drawn up, the overall tax burden on a married couple could end up being more than it should. If property passes entirely to the spouse, it must be included in the surviving spouse's taxable estate. Assuming the survivor dies without depleting the estate, that second estate will be subject to tax on the full inherited amount plus its appreciated value. A better policy is to allow part of the property to be passed on through the lifetime $675,000 exclusion to a son or a daughter through a revocable living trust (to be discussed later).

Life Insurance Is a Significant Part of Your Wealth and Should Be Kept Out of Your Estate

Life insurance proceeds will not be considered part of your estate if you did not own the policy. A simple way to arrive at this is to have your spouse own the policy and pay the premiums. You can give your spouse the money to make the payments as long as the money is kept separate from your account and the spouse writes a separate check for each premium payment.

You can do the same thing with a child. Alternatively you can also create an irrevocable life insurance trust. The trust owns the insurance policy but you can make a gift to the trust each year that is used to pay the premium. When you die, the proceeds are paid to the trust, which in turn pays them to the beneficiaries according to stipulations set up in the trust.

Types of Assets That Compose Most Estates Fall into Six Categories

Most estates have assets that fall into the following six categories.

1. Your residence.
2. Tangible personal property, such as furniture, jewelry, paintings, cars, and boats.
3. Investment real estate, such as houses or buildings not occupied by the owners but rented to tenants.

4. Your closely held business, whether it's a sole proprietorship, an interest in a partnership, or an interest in a controlled corporation.
5. Checking accounts, savings accounts, certificates of deposit, stocks, and bonds, the sum of your liquid assets except for insurance proceeds.
6. Proceeds of life insurance.

See Exhibit 7.1 for the estate-tax return Form 706 to examine how assets should be precisely listed on this form.

The Estate-Tax Table

The estate-tax table, with the current rates of taxation, is shown in Exhibit 10.1.

Although the tax law gives everyone a $675,000 exemption (2001) from estate taxes, the IRS considers a married couple to be the same as *one person* for the purposes of determining this exemption! In order not to be confined to only one exemption, a couple must take specific action to separate and identify their assets by creating a revocable living trust.

Create a Revocable Living Trust to Separate the Assets of a Married Couple

The way to accomplish this is as follows: It would be written in the living trust documents that upon the death of the first spouse, the estate would be separated into two parts. The first part would represent exactly $675,000 of property, the amount exempt from estate taxes. This $675,000 can be handled in two ways:

1. It can be given directly to your heirs upon the death of the first spouse, with the balance of the estate going to the surviving spouse.

EXHIBIT 10.1 Estate-Tax Table

Size of Taxable Estate	Amount of Tax	Plus % of Excess
$ 100,000	$ 18,200	28%
150,000	23,800	30
250,000	38,800	32
500,000	70,800	34
1,000,000	248,300	39
2,500,000	780,800	45
3,000,000	1,025,800	55

2. It can be put into another living trust so that the heirs will have title to the assets but cannot touch them while your spouse is still living. Thus, your spouse can receive income from the investments while alive. In addition, the home could be included in this living trust so that the spouse could continue to live in it.

The second part of the first estate is the balance beyond $675,000. This can represent any amount of money, be it $5,000 or $1,000,000. The point, though, is that because you have set up a revocable living trust and separated the assets of the two spouses before the death of either spouse, you have essentially created an additional $675,000 unified credit exemption.

If you had not created this revocable living trust and you had allowed all the assets to be transferred to your spouse as part of the unlimited marital deduction, then you (the couple) would be considered to be one person for the sake of the exemption. The unlimited marital deduction rule simply means that the government will defer tax on a couple's estate until the death of the second spouse. The government then collects on what are now the combined remaining assets of the couple before anything goes to the heirs.

With the formation of this type of trust, $675,000, the initial part of the first deceased spouse's assets has already been removed from the combined assets with no estate tax. Upon the later death of the second spouse, an additional $675,000 will become exempt from estate taxes. What this has effectively done is to have created a unified credit of $1,350,000 as opposed to simply $675,000.

This is a perfectly legal and simple strategy that can save you up to $192,800 in unnecessary estate taxes. It is not common knowledge that this strategy is necessary or available, and furthermore, those who are aware of it often will not want to pay the expense of setting up a trust such as this. Yet when you put the tremendous tax savings that can be achieved from the establishment of a revocable living trust against the cost to set the trust up, there is no comparison. I would suggest that you utilize all that is available to you under the current tax law for planning your estate-tax strategy.

Considerations for Unmarried Taxpayers

Unmarried taxpayers need an estate plan more so than do married couples. Most single people prefer to distribute assets among a number of beneficiaries, whereas married people generally leave property to the surviving spouse and children. And if you are unmarried, you will not get the benefit of the marital deduction to reduce estate taxes. Therefore, estate planning is vital to ensure that the bulk of your property goes to beneficiaries and not to the government or to the administration of your estate.

Cohabitation presents a special set of problems when most of the estate is left to the cohabitant. A lawsuit by family members could consume most of the estate's assets. A solution to this, if you expect hostility from family members, is to have a lawyer draft a will that disinherits anyone who contests the will. You should also prepare evidence that you were not subject to undue influence or duress when writing the will. This is particularly important when you are significantly older than your cohabitant or if you were ill at the time the will was drawn.

A better solution to this problem would be to create an irrevocable lifetime trust and to make use of your $10,000 per year, per person gift-tax exclusion while you are still alive.

Conclusion

Bear in mind that being wealthy does not exempt you from estate tax problems, and in fact can be the cause of them. Some of the most prominent and wealthy people of this generation, Groucho Marx, Jackie Kennedy Onassis, Elvis Presley, as well as the most educated of congressmen in this field, Senator Robert S. Kern, all had devastating estate-tax problems. The same situation could happen to you, even if you have a will. Federal estate taxes are levied on any estate beyond the $675,000 unified credit amount. The tax rate quickly rises from a low of 37 percent to the maximum 55 percent rate.

In this chapter I have given you a basic background on estate planning and the considerations involved. It is up to you to protect your assets from the IRS and the attorneys in the event of your death. To ensure that the maximum wealth is passed down to future generations, it is necessary for you to seek professional counseling in this area more than any other.

SIXTEEN CRUCIAL DEFINITIONS

1. *Unified Credit.* A unified estate-and-gift-tax credit may be used to offset gift taxes on lifetime transfers and, to the extent not used during one's lifetime, to offset estate taxes.

2. *Unified Estate-Tax and Gift-Tax Rates.* Estate-tax and gift-tax rates are combined in a single tax-rate schedule. Lifetime transfers are subject to the gift tax and are also added with transfers made at death to determine the estate tax and the estate-tax rate.

3. *Taxable Transfers—Either Taxable Gifts or Taxable Estates.* Taxable transfer means the total amount of gifts that is made during any calendar year by the gift or that is reduced by $10,000 per person annual gift-tax exclusion ($20,000 for a split gift made by married people) and unlimited gifts to a spouse (within certain limitations). Unlimited transfers made on behalf of one person for educational or medical expenses and certain other allowable deductions are also gift-tax and estate-tax free.

4. *Taxable Estate.* This is the gross estate minus the marital deduction for property passing to one surviving spouse, minus all other allowable deductions.

5. *Calculation of Estate Tax.* The estate tax is determined by computing the tentative tax under the unified credit on the total taxable estate and all post-1996 gifts (other than those includable in the decedent's gross estate), and then subtracting the following six items from this:

1. Total gift tax payable on post-1976 gifts.
2. Credit for any state inheritance tax.
3. The unified credit.
4. Credit for federal estate taxes paid by prior estates on the same transfers.
5. Credit for gift taxes on pre-1977 gifts.
6. Credit for foreign debt taxes paid.

6. *Phaseouts.* The benefits of these graduated rates and the unified credit are phased out for estates over $10 million and less than $21 million by a 5 percent surtax. Therefore, the effective rate on these estates is 60 percent.

7. *Generation-Skipping Transfer Tax.* An additional tax is imposed on certain generation-skipping transfers assessed at the maximum estate-tax and gift-tax rate of 55 percent.

If the transfer is made between generations that are out of sequence, there is an additional surtax on transfers above the annual exclusion. The annual exclusion is one of the ways that the wealthy fund their transfer strategies. In other words, if a grandparent transfers an asset to his or her grandchild without first gifting it to a child and then having the child gift it to the grandchild, the transfer will be subject to the surtax. This additional tax is imposed on generation-skipping transfers assessed at the maximum estate-tax and gift-tax rate. This rate is 55 percent *in addition* to the 60 percent estate-tax rate.

8. *Generation-Skipping Transfer-Tax Credit.* There is a $1,000,000 lifetime exemption per person making the gift. Anything else is basically

taxed at a 55 percent additional rate. Essentially, the government does not want to bypass one level of taxation on a transfer of wealth between generations.

9. *State Estate Taxes.* Most states also have separate gift and estate taxes that are not included in *Don't Dare Die* illustrations because they vary so much from state to state. The taxes would make the illustrations too complex to understand. However, they are a significant factor, as are legal expenses such as probate, executors fees, and other costs of dying.

10. *Unlimited Marital Deduction.* There is an unlimited amount of transferability between spouses, both during one's lifetime and at date of death. However, there are two problems that arise from this plan. If a couple has a $1,350,000 estate and does not utilize at least one of the unified credits, $675,000 of that amount will be taxable at date of death of the second spouse. In other words, in order to utilize fully a couple's unified credit, they must separately own assets and take advantage of separate unified credits at dates of death.

Most people think that they don't need estate planning because when they die the assets will transfer 100 percent free of tax to their spouse. This is exactly the wrong way to go about estate planning and the way most couples lose a lot of money to the government, through the estate tax, when they die. In other words, lack of proper estate-tax planning is the biggest reason the government has such a large pay day. It is estimated that over the next 20 years there will be transfers of approximately $8 trillion between generations that may be subject to estate tax. This is a huge pay day, and the government is drooling over it.

11. *Stepped-Up Basis.* When you die, the capital assets that are transferred to your heirs get a new cost basis. This basis is equal to the value that was declared on your estate-tax return. For this reason, if the assets are sold after they transfer ownership through the estate-tax return, they will retain the basis on the date of death or six months subsequent to the date of death (alternate date valuation).

When a gift is made, however, the old basis is transferred along with the gift. This makes for a big difference in planning your estate and gifting strategies.

12. *Charitable Deductions.* Charitable giving is a useful tax-planning tool and very important to our society. Gifts that are made through your will are deductible against the estate taxable income. This is a very useful tool, which will be addressed later in this book.

13. *Probate.* This is a court proceeding in which a determination is made that will be submitted to the court stating that the will is correct

and that assets are inventoried. Notice is published inviting creditors to make claims, legitimate creditors are paid, and the balance is distributed to the people named in the will. Only items that are owned by a person at the time of his or her death go through the probate process.

14. *Executor.* This is a person whom you designate to manage your estate, including gathering the assets, paying expenses and taxes, and making distributions to beneficiaries.

15. *Executor's Fees.* The executor is paid a fee for performance of his or her duties. These fees are limited under statute (often governed by the state), which indicates how much an executor should be paid.

16. *Legal Administrative and Accounting Fees.* This includes all miscellaneous fees associated with the probate and settlement of an estate. These fees often amount to a great deal more than you would think and contribute immensely to the high cost of dying in the United States.

As you will see in the strategy section, these definitions are essential in enacting concurrent strategies. A good part of immediate tax planning is inseparable from retirement and estate-tax planning. They work in tandem.

11

The Double Play: To Give Is But to Receive!

BACKGROUND

The next strategy that we will discuss is that of the *trust,* starting with a type of trust that is crucial in setting up your estate plan. It is called the *charitable remainder trust* (CRT).

John D. Rockefeller made one of the wisest statements ever: *"The best way to circumvent taxation is to give it all away."* The CRT is a prime example of how this principle works. In order to better understand why the government is willing to give you the benefits that we'll be discussing and why charitable-trust planning is so unique, it is important to go back and examine how the charitable trust came to be.

During World War I, the government came up with one of the most ingenious ideas in the creation of mankind. They needed a way to raise revenues to support the war effort. And so they created the first income tax for American citizens. The Tax Reform Act of 1917 not only included the first income taxes but also included the first charitable deductions. Even back then the government realized that charities should not be negatively impacted by the new tax. Income taxes and charitable deductions have been linked inseparately ever since.

The question is, who provides social benefits more efficiently—the government or charities? There's a consensus of opinions, including my own, that charities can provide social benefits much more efficiently than the government. In fact, studies have shown that if the charity provides $1.00 of social benefit, it would cost the government about a $1.50 to provide the same benefit value.

Aren't our tax dollars just a way of providing social benefits and reallocation of wealth? If we provide for the military, for scientific research, and for schools, aren't those social benefits paid for by tax dollars?

Charities provide social benefits. If a charity feeds the hungry, clothes the poor, and pays for college education, aren't they providing *social* benefits? So, it really makes a great deal of sense for the government to treat charities favorably. They are aware that they should not put the charity at a disadvantage just to raise tax revenues to provide less-efficient social benefits. What the government has had to do is to turn around and provide for the charities that can support benefits not provided by tax dollars.

The government wants these programs to exist because they make sense. Charitable trusts were written into the tax law way back in 1969. Not much has happened regarding charitable-trust planning because there have always been many other ways to avoid taxes. I'm sure you can remember the days of oil and gas tax shelters, real estate limited partnerships, and many other tax-avoidance strategies that were established in the 1980s. The government did away with these schemes because they did not provide any legitimate social benefit. There was no benefit at all to society.

It has only been since 1986 or so that the charitable trust has really taken off. This is because we have had to use high-powered computers and software programs to be able to calculate the precise benefits of CRTs. Before that time, the laws were on the books, but there was no practical way of illustrating their benefits. Just calculating tax deductions received when you gift into a CRT requires quite a few computations. The best way to illustrate the benefits of CRTs is to illustrate the differences between establishing a trust and not establishing a trust, side by side, on all levels. To do these types of comparisons, we need high-powered computers, which are now readily available.

In the 1990s, CRTs have literally exploded, growing at a rate of 100 percent a year or more as people are becoming aware of the advantages offered by this unique planning tool, but the planning is still in its infancy. In the first decade of the twenty-first century, tax attorneys, CPAs, and financial planners will have to become very familiar with the benefits of CRTs.

With CRT planning, you cannot take a myopic approach. You must have accountants who work with the numbers, attorneys who work with legal aspects, and financial planners who work with investments and various insurance aspects of these programs. You need to incorporate all of this expertise and form a synergy in order to come out with a good, finished product. *If you can find an accountant who is also a financial planner and well versed in the insurance and legal field, you have a real winner.*

The complicated structure of the CRT requires a team approach. My hope is that, in this section, I will be able to convey the advantages of a CRT to you.

As I mentioned earlier, CRTs provide social benefits. Because of this, there are tax breaks available in the IRS Code for setting up CRTs. The income tax system also allows a tax credit if you invest in certain types of low-income housing. It does so because if a company builds and maintains low-income housing, the government doesn't have to build or maintain these buildings. But it allows a tax credit to private investors who then provide social benefits.

It's interesting that both houses of Congress unanimously passed the low-income-housing tax credit now in the tax law. This is because the Republicans liked the fact that the private sector is providing these benefits, and the Democrats liked the fact that low-income people are afforded shelter.

This is the same logic that has allowed both houses of Congress to unanimously approve CRTs and charitable contributions. Charities provide such services as feeding and clothing the hungry, cleaning up environments, and educating college students. By supporting these organizations, the private sector will lessen the government's burden in trying to fulfill these social obligations, and, as I have shown you in a previous chapter, the government squanders enough of our money doing this inefficiently. It costs the government 50 percent more than the private sector to provide social benefits. For this reason, CRTs are not tax schemes. They are socially responsible mechanisms for providing social services.

I've never had a client who has objected to giving money to charity if they could afford to do it. The problem is that most people have not been in that position. This is where the distinction needs to be made between charitable intent and charitable capacity. The beauty of CRTs that are properly structured is that not only will all the benefits go to charity but *you* will be better off financially as well. The CRT is a well-thought-out vehicle that allows for both of these objectives to be met. In my opinion, this is salient tax legislation.

A Way to Give Back to Society—and Reap Personal Tax Benefits as Well

Now, let's look at what benefits the CRT holds for society. I've hinted many times that CRTs can help you as well as the charity. So let's look at those situations where you will benefit as well as the charity. Let's look at a true scenario, the case of one of my clients who benefitted by setting up a CRT several years ago. The client, for the purpose of this illustration, will be called Mr. Made-It-Big (MIB). MIB had a little company that did quite well. The more that people found out about it, the more they wanted to invest in it. MIB at one point decided to take the company public. Years went by, and the company continued to prosper.

So MIB developed a fortune of approximately $2 million in stock with literally no cost basis. What this meant was that MIB paid nothing for the stock, and when he sold it, he would be exposed to all of the capital gains on it. The company paid no dividends, so MIB needed to sell stock in order to generate any income. He was 63 years old at the time he came to me and stated that he had decided to retire and wanted to use his stock as a retirement-funding tool.

After discussing the capital gains problem with MIB, I determined that if he sold the $2 million of stock, he would pay roughly $600,000 in capital gains tax and would be left with $1.4 million, which he could reinvest for retirement.

If you think about it, there are really only four things you can do with an asset: (1) keep it; (2) sell it; (3) spend it; or (4) give it away.

In this case MIB had a dilemma. He would have to take a huge tax hit and pay $600,000 in taxes if he sold the stock. He could hardly swallow that situation.

I suggested to him that another approach would be that he sell just enough stock each year in order to generate income on which he could live. This meant, however, that he would put most of his assets at risk because they would all be in one place. (Remember, diversification is one of the primary tenets of estate planning.) Obviously, he did not want to have all of his eggs in one basket, certainly not when it pertained to his retirement assets—especially if invested in one *small* company.

I've heard many clients tell me over the years, "Oh, that's okay. I only have one stock, but it's IBM, and IBM would never let me down. It's the best place anyone can have their money."

Well, I wouldn't have wanted to be one of those clients when IBM went from 180 down to 40 a few years ago; and although it's back around 150 now, holding only one stock still lacks the diversification one's portfolio should have. Risk is thereby increased tremendously.

The bad news for MIB was that he had a dilemma. He could either pay $600,000 in capital gains tax and re-allocate his assets or he could sell just enough each year to live which would mean the entire asset would be exposed in one investment.

When I spoke to MIB, I presented one other scenario for him and that was the possibility of setting up a CRT. We determined that the benefits of this trust would be that any stock he put inside of the trust could be sold without paying capital gains tax. If he established a CRT and put $2 million of stock into the trust, he could name himself and his wife as co-trustees and would be able to control the assets for the rest of his life. He would then be able to select a portfolio of no-load mutual funds that would be best suited for his income objectives.

So that's exactly what MIB did. He put the $2 million of stock inside a CRT that he had created, with himself as trustee of this trust for the rest of his life. Should he pass away, his wife would then become trustee. As trustee, MIB sold the $2 million of stock and had $2 million of cash to invest.

This was because in the CRT there was *no capital gains tax erosion* on $2 million. Then, as trustee, MIB selected a series of no-load mutual funds, stocks, bonds, and a whole other array of investments that he felt best suited his needs. At this point, he now had $2 million invested inside the trust instead of $1.4 million that he would have had had he not utilized the CRT.

The MIB case demonstrates the principle of separation of ownership and beneficial interest that I spoke about in the introduction to this book. My own feeling is that I would rather own nothing and control everything. By having control, I can take the money out, spend it, but not own it. MIB has given up ownership of the stock; yet, he has maintained control over what he is going to do with the stock and the subsequent cash from the sale of the stock.

Remember this principle: You don't want to *own* things, you just want to *control* them. *The price of ownership is taxation.*

Now, if this was the end of the story, I probably wouldn't have MIB as a client today. Just because he saved capital gains tax by gifting the money to a trust would not be appealing if he couldn't get the money out.

I'm sure you've heard the old expression: If it sounds too good to be true. . . . The standard ending to this sentence has always been, "Then it probably is."

I'd like to provide you with an alternative ending—one that I discovered in spades since I have researched the tax law, especially the sections applicable to estate planning: "If it sounds too good to be true, either it *is* too good to be true, or *it's a government program.*"

In this case, the government *requires* that you *take income* from this trust. In fact, the IRS Code states that you must take out a minimum of 5 percent of the income each year from a CRT. (I actually structure most of the trusts to take out between 5 and 10 percent a year.)

So, you have access to your money, which is inside the trust, and you have income that you can take out at, say, 10 percent a year. In fact, I have found that working with the 10 percent figure is advantageous and also very easy to illustrate. Now, this 10 percent a year can be 10 percent of income or of income in principal. It depends on how you structure the trust.

What if the trust only earns 3 percent a year? Am I saying that you can take out 10 percent even though you've only earned 3 percent? Yes, you can. In fact, you can take the other 7 percent out of principal.

Many people I speak to don't believe that this truly exists. Why is the government going to allow you to deplete this type of trust? Well, it's really not in your best interest to deplete the trust. Remember, whatever is inside is growing, free of income tax. You don't want to deplete the trust if you don't have to. You want the assets to compound, tax free, so that you can take out a greater amount later.

So, it's really to your benefit *not* to deplete this trust and *not* to take out principal. In fact, the way that you should determine how much income you can get out of the trust each year should be based on the realistic expectations of what the trust will earn. If you can realistically expect that you can actively trade the trust and earn up to 15 percent a year, then you should select a 15 percent income interest in the trust so that you can take out this amount. In some years the trust might only earn 3 percent or even nothing. You can still take up to 15 percent if you set it up this way.

Some years the trust may earn 35 percent. But again, if you structure it in a trust agreement whereby you can only take out 15 percent, then that's okay because the next year you're going to have a larger amount in the trust to invest, and you will be able to take out *15 percent of a larger number.*

In MIB's case, we designed the trust so that he could have access to 10 percent of the trust assets each year—with $2 million in the trust he had access to $200,000 each year without any capital gains erosion. Let's look at what would have happened if MIB had not utilized the trust. His $2 million would have been whittled down, *through the modern miracle of taxation,* to $1.4 million. If we assume the same 10 percent payout, MIB would have only received $140,000 a year in income.

You might say 10 percent a year growth rate is too high. The growth rate is unimportant. I am setting this example up with a 10 percent rate because it is easy to illustrate. It doesn't matter whether the trust earns 10 percent, 8 percent, 5 percent, or 35 percent. I'm just trying to convey the concept now. The trust will provide benefit at any level of income, much more so than a nontrust alternative. Remember, in this case, it was $140,000 versus $200,000 of income per year.

Summary: The CRT Is a Gift to Society Which Is Also a Gift to You!

So, if you're looking for increased income and this is your primary motivation, the CRT is the best planning alternative for providing additional income. There are other aspects of CRTs that you need to consider. But purely from a selfish standpoint, the CRT is almost always better than the non-CRT alternative. Wouldn't you rather have $200,000 a year instead of $140,000?

With a properly structured trust, you could determine how much you would like to take out on a yearly basis. This sounds complicated but really isn't. Basically, you can have flexibility in taking your annual income from the trust. You may take out 5 percent if it earns

5 percent or 10 percent if it earns 10 percent—or any amount in between. This assumes that the trust is properly set up to meet your objectives and that it uses the correct funding vehicles.

The tax code says that you have to select either 5 or 10 percent, but that's not a static amount. By using the net income trust with makeup provisions, as I will now discuss, there's a lot more flexibility in how much you take out of these trusts annually.

My favorite trust is the Charitable Remainder Unitrust, which we will call a NIMCRUT (Net Income with Makeup Provisions—Charitable Remainder Unitrust). This income trust has makeup provisions, and it allows you to take out nothing in any given year if you so select. Yet the money in the trust is *owed to you.*

In this example, MIB could take out $200,000. But if he elected one year not to take the money out because he would like to leave it in to compound, tax free, he could do so. The next year MIB could take out 10 percent of the value—now $2,200,000—so he could take out $220,000.

But wait—the trust still owes him the $200,000 that he elected not to take out in the first year. So he could now go back, if he needed to, and take out the money that he had elected not to touch in the first year. During the second year, MIB could actually take out $420,000 ($220,000 plus the $200,000 he didn't take out in the first year). By not taking income out, you can allow your trust to grow quite rapidly because of tax-free compounding.

TO FURTHER COMPOUND THE SITUATION

Albert Einstein once stated: "The greatest concept conceived by man is *compound interest."*

I have always said: *"The greatest concept conceived by man is* tax-free *compound interest."*

You can see how tax-free compound interest works quite well within the trust. Keep in mind that all assets inside a CRT are the property of the charity (ownership). However, this charity is not going to receive the assets until you die (beneficial interest *after* your death). The charity does not even need to know that it is the beneficiary of whatever is in the trust when you die. In fact, you can change the name of the beneficiary charity subsequent to setting the trust up—*most people don't know this!*

You can also elect that this trust continue 20 years after you and your spouse have been deceased. So, in fact, you have two options. You can either have the trust terminate when you and your spouse die, or you can continue it for another 20 years. In this case, your kids can be the trustees, and they can receive the income (10 percent a year) for another 20 years. As long as you live, you're going to receive income from the trust (beneficial interest during your life), and you're going to *control* the trust. It is only at your death that the assets go to the charity. The hardest job I have working with clients is convincing them that the money they give to a charitable trust benefits them as much as the charity.

John D. Rockefeller said: "The greatest tax dodge of all is to give it all away." Maybe the CRT is what he was talking about. My job here will be to convince you that the *more* money you give away, the *better off* you will be.

Let's recap what we know about CRTs so far:

1. You've set up a CRT.
2. You've gifted stock to the trust.
3. You've elected to maintain control of the trust as trustee for your lifetime.
4. You've then sold the stock.
5. You paid no capital gains tax because this is a CRT.
6. The charity will get all of these funds eventually.
7. You reinvest those assets into no-load mutual funds and other types of investments that are comfortable for you.
8. Because these assets are in a CRT, they will grow and compound, tax free, for the rest of your life.
9. You receive distributions from the trust for your life, your spouse's life, and even another 20 years (of the life of your child).

Remember, that means that as long as the assets are growing in the trust, there will *never be taxation* of any kind. Many clients ask me, "Do you mean that if I don't take the money out it's going to keep growing and I owe no taxes?" That's right. If you want tax-free compounding on your investments, just leave them inside the trust.

In the case of MIB, he elected to take a 10 percent payout of the value of the trust each year. So each year the trust paid MIB 10 percent of its value on January 1—the date that an audit was done and the date that the value of the trust was set. MIB elected to take interest out each year, which we arbitrarily presumed would be 10 percent a year, and then the remainder would go directly to the charity upon the couple's demise. He was thus able to give back something to society for all the benefits he received during his lifetime.

A CRT AND YOUR HEIRS

The next question I hear usually is, *"What happens to my kids?"*

By not using the CRT, MIB would have had $1.4 million at his death. But remember, he now would be subject to estate taxes, so his kids may only have received about $700,000 after tax. If he doesn't do the trust, the kids will get $700,000 when he dies. *If he does the trust, the kids get nothing.* Isn't this the best planning tool you've ever seen if you'd like to disinherit your kids?

Seriously, though, I'm sure most of you like your kids, and if not, you probably have some grandkids you care about or are even quite fond of. I've never had anybody set up a trust with the intent of depriving their children of an inheritance.

Let's assume that you even want to leave more money to your children than if you hadn't set up the trust. In order to understand the benefits of CRTs with regard to estate planning, I think that it's important to look at what would happen if you didn't utilize the CRT. Remember, the kids would have received $700,000, and with the trust they receive nothing. But if you die without a CRT, your assets will go through estate taxes, and you've already seen how estate taxes can ravage an estate.

So, in MIB's case, let's assume that the $2 million of stock less the $600,000 capital tax would have left him $1.4 million. At death, 50 percent of this $1.4 million would have gone to the government and the rest to his heirs. So let's assume his heirs would have gotten $700,000 out of the original $2 million.

Now, let's go back to the CRT and look at the alternative afforded in this type of estate-tax planning. We must remember that $2 million of principal inside the trust will eventually go to the charity. Nothing will stop that from happening. The way we protect our children is by creating a separate trust—the *irrevocable life insurance trust (Crummey trust).*

A CRUMMEY TRUST IS NOT SO CRUMMY!

I've also heard this trust referred to as a *wealth replacement trust.* It is called a wealth replacement trust because it is created to replace or to increase your wealth and to pass it on to your heirs. This trust is created totally separate from the CRT. This trust is irrevocable. This means that once you have set it up and it is in place, you can never change it. Keep in mind that we're talking about a wealth replacement trust, and not a CRT. These are two totally separate entities.

So, we set this trust up, keeping in mind that you may gift $10,000 a year to anybody you want under the current tax laws. This also means that you and your wife can gift $20,000 a year jointly to anybody you want.

In this case, let's assume you have three children. You would give each child $10,000 a year, or as a couple, $20,000. So, as a whole, because you have three children, you could gift each child $20,000 a year, and a total of $60,000 per year for all three children would go into the wealth replacement trust. Now, this trust would name your children as beneficiaries; however, *you cannot be the trustee.* If you are the trustee, this trust is considered to be part of your estate. You would then have what the government refers to as *incidents of ownership* in this type of trust.

Everything inside of your estate will be taxed at your death. If you name your brother or your sister or a grown child as trustee of the wealth replacement trust, it is not part of your estate. What you would do is gift the money to the trust. When you die, because you have no control of this trust, the government does not consider it to be part of your taxable estate. If it is not part of your estate, you don't owe any estate tax on the asset. So anything in the trust will go to your children without estate taxation. There is no 37 percent estate-tax rate, no 55 percent estate-tax rate, no estate-tax rate at all on this money.

Now, the only problem with the wealth replacement trust, apart from the fact that you can't make any changes to it, is that you can only put in a finite amount of money each year. Remember, you can only gift $10,000 or, for a couple, $20,000 annually. But if you have used the CRT and you have given $2 million to charity like MIB did, how are you possibly going to get $2 million into this wealth replacement trust? If you did it only this way, it would take an extremely long time to get the $2 million in there.

The simple solution to this problem is in funding the trust with a *second-to-die* insurance policy, also known as a *wealth replacement policy* or an estate-tax policy.

TO GIFT IS BUT TO RECEIVE

Now, remember, you don't pay estate tax until both you and your spouse are deceased. Also, remember, that your CRT is going to be paying both you and your spouse income until you both die. So you don't need an insurance policy. What you need is a *second-to-die* policy. This is a special type of insurance, offered by many companies, that insures two lives. It insures both spouses. It doesn't pay any benefit when the first spouse dies, unlike a normal policy. It only pays benefits when the second one dies. When you are both deceased, the insurance benefits are paid to the trust. Remember that there are no estate taxes due, and you don't lose your income from the CRT until both of you are deceased. (If you are single, you would get a single life policy, not a second-to-die policy.)

The advantage to the second-to-die policy is that the premiums are *much less expensive* because the probability of two people dying actuarially is far more remote in any one given year than one person dying. We're all going to die, but the probability of you dying this year is remote compared to the probability of you dying, say, in 20 or 30 years; and the probability of both you and your spouse dying this year is *highly* remote. So these policies are very, very efficiently priced because they are based on joint life expectancies (two, not one).

I'm going to ask you to keep an open mind regarding insurance. I've heard many times from my clients, "Oh, I hate insurance, I hate insurance companies, and I hate insurance agents." I don't care if you hate insurance companies or insurance agents, but please keep an open mind about insurance. Many of you already realize the benefits provided by these types of policies. Many of you don't. However, if you can't open yourself to the possibility, you will not be able to expand your knowledge.

It has been said that "A mind is like a parachute, it only works when it's open." You must keep an open mind regarding insurance because in this case, I don't care whether you call it insurance, call it an investment, or call it whatever else you like, it will be of tremendous benefit to you and your estate.

Using this type of vehicle, you're going to be allowed to purchase a dollar's worth of benefit for your estate (your kids and grandkids), and it's only going to cost you eight to ten cents on the dollar. So, for eight to ten cents of insurance premiums, your estate will give your heirs one dollar.

This is what is known as leverage. And anybody who has ever made money understands leverage. In fact, this is the best leverage vehicle for *replacing* or *building* wealth in an estate that exists today!

PREPAY YOUR ESTATE TAX FOR PENNIES ON THE DOLLAR

Remember, I discussed paying retail versus wholesale. The estimated discount is proportional with age; but they will give you a fair idea of how a second-to-die policy can save you money *and* replace your wealth. The only thing better than this scenario would be if *somebody else* paid the premiums for you.

What if I told you there was such a program, and what if I told you that it was one of those *too good to be true* programs? In fact, it is. It is a program that sounds too good to be true and, therefore, either *must* be too good to be true or must be *sponsored by the United States government*! In this case, the government has a program whereby every time you put your assets into a CRT, they will *buy insurance to replace your assets for you.* This program is called the *charitable income tax deduction.*

Remember, you're going to be gifting money to charity by setting up a CRT. When you gift money to charity, you receive a tax deduction. If, like MIB, at aged 63 you put $2 million into a CRT, depending on several different factors, you will receive roughly about $600,000 in income tax deductions. This figure will be subject to such factors as the way the trust is structured and your life expectancy.

It is far easier to understand this concept if we work with simple numbers, so let's assume that out of a $600,000 write-off, you will net about a third, or $200,000, in tax savings, which you will have to spend. Let's also assume that you take this money and gift it into the wealth replacement trust. You can then use this tax credit to fund a second-to-die policy and replace most, if not all, of the wealth you have given away to charity.

Now, this deduction varies. It takes into consideration many factors, such as how much income you elected to take out of a trust, how old you are, and the life expectancy rates. The 10 percent a year that you decide to take out, such as MIB did, gives you a smaller deduction than if you elected only an 8 percent a year payout. Remember, if you take out 10 percent a year, there's going to be less at your death, and that's when the money goes to charity. Your age is another factor. If you're 30 years old when you set the trust up, the charity probably can't expect to receive the money for another 50 years. However, if you're 60 or 70 when you set up the trust, the charity can reasonably expect to get the money within the next 20 years. So you get a much higher deduction.

On the other hand, the cost of insurance will vary inversely: It will cost far less to insure two 30-year-olds for $2 million than two 60-year-olds, *so the net effect will be about the same.*

In this illustration, let's say that MIB received a $600,000 tax deduction when he contributed the $2 million into the trust. Assuming a 30 percent tax bracket, this meant that MIB saved $200,000 in taxes (a $600,000 deduction at 30 percent saved him $200,000 in taxes).

That $200,000 is money he didn't have to pay the government. Remember, I promised that the government will buy your insurance?

Well, let's take those tax deductions (the $200,000 of savings) as MIB did and gift it to that newly created wealth replacement trust; $200,000 would buy about $2 million of insurance on a 63-year-old couple, assuming reasonably good health and qualifying this with the concept of BOCA (*based on current assumptions,* such as mortality costs, insurance costs, and interest rates).

Did you follow what we just did? We took our tax deduction and purchased $2 million worth of insurance that the children will get. These deductions will now purchase an insurance policy placed inside the wealth replacement trust. This $2 million of second-to-die estate-tax insurance will go directly to your kids at your death and will not be subject to taxation of any kind!

Insurance benefits are *income-tax free;* and because these benefits are in the trust (the wealth replacement trust), they're also *estate-tax free.* They are part of the trust, you owe no taxes (if structured properly), and your children owe no taxes when they receive the money. Two million dollars will go directly to them, tax free, and that's exactly what MIB did.

MIB gave $2 million to his CRT, retaining the income rights to the $2 million. He elected to pay himself 10 percent of the trust assets each year. MIB received $200,000 the first year, which he could then either take out or leave in the trust to compound tax free. All of his money, for the rest of his life, can, in fact, grow tax free inside the trust. He can buy, sell, and trade securities all day long and never pay one penny of capital gains tax.

He also got a tax deduction for giving the $2 million to charity. He created a wealth replacement trust, took the tax deduction, gave the money he saved in taxes to the wealth replacement trust, and named his three children as beneficiaries.

In this case, it took several years to contribute the money into the wealth replacement trust so that he avoided gift-tax implication or using up his unified credit. He could have, however, taken the tax deduction all at once and gifted it to the trust. He could have done this by using some of his unified credit, but in this case he chose not to. This was fine.

Most insurance companies will allow you to spread out the premiums over a period of time and still maintain the full face value of the policy.

When MIB's wife dies, $2 million goes to the charity of his choice from the CRT and $2 million goes tax free to his children from the wealth replacement trust. Compare this to the situation if MIB hadn't done anything with the CRT: He was going to sell that asset—the stock—and pay the tax. If he had done that without using the CRT and wealth replacement trust programs we've just discussed, he would only have left $700,000 to his children. He would only have had $1.4 million growing, *taxable,* after he paid the capital gains tax. Consequently, he would only have had an income of $140,000 a year versus the $200,000 a year income from the trust.

MIB is now far better off than he would have been; the charity is better off; and his children are far better off after he instituted these strategies. This multilevel structure is one of the key components of estate-tax planning.

Frank Corn, CLU, Chartered Financial Consultant and a renowned authority in the estate-planning arena, has described second-to-die insurance as being, "the most effective vehicle for wealth preservation and the transfer of assets between generations ever developed." I would have to say that I agree with this analysis.

The CRT/wealth replacement trust strategy is a solid leg in our estate-planning tripod. It is the first part of a solid financial foundation that you should seriously consider if the circumstances merit. You must understand these concepts in order to get ahead in the financial arena. Please reread the preceding section, if you need to, until it makes sense to you.

THE DOUBLE PLAY—SUMMARY

1. Set up a charitable remainder trust.
2. Donate highly appreciated assets to it.
3. Get an up-front tax deduction.
4. Sell the asset in the trust.
5. Pay no capital gains tax on the sale.
6. Draw a stream of income (higher than would be possible if you paid tax on the sale of the asset and reinvested the proceeds) for your life and the life of your spouse.
7. Asset goes to the charity upon second death.
8. Set up a Crummey trust with your children as beneficiaries.
9. Use cash from tax savings to buy a wealth replacement insurance policy to replace assets in your estate.
10. Proceeds from this policy go to your children free of estate tax.

12

The Layup: It's Just a Matter of Trust

HOW AND WHY TO SET UP A TRUST

Let's now discuss one more issue—whether or not the family-limited partnership is a good alternative vehicle to the trust with respect to holding life insurance used for estate-planning purposes.

In Chapter 11, we discussed the Crummey trust (aka wealth replacement trust and irrevocable life insurance trust) as a means of using second-to-die life insurance to replace the wealth in your estate after gifting whatever assets you had to a charitable remainder trust (CRT). We must at least consider a partnership as an alternative to this irrevocable life insurance trust for several reasons: first is the ability for you to maintain control over the entity, second is the issue of increased flexibility.

An irrevocable life insurance trust is by its very nature irrevocable—you can never get back what you put in nor can you change the terms of the trust. In setting up an irrevocable life insurance trust, you have thereby lost both control and flexibility. A partnership, on the other hand, is a creation of state and contract law and, therefore, much more flexible. Tax laws that are created for partnerships are more favorable than the laws for trusts, especially in light of the 1997 Tax Relief Act. For instance, if the parties involved in a partnership decide that the partnership contract should change, they can do so quickly and easily. If you wish to change ownership on the policy, you can change the contract that governs the family-limited partnerships. Recall that a partnership is like a *magic hat:* much more flexible than trusts, which are more like *strong boxes.* If instead of a Crummey trust you set up a family-limited partnership to hold your insurance policy, you can change the beneficiary and maintain much more control over the policy without having it be included in your taxable estate.

If your life insurance policy is owned by a family-limited partnership, you could indirectly provide cash to pay the premiums merely by making contributions of capital to the partnership in return for an enlarged interest or additional units in the partnership. You can then gift away all or a portion of these additional units outright to family members who qualify for the family exclusion.

To restate, your transfer of cash to the partnership would not be a gift because you would be receiving units of equal value to the cash contributed. However, at some point you will be giving these units to your children. Therefore, with no strings attached, this would clearly qualify for an annual gift-tax exclusion. Alternatively, you could give the children the cash. They, in turn, could contribute that cash to the partnership in return for an increased interest in the partnership that would own your insurance policy.

To summarize, the procedure to place your insurance policy into a partnership is as follows:

1. The family-limited partnership applies for an insurance policy on your life.
2. The family-limited partnership owns, pays premium on, and is beneficiary of the policy.
3. The premiums are paid through the family-limited partnership, and there are many options:
   - Premiums could be paid from investments or business proceeds.
   - You could put capital into the family-limited partnership to pay the premiums.
   - The partners themselves can contribute capital to the partnership, and that cash can be used to pay the premiums.
4. The general partner makes decisions about partnership operations and investments that include, of course, the purchase and maintenance of life insurance on his or her life.
5. You could, on behalf of the firm, purchase life insurance on others, assuming that you have an insurable interest.
6. At the death of the insured, the partnership receives the insurance proceeds and allocates that money to each partner's account according to his or her respective interest.
7. The partnership can then use cash derived from such insurance proceeds to purchase assets from the deceased partner's estate or to make a fully secured interest-bearing loan to the estate to pay the estate tax.

8. That would give the partnership valuable assets with a stepped-up basis.
9. The estate now has cash that it uses to pay administrative costs, debts, and taxes.
10. When a partnership dissolves, any money or assets that are not already distributed are paid out to the partners according to their respective interest.

The neat thing about this structure is that there are many alternatives to accomplish the same objective. For instance, you could set up a life insurance trust as we discussed in Chapter 11. However, you can name the trustee of that irrevocable life insurance trust as a limited partner in the newly formed partnership merely by giving an interest in the partnership to the trustee. Distributions of cash from the partnership are therefore legitimately payable to the trust as a limited partner, or the cash flow can be used as a source of premiums for the life insurance owned by the trust.

Another concept is *insurable interest.* With respect to a life insurance policy, the person or entity purchasing the policy must have an insurable interest in the person to be insured. Here are some of the general guidelines:

- Typically, a partnership will have an insurable interest in its general partner's life.
- The facts of the case will determine how much insurance will be issued.
- Typically, a partnership will not have an insurable interest in the life of an employee that is merely working for the partnership. However, to the extent that the business can incur a loss at the key employee's death, there should be no problem. So if the proposed insured is neither a general partner nor a key employee, you may have a problem with insurable interest.

You may ask about the effect, from a tax perspective, of payment of premium when life insurance is owned by a partnership. There is no effect on profits because premiums are not an income tax deduction for either the partnership or its partners. However, because of this, the proceeds are not income taxable upon the death of the insured. Upon dissolution of the policy, there may be a taxable event. The insurance proceeds would then be allocated to the partners in proportion to their interest in the entity.

Let's look at an example. Say you had a 4 percent general partnership interest and a 6 percent limited partnership interest (a total of 10 percent). Now let's assume that there was a $1 million policy payable on the death of the general partner. When the general partner dies, you would increase your basis by 10 percent of the $1 million, or $100,000, and the cash would go into the partnership.

If the partnership cashed in the policy during the insured's life, there may be a partnership gain. This would be the difference between the payment received and the net premiums paid by the partnership. The difference would then be reportable by each partner in proportion to his or her share in the partnership as income. When the gain is reportable by the partners, their shares in the partnership increase by that amount just as if they had contributed cash to the firm.

One very important word of caution: In my opinion, a partnership would not be recognized as a family-limited partnership if its *only purpose* is to purchase or hold life insurance policies. There has been a private letter ruling saying that a family-limited partnership can hold life insurance, but it is only a private letter ruling and, in my opinion, does not adequately protect you from structuring a partnership this way. I feel very strongly that there must be some type of business or profit purpose to the partnership, and the insurance policy will be held as an ancillary act.

Again, this is my delineation between grey areas and black-and-white areas. Why take the chance? The stakes are too high for you to become a famous name in IRS Tax Court history. If the IRS refuses to recognize the existence of a partnership, then the entire proceeds would be includable in the insured's estate.

There is another consideration, and that is the fact that if you structure the partnership properly, IRS Code Section 2035—three years of death transfer rules—will not apply. You do this by having your partnership buy an existing policy on the partner's life for a fair value. Section 2035 applies only to gratuitous transfers. So if the partnership pays a fair market value for the policy, the three-year rule should not apply. (For those unfamiliar with the three-year transfer rule, it states that if an insured dies within three years of making a transfer gratuitously to another entity, then the proceeds would still be included in the insured's estate.)

Let's look at another example: the *buy-sell agreement* using an insurance policy to fund it. As you know, a buy-sell agreement is an essential tool in estate planning to both the partners and the partnership in an entity agreement where the partnership is the purchaser. There are income tax implications.

Each premium paid by the partnership is treated as a distribution to the partner. As I mentioned before, that reduces the partner's basis in proportion to his or her interest in the partnership. Any death benefit the partnership receives is then totally free of income tax for both the partnership and its partners.

When the partnership receives the insurance proceeds and buys the decedent's shareholder interest, basis is split between a decedent's estate and the surviving partners. That gives the surviving partners at least a partial interest and basis for the firm's payment to the decedent's estate in return for his or her interest. An allocation of basis to the decedent's estate means that the basis will be wasted. Its share of the purchase already has received a stepped-up basis at the partner's death. So if you make a special allocation, you've gained everything and given up nothing. However, you can suggest that there be a provision in the partnership agreement to allocate *all of the basis to the surviving partners.*

In a *cross-purchase agreement,* each partner is obligated to purchase the interest of every other partner upon death or disability or retirement. Let's once again look at what happens with respect to premiums, proceeds, and basis.

In a cross-purchase agreement, each premium paid by the partnership on behalf of the individual partners is treated as if the entity paid out a distribution of cash in an amount equal to the premium paid to the policy-owning partner. This will increase the partner's basis, dollar for dollar, and this results in a different basis adjustment because the premiums of the partners are likely to differ.

As far as the proceeds go, death benefits are income tax free to the surviving partners. With respect to basis, each partner who pays for the interest of a deceased or disabled or retiring partner receives a dollar-for-dollar increase in basis.

THE LAYUP—SUMMARY

1. Use a family-limited partnership to hold a life insurance policy.
2. Use the annual gift-tax exemption to gift shares in the family-limited partnership to other family members.
3. The policy ownership passes estate-tax free to the owners of the partnership.
4. Estate tax is avoided.

13

The Home Run: A Way to Double Your Exemptions

THE BASICS

As you recall, everyone gets a one-time unified credit exclusion for gifting and for passing wealth through an estate. Most couples don't take advantage of this properly because they figure there is an unlimited marital exclusion. They simply pass all the wealth down to their spouse. This is exactly the wrong way to do it!

Let's look at an example. If a couple has $1,350,000 (2001) and the first spouse dies, all of the $1,350,000 passes to the second spouse. The second spouse will be taxed on $675,000 of it (per 2001 rates) when he or she dies. They didn't use the unified credit when the first spouse died, so they lost it. This is a prime example of the precept, "Use it or lose it." The second spouse then gets taxed on an amount of money that would have been tax free if the first spouse had made use of the credit.

A far better way to do this is to establish a trust before the first spouse dies in which $675,000 of the money enters into the trust, and beneficial interest passes to the heirs of the first spouse at the time of his or her death. However, a stream of income from the trust is retained by the second spouse for his or her lifetime. This will ensure that the second spouse is taken care of, as well as the children.

THE HOME RUN—SUMMARY

1. Use the double unified credit to pass twice the wealth down to your heirs.
2. Use a trust to hold title to the assets of each spouse separately.
3. Let the remaining spouse get a stream of income for life off the trust.
4. When the second spouse dies, the assets pass estate-tax free to the children.

14

Modern-Day Miracles—Chalk Up a Few for the Good Guys

TRADER STATUS AUDIT VICTORIES I HAVE HAD

"Sam the Sham" and the Pension Audit

> Dear Ted,
>
> Your strategy worked like a charm. We left the auditor alone, and he dug his own grave. I would like you to handle my account from now on, as my CPA doesn't really understand the difference between a non-floor trader and floor trader. Please contact me about getting started on this year's tax work.
>
> —A former floor trader, currently filing under Trader Status, who successfully withstood a pension audit by a supposedly "experienced" IRS pension auditor.

My first book, *The Serious Investor's Tax Survival Guide,* began with a series of articles that were published in the *AIQ Opening Bell* magazine. An old acquaintance of mine had just begun his very short stint as editor-in-chief of this publication, and he was hard-pressed for articles. He asked if I had anything I could contribute, and I gladly obliged. Never being one to shun publicity or acclamation, I set forth to write a series of articles that examined the tax aspects of trading. It was an unusual series for this particular publication, but it went over quite well.

I began receiving calls from all over the country inquiring into the concept of Trader Status. A few months later, I ran into my first publisher, Trader's Library, at a Bill Williams' seminar in Chicago, and

Chris Myers approached me about doing a book on the subject. The rest is history.

One of the by-products of this series of articles was that it put me in touch with a large group of traders and among them was Sam Muller (name changed), an elderly gentleman who had been profitably trading for the past 50 years. He had been a professional for the bulk of his life, but when he retired from the floor, he began trading his own account. He did quite well for himself, amassing a small fortune in assets, and was living quite comfortable in his "retirement."

He had a CPA who had filed his tax return for many years while he traded, but who unfortunately was not aware of the distinction between a floor trader and one that traded off the floor (Trader Status). For this reason, the CPA had filed Sam Muller's tax return just as he had when Sam still traded on the floor—taking a pension deduction against trading income.

The return was being audited by an experienced IRS pension auditor, but one who, fortunately for us, knew less about Trader Status than the former CPA did. Sam had read one of my articles in 1991, and he called me up to ask for my input on the situation.

I was delighted to give my advice and to learn the facts of this audit, as it was one with which I had not had much experience at that time. I had participated in many audits with regard to Trader Status, but only one or two in the specific area of whether or not a trader is entitled to a pension deduction.

I told Sam that I could do one of two things: (1) take over the audit (take a retainer, obtain power of attorney, and begin the fight from my vantage point) or (2) watch from afar, see how it was going, and, if need be, take over at some future time. I suggested the latter because the audit hadn't yet gotten into full swing, and I felt Sam should save his money on my fees until we really determined whether or not I was needed. He liked this idea—a lot!

From my perspective it was worth monitoring with no fee because I wanted to see the outcome, glean more experience in this area, and perhaps at some point have it as material for a new book. Well the gamble paid off—in all aspects.

The former CPA knew just enough to confuse the auditor, who had never handled a Trader Status case. The IRS auditor had handled "Floor Trader" pension cases and was thoroughly confused. When Sam's former CPA put down "Trader" as occupation, the auditor simply assumed Sam was still a floor trader and allowed the deduction in full. The deduction, although *not* warranted, *was allowed!*

This reinforced a basic tenet to which I have always subscribed in handling IRS auditors: When there is a question and it looks like the auditor has misunderstood the situation with at least some chance of it being resolved in your favor, keep quiet—loose lips sink ships. This is one case in which an IRS auditor's misunderstanding, misinformation, and, quite bluntly, ignorance worked fully in my client's favor.

An Appealing Case of Trader Status

> Dear Ted,
>
> I just received my $38,000 refund check for 1991 taxes, after the auditor initially rejected your amendment of my 1990 and 1991 tax returns. I guess the position you took in appeals was ultimately upheld and agreed to by the IRS. Coupled with the $19,000 I received last week, this was quite a pleasant surprise.
>
> I had almost given up—I don't believe it.
>
> Another thirty-eight f . . king thousand dollars—this is incredible!
>
> —A current client, $150,000 richer due to Trader Status.

One of my greatest victories in 25 years of dealing with the IRS came in 1999. It was a gift that I had not anticipated would be delivered to me with so little fighting. I won't say with "so little work" because it was in fact quite an ordeal; however, the reward of staying the course and seeing this audit through to its conclusion was quite substantial.

Here is a brief history:

This client had been referred to me in 1992 by a prominent figure in the trading arena. My new client, "Double E," had a significant tax problem. He had filed his 1990 and 1991 tax returns as an *investor*, compromising his position significantly. He had, in fact, given away over $100,000 in tax refunds by filing as an investor (and another $30,000 to New York City and New York State).

This trader had been a subscriber to Bloomberg Market Service and Quotes, Futuresource, C.Q.G., and many other top-line market services, including trading newsletters, trading advisory services, and so on. He had also spent many thousands of dollars building a trading room in his house. Then there were the new computer systems and other such equipment that would be used exclusively in his primary endeavor—trading. When I met with Double E in 1992, he had not yet filed his tax return for 1992.

He filled out one of my Trader Questionnaires; after reviewing it, I informed him that according to everything that I had seen about his business and activities he was in fact a trader. Accordingly, he was entitled to significant write-offs that he had foregone.

The Caveat: Amending an Investor's Tax Return as a Trader

However, there were *two small problems* as I saw them:

1. He had already filed his 1990 and 1991 tax returns. To amend these years and to ask for a refund of somewhere in the neighborhood of $100,000 would certainly raise a flag.

The IRS is a lot less prone to refund your money once they have it in their coffers. Certainly, two amended tax returns requesting over $100,000 would pass by more than one audit desk. I told him that he should expect an audit and also informed him that I felt he was 100 percent entitled to get the money back.

I asked him if he was up to a fight, and he said, "Ted, you're the boss. I'll let you decide what our chances are of winning this thing, and then let's evaluate the risk-reward of doing it."

I told him what my fees would be for amending the returns, and I gave him a ballpark range of what it would cost to fight this thing in audit. The audit cost is the largest variable, however, because you never can be sure how cooperative the Internal Revenue Service will be.

When we looked at the stakes and evaluated the downside, we both agreed without hesitation that it would be worth amending the returns because, in addition to the federal refund, we would also amend the returns for New York State and New York City. In total, for the two years, I calculated his refund, including interest, to be somewhere in the area of $140,000 to $150,000.

2. Although 1992 had been a slightly profitable year for Double E, 1990 and 1991 had not been. They were his first two years trading full time, and as most of you realize, there is a cost of learning the trade. The tuition that most of us survivors have paid has been one, two, and sometimes more years of loss—many times, significant loss.

Double E had a similar situation in 1990 and 1991; he had lost some money in honing his craft. The losing years could present a problem. Most likely the IRS auditor would challenge the fact that he had two consecutive losing years, and they might think this was not a business but rather a hobby.

I told Double E that if he did not make money in 1992, it would add to the auditor's case.

For those of you not familiar with the *hobby-loss rule* review Chapter 6 which discusses the supposition that a business will make money after three years. If you reread this section you will see that my views differ widely from the general perception of the IRS.

Again, the hobby-loss rule is merely a supposition. Nowhere in the IRS Code does it say that a business has to be profitable in its third year of operation, and I have been successful in defending this many times in audit. Thus, with these two problems in mind and with the determination of getting back some money, we forged on.

We proceeded to amend the returns, filing two years of federal and state amended tax returns. New York State was wonderful; within eight weeks they sent us two checks totaling approximately $43,000. Double E was thrilled, he said, "My God, Ted, this is much easier than I thought. Perhaps the IRS will follow suit."

Several "Gifts" from the IRS. Well, lo and behold, within the next several weeks, a check arrived from the federal government for approximately $52,000 plus interest. This was for the tax year 1990.

Once again, Double E was quite delighted. Because my fees for preparing these amended returns had only been several thousand dollars, he figured this was quite a good cost/benefit and in fact a marvelous way to spend his money! He anxiously awaited the next $45,000 from the feds. And he waited . . . and waited . . . and waited.

When the next envelope from the IRS finally arrived, he rushed up to his apartment and trading room and ripped it open, joyfully expecting another "multithousand dollar present" from the IRS. His anticipation, however, quickly evaporated and changed to consternation.

It was not a check but rather an invitation from the IRS to "come on down" for a get-acquainted visit regarding tax years 1990 and 1991. They also advised him that they were in fact holding up the processing of his refund request for 1991 subject to the outcome and determination of the audit of his 1990 and 1991 tax returns. This was pretty much what I had anticipated, and I told Double E not to worry. We were prepared for the fight.

The Audit Begins. On my first visit *downtown* several weeks later, I was blessed with another IRS "gift." I was once again given an auditor whom I needed to educate on the issue of Trader Status. Unfortunately, however, this auditor knew just enough to be dangerous. He "thought" he understood what a trader did, however, in reality he had no clue. I spent the next several months sending him articles that I and other people had written, together with court cases and sections of the Code that substantiated my position. Finally, I believed I had made headway.

Mr. C, "frontline IRS desk auditor," had finally understood what a trader does, and furthermore he came to understand who qualifies as a trader—or so he said. He informed me that he now must proceed with the normal course of the audit, which was examining all income and expenses for the tax year 1990. In my mind, I assumed that everything was proceeding just fine.

I told Double E to begin putting together packages of receipts, canceled checks, credit card statement, brokerage statements, bank confirms, bank statements, and the normal substantiation that I have learned will satisfy the most tenacious of IRS auditors. On my next visit to New York, I marched in with what could best have been described as a steamer trunk full of substantiating documents.

I used one of those airport carriers with wheels to secure the trunk and wheeled it up to the third floor of the Manhattan district office of the Internal Revenue Service. I proudly put the trunk down in Mr. C's office and opened it up, saying "Let's go!"

At that first meeting, we went through most of the material in a cursory manner. I convinced Mr. C to select two months as an audit sample and to audit everything in those two months, but to leave the remaining 10 months alone.

He reluctantly agreed to do so on the expense side, however, he insisted on verifying every penny of income and every single trade. Knowing that my client was one of the most anal record keepers I had ever handled, this would be no problem; so I agreed to his conditions.

We then proceeded to go through the income side of 1990. After several hours I left the materials with him, taking copies for my own files. He indicated that he would continue to go through the trade confirms and brokerage statements tying out the trades and income/loss for the year.

The Audit Continues. Over the next few weeks, I received many phone calls from Mr. C asking questions about trading and about the profit or loss. I could see from these telephone calls that he was not very clear on what a trader did and what trades were; however, I was cooperative in the hopes that I could convince him and sway him to our side.

Several months later, I flew up to New York for my next appointment with Mr. C. We spent several hours going through the rest of the income, with several questions to go back to my client for answers.

When it was time to make a selection of the two-month audit sample of expenses, Mr. C decided to do both a random and high-dollar value sample. He selected the highest month—the month in which my client had the greatest number of expenses—and another month at random. The two months that were selected were February and June of 1990. He then proceeded to look at every single expense in those two months.

The major expense, other than data feed, was margin interest, or in this case trading interest. This was a rather complex calculation in that my client had been an expert in borrowing money to finance his trading business. He used lines of credit, credit cards, home equity loans, and just about any form of borrowing he could possibly use; and he had the records to trace this borrowing to his trading account. Fortunately for my client, but unfortunate for us, he had also moved these lines around significantly, repaying and reborrowing as often as once or twice a week to get the best rate.

To say the least, trading interest and tracing trading interest for even just a month or two was a nightmare. This took many months and several additional trips to New York to accomplish, not to mention the numerous phone calls.

Finally, however, after almost a year of going back and forth to New York, telephone calls to Mr. C, and telephone calls and answers from Double E, we had tied in all but about $300 worth of interest for the two months in question. This was $300 out of $20,000 and a modern-day miracle.

It was now time to look at some of the other expenses, such as $6,000 per month for Bloomberg, several thousand dollars a month for C.Q.G. and Futuresource, many thousands of dollars in trading advisory services, and so on and so forth. This consumed the next eight months.

It was now late 1995—almost three years after I filed those two amended tax returns. We were now finally wrapping up the first of the audits that I had anticipated.

Double E was still waiting for his $45,000 (plus interest) refund check from the U.S. government, but he had the use of the $100,000 that he had received from the Feds and New York state for the past three years.

My fee for doing the audit, including travel expenses to New York and all the time I spent with Mr. C, approached five figures. This is not the type of work I like to do. I find it draining, demanding, and a waste of my talent and resources; but I thought it had been time well spent. I felt that we had made many inroads in dealing with a hardline IRS auditor who I believed at this point had been converted.

It Was Going Too Smoothly! What's Up? There was a gnawing suspicion in the back of my mind, however, that something was awry. Mr. C smiled too much. He was all too pleasant and all too agreeable. As he tied the numbers in, I had the sneaking suspicion that he had to have something else up his sleeves. The numbers were falling into place too well for us for him to be this happy. By agreement I signed the mandatory 872 statute extension. In November 1995, he laid the next bomb on me. He said, "Well, Mr. Tesser, it looks like we have just about finished tying out all of the expenses for 1990. When do you think it would be possible for myself and my supervisor to come down to visit you and Mr. Double E in his trading room and to spend a few hours with him to see what kind of business he is really conducting."

The light went off in my brain. I then realized that although he *seemed* like he was convinced, it had only been a charade. He was still holding an ace up his sleeve—the Trader Status issue.

He was smiling as he allowed our deductions because he knew in the back of his mind that he might still be able to disallow this entire case based on his questioning of the trading business. And now, he was not only going to do it himself, he was going to do it with his supervisor. I had seen this before. He will most likely put on a scenario of "good cop/bad cop" so that he could come back to me and tell me that he tried everything he could but his supervisor would not allow the Trader Status issue. And that is exactly what occurred.

I was not going to let him get away with it this easily though. I instructed Double E to do exactly what he did every day of his life—*Trade!* But what we decided was that we would give Mr. C the show of his life. We would, in fact, show Mr. C just what a trader did. In case he didn't already know, *a trader trades*—thank you, very much!

In addition to just calling his trades in and watching the screen, we carefully orchestrated calls from various people asking trading advice. We set the stage for several more players: we brought on more administrative help that day then he had in reality, and in fact we did everything we could so he would look twice as busy as he normally did.

When the auditor and his supervisor came to visit on that fateful day in February 1996, we were prepared. Everything went like clockwork—and in fact it was a profitable day for my client. By the time Mr. C and his supervisor left, I was starting to believe that they could still be convinced.

The Chips Fall. This belief, however, was short-lived. Several weeks later, we received a notice from Mr. C stating that although the deductions tied out and the income was substantiated, he regretted that he must disallow all of the deductions as trading expenses and move them back to Schedule A as itemized deductions. This was because, as I suspected, he felt that the activity my client was engaged in was not trading but rather investing.

I must tell you, I feel this was one of the most ludicrous decisions I have ever been given on an audit, and I was not for a minute going to accept it without a good fight. I was not, though, unprepared for this decision. In fact, I had a letter already started, and I finished it up and sent it off the following day. It was a four- or five-page letter going through the process of the audit over the past two years, recounting to him what he had made us prove, what we proved, and restating what the taxpayer did and the basis I had for filing him as a trader. I sent a certified copy of this letter to his supervisor with a cover sheet. The response I got was not totally unexpected.

They both confirmed that it was their opinion that this was not a trading business but rather an investment activity and that they were disallowing the refund claim. In fact, they were requesting the $50,000 back plus interest. They informed me that they would also let New York State know about their decision, just in case they might want to follow suit.

Along with this letter came a second letter—certified, of course—informing us that they were now ready to start the audit of the 1991 tax return! This was infuriating to me. Not only had they blatantly disregarded everything that I had put forth in the prior two years, but they had wasted Double E's money and my time for two years when in fact they really never had to tie out one penny on the return. They could have just disallowed everything on the basis of Trader Status from day one. And now they were about to begin again the exact same charade for 1991!

The Ultimatum. I called Mr. C back and asked him why in the world he thought I would spend the next two years doing what I had done for the prior two. I questioned him as to why he thought that I would waste my time, my client's money, and in fact the taxpayers' money by having him sit there and examine every expense and deduction on the 1991 tax return. Would he then disallow it again as he had for 1990 based on grounds of non-Trader Status?

His reply to me was, "Well, Mr. Tesser, we have to look at each and every year individually. Each case stands on its own merit or falls on its own merit. Therefore, 1991 is fully independent of 1990."

My reply to him was "Mr. C, if you didn't think that Double E traded in 1990, then you're not going to think that he traded in 1991 because everything that he did in 1990 was done in 1991 once again. And if you feel that the activity in which he engaged in 1990 was investing, then I have no doubt that you will come to the same conclusion about the 1991 activity."

He said to me: "I'm sorry, I have no choice. This is the decision my supervisor has made."

I now used some ingenuity.

I made some phone calls. I spoke to some people who are allies and who had been either former IRS agents or who are currently working with the Internal Revenue Service. I formulated my approach, mapped out my attack.

It took several months and, in fact, several postponements of my initial appointment for 1991. In the interim, I received a letter informing me that 1994 was now under audit as well.

What happened to 1992 and 1993? I figured these had just somehow slipped through the cracks—those were pretty big cracks. Double E had already received refund checks for those two years totaling in excess of $150,000 (refunds of withholding tax from his wife's salary).

So, I thought, "1990 disallowed; 1991 under audit; and now they want to look at 1994." Even if this looked pretty grim, and even if it turned out for the worse, we had not been totally defeated. We still had an additional $150,000 that we would not have had if the Trader Status issue had been overlooked.

I formulated my approach after several months of thought and consultation with other knowledgeable and experienced people in this area. The letter I sent was actually in response to a request for a statute extension for 1991.

They wanted me to give them another year and a half on the 1991 tax return by having me sign an 872 form. This 872 allows the IRS a certain period of time beyond the normal three-year statute of limitations to audit a return. I was not going to be had so easily.

The letter I wrote informed them in no uncertain terms that I would not sign the 872 unless they agreed to the following:

1. They would agree to waive the question of Trader Status for 1991 and 1994; *and* they would submit 1990 to appeals.

2. They would disallow 1991 and 1994 immediately and send all three returns to appeals on the Trader Status issue—forgetting about the substantiation of expenses and deductions until they decided on the nature of the business.

Furthermore, I informed them that I would not participate in their charade for another two or three years, and that I refused to waste my time and my client's money to see them waste the taxpayers' time and money by having us parade a wealth of documentation in front of them supporting and substantiating every figure on the return, only to have them disallow it on the grounds of non-Trader Status.

I told them that if they wanted their statute extension, they would have to agree to one of my conditions. They did. They chose "Door #2."

They said "Okay, Mr. Tesser, have it your way. If you want to play this game with us, we will just disallow all three years, ask for our money back, and you can just deal with appeals." If I hadn't been as confident about this situation as I was, I probably would have been quite intimidated by this eventuality. I was not, however.

An Appealing Alternative. The case went to appeals, and I signed the 872 statute extension.

It was now the middle of 1997 and the returns had been in appeals for quite some time. I had still heard nothing from them other than a brief introductory letter confirming for me that the returns had in fact been put into appeals. The letter also stated that the issue was the disallowance of all deductions and expenses as Schedule C items for the three years in question.

Not only hadn't we gotten our 1991 refund, but the IRS was now asking for over $100,000 in back taxes (1994).

I must admit, however, that having the returns sitting in appeals for a year without any word from the appeals department was somewhat unnerving. Through my connections, I found out who was handling the appeal of these three years tax returns, and I called and left him several messages asking to please advise us as to the status of the appeal.

About a month later, I received a call from Mr. George Simpson, Chief Appeals Officer of the Manhattan District office. Mr. Simpson informed me that he was aware of the appeal, and that the returns were sitting on his desk waiting for his review. He had, in fact, been through them once, and quite frankly "off the record" he had tabled them for a while because the appeals department was very overworked and had a huge backlog of matters to deal with.

He further informed me, "off the record," that it was the practice of his department to promptly handle those cases that he was more likely to win because it was in fact a revenue game and he wanted to handle the ones that would bring revenue to the government in the quickest manner. He also told me, "*very* off the record," that after his first look at the returns it appeared that the IRS "did not have much of a case." And because of that, he had been postponing the final review of these tax returns.

I indicated to him that we had been involved in this audit for a good number of years, that many thousands of dollars had been expended, and that my client was awaiting a refund check. He replied "Yes, I know that, and I will get to them as soon as possible."

It was now the beginning of 1998, I made several more calls and got a similar response from him that yes, they were backed up but that they would be getting to our case shortly.

It was not until October of 1998 that the letter of determination finally came through. It stated:

> Dear Taxpayer,
>
> We have reviewed your returns for the tax years in question and have found to uphold your position. We have ruled no change in any of the years. You will soon be receiving your refund check.
>
> Very truly yours,
>
> George Simpson,
> Chief Appeals Officer

It took several more months for the checks to come through, but once they did, it was well worth waiting for.

Risk-Reward Revisited. The total cost to Double E including amended returns and the handling of the audit was approximately $15,000—a lot of money. Total refunds received were in excess of $150,000 for tax years 1990 and 1991 and $48,000 for 1994—a lot more!

This was in fact an unusual situation. In my experience, I have rarely had as much difficulty in dealing with the IRS. Usually, if the case is worth fighting, we fight it and we fight it well. We generally win in the first or second line, that is, with the frontline auditor or with his or her supervisor.

If the case is not strong enough, we usually do not go to appeals because of the cost of the travel expenses and my time in substantiating expenses that shouldn't have been substantiated when the issue was really Trader Status. This audit was excessive in cost; but, as you can see, the reward for staying the course and completing the audit was well worth the expense.

The conclusion I have come to in dealing with the IRS is that if you are right, hold your position. There is usually some reasonable person in the line that will hear what you have to say.

Like all trades, it is always a risk/reward, cost/benefit situation. Always evaluate the money at stake before you put the money into defending your position.

In this particular case we had several hundreds of thousands of dollars in tax refunds at stake; and because of that it was well worth the expense of defending. Furthermore, as a result of doing so, we allowed two more years to slip through the cracks without question during the process, those years also yielded a substantial tax refund for Double E.

In my 25 years, I thought I had seen it all—I hadn't. But I have found this case to be one of my fondest victories in dealing with the IRS.

Postscript: Don't These Guys Ever Give Up? Well, just when we thought we were out of the woods, it didn't take them long to spoil our celebration. Soon after we received the big refund check from the IRS we received another "surprise" in the mail.

This surprise was not expected and was equally as unpleasant. I will paraphrase the letter we received:

> Dear Double E,
>
> I guess you were feeling pretty good from your last victory in the tax years 1990, 1991, and 1994. But guess what? We would now like to take a look at 1995!
>
> Please appear downtown with all your records, receipts, checks, credit card vouchers, blah, blah, blah for the tax year ended 12/31/95. You have the right to be represented by a competent tax professional, you have the right to remain silent, you have the right to shoot yourself . . . " [Well, those weren't the exact words, but you get the drift.]
>
> Sincerely,
>
> Your friend,
>
> Mr. C,
> Frontline IRS auditor

They're back! How could I have been so foolish as to think they would go away so easily—after only five years of fighting, and after they lost all three cases—these guys want another shot! Okay then come on make my pay (or was that day?).

I wrote them back a short, courteous, but to the point letter using the magic word I encourage everyone to use when dealing with the IRS—"NO."

I told them *no.* We are *not* coming downtown. We are *not* bringing any records, we have already been that route. JUST DISALLOW IT ALL (1995) AND WE WILL GO STRAIGHT TO APPEALS. We have already beaten you there, and if you want, we will do it again.

I got the same lingo back from Mr. C that I heard with the prior tax return examinations. "Well, Mr. Tesser, each year is considered a separate entity, we have to look at it separately. You know that is not my decision, it is what the big boys want me to do. Etc., etc., etc."

Internal Revenue Service
District Director

Department of the Treasury
PO Box 4645
Grand Central Station
New York NY 10163

Date: OCT 0 5 1999

Form:
1040
Tax Periods Ended:
9512
Person to Contact:
[redacted]
Contact Telephone Number:
[redacted]
Fax Number:

[redacted]

We are pleased to tell you that our examination of your tax returns for the above period(s) show change is necessary in your reported tax. However, our examination may not reflect the results of examinatio flow-through entities (Forms 1120S, 1060, 1041) in which you may have an interest.

If you have any questions, please write to the person whose name is shown at the top of this letter, or may call that person at the telephone number shown. If the number is outside you local calling area, there will long-distance charge to you. If you prefer, you may call the IRS telephone number listed in you local directory employee there may be able to help you, but the office at the address shown on this letter is most familiar with case.

If you write to us, please provide your telephone number and the most convenient time for us to call in we need more information. Please attach this letter to any correspondence to help us identify your case. Keep copy for your records.

Thank you for your cooperation.

THANK YOU FOR YOUR COOPERATION!

Sincerely yours,

[redacted]

District Director

Enclosure:
Copy of this letter

[redacted]

Letter 590(DO) (Rev.12-8

"So let me speak to the big boys!"

"Well you know Mr. Tesser, I can't do that. Just write to me and I will forward your correspondence on to my supervisor." RIGHT!

Again I told them, "Well if you didn't like 1990, 1991, or 1994, you are not going to like 1995. Because it is more of the same. The same, by the way that Appeals ruled in our favor on. Give it a rest—enough already."

This jousting went on for a few months. Them setting appointments, and me telling them I was not coming in—"just send it to appeals."

Quite frankly I did not know what the outcome would be. I just stood my ground, because I knew we were right. Finally, in October 1999 we heard from them in letter form. And I will let a picture do the talking.

On page 217 is what I received as the final (I hope) response from the IRS. Without even looking at the 1995 tax return, we got a "No Change" letter!

The Case of the Amended Fly Through

Dear Mr. Tesser,

I have just received my refund check in the mail totaling more than $2,800. I thank you for your fine books and counsel. My amended return was accepted with no change by the IRS, and I recently received my refund in the mail.

Once again, I appreciate your efforts in this regard.

Sincerely,

B.H.
Sedona, AZ

In this case, an amended return was filed. The person reviewing the return for the IRS made a call to B.H., who referred the call to me. This situation was a layup, compared to Double E.

I simply forwarded articles and court cases to the IRS auditor and held two or three phone conversations with her. The check was then issued.

We then heard, once again, the two most desirable words to be uttered in an IRS audit—"No change." This basically meant goodbye to the IRS, we are going home now!

WHAT WE CAN LEARN FROM ALL OF THIS

I could go on. I have handled approximately 30 audits in my 15 years of having my own practice. I have consulted with other professionals on another 25 or so. The outcomes have been the same.

In my 15 years experience of handling Trader Status audits, I have discovered that there is a large degree of humanity in the audit process—a great deal depends on the circumstances, who you get, and what kind of evening he or she had the night before.

I have encountered two kinds of auditors: those familiar with Trader Status and those who are not. Of those not familiar with Trader

Status, there are some you can convince, and some you cannot. Sometimes having someone not familiar with this distinction can actually work in your favor. In other words, having an auditor who doesn't know what he or she is doing can sometimes be beneficial—you can educate the auditor. But sometimes it can be a killer!

I have found, though, that whatever the situation, if you want to win badly enough, chances are you can—if you really qualify for Trader Status. We have gone to appeals, but I have never had to go to Tax Court. There has never been a case that I have lost that has had the merit and the stakes to undertake this endeavor. Also, if you recall from my section in this book, you can, if need be, go to small claims Tax Court.

I do have friends who have tried their cases in Tax Court, and the results have been mixed. I say that because of the strength or lack of strength of their case.

It has been my experience that in filing Trader Status for the past dozen years, there is no higher incidence of audit in a trader's tax return than in any other category. The audit process is the same—trader or not. I have also found that the risk-reward ratio of filing as a trader if you qualify is well worth the effort: there is a very high reward potential with a comparatively low risk. Therefore, after some experience in the trenches, I can assert that Trader Status is very much alive and a viable tax strategy to keep in your trading arsenal.

15

Knowing Your Limits: How Far Can You Go?

QUESTION OF LEGALITY

Government officials have talked about what motivates taxpayers. Ask most IRS employees, off the record, and they will agree that the most effective method through which they can achieve tax compliance is by instilling fear. This four-letter word, *fear,* is what keeps most people from utilizing the tax law to their fullest advantage.

Many of my friends have either worked for the IRS or are acquainted with someone who has. They tell me that unless you are an outright tax cheater, you have little to worry about. Many people have an irrational fear about going to jail or losing everything they have because of the IRS.

The IRS likes it this way. Believe me, it is a far better position for them. But when you look at the nature of the penalties for all types of offenses, from a simple mistake to undeniable fraud, you will see that this fear is not based entirely in reality.

Don't get me wrong, you want to avoid penalties for several reasons. They can be costly, they make your return more susceptible to audit, and, if serious enough, the penalties can involve prison terms. But on balance, the two most serious penalties, those for fraud and for negligence, are well defined and fairly easy to avoid.

As you will see in the following summary, penalties are not given arbitrarily or used to punish taxpayers without reason; rather penalties are used as a threat to taxpayers who intentionally try to cheat or to hide unreported income. Interest and penalties are assessed only on the taxes that are currently due, not on the total tax that has been paid, nor on your total taxable income.

Honest taxpayer mistake, another event for which a penalty is imposed when filing of your tax return. Your tax return is due, except for certain extenuating circumstances, by April 15 of each year. You may file an extension for a return by the due date. If you do not, the late-filing penalty is 5 percent per month up to 25 percent maximum of the tax due. Generally there is no penalty unless you owe money.

Interest and Penalties on Tax Returns

Interest. Interest currently charged for underpayment of tax is the three-month Treasury bill (T-bill) rate plus 3 percent.

Penalties. Currently charged by the IRS (note that some of these penalties are overlapping, i.e., one type will often reduce the other):

- Unpaid taxes: 5 percent per month up to 25 percent plus interest.
- Negligence: 5 percent of underpayment plus interest.
- Failure to file return: $100 or taxes due (60-day grace period).
- Bad-check charge: 1 percent of check.
- Frivolous or incomplete return: $500.
- Frivolous lawsuit against the IRS: $5,000.
- Overvaluation of property: 10 percent to 30 percent of underpayment.
- Intent to evade taxes: 75 percent of underpayment plus additional 50 percent of interest due.
- False withholding information: $500.
- Failure to file partnership return: $50 each partner per month, maximum five months.

Criminal Violations

The following activities are deemed criminal:

- Willful failure to pay or to file: Up to $25,000 plus one year in prison.
- Willfully falsifying return: Up to $100,000 plus three years in prison.
- Intent to evade taxes: Up to $100,000 plus five years in prison.
- False withholding information: Up to $100,000 plus one year in prison.

"ONLY THE LITTLE PEOPLE PAY TAXES"

The question most often asked during the week that Leona Helmsley was sentenced to five years in jail was: "Why has Harry Helmsley dimmed the lights at the top of the Empire State Building all week?"

Some people answered, "He did it in deference to Leona and to show his disgust with the penalty given to his wife." But the true answer I hear, from those who really know about such things, is that Harry turned down the lights at the top of the Empire State Building so that Leona couldn't find her way back to New York.

Why was Leona Helmsley convicted of tax evasion? Was it because she was so flagrant a tax evader that the government had to teach her a lesson? Or was it because she was such a well-known figure that the government could not let anyone believe that she could get away with it and, therefore, had to make an example out of her? It was alleged that she broke the law. It is true that Leona remodeled her estate, purchasing many hundreds of thousands of dollars of new items. This is no crime. The crime was that she apparently wrote these items off as business expenses. In other words, she purchased them through the business, for personal use, but nonetheless took them as valid business expenses. This reduced the taxable income of the business that she and her husband own and, consequently, the tax payable on that income.

I believe the answer to the question of why she was convicted and given what many people consider an extremely harsh jail sentence for a woman her age was a combination of factors. Yes, she was a convicted tax evader; yes, she overstated deductions and understated income; and yes, she was a well-known figure. But I feel that the clincher was the six little words that comprise the title of this section: "Only the Little People Pay Taxes." Leona was saying that people of her class—a class into which she married—did not have to pay taxes, and those six words locked in a jail sentence for Leona Helmsley. An ex-employee's testimony that Leona made that statement whenever questioned about taxes was so damaging that it mandated prison time. The government could not afford to let someone walk away from tax evasion rubbing the "little people's" collective faces in the mud. It would have been far too damaging a blow to the legal system in general and to the IRS specifically.

I have been told that the IRS is generally obsessed with keeping taxpayers and tax preparers nervous and honest. Often, the IRS is quite willing to spend $50,000 to prove a $2,000 intentional omission.

HOW THE IRS BUILDS A CRIMINAL CASE

In an *IRS Confidential Report* article entitled "How the IRS Builds a Criminal Case," R.B. Blaustein stated that criminal tax investigations are the ultimate weapon in the IRS enforcement system. They are conducted by IRS special agents who can show up at a taxpayer's home or business without any notice. They usually work in pairs so that they can corroborate one another's testimony about facts or statements that the taxpayer makes.

They will usually give you a Miranda warning to let you know that anything you say can be used against you in court and that you do not have to answer questions without an attorney present. However, many taxpayers are afraid that they will appear guilty if they do not answer a question. In addition, the agents are very persistent and will usually press for answers. As a result, the taxpayer will often make statements that he or she later regrets.

The special agents will ask questions such as: Have you reported all of your income? Where do you keep your savings and checking accounts? What is the procedure for reporting sales in your business? What kind of car do you own? Do you gamble? and other seemingly low-key questions. They will try to convince you that if you help them, they will close your case and you will be done with them. Guess again!

Be extremely wary of these IRS interviews because any false or misleading statements you make in answering questions may be a crime. What the agents are trying to establish in this particular kind of investigation is whether a taxpayer failed to report income or misreported income and whether any error or omission was done willfully. They will ask for copies of your checking account statements, canceled checks, saving account booklets, and/or deposit and withdrawal tickets.

They may speak to neighbors and business associates and will look at public records to find out whether a taxpayer owns real estate, cars, boats, or any other large, expensive items. They will also examine insurance records that indicate possession of furs and jewels. The IRS will also use mail surveillance to try to determine who a businessperson's customers and suppliers are. Although they will not open your mail, they can obtain a great deal of information just by looking at the outside of the envelope.

Mr. Blaustein also discussed a procedure used to analyze a taxpayer's net worth. The agent will take the value of all the taxpayer's property at the beginning of the year and subtract from it his or her end-of-year assets. The difference between these two figures, with adjustments for nontaxable items and other factors, represents the increase in net worth for the year. It is generally correct to assume that the taxpayer had income that was at least enough to generate that increase in net worth.

Blaustein revealed a technique that often incriminates the taxpayer. Sometimes during the initial interview with the IRS agent, a taxpayer is asked how much cash and property he or she had at the beginning of the year. A taxpayer who does not want to appear very prosperous may state that he or she only had a few hundred dollars and no other property to speak of. This allows the IRS to then claim that everything that was owned at the end of the year was acquired during that year and, hence, should have been reported as income.

Sneaky! Very sneaky, but effective.

The way to deal with this type of investigation is to give the special agent as little information as possible when you are asked questions about your opening net worth. The IRS does not have as much information on most individuals as we believe. It must get information from the taxpayer or from other knowledgeable third parties. The most effective legal strategies for dealing with the IRS focus on keeping information out of their hands.

THE TAXPAYER BILL OF RIGHTS

Over the years, the IRS has had a public relations problem and has recently taken steps to spruce up its image. As a result, the IRS has formally given the public certain rights ensuring that they are treated fairly.

The first indication that something has changed is evident whenever you receive correspondence from the IRS requesting payment of delinquent taxes. Enclosed along with the bill is a four-sided document entitled "Your Rights as a Taxpayer." This is put out by the Department of the Treasury, Internal Revenue Service, and is called "Publication No. 1."

Publication No. 1 states, "As a taxpayer you have the right to be treated fairly, professionally, promptly, and courteously by Internal Revenue Service employees. Our goal at the IRS is to protect your rights so that you will have the highest confidence in the integrity, efficiency, and fairness of our tax system. To ensure that you always receive such treatment, you should know about the many rights you have at each step of the tax process."

This document contains a great deal of information, and you should, if ever given the chance, read these four pages carefully. It goes into subjects such as the type of assistance available to you through the IRS in preparing your tax returns, including many valuable publications, and how to obtain information on the Volunteer Income Tax Assistance (VITA) program in your area.

The VITA service is offered above and beyond the direct assistance of IRS employees who are available to answer questions by phone (but in whom I have little confidence). Studies (e.g., *1995 General Accounting Office Study*) have shown that IRS employees will disseminate inaccurate information more than 50 percent of the time. The VITA program, on the other hand, is composed of tax professionals in private practice as well as other knowledgeable tax preparers who are generally better informed than IRS employees. In fact, I used to be among the ranks of VITA tax preparers.

Also contained in Publication No. 1 are facts about your rights to privacy and confidentiality, representation by someone else to the IRS, the line of authority you can access to appeal a decision you believe is unfair, the rights you have as a taxpayer to set up payment arrangements with the IRS, and your responsibility to the IRS if such arrangements are established. This publication also informs you of your right to the cancellation of penalties such as the ones referenced previously for certain mitigating circumstances. It states:

> You have the right to ask that certain penalties (but not interest) be canceled (abated) if you can show reasonable cause for the failure that led to the penalty (or can show that you exercised due diligence, if that is the applicable standard for that penalty).
>
> If you relied on wrong advice you received from the IRS employees on the toll-free telephone system, we will cancel certain penalties that may result. But you have to show that your reliance on the advice was reasonable. If you relied on incorrect written advice from the IRS in response to a written request you made after January 1, 1989, we will cancel any penalties that may result. You must show that you gave sufficient and correct information and filed your return after you received the advice.[1]

The best way to have the IRS accept responsibility for the conveyance of inaccurate information is to have them state it to you in a written document. From my own experience, I have learned it is very difficult to establish a case that you were given misleading information verbally from an IRS official, even if you record the name of the employee and the date on which you spoke with him or her.

An alternative to this is to request a written response to the question by telephone or a written inquiry by you in lieu of a telephone call. The safest method of all is to never ask the IRS anything. Get your information from a qualified tax professional in the field.

Another publication on taxpayer rights and penalties is "Notice No. 746" also put out by the Internal Revenue Service. It states:

> **Elimination of Penalty—Reasonable Cause.** Except for certain cases of the Underpayment of Estimated Tax Penalty and for Fraud and Negligence penalties, the law provides that the penalties explained below can be removed if you have an acceptable reason. If you believe you have a good reason but have not yet sent us an explanation, please send it to us. The explanation should be signed by the taxpayer or person having a

power of attorney. We will review your explanation and let you know what our decision is. If a penalty or any portion of a penalty is the result of written advice of the Internal Revenue Service, that penalty or portion of the penalty will be "removed." To have the penalty "removed," you should complete Form 843, requesting that the penalty be removed. Submit the Form 843 to the service center where your tax return was filed for the tax year in which you relied upon erroneous advice from the IRS. Attach the following documents to the Form 843: a copy of your original request for written advice from the IRS; a copy of the erroneous written advice you received from the IRS; and a notice (if any) showing assessment of the penalty that you wish to have removed.[2]

SPECIFIC MITIGATING CIRCUMSTANCES

In the March 1992 issue of *Tax Avoidance Digest,* there was an article entitled "File Two Years Late and Not Pay a Penalty?" This article stated that you don't always have to get hit with penalties when a tax return is filed late. As spelled out in "Notice No. 746," a late-filing penalty can be waived for reasonable cause. In fact, IRS regulations state that late filing will be excused if you "exercised ordinary business care and prudence and were still unable to file on time."[3] Specific instances considered reasonable causes are discussed there.

One generally accepted reasonable cause is that of *illness.* If you are very ill or a close relative is gravely ill, the IRS usually excuses late filing of a tax return until that person either recovers or dies. As you can see, death is not a reasonable cause! In addition, the IRS considers only a spouse, a child, a parent, or a sibling as a close relative. If you are unusually close to a friend or a cousin, you may have a problem with reasonable cause.

I have done a good deal of work with taxpayers who are recovering alcoholics and consequently have not filed tax returns for several years. The approach I take when filing past-due tax returns is to be totally honest with the IRS and to reveal to them the extenuating circumstances surrounding each particular case. I go in with the goal of helping the taxpayer "wipe the slate clean." Generally, the IRS cooperates. They usually agree that alcoholism is an illness and demonstrates reasonable cause. The results do vary, however, based on the mitigating circumstances and also on the agent handling the case.

Another reasonable cause cited in the March 1992 article is *not having documents available.* If your tax records were destroyed in a fire, storm, hurricane, or war, your penalties will probably be waived until you have had a reasonable opportunity to reconstruct them. Also, if you are dependent on someone else to generate items such as a W-2 or a 1099 and that information is late, you usually are given a waiver of penalty. If you did not get around to organizing and putting together your tax records, however, that is *not* reasonable cause!

Travel may be a reasonable cause when it results in an *unavoidable absence*. Business and vacation travel are not reasonable causes, no matter how important. You are expected to plan around these absences. But, if you have to go out of town to care for a sick or dying relative, the IRS will sympathize. The article did state that "if you are out of the country on business and get stuck in a civil war, you can probably get the penalties waived."[4] This has never happened to me, so I can't say for sure that it is true; yet it seems to make sense.

Other reasonable causes listed in this article include: mailing the return on time, but with insufficient postage; filing a return with the wrong IRS district address; getting erroneous information from an IRS official; not receiving the requested forms from the IRS; and unsuccessfully trying to get assistance from the IRS after personally visiting an IRS office.

Another reasonable cause that usually works is blaming a tax professional. This is one reasonable cause I would generally not recommend you use, especially if you are my client! However, many businesses get penalties waived for poorly prepared tax returns as well as for lateness of filing other required documents by saying that the filing was left up to their accountant or that failure to file was based on professional advice.

The article summed it all up by stating that "there is no foolproof way to get penalties waived. Some IRS employees seem to waive penalties if you offer almost any excuse. Others don't ever want to waive penalties. The point is that you should not meekly accept a penalty no matter how late your return is. State your reason to the IRS employee and you might get the penalty waived."[5]

I will conclude this section on penalties by relating a true story about a situation I was involved with several years ago. I had just started working with a competent tax manager in a relatively new position in the tax department of an accounting firm. This man was an amazing worker and, in fact, did the work of about three people. This was both a blessing and a curse for the department because it meant that several other people in the firm got by without necessarily pulling their own weight.

Because of his diligence, he was overworked, overstressed, and overburdened. This naturally affected his health, and when he became suddenly ill on April 13 one year in the middle of filing extensions for some hundred clients, no one in the department knew what to do. And because I had very recently joined the firm, neither did I.

But there I was, on April 13, with more than a hundred federal extensions and corresponding state extensions to file by midnight

April 15. I was familiar with some of these clients, but not on top of all their tax situations. I rounded up whatever people I could to help me with this task and within two days we filed all of the federal and state extensions.

The one problem, however, was that some of the estimated tax liabilities we claimed were incorrect. They were the best we could do under the circumstances, but, in some cases, the amounts were grossly insufficient to cover the amounts actually due.

You should be aware that an extension to file your tax return does not constitute an extension to pay your tax liability late as well. When you extend a tax return, both for federal and state purposes, you are expected to pay your full tax liability. If you do not do this and underpay your liability by more than a certain amount (usually 5 percent), you will invalidate the extension that was granted and create penalties for underpayment of taxes as well as for late filing.

We had a hundred or so taxpayers being granted automatic extensions. But a good part of these extensions would become useless because of underpayment of estimate tax liabilities due. Thus, these taxpayers could owe a great deal of money in penalties and interest.

After the returns had been filed and the IRS and the states sent us notices of deficiency for the penalty amounts, we responded. We advised them of the extenuating circumstances surrounding the filing of these extension requests. We also told them that we felt these circumstances constituted reasonable cause for the waiving of any related penalties. We sent explanatory letters to the IRS centers and the various state offices in all parts of the country. These taxpayers were scattered throughout the United States and had been required to file in many different locations.

The results of requesting almost 50 of these penalty waivers was as follows: We were *not denied* the waiver of one single penalty by any *federal* agent who reviewed the case at *any* IRS center. They were all waived. However, we were *not granted* the waiver of one single penalty by any *state* we applied to. That's right, the IRS granted every one of our requests and every state we applied to denied them! And, if my memory serves me well, this included approximately 15 states.

So, if you always thought that the IRS was tougher to deal with than state tax departments, you are wrong. The IRS is generally more understanding of such matters, whereas state and local governments are not so flexible.

This was an important lesson for me to learn. It taught me that if you are honest and treat the IRS fairly, they will usually do the same for you. It is the state and local governments that are the real problems whenever you have a situation that requires a judgment call!

YOUR NEW RIGHTS AS A TAXPAYER

Another excellent publication put out by Agora, Inc., the publishers of the *Tax Avoidance Digest* newsletter, is called *Tax Liberty* by Robert Carlson. This publication lists "199 loopholes that accountants overlook, ignore, or refuse to use." It also talks about the new bill of rights that taxpayers now have:

> **One of the most significant actions Congress took in 1988 was passing the Taxpayer Bill of Rights.** Though this is a watered-down version of what was originally proposed and what is needed, the law makes a number of significant changes.
>
> Taxpayers now have some important protections that were not available a year ago, and some of the worst IRS abuses now are curbed. More importantly, Congress has sent a message to the IRS. The message is that deficit reduction is not so important that the IRS can do whatever it wants to the taxpayers.
>
> Most of the Taxpayer Bill of Rights provisions became effective over the last few months, and the IRS has issued some rules in this area, so this is a good time to review what your new rights are. There are so many provisions of the Taxpayer Bill of Rights that we cannot cover them all in one article. Here are the major benefits.
>
> **Knowing your rights.** The first big change is that the IRS actually has to describe your rights in writing at the beginning of an audit or other interview. In the past, many people thought they had to talk to the IRS and didn't know that they could refuse to say anything or turn over evidence. The IRS plans to give everyone a copy of Publication 1, "Your Rights as a Taxpayer," to meet the requirement. The publication explains both the audit and collection processes and what your rights are during each process.
>
> **Audits and interviews.** The new legislation also makes clear that you can be represented at an IRS proceeding by anyone who is qualified to represent taxpayers before the IRS. This means attorneys, CPAs, and enrolled agents. In fact, you are allowed to seek representation at any time, and the IRS is required to suspend an interview if you so request to allow you to consult with your representative.
>
> Most importantly, in most cases you do not have to appear at an audit. That had been the IRS's longstanding policy. But a few years ago the IRS tried to change the policy, particularly when business taxpayers were involved. The IRS manual told agents that taxpayers were likely to make misstatements and other mistakes at an initial interview, so taxpayers should be told to attend the initial meeting themselves even if a representative would be handling most of the audit.

The IRS Ombudsman is an important change for many taxpayers who have problems with the IRS. A common complaint among taxpayers who have been burned by the IRS is that their problems could have been resolved quickly, but the IRS employees involved did not pay attention to important facts until many months had passed. The result was a lot of headaches for the taxpayers and perhaps a loss of the taxpayer's business.

The Problem Resolution Office was set up a few years ago to deal with such problems, but that office had no real powers. Now each PRO has an Ombudsman. This employee can intervene in any IRS enforcement action when the taxpayer is "suffering or about to suffer a significant hardship as a result of the manner in which the Internal Revenue laws are being administered." The Ombudsman can issue a Taxpayer Assistance Order, which is legally binding on the IRS.

If you have a problem that you think requires the Ombudsman's help, you should look up the PRO of your IRS district office in the telephone book under "United States Government, Internal Revenue Service." Call or write the PRO and ask for Form 911. When you receive the form, complete and return it according to the instructions. The Ombudsman will then look into your situation and decide what, if any, action should be taken.

But be warned that the PRO will act only in extreme situations. The IRS recently reported that over 50,000 requests for action by the Ombudsman had been received so far, and the Ombudsman had taken action in less than 100 cases.

Suing the IRS. You can sue the IRS when certain specified conditions are met. The general rule is that a government cannot be sued except when it specifically gives consent to be sued. The government has agreed that it can be sued when the IRS knowingly or negligently fails to release a lien when there was an error in the filing of the lien. The IRS also can be sued when an IRS employee acts recklessly or negligently in disregard of any provision of the tax code or regulations. But you can only recover actual economic damages and court costs under this provision, and your reward is limited to $100,000.

These are the major provisions of the TBR. Taxpayers are no longer faced with a completely one-sided system that is stacked against them, though the IRS still is in a better position than the taxpayer. It is possible that IRS abuses will continue and another TBR will be needed in the future.[6]

SIGNIFICANCE TO THE INVESTOR AND THE TRADER

What does this all mean to you and me? My interpretation of all this new tax legislation is that the IRS wants to be perceived as a more flexible institution. Although it will still maintain an intimidating appearance in pursuing all tax fraud perpetrators, it will, I believe, listen to reason.

Therefore, it is necessary, as I've mentioned many times in this publication, to acquire as much tax-law knowledge applicable to your situation as is possible. Armed with this knowledge, you will be in a strong position to support any position you take within reasonable limits.

Charles Givens discussed this subject further in his book *More Wealth without Risk*. He said that in pursuing the objective of lowering one's taxes, it is never necessary to resort to tax cheating or loopholes. He further stated that there is a tremendous difference between cheating, taking advantage of loopholes, and using tax strategies. I firmly concur with Mr. Givens. He defined *tax cheating* as understating your income and claiming deductions for assets you don't own for expenditures you never make. Leona Helmsley, of course, is a glaring example of such abuse.

Loopholes, as defined by Mr. Givens, are gray, untested areas of the tax law that allow you to claim deductions that Congress and the IRS might have ruled against had they had the foresight to see the potential for abuse. Because a specific "no" does not exist, you create a loophole by saying "yes" to a shaky deduction. Loopholes are often sought out by desperate, high-income taxpayers who have never taken the time to plan their tax situations. Some loopholes are used entirely out of greed, and others are taken because of the taxpayers' gambling instincts. Chuck Givens stated unequivocally, and I once again concur, that there is only one "do" about loopholes, and that is "don't."

Tax strategies on the other hand, as defined in this book, are positive and legal uses of the tax laws to reduce your income taxes. Tax strategies arise from knowledge of the tax law. They are actions taken to automatically and legally qualify a taxpayer for additional deductions. These strategies can include opening up a retirement account, starting a small business, or buying a rental property, among many other options. Many of these possibilities are straightforward and obvious. Other methods, such as traveling on tax-deductible dollars or creating a tax-deductible college education for your children, are just as legal and just as easy to use, but less understood. Mr. Givens stated:

> One question I am asked over and over again: "Is paying less taxes really legal, patriotic, and moral?" For some reason many people seem to confuse our tax system with the United Way Fund, whose slogan is "Pay your fair share." By following the tax laws and regulations when you use tax strategies, you automatically pay your fair share, even if your share amounts to zero. Two neighboring families, each with a $30,000 annual income and two children, could both be paying their fair share of income

taxes, even if one family paid $5,000 and the other paid nothing at all. It's the way the American tax system was designed.

We have a system that imposes taxes, not on your total income, but on a far smaller amount known as your taxable income, your residual income after you subtract your exemptions, adjustments, and deductions. Within the difference between total income and taxable income lies your opportunities for applying legal, powerful tax-reducing strategies.

Not long ago on the *Donahue* show, during one of the best national discussions on tax strategies in which I have ever participated, a lady caller said she thought reducing your taxes was cheating. She made $15,000 working, didn't have an IRA, and her husband was even a tax attorney! Her feeling was that she wanted to pay taxes to help the homeless. This may come as a surprise to you, as it did to her, but very few of your federal tax dollars go to the homeless or many other places you might prefer the money to go. By learning legal strategies for reducing her taxes, she could have given her tax savings directly to the homeless herself.

Another woman in the studio audience felt that paying more taxes was patriotic. The courts say that paying taxes has nothing to do with patriotism whether you pay a lot or none at all. The money goes into the economy whether paid to the government or used by you for a deductible purpose. The question of legality and morality of tax deductions was settled once and for all over 40 years ago by the U.S. Circuit Court of Appeals in an opinion written by Judge Learned Hand. "Anyone may so arrange his affairs that his taxes shall be as low as possible. He is not bound to choose a pattern that will best pay the Treasury. No one owes any public duty to pay more than the law demands."[7]

The decision as to how to handle your tax affairs should directly influence your tax plan and attitude. Rearranging your affairs to create deductions where you had none before is the secret to paying less taxes. I discuss several general and quite a few specific tax strategies in this book. Which you use is your choice and depends on which one best suits you. Mr. Givens further stated his own opinion about deducting expenses. As he put it:

Most taxpayers think they are doing themselves a favor by being ultra-conservative in taking deductions. Nothing could be further from the truth. If you are tax deduction shy not only do you end up spending thousands of dollars in unnecessary taxes, you don't even reduce your chances for audit. Most audits are done at random and have little to do with whether you take all of your allowable deductions or only a few.

If you want to reach your financial goals you must adopt the winning tax strategy: WHEN IN DOUBT, DEDUCT IT. Take everything the law allows. Follow the rules, but deduct all gray areas in your favor. Gray areas are not loopholes or an attempt to get around the tax laws, but are areas of ambiguity and uncertainty about what Congress or the IRS really meant. You have just as much chance of winning your point as the IRS does. You'll be surprised, as you learn about taxes, at how much of the code is ambiguous. Simple record keeping and tax strategies will always have you prepared to win your point.[8]

MICHAEL MILKEN

A discussion of legality would not be complete without a brief glance at one of my favorite criminals, Michael Milken. As investors, you should recall that Mr. Milken was convicted on several counts of fraud relating to the sale of junk bonds. Without going into too many of the details of his case, Mr. Milken became a hero to some and a nemesis to others, depending on where you got in on the purchase of these bonds. Some of his closest friends apparently made millions; and some who were not lost an equal amount.

But there is a relevant issue directly related to the discussion of legality of deductions. As you may recall, Mr. Milken, as part of the settlement with the courts, agreed to pay approximately $500 million to settle a securities fraud suit. If this amount of money is considered a *fine* or a *penalty*, then it would not be deductible on Milken's tax returns. But because Michael Milken declared all of his misbegotten income on his tax return, and consequently paid taxes on it, he was not indicted for tax evasion. And, because he paid taxes on income that he must now return, should he not be entitled to either a credit on future tax returns or a return of the tax he paid on this income?

The law states that a taxpayer cannot deduct a fine or a penalty, but it does say that he or she can deduct the return of misappropriated funds that were previously included in income. According to the tax code, because this payment is not considered a fine or penalty, the $500 million should apparently be deductible.

What this ultimately means is that if the deduction is allowed, Mr. Milken will not pay taxes again for a very long time. It is expected that he will request a ruling from the IRS before finalizing the settlement.

HOW TO PLAY FOR KEEPS WITH THE IRS

This solution deals with an unpleasant but necessary situation—what to do in case you are audited. The first part of this chapter discusses *who* gets audited, the second part presents methods to *lessen your chances* of an audit, and third part addresses *what to do* in case you are audited. I will summarize some of the concepts and ideas already discussed throughout this book and will add many new ones. Even the most conservative taxpayers are selected for IRS audits through no fault of their own. I will put together a workable plan of attack on what to do if, or perhaps when, your return is examined.

WHAT CRITERIA ARE MOST IMPORTANT IN THE SELECTION OF TAX RETURNS FOR AUDIT?

No one I know can say for sure what factors are directly responsible for your tax return being selected for audit. People often try to avoid an audit by being overly conservative on their tax returns and sometimes not even taking those deductions to which they are entitled. This is a mistake and may, in fact, not even help lessen the chances.

Audited returns are analyzed afterward from all angles so that we might figure out the factors that contributed to their having been selected. Several of the ways that have been classified follow.

Audit Chances Based on Income

What are your real chances for being audited in one year? Out of approximately 100 million individual tax returns, less than 3 million returns are audited. Even so, it is important to know the rules of the game. Based on past performance of the IRS, here are your percentage chances for being audited by income and profession.

Your Income/Professions	Chance for Audit[9]
Under $50,000	2%
Over $50,000	8
Professionals	25
Known criminals	50

Other Targeted Occupations

An interesting table comes from another of my favorite publications, *The IRS Confidential Report*. This table gives some idea of how specific professions are rated as far as probability for audit. This table is called "The IRS Hit List" and was prepared by Ralph J. Pribble, former IRS agent and president of the Tax Corporation of California.[10]

In addition to doctors, dentists, lawyers, and CPAs, who are all good targets for the IRS due to a generally high income level, the following list represents other professions that are also subject to investigation and the areas most likely to be examined:

- *Salespeople:* Outside and auto salespeople are particular favorites. Agents look for, and often find, poorly documented travel expenses and padded promotional figures.
- *Airline pilots:* High incomes, a propensity to invest in questionable tax shelters, and commuting expenses claimed as business travel make them inviting prospects.
- *Flight attendants:* Travel expenses are usually a high percentage of their total income and often aren't well documented. Some persist in trying to deduct pantyhose, permanents, cosmetics, and similar items that the courts have repeatedly ruled are personal rather than business expenses.
- *Executives:* As a group they are not usually singled out. But if the return includes a Form 2106 showing a sizable sum for unreimbursed employee business expenses, an audit is more likely. Of course, anyone whose income is over $50,000 a year is a higher-priority target just because of the sums involved.
- *Teachers and college professors:* Agents pounce on returns claiming office-at-home deductions. They are also wary of educational expense deductions because they may turn out to be vacations in disguise.
- *Clergy:* Bona fide priests, ministers, and rabbis aren't considered a problem group. But if W-2s show income from nonchurch employers, the IRS will be on the alert for mail-order ministry scams.
- *Waitresses, cabdrivers, room attendants, and so on:* Anyone in an occupation for which tips are a significant income factor is likely to get a closer look from the IRS nowadays.

(Doesn't look like traders are here, does it? Guess what—they're not!)

Audit Selection by Geographic Location

Depending on where you live, your risk of audit will vary. In the Manhattan district, for example, several years ago, 1.98 percent of all individual tax returns filed were audited, whereas in Dallas the rate was only 1.2 percent. The following table, taken from "The IRS Commissioner's Annual Report,"[11] shows the percentage of returns audited in various IRS districts. It will give you an idea of which areas are the most audit prone in the country.

IRS District	Percent of Returns Audited
Albany	0.88%
Anchorage	2.48
Atlanta	1.21
Baltimore	0.99
Boston	0.69
Chicago	0.98
Cincinnati	0.75
Dallas	1.20
Denver	1.37
Detroit	0.90
Jacksonville	1.36
Los Angeles	1.88
Manhattan	1.98
Nashville	1.14
Newark	1.34
New Orleans	1.30
Philadelphia	0.82
Salt Lake City	1.97
San Francisco	2.17

TYPES OF AUDIT-SELECTION PROCESSES

The selection process is done in several ways, both by computer and manually. And, as I said before, no one knows for sure exactly how returns are selected. However, the following four procedures are generally believed to constitute most of the selection process:

1. *Random selection.* This is what is commonly known as the TCMP audit, or *taxpayer compliance measurement program* audit. In this case it does not matter what your income level is or what deductions you take. Everyone has an equal chance of being selected for a TCMP audit. Reports state that approximately 40,000 to 50,000 out of 100 million returns were selected for the TCMP audit last year.

The IRS has used this type of audit to discover where taxpayers make mistakes or tend to cheat on their tax returns. The IRS has made taxpayers prove everything on the tax return—even the children you claim. This audit has been described as the most grueling type imaginable because of the thoroughness of it.

It is also true, however, that a good percentage of people selected for the TCMP audit actually have received a refund as a result of this audit. As of 1996, Congress has mandated that the IRS discontinue this type of audit temporarily. We will see if they do, and for how long.

2. *Target group selection.* This is the second group of taxpayers that is regularly selected for audit. The IRS has found that certain professions tend to provide the greatest amount of income for them per employee-hour spent on an audit. In other words, the IRS feels that it can collect the most tax dollars from these groups with the least amount of audit work. As I previously mentioned, these groups include doctors, dentists, lawyers, accountants, and other high-income groups.

3. *Discriminant function system.* This is a point system the IRS has developed as a third criteria for audit selection. Deductions on your return are compared to what the IRS considers to be normal for a person of your profession in your area of the country and with your income. The greater the difference between your tax return and what is considered normal, the higher the number of points you are assigned. If your discriminant function system (DFS) score gets too high, you may be chosen for an audit.

If you are selected by the discriminant function system by computer the story goes that two IRS employees must agree that there is a good chance of collecting additional taxes before you are actually sent an audit notice.

4. *Document compliance system.* You may be selected through what I call the document compliance selection process (DCS). This is possible because other entities, such as businesses or banks, report income to the IRS through the processing of such forms as W-2s (for salary) or 1099s (for commissions or interest). A computer-matching process is performed at the IRS, and if you do not report these amounts on your tax return, it may result in some form of an audit. Many times a nonmatch will only lead to a desk audit. A desk audit is generally done through the mail and can be as simple as a request by the IRS for more information on the breakdown of a figure, such as interest, on your tax return.

It goes without saying that the more unreported items the IRS finds, the greater the chances of triggering a full-scale audit of your tax return. If several items are missed, it would indicate carelessness or sloppy preparation of your tax return to the IRS.

TEN WAYS TO REDUCE YOUR CHANCES OF BEING AUDITED

Although, in general, the greater the income, the greater your chances of an audit, some specific methods have been proven over the years to help the taxpayer avoid being audited. These methods do not guarantee nonselection in the audit process. But, if two returns are identical in certain areas, steps can be taken to ensure that the other one is the more likely to be selected.

1. *Be specific in categories that are apt to be questioned.* Suppose you have freelance income of some kind, and it is merely reported as "other income." It would be to your advantage to put down the specific source of this income, such as non-1099 Income—"Income from Investment Seminars."

One school of thought believes it is best to avoid Schedule C (form for reporting business income from self-employment). These people believe that if the expenses associated with this income are minimal, it is best to not report it as a business, but rather as simply "other income" with detail as just explained. Nonetheless, I know of many instances when Schedule C can provide much greater benefit than exposure. This is discussed further in "The Schedule C—Born to Be Filed" section in Chapter 2.

2. *One way to avoid the Schedule C problem is by incorporating or finding a partner if you are self-employed.* There are several advantages to doing this, the most significant being that as a corporation or a partnership you will be a small fish in a big pond, whereas nonincorporation may put you in a more conspicuous situation as your income grows. The IRS generally concentrates its corporate auditing on the very largest corporations. There are pros and cons to the incorporation process, and it is best to have an attorney handle the formality.

If you do not incorporate, *attach any explanation* to the return when your total income does not equal the sum of your W-2s and/or 1099s. For example, many businesses mail their checks on December 31 to get the deductions in the current year, and they will include these payments on the 1099s filed for that year. However, if a check is received by you in the next year, and you report income on a cash basis, you are not required to report the income until the year you receive it.

The way to deal with this is to reconcile the figure reported on your tax return with the 1099(s) filed on your behalf. This will demonstrate to the IRS that you are not understating your income, but rather are reporting it consistently from year to year. Be absolutely certain that your federal income tax returns are consistent with state income and sales tax returns. The IRS is able to examine these reports in many states without even notifying you.

3. *File your tax return as late as possible.* The later a return is filed, the less chance it has of being selected for audit. This is not what most

non–tax professionals believe. I have heard many clients whose return I have extended say, "But won't filing after April 15 make my return look suspicious and thereby increase my chance of an audit?"

This could not be further from the truth. A tax return filed on or before April 15 generally has a greater chance of being audited than one being filed on October 15 (the last extension date). This is because the IRS schedules audits about a year and a half in advance. As returns are filed and scored according to the methods I have discussed, local IRS offices submit their forecasts for returns with audit potential.

Before the computer age, it was probably best to file your return between April 1 and April 15, just about when half the returns are filed. At that time the IRS was generally inundated with returns, and your tax return had the best chance of being overlooked in the audit-selection process.

But because the computer now does the bulk of the selection process during this period, filing between April 1 and April 15 will not reduce your risk of audit but, rather, will increase it. As I mentioned, each year the IRS establishes an estimate of what percentage of returns should be audited. The ones that are filed first are the ones first chosen. Therefore, the later your return is filed, the greater the chances are that the quotas for returns in your particular category will have already been met.

You would think that the IRS would be wise to this ploy. But even if they were and tried to make the selection process as fair as possible, they could not fully accomplish it. Therefore, it makes sense to try to be part of the group that has the smallest chance of being audited.

In a prior issue of *Tax Avoidance Digest,* it is reported that the IRS recently did a study that confirmed that it was not worth the cost to try to change its audit procedures. They stated:

> It's better to get an automatic extension to August 15 using Form 4868, and even better to get an additional two-month extension to October 15 for "reasonable cause" on Form 2688. By the time your return gets into the computer and gets an audit score, chances are the IRS employees will already have more returns assigned to them than they can handle in that audit cycle. A few years ago when the IRS saw that the number of returns seeking extensions was rising, it did a study to see if audit-selection procedures should be adjusted to include these returns. Then the number of extension requests started dropping, and the IRS concluded that it did not need to change its audit procedures.[12]

4. *Avoid certain items that are universally thought to trigger special IRS scrutiny.* One of these such deductions is Home-Office Expense. There are instances, however, where these deductions are absolutely justified, and when they are, they should be taken.

One of these exceptions is when declaring Trader Status. Having an office is in fact a prerequisite for being a trader; so if you don't rent an outside office, you better have a place to do business.

Whenever I have an item that is apt to raise a red flag, such as Home-Office Expense, I will generally *put an explanation right on the tax return* to justify my reasons for taking the deduction. I also do this when an item appears to be out of line, in the sense of being too large or too small.

For example, a client who had a son with mental retardation spent many thousands of dollars to send him to a special school for the disabled. This deduction qualified under the tax code as a valid medical expense. For a taxpayer in her tax bracket, the expense appeared to be inordinately large, especially because she had deducted significant sums of money for medical insurance.

The medical insurance did not, of course, cover the tuition, and I attached the explanation and even included documentation in the form of a copy of the paid bill to the special school. This technique reduced the possibility of an audit for the taxpayer and avoided further questions from the IRS.

Another example of the way I handle certain large dollar amounts for red-flag expenditures is to attach an explanation, with a reference to "See Statement 1." I then attach this statement to the return to further explain and break down these expenses.

If, for example, I am an investor who spends substantial amounts on investment software, data retrieval, and on-line data fees, I will provide further explanations on "Statement 1" as to the nature of these expenses and their relevance in the production of income.

I have been using this technique for years. It makes sense to let the IRS know that you pay attention to details and are familiar with the tax law. Any explanation or breakdown of figures on your tax return that shows how they were calculated will help convince the IRS that you knew what you were doing. Therefore, they will (we hope) be convinced that there is no reason to spend any more time on your return than they already have!

Other areas that might raise questions include taking large expense deductions as Unreimbursed Employee Business Expenses and Casualty Loss Deductions. Historically, these deductions have triggered audits. If you have a reason for taking them, include an explanation as I have just discussed.

In addition, you should try to have your employer reimburse you for as many of these expenses as possible, rather than taking them as deductions. You can attempt to work out an arrangement with your employer that would reduce your salary by a corresponding amount.

If you have casualty losses, make sure that they are properly documented; and be aware that the IRS may be able to make a case that you actually received a gain from the insurance proceeds, even though you believe you had a loss.

5. *Choose your tax return preparer carefully.* When the IRS suspects a tax preparer of incompetence or other wrongdoing, it can force them to produce a list of their clients. You would not want to be on this list, regardless of how honest you are in preparing your tax return.

6. *Answer all questions on your tax return completely.* The IRS computer generally flags returns with unanswered questions or inconsistent answers. For example, on Schedule B, there are questions asking you about foreign bank accounts. It is important, even if you do not have foreign bank accounts, to answer these questions. You do not want to make anyone at the IRS *have* to look at your tax return more than once.

7. *Fill in your return neatly and carefully.* A sloppy return may indicate a careless taxpayer to the IRS. Furthermore, if they cannot clearly read any figure on your return, it will make your return subject to further scrutiny. The IRS may continue to examine the return to make sure that the carelessness did not lead to any other mistakes. As I said before, you do not want to make anyone at the IRS look at your tax return more than once.

8. *Avoid putting large amounts of money in general categories, such as "Miscellaneous Income" or "Miscellaneous Expense," without a more detailed explanation.* Avoid such terms as "miscellaneous," "general," "sundry," or "various" on your tax return. If you cannot be specific about a deduction, the IRS may decide that you cannot substantiate it.

9. *Avoid round numbers on your tax returns.* A deduction rounded off to the nearest hundred or thousand may raise IRS suspicions. It will appear as if you are guessing at the deduction instead of determining it from accurate records.

10. *Take all your entitled deductions.* Not taking all your deductions actually increases your risk of an audit. According to *Tax Avoidance Digest,* many people believe that it is better to leave off legitimate deductions. In truth, it is not. The IRS is trained to look at tax returns that are out of the ordinary. Missing deductions is out of the ordinary.

For example, the *Digest* described an automobile dealership. The owner knew that entertainment deductions increased the chance of an audit, so he didn't take any. The return was referred to an auditor who decided to examine the auto dealer's books in detail. This probably would not have happened had a reasonable amount been deducted for entertainment expenses. The auditor went through the books and eventually found other deductions that were not appropriate, and he disallowed them.[13]

The IRS knows that a sales business should have entertainment expenses and expects to see them deducted. Another example of this, which supposedly comes straight from the IRS manual, shows that someone reporting capital gains from the sale of stock most likely has dividend income to report; someone reporting property-tax deductions most likely has a mortgage-interest deduction; and someone who deducts medical insurance premiums should probably not have large medical-expense deductions. If you do not have corresponding deductions when you should or if you have them when you should not, an explanation is appropriate.

I want to mention one more thing in this section before I move on to discuss specific strategies for handling the audit. Many people have asked me when they can be sure that they have not been selected for an audit. Generally, the IRS will not audit you more than three years after April 15, or the date your return was filed, whichever is later.

The normal audit policy is to send out the majority of notices approximately 18 months after April 15 of each year. Audit notices for tax returns filed by April 15, 1998, should be sent out by the fall of 2000. You can begin to feel good about not being audited about 20 months after the return has been filed.

PLAYING IN THE MAJOR LEAGUES WITH THE IRS

I have heard that if you take the entire IRS Tax Code and place it on a shelf along with the tax regulations, it would stretch out to approximately 50 feet, or about 60,000 pages. This is the reason informed people consider the system to be such a mess. The IRS itself is even confused by the tax laws.

As I previously stated, IRS representatives have a reputation for providing incorrect information over the telephone. It was reported in a survey taken by *USA TODAY* that this is indeed the case. The publication hired CPAs to call the IRS with a list of 10 questions. The IRS gave the wrong answer to these questions 40 percent of the time. Although these facts are not particularly comforting, they do demonstrate that IRS professionals are human beings and make mistakes just as you or I do. With this in mind, we can deal with the potential audit a bit more comfortably.

AUDIT DO'S AND DON'TS

A significant part of this book has covered the audit process. Here are some more pointers:

- *Delay the audit as long as possible.* Federal laws allows that the time and place for an audit must be convenient to both parties. Your best strategy is to delay the audit for as long as possible.

  I would send a registered letter to the IRS letting them know that I could not meet with them at the time they had set.

  This response will automatically postpone the audit; and after several postponements, you will receive a non-computer-generated letter or a call from an IRS employee. At the very least, this will give you much more time to prepare your records.

  Once the audit has begun, the postponements will put pressure on the auditor to finish. Auditors usually have their time blocked out for them by their supervisors; and due to inadequate staffing, they have fairly tight schedules. In other words, they must meet deadlines, just like you and me.

  In addition to the time constraints, continual postponements tend to wear an auditor down. Consequently, he or she may be in the mood to compromise more readily in certain areas.

  Ted Colson, one of ex-President Nixon's henchmen, was no favorite of mine. However, I'll always remember him for one thing and one thing only: he had a sign on the wall behind his desk quite visible to anyone entering his office. It said, "When you have them by the balls, Their hearts will follow." Doug believed this was particularly true of the audit process.
- *The IRS is a business and should be treated as such.* Granted it is a big collection business, run by the government, but nonetheless its existence depends on its ability to generate income for itself. The IRS auditor is an employee who would like to please his or her supervisor. The way this can be ensured is by creating revenue for the business.

  With this in mind it is much easier to approach the audit because you are now aware of a major motivating factor involved in the audit process. Auditors must, at some time, evaluate their chances of winning on each point. Contrary to popular opinion, they are willing to trade allowances and disallowances of certain items if it will help achieve their overall success.
- *Keep talking; try to get the auditor to see things your way.* Don't expect to walk out of an audit without owing anything. *Set your sights on the large, important items and be willing to compromise on*

some of the smaller ones. If you are convinced that an item that the auditor would like to disallow is an appropriate deduction, be firm.

Don't give up until the auditor reduces the adjustment. Even the most stubborn auditor will give in somewhat if you stand your ground. Keep in mind that the auditor's ultimate goal is to close the case, obtain some additional taxes from you, and move on to the next audit.

- *If you're at an impasse, let the auditor know that you are willing to go above his or her head if necessary.* It is best never to outwardly threaten or antagonize an IRS agent. This would be more aggravation than it's worth; however, this technique can be accomplished in a much subtler manner.

  At the end of this section I will discuss the various ways you can handle an audit in which you feel that you have not been treated fairly and the different levels to which you can take it ("Other Winning Audit Techniques").
- *Never give auditors original documents to take with them either to photocopy or to take back to their office.* The IRS is not responsible if the original documents are lost, regardless of how it happens. If by some chance an auditor misplaces the documents, that will not excuse you from having to produce substantiation.

  In addition, you do not want the auditor to have possession of anything more than he or she is entitled to. Only give what is asked for, and never give an auditor free rein of your documents or backup material.

  Only let the auditor look at each of your documents once. Under a recent court ruling, if the auditor wants to look at your papers a second time, written permission must be obtained from the U.S. Secretary of the Treasury. This can be done, but the auditor usually will not go to the trouble if you mention the rule.
- *Use alternate documentation if the substantiation requested by the auditor is not available.* If, for example, an auditor requests an original invoice for the purchase of one of the items you have deducted and you cannot locate that invoice and cannot get the store to reproduce it, an auditor will usually accept a credit card statement and receipt (chit) that specifically itemizes the expenditure.

  The canceled check used to pay the credit card bill for this item is also documentation. This is not necessary, as you do not have to actually pay the credit card company in the year of the purchase to be entitled to a deduction. However, the more documentation you can provide to substantiate an expenditure, the more believable it will be to the auditor. As a result, the more probable the chances will be of having the auditor accept the alternate documentation.

- *When preparing a return, never consciously omit deductions to which you are entitled.* However, on reviewing a return in audit, *if you discover that deductions were inadvertently overlooked or calculations were made on a very conservative basis, make note of it.* This can provide a bargaining chip for you if needed in reaching a settlement with the auditor.
- *If a trip for business, charity, or medical purposes is challenged, be prepared to provide proof of the nature of the trip.* For example, if, as a trader, you had to travel to Chicago for a trading seminar, you would want to provide backup on the seminar and why it was necessary for your business. The syllabus, notes, and manual should be kept on hand for substantiation.

  If you are traveling for business or charitable reasons, provide documentation that the work was actually performed. An example of this was a client I had who organized renovating projects for various underprivileged area facilities throughout the country. When the expenses for travel were deducted as charitable contributions on the client's tax return, the deduction was questioned. We provided photos of his group renovating a drug rehabilitation center located several hundred miles from the taxpayer's residence.
- *Save the toughest items to substantiate for last.* As the audit progresses and the auditor gets closer to a settlement, he or she may be willing to compromise or to overlook some items. Provide documentation for the easiest items first. In addition to delaying the process of investigating the questionable items, this will help convince the auditor that you have done a tight job in keeping your backup.

  First impressions are generally strongest, so provide your tightest and neatest backup first. You want to start with the auditor thinking that you are a good record keeper.
- *Never invite an auditor to lunch.* Auditors are not supposed to accept gifts or favors from taxpayers. Besides, you do not want to spend more time with an auditor than you must because you might say something that could work against you. In addition, it would look bad if somebody familiar with the auditor spotted the two of you having lunch or socializing. It also might make you look like you have something to hide if you try to be too nice to the agent.

OTHER WINNING AUDIT TECHNIQUES

The following points are a compilation of ten strategies I have learned in dealing with the IRS. Some of these are original and some I have borrowed from other sources (as noted).

1. *Try to schedule an audit before a three-day weekend if at all possible.* The auditor may be less interested in the audit than in the holiday.

Another good time to schedule an appointment is at the end of the month. If an auditor has not closed enough cases that month, he or she may be inclined to go easy on you to gain a quick settlement and to close another case. For the same reasons, an auditor may be willing to compromise on certain points.

In her book, *How to Best the IRS,* Ms. X., Esquire, a former IRS agent, stated:

> Although the timing of an audit may seem ridiculous, in fact it may provide you with a real advantage.
>
> As for the best time of day, most experienced tax professionals like to start an audit at about ten o'clock in the morning. By the time it comes to discussing adjustments with the auditor, it will be close to lunch time. If you are persistent, the auditor may be willing to make concessions just to get rid of you so as not to interfere with lunch.[14]

2. *Good records are the key to success and should be as complete as possible.* However, do not concede an issue if the paperwork is not perfect. Philip Storrer, in *The Tax Fighter's Guide,* stated:

> Under the "Cohan Rule," you are allowed to use approximations in determining deductible expenses. You must, however, establish that you did legitimately incur the expense, and that your records are incomplete and unavailable. Many agents will not be open about the Cohan Rule and will try to disallow some of these expenses. Do not accept a disallowance which you think should be allowed.[15]

The Cohan Rule does not apply to expenses for overnight travel, business entertainment, or gifts. These must be fully documented to sustain a deduction. The documentation does not necessarily have to be in the form of receipts. Many times it is acceptable to provide a diary with the expenditure written in with details in the appropriate slot, especially if it is for an amount of $75 or less.

3. *Try to get the audit transferred to another district if it is at all possible.* You would not want to ask for a New York case to be arbitrarily transferred to Fresno, California, without some believable reason. But if you have a client being audited in a local branch of the IRS, say an hour or

so away, you would be best off not making the drive to have the case done there. If they will agree to it, you should try to bring it to *your* local office.

The *IRS Confidential Report* by Boardroom Books stated:

> Don't expect the IRS to admit it, but transferred cases often fall between the cracks and never get worked on, even though the taxpayer has been notified of the examination. Delays caused in processing the case file between districts, combined with the fact that the case is likely to go to the bottom of the pile when it is assigned to a new agent, may bring help from the statute of limitations. Rather than asking the taxpayer to extend the statute of limitations, as is the usual practice, many agents are inclined to take the easy way out and close transferred cases without auditing them.[16]

One of the first questions I am usually asked when a new potential client calls me to inquire about my handling their account from out of state is, "How will you be able to handle this account if my tax return is audited?"

My response, in addition to telling them that there is little chance of an audit just for filing as a trader, is that we can usually handle any IRS inquiries by phone or mail. If that doesn't work, the next best strategy is to have the audit or inquiry transferred to my district (Southern Florida).

In addition to allowing me to handle it locally, at less cost to the taxpayer, it will sometimes work in the taxpayer's favor by possibly allowing the tax return to fall to the bottom of the pile. In this case, many times the statute will have expired by the time the new auditor gets around to it.

4. *Do your homework, and be adequately prepared for the audit.* Make sure that each paper that supplies detailed figures of amounts on your tax return adds up correctly and ties in to the exact amounts on your tax return.

Take the time to provide added details on this backup, as appropriate, such as how and when you made the expenditure or how and when you earned the income. By meticulously preparing whatever records you have available, you will establish your credibility with the auditor. In an audit, credibility is everything. It will thereby become a bit easier for an auditor to accept nondocumented items.

5. *Try to limit the items the auditor examines by persuading him or her to do a test check of your expenses.* Let the auditor choose a three-month period for detailed examination. Or talk the auditor into limiting the audit to items over, say, $100. Make sure you can document all items in the test-check period or in the amount being examined.

Travel and entertainment is a common expense chosen for audit. The test-check technique works extremely well in this and provides a double benefit. This cuts your work in assembling backup data, and it prevents the auditor from rummaging through all your travel and entertainment expense, which can be quite time consuming.[17]

6. *If an IRS field auditor comes to your door, unannounced, do not invite him or her in.* The IRS has issued new guidelines as to what field auditors can do when visiting a taxpayer's home or place of business. Auditors may enter premises only when they are invited in by the rightful occupant. This rule has arisen from the IRS's concern about taxpayer lawsuits for violation of privacy rights.[18]

7. *Never go to an audit until you are advised of the reasons for the audit in writing.* The IRS is obliged to provide you with written answers to questions concerning a proposed audit of your tax return.

- They must tell you *why* they are auditing it.
- They must tell you *which* parts are being audited.
- They must tell you *what* they want to see.

Try to look relaxed, even if you're not. Body language and nonverbal communication is extremely important in any business interaction but particularly in the case of an audit. An auditor will try to ascertain your credibility as part of the audit process. Say little, smile a lot, and never volunteer information.

8. *Let the auditor know if you have been audited numerous times in the past few years.* The IRS is not allowed to engage in a *hassle audit.*

If you are audited on any part of your return and the audit produces no change or only a small change, you should not be audited on the same part of your return for at least three years. The IRS should be made aware of this situation if it exists, as oftentimes they are not.

9. *If you are unfairly treated or if you feel you can justify items disallowed by the auditor, go over his or her head.* The first level above the IRS auditor is the *immediate supervisor.*

Auditors will generally make decisions in favor of the IRS in unclear areas. Supervisors generally will be more open to ruling in favor of the taxpayer. In addition, supervisors are generally more knowledgeable and familiar with the subtler nuances of the tax code.

Whenever an auditor shows some uncertainty as to an area of the IRS Code that I feel should be in my favor, I immediately request that it be discussed with the supervisor. I do this before the auditor has had a chance to make a decision that may be against the taxpayer.

In a recent audit of one of my clients at an IRS branch office, I dealt with a field auditor who appeared to be quite inexperienced. Several complicated areas of the Code were being questioned, and I was fairly certain that my interpretation was correct in each of these areas.

The first question the auditor raised was on the propriety of handling OEX options as commodities, that is, marking them to market at year-end and reporting them as Section 1256 transactions. I was quite experienced in this area and could tell that she did not know what I was talking about.

I was very respectful and did not take the attitude "I know more than you, so why don't you go check it out," but rather "I believe I am correct, and perhaps we should discuss this with someone more knowledgeable on this subject, just to be sure." This was my tactful way of requesting additional input from a higher-level official. Her supervisor intervened and ruled in my favor, as I thought he would.

The next level, beyond the supervisor, that you can contact is the *Problem Resolution Office* (PRO), which was set up to keep the IRS from going to court if possible. They have the power to compromise on issues and to resolve any dispute you may have with an auditor or supervisor. Each local district of the IRS should have its own PRO. It is easy to obtain the phone number by either requesting it at your branch or by looking it up in the phone book under United States Government, Internal Revenue Service, Problem Resolution Office.

Many times I have contacted the PRO to help resolve issues that could not be settled at the local office level. I have found them to be particularly helpful in cases involving more than one district office where I could not pin down the center of authority on an issue.

The next step, should you need it, is to take the IRS to court. The big dollar settlements can only be made in *Tax Court,* and you would be required to have an attorney to present your side of the argument. This is often a costly and time-consuming endeavor and should only be done in cases that warrant such expense. The IRS publications on appeals and review procedures outline this process in greater detail.

Cases with under $10,000 at issue can be settled in *Small Claims Tax Court.* The judgment is final here, and appeals are not permitted. But the cost for pursuing this avenue is small, so it is a trade-off.

This section has presented a summary of ideas on how to deal with the IRS at various stages. The strategies provided here will facilitate your interaction with them before, during, and after the audit process.

16

101 Tax-Reduction Strategies

As part of my plan to maximize the benefits available to traders and investors under the new tax law, I have put together a compilation of 101 of my favorite strategies for reducing tax liability. All of these strategies, if correctly applied, can help reduce your tax burden. Actually, they are more than simply pointers; they are part of an overall strategy for tax reduction. For this reason I call them *strategies* as well as *tips,* because in this context the two words are synonymous. Regardless of what they are called, use the ones that most appropriately fit your tax situation; in doing so, you will increase your investment yield through implementing a maximization of Total Return Investment Planning (TRIP).

Tax Strategy #1

Establish a trading business and use the Triple Crown Strategy to significantly reduce your tax liability. If you qualify as a trader, report your trading income on Schedule D (unless you elect IRS Code Section 475). Your expenses are reported on Schedule C. Aside from bypassing the 2 percent and 3 percent floors for itemized deductions, you will be able to deduct many expenses that you are presently incurring but haven't deducted.

Now more than ever, it is important to qualify for Trader Status. This truly is the best tax shelter available for traders who meet the requirements. And with the increased tax rates, and lower deduction and exemption phaseouts, you need as many deductions as possible.

The new tax law has added validity and even flexibility to the declaration of Trader Status by the introduction of Section 475 to traders of their own accounts.

This strategy allows you to capitalize on some of the perks from the new tax bill. You can now purchase up to $18,000 in equipment and get an immediate write-off. As long as you have income to cover it, you can deduct 100 percent of this amount on your tax return. Any computer, business machine, fax, phone, or auto used in business can qualify.

If you are shrewd, you can time your purchase at year-end and buy some of the items on December 31 of one year and the rest on January 1 of the next year in order to maximize the write-off for your situation. Remember, you can charge these items on a credit card or on a store charge account and thus have a record of the purchase on the day the transaction takes place. They do not have to be paid for at that time.

Tax Strategy #2

Here's one I bet you didn't think of before. If you qualify as a trader (or even if you have another business), it is a good idea to hire your son or your daughter to work for you and deduct his or her allowance as salary payments.

Hire them as either a salaried employee or a consultant. Any service they may provide for you relating to your business will qualify them to receive deductible compensation from you for this service. Jobs such as straightening up your desk, sweeping the room, carrying out your trash, and servicing and updating your computers can be valuable services to your business. In setting the situation up like this, you can legally deduct allowance payments you may already be making to them but are not able to deduct. They will, of course, have to declare this money as income, but chances are it will be taxed at a lower rate. And, unless they have income above a certain level, they will not be taxed on it at all. This is a good method of shifting income among your family members to lower tax brackets. There may be some payroll tax due, so have someone familiar with this statute help you set it up—it will be well worth it.

Tax Strategy #3

Become knowledgeable on the new tax laws that affect traders, investors, and taxpayers. Many taxpayers make the mistake of thinking this is their accountant's responsibility. Ultimately you have to sign the tax return and pay whatever tax is due. It is imperative for you, therefore, to know what you are doing. A good accountant or tax adviser will help you to stay aware of the pertinent issues; however, do not think that your adviser is responsible for your tax education.

There are plenty of good services around to which you can subscribe that will help you maintain a competitive edge in this area. Take advantage of them! These services include BNA, Commerce Clearing House, Research Institute of America, J.K. Lasser, The Tax Hotline (Boardroom Books), Agora's Tax Wise Money, and the list goes on.

Tax Strategy #4

Once you have learned how the changes in the new law affect you and are familiar with your available options, you must take full advantage of them. There aren't that many left, and the new law further restricts many of the ones we have left after the recent tax acts. However, some provisions were put back in or expanded, such as charitable gifting advantages and Section 179 depreciation. Others still remain, such as retirement and estate planning, that should be utilized to their fullest advantage.

Many taxpayers still make the mistake of thinking that fewer deductions equal less chance of an audit. You should know by now that that simply is not true. I am not talking about loopholes or gray areas of the law, but rather about the use of knowledgeable tax strategies to reduce your tax liability.

Also, do not equate good tax planning with tax preparation. Effective tax strategies start January 1 of each year, not April 15 of the next year. Your best financial plan is a sound tax plan.

Tax Strategy #5

Now that the tax laws have changed, you must reevaluate every investment in your portfolio to recalculate true yield. A small change in tax rate will greatly affect your rates of return, and this was by no means a small change. This is especially true for investments that compound over the years.

Also, the normal yields on Treasuries, municipal bonds, and all other interest-bearing instruments have changed significantly in the past year, irrespective of the new tax law changes.

A mistake people frequently make is not quantifying the tax consequences of their investment portfolios on an ongoing basis. This is critical when there has been a change in the tax law or significant changes in interest rates; and as you know, both have occurred recently.

Tax Strategy #6

Growth stocks may once again become favored investments. Even with the additional restrictions on deductibility of investment interest, the 20 percent maximum tax rate is quite a savings as the top federal tax bracket approaches 40 percent (a spread of 20 percent and a 50 percent tax savings)!

Although certain investors, such as retired people, generally think in terms of conservative, income-oriented equities, it may be wise to increase holdings in something like a *quality* growth mutual fund. This would increase the percentage of capital gain income to ordinary income, and it will combat both increased tax rates and potential inflation, likely to increase in the next several years.

Tax Strategy #7

Consider investing in a Real Estate Investment Trust (REIT). Real estate should recover nicely under the next few years for two reasons: (1) with interest rates at historic lows, the real estate market should recover, and (2) the new tax law has some favorable real estate provisions in it, as I mentioned. As you recall, real estate activities are no longer passive activities in every case. Each real estate property is now judged on its own merits.

Tax Strategy #8

Always review your investments periodically to determine which, if any, can be written off. Keep all documentation relating to the potential worthlessness of an investment, such as an attorney's letter or a news article, in a special tax folder as backup. There are no specific standards toward which the IRS will look as a precondition for worthlessness of an investment. Discretion is reserved for each situation. An investment deemed worthless can be taken as a short-term capital loss, subject to the same capital-loss restrictions as other types of capital losses per Section IRS Code 1221. The tax law allows you to write off an investment in the year in which it becomes completely worthless (IRS Code Section 165[g]). Bankruptcy of a company is not a precondition if worthlessness is evidenced through other substantiation.

Tax Strategy #9

Always review your portfolio toward year-end to determine if sales of securities will be beneficial to your tax situation. Should you have a realized loss on the sale of stock during the year that exceeds $3,000, you may want to sell another investment that has an unrealized gain at that time. You might want to invest in something else, or simply reinvest in the same stock, but want a higher tax basis for gifting or contribution purposes. *Wash sale rules* do not prohibit you from selling your stock at a *gain* and then repurchasing it within 30 days. This is only true if there is a loss on the sale of the stock (IRS Code Section 1091[a]). Remember wash sale rules are not relevant if you elect Section 475, mark-to-market.

Tax Strategy #10

Instead of selling a stock at year-end to protect a gain, you may consider the alternative of buying puts to protect against erosion in your position while you avoid paying capital gains tax on it. By purchasing a put on your stock or an OEX put, you could ensure that a loss in value could not go beyond a certain amount while still owning the stock.

For instance, say you purchased General Grits for $80 in November, and the stock goes up to $100 by December 31. You believe the stock is basically worth holding but feel the market is due for a correction. You may do the following: Purchase the January, $95 puts for approximately $2 per put, guaranteeing you receive no less than $95 per share for your "Grits," or $15 per share profit. Even in the event of a serious market decline, the premium of $2 per share, or $200 per 100 shares, would protect you against any erosion in value beyond $5 per share.

Tax Strategy #11

If you feel that the market is *not* in for a serious decline, but rather a minor pullback, you can sell the January calls on your stock to protect against the erosion in value of only several points. You would not have to declare income on these calls until they expired the following year. Another somewhat more advanced strategy would be to put on an OEX January call credit spread. This might be preferable due to the tax considerations and could actually be managed more aggressively to result in your taking out some profit even in a sideways move.

Tax Strategy #12

If you are expecting a severe market decline and if you have a similar situation as in Tip #10, another course of action would be to "short General Grits against the box." When you *short against the box,* you are basically borrowing somebody else's stock to sell in the market, instead of selling yours. This will allow you to postpone the gain until the following year when you can use your stock to pay back the borrowed shares and complete the transaction. At this point you would report the gain or loss from the shorting of the stock, as well as the gain or loss from your original purchase (see Chapter 4—regarding restrictions and safe harbor rules on shorting against the box).

Tax Strategy #13

Earmark shares of stock and mutual fund purchases so as to maximize your tax advantage when these items are sold. When shares are purchased over a period of time, they may be purchased at different prices. At the time shares are sold, you can control which shares are considered to have been sold.

You can earmark shares sold to have either the highest or the lowest cost basis, depending on whether you want to recognize more or less income in the year of the sale. For example, suppose you bought 1,000 shares of a stock at $20 per share and later bought another 1,000 shares at $30 per share. In the future, if the price goes up to $35 per share and you want to sell half of your position, you have a choice of which 1,000 share lot to sell.

If you tell your broker to sell the second thousand shares, your gain is $5 per share. But, if you do not designate which shares you want sold, the IRS will treat it as if the first shares purchased were the first shares sold (IRS Code Section 1012-1[c]).

The gain would be $15 per share, or in this case $15,000 as opposed to $5,000. Your broker should be notified in writing with instructions for selling specific lots of stock. A copy of this letter should be kept in your tax file.

Tax Strategy #14

Get the IRS to absorb some of the cost of the sales load when you buy into a mutual fund. The way to work this is to first find out at what point the fund charges the load. If it is a front-load fund, meaning the fee is charged upon entry, put your money into a money market fund first. Then switch your investment to the fund in which you want to invest, for example, the growth fund. When you sell out of the money market, you will have realized a small loss, which is the load you were charged for the original purchase. When you report this transaction on your tax return, the result will be a loss equal to the amount of the load. In this manner, you get to deduct the sales fee from your tax return immediately.

Sometimes the load is charged on the sale of only an equity fund. If this is the case, go into the equity fund first, switch to a money fund, and then back to equity. Be careful not to violate any wash sale rules in doing so. The objective here is to turn a charge into a realized loss, so that it can be deducted currently on your tax return.

In a recent ruling, the IRS made this process more difficult by claiming that it was a "step transaction" and disallowed the loss. However, the way it stands, if you wait 90 days, you should have no problem.

Tax Strategy #15

Use swapping to defer gains on exchanges of capital assets. The tax swap is an action that generates paper losses. Perhaps the investor finds in his or her portfolio that some securities have decreased in value since being acquired. The investor sells these securities to generate the loss and then immediately reinvests the sale proceeds to purchase *similar* securities. The sale generates a capital loss that can be used to offset any capital gains received during the year, plus up to an additional $3,000 loss against ordinary income. But the loss is really only a paper loss because the value of the investor's portfolio remains approximately the same.

By similar, I mean *similar and not identical.* If a bond were to be sold, a similar bond might be one of a different company with the same coupon, maturity date, and credit rating. When a stock is sold, a similar stock might be that of a different company in the same type of industry. Be certain not to invest in the same exact item unless you wait a full 31 days before doing so. Otherwise, the loss will be disqualified due to the wash sale rule.

That same provision, however, does not apply if you sell a security at a gain. So, if you already have a loss this year, you could sell a security at a gain, shelter the gain with the loss, and then immediately buy back the same security, avoiding future tax that would have been otherwise due on its appreciation.

Tax Strategy #16

Make a tax-deferred exchange of real estate or insurance policies. If you would like to sell real property on which you have a gain or if you would like to get out of an insurance policy but don't want to recognize the gain, you may be able to use what is known as a deferred tax swap of like-kind property. The rules for doing this are rather complicated, but many people can meet these criteria. No tax will be paid, regardless of the amount of gain involved if you qualify. You should consult with your investment-tax adviser as to what is necessary to qualify for this tax treatment.

Tax Strategy #17

Make use of the installment sale method of selling certain types of capital gain items. The *installment sale rules* have been modified significantly with the Tax Reform Act of 1986. Publicly traded items such as stock cannot be sold on installment. However, there still is the opportunity to use such a method of recognizing your gain over a longer period of time than simply when the sale is made for other capital items such as real estate. Check into the opportunities for availing yourself of this treatment before you make a large sale of property.

Tax Strategy #18

Prepay your state estimated taxes prior to the end of the year. Although the fourth-quarter estimated-tax payment is not due until January 15 of the following year, if you mail it out prior to December 31, you may deduct it on that year's tax return.

A caveat here is that you have to be aware of potential alternative minimum tax (AMT) liability if the payment is very large or if you have a great many "preference" items. The deduction for state taxes paid is now an AMT addback. Also, do not *overpay* your state taxes just to get the deduction. Make sure it is close to the amount due. If you overpay, the IRS can penalize you for overpaying and deducting an unreasonable amount.

Tax Strategy #19

Another good tax strategy is to time the disbursement of expenses each year with the objective of alternating between itemized and standard deductions.

This is really a great technique if you qualify for doing it. The way this is done is to double up on your state income tax, your real estate tax, and certain other itemized payments *every other year.* You take the standard deduction in the year you do not make the payment.

For example, let's say, in the simplest case, that for the next two years you owe approximately $4,500 each year in real estate taxes, your only itemized deduction. If the standard deduction is now $4,400 per year, you have two choices.

You can pay the $4,500 real estate tax each year when it is due and take the itemized deduction in both 2000 and the year 2001. The total deduction you would get over the two-year period would be $9,000 ($4,500 in 2000 + $4,500 in 2001).

Your second option would be to pay all the tax in 2000. You would make one payment in the beginning of the year, and the next payment on December 31, 2000. By doing this, you would get the entire $9,000 write-off up front in 2000 and be qualified for the standard deduction of $4,500 (estimated) in 2001. In addition to getting the deduction sooner and reducing the immediate tax to be paid, you would also increase the total amount of deductions you get over the two-year period.

	2000	2001	Total
Without strategy	$4,500	$4,500	$ 9,000
Utilizing strategy	9,000	4,400	13,400

As always, you will need to evaluate the situation and take into consideration such factors as the AMT, which adds certain deductions back to income and recalculates the tax.

Tax Strategy #20

If you own vacation property, consider renting it out for two weeks or less per year to collect income that does not have to be reported on your tax return. IRS Code Section 280A specifically states that if a property is rented for less than 15 days a year, no rental income needs to be reported.

Tax Strategy #21

Instead of having one or two retirement plans that contain the bulk of your funds, consider breaking them up into six different smaller ones. If this is done properly, you can roll over a plan each month and, in effect, have a tax-free, interest-free, permanent 60-day loan from your retirement plans.

A taxpayer is allowed to withdraw money from an IRA for up to 60 days once every 365 days (IRS Code Section 402(A)(5)). This provision is designed to let you move funds from one IRA sponsor to another. But there is no restriction on what you do with the money during the 60-day period, as long as you redeposit it into an IRA within that time period.

Tax Strategy #22

Gift assets with *low current income streams* to children under the age of 14. This would be done to keep them from having investment income above $1,200, which would subject them to the kiddie tax. This method of shifting assets should be done on an annual basis to provide for maximum passage of tax-free wealth from one generation to the next.

Tax Strategy #23

Gift assets with the *lowest cost basis* to the youngest heirs. This strategy is similar to Tip #22 in purpose. By transferring the lowest cost basis stocks and other assets to the youngest heirs, you are, in essence, gifting those assets with the highest potential appreciation to them.

Tax Strategy #24

Take advantage of the gift-tax and estate-tax breaks that now exist. Create various trust instruments to shelter assets from estate taxes, for example, charitable remainder and credit shelter trusts. This section of the law is particularly complex, and you should seek the advice of a professional.

But act now! Although the rate was moved back up to 55 percent, the unified credit and gift-tax exclusions weren't touched.

I will remind you once again, as I have in prior chapters, many taxpayers mistakenly avoid estate-tax planning as part of their overall financial plan. Do not fall into the trap of putting off estate-tax planning because thinking about death, especially one's own death, is not pleasant. Also, it is a false assumption that it is not necessary to do because all the assets pass to the spouse tax free or because the first $675,000 (in 2001) is covered by the unified credit.

Tax Strategy #25

Your estate may, in fact, be pushed far over the $675,000 (in 2001) amount by assets that you don't think of, such as life insurance proceeds, the value of retirement accounts, or the appreciation in value of real estate (primary, secondary, or vacation homes). Also, passing the full value of your assets to your spouse can be a costly mistake, because your spouse will be able to pass no more than $675,000 tax free to the next generation, whereas the two of you could pass a total of $1,350,000 separately.

Tax Strategy #26

One of the benefits of good estate planning is that it can be done in connection with your inter-vivos tax planning; that is, the steps you take to plan for this can also cut your tax bills while you are alive. One example of this would be the gifting of current high-income securities to children over the age of 14 who are in a lower tax bracket.

Tax Strategy #27

An additional step to consider is to have the insurance on your life owned by a child or by a trust that benefits family members. You can provide the premiums for it through your annual tax-free gifts. When you die, the insurance proceeds will not be part of your taxable estate.

Tax Strategy #28

If you own more than $675,000 (in 2001) of assets, you should pass some of these directly to your children while you are alive to take advantage of the unified credit exemption.

Tax Strategy #29

An alternative method for utilizing your $675,000 exemption would be to set up a trust that pays income to your spouse for the duration of his or her life, and then distributes its assets to your children, while leaving the rest of your assets to your spouse directly. The $675,000 (in 2001) credit would be available for the passing of property to your children from both you and your spouse—a sum total of $1,350,000.

Tax Strategy #30

Another tax strategy is to make use of the $10,000 per person (now indexed for inflation), $20,000 per couple, annual gift-tax exemption. Gifts of income-producing assets to children over the age of 14 will also help to cut family taxes as well.

Keep in mind that a married couple can gift to another married couple up to $40,000 per year tax free ($10,000 from each of you to each of them) without using up any of the unified credit. For example, you and your spouse could leave your son and his spouse $40,000 each year tax free.

Tax Strategy #31

Make use of wealth replacement insurance. At a low cost that varies with your age and health status, you can use this to cover the potential tax liability of your estate.

Tax Strategy #32

The marriage penalty may take a bigger bite for those married filing separately. You may want to consider filing jointly, even if you have filed separately in the past. There is a significant marriage penalty under the new law that was not in effect under the old one. This was accomplished by increasing the rate at which you pay tax when filing separately.

The extent of this penalty is determined by:

- The amount of income and its split between the taxpayers.
- The amount of itemized deductions and its split between the taxpayers.
- The number of dependents.
- Their eligibility for earned income credit.
- The alternative minimum tax implications.
- Self-employed versus employee status.

The change in the 2001 Tax Act makes this strategy even more relevant, as the married filing joint tax classification has now become even more beneficial.

Tax Strategy #33

Avoid tax on dividends by selling mutual funds before dividends are declared and repurchasing them afterward. Most mutual funds declare dividends only once a year, in late December. You can usually determine when these dividends will be declared by calling the fund and asking them. You can then sell the fund and transfer the proceeds to a money market fund shortly before the dividend is declared.

After the dividend is declared, repurchase the fund immediately. You will have to consider the advantages and disadvantages of such a strategy depending on your capital gain or loss situation for the year.

Such a sale is a capital transaction, in most cases, and consequently will generate a capital gain or capital loss. But if you are in a tax situation in which you have a capital loss in another investment not fully being used and a capital gain in the fund, this strategy can save you considerable tax dollars. Instead of having to recognize a taxable dividend from this fund, you can convert it into a capital gain, which can then be offset by the capital loss, which you otherwise may not have been able to utilize that year.

Furthermore, even if you must pay tax on the gain, it may be at the lower rate of 28 percent. This would occur if you have held the fund for a year or more, thus generating a long-term capital gain. If a dividend is received, it would be taxed at the ordinary rate, which can be as high as 39.6 percent.

Tax Strategy #34

If you have contributed the maximum deductible contribution to your retirement plan for the year, consider investing in a tax-deferred annuity. Although these plans are not *tax deductible,* they are *tax deferred.* This means that any income generated by them will not be taxed until the money is withdrawn.

Tax Strategy #35

If you have a business or can start one, hire your spouse and create a deductible IRA. No matter what you do, you can hire a nonworking spouse, pay them, and create a $2,000 tax deduction from your total income. This is assuming that you qualify for a deductible IRA contribution as outlined in Chapter 6, Planning for a Wealthy Retirement.

You can also hire elderly parents or other family members to work for you. In addition to the benefits of putting away deductible money for them, you can provide such items as company-paid life insurance, health insurance, and tuition for job-related education, travel, and entertainment, which may be deductions to your business. As mentioned in Tip #2, there may be payroll tax considerations and possible compliance with various statutes, so have a CPA or someone knowledgeable in this area assist you in setting it up.

Tax Strategy #36

Parents should consider reporting their children's investment income on their own tax return. If your child is under age 14 and has investment income over $1,250, you can avoid the hassle and expense of filing a separate tax return and kiddie tax form for the child by including his or her income on your tax return.

Tax Strategy #37

Use the *long form* to file your tax return, even if you do not itemize your deductions. Some deductions are taken as "adjustments" to income and are known as "above-the-line" deductions. These are available even if you do not itemize your expenses. They are not available to those who file a short form.

Such subtractions to which you may be entitled are: retirement plan contributions, penalties on early withdrawal of savings, alimony payments, deduction for self-employment tax and health insurance, and disability income exclusion.

Tax Strategy #38

Sometimes you can save money by not filing a joint tax return if you are married. As explained throughout this book, several types of expenses are deductible only when they exceed a percentage of adjusted gross income. If one spouse has a high amount of these expenses and a lower gross income, it might make sense for the couple to file separate returns.

Also, if the combined income is over $250,000, it may pay to look into married filing separately. The reason for this is that if the spouses file jointly, both incomes would be taxed at the surtax, whereas if they file separately; the second spouse (with the lower income) may still get the advantage of a lower tax rate.

Tax Strategy #39

The IRS allows a deduction of 32.5 cents per mile for business-related automobile use. This would include actual business travel, as well as trips for the purpose of business promotion. Medical mileage is deductible at 10 cents per mile, and mileage attributed to charitable work is deductible at 14 cents per mile. Mileage associated with a business-related move is also deductible at a rate of 10 cents per mile. There is one caveat regarding this deduction—you must maintain detailed and accurate records of all such automobile use with reference to purpose, location, and actual mileage.

Tax Strategy #40

If you are holding bonds that have increased in value since you purchased them, use that gain to offset a realized loss you may have on another item that may be more than $3,000. Many investors may have bonds with a higher yield than the interest rates on the newer bonds offered today. If this is the case, the bonds will be worth a premium over their face value.

Sell your bonds and realize the gain. Then buy the same bonds back at a premium. The law allows you to amortize the premium over the life of the bond, so you get an annual deduction from the interest earned. The wash sale rules do not apply here, even if you purchase the same bonds back the day you sold them, because you have a *gain.*

Tax Strategy #41

Create a trust to avoid the huge costs of probate. In addition, as described in Chapter 10, New World Estate Planning, you can increase your unified credit per married couple from $675,000 (in 2001) of assets to $1,350,000 of assets.

Tax Strategy #42

Open an IRA and/or a KEOGH. Even if your income is too high to qualify for the IRA deduction, you will still benefit by making nondeductible contributions. Interest, dividends, and capital gains grow and compound tax free inside the retirement plan.

Tax Strategy #43

Deduct the full contribution to an IRA even though you have not yet contributed. The full amount must be deposited by April 15 of the following year. If you file early enough in the year to receive a refund by the date the contribution is due, you can use this refund to partially fund the IRA.

For example, suppose you have an IRA and are eligible for a fully deductible contribution of $2,000. You file your 1999 tax return in early January of 2000, deducting $2,000 for an IRA contribution that you have not yet made. Assuming you live in New York City, where the combined federal and state tax rate can be in excess of 50 percent, the tax saving on such a contribution would be approximately $1,000. When you receive your refund, assuming it is prior to April 15, 2000, you use this $1,000 to partially fund the IRA.

Thus, the government essentially matches your retirement contribution dollar for dollar ($1,000 in tax savings for every $1,000 you put in). This is a gift from Uncle Sam and should be accepted graciously.

Tax Strategy #44

Make retirement plan contributions *early in the year* to shelter the earnings from tax. Most people wait until late in the year to make their contributions to retirement plans. The due date for contribution to an IRA is the following April 15; and if the taxpayer files for an extension, the contribution date on a KEOGH plan or SEP can be extended until the following October 15. Do not wait until those dates to make your contribution. Rather, if you can, make them as early in the year as possible. Over the long run, the tax deferral obtained for the compound retirement plan earnings can be more valuable than the contribution deduction itself! This is particularly true now because of the new higher tax rates for most individuals.

For example, a $2,000 IRA contribution will save $800 for a person in a 40 percent combined federal and state tax bracket. But a contribution made early in the year will also earn tax-deferred income within the account during the year. If the IRA earns an average 10 percent annually, $2,000 contributed a year before the deadline for just one year, will earn $200. Over 30 years, this $200 will compound to $3,490. And each time you do this, over the 30-year period, you will compound a similar amount. If this is done on a regular basis each year, the increase in total retirement funds available will be significant. As of 1996, the spousal IRA contribution has been increased from $250 to $2,000. So now the total contribution for a couple, where one spouse works and other does not, has been increased from $2,250 to $4,000.

Tax Strategy #45

You get an instant deduction on a stock you are carrying at a loss without giving up the stock. Under most circumstances, the wash sale rules would deter you from selling a stock for a loss and then buying it back again within 30 days.

However, you could sell it out of your regular portfolio for a loss (which you could take as a capital loss on your tax return) and contribute the cash to your retirement plan. If you then repurchase it in your retirement plan, it is treated as a new purchase by another entity and the wash sale rules do not apply.

Tax Strategy #46

Make use of the new gold and silver bullion coins minted by the U.S. Treasury as investments for your retirement plan. As was discussed in Chapter 4 in the section Holding Periods and Rates, most collectibles are not permitted as investments for retirement plans. The exception to this rule are these bullion coins; and although you cannot put other forms of gold or silver into your IRA, these coins are now permitted as IRA investments.

Tax Strategy #47

If your child or grandchild is of college age, consider purchasing a small apartment building or multibedroom house in the college town. It would serve as an investment for you and could provide additional tax benefits and help pay for tuition.

Assuming your child or grandchild goes away to college, the proper way to handle this from a tax point of view would be to have him or her live in the apartment and serve as manager. He or she would live in the apartment rent free and be paid a salary for doing this. The salary, as well as the building upkeep and the depreciation, would be deductible. In return, the student would mow the lawn, collect the rent, supervise any repairs and maintenance of the property, and so on. Of course, he or she would have to pay income tax on the salary, but the first $3,400 of compensation escapes federal taxation, and the remainder, net of deductions, would probably be taxed at a 15 percent tax rate. This is a lower tax rate than you would pay on the same money, and he or she could use it to pay for tuition.

Tax Strategy #48

Evaluate the basis of a gift asset before gifting it to a relative. When the gift is made, it takes on the lower of the market value or the original basis of the gift. When the asset passes through an estate at the time of the one's death, it gets a stepped-up basis to either the fair market value or the alternate valuation, six months after death. Give away your highest basis assets first in most cases.

Tax Strategy #49

Assets you are holding at a loss should never be gifted. In doing so, the loss could never be recognized by either person. The asset would take on the market value at the time of the gift because it is lower than the cost. Rather, a person should sell the asset, recognize the loss on his or her tax return, and then gift the money from the sale of the asset. The value given away would be the same, but the giftor would get the benefit of a tax loss.

Tax Strategy #50

Give away appreciated assets to charity. Suppose you wanted to give $10,000 to your favorite charity: Consider making the gift in the form of appreciated property that you have. In this fashion, you avoid paying the capital gains tax on the appreciation. Because of the change in the tax law this year, you will not be subject to the alternative minimum tax on the appreciation in value of the item contributed.

Tax Strategy #51

If the end of the year has arrived and you have not made any provision for retirement planning, it's not too late. Assuming you meet the criteria, you can still establish an SEP for *last year* up until the valid extension date of your tax return this year. Even if you do not have the available cash to currently fund it, you could extend your tax return until October 15. If you make the contribution by then, it can still be deducted on what is essentially last year's tax return.

Tax Strategy #52

Invest in Series EE savings bonds to save for a child's college expenses. The interest on such bonds issued after 1989 will be tax free when it is used to pay for college.

Tax Strategy #53

Use margin accounts only to purchase taxable investments. If the investment you purchase on margin is tax free, the margin interest you pay is not tax deductible.

Tax Strategy #54

Never purchase tax-free instruments in a retirement account. The return on a tax-free instrument reflects its tax-free status, and it usually pays a much lower yield. If you are purchasing an asset for your retirement plan, there is no further benefit to purchasing one that is tax free. Everything earned within the plan is tax deferred; thus, yield should not be sacrificed for favorable tax status.

Tax Strategy #55

Move to a lower-tax state to save substantial state taxes. The range of state income tax rates goes from a high of approximately 13 percent (New York City/New York State) to a low of zero. The larger municipalities, such as Washington, D.C., and New York City, have the highest state and city income tax rates, whereas states such as Texas and Florida have none. *Money* magazine published a survey of the tax burden of all 50 states. The "tax" consisted of a composite tax on income, sales tax, gasoline tax, and real estate taxes. According to the article, state taxes rose an average of 116 percent since 1980—almost twice the federal increase.

The difference between states is significant. A two-wage-earner family of four, earning $69,275 (median *Money* household) would pay over twice the state and local tax in New York City ($8,841) as the same family would in New Hampshire ($4,345).

Several of the states that have no or very low income tax are Florida, Texas, Nevada, Washington, Tennessee, Alaska, and New Hampshire.

In fact, Alaska even gives you a tax rebate for living there (a share of the profit from the fuel pipeline).

Tax Strategy #56

Never apply an overpayment to the next year's tax return or you will be giving the government a tax-free loan. Regardless of how low the rate of return on that money would be in your hands, it is greater than getting absolutely nothing by letting the government hold it for a year.

Tax Strategy #57

Establish a charitable remainder trust (CRT) to generate a charitable contribution deduction and to avoid capital gains tax on appreciated assets. By transferring growth stocks to a CRT, you get an up-front charitable deduction, avoid capital gains on the sale of the assets, and avoid estate taxes. In addition, you can change the beneficiary to any charity you choose should your preference change during your lifetime.

With this type of trust, you continue to get the income from the investment for the duration of your life, and when you die, the assets go to charity. Furthermore, you can replace any asset with a *higher-yielding current investment* by selling it within the trust. You do not have to pay capital gains on the sale of this appreciated capital asset. The goal would be to sell whatever you donate and replace it with the currently highest-yielding investment available, such as a high-income mutual fund.

Tax Strategy #58

If you establish a CRT, you can still leave an amount equal to the donated property to your heirs, free of federal estate taxes. This is accomplished by the establishing of a wealth replacement trust (irrevocable life insurance trust). You can use the additional income generated by the greater yielding investments purchased in the CRT to fund this trust.

The actual administration of these two trusts must be done by an attorney, as it is somewhat complex. However, I have coordinated several of these, and the benefits are well worth the effort.

Tax Strategy #59

Protect your estate from taxes by purchasing a second-to-die insurance plan. It would cost you approximately 1 percent of your total net worth to purchase a joint-last-survivor insurance policy. The insurance company pays nothing until the second spouse dies. The unlimited marital deduction will pass all the assets to the surviving spouse, and at his or her death, the insurance company provides cash to pay the estate taxes.

Tax Strategy #60

Give property to a parent who does not have a large taxable estate. If you have an investment that has appreciated in value, gift it to your parents using the annual exclusion. This can be done with annual gifts of any item, say a partial interest of ownership in a house or a property or part of a portfolio of stocks. When the parent dies, it will become part of their estate and get a stepped-up basis. If the parent has an estate under $675,000 (in 2001), the property will pass through without any federal tax to anyone in the will with a higher tax basis. An agreement can be made whereby the property will come back to you at a higher basis. It can then be sold without capital gain.

Tax Strategy #61

If you are self-employed and pay for your medical insurance, you receive an additional benefit. Aside from an itemized deduction (subject to a 7½ percent floor), you will be entitled to deduct a percentage of the cost directly from income (eventually going up to 80 percent). It is allowed as an above-the-line deduction, which is more beneficial.

Tax Strategy #62

Defer interest to subsequent years by the purchase of Treasury bills. If you are in a high tax bracket currently but will be in a lower bracket the following year, you will want to postpone as much income as possible until then. One way of doing this is to purchase Treasury bills (T-bills) with maturity dates in the next tax year.

With most regular bonds, you must recognize interest when it is accrued. With T-bills, you do not have to recognize the income until the bill comes due and you receive the cash. This would be in three, six, nine, or twelve months, depending on how long a T-bill you purchased.

Tax Strategy #63

Defer interest to subsequent years by the purchase of a certificate of deposit (CD). Another method of postponing income is through the purchase of a CD that allows you to elect to leave the interest with the bank until maturity. This type of arrangement will defer tax until the interest is received.

Tax Strategy #64

If you have passive activities that are generating passive activity losses (PALs) that cannot be used, consider investing in a passive income generator (PIG).

Explore the purchase of a parking lot or a partnership owning parking lots. They generally provide a steady source of income, and there is no question as to their passive activities status. Also, a good real estate property or partnership that generates income will be passive to you if you do not materially participate in the management of it.

Tax Strategy #65

If you have implemented the strategies reviewed in this book, your tax liability will decrease significantly. Because you are legally allowed to increase the number of allowances you claim, you will reach a break-even point with the IRS. Don't let your money sit with the government without earning interest.

Increase the number of allowances on your W-4 so that less withholding tax is taken out of your pay each week. You can do this anytime in the year by advising your employer. Do so in writing, and the employer is required to provide you with another W-4 to complete.

The number of allowances is not contingent entirely on your dependents. If you are in the 28 percent tax bracket, every allowance you add will increase your monthly take home by approximately $50. If you are in the 15 percent bracket, it will increase it by about $25. You should fine-tune your withholding to the point where you get no refund and pay very little or no tax on April 15.

Tax Strategy #66

If you are married and your combined estate is more than the exemption amount, check to make sure that your will or trust uses a formula to capture the exemption amount. The formula, rather than set amounts, will be effective regardless of the year.

If, on the other hand, your will specifies a dollar amount, you should have the will revised to incorporate a formula that will enable you to take full advantage of the escalating tax-free amounts.

Tax Strategy #67

If you've already made gifts that have used up the current exemption amount, you'll be able to make more tax-free gifts in the future. From

1999 through 2010, you can make additional gifts to bring you up to the new exemption amounts. Make plans now for gifts that you'll make next year.

Tax Strategy #68

You can currently gift up to $10,000 annually to each of as many relatives or friends that you choose. (It is $20,000 to each individual if you are married and your spouse consents to the gift.)

For example, if you are a widow with four grandchildren, you can give them a total of $40,000 this year ($10,000 per grandchildren multiplied by four, without owing any gift tax to the IRS). If they are married, you can gift up to $160,000 ($20,000 per couple). And if you remarry, that figure becomes $80,000 ($320,000 to four married grandchildren) from both you and your spouse.

Under the 1997 Tax Act, starting in 1999, the $10,000 annual gift-tax exclusion has been indexed for inflation, as stated in Tip #67, allowing you to make even larger tax-free gifts.

Tax Strategy #69

If your motive for making gifts is to reduce the size of your taxable estate, then you should consider gifting assets that are expected to appreciate in value. This will shift the appreciation out of your estate along with the asset.

Tax Strategy #70

In planning gifts of business interest to children or others, make sure that your estate will qualify under the 50 percent business-ownership test. If the exemption is applicable to your estate and within 10 years of your death, your heirs fail to materially participate in the business or give away or sell parts of the business, an additional estate tax will be imposed as a *recapture* of the tax saved by this exemption bonus for the family business.

Tax Strategy #71

Although the tax law has always encouraged savings for retirement, until now it has penalized those who were successful in doing so. The penalty used to be a 15 percent additional estate tax on what the law determined to be excessive retirement plan accumulations in an estate and a 15 percent income tax penalty on excess retirement plan distributions.

The new law permanently repeals both of these penalties. The repeal applies retroactively to estates of people who died after December 31, 1996, and, for income tax purposes, to distributions received after that date. The strategy, therefore, is to make the most money you can in your retirement account without any consideration to overfunding it!

Tax Strategy #72

Charitable remainder trusts, as discussed in Tips #57 and #58, allow individuals to receive income for life (or for a fixed number of years), and then the charity receives the trust assets when the trust terms end. CRTs can be set up into two different ways:

1. Annuity trusts, where the income payments are fixed.
2. Unitrust, where the income payments are a percentage of the value each year of the assets in the trust.

The government perceived that certain individuals have abused these trusts using rules to claim large deductions for charitable contributions without really benefiting the charity. The new law cracks down on this abuse by putting new limits into place. These new limits are:

1. The value of the annuity or unitrust interest must not be more than 50 percent for trusts set up after June 18, 1997.
2. The value of the interest passing to the charity must be at least 10 percent of the initial value of the property placed in the trust for most transfers after July 28, 1997.

Take advantage of these new widened limitations. Speak to a professional about utilizing this most advantageous vehicle. As John Rockefeller used to say, "The best way to avoid taxes is to give it away."

Tax Strategy #73

The generation-skipping transfer tax essentially imposes that tax that would have been paid had the property passed in an orderly fashion from one generation to the next. In other words, when an asset passes from a grandparent to a grandchild rather than going from the grandparent to the child to the grandchild, this is considered to be a generation skip. The government wants to get money from every transfer, and this tax generally affects individuals who are wealthy because the first $1 million of property transfers are exempted from this tax. However, many more people are falling into this trap.

The new tax law now indexes the $1 million exemption amount to inflation for individuals who die or make life-time transfers after 1998. But the exemption will not increase until inflation pushes the figure up by $10,000 or more. Use this tax break!

Tax Strategy #74

Be sure that your will with the generation-skipping provision is phased in terms of a formula (rather than a dollar amount) so you will get the benefit of this new indexing. Wills without formulas should be revised.

If you have any concerns about your current estate tax needs or want to know how to benefit from the new law, schedule an appointment with your estate-planning adviser.

Tax Strategy #75

Using income shifting and gifting assets to children or other family members in lower tax brackets with a view toward reducing the family's overall tax bite on the assets has already been excellent strategy. With the new capital gains tax rate of 10 percent for those in the 15 percent tax bracket, income shifting is now even more attractive.

For example, in 1997, a child remains in the 15 percent tax bracket until his or her taxable income exceeds $24,650. If parents can give to a child stock worth $20,000 that has a basis to them of $5,000, the child (assuming he or she is still in the 15 percent tax bracket) will pay only 10 percent of the $15,000 gain, or $1,500. The parents would have paid 20 percent of the $15,000 gain, or $3,000. Therefore, tax savings under this strategy would be $1,500.

Tax Strategy #76

Make full use of income shifting to maximize your tax benefit. For example, gift appreciating securities to your child in trust for use for future college education.

Caveat: If the recipient of this gift and the implementor of this strategy is 14 years or younger, you may have to consider the kiddie tax implications with minors receiving more than $1,250 of unearned income in any one year. Consult your tax professional for the specifics.

Tax Strategy #77

Once popular retirement-plan vehicles, variable annuities may have lost a good deal of their appeal. Gains realized inside a variable annuity will be taxed at the highest tax rate (currently a maximum 39.6 percent plus state tax) when they are withdrawn. In doing so, you lose the benefit of the new 20 percent capital gains tax rate. You should consider variable annuities only if you're sure you will not need the cash for at least 20 years or more (an arbitrary figure that may vary depending on your own tax situation).

The strategy now is to purchase variable life insurance. Variable life insurance is an insurance product that affords protection on one's life while also allowing the person to invest the cash buildup inside the policy in a market-related product.

Tax Strategy #78

The *annual* strategy here is that you are allowed to compound and grow your cash buildup in the policy in a way that will give you capital gains growth through participation in the stock market. The *long-term* strategy here is to build up a significant value within the insurance policy and then at some future date, to borrow against the variable policy and to use the cash as a permanent loan.

Tax Strategy #79

New tax-law savings for home owners may, in some way, change the strategies that have previously been adhered to for estate planning:

The new tax law on home sales is truly tax simplification. It will give people a lot more freedom and flexibility in selling their homes than ever before. The new tax law will allow many people who are ready to move into smaller houses an opportunity to take tax-free profits on their big houses. Also, the new tax law will relieve a lot of people of record keeping because every time you move you start with a clean slate. Under the old law you were able to take a $125,000 once-in-a-lifetime exclusion on capital gains if you were 55 years of age or older. Also, under the old tax law, you were allowed to avoid capital gains on the sale of a principal residence as long as it was replaced with a new one costing as much or more within two years of the sale.

Under the Taxpayers' Relief Act of 1997 couples are now allowed to exclude from income a gain of up to $500,000 on a sale of a principal residence. Single people are allowed to exclude gains of up to $250,000. This replaces the prior exclusions that I just mentioned.

Generally, people are allowed to take an exclusion each time they sell a principal residence. The majority of people who sell their principal residences do not end up with a gain of more than $500,000, so all the profit they realize will be tax free. You can now take such a tax-free gain as often as every two years; but in order to be eligible, you are required to have owned and lived in the home for two of the preceding five years.

The old tax law generally created pressure on home owners to trade up when they moved to defer tax. Now they can move about as they please. The new exclusion amounts apply to profits on homes sold on or after May 7, 1997.

Most people who sell their homes will be winners under the new tax law, although there will be some losers, mainly the people who have gains of more than $500,000 due to a lifetime of trading up and rolling over their gains. Empty nesters or people who are downsizing today sometimes want to move into condos because they want to travel more or they just don't want all the work of maintaining a big house. Previously, the choice these people faced was to pay a large capital gains tax on the house or to wait until they were 55 years to get the $125,000 exclusion. Things have changed dramatically for these people under the new law.

For example, a couple in their late forties who have two children in college and a $600,000 home for which they paid $200,000 can now sell the home, pay no capital gains tax, and use some of that $600,000 to buy a condo and to pay for the kids' education. This couple will still have money left over to invest for retirement.

Tax Strategy #80

People who use these strategies can now buy what they actually need and invest the surplus profits. A good tax-planning and estate-tax-planning vehicle is to invest surplus money in a variable or fixed-life insurance product. This will ensure that there is a buildup of cash while affording protection and prepaying estate taxes at a large discount. If the financial markets continue to outperform the real estate market as they have done in recent years, you can build up a larger amount of cash in a variable life insurance product.

Tax considerations will no longer dictate personal choices in these cases. For years, when two older people thought about getting married and combining households, they saw their accountant first to find out what to do about the extra home and then their clergyman later. "Do we sell before or after we get married?" was generally the question they asked. If both were over age 55, we had to ask if either had used up their one-time $125,000 exclusion. If so, the other needed to sell before the wedding or give up his right to the exclusion forever. This was generally referred to as the "tainted spouse" doctrine.

Now people who plan to remarry don't have to worry about that any more. They can sell whenever it is most convenient, before the marriage or after. And if they want to sell both homes and buy a new one, unless they have very large gains, they can usually do so.

Caveats: One trap that might be worthy of consideration is the home office. The home office deduction has long been something that Americans have taken frequently. Now there is another reason to be wary of the home office deduction. Taxes that have been avoided as a result of depreciation deductions will now be recaptured as taxable income when the home is sold.

Also, renting out your home may not have been a good idea under the new tax law. Any taxes that have been avoided due to depreciation deductions over the years will now be recaptured when the home is sold. These new rules do not apply to vacation homes or to rental properties, both of which involve a separate application of tax rules.

Tax Strategy #81

Wait until next year to decide if you want to elect Section 475 as a trader. Although technically you are required to declare your intention in the minutes of the Board Meeting by the middle of the third month of the first year you do business, you can wait until the next year to do so officially with the filing of the first tax return of the entity. The way to get this extra year is to start a new entity in which to trade.

Tax Strategy #82

Use the time you gained by using Tip #81 to evaluate whether or not the Section 475 election is right for you.

Tax Strategy #83

If you have a loss at year-end, elect Section 475 to take the loss as ordinary. If not, you may not want to elect Section 475.

Tax Strategy #84

If you are a commodity trader with Section 1256 income (60 percent long term), you will not want to make the Section 475 election. Electing 475 would negate the ability to take 60 percent of your gain as long term because the entire gain would then become ordinary income to you. The difference in tax rates could be as high as 12 percent (39.6 percent versus 28 percent).

Tax Strategy #85

If you have large unrealized gains at year-end, do not make the Section 475 election. This would add to your income for the year.

Tax Strategy #86

If you have large unrealized losses at year-end, make the Section 475 election. By doing so, you can actually recognize losses on your tax return that have not yet been realized.

Tax Strategy #87

If you have wash sale losses that you cannot take without the Section 475 election, make the 475 election. This will enable you to recognize losses that you would not have been able to take without the 475 election.

Tax Strategy #88

Use the strategy of waiting until next year to decide on the Section 475 election for this year on an annual basis. This can be done by forming a new corporation, family-limited partnership, or limited liability company each year in which to trade. The extra cost of starting a new entity will be more than offset by the advantages of having the extra time in which to evaluate this election. Remember, new entities do not have to officially make the 475 election (filing Form 3115 with the IRS) until the first tax return is filed. This can be as late as October 15 of the following year, if the tax return is extended.

Tax Strategy #89

Avoid having to ask the IRS for a rescission of the Section 475 election by forming a new company every year in which to trade. Normally you cannot change back from a 475 election to a non-475 election, and this is a way around it.

Tax Strategy #90

As a trader, use the Section 475 election to change your trading income to ordinary. This way you can use for-employee benefit plans.

Tax Strategy #91

Use a Nevada corporation to loan money to your entity in a high-tax state to get some of the money out of a taxable state into a tax-free state.

Tax Strategy #92

Use a Nevada corporation to contract with your "taxable state corporation" and provide services to the taxable corporation. In this manner you can get money out of the taxable state into Nevada. Some of these services can be for advertising, for consulting, or for the rental of equipment.

Tax Strategy #93

Set up a children's trust, and gift business equipment to your children. They can then lease the equipment back to you, and you will get a deduction at a higher rate than the one at which the children (lower tax bracket) will be taxed.

Tax Strategy #94

Use a medical spending account (MSA) to accumulate tax-deferred, tax-deductible wealth. The money can be used at any time to pay for your future medical expenses. Until that time, you can grow the money in a tax-deferred environment, eventually augmenting your retirement accounts.

Tax Strategy #95

Use your multi-entity structures by putting your children on the payroll, and then set up tuition-reimbursement plans. You can then pay for part of your children's education. Although technically you cannot use this to fund a college degree, you can send them to a class if it helps them with their job. Make sure you document the business orientation of these classes.

Tax Strategy #96

Set up a medical cafeteria plan to cover the employees of your corporation, and then hire your family. In doing so, you can cover 100 percent of their medical costs rather than just a portion of them.

Tax Strategy #97

Start a meal-reimbursement plan for your employees (including you and your family), and have the company pay for some of your meals when you work overtime.

Tax Strategy #98

Never take a vacation! Always take a *business trip.* If a trip is predominantly for business, there is no rule against enjoying it as well. Especially well-suited are trips that take you out of town for business but must include a weekend stay. Many times the entire cost of the trip will be deductible, even if some of the days are not spent working.

Tax Strategy #99

Use the VEBA to cut your tax debt in half this year by making a contribution equal to half your taxable income.

Tax Strategy #100

Write off this book! It is both an investment and a tax guide, and consequently it is a legitimate tax deduction. Most taxpayers would deduct it on Schedule A, line 20, as a miscellaneous itemized deduction. If you qualify as a trader and file Schedule C, it should be deducted on Schedule C to avoid the 2 percent and 3 percent floors on the miscellaneous itemized deductions.

In any event, this book has provided you with information that has increased your investment and tax expertise. Within this context, save your receipts, canceled checks, and credit card statements, and remember to write them off!

Tax Strategy #101

Call Dr. Kevorkian—now.

As I stated in the Preface to this book, one of the clearest cut, unambiguous sections of the new Tax Act is the government's intended repeal of the estate tax in 2010. Quite frankly, I have my doubts as to whether we will ever see that repeal actually go into effect, but we must act as if it will, in order to set up some tax planning strategies. For that reason, there is ony one obvious course of action—dying in 2010. From what I hear, he is close to being booked up for that year, so do not delay—call Dr. K. today!

CONCLUSION

Some of the rules as they apply to these tax strategies are quite complex. Still others will be refined and parameters put forth which will impact them through either judicial interpretation or further legislative action. To stay one step ahead of the game, call our office at (800) 556-9829, and we will provide you with more information on any of them.

Appendix A

Investment/Trading Vehicles and How to Report—Tax Consequences

STOCK

Generally, a shareholder who sells or exchanges stock for other property realizes a capital gain or loss. Whether it is a long-term or a short-term gain or loss depends on how long the investor held the stock before selling or exchanging it.

When shares are sold, the gain or loss is the difference between the investor's tax basis (the purchase price or adjusted purchase price) and the selling price. If stock is exchanged for similar stock in the same corporation, it is considered to be a like-kind exchange, and no gain or loss is required to be reported on the tax return.

When stock is all purchased in one lot or purchased at the same time and cost as other lots of the same stock, there is no problem with establishing date of acquisition. When holdings of the same stock have been acquired in several lots (at different dates and/or for different costs), the investor has to determine the date of acquisition and the tax basis of the stock. This information is necessary to report the sale.

Investors can use a *first-in first-out* (FIFO) method, whereby the first lot purchased becomes the first lot sold. Or they can use a method of specifically identifying the lot they wish to consider sold. By using *specific identification,* investors can sell a higher-priced, subsequently purchased lot of stock first to postpone the potential recognition of a capital gain.

For example, suppose an investor purchased 100 shares at $100 per share and a month later purchased another 100-share lot at $110 per share. If he or she sells 100 shares (half the holdings) two months later at $120 per share, the investor can determine his or her tax basis for the 100 shares sold in two ways:

1. Using the first-in first-out method, the investor would first sell the 100 shares purchased at $100 per share. The gain would then be $20 per share, or $2,000.

2. Using the specific identification method, the investor could specifically identify the second lot, purchased at $110 per share, as the lot that he or she wishes to sell. In this case, the gain would be $10 per share ($120 – $110), or $1,000. If, on the other hand, the investor purchased the first lot for more than the second, he or she could use the first-in first-out method to reduce the gain.

How to Report

Both gains and losses are reported on Schedule D. If the gain or loss is short-term, it is listed on Part I, line 1a; if the gain or loss is long-term, it is reported on Part II, line 9a.

EQUITY OPTIONS

If an option is not exercised, but rather sold before it expires, the tax treatment is the same as that of an ordinary equity—the calculation of the gain or loss is based on purchase price (or tax basis, if different) and sales proceeds. Short- or long-term status is based on date of purchase and date of sale. There is no marking to market at year-end for a holder of an equity option, as will be illustrated in the case of a non-equity option, to be discussed in the next section.

For the holder of an option that expires worthless, a loss is recognized for the amount of premium. For the writer (seller) of an option that expires worthless, a gain is recognized for the amount of premium received (less commission costs). If the option is *exercised,* the tax treatments affecting the writer of the option and the purchaser of the option are different.

For the trader who exercised the option, the cost of the option is not deductible but, rather, affects the price of the stock. The following two scenarios can occur:

1. The option holder has long calls and exercises them to purchase stock. In this case, the cost of the option is added to the cost basis of the security. Gain or loss will be calculated on the stock when it is sold.

2. The option holder has long puts and exercises them to sell stock. In this case, the cost of the put reduces the proceeds received for the stock.

For the writer of an option exercised before expiration, the proceeds from the sale of the option are not recognized alone as income but, rather, affect the price of the stock being called or put. The following two scenarios can occur:

1. The writer of a call has the stock called away from him or her. In this case, the proceeds of the sale of the stock to the option writer are increased by the option *premium* received.

2. The writer of a put that has been exercised must now purchase the shares of stock for a certain price. In this case, the cost of the stock to him or her is reduced by the option premium received for the put.

How to Report

Both gains and losses are considered short-term for options that expire worthless, unless the person is in the business of equity options (market maker).

In cases in which an option is exercised, a short- or long-term gain or loss is determined by the holding period of the stock, not the option.

INDEX OPTIONS AND FUTURES CONTRACTS

Index options, such as OEX calls or puts, are generally treated as a commodity (futures contract), a non-equity option, for tax purposes. In this regard, it is marked to market at year-end, and the purchase or sale is viewed as a complete transaction at that time (December 31). The closing price on December 31 is considered to be the price received or paid to complete the transaction and is also used in calculating the new basis for the following year. The treatment of various futures and options contracts are specific to the contract. You must check with the exchange they trade on if you are not absolutely sure about how they are handled.

Other types of investment vehicles treated in this manner include Nikkei put warrants, foreign currency contracts, and dealer equity options.

How to Report

Any capital gains or losses arising from these transactions are treated as if they were 60 percent long-term and 40 percent short-term, without regard to their holding period. They are reported on Form 6781,

Part I, line 1. They are then carried to Schedule D. Again, it does not matter how long the option or futures contract was actually held.

U.S. TREASURY BILLS

Interest on Treasury bills (T-bills) is taxable on the federal tax return but usually tax free on the state return. If held to maturity, the interest is included in the proceeds received and is reported at the time of receipt for cash-basis tax payers (99 percent of all individuals).

There is no capital gain or loss on a T-bill held to maturity. The difference between the purchase price and the proceeds received is deemed to be interest.

If a T-bill is sold before the maturity date, the proceeds must be split between interest and capital gain or capital loss. The amount of interest accrued to date of sale is calculated based on its original rate and is reported as the interest (nontaxable to state) on Schedule B if necessary or simply on line 8a, page 1, of Form 1040. The cost plus this amount is used as your tax basis to calculate your gain or loss when subtracted from the proceeds received.

How to Report

Interest is reported as federal interest on Schedule B (if total interest is over $400) or simply on line 8a (total interest $400 or less) of Form 1040. On most state tax returns, you pick up the full amount of interest reported to the IRS and put down "federal interest" as a subtraction from state income.

Gains or losses are reported on Schedule D, Part I, line 1a, and Part II, line 9a. The capital transactions are treated as gains or losses for most state tax returns, even though the interest is not generally considered income.

TREASURY NOTES

The interest on Treasury notes is taxable on the federal tax return but is usually tax free on the state. Just as with T-bills, it is taxable when received, but, in this case, payments are usually received twice a year. If a premium was paid for the note, a portion of it gets subtracted from interest each year *(amortization).* If the note was purchased at a discount, a portion of the discount gets picked up as additional income each year. If a Treasury note is sold before maturity, there could be a gain or loss on the disposition, depending on the price paid and on the amount of amortization taken to that point.

How to Report

The tax treatment of Treasury notes is virtually the same as with T-bills, the only difference being that the income is reported throughout the life of the note as it is received. Interest is reported as federal interest on Schedule B (if total interest is over $400) or simply on line 8a (if total interest is $400 or less) of Form 1040. On most state tax returns, you pick up the full amount of interest reported to the federal government and put down federal interest as a subtraction from state income, as done for T-bill interest. Gains or losses are reported on Schedule D, Part I, line 1a, and Part II, line 9a. The capital transactions are treated as gains or losses for most state tax returns even though the interest may not be considered income.

U.S. SAVINGS BONDS

The taxpayer has the choice of declaring savings bond interest for tax purposes at the time it is received, when the bond is redeemed, or amortizing it throughout the life of the bond. There is also an exclusion for college tuition as was discussed earlier. If the interest is taxable, it is taxable on the federal tax return but is usually tax free on the state, just as with T-bills and Treasury notes. If a savings bond is sold before maturity, there could be a gain or a loss on the disposition, depending on the price paid.

How to Report

Interest is reported as federal interest on Schedule B (if total interest is over $400), or simply on line 8a (if total interest is $400 or less) of Form 1040. On most state tax returns, you pick up the full amount of interest reported to the federal government and put down federal interest as a subtraction from state income. Gains or losses are reported on Schedule D, Part I, line 1a, and Part II, line 9a. The capital transactions are treated as gains or losses for most state tax returns even though the interest is not generally considered income.

MUNICIPAL BONDS

The interest on municipal bonds is usually exempt on the federal tax return (except for private activity bonds, which are subject to the alternative minimum tax), exempt on the investor's state tax return if it is the state issuing them, and taxable on the tax return of a state that is not the issuer. If a municipal bond is sold before maturity, there could be a gain or a loss on the disposition, depending on the price paid.

How to Report

Interest is reported as tax exempt on Schedule B and is not included in the total carried to line 8a (if total interest is over $400) of Form 1040 or simply to line 8b (if total interest is $400 or less). On in-state tax returns, you pick up the full amount of interest reported to the federal government (without the amount of municipal interest in the total). You do not have to deal with any addback or subtraction because it is also tax free in the state of origin.

If it is an out-of-state issue, you must start with the federal income and add back the out-of-state municipal interest.

Gains or losses are reported on Schedule D, Part I, line 1a, and Part II, line 9a. If the bond is sold before maturity, the capital transactions are treated as gains or losses for federal tax purposes, even though the interest is not generally considered income. If it is held to maturity, a gain can be recognized, due to a purchase at a discount. However, a loss cannot be taken for bonds purchased at premium.

One final word: You cannot deduct margin interest expense paid to carry tax-free notes. If an investor has paid margin interest to carry a mixed portfolio for any one tax year (a portfolio containing both taxable and nontaxable items), he or she must allocate the amount of margin interest as to deductible and nondeductible.

NIKKEI PUT WARRANTS

These warrants are treated as commodities and marked to market at year-end for tax purposes. They are reported as are other commodities (see the previous section "Index Options and Futures Contracts").

CALLS OR PUTS ON THE FTSE 100

These are treated as equity options to nondealers and not marked to market. They are reported as are other equity options (see the previous section "Equity Options").

STOCK DIVIDENDS

A *stock dividend* is a dividend paid to the stockholder in stock rather than cash. This distribution may also be paid in warrants or other rights to acquire stock.

Generally a stock dividend is not a taxable event; but, rather, the investor's tax basis of the lot of stock is reduced by some factor. For example, if an investor paid $100 per share for 50 shares of a stock, the basis for the entire purchase would be $5,000. If the investor sold any shares, the basis for each one would be $100 per share.

Assuming a nontaxable stock dividend of one share was paid for every one share held, the taxpayer would have 100 shares for which he or she paid the same $5,000. The basis per share, assuming he or she sold any of them, would go down to $50 each (reduced by a factor of one-half). In this way the dividend will be reflected when the stock is sold.

Stock splits are treated essentially the same as stock dividends for tax purposes.

RETURN OF CAPITAL

If a corporation makes a distribution that is more than the accumulated profits of the company, it is considered to be a return of capital. In this case, also, there is no taxable event. Rather, the investor's tax basis is reduced by the amount received. In this way, the return will also be reflected when the stock is sold.

How to Report

Any return of capital above the original investment in the stock (the investor's tax basis) is usually treated as a capital gain and is reported in the same manner as other capital gains on Schedule D.

DIVIDEND REINVESTMENT

Although the dividend is reinvested, it is usually taxed as an ordinary dividend and reported on Schedule B (if over $400) or simply on the front page of Form 1040, line 9. In this case, if a dividend is reinvested and taxed, the investor's basis for the stock would be *increased* to reflect such a taxable event. This would avoid paying taxes on the dividend when received and then paying taxes on it again as part of the sale. If an investor did not increase his or her tax basis, the proceeds from the additional stock or mutual fund shares reinvested would be considered an additional gain.

For example, if an investor owns a mutual fund in which he or she reinvests dividends and the mutual fund pays a $401 dividend at year-end, the taxpayer reports the dividend on Schedule B. But when it comes time to sell the mutual fund, the tax basis is increased by the dividend amount. In this way, the tax paid on the dividend is reflected in the cost per share of the fund. The investor will then have that much less of a gain or more of a loss on the sale of the mutual fund.

MUTUAL FUND SWITCH FROM EQUITY TO CASH

Every time an equity fund is redeemed and put into cash, a taxable event takes place—unless the mutual fund is part of a retirement plan.

Thus, every time a switch is made from equity to cash, it translates into the sale of equities for tax purposes just as if the investor owned the stocks outright and sold them all. Every time a switch is made to equity from cash, it translates into the acquisition of tax basis as with the purchase of individual stocks.

Many investors who regularly switch between cash and equity in a nonretirement, no-load mutual fund are generating taxable transactions every time a switch is made. For this reason, detailed records must be maintained because all of these transactions must be reported on the tax return.

How to Report

Both gains and losses are reported on Schedule D. If they are short-term, they are listed on Part I, line 1a. If the gain or loss is long-term, it is reported on Part II, line 9a.

SHORT SALES OF STOCKS AND SHORTING AGAINST THE BOX

A *short stock sale* occurs when an individual contracts to sell stock that he or she either does not own or does not wish to deliver at the time of the sale. A short sale seller usually borrows the stock for delivery to the buyer.

At a later date, the short seller will repay the borrowed shares by either purchasing those shares or relinquishing the shares he or she already holds but did not want to give up at the time the short sale was made. The short seller will usually pay interest for the privilege of having borrowed the stock to sell short. This will be treated as an ordinary investment-interest expense for tax purposes.

If a short seller *shorts against the box,* he or she already owns the stock at the date he or she shorts it but chooses to short shares other than the ones he or she owns. A shorting-against-the-box transaction is treated identically to that of simply shorting the stock.

The act of delivering the stock to the lender (repaying) and shorting against the box is called "closing the short sale." In both cases, this is the point at which the taxable event occurs.

When a stock is sold short and the transaction is closed, a seller will realize a gain on the transaction if the price that the seller pays for the borrowed shares is lower than the price for which he or she sold them. If the seller covers at a higher price, he or she will realize a capital loss.

In other words, it is possible for investors to short a stock even if they own it at the time. This allows for the locking in of gains on a stock without actually selling that stock. In doing so, investors would postpone the realization of capital gains that would then be incurred and reported by the outright relinquishing of the stock.

How to Report

Both gains and losses are reported on Schedule D. If they are short-term, they are listed on Part I, line 1a. If the gain or loss is long-term, it is reported on Part II, line 9a.

The only distinction in the way a short sale is reported is when the sales date comes before the purchase date. Whether a gain or loss is long-term or short-term will generally be determined by how long the seller held the stock used to close the sale.

Read Chapter 4 on the new tax law to be sure you do not violate any of the safe harbor provisions of the law. Shorting against the box has been tightened up now and, in most cases, is not an effective hedge against taking capital gains—but in some instances, the gain can be put off until the next year.

INCENTIVE STOCK OPTIONS

An *incentive stock option* is an option granted to an individual in connection with his or her employment to purchase stock in the employer's corporation. No income is realized by the employee when the incentive stock option is granted if it is a qualifying transfer (certain conditions must be met by the employer). In addition, if it is a qualifying transfer, no income will be recognized when the option is exercised to obtain the stock.

How to Report

The income or loss will be recognized at the time of the sale of the stock and is determined by subtracting the tax basis from the proceeds realized. Both gains and losses are reported on Schedule D. If they are short-term, they are listed on Part I, line 1a. If the gain or loss is long-term, it is reported on Part II, line 9a.

Any reduced cost of the stock due to an incentive stock option will be reflected at that time as an additional gain (or reduced loss) on the sale of the stock because it will have resulted in a reduced tax basis of the stock.

Appendix B

Deductions Related to Investment and Trading Activities

Many expenses incurred in trading activities are deductible, in full or in part, in calculating taxable income. Investors take their expenses as itemized deductions, whereas dealers and traders take their expenses as business deductions. Except as noted, these items have not changed with the 2001 Tax Act.

COMMISSIONS

Commissions are frequently the most significant expenditures associated with trading activities. For an investor or a trader, commissions are included in the calculation of gain or loss; commissions may *not* be taken as a deduction. For a dealer or a hedger, commissions may be deducted as a business expense.

CARRYING CHARGES

No deduction is allowed for interest and carrying charges allocable to personal property that is part of a straddle, except to the extent that the position generates ordinary income. Carrying charges consist of interest, storage charges, insurance premiums, and similar expenditures. Hedging transactions are exempted from this rule. Any amount not allowed as a deduction can be capitalized and will thus enter into the calculation of gain or loss when the position is closed.

DEDUCTIONS OF INVESTORS

Investors are not "in business"; but they incur expenses for the production and preservation of income, so their investment expenses are deducted as miscellaneous itemized deductions. The taxpayer does not benefit unless the tax return uses itemized deductions. Furthermore, there are limitations on itemized deductions. First, miscellaneous itemized deductions are reduced by 2 percent of adjusted gross income; if the miscellaneous itemized deductions are less than 2 percent of adjusted gross income, then the taxpayer gets no tax benefit from the deduction. Second, there are limitations on the deductibility of interest expense. Third, individual taxpayers whose adjusted gross income exceeds a threshold amount have the allowable amount of certain of their itemized deductions reduced by 3 percent of the excess of their adjusted gross income over the threshold amount.

Interest expense related to trading activities is classified as investment interest. Investment interest is deductible only to the extent of net investment income; interest that is disallowed because of the limitation is carried over to the succeeding tax year. *Net investment income* is defined under the law as the excess investment income over investment expenses; investment income consists of income from dividends, interest, rents, and royalties. For 1993 and subsequent years, net capital gain from investment property is not considered investment income; however, individual taxpayers may make an election to treat all or a portion of their net capital gain as investment income. If the election is made, the portion of the net capital gain treated as investment income is taxed at ordinary income rates rather than at the long-term capital gains rate.

DEALERS, TRADERS, AND HEDGERS

Dealers, traders, and hedgers are all "in business," so ordinary and necessary business expenses of a reasonable amount are deductible in the calculation of adjusted gross income.

Members of commodities and securities exchanges may deduct their expenses of membership. Common expenses of membership include exchange dues and fees, licenses, printing of trading cards, interest on membership loans, trading jackets, and laundry. Employee salaries, related payroll taxes, and employee benefits costs are also deductible. Exchange members are subject to self-employment tax on their net trading income, whereas traders are not; they are also eligible to establish qualified retirement plans for themselves and their employees, whereas traders are not (on capital gains income).

COMMON DEDUCTIBLE EXPENDITURES

Investors may deduct their expenses as described in "Deductions of Investors." Expenditures for market information—subscriptions to chart services, weather and crop information services, market advisory services, quotation devices, and the like—are the most common deduction. A great deal of market information is available in various computerized formats. Data may be used as received or further processed to facilitate market decisions. Expenditures for computers and software are deductible. Computers are capital assets, and deductions are taken in the form of depreciation. Computer software is considered an intangible asset; it may be capitalized and amortized over a period of five years or less if a shorter life can be established.

Fees for professional services paid to accountants or attorneys or professional fees incurred for tax counsel or in the determination of a tax liability are deductible if they are ordinary and necessary.

This list of common deductible items is not conclusive; it should be viewed as indicative of the types of deductions commonly encountered. Once again, the reader is urged to seek professional counsel regarding the application of tax law to his or her particular set of circumstances.

Appendix C

The VEBA—Code Sections

Internal Revenue Code Section 501(c)(9) created tax-exempt VEBAs (voluntary employee benefit associations), provided that the organization has received a favorable IRS determination letter.

SECTION 501

Section 501 describes the exemption from taxation, which lays out that an organization described in subsection (c)(9) shall be exempted from taxation if it is one of the following: "Voluntary employee benefit associations *providing for the payment of life, sickness, accident, or other benefits* to the members of such association or their dependents or designated beneficiaries, *if no part of the net earnings of such associations inures (other than through such payments) to the benefit of any private shareholder or individual.*"

Note that this Code Section was first enacted in 1928 as Section 103(16) of the Revenue Act of 1928.

INTERNAL REVENUE REGULATIONS 1.501(c)(9)-1

Internal Revenue Regulations 1.501(c)(9)-1 deals with the qualifications of a VEBA. It states that to be covered by Section 501(c)(9), an organization must meet *all* of the following requirements:

- The organization must be an *employee's* association.
- Membership in the association must be *voluntary*.

- The organization must provide for the *payment of life, sickness, accident, or other benefits* to its members or their dependents or designated beneficiaries, and substantially all of its operations must be in furtherance of providing such benefits.
- *No part of the net earnings* of the organization other than by payment of the benefits referred to in paragraph c are to *benefit any private shareholder or individual.*

INTERNAL REVENUE REGULATIONS 1.501(c)(9)-2

Internal Revenue Regulations 1.501(c)(9)-2 deals with membership in a VEBA, employees, and a description of the VEBA.

Membership must consist of individuals who are *employees* and whose eligibility for membership is defined by reference to objective standards that constitute an employment-related common bond, such as a common employer or affiliated employers.

In addition, employees of one or more *employers engaged in the same line of business in the same geographic locale* will be considered to share an employment-related bond for purposes of an organization through which their employers provide benefits. Employees can include nonemployees, so long as they share an employment-related bond, such as a sole proprietor or a partner whose employees are members of the association; however, total membership must consist of no less than 90 percent of the employees at least one day of each quarter of the year.

Eligibility may be restricted by geographic proximity or by objective conditions or limitations reasonably related to employment. Objective criteria may not be administered in a manner that limits membership or benefits to officers, shareholders, or highly compensated employees or that gives them benefits that are disproportionate.

An employee is *defined* by reference to the legal and bona fide relationship of employer and employee.

There must be an entity having an existence independent of the member-employees or their employer. Membership must be voluntary, and an affirmative act is required on the part of the employee to join. However, an association is considered voluntary although membership is required of all employees, provided that the employees do not incur a detriment as the result of membership (e.g., deductions from pay).

The *VEBA must be controlled* by (1) its membership; (2) an independent trustee, such as a bank; or (3) by trustees, at least some of whom are designated by the membership.

There must be an independent trustee.

INTERNAL REVENUE REGULATIONS 1.501(c)(9)-3

Internal Revenue Regulations 1.501(c)(9)-3 deals with the benefits allowable in a VEBA, life, sickness, accident, and/or other benefits.

Life benefits mean a benefit payable because of the death of a member or a dependent. A life benefit may be provided directly or through insurance. The benefit must consist of current protection but also may include a right to convert to individual coverage on termination of eligibility for coverage through the association, or a permanent benefit as defined in the regulations under Section 79. Life benefit does not include a pension, an annuity, or other similar benefit.

Sickness and accident benefits mean amounts furnished in case of illness or personal injury to a member or a dependent. Benefits may be provided through reimbursement or through payment of premiums to a medical benefit or a health insurance program. These benefits may also include sick pay during a period in which the member is unable to work due to sickness or injury.

Other benefits include only benefits that are similar to life, sickness, or accident benefits. The benefit must be intended to safeguard or improve health or to protect against a contingency that interrupts or impairs a member's earning power.

There are several examples of other allowable VEBA benefits:

- Paid vacation benefits.
- Vacation facilities and expenses.
- Subsidizing recreational activities.
- Child care facilities for preschool and school-age children.
- Job readjustment allowances.
- Income maintenance payments for economic dislocation.
- Temporary disaster grants.
- Supplemental Unemployment Benefits (SUB).
- Severance benefits.
- Education or training benefits.
- Personal legal service benefits.

There are several examples of nonallowable VEBA benefits:

- Commuting expenses.
- Homeowners insurance.
- Malpractice insurance.
- Loans to members (except for distress).
- Savings facilities.
- Benefits similar to pensioner annuity—payable at the time of mandatory or voluntary retirement.

- Deferred compensation or other benefits that become payable by reason of the passage of time, rather than as a result of an unanticipated event.

INTERNAL REVENUE REGULATIONS 1.501(c)(9)-4

Internal Revenue Regulations 1.501(c)(9)-4 deals with prohibited transactions.

No part of the net earnings of a VEBA may inure to the benefit of any private shareholder or individual. Of course, the payment of benefits permitted to *all* employees are not prohibited.

There can be no disposition of property or the performance of services for less than fair market value or cost. There can be no unreasonable compensation paid to trustees or employees of the VEBA.

There can be *no payment of disproportionate benefits to any member,* unless pursuant to objective and nondiscriminatory standards. Payments to highly compensated personnel or to officers and shareholders may not be disproportionate in relation to benefits received by other members. Any differences as to payments in kind or amount must be justified based on objective and reasonable standards.

Upon termination of a VEBA, assets remaining after satisfaction of all liabilities must be applied to provide (directly or through purchase of insurance) benefits pursuant to criteria that *do not provide for disproportionate benefits* to officers, shareholders, or highly compensated employees.

INTERNAL REVENUE CODE SECTION 162(a)

Internal Revenue Code Section 162(a) is an applicable provision of the Code to discuss because it deals with the deductibility of a trade or a business expense.

A deduction is allowed for all ordinary and necessary expenses paid or incurred during the taxable year in carrying on any trade or business.

The requirements for deductibility are that the expense must be:

- Paid or incurred during the tax year.
- An expense of carrying on a trade or a business.
- A "necessary" expense.
- An "ordinary" expense.

Note that court decisions indicate that the expenses must also be "reasonable" in amount. Also, it is important to realize that an expense, in order to be deductible, must be 100 percent legal. *There is no problem in this case.*

INTERNAL REVENUE REGULATIONS SECTION 1.162-10(A)

Internal Revenue Regulations Section 1.162-10(A) deals with the deductibility of a VEBA contribution. It states that certain employee benefits can be deducted:

> Amounts paid or accrued within the taxable year for a sickness, accident, hospitalization, medical expense, recreational, welfare or similar benefit plan, are deductible under Section 162(a) if they are ordinary and necessary expenses of the trade or business. However, such amounts shall not be deductible under Section 162(a) if, under any circumstances, they may be used to provide benefits under a stock bonus, pension, annuity, profit-sharing, or other deferred compensation plan.

INTERNAL REVENUE CODE SECTION 419(e)

Internal Revenue Code Section 419(e) deals with the rules for a welfare benefit fund.

In general, *welfare benefit fund* means any fund that is part of a plan of an employer and through which the employer provides welfare benefits to employees or their beneficiaries with some exceptions as described in the Code.

INTERNAL REVENUE CODE SECTION 419(A)(f)(6)

Internal Revenue Code Section 419(A)(f)(6) deals with the 10-or-more employer rule and the exceptions for 10-or-more employer plans.

Certain restrictions will not apply in the case of any welfare benefit fund, which is part of a 10-or-more employer plan. For the purposes of this subparagraph, *10-or-more employer plan* means a plan to which more than one employer contributes and to which no employer normally contributes more than 10 percent of the total contributions contributed under the plan by all employers.

INTERNAL REVENUE CODE SECTION 505(b)

Internal Revenue Code Section 505(b) deals with the nondiscrimination rules.

In general, each class of benefits provided under a classification of employees must *not be discriminatory* in favor of the highly compensated, and each of such benefits must not discriminate in favor of the highly compensated.

For the purposes of this Code section, you *may* exclude from consideration the following:

- Employees who have not completed up to three years of service.
- Employees who have not attained the age of 21.
- Seasonal employees or less-than-half-time employees.
- Employees not covered in this plan who are included in a unit of employees covered by a collective-bargaining agreement (such as unions).
- Employees who are nonresident aliens and who receive no earned income from the employer, which constitutes income from sources within the United States.

This Code section also deals with the aggregation rules whereby, *at the election of the employer,* two or more plans of such employer may be treated as one plan for this purpose.

Also, *highly compensated individuals,* for the purpose of this subsection, shall be determined under rule similar to those rules that determine whether an individual is highly compensated and shall be limited to compensation of *$160,000 or less.*

Appendix D
The VEBA—Court Cases

GREENSBORO PATHOLOGY ASSOCIATES, P.A. V. U.S., 698 F.2D 1196, 83-1 USTC ¶ 9112 (FED. CIRCUIT 1982)

The Court of Appeals—Federal Circuit in 1982 stated: Contributions to an educational benefit trust established for the children of employees were deductible under Internal Revenue Code (IRC)-Section 162. Benefits were available to all employees, not to just owners or key employees. The plan was not a deferred-compensation plan subject to Code Section 404; rather it was a welfare or similar-benefit plan as described in Regulations Section 1.162-10.

Funds contributed to the plan would not revert to the benefit of the taxpayer. The benefits were not dependent on the earnings of the taxpayer. The plan was not intended as a substitute for an increase in salary. The corporation had actually spent the money it wished to deduct.

An independent trustee, who was not controlled by the employer, administered the plan. The employer did not retain an inordinate amount of control over the funds.

BRICKLAYERS BENEFIT PLANS OF DELAWARE VALLEY, INC. V. COMMISSIONER, 81 TC 735 (1983)

Tax Court of the United States in 1983 stated: The taxpayer was not an association of employees. Its members were tax-exempt welfare and pension funds, not individual employers. The taxpayer was in essence a cooperative of tax-exempt organizations and not an association of employees within the meaning of Section 501(c)(9). Therefore, the taxpayer was not a VEBA and did not qualify for exemption under

Section 501(c)(9). Membership must be composed of individuals, not organizations.

The organization provided for the payment of pension benefits, and it was not an association of employees. Pension benefits are not similar to life, sickness, or accident benefits. IRS regulations under Section 501(c)(9) were held to be reasonable and consistent.

Note: This case was decided prior to enactment of DEFRA in 1984, which added Section 419A(f)(6) to the Internal Revenue Code, providing for multi-employer VEBAs.

WATER QUALITY ASSOCIATION EMPLOYEE'S BENEFIT CORPORATION V. U.S., 795 F.2D 1303, 86-2 USTC ¶ 9527 (7TH CIR. 1986)

Court of Appeals—7th Circuit in 1986 stated: The "same geographic locale" provision of Regulations Section 1.501(c)(0)-2(a)(1) was held to be invalid. This provision restricted membership in tax-exempt VEBAs to employees engaged in the same line of business in the same geographic area. The court found that the provision was unduly restrictive and impermissibly excluded VEBAs that the statute otherwise exempts. Geography alone has no reasonable or local relation to the establishment of an "employment-related" bond to distinguish true VEBAs from commercial insurance ventures. The absence of geographically limited words within Section 501(c)(9) reveals a congressional intent that exempt status was to be granted to VEBAs generally.

Note: In Proposed Regulations Section 1.501(c)(9)-2, effective August 7, 1992, the IRS gave in to the holding of this opinion by allowing a three-state "safe harbor." This provides that an area will be recognized as a single geographic area if it does not exceed the boundaries of three contiguous states that share a land or river border with each of the others.

Therefore, a complete coverage of 50 states requires 17 separate VEBAs, each covering three states.

SUNRISE CONSTRUCTION COMPANY, INC. V. COMMISSIONER, 52 TCM 1358, T.C. MEMO 1987-21 (1987) AFF'D. (9TH CIR. 1988) UNPUBLISHED OPINION

Tax Court of the United States in 1987 stated: A VEBA plan was maintained in which the corporation claimed exempt status under Section 501(c)(9), but the IRS refused to issue a favorable determination letter because the net earnings of the fund inured to benefit the sole shareholder.

The Tax Court held that the VEBA was not tax exempt, where:

- The amounts contributed far exceeded the amounts reasonable for the stated purposes of the contribution.
- Excess funds were invested at the direction of the shareholder in a nonfiduciary manner.
- The terms of the organizing agreement were not honored upon termination of the plan.

The plan was actually a separate fund controlled by the sole shareholder for his own benefit.

AMERICAN ASSOCIATION OF CHRISTIAN SCHOOLS VOLUNTARY EMPLOYEES' BENEFICIARY ASSOCIATION WELFARE PLAN TRUST V. U.S., 663 F.SUPP. 275, 87-2 USTC ¶ 9328 (M.D.ALA. 1987), AFF'D. 850 F.2D 1510, 88-2 USTC ¶ 9452 (11TH CIR. 1988)

Court of Appeals—11th Circuit in 1988 stated: A trust established by a tax-exempt association of churches to provide a variety of insurance benefits to member school employees was denied tax-exempt status. The association covered over 1,000 participants in all 50 states. The association was not a VEBA.

Moreover, the trust failed to qualify under Section 501(c)(3) because it was not operated exclusively for religious purposes. The trust was not a religious organization because it operated as an insurance company with required premiums rather than voluntary contributions.

The trust also did not qualify as an organization operated exclusively for the promotion of social welfare. The trust did not qualify as a VEBA because it was not controlled by the employees through a trustee selected by the employees, and it granted higher-paid employees disproportionately greater benefits than lower-paid employees. The trust did not qualify for exemption as an association of churches that provides welfare benefits for its employees because it was established before the effective date in 1985 allowing for such an exemption.

WADE L. MOSER V. COMMISSIONER, 56 TCM 1604 (1989), AFF'D. ON OTHER ISSUES, 914 F.2D 1040, 90-2 USTC ¶ 50,498 (8TH CIR. 1990)

Tax Court of the United States in 1989 stated: The corporation was entitled to a $200,000 deduction for a contribution to its VEBA as an ordinary and necessary business expense, under Regulations Section 1.162-10(a). No taxable income to the officers and directors resulted.

Although there was scant authority governing the deductibility of an employer's contribution to a VEBA, the terms of the association were found to be structured in accordance with all relevant regulations. There was no statutory or regulatory provision that prohibited a deduction for a contribution to the plan merely because a high portion (90 percent) of the costs of the insurance premiums and costs of the full funding of the severance benefit were for benefits attributable to the officers and directors. The fact that the officers could effect amendment or termination of the association did not give them total unfettered control of the assets. Finally, the VEBA was operated in accordance with the plan provisions, and the assets did not revert to the employer or any shareholder, except as permitted pursuant to the plan provisions.

The severance benefit was computed as a function of a uniform percentage of compensation and years of service. There was an independent trustee, a trust company.

LIMA SURGICAL ASSOCIATES, INC., VEBA V. U.S., 20 CLS.CT. 674, 90-1 USTC ¶ 50,329 (COURT OF CLAIMS, 1990), AFF'D. 944 F.2D 885, 91-2 USTC ¶ 50,473 (FED.CIR. 1991)

Court of Appeals—Federal Circuit in 1991 stated: A plan and trust set up to provide severance pay to employees of a medical corporation did not qualify as a VEBA because it made payments of retirement benefits. Benefits were based on level of compensation and length of service. Severance payments provided under a VEBA plan must qualify as life, sickness, or accident benefits or as similar welfare-type benefits. Any benefit that resembles a pension or an annuity payable at the time of mandatory or voluntary retirement is a nonqualifying benefit for VEBA purposes. This deferred-compensation plan was similar to a pension or an annuity because it became payable by reason of the passage of time rather than as a result of an unanticipated event.

The plan was set up when the employer ended its preexisting retirement plan. The only participant in the plan to obtain benefits did so upon retirement. By paying retirement benefits as part of its alleged severance pay arrangement, the plan was both organized and operated to pay nonqualifying benefits. The benefits provided under the plan were not limited to the type of benefits specified in the VEBA regulations [Reg. Section 1.501(c)(9)-3].

The benefit scheme established under the trust provided disproportionate benefits to the doctor-owners, which violated the prohibition against private inurement.

JOEL A. SCHNEIDER, M.D., S.C. V. COMMISSIONER, 63 TCM 1787, T.C. MEMO 1992-24 (1992)

Tax Court of the United States in 1992 stated: A doctor, the sole shareholder of a medical service corporation, established three separate trusts for the corporation's employees and claimed that they were VEBAs. The trustee was an independent bank. Assets held in the trusts were dedicated to providing the employees, and not the employer, with benefits. *Plan benefits attributable to the doctor exceeded 95 percent of the aggregate benefits.* The doctor retained the right to terminate the trusts.

The IRS challenged the claim that the trusts were VEBAs and claimed that retention of the right to terminate constituted impermissible control over the trusts, making them investment vehicles for the owner and not VEBAs. The Tax Court rejected the IRS argument and stated that control was not too much, so long as funds may never revert to or inure to the benefit of the employer. The minimal retention of control was not enough to make the benefits of the plan in any way illusory.

Contributions to plans that were designated to provide death, disability, termination, and educational benefits were currently deductible business expenses, rather than capital expenditures or prepaid expenses. Neither the retained power to amend or terminate the trusts nor the benefit to be derived from employee loyalty resulted in a finding that the employer would realize a direct and continuing economic benefit or advantage of the sort that would require a capitalization of expenses. The contribution to each plan for a particular year related only to the year in which the contribution was made.

HARRY WELLONS, JR., M.C., S.C. V. COMMISSIONER, 643 TCM 1498, T.C. MEMO 1992-74 (1992), AFF'D. 31 F.3D 669, 94-2 USTC ¶ 50,402 (7TH CIR. 1994)

Court of Appeals—7th Circuit in 1994 stated: A medical service corporation that established a severance pay plan for its employees could not deduct its plan contributions as ordinary and necessary business expenses. It had to deduct the contributions in the years that plan benefits were actually paid to the plan participants. The plan did not have an exemption letter from the IRS under Section 501(c)(9). The plan was in substance a deferred-compensation plan. *Its participants received the benefits only after the termination of their employment.*

Moreover, the amount of benefits received by a participant was contingent on the length of time the participant had been in the corporation's employ and on the amount of the participant's compensation while in such employ. Five years' service was required, and benefit amount was linked to the level of compensation and the length of service. The plan calculated the benefits paid based on each participant's compensation, *just as a retirement plan would.* Because the benefits were deferred compensation, the deduction provisions of Section 404(a), not the deduction provisions of Section 162, apply.

The plan permitted voluntary severance of an employee, and the definition of severance did not exclude retirement from the events triggering the benefit.

GENERAL SIGNAL CORPORATION V. COMMISSIONER, 103 TC #14 (1994)

Tax Court of the United States in 1994 stated: A corporation set up an individual VEBA to provide welfare benefits for its employees. The VEBA applied only to the employees of General Signal Corporation, its 40 domestic subsidiaries and 49 foreign subsidiaries, involving many thousands of employees. The amounts contributed were used primarily to satisfy benefit claims in the year following the year of contribution. Postretirement benefits were also provided, but there was no reserve established for the purpose of paying such benefits.

The corporation *had to meet the limitations and restrictions of Section 419 because it was not a multi-employer VEBA* exempted from these provisions by Section 419A(f)(6). For example, the "account limit" on a "qualified asset account" for a taxable year is the amount reasonably and actuarially necessary to fund claims incurred but unpaid for such benefits, as well as administrative costs.

Because this case does not involve multi-employer VEBAs under the 10-or-more employer rule, the holdings of this case are not applicable to plans that qualify for exemption under Section 419A(f)(6).

PRIME FINANCIAL CASES

Tax Court of the United States in 1998: *Decision just decided!*

There were nine cases being litigated in the Tax Court in Phoenix, Arizona. These were all plans sponsored by the Prime Financial group.

These were taxable trusts, which did not have a tax exemption letter from the IRS under 501(c)(9) and were not multi-employer VEBAs under 419A(f)(6). There are many complicated issues in these cases, some of which are not applicable to multi-employer VEBAs, which are tax exempt.

The basis of the IRS disallowance of the deduction was as follows:

- The plan was not a welfare plan but was one that provided deferred compensation.
- The plan was alleged to be experience rated.
- The plan was not a single plan.
- The plan contained no substantial risk of forfeiture.
- P.S. 58 costs must be included in the annual income of the participants.

As was hoped, Judge Larro's decision provided long-overdue guidance with respect to Section 419(a)(f)(6), welfare benefit plans. The bottom line in this landmark decision is that VEBAs are viable employee benefit plans with favorable tax treatments. The decision stated:

- Prime Trust is a welfare benefit plan, not a plan of deferred compensation.
- The taxpayers had substantial authority for the tax deductions taken. Therefore, no penalties were levied.
- However, the Prime Trust was found to be an aggregation of individual plans because the assets for each employer were segregated. Segregated assets were found to be an experience-rated arrangement.

The bottom line to this decision is that we now have a very clear definition of what works in a welfare benefit plan. The Prime Trust plan was not viable in its current form, and it is debatable whether any simple 419(a)(f)(6) plan is. This decision says that the plan must meet the multi-employer requirements by having 10 or more employers. If the assets are contributed to a single pool, the valuation of the plan is done as a whole (i.e., files one 5500 tax form) and not as separate employee groups. This is if the plan pools all claims within the trust.

This decision stated that the Prime Trust plan was distinguishable from Wellons. It says that the Prime Trust plan provided real employee benefits and that severance benefits were not "payable upon a certainty but more closely resembled insurance payable only in a case of an uncertainty." The decision also stated that an employer had the right to voluntarily terminate its participation, *that this was an acceptable provision of a welfare benefit plan.* The decision more fully defined the term "experience rating" and provided insight into how the Tax Court views the intent of Congress in having written the statute. "The essence of experience rating is the charging back of employee claims to the employer's account."

The acceptability of the provision making this a welfare benefit plan has been our position all along, and it is very clear that welfare benefit plans that allow segregation of employer assets must have their trust structure revised and their legal opinions updated. It may not be possible to make such sweeping changes in most plans. Plans not conforming to the descriptions provided by Judge Larro's decision will be subject to losing deductions and incurring penalties for their participants if the contributions are accepted after this decision is published. Most welfare benefit plans are not in compliance. However, VEBAs that we use meet the requirements of a bona fide welfare benefit plan, as written in Larro's opinion and, of course, already have letters of determination. I believe that properly structured VEBA plans will be more readily embraced by tax advisers and small business owners now that the cloak of doubt has been substantially removed.

In our opinion, the IRS position in the Prime Trust case with regard to this issue is incorrect. An analysis of the government's memorandum of issues in the Prime Trust case, as well as Notice 95-34 (the only IRS pronouncement on 419(a)(f)(6), plans for date), shows that the IRS's reasoning was completely in error regarding their reliance on Wellons. The IRS's unsupported contention was that, "If a plan has features of both the welfare benefit plan and a deferred-compensation plan, the entire plan is treated as deferred compensation." This position also was set forth in Notice 95-34 and is clearly erroneous now that the Tax Court has rejected the IRS argument. It is the position of the Tax Court that a plan can be a welfare benefit fund if it intends to provide employees with real welfare benefits. Those payable upon an event occurrence that is uncertain are truly welfare benefits. As such, the welfare benefit fund should resemble insurance payable only in a case of such an uncertainty. Clearly, the provision of a preretirement death benefit funded by life insurance, as is the case of an employer's adoption of a well-constructed VEBA, is the truest form of an uncertain event.

The Tax Court stated that the commissioner was misreading Wellons by attempting to characterize any plan that has features or elements of both deferred-compensation plans and welfare benefit plans as a plan of deferred compensation. The Tax Court goes to some length in criticizing this position by the IRS as an abuse of taxpayer rights to avail itself of the tax attributes of a welfare benefit plan. Our opinion on VEBA plans echo these arguments and limit the reading of Wellons to cases where the plan at issue is "more akin to deferred-compensation plans than the sort of welfare benefits arrangement contemplated by the regulations (108 TC 25). Obviously, the Tax Court agrees with our position that in order for the plan to be deferred compensation under Wellons, it must have provisions that are more akin to those of a pension, profit-sharing, stock, or bonus plan or other similar arrangement. Although we believe that Prime Trust's dismissal of wage benefits met many of the criteria for deferred-compensation treatment, the Tax Court's decision to hold that the plan was a welfare benefit plan is very clearly a good result for VEBAs because of the fact that most VEBAs provide nothing more than preretirement death benefits. There are several aspects of the decision, however, that are even more favorable for VEBAs and clearly support the conclusion that we have gone by all along. For example, one concern has been the ability of an employer group to terminate participation in the plan and thereby cause the excess assets to be paid to the employees of that group. It has always been our position that an employer's right to terminate is clearly supported by the Code. The Tax Court decision clearly states that there is "no requirement in the applicable statutory and regulatory provisions that will limit welfare benefits to cases in which an employer could *not* voluntarily terminate its participation in the plan."

In fact, the court refused the IRS request to put such a requirement into the legislation. The Tax Court did so in a manner that should prevent the Treasury from enacting future regulations, stating that the legislation does not call for such limitation.

This result is reached as a part of a rejection of the IRS's contention that an employer could thereby control the timing of distribution of income to employees. The Tax Court rejects this concern as being misplaced. In short, this is an endorsement of a well- constructed VEBA-termination provision that requires determining authority to be an independent trustee without making the VEBA a deferred-compensation plan. However, they allow the decision to be with the company that has put the VEBA in place. Furthermore, a well-constructed VEBA's distribution of life insurance policies only upon an event of termination complies with the prior general counsel memorandum regarding a VEBA, in which the Office of the Treasury General Counsel held that distribution of policies is not a deferred-compensation arrangement (General Counsel Memorandum 39818—May 10, 1990).

In reviewing the Tax Court's analysis of the multi-employer exception in 419(a)(f)(6), it is clear that these provisions of a well-constructed VEBA are in compliance with the spirit and the letter of the Tax Code and the legislative history that accompanies the enactment of the Code. The Tax Court stated that Congress enacted 419 and 419(a) with the understanding that the principal purpose was to prevent employers from taking premature deductions for expenses that have not yet been incurred by the establishment of an intermediary organization, which holds the assets in order to provide benefits to the employees of the employer (108 TC 25).

Clearly, Congress was concerned that there was no standard available up to that point regarding VEBAs and welfare benefit funds to preclude their use in providing substantial, nonqualified deferred-compensation funding. Congress took exception to the segregation of funds and assets by employer groups in a plan that claimed to be a multi-employer arrangement. The true test of whether a plan is a multi-employer plan is whether there is a true shifting of risk between and among employer groups and whether all assets of the entire pool are available to pay all claims for the benefits within the plan.

CONCLUSION

The basis for Prime Trust's loss in Tax Court only reinforces our belief that a well-constructed VEBA should be successful if challenged by the IRS. The Prime Trust plan failed several crucial tests which are satisfied in well-constructed VEBAs. The Prime Trust plan provided for the following seven damaging factors in the Tax Court's opinion:

1. Prime Trust was required to maintain separate accounts and a separate accounting for each employer group (the employees of a single employer).
2. The trust agreement limited an employee's right to benefits under the plan to the assets of his or her employer group.
3. An annual evaluation was performed for each employee group's account, but such evaluation was never performed for the trust as a whole.
4. The summary plan description was prepared separately for each employer group.
5. Each employer's contribution benefited primarily its employees and not the employees of the other employers because nothing other than a suspense account of forfeited items and experience gains was ever available to supplement shortfalls of any employer group in the payment of benefit claims.
6. The trust agreement provided rules under which an employee's benefits would be reduced in the event of a shortfall in his or her employer group's account without any subsidiary from the trust as a whole (only the suspense account).
7. The Prime Trust plan did not pool all the claim risks within the trust, which caused there to be a lack of risk shifting in the plan.

In short, the Tax Court found that the assets of all participating employer groups were separate from one another with no true shifting of risk and no sharing of gains and losses within a multi-employer pool. In the opinion of the Tax Court, this situation caused the trust to be "an aggregation of single entity plans rather than a true multiple employer plan." As the legislative history states, there must be a shifting of risk, and the assets must be held by the trust so that the relationship of each employer group is essentially the same as the relationship of an insured to an insurer. Without this shifting and sharing of risk and without the availability of all assets of the trust to pay all the claims for benefits, the employer relationship to the group is really that of an employer to its own fund rather than that of an insured to an insurer.

Under Section 419(a)(f)(6), the exception for 10-or-more employer plans does not apply to any plan that maintains experience-rating arrangements with respect to individual employers. According to the Tax Court, Prime Trust's plan had mechanisms for adjusting the employee benefits to equal its employer's contributions without access to the assets of any other employer group (or even a suspense account). This caused there to be an experience-rating arrangement that was maintained between every employer group and the trust on an independent basis. This represented the ability to achieve "an experience rating which is the charging back of employee claims to the employer's account." In sum, the Prime Trust plan filed separate 5500 forms for each employer group, rather than one for the trust as a whole. The provisions of a well-constructed VEBA plan preclude this from happening because there is a true risk sharing and an availability of all assets to pay all claims for benefits. In addition, all items of gain or loss are pooled between and among the employer groups on a proportional basis. The account values represent those of the employer's allocable share of the trust overall investment gains, losses, and experience gains and losses. All reporting of account values to the employer groups is in accordance with this allocation, and a single form 5500 is filed for the plan as a whole.

In light of the Prime Trust decision, as well as other decisions that have come out of Tax Court, it is our opinion that a well-constructed VEBA plan meets all the requirements of Section 419(a)(f)(6)—a multi-employer plan.

The bottom line to this decision is that we now have a very clear definition of what works in a welfare benefit plan. The Prime Trust plan was not due-able in its current form, and it is debatable whether any simple 419(a)(f)(6) plan is (although a VEBA is). This decision says that the plan must meet the multi-employer requirements by having 10 or more employers. If the assets are contributed to a single pool, the valuation of the plan is done as a whole (i.e., files one 5500 tax form) and not separate employee groups, and if the plan pools all claims within the trust.

It has been our position all along and it is very clear that welfare benefit plans that allow segregation of employer assets must have their trust structure revised and their legal opinions updated. It may not be possible to make such sweeping changes in most plans. Plans not conforming to the descriptions provided by Judge Larro's decision will be subject to deny deductions and penalties for their participants if the contributions are accepted after this decision is published. Most welfare benefit plans are not in compliance.

However, VEBAs that we use meet the requirements of a bona fide welfare benefit plan, as written in Larro's opinion, and, of course, already have letters of determination. I believe that properly structured VEBA plans will be more readily embraced by tax advisers and small business owners now that the cloak of doubt has been substantially removed.

Appendix E
Other VEBA Rulings

PRIVATE LETTER RULING—9115035—1991

Corporation created a tax-exempt VEBA in 1985. In 1986, corporation decided to stop funding the VEBA directly and to pay claim reimbursements and administrative fees directly to the administrator. No reserve fund was set up.

In 1989, corporation formed a new tax-exempt trust and terminated the prior VEBA. Corporation proposed to transfer prior VEBA's cash to the new trust, to provide Section 501(c)(9) benefits to participants, and to pay administrative fees. Participants of the VEBA are participants under the trust. Any termination surplus of the trust may be used only to provide benefits to participants or their dependents.

IRS ruled that transfer of VEBA's assets to the trust did not adversely affect trust's exempt status under Section 501(c)(9) or the exempt status of the VEBA. No prohibited inurement has occurred; no impermissible benefits will be provided. Transfer will not result in realization or recognition of gross income to the corporation. Finally, a trustee-to-trustee transfer will not subject the corporation to the 100 percent excise tax under Section 4976.

PRIVATE LETTER RULING—9401033—1994

Corporation entered a collectively bargained agreement to provide SUB (supplemental unemployment benefits) to its employees in 1973. Trust was created and was ruled exempt by IRS under Section 501(c)(17).

In 1989, corporation amended the agreement to provide other benefits. IRS ruled that the trust was an exempt VEBA but would not rule that the trust's proposed benefit was a permitted severance benefit for purposes of Section 501(c)(9).

In 1992, corporation decided that VEBA would no longer be funded, VEBA would terminate, and all assets would be distributed to all participating employees in proportion to their respective account balances on the termination date.

IRS ruled that account limits prescribed in Section 419(c) do not apply to the VEBA. Because the VEBA is a Section 501(c)(17) exempt trust, it is also a find under Section 419(e)(3)(A). Therefore, it is a welfare benefit find under Section 419(e)(1) because the fund provides SUB to its employees. All funds contributed for this purpose constitute a qualified asset account. In addition, set-aside limitations of Section 512(a)(3)(E)(I) do not apply to the fund. Further, the distribution will not constitute inurement under Section 501(c)(9). *Finally, the fund will not provide any disqualified benefit resulting from pro rata distribution because the corporation will not participate or receive any portion of the fund's assets.*

PRIVATE LETTER RULING—9406008—1994

The IRS ruled that the transfer of group term life insurance policies and amounts held in the retirement funding accounts for the benefit of retired employees did not result in taxable transactions.

IRS held that such a transfer does not result in the recognition of gross income or gain to participants or their beneficiaries, the corporation would not realize gross income or gain, and the transfer would not be considered a reversion subject to the 100 percent excise tax under Section 4976. This is *because the transfer does not give participants access to any portion of the assets transferred, nor do they have control over the assets.*

Additionally, participants have no active participation in the execution of the transfers, and no parts of the transferred assets are to be paid directly or constructively to them. Rather, the contracts are earmarked solely to provide group term life insurance benefits to the participants.

This ruling applies to term insurance. However, under General Counsel Memorandum (G.C.M.) 39440, whole-life policies are treated similar to term insurance, provided they meet the requirements set forth in that G.C.M.

PRIVATE LETTER RULING—9414011—1994

VEBA proposed to transfer all its assets to another VEBA. The surviving VEBA would hold all assets of the prior VEBA to be used to provide possible benefits under Section 501(c)(0) to eligible employees of the employer. The surviving VEBA's trust agreement permits the employer to terminate the VEBA, provided that any trust funds remaining after payment of all claims be applied to provide various insurance benefits to employees.

IRS ruled that *transfer of assets from one VEBA to another VEBA will not cause either VEBA to cease to be recognized as exempt under Section 501(c)(9)* and will not result in the realization or recognition of gross income to the employer. IRS further ruled that the employer is not liable for excise tax under Section 4976 as a result of the transfer.

PRIVATE LETTER RULING—9438017—1994

Several funds are exempt as VEBAs under Section 501(c)(9) and provide health benefits to employees. In order to streamline and improve the administration of benefits, to reduce administrative costs, and to have a uniform benefit policy for all employees, the funds will be merged into a master fund that is also an exempt VEBA.

IRS ruled that *the merger of funds would not adversely affect the Section 501(c)(9) tax-exempt status* of the merging funds or the master funds. Also, the transfer of assets to the master fund would not be subject to excise tax under Section 4976.

PRIVATE LETTER RULING—9446036—1994

An exempt business league created a VEBA for its employees. Purpose of the VEBA was to provide employees of the members of the league with medical, dental, sickness, disability, and life insurance benefits.

VEBA was inactive from 1989 to 1994, but it plans to reactivate by using up its remaining assets to provide benefits to the current employees. The assets will be used to purchase insurance policies that will provide accidental and disability benefits as well as long-term care benefits. When the assets are exhausted, the VEBA will terminate.

IRS ruled that the benefits of the VEBA are permissible benefits under Section 501(c)(9). *The proposed use of the VEBA assets will not adversely affect its exempt status.* The transaction will not result in the realization of gross income to the league or its members. IRS further ruled that the league members would not be liable for excise tax under Section 4976.

PRIVATE LETTER RULING—9505019—1995

A VEBA qualified as tax-exempt under Section 501(c)(9) plans to create two new VEBAs, one for union employees and another for nonunion members. Existing VEBA will provide the initial funding for both new VEBAs by transferring assets to them. The two new VEBAs will assume all the existing VEBA's liabilities.

After the transfer and assumption, the existing VEBA will terminate. Benefits that the existing VEBA currently provided to a group of employees will continue to be provided by the new VEBAs.

IRS ruled that *the transfer of assets to the two new VEBAs would not adversely affect the exempt status of any of the VEBAs.* The transfer will not result in any taxable income to the existing VEBA or the two new ones. The transfer and assumption of liabilities will not result in any taxable income to the employer and will not subject the employer to excise tax under Section 4976.

GENERAL COUNSEL MEMORANDUM—39052—1983

The transfer of assets from one VEBA to another VEBA is permissible, without jeopardizing the exempt status of either VEBA, so long as otherwise applicable provisions relating to each of the VEBAs have been satisfied.

The transfer of assets by one Section 501(c)(9) trust to another will not result in inurement of net earnings to the benefit of any private shareholder or individual in this case. No trust assets would revert to any of the participating employers. The benefits will not result in prohibited inurement when such payments are pursuant to objective and nondiscriminatory standards, under Regulations Section 1.501(c)(9)-4(b).

IRS ruled that *the transfer of funds would not affect the exempt status under Section 501(c)(9) of either VEBA.* IRS provided the following four guidelines, which, if met, will prevent prohibited inurement from occurring:

1. Both trusts are exempt under Section 501(c)(9).
2. The transferred assets will be used to provide permissible benefits.
3. The participants of each trust share an employment-related bond.
4. The transfer is not used to avoid the applicable requirements of Section 501(c)(9) and the regulations thereunder that otherwise would apply to each VEBA.

GENERAL COUNSEL MEMORANDUM—39440—1985

Generally, only term life insurance under Section 79 is permitted in a VEBA, qualifying as a "life" benefit. The IRS ruled that *employer-funded whole-life policies not subject to Section 79 could be used to fund benefits of VEBAs if the whole-life benefits meet three guidelines:*

1. The policies must be owned by the VEBA.
2. The policies are purchased through level premiums over the expected lives or working lives of the individual member.
3. The accumulated cash reserves accrue to the VEBA.

IRS ruled that so long as the policies meet these guidelines, the use of such policies to fund VEBA benefits is not necessarily inconsistent with the regulations under Section 501(c)(9) and need not preclude qualification under Section 501(c)(9).

But a VEBA will not qualify if the employer or the employer's committee (as opposed to the members of the organization) designate the beneficiaries. A VEBA will qualify if the life benefits provided are offset by the pre-retirement death benefit described in this case.

GENERAL COUNSEL MEMORANDUM—39774—1988

The transfer of the excess assets of a VEBA attributable to employer contributions to another VEBA for the continued provision of employee medical benefits does not constitute a reversion to the benefit of the employer under Section 4976(b)(1)(C).

Because the assets are to be transferred directly from a first VEBA to a second VEBA, there is no other reason to view the transfer as a reversion for purposes of Section 4976. The 1984 Act (DEFRA) explains in the Bluebook: "If an amount is paid by a fund to another fund for the purpose of providing welfare benefits to employees of the employer, then the payment is not to be considered a reversion."

GENERAL COUNSEL MEMORANDUM—39818—1990

VEBA benefits *did not favor owner-employees of small, closely held companies where benefits were determined on the basis of a percentage of compensation and the plan occasionally imposed a length of service restriction.* However, the IRS cautioned that a VEBA that does not provide for the common welfare of all employees may be disqualified from tax-favored status and forced to distribute its assets on a taxable basis. Here, the trust violated the inurement proscription of Section 501(c)(9) because a dominant share of aggregate benefits is allocated to the owner-employee *who maintains effective control over the trust.* Therefore, the trust does not qualify for exemption as a VEBA under Section 501(c)(9).

Each of the seven organizations is a professional service corporation, employing a small number of employees (two to seven). Each provides a dominant share of aggregate benefits to a single highly compensated owner-employee. *A uniform percentage of compensation is a permissible restriction* on eligibility for such benefits even if applied to a small membership group composed of employees receiving widely disparate levels of compensation.

A length of service requirement may constitute a permissible restriction on eligibility for severance benefits if it does not have the effect of allowing disproportionate benefits to be provided to members of the prohibited group.

Appendix F

166 Frequently Asked Questions and Answers

1. *If dividends are received on part of my portfolio—either the investment part or the trading part—on what section of the tax return would I declare the dividends?*

You will always put dividends on Schedule B because dividends are not trading income. The proper way to report all of your trading profits, the income part, is on Schedule D. The expenses go on Schedule C.

2. *How do I get around the fact that after the third year the IRS wants to see a profit in the business?*

There is nothing in the law that says that if your business runs a loss for more than two years, it is no longer considered a business. The primary purpose of most (if not all) businesses is to generate profits. When a "business activity" continuously shows losses, the IRS may not view it as a business at all but rather as a hobby. They have established the "hobby-loss" rule whereby they take the position that if you don't have a profit in the business after three years, you are presumed to have a hobby and not a business, thus disallowing the loss deductions. This "rule" is actually merely a presumption on the part of the IRS—there's nothing written in stone. However, it shifts the burden to the taxpayer to prove that the activity actually is a business and not a hobby. Chances are that if you don't put a note down on your return as to what you're doing, they will call you in and ask you for an explanation. There have been circumstances—not even trading circumstances—in which people have run losses for three, five, and even ten years before showing a profit; and I've been called down to justify the legitimacy of the business enterprise, and I've done it! Basically, you have to demonstrate that this is a business. In a trading business, you must reference the fact that only your losses are reported on Schedule C and that the income is being reported on Schedule D.

3. *Does that mean that Schedule C will always show that there's going to be a loss?*

Yes, unless you are a floor trader.

4. *Because of this loss every year on Schedule C, I will never have to report self-employment tax, right?*

So long as this income is still capital income, you will not have to pay self-employment tax on it; however, you will also not be allowed to take a pension deduction against it. Now, there are certain circumstances in which this will not be the case. There are ways that you can set this up so that you can have it both ways; for example, through utilizing a subchapter S corporation to conduct your business, you will be permitted to set up a pension plan; and because your personal income from the corporation is in the form of "salary income," you will be subject to self-employment tax. Keep in mind that this is not a hard-and-fast rule—there are exceptions. You will need to consult with your tax professional to see if this applies to your particular circumstances. Now, if you're a member of a nationally recognized commodity exchange, you still report the income on Schedule D, but you are required to take self-employment tax against that income. Anyone who's a member of a nationally recognized commodity exchange must pay self-employment tax even though that income is capital. This is true even if you elect Section 475 (marked-to-market). (Note: The Blue Book Committee has determined that the income generated from a Section 475 election, although ordinary, should not be treated as self-employment income just by virtue of the fact that it is ordinary due to a 475 election.)

5. *On Schedule C, can I merge two variant small businesses that I run?*

The accurate answer to that is no. You must keep every business that you have separate. The IRS is very insistent on segregation of assets, segregation of income, segregation of funds, segregation of bank accounts, and so on. They don't like to see everything merged together because it makes it very hard for them to figure out what is a real expense and what isn't. So the law requires that you must separate various business interests on your tax return; for example, if you're a trader as well as a weekend car mechanic, as well as a consultant in something else, you should [must] file three Schedule Cs. If the businesses are somewhat related, however, you may have more room for combining them. (Note: In actuality, many people do combine them, and I have not seen any dire consequences as a result of this.)

6. *What are the advantages and disadvantages of operating as a subchapter S corporation?*

I could devote an entire book to that question alone, but let me see if I can summarize quickly. Some of the advantages are: (1) as a subchapter S, you are sheltered from a lot of personal liability because you are in fact a corporation; (2) the corporation is only limited in liability to the extent of the corporation's assets; (3) the corporation can set up a pension plan through the subchapter S; (4) the subchapter S allows all income and expenses to flow through to the individuals that own it for reporting on the personal tax returns of the owners. The major disadvantage is that the *advantages* only apply so long as the corporation is conducted as a corporation. If the IRS, creditors, or others can demonstrate that the corporate entity is a sham and are able to "pierce the corporate veil," then the individuals who own the corporation may be held liable for the debts, liabilities, and actions of the corporation. Thus, it is very important that even a subchapter S corporation be conducted in a corporate manner—the owners should receive "salaries" with deductions, not just draws; there must be shareholder meetings; major decisions must be made by written resolutions; and the corporate book *must* be maintained.

Generally, a subchapter S is a hybrid between a regular corporation (subchapter C), which is taxed as an entity unto itself, and an individual who is taxed personally. The sub-S does not pay any tax, but there are things that you can do in the sub-S that you can't do as an individual, such as set up a retirement plan against trading income. There are other provisions such as a VEBA that you can more easily conduct through the sub-S.

7. *What does TCMP mean?*

Travel to Canada or Mexico Promptly! No, seriously, TCMP stands for Taxpayer Compliance Measurement Program—a type of audit. The IRS called you down and looked at everything on your tax return. They even looked at the birth certificates of your children. It was a real pain. Congress stopped them from doing this a few years ago.

8. *Is there really a "taxpayer bill of rights"?*

Yes. The taxpayer bill of rights is found in IRS Publication No. 5. You can request it by writing to the IRS or by calling their taxpayer assistance phone number. They did not produce this document because they wanted to. In 1989 Congress passed a law that essentially said, "You must provide taxpayers with a bill of rights." And so, begrudgingly, the IRS issued this document.

9. *How long should we maintain personal tax returns and backup information on those returns?*

Tax returns should be kept forever. Documentation of deductions should be retained for at least three years after the return is filed because the IRS can go back three years to audit deductions. If you omit income on your return, you can be taxed on it up to six years after the return has been filed so it would be prudent to retain income documentation at least that long. Keep in mind, however, that if they suspect fraud—underreporting of income by 25 percent or more—the IRS can go back to the beginning of time!

10. *If I'm making money through a business, be it trading or anything else, throughout the year on which the IRS is not withholding tax, am I required to pay quarterly estimates?*

Generally yes. There are, however, certain circumstances in which you can avoid being penalized for not paying quarterly estimates. Basically, if you cover at least 90 percent of this year's tax liability or 100 percent of last year's liability through either estimates or withholding tax, you can avoid the penalty. This year, though, there's another provision whereby if you're earning $75,000 or more in income and that is $40,000 more than last year's income, those exceptions will not get you out of the penalty. Check in Chapter 4 on the new tax law changes in this book.

11. *If somebody employs your services, how would you handle an audit which is in a city distant from those cities in which you maintain offices?*

The first thing I would do is to request that the audit be transferred to a service center near me. This is a very good strategy because many times during the transfer the file will fall through the cracks; and when it doesn't fall through the cracks, it is put at the bottom of the pile at the new service center. In either event, it gives us more time in which to prepare for the audit. The IRS is *obliged* to transfer audits to a service center with which I can deal as a practitioner. The transfer is one of my rights—one of your rights. Additionally, a lot of times I have seen it happen that a file would fall through the cracks for such a long period of time that the statute of limitations for the tax year would run out, thus precluding the IRS from proceeding. So having your audit shifted between service centers is actually a very good strategy. But that's how I handle it for out-of-town clients. Many times, however, we can handle matters with the IRS by phone and mail. And if I have to, I can go to your IRS district. I have clients all over the country and travel quite a bit.

12. *If I meet the qualifications of a trader but I have another job, would I still file Schedule C as a trader?*

Yes. If you recall in Chapter 2 I listed seven criteria that the IRS uses to determine if you are a trader. Nowhere in those seven criteria did I say that trading has to be the only thing you do, because the courts haven't said that. It helps if you earn your living through trading and nothing else, in which case they would be hard pressed to say you're not a trader. I mean, if that's the only thing you're doing, it is harder to disallow it. Obviously, they're looking for you to put time into this activity, so you've got to demonstrate that you devote significant time to trading, watching the market, and maintaining financial records. Keeping a log is one of the ways to do that. I recommend a prudent course of action by assuming that sooner or later everyone's tax return is going to be checked. So what you want to do is to avoid sticking red flags in your returns so that it will be later rather than sooner. If they do look at your returns, how are you going to substantiate what you say on the return? *Logs!* Use the logs in this book.

13. *How about an investor who is also a trader? How does Trader Status affect somebody who has holdings that are longer term but part of his portfolio he trades?*

In that case you are both an investor and a trader. One category does not disallow the other one. They're not mutually exclusive. What you would have to do is to allocate a portion of your expenses to the longer-term holdings and a portion to the trading. There are no fixed rules on how to do that. You can allocate it based on a percentage of total capital; you can allocate it based on hours spent. Perhaps you can come up with a formula that allows you to allocate a portion of your computer expense to investing and a portion to trading; or you can determine the portion of your data that is used by each activity. Any reasonable method of allocation should be acceptable. Again, use those logs!

14. *On the log, should I list both business and personal use of business assets such as computers and automobiles?*

Listing both would be wise. What they want you to do is to come up with a percentage of business use. If you can substantiate that you used the computer 80 percent for business, then how can they refute it? Do they have a log that shows that you didn't use it 80 percent of the time for business? No, but you do have a log. If you put down every use of that computer (car or other asset), be it personal or business, you have documentation as to what percentage of that use is deductible as a business expense.

15. *Is "traders" one of those specific categories that the IRS targets for audits?*

I have not found that to be the case. Rather, it depends on your income level. They recognize that certain types of professions and occupations are more likely to fail audits (thus generating income for the government) and they pull those for examination. "traders," per se, is not one of those.

16. *If the unified credit were to be reduced to, say, $200,000, or if it were eliminated, would a living trust still go by the old rules if the trust were established before the change?*

We believe it will, though we can never be sure. The reason we aren't sure is because the IRS is attempting to take it back. One of the issues that is currently being contested in the courts is the fact that they had decreased the maximum estate-tax rate from 55 percent to 50 percent, so people who died in the first half of 1997 and who filed the estate-tax returns only paid 50 percent as a maximum rate. Now as part of this tax bill, as part of the deficit reduction plan, what they've said is, "Sorry, we said it was going down to 50 percent, but it's not. It was 55 percent all along and we made a mistake." Now people are challenging that position. In the past, the courts have held that a tax that is triggered by a single event like death *cannot* be made retroactive, whereas taxes levied on income you've earned over the course of, say, six months can be retroactively applied by changes in the tax laws. So there are going to be court challenges in the coming months and years. Keep your eyes and ears open and tuned in.

17. *If Congress can just say, "Sorry, no grandfathering," to an old tax law, how can there be any predictability in tax planning?*

Congress passes many laws, but the courts have the final say. What I am saying here is that in the past the courts have held that a tax on a single event, such as a transfer or a death, will not be challenged—cannot be changed as the result of a subsequent change in the tax laws. This is what law has shown us; and until the courts render another decision, that's what it's going to be. On the other hand, that's the courts. Look at the way you can deduct real estate deductions, and look at what happened in 1986. Even though you bought the property years ago with the understanding that you could take unlimited ordinary losses forever, they said, "Sorry. Starting now, even though you made that decision, there's no grandfathering to an old law." That's acceptable. They can do that.

18. *If the unified credit law is going to change, can grandparents each give $675,000 to their grandchildren now?*

No. The $675,000 unified credit is a one-time exemption (a total) for each person. When you use it up, it's gone. The other exemption is the *annual gift-tax exemption,* which is $10,000 per person to any other person. There is also a separate generation-skipping transfer tax that is apart from this of which you are probably thinking. See Chapter 10.

19. *Have you ever had to go to appeals to win a Trader Status case?*

Yes, we have had to go to appeals several times, but have won every time we have gone.

20. *If I mail my tax return using the preprinted address label that the IRS sends inside the form book, does it increase my chances of being pulled for audit?*

Interesting concept. I've heard that before, too, but I have no proof or reason to believe it is true.

21. *How many times can the IRS audit me before it becomes discriminating?*

Well, the IRS basically makes up the rules as far as that goes. If you get away with very little change on your tax return, they shouldn't audit your return for another three years, or at least they shouldn't audit that same section of your return for three years. If you feel you are being wrongly singled out, you can file a complaint. The IRS now has an ombudsman, and you can write to him or her if you feel you are being harassed. If you send the letter and it is found that they have harassed you, they will stop doing so; but technically they can continue to audit you as frequently as they wish unless you complain. So complain! If they pull your return and they haven't found a change and they audit you next year in the same category, write a letter.

22. *Do I have to list all of my trades on my return when I file?*

My experience is that you don't, but be sure you can prove all of your transactions if requested to do so. I had a client once who was a day trader who traded at least 10 times a day, sometimes as often as 20 times daily. When I started to prepare his return, I looked at the year's worth of confirms and I said, "I can't list all these trades on the return. It will take me all year to file this return. I won't be able to do anybody else's." So I summarized them with a tape, and I put the totals on the return. I also attached a little note that said "These are the totals, and enclosed are the statements." And I mailed the return with a box full of statements. They wrote me back and said, "Thank you very much, we're returning the statements. We don't want them." So from then on, whenever I do anything like that, I say, "Statements with client. If you need them, let me know." Make sure though you tie in gross proceeds to the 1099B.

23. *Can I be a trader if I trade in a retirement plan?*

Probably so. The reason I say "probably" is because the IRS hasn't said that you can or you can't. Nowhere, in any case that has been handed down, does it say that the income has to be currently taxable—nowhere. Okay? They will tax that income eventually. You can't write it off as a trader 10 years from now when it's taxable if you have the expenses today. So when else are you going to do it? I would say yes you can be a trader. There may be a problem, though, with the retirement plan—if they see it as a business, they may disallow it as a retirement plan. You can't run a business in a retirement plan.

24. *What is the business code for traders? Is there one?*

There is no business code that says "trader," although there are several categories that you can use. The code we currently use is 523900, but these change frequently. So check with your tax adviser.

25. *If you're classified as a trader can you still utilize long-term capital gains treatment on the investments portion of your portfolio?*

Yes, you can.

26. *With the passage of the Tax Reform Act of 1986 as amended in the 1993 Tax Act, are the meals I eat while attending investment seminars deductible?*

If you're an investor, there is no investment expense deductibility—not for the seminar, not for your hotel, not for your travel, not for your meals—none. If you're a trader, on the other hand, you can deduct those expenses subject to whatever restrictions there are.

27. *The investment-interest expense deduction or margin interest was limited to the amount of investment income for all investors. This means that if an investor has no investment income for the year, he or she cannot deduct any margin interest. Is it true that a trader, on the other hand, is entitled to deduct 100 percent of this interest, regardless of the profit or loss for the year?*

Yes.

28. *I own 1,000 shares of stock in a public company, which I purchased at $39 per share last November. With the stock at $50 per share, can I now call the broker who holds the stock, sell the 1,000 shares, and still not pay any capital gains tax on the sale this year?*

No. Shorting against the box was essentially eliminated in the 1997 Tax Act.

29. *Is it true that one of the most favorable provisions of the Taxpayers' Relief Act of 1997 was that the government lowered the maximum tax rate on certain types of long-term capital gains from 28 percent to 20 percent?*

If you hold the position for 12 months or more, the rate is 20 percent. Keep in mind, however, that the maximum rate on capital gains for positions held under a year is still 39.6 percent.

30. *Is it true that another favorable provision of the 1997 Taxpayers' Relief Act was that I can now exclude $500,000 of capital gain on the sale of my personal residence from tax, assuming I have reached 55 years of age by the time the house is sold?*

You don't have to be 55 years of age. The law used to be that if you were 55 years or older, you got a one-time, $125,000, tax-free exclusion. You could also roll your gain over into your new residence. Those two provisions have been eliminated. In their place, Congress has created the $500,000 capital gains exclusion on the sale of a *primary* residence. It can be used every two years, and it is a very good opportunity for people to take advantage of this now and to get rid of gains that are built into their residences and to put the profits into growth assets.

31. *Is there a new educational IRA that allows me to contribute up to $1,000 per year and withdraw it totally tax free, presuming I am 59½ and use it for my child's college?*

Yes, there is, but you don't have to be 59½.

32. *Did they also substantially increase the income limit to fund a regular IRA from $50,000 to $80,000 for those with other pension plans?*

That's exactly what they did. The $80,000 will be phased in over a number of years. Under prior law, you couldn't deduct an IRA if either you or your wife had a separate pension plan through any employer. An employer-sponsored pension for either one of you precluded the other from funding a tax-deductible IRA. You couldn't deduct the IRA (1) if your income, if you were single, was between $25,000 and $35,000, phased out totally at $35,000; or (2) if your income, if you were married, between $40,000 and $50,000, phased out totally at $50,000. That's the phaseout that I just mentioned that's now going to be raised to $80,000.

33. *Is one of the new "relief provisions" of the 1997 tax act that taxpayers are now relieved of being able to short against the box?*

Yes!

34. *Was the onerous estate-tax rate significantly reduced from the 55 percent maximum rate that was previously in effect?*

Yes, in the future. See the schedule I have detailed in the Preface.

35. *Has the charitable remainder trust, a tool so important to many wealthy tax-wise individuals, now been removed from their arsenal?*

No. The charitable remainder trust (CRT) is still a very useful tool, not just for the very wealthy, but for everybody. In fact, they liberalized some of the provisions, such as gifting appreciated securities to a private foundation when a CRT has been set up for the foundation's benefit.

36. *I understand that traders of OEX options can no longer take 60 percent of their gain as long term unless they hold the position for at least one year. Is that true?*

No. They still can, and there is no minimum holding period.

37. *I purchased a computer on December 31, 1999, for $15,000 and plan to use it to keep track of my trades. Although it has a depreciable life of five years and I've never used it in 1999, can I deduct 100 percent of the cost of this computer on my 1999 tax return and a full deduction against trading income.*

Yes. You don't even have to have paid for the computer. You can charge it and still write it off. This requires, however, that you qualify as a trader for tax year 1999. If you are an investor and not a trader, no part of the expenditure will be either deductible or depreciable either in the current year nor at any time in the future.

38. *Do wash sale rules prohibit me from selling stock at year-end and then repurchasing it within 30 days?*

Only if you have a loss. If you have a gain, you can do it all the time. Also, the wash sale rules will have no consequence if you do not own the stock at year-end or if you repurchase it again within 30 days of year-end. Many people get that confused.

39. *As a trader, can I deduct my son's $25 per week allowance as a business expense if he has helped out with some business-related chores? Can I deduct 100 percent of his weekly allowance on Schedule C?*

Yes.

40. *Is the alternative minimum tax an alternate way of calculating your tax that allows you to deduct alternative items in the calculation of your tax at the* lower *of two rates.*

If you believe that I have a beautiful bridge to sell you in Brooklyn! The IRS doesn't let you take the lower. You have to calculate a second way to pay—and take the higher of the two amounts.

41. *A $5,000 investment I made two years ago in Crap Co. has done nothing but go down in value. The corporate attorney has written to me stating that although my investment is totally worthless, the company is still not filing for bankruptcy, and he urges all shareholders to keep the faith. Can I write off the stock as a loss on this year's tax return?*

Yes, you can. You have reasonable basis to believe that the investment is worthless.

42. *Each spouse has a $10,000 gift exclusion—a total of $20,000 per couple. Does it make any difference which spouse actually gives the money?*

No. If you and your spouse sign a joint tax return, it doesn't matter whose money it is. The money is considered joint because there's a tax-free transfer between spouses.

43. *Do you have to pay FICA (social security or self-employment tax) on trading income?*

Not unless you rent or own a seat on an exchange.

44. *I have income from other businesses, including real estate. Will this disqualify me as a trader?*

Not necessarily. Qualifying as a trader depends on the nature and the extent of your trading activity. You must look at your trading activity independently. If you have expenses that cover all of your businesses and you allocate them all to trading expenses, you may be disqualified for not appearing credible. If, on the other hand, you consider your other businesses and you allocate the expenses appropriately among all of your business ventures, the mere fact that you receive income from businesses other than trading should not disqualify your Trader Status.

45. *Are there better entities to set up, from a tax point of view, if I'm going to trade within them, such as an S corp, a C corp, or an LLC (limited liability company)?*

From a tax point of view, you don't want to set up a C corp if all you do is trade. This is because you may be classified as a "personal holding company," in which case all you have is unearned income and you would be subject to a surtax on your regular tax. (This has been changed somewhat because now you can elect Section 475 and circumvent that caveat.) From a tax standpoint, it would be better to set up as an S corp or as an LLC. LLCs are the newest entities with the widest variations. They are basically a cross between a corporation and a partnership. In fact, in some states, you're allowed to be a one-person LLC. LLCs give you the same legal protection that a corporation does, but they are taxed like a partnership. There's less compliance involved with LLCs than with S corps (see Question 6). S corps were hot a few years ago, but now LLCs are becoming more and more popular.

46. *What do you think of using offshore corporations to conduct trading activities?*

We've set up offshore corporations and accounts where the circumstances required. Let me give you the pros and cons of offshore corporations. It is possible to set up an offshore corporation through which your trading can be conducted. I know of people who have set up a trust that owns corporations, and they insulate themselves with several different layers of entities so that the government can't find them and so that they have all sorts of privacy. The *benefit* is that as long as you leave your money offshore, in certain places around the world where there are favorable tax treaties with the United States, you can avoid U.S. taxation. The *problem,* however, is that when you bring that money into the United States, you are going to be killed with taxes. Now, I do know of people who are setting up corporations offshore; doing business offshore; and having those corporations issue them credit cards to do business in the United States, buy them cars in the United States in which to do business, and buy houses in which to live. There's all sorts of things that are being done. You've got to be very careful, though, because if you start doing that, the government can come in if they find out about it and construe that you are constructively bringing that money in. Then, they will not only tax you very heavily on it, they will penalize you on that as well.

Yes, it is possible to do, especially if you're thinking about leaving the United States at some point, maybe for your retirement, and you want to build up money offshore. But if you're going to trade offshore and try and bring the money back in, you've got to be very careful. I don't recommend offshore corporations for the purpose of avoiding tax. There are too many risks and too many onshore opportunities of which you can take advantage. Offshore corporations might work for asset protection or for compliance reasons, but not for tax avoidance. The government, in many cases, considers the money to have been brought in and requires tax to be paid on it. That is why most offshore schemes require you to hide your ownership. The subject is far too complex for a thorough discussion here, but in most cases I advise against it for tax avoidance.

47. *What if I spend a lot of money this year learning to trade, setting up my business, but I have no trades or very few trades? Can I deduct these expenses as a trader?*

Well, let's look at the factors. The factors are frequency of trades, number of trades, holding period of trades, . . . Are you starting to see a pattern here? Trades, trades, trades. You're going to have a lot of trouble declaring yourself as a trader this year without any trades. So what can you do about it? Well, you can buy stuff and not put it into your business until next year. So, let's say you spend a lot of money buying computers, and trading systems, fixing up an office, and buying furniture. You cannot write these costs off this year because you're not a trader; you're not doing business. But if you start trading next year—you start having a lot of trades and trade frequently—you can bring the stuff into your business in that year and write it off. There are some disadvantages to that. You can't Section 179 material that you bought last year and started using this year. You can depreciate it. So, you lose certain advantages, but not all of them.

48. *Are exchange fees and brokers commissions deductible as ordinary expenses on Schedule C?*

Commissions paid to brokers are part of your gain or loss from trading, and they do not go on Schedule C. Without a Section 475 election, they're a subtraction from your capital gain or an addition to your capital loss; so they're not deductible on Schedule C. If you are talking about the dollar or two dollars per trade that are allocated to the exchanges, then the answer is that these are part of the cost of trading. They are part of your capital gain or loss and thus nondeductible. The exchange fees that you pay as part of your online data feed are deductible as ordinary expenses on your Schedule C.

49. *What sort of entity would I set up as a commodity pool operator?*

I think you have more considerations than just the tax consequences. I think that your foremost consideration will probably be your legal consequences; and you're probably going to insulate yourself in some sort of a structure—a corporation or an LLC—that will protect you legally. The tax consequences of running a pool are very similar to those of a trader. You would have virtually the same benefits from operating the pool from within a corporation or an LLC. As an S corp or a partnership, you would be taxed as an individual because the profits or losses would flow through to the individual partners—though of the two, the S corporation would provide you with more liability protection.

50. *If I ask the IRS for a printout of my IRMF file, will it trigger an audit, or will the IRS send an IRS agent to my house?*

No. A lot of people are now turning on to the fact that they can request an IRMF. You have the right to know what the IRS knows about you (IRMF stands for individual reporting master file—sometime also called an IRP).

51. *What kind of stuff is on the IRMF report?*

That's your master file. You will learn exactly what the IRS knows about you. If the IRS has an audit planned for you next year, it will be on this report.

52. *Can you request this every year?*

You can request it every quarter!

53. *Does the IRS act frivolously in accusing people of fraud?*

The IRS is liable to suits. You have the right to sue the IRS in court for frivolously going in and auditing your return without reasonable cause. So, it can do it, but it is a lot more cautious about doing it now, since you have the right to sue the IRS. It will have to pay for your attorney's fees if you are right.

54. *If I elect Trader Status on my return, is that more likely to trigger an audit?*

If you do it properly, no, it's not likely. In a lot of cases, the IRS won't know what you're doing if you elect Trader Status—in fact, in 90 percent of the cases. Most IRS field agents don't understand Trader Status anyhow!

55. *If I use a computer program like Quicken to enter my checks and to sort them into various expense categories and to write reports on a weekly or monthly basis, do I still need a backup to that?*

You probably should keep your backup, your checks, for the safest way to prove your expenses. If you do not have them, the reports are much better than nothing. A way to make your backup even better is to use the number-six type of documentation that I put down, which is *sworn testimony* (see statement in the logs section of this book). For this, you can take something like a Quicken printout or your logs or your journals, and at the end of the year, bring them to a notary and have them notarized with a statement on them—something that states, unequivocally, that these logs were kept contemporaneously by you for this purpose at this time. Then the IRS cannot come back three years later and say, "You made this stuff up." (A lot of people, the night before the audit, get little diaries from two years ago, sit with 14 different-colored pencils, and invent a log.) If you go in with all your documentation, such as these diaries, notarized and dated at year-end, you'll be in a very good position. There have been court cases for people who have brought in such notarized documentation and had nothing else, and they have gotten through. So, the answer to your question is, it's always better to keep as much as you can. There should be no unclear statements or ambiguities in your logs. They should contain specific dates and times—not approximations.

56. *How do I set up a sworn testimony statement?*

I would put it somewhere on the documentation, somewhere on the log. If you have a book, put it on a page in the book. If you need to, you can always attach it, but make specific reference, if it's a separate sheet of paper, as to what it is that you are swearing to, say, this journal of home/office use. Chits from charge cards are good forms of documentation; they are a good way to substantiate your expenses. The more substantiation you have the better. If you keep it organized and in a safe place and if you know what's there and use it to your best advantage, you will free yourself to a large extent from much of the burden of taxation. Knowing what to deduct and how to deduct it is the best way to cut down on your tax expense.

57. *If I make $100,000 investing and incurred $3,000 in making this money, I've spent $3,000 to make $100,000. The IRS will tax $100,000 and not let me deduct $3,000. They will say, "We are first taking 2 percent of the $100,000 off of the $3,000 before you can deduct it." That gives me only a $1,000 deduction. Is that fair?*

Who ever said life and taxes were fair? No, it's not really fair. Expecting the IRS to treat you fairly because you are a good person is like expecting the lion not to attack you because you are a vegetarian! What happened in the 1986 tax act is that when they simplified things, they introduced a lot of these floors and limitations. They made it simple. You can't deduct many things anymore—TRUE TAX SIMPLIFICATION! What the courts have done over the years is to determine that certain investors trading their own accounts do so at such a high level of activity that they can call themselves businesses. Therefore, any expenses that they had in generating income can be taken as ordinary—it's called Code Section 162 business expenses on Schedule C, which is not subject to the 2 percent limitation. They can deduct it dollar for dollar. What the courts didn't do is define what *level of activity* is. Nowhere in the IRS Code, although it talks in Code Section 162 about business expenses and about deducting them, does it tell you what you have to do to be a business. It does not tell you how much activity is enough activity to be a trader. The courts have not defined this clearly.

58. *In order to receive Trader Status, am I required to conduct the "business" in some entity other than in my own name as an individual?*

No, you are not. There is no requirement that the business be conducted in any particular manner, whether corporation, partnership, or otherwise, in order to receive Trader Status. You can do it as a sole proprietorship under your own name. S corporations and limited partnerships, however, do have certain advantages that I've addressed in the body of this book.

59. *Should I declare Trader Status on a C corp?*

If you conduct your trading business in a C corp and derive most of your income from trading, you may be subject to a personal holding company surtax because most of your income will be from trading or nonactive (i.e., passive) activities. This may not be the case if you elect Section 475. A lot of people don't realize that. The only way to safely obtain Trader Status through a corporate entity is under an S corp or by electing Section 475 in a C corp.

60. *What if the corporation pays the surtax? Can it be deducted as a business expense?*

The company cannot deduct the surtax.

61. *Who qualifies as a trader?*

As I said before, it is not clearly defined in the code. We've looked at all of the cases that have come out of the courts—the Tax Courts—and have tried to glean from this what is necessary for you to qualify as a trader. The primary criteria is the number of trades and the average holding period of whatever it is you're trading. Are you holding something for five minutes, ten minutes, a day, a month, a year? Are you turning them over to make quick profit in the market? That's what a trader does. A trader uses the market swings to make money. He or she buys and sells frequently and quickly. That's what the courts are looking for. How many trades do you have? Do you have five trades a month? Do you have 20 trades a month? Do you have 50 trades a month? Are you *trading?* The term *trading* implies activity. Some court decisions have come down in which Trader Status was disallowed for too *few* trades. You don't necessarily have to be day trading; however, the more trading you do the better. The shorter the holding period, the better. The courts look at your return to see if you have a lot of dividends. If you have a lot of dividends on your return and the stuff that you're holding generates dividends, they're going to say that you're not a trader but an investor. They don't like to see a lot of dividends on a return. Is your intent to derive profit from frequent trading? Also, they look for the presence of Schedule C in your tax return. If you're claiming Trader Status, you should file a business form, Schedule C. In a court case a few years ago, *Purvis v. The Commissioner,* an attorney was disallowed Trader Status because he did not file Schedule C. The court essentially said, "If you don't tell us you're a business, then you're not a business." Finally, they like the existence of an office—a place to do business. If you have a business, where are you doing business? Even a home office is sufficient, provided that you meet the criteria to substantiate a home office.

62. *What if I have a large chunk of interest from treasury bills (T-bills) that I'm using as margin?*

You may have to go in and prove that's what it is. It may trigger some disbelief on their part if they see too much interest. They may say that too big a chunk of your income is from interest. It doesn't necessarily disqualify you, but it might raise some eyebrows. There's nothing set in concrete that will say definitively yes or no.

63. *If I have an S corporation, does it make any difference whether I trade my own account in the corporation or as an individual?*

There are pros and cons for setting up an S corp. Theoretically, it shouldn't make any difference how you do it—whether you trade as a sole proprietorship or an S corp. The requirements for Trader Status are supposedly the same. I will tell you that in my experience it's a lot easier to get by through Trader Status in an S corp, at lower levels of income and expenses. One of the reasons is that they will look at S corps a lot less than they will personal returns with the same level of income. As a corporation, you will be a small fish in a big pond—depending on what your income is. You're less likely to be looked at in a corporation, but there are other reasons for doing it, not just that. If you want to set up a retirement plan and deduct it against your trading income, the only way to do this is in an S corp. You cannot do this on Schedule C. If you're making money, you don't want to pay tax on your income. You want to set up as a deductible retirement plan—a Keogh, a SEP-IRA. The only way to do it right is to do it in a corporation. The way you do it is you draw a salary from the corporation. You turn some of the income back to ordinary income within the corporation so that you can deduct a retirement plan against it within the corporation. With corporations, you have compliance requirements. Keep in mind that different states have different requirements for filings, for minimum taxes. So there is more compliance, and it will be a little more costly to stand up and to comply; but in a lot of cases, it's worth it. You may not be able to trade within a C corp and avoid personal holding company tax unless you elect Section 475. If you set up a C corp, there's something known as a personal holding company that will subject you to an additional surtax on any money you make in that company. If you trade in a C corp, it may be considered a personal holding company.

64. *What is the biggest cost of conducting a trading business? Is it computers, trading systems, seminars, education, books?*

None of the above. It's taxes! That may come as a surprise to some of you, but many, many people are already in the 50 percent bracket in this country, which means that they're giving half of their net profit over to the government. And I ask you, what good is making money if you lose half of it? If that's your biggest expense, your business is basically tax residual because almost half of it goes to the government at a certain level. Using the strategies I've outlined in this book can drastically reduce your tax liability—frequently by as much as half and sometimes more.

65. *Can I deduct the price of an investment seminar as an investment expense?*

Investment seminars are not deductible. Surprised? Not if you're an investor! As a trader. That's right. Up until 1986 an investor can deduct investment seminars as part of the cost to learning how to invest. You can't do that anymore. If you're an investor—okay?—forget about 2 percent limitations—you get zero deduction for a seminar like this. If you're an investor and you don't have a Schedule C as a trader, you cannot deduct this seminar as an investment expense; they're not deductible. Okay? A lot of people don't know that. As a trader, you can deduct 100 percent of this seminar, dollar for dollar; 100 percent of your travel expense of getting here; of your educational materials here—all deductible. Fifty percent of your meals—that was limited in 1990 to fifty percent (it used to be eighty percent). It's now fifty percent.

66. *Are options or futures also considered as 60/40 tax treatment?*

Yes. See questions 67 and 76.

67. *Are options on the SPX considered as Section 1256 assets?*

Yes, they are. Certain types of index options are considered to be commodities also. OEX contracts are considered commodities. Although the OEX is an index, it's considered to be a 60/40 transaction and treated just like commodities, whereas equity options are considered to be equities.

68. *For equities, is the one-year holding period still effective?*

Yes. You must hold an equity for a year or more to get long-term capital gains treatment, to get the 20 percent rate.

69. *Do I automatically get Trader Status as a corporation?*

No. You have to still qualify as a trader regardless of the entity, be it corporate, partnership, or individual. There are certain guidelines but no hard-and-fast rules. One of the things you have to look at as a corporation, especially if you're trading as a C corp, is whether you will be considered to be a personal holding company. I don't want to even get into that here because if you're a C corp and you do nothing but trade, you should realize that most of the income is capital gains income, and you may incur all sorts of surtaxes.

70. *If I use bond holdings as margin for trading, will that work against me in Trader Status?*

No. If you can show that you've only held the position to use it as margin, then it won't work against you. What you should do is to allocate some of that expense to investment expense. Paoli's mistake (see Chapter 3) was that although he had 50 percent or so in long-term income and 50 percent in trading income, he took all of his expenses as trading expenses. The courts didn't like that.

You can be an investor and a trader. Being one doesn't keep you from being the other, but you had better allocate your expenses properly because the courts don't go kindly on people deducting all their expenses as trading expenses if they're also investing.

71. *If I work for salary and trade, is there a certain percentage of income that I must derive from trading in order to have Trader Status?*

No. They've never come out with a certain formula saying, "Well, you've got to earn 50 percent of your income from trading." They've never come out and said suggestively or quantitatively that a certain dollar-value level makes you unequivocally one thing or another. That vagueness is deliberate—a little side view—because if something is stated in the tax law, then everybody would know exactly what his or her rights were. And I feel that a lot of what the government has done—and this is just my opinion—is to make certain things very subjective so that it can come in and audit people, and people can't say unequivocally,

"The Code says this, this, this and this." For example, the Tax Code never states what proper documentation is for anything. But you've heard of "proper documentation," and for audit, you had better have it.

With regard to trading, the government has said that you've got to put substantial time and effort into your trading activities. What is "substantial time and effort"? I don't know. All I can do is look at the court decisions that have come out and evaluate each client's case on an individual basis.

72. *Can slippage be considered an expense for doing business as opposed to capital loss?*

No, it can't, because slippage is part of your gains or losses.

73. *Does owning an exchange seat put me in a better position to be classified as a trader?*

The long and short answer to that is, "Probably," that is, if you use the seat to trade. But keep in mind that if you own a seat on a commodity exchange, you're subject to self-employment tax on that income—on the trading income—just like any broker-dealer would be.

74. *Does CTA status affect my position as a trader?*

I would have to say that the IRS is more interested in what you do, not what your title is. There are a lot of CTAs who don't do anything. The important thing to remember is that to be considered a trader you must *trade!*

75. *What is slippage?*

Let's say you put an order to sell something at the market. The market is trading at a certain price, and you get billed at a lower price. The difference between that certain price and the price at which you get billed is *slippage.*

76. *Is there a difference between the short- and long-term capital gains rate at this point?*

There is. The tax rates for both increase as your tax bracket increases. The short-term rate, which generally applies to positions held less than a year, can be taxed up to a maximum rate of 39.6 percent at the highest tax bracket. Long-term capital gains, which apply to positions held for a year or longer, max out at 20 percent at the highest tax rates. Commodity positions, however, are split between long-term and short-term considerations, with 60 percent of the position being considered short-term and 40 percent being considered long-term.

77. *Is there any advantage to listing myself as a trader if my expenses are not great?*

The greater your expenses, the greater the advantage. That's the answer to that question. If you qualify as a trader, you should file as a trader. There are no *disadvantages* to doing so. It is only by declaring your Trader Status that you will be able to take advantage of writing off your trading expenses. Otherwise you will be subject to a 2 percent limitation, which isn't that much. If you qualify, declare your Trader Status. There are many other advantages as well (see Chapter 2). Also, by declaring Section 475, you can, as a trader, take all your losses as ordinary (not be limited to $3,000).

78. *If you are considered a trader in one year does that do anything to establish a precedent for you in the next?*

The IRS looks at each return on a case-by-case basis. It reserves the right to examine your returns (and status) each year. However this applies to everyone.

79. *Do I have to qualify as a trader to be able to trade my retirement plan?*

No. There are many firms that will allow you to trade a retirement plan—I do it.

80. *Can a Keogh be traded?*

Yes, but only if it is permitted within the terms of the Keogh plan. If your current plan does not permit it, then you can write your own Keogh plan. Have an attorney draft it, and get it approved by the IRS. I have established many such plans for my clients that have been approved by the IRS; and the clients are trading them quite successfully. There's nothing that prohibits you from trading commodities in a retirement plan.

81. *If I'm trading a retirement plan, is it correct that I am not paying taxes on it regardless of how much money I'm making?*

That is correct. Anything that's in a tax-deferred retirement plan is not taxable until you withdraw the money. And if you withdraw the money after age 59½, there's no premature withdrawal penalty. If you withdraw money from a retirement account before age 59½, you will be subject to a 10 percent surtax.

82. *Can you contribute to a Keogh if you have a 401(k) or an IRA from another source?*

Possibly. It depends on your income level. With the Tax Reform Act of 1986, Congress provided that any single person with annual income over $35,000 (or married couple with joint income over $50,000) cannot have a tax-deductible Keogh and an IRA. You can have a *nondeductible* IRA with a Keogh—but if you earn over the income limit, you can't deduct both of them. And the deduction is phased out at income levels above $32,000.

83. *Is there anything in the law that would prevent the government from taxing retirement plans?*

There is nothing in the law that prohibits the government from taxing anything (or for doing most things for that matter!). Even if there were, it doesn't matter because the government can change the law. That's exactly what happened in 1986. Prior to 1986, the government said that if you invest in real estate, you will have this tremendous tax benefit for the rest of your life; you will be able to deduct tax and losses against your other income. Then in 1986 they said, "Forget what we told you. We're changing that law—we're no longer letting you take these losses against other revenue or income." So it doesn't matter what they tell you. If they change the law, they can change what's taxable and what's not.

84. *So you have a strong reason to believe that they will not tax retirement plans?*

I don't know if they will or will not, but I do know that you can get the exemption today, and it's my strategy to defer as much tax as possible. So if they tax a return at some time in the future, let them tax it. Right now you can get a deduction for it.

85. *If a person has a joint commodity account with someone to whom he or she is not married, does the person have the ability to pass a certain percentage of the profits to either one?*

Yes. First, though, the person whose Social Security number is on that account must report the full amount of profits on his or her tax return and then pass out the portion on his or her return to whomever else you want and designate the receiver's Social Security number so the IRS will know where to look for that income. A better and cleaner way to pass on the profits is to set up a partnership and to pass the profits through.

86. *Can I qualify as a trader if I only trade retirement accounts?*

Technically, yes, you would qualify as a trader because that's what you're doing—you're trading the account; you're engaged in the activity of trading the account. Even though the income is not taxable now, it will be taxable at some point in the future, so the expenses associated with it should be deductible. There's one slight problem with that. If you trade a retirement account, the government has the right to come and say that it's no longer a retirement account because retirement accounts are not meant to be traded. So I wouldn't advise it as the only thing you trade.

87. *Does the IRS have the right to say that I can't trade retirement accounts?*

They've never had any court cases against trading retirement accounts. I've been in touch with the specialized financial instruments department of the IRS in Chicago, and they said that it's possible that they can disallow it, although they have never done so. Retirement accounts can in fact be traded; I mean, mechanically you can set up an account and trade it. I've never had any problem with it, but you should be aware that you are taking a risk in doing that.

88. *Can I write off certain losses against other certain gains, say, long-term and short-term?*

Yes. They are all capital transactions. You can offset them. It doesn't matter if they're different—one's real estate and one's trading—as long as they're capital transactions.

89. *As for trading within an IRA, what becomes of my losses and my expenses?*

The losses are not deductible because your income is not taxable. Your expenses can be deducted either as investment expenses or as trading expenses, depending on what you do, subject to the qualification I mentioned before, which is that the IRS may at some time take a long, hard look at that—they haven't at this point, but they may.

90. *But you say I can take my deductions as investment expenses?*

You can take them as an investment expense, absolutely, on Schedule A.

91. *If Hillary Clinton was still trading commodities, how much money would she have made today?*

Enough money to pay off the cumulative national debt. That's what somebody calculated, based on the length of time she traded.

92. *How much of the Social Security account is spent on other projects?*

$65 billion, according to what Alan Greenspan said in Congress in 1997.

93. *How much of my Social Security account is left for my retirement?*

Zero. You have no Social Security account with your name on it—anything else is a hoax! It is a general tax, now used to fund other general projects!

94. *How much did Congress spend on mohair sheep farm subsidies in 1995 under a World War II program?*

$385 million for World War II uniforms.

95. *What does the average audit net for the IRS?*

The 1996 estimate was $5,000 in penalties and tax.

96. *What percentage of tax notices are erroneously sent out with the full knowledge of the IRS?*

In a 1993 audit of the IRS, 48 percent. The General Accounting Office told them that they were sending out almost 50 percent wrong notices. And you know what they did? Nothing. They still sent them out.

97. *By what year does the government want to audit every return at least once under a bill called "Compliance 2000"?*

It was supposed to have been by the year 2000.

98. *How much did your average trader client save by filing as a business instead of as an investor?*

In 1998, the average dollar-for-dollar savings of my trader clients was $4,300 over filing as investors. And some people saved a lot more, so think about Trader Status quite seriously!

99. *As a trader, how much of my trading seminars are deductible?*

One hundred percent. As an investor, it's zero.

100. *What is a VEBA?*

A VEBA is a Voluntary Employees Beneficiary Association, described in Section 501(c) of the 1986 Internal Revenue Code (IRC). A VEBA is an organization that has received a letter of tax exemption from the Internal Revenue Service. Generally, this type of organization guarantees the payment of life, sickness, accident, or other benefits to its members, their dependents, or specifically designated beneficiaries. The VEBA is a nonprofit corporation or a trust, normally having a bank or a trust company as its trustee.

101. *What is the role of the VEBA?*

The role of the VEBA is to provide the means by which employers may provide certain specified "current" (as opposed to "future") welfare benefits to a group of employees, as determined by the employer. The employer makes annual contributions to the VEBA to pay for or to fund the benefits provided, and receives a *full* tax deduction for all current contributions as they are paid to the VEBA.

102. *What is a multi-employer VEBA?*

A multi-employer VEBA is a welfare benefit plan that is part of a 10-or-more employer plan that qualifies under Section 419A(f)(6) of the 1986 IRC.

103. *How is favorable tax treatment of a VEBA provided by the IRC?*

Favorable tax treatment of a VEBA is provided by the IRC as follows: Section 501(c)(9) provides for the tax-exempt earnings power of a VEBA; Section 419A(f)(6) provides the qualifications, operating rules, and tracing rules for a properly designed multi-employer VEBA; and Section 162 allows for the deduction of the annual contribution made by the employer to the VEBA.

104. *Why is a VEBA not subject to the IRS rules for qualified retirement plans?*

A VEBA is not subject to the IRS rules for qualified retirement plans because it does not fit the definition of a retirement plan in that it does not provide "future" benefits.

105. *Why is a VEBA not subject to the rules for nonqualified compensation plans?*

A VEBA is not subject to the rules for nonqualified compensation plans because it is not set up to pay benefits at a specific time in the future and it does not provide benefits only for highly compensated or key employees. A VEBA is a plan that benefits all employees, and the current contributions made by the employer are deductible under IRC Section 162.

106. *Do the rules of the Employee Retirement Income Security Act of 1974 (ERISA) apply to a VEBA?*

Yes.

107. *What businesses should consider adopting a VEBA?*

VEBA adoption should be considered by businesses and individuals who would like to protect their assets from creditors, especially individuals who are in high-risk businesses, such as surgeons, contractors, real estate developers, manufacturers, and traders; companies whose owners have estate-tax problems and wish to minimize estate taxes and state inheritance taxes; companies that no longer make contributions to their qualified retirement plans because the plans have been overfunded; and companies that have pension plans no longer favorable to the business owners, due to the $170,000 cap on compensation.

108. *Is a VEBA available to a partnership or a sole proprietorship?*

Under certain conditions, yes, but generally no. In order for a VEBA to maintain its tax-exempt status, 90 percent of the total number of participants in the VEBA are considered employees for the purposes of this rule, although regulations permit them to be covered by the VEBA as they share an "employment-related bond" with the employees who are covered. The 90 percent rule is based on the total coverage of the VEBA, not on an employer-by-employer basis. A sole proprietorship or a partnership adopting a VEBA must have at least one participant qualifying as a true "employee."

109. *How is the VEBA organized?*

A VEBA is organized as either a trust or as a nonprofit corporation.

110. *What qualifications are required to join a VEBA?*

Participation in a VEBA consists of people allowed to participate by reason of being "employees."

111. *What are the geographic restrictions of a VEBA?*

The IRS in its regulations considers employees of several employers engaged in *the same line of business* and in the *same geographic locale.*

112. *Must all of the members of a VEBA be employees?*

No.

113. *May a VEBA member be a non-employee?*

Yes.

114. *Can VEBA members be retirees or former employees?*

Retirees and other former employees can be members of the VEBA and can be counted as employees for the purpose of the requirement that 90 percent of the total membership must be employees.

115. *Can spouses and dependents be VEBA members?*

Spouses and dependents of active employees cannot be VEBA members, although they can participate in the VEBA's employee benefit plans.

116. *What are the means by which an employer meets the VEBA membership requirement?*

Membership in a VEBA is considered to be voluntary.

117. *Who controls a VEBA?*

A VEBA must be controlled by anyone of the following: its membership; an independent trustee, such as a bank; trustees, at least some of whom are designated by or on behalf of the membership. As a general rule, in order to operate conservatively, an independent bank trustee should be appointed in all cases.

118. *Who may not control a VEBA?*

The employer may not control a VEBA *under any circumstances.*

119. *What benefits can a VEBA provide to its members?*

There are numerous types of plans, but only one type I recommend. The cleanest form is death benefit only, which is virtually all we do.

120. *What constraints apply to the disposition of VEBA assets upon termination?*

The prohibited inurement rule affects how VEBA assets may be dispersed when the VEBA adopted by an individual business is terminated. The same rule applies when the VEBA organization itself terminates.

121. *What is the tax status of a VEBA?*

A tax-qualified VEBA (one that has an IRS exemption letter under IRC Section 501(c)(9)) is exempt from federal income tax.

122. *Is it permissible for a VEBA to discriminate in favor of highly compensated employees?*

No.

123. *What are the nondiscrimination requirements for a VEBA?*

The general rules are that each class of benefits under the plan must be provided under a classification of employees set forth in the plan that does not discriminate in favor of highly compensated individuals.

124. *What is the maximum compensation that may be used as a base for VEBA benefits?*

The maximum compensation is an indexed figure of $170,000 (as of 2002), which presumably will be increased by a factor equivalent to the cost-of-living increase, in the range of 3 percent to 4 percent.

125. *What happens when a VEBA secures an IRS approval letter?*

The income earned by the assets in the VEBA will not be subject to current income tax.

126. *Is it permissible for the contributions to a VEBA to vary from year to year?*

Yes.

127. *What is the latest date for an annual VEBA contribution to be made so that it is tax deductible?*

A VEBA contribution that is made by the last day of the calendar year, or the last day of the employer's fiscal year if other than the calendar year, is deductible in that year.

128. *What are the start-up costs for installing a VEBA?*

Initial annual administration fee and setup vary, but are usually around $1,500; there is also a small maintenance fee, depending on the number of employees.

129. *If participation in a VEBA is terminated, how are benefits taxable to the participants?*

When the participants receive their VEBA benefits from the plan, ordinary income tax is due in the year of receipt.

130. *How are VEBA death benefits funded?*

The death benefit is generally funded by permanent or ordinary life insurance.

131. *What are the income tax consequences to the VEBA participant's beneficiary when the proceeds of the policy are received?*

None, if the VEBA is properly structured and it is fulfilling its primary objective.

132. *What are the estate-tax consequences to a VEBA participant upon death and payment of the proceeds of the policy?*

Insurance is taxable for estate-tax purposes provided that the insured possessed any incidents of ownership or had the right to designate the beneficiary of the policy. The adoption of a proper planning technique should insure that there will be no estate tax payable at the time of his or her death.

133. *How does an irrevocable beneficiary designation prevent any potential gift taxes?*

If the irrevocable beneficiary designation is executed prior to the employer's funding of the VEBA and payment of the initial premium, then there is a taxable gift with a value of zero, and thus no gift tax is payable. The unified exemption should not be invaded as a result of this gift.

134. *How are the funds paid out to the participants if participation in the VEBA is terminated?*

Under the terms of the VEBA, no funds can ever revert to the employer. This means that in the event of termination by the employer, the funds must be distributed to the remaining participants on a pro rata basis. A calculation is made at the time of the termination, attributing all compensation paid to each employee during the entire term of the existence of the VEBA. With normal turnover, the owner group should derive the most significant portion of the fund because that group has been employed the longest and, additionally, has received the largest portion of compensation.

135. *Are the VEBA assets safe against claims of creditors of the employer or the participants?*

Yes.

136. *Is there any reason why an employer cannot maintain both a VEBA and a qualified plan and make deductible contributions to both?*

No. There is no reason why both plans cannot operate in tandem in the same corporation because each accomplishes its own separate purpose.

137. *Why should a business adopt a VEBA Health and Welfare Plan?*

A VEBA is one of the last, best, legal tax shelters available.

138. *Must a company incorporate to have a VEBA?*

No.

139. *What is the Employee Retirement Income Security Act?*

The Employee Retirement Income Security Act of 1974 (ERISA) is a law that protects participants in pension plans and employee welfare benefit plans. ERISA established a set of rules for participation in plans, added mandatory schedules for the vesting of benefits, fixed minimum funding standards, set standards of conduct for plan administration and for handling plan assets, required disclosure of plan information, and enacted a system for payment of pension benefits. It basically killed the qualified plan.

140. *Does the adoption of a VEBA by an employer constitute a contractual obligation to maintain the plan?*

No. Although an employer must have some intention of continuing a plan to prevent it from being considered illusory, continuance of the plan is voluntary.

141. *Must the employer contribute each year once it initiates the VEBA?*

No, there is no such requirement, as long as there is cash value to adequately fund the insurance policy.

142. *Must a VEBA include all employees?*

No.

143. *Can an employer establish more than one VEBA plan?*

Yes, and there may be significant advantages in having more than one VEBA plan.

144. *Is a contribution to a VEBA that is adopted on the last day of the taxable year fully deductible?*

Yes.

145. *How large can the deductible contribution to the VEBA be for any one year?*

Deductions are permitted if they are "ordinary and necessary." Because VEBA benefits also bear some resemblance to compensation, the amount of benefits and the cost thereof must be considered in light of all compensation; the total must be "reasonable."

Generally speaking, there are no limits, so long as income-replacement-type benefits, such as life, disability, and severance benefits, bear a uniform relationship to compensation for all eligible employees.

Basically, the permitted deduction depends on facts and circumstances. It is clear that a contribution comprised of the actual cost of insurance needed by the plan and a reasonable allowance for plan expenses would be deductible.

146. *How much am I obligated to contribute to the VEBA each year?*

You are not obligated to contribute anything. The plan is extremely flexible. After the initial first-year contribution, your business must contribute just enough to keep any insurance policies for death and other benefits in force.

147. *How does the employer's cash position affect its decision to implement a VEBA?*

Because adoption of a VEBA entails a commitment to fund the plan, a company experiencing a weak cash position would not be advised to establish a VEBA.

148. *What happens to the cash value in the life insurance policies upon plan termination?*

The cash value is paid out to current plan participants in the proportion that their total compensation while participating in the plan bears to the total compensation paid to all of the participants in the VEBA at the time of termination.

Obviously, the participating employees who have earned a higher percentage of income would receive a higher percentage of plan assets upon termination.

149. *Can the cash value in the life insurance policies be used for other VEBA benefits?*

Of course. The cash value (aka side fund) functions as the source for all other benefits.

150. *Is a VEBA benefit subject to the same complex rules that govern pension and profit-sharing plans?*

No.

151. *Why is a third-party trustee necessary?*

There is one major reason why a third-party trustee is necessary. A VEBA must not be controlled by its employees.

152. *Can an employer require employees to contribute to the cost of VEBA benefits?*

Yes.

153. *Is the VEBA subject to rules against discrimination?*

Yes. Section 505 contains general nondiscrimination requirements.

154. *Must one include employees from related companies in a VEBA?*

The answer to that question is unclear. As stated previously, the rules applicable to qualified retirement plans do not apply to VEBAs. However, in the summer of 1994, an IRS official admitted publicly that the affiliated-service-group rules probably do not apply to VEBAs.

155. *Can the benefit formulas of a VEBA change from year to year?*

Yes.

156. *Is there any risk of losing favorable tax treatment?*

The tax rules are covered by Code Sections 501(c)(9), 419A(f)(6), and 162. The Congress may change these rules in the future to reduce or remove the plan's favorable treatment. However, in similar situations in the past, the adverse tax changes have often been applied only to future funding of products or plans. If history is any guide, any changes will probably be applied prospectively.

157. *Suppose the VEBA is disqualified. What would happen?*

To answer this question, we will assume that the VEBA benefits would remain unvested until payment. Loss of Section 501(c)(9) qualification will not, in itself, result in certain deductions for VEBA benefits being disallowed currently. However, loss of Section 419A(f)(6) treatment could result in disallowance. The deductions would not be lost entirely. Rather, they would be deferred until employees took the VEBA benefits into income. The VEBA would probably be recharacterized as a nonqualified deferred-compensation plan, and still be subject to ERISA.

158. *Would a VEBA be considered a tax shelter?*

Yes. The term *tax shelter* means a program designed to protect income from taxation. The VEBA does this in two ways: (1) As a "deferral shelter," a VEBA offers an environment for contributions to grow tax free as cash value in an insurance policy. The tax on that growth is deferred until subsequent years. (2) As a "conversion shelter," a VEBA converts deductions from taxable, ordinary income into tax-free life insurance proceeds.

159. *Aside from its value as a tax shelter, how else is a VEBA beneficial?*

For employers, a VEBA offers a number of nontax benefits. A VEBA can serve as the central plan for a variety of health and welfare benefits.

160. *Can an employer operate a plan for his own company rather than join a multi-employer VEBA?*

The law does not prevent employers from having their own single-employer plan. Many large companies have them. Such plans are, however, subject to strict deduction limitations contained in Sections 419 and 419A, which came into the law in 1984. These restrictions make the plans not very advantageous for small businesses. If the plan qualifies as a "10-or-more employer plan" as defined in Section 419(A)(f)(6), the restrictions do not apply. Most small businesses desire the ability to make large tax-deductible contributions during favorable economic trends.

161. *What is a 10-or-more employer plan?*

In 1984, Congress enacted Section 419A(f)(6), which defines a special type of VEBA, called a "10-or-more employer plan" (or "TOME" for short). In order to qualify as a TOME, the plan must satisfy three basic requirements: (1) it must be a single plan; (2) no employer can regularly contribute more than 10 percent of the total annual contribution to the plan made by all participating employers; (3) the plan cannot maintain experience rating with respect to individual employers. Congress said in its Committee Reports that the relationship between an employer and the plan must be more like the relationship between an insured and an insurer than that between a participant and a fund.

162. *Must a 10-or-more employer plan have 10 employers at the inception of its operation?*

No. The statute says that a TOME is a plan to which no employer regularly contributes more than 10 percent of total annual contributions of all employers. This would obviously be satisfied if 10 employers contributed equal amounts to a VEBA during a given year.

163. *Must a welfare benefit plan qualify as a VEBA under Section 501(c)(9) to obtain the benefits of Section 419(f)(6)?*

No. A nonqualified plan can theoretically enjoy the benefits of classification as a TOME.

164. *Why is qualification as a VEBA important?*

There are several important reasons why VEBA qualification is important. Once a plan has been qualified, it will be difficult for the IRS to attack deductions for plan contributions as disguised deferred compensation. This is because the IRS will not give a favorable VEBA ruling if it determines that the plan is similar to a pension, profit-sharing, annuity, or other form of deferred-compensation plan. The ruling letter issued by the IRS is a little bit of insurance. Second, we have over 60 years of law to rely on in the area. VEBAs came into the law in 1928, so we know much about how they are supposed to operate. Third, VEBA qualification provides a justification for prefunding of benefits through large, tax-deductible contributions.

165. *Why must VEBA assets be invested in insurance contracts?*

There are at least three reasons for this: (1) Section 514 of ERISA allows states to regulate multi-employer welfare arrangements as insurance companies unless all benefits are fully insured. If state regulation occurred, the benefits of the VEBA would surely be destroyed. (2) Using annuities or other funding media can create problems with the IRS. Remember that a VEBA cannot contain a profit-sharing, pension, annuity, or other form of deferred compensation. The IRS could look through the trust at the funding media to allege that the nature of the plan is nondeductible deferred compensation. (3) The risk-sharing relationship required under Section 419A(f)(6) would create a massive problem if insurance were not used. It would be very difficult to police the contributions of employers, and demanding certain levels of cash funding might be considered prohibited experience rating. Insurance policies give participating employers assurance that the benefits relating to the employees of other employers have been appropriately funded. This is part of the risk-minimization strategy that attracts employers to the VEBA and assures the ability of the plan to perform as designed.

Modern insurance contracts produce investment results that are comparable with many other types of financial instruments. The VEBA plan has been submitted to the IRS and approved to use modern insurance contracts based on mutual funds.

166. *What about this "stuff" I have heard about new tax legislation making VEBAs illegal?*

First of all, stuff is what my kids throw in their closets! Second, it would be unlikely for Congress to eliminate the VEBA altogether. There are too many unions and other forms of big business that currently use them. Eliminating the VEBA could be political suicide. There may be some reform and changes in what you can and cannot do within the VEBA in the future. We have always used only the most conservative VEBAs available—funding for death benefit only. With these you can still accrue a large future benefit as well as current benefits.

The type of funding may change, but there will always be ways to accomplish the objectives. The point here is to get started today. Almost all legislation has grandfathered the previous law. With the VEBA, we do not know for sure what is to come, but we do know what is available today. Don't hesitate. To wait is to be left behind!

Appendix G

Trader Tax Return Examples and the 475 Election

PREPARING YOUR OWN TAX RETURN IS LIKE PERFORMING OPEN HEART SURGERY ON YOURSELF—BUT IF YOU INSIST. . . .

The Federal Tax Code and supplementary regulations are perhaps the most complex legislative and regulatory boondoggle ever devised by man. In particular, the taxation of traders, investors, and other people who are involved in the financial markets is quite convoluted. The accounting, tax planning, and ultimately the tax return preparation should only be entrusted to a competent tax practitioner with a great deal of experience in these areas. I have stated this before, and I will once again: "Trying to prepare your own tax return and related endeavors in this complex area is akin to someone with a heart attack trying to perform open heart surgery on himself or herself." I do not suggest it.

A change in any one of a number of essential variables is likely to have a profound effect on your bottom line and either be squarely in or out of compliance with the Tax Code. Being out of compliance will have severe consequences on your financial well-being. It will directly impact just how much the government ultimately extracts from your trading profits.

With that being said, I will give some examples. I want to lay out a fact scenario in which we have a trader/investor who is a single man and who had the following set of financial information for 2000.

1. We have a trader who is earning a salary as well as trading.
2. He has a job that pays him $200,000 annually, from which $60,000 in federal taxes have been withheld.

3. He is a participant in an S corporation, which earns him $200,000 as well.
4. He has had an overpayment of $50,000 applied from 1999 to his 2000 tax return. This means that the total withholding to be applied against his tax liability is $110,000.

We will now look at different examples of this taxpayer who is either a trader or an investor, depending on the situation in which he either:

1) Earned $301,519 from
    a) trading or
    b) investing income

   from either
    a) stocks or
    b) commodities or has
2) Generated a $100,000 loss from
    a) trading or
    b) investing income

   from either
    a) stocks or
    b) commodities

We will now look at 12 different scenarios utilizing this same information and then a summary page comparison:

Example 1 Investor with profitable year made $301,519 from trading stocks.

Example 2 Trader with profitable year made $301,519 from trading stocks.

Example 3 Trader with profitable year made $301,519 from trading stocks utilizing a mark-to-market accounting method—Section 475 (assumes no open positions at the end of 1997 to make a Section 481 adjustment).

Example 4 Investor had a bad year and lost $100,000 trading stocks.

Example 5 Trader had a bad year and lost $100,000 trading stocks.

Example 6 Trader had a bad year and lost $100,000 trading stocks but elected Section 475 (again no 481 adjustment was necessary for our illustration).

Example 7 A profitable investor invested in commodities and made $301,519.

Example 8 A profitable trader invested in commodities and made $301,519.

Example 9 Trader elected mark-to-market Section 475 and has made the same $301,519 trading commodities (no Section 481 adjustment was necessary for our example).

Example 10 Investor investing in commodities and lost $100,000.

Example 11 Trader traded commodities and lost $100,000.

Example 12 Trader traded commodities using the Section 475 mark-to-market accounting method and lost $100,000 (no Section 481 adjustment was necessary in this example).

Let's go into the comparison of these 12 examples, first the 6 stocks examples.

In Example 1, the investor will end up owing $99,895 in taxes. Traders get much greater write-offs, and the trader will only owe $64,261 (Example 2). In Example 3, a trader electing Section 475 will have the exact same outcome as in Example 2—he will owe $64,261 (no significant advantage to a trader without a loss, no unrealized losses, or disallowed wash sales).

In Example 4, the investor will get a refund of $2,340. However, as a trader, the same person (Example 5), losing the same amount of money, will get a refund of $46,625. If the trader elects Section 475 (Example 6) and gets a full $100,000 write-off of his losses, he will receive a refund of $81,135. We now see the beauty of a 475 election under the right circumstances—this is some difference!

We now look at the results for commodities situations.

As an investor, in Example 7, this person will end up owing $64,437. As a trader (Example 8), the tax will be reduced to $28,802 (because of the added write-offs). It is interesting to see that as a profitable commodities trader electing Section 475 (Example 9), this will actually work against him, and this trader will owe $64,261. This is because for a trader electing Section 475, a portion of the commodity income that would be taxed as long-term capital gain is now taxed as ordinary income. If you elect Section 475, it is all taxed as ordinary income.

In Example 10, the investor lost $100,000 in commodities. He will get the exact same refund as the investor who lost $100,000 investing in stocks ($2,340). In Example 11, the trader lost $100,000 trading commodities and, again, will get a refund equal to the refund he would have gotten had he been trading stocks ($46,625). In Example 12, the trader elected Section 475 and has lost $100,000 trading commodities; he gets $81,135 as a refund, the same amount that a stock trader would have gotten with a Section 475 election. This is again a tremendous difference over a non-475 trader with a loss (refund of $46,625), or an investor (refund of $2,340).

It should be noted, however, that the non-475 trader who has a commodity loss could be eligible for a three-year carryback if he had profit in any of the prior three years from (Section 1256) commodity contracts.

If you look at Example 13, you will see a comparative summary of the 12 different investors and traders and the differences in the stocks/commodities losses/gains throughout as investors, traders, and traders electing Section 475.

You will also note that there are huge differences in the amount of itemized/standard deductions, exemption phaseouts, alternative minimum tax due, investment interest-expense deductible, depreciation allowed, and numerous other significant and subtle differences. Go through the forms, run the numbers, compare the differences; but to maximize your refund and to minimize your tax liability due, consult a competent tax professional. It will be worth the cost.

HOW TO ELECT MARK-TO-MARKET

Electing mark-to-market is an automatic election for a change in accounting principles and is done by filling out Form 3115. It is an automatic election; however, this form must be filed by certain deadlines. It also must be filed in duplicate, the first by itself with the national IRS office and the second attached to the tax return when filed.

For years beginning in 1999 and subsequent to that, the election must have been made in all *preexisting* entities by the time the previous tax return was extended, or by April 15, for individuals and by March 15, for corporations in the year you are electing or the date the previous tax return was filed—whichever comes first. For new entities, a notation and a record must be placed in the corporation's board of directors minutes within 2½ months of the beginning of the tax year.

Strategy: If you have missed the election deadline for this year for the entity that you currently have, you can start a new entity and still elect Section 475. You can do this by putting it in the minutes within 2½ months of the beginning of the tax year.

This means that if you are in the middle of 2002 and decide that you want to elect Section 475 for 2002, you can form a new corporation and put a notation in the board of directors minutes within 2½ months of the beginning of the year in which you are making such an election.

The election does not have to be made until the first tax return is filed, which can be as late as October 15 of the following year. Example 14 shows Form 3115 filled out for A. Trader.

Example 15 shows explanatory notes that I use when filling out Form 3115, electing Section 475.

SECTION 481 ADJUSTMENT

A Section 481 adjustment is generally necessary when electing Section 475. Basically a Section 481 adjustment is a one-time adjustment that has to be made, as a result of last year's open positions, to bring the taxpayer into compliance with making a 475 election this year. This year, this is a catch-up adjustment that will restate the return as if the mark-to-market accounting method had been followed forever.

What this means to the trader making a 475 election is that if there are open positions at the end of the preceding year, they must be marked-to-market at the beginning of the year in which the Section 475 election is made. The difference in marking those positions to market is the 481 adjustment that must be made on your tax return.

If the amount of 481 adjustment is $25,000 or less, you have the option of including it in the year in which you are making the Section 475 election. If it is more than $25,000, you must spread it out over a four-year period.

I have seen an incredible amount of misinformation written on this subject—some of it coming from supposedly competent tax professionals in this field. I have recently read a book written by someone who is reputedly a "Trader tax expert" CPA who states that "the Section 481 adjustment should include wash sale losses taken in the year of the 475 election; the difference between the $3,000 capital loss that would have been allowed and the ordinary loss actually taken in the year of the election; and the amount of gain or loss from positions marked to market in the year of the 475 election."

I have been informed by my contacts at the IRS, and also by the chief issues specialist at the IRS on this matter, that as of the date of writing this book, these statements are inaccurate. The only Section 481 adjustment associated with this election is the adjustment to be done to open positions in the year prior to the election—to mark them to market at December 31 of the *prior* year. This is a very complicated section of the Internal Revenue Code, and I strongly suggest that you consult with your tax professional prior to doing this yourself.

Example 1

FORM 1040 Department of the Treasury – Internal Revenue Service
U.S. Individual Income Tax Return 2000 (99) IRS Use Only – Do not write or staple in this space.

For the year Jan. 1 – Dec. 31, 2000, or other tax year beginning , 2000, ending , 20 — OMB No. 1545-0074

Label (See instructions on page 19.) Use the IRS label. Otherwise, please print or type. LABEL HERE

Your first name and initial / Last name	Your social security number
N. VESTOR-PROFIT	123-45-6789
If a joint return, spouse's first name and initial / Last name	Spouse's social security number
Home address (number and street). If you have a P.O. box, see page 19. Apt. no.	▲ **IMPORTANT!** ▲ You **must** enter your SSN(s) above.
C/O TED TESSER-6274 LINTON BLVD. #102	
City, town or post office, state, and ZIP code. If you have a foreign address, see page 19.	
DELRAY BEACH, FL 33484	

Presidential Election Campaign (See page 19.) **Note.** Checking "Yes" will not change your tax or reduce your refund. Do you, or your spouse if filing a joint return, want $3 to go to this fund? ▶ You: ☐ Yes ☒ No Spouse: ☐ Yes ☐ No

Filing Status (Check only one box.)

1 [X] Single
2 [ ] Married filing joint return (even if only one had income)
3 [ ] Married filing separate return. Enter spouse's soc. sec. no. above & full name here ▶
4 [ ] Head of household (with qualifying person). (See page 19.) If the qualifying person is a child but not your dependent, enter this child's name here ▶
5 [ ] Qualifying widow(er) with dependent child (year spouse died ▶). (See page 19.)

Exemptions

6a ☒ **Yourself.** If your parent (or someone else) can claim you as a dependent on his or her tax return, **do not** check box 6a.

b ☐ **Spouse** — No. of boxes checked on 6a and 6b: 1

c **Dependents:**

(1) First Name Last name	(2) Dependent's social security number	(3) Dependent's relationship to you	(4) Chk if qualifying child for child tax credit (see page 20)

If more than six dependents, see page 20.

No. of your children on 6c who: ● lived with you ● did not live with you due to divorce or separation (see page 20) — Dependents on 6c not entered above — Add numbers entered on lines above ▶ 1

d Total number of exemptions claimed

Income

Attach Forms W-2 and W-2G here. Also attach Form 1099-R if tax was withheld. If you did not get a W-2, see page 21. Enclose, but do not attach any payment. Also, please use Form 1040-V.

Line	Description		Amount
7	Wages, salaries, tips, etc. Attach Form(s) W-2	7	200,000
8a	**Taxable** interest. Attach Schedule B if required	8a	
b	**Tax-exempt** interest. **Do not** include on line 8a ... 8b		
9	Ordinary dividends. Attach Schedule B if required	9	
10	Taxable refunds, credits, or offsets of state and local income taxes (see page 22)	10	
11	Alimony received	11	
12	Business income or (loss). Attach Schedule C or C-EZ	12	
13	Capital gain or (loss). Attach Schedule D if required. If not required, check here ▶ ☐	13	301,519
14	Other gains or (losses). Attach Form 4797	14	
15a	Total IRA distributions ... 15a / b Taxable amount (see pg. 23)	15b	
16a	Total pensions and annuities ... 16a / b Taxable amount (see pg. 23)	16b	
17	Rental real estate, royalties, partnerships, S corporations, trusts, etc. Attach Schedule E	17	200,000
18	Farm income or (loss). Attach Schedule F	18	
19	Unemployment compensation	19	
20a	Social security benefits ... 20a / b Taxable amount (see pg. 25)	20b	
21	Other income.	21	
22	Add the amounts in the far right column for lines 7 through 21. This is your **total income** ▶	22	701,519

Adjusted Gross Income

Line	Description				
23	IRA deduction (see page 27)	23			
24	Student loan interest deduction (see page 27)	24			
25	Medical savings account deduction. Attach Form 8853	25			
26	Moving expenses. Attach Form 3903	26			
27	One-half of self-employment tax. Attach Schedule SE	27			
28	Self-employed health insurance deduction (see page 29)	28			
29	Self-employed SEP, SIMPLE, and qualified plans	29			
30	Penalty on early withdrawal of savings	30			
31a	Alimony paid. b Recipient's SSN ▶	31a			
32	Add lines 23 through 31a			32	0
33	Subtract line 32 from line 22. This is your **adjusted gross income** ▶			33	701,519

KFA **For Disclosure, Privacy Act, and Paperwork Reduction Act Notice, see page 56.** IF0US1 11/07/00 Form **1040** (2000)

Form 1040 (2000) N. VESTOR-PROFIT 123-45-6789 Page 2

Tax and Credits	34	Amount from line 33 (adjusted gross income)		34	701,519
	35a	Check if: ☐ **You** were 65 or older, ☐ Blind; ☐ **Spouse** was 65 or older, ☐ Blind. Add the number of boxes checked above and enter the total here ▶ 35a			
Standard Deduction for Most People Single: $4,400 Head of household: $6,450 Married filing jointly or Qualifying widow(er): $7,350 Married filing separately $3,675.	b	If you are married filing separately and your spouse itemizes deductions, or you were a dual-status alien, see page 31 and check here ▶ 35b ☐			
	36	Enter your **itemized deductions** from Schedule A, line 28, **or standard deduction** shown on the left. **But** see page 31 to find your standard deduction if you checked any box on line 35a or 35b **or** if someone can claim you as a dependent		36	115,092
	37	Subtract line 36 from line 34		37	586,427
	38	If line 34 is $96,700 or less, multiply $2,800 by the total number of exemptions claimed on line 6d. If line 34 is over $96,700, see the worksheet on page 32 for the amount to enter		38	0
	39	**Taxable income.** Subtract line 38 from line 37. If line 38 is more than line 37, enter -0-		39	586,427
	40	**Tax** (see page 32). Check if any tax is from a ☐ Form(s) 8814 b ☐ Form 4972		40	209,895
	41	Alternative minimum tax. Attach Form 6251		41	
	42	Add lines 40 and 41 ▶		42	209,895
	43	Foreign tax credit. Attach Form 1116 if required	43		
	44	Credit for child and dependent care expenses. Att. Form 2441	44		
	45	Credit for the elderly or the disabled. Attach Schedule R	45		
	46	Education credits. Attach Form 8863	46		
	47	Child tax credit (see page 36)	47		
	48	Adoption credit. Attach Form 8839	48		
	49	Other. Check if from a ☐ Form 3800 b ☐ Form 8396 c ☐ Form 8801 d ☐ Form (specify)	49		
	50	Add lines 43 through 49. These are your **total credits**		50	
	51	Subtract line 50 from line 42. If line 50 is more than line 42, enter -0- ▶		51	209,895
Other Taxes	52	Self-employment tax. Att. Sch. SE		52	
	53	Social security and Medicare tax on tip income not reported to employer. Attach Form 4137		53	
	54	Tax on IRAs, other retirement plans, and MSAs. Attach Form 5329 if required		54	
	55	Advance earned income credit payments from Form(s) W-2		55	
	56	Household employment taxes. Attach Schedule H		56	
	57	Add lines 51 through 56. This is your **total tax** ▶		57	209,895
Payments	58	Federal income tax withheld from Forms W-2 and 1099	58 60,000		
If you have a qualifying child, attach Schedule EIC.	59	2000 estimated tax payments and amount applied from 1999 return	59 50,000		
	60a	**Earned income credit (EIC)**	60a		
	b	**Nontaxable earned income: amt.** ▶ **and type** ▶ No			
	61	Excess social security and RRTA tax withheld (see page 50)	61		
	62	**Additional child tax credit. Attach Form 8812**	62		
	63	**Amount paid with request for extension to file** (see page 50)	63		
	64	Other payments. Check if from a ☐ Form 2439 b ☐ Form 4136	64		
	65	Add lines 58, 59, 60a, and 61 through 64. These are your **total payments** ▶		65	110,000
Refund Have it directly deposited! See page 50 and fill in 67b, 67c, and 67d.	66	If line 65 is more than line 57, subtract line 57 from line 65. This is the amount you **overpaid**		66	
	67a	Amount of line 66 you want **refunded to you** ▶		67a	
	b	Routing number ▶ c Type: ☐ Checking ☐ Savings			
	d	Account number			
	68	Amount of line 66 you want **applied to your 2001 estimated tax** ▶	68		
Amount You Owe	69	If line 57 is more than line 65, subtract line 65 from line 57. This is the **amount you owe.** For details on how to pay, see page 51 ▶		69	99,895
	70	Estimated tax penalty. Also include on line 69	70		

Sign Here
Joint return? See page 19. Keep a copy for your records.

Under penalties of perjury, I declare that I have examined this return and accompanying schedules and statements, and to the best of my knowledge and belief, they are true, correct, and complete. Declaration of preparer (other than taxpayer) is based on all information of which preparer has any knowledge.

Your signature	Date	Your occupation	Daytime phone number
Spouse's signature. If a joint return, **both** must sign.	Date	Spouse's occupation	May the IRS discuss this return with the preparer shown below? (see page 52)? ☒ Yes ☐ No

Paid Preparer's Use Only

Preparer's signature	Date	Check if self-employed ☐	Preparer's SSN or PTIN
Firm's name (or yours if self-employed), address, and ZIP code	Waterside Financial Serv., Inc 6274 Linton Blvd., Suite #102 Boca Raton, FL 33484	EIN 65-0664126 Phone no. (561) 865-0071	

IFOUS1A 11/22/00 Form **1040** (2000)

SCHEDULES A&B (Form 1040)
Department of the Treasury Internal Revenue Service (99)

Schedule A – Itemized Deductions

▶ Attach to Form 1040. ▶ See Instructions for Schedules A and B (Form 1040).

OMB No. 1545-0074
2000
Attachment Sequence No. 07

Name(s) shown on Form 1040: N. VESTOR-PROFIT
Your social security number: 123-45-6789

Section	Line	Description	Line no.	Amount	Line no.	Total
Medical and Dental Expenses		**Caution.** Do not include expenses reimbursed or paid by others.				
	1	Medical and dental expenses (see page A–2)	1			
	2	Enter amount from Form 1040, line 34 … 2				
	3	Multiply line 2 above by 7.5% (.075)	3			
	4	Subtract line 3 from line 1. If line 3 is more than line 1, enter -0-			4	0
Taxes You Paid (See page A–2.)	5	State and local income taxes	5			
	6	Real estate taxes (see page A–2)	6			
	7	Personal property taxes	7			
	8	Other taxes. List type and amount ▶	8			
	9	Add lines 5 through 8			9	0
Interest You Paid (See page A–3.)	10	Home mortgage interest and points reported on Form 1098	10			
	11	Home mortgage interest not reported to you on Form 1098. If paid to the person from whom you bought the home, see page A-3 & show that person's name, ID no. & address ▶	11			
Note. Personal interest is not deductible.	12	Points not reported to you on Form 1098. See pg. A–3	12			
	13	Investment interest. Attach Form 4952, if required. (See page A–3.)	13	51,357		
	14	Add lines 10 through 13			14	51,357
Gifts to Charity	15	Gifts by cash or check. If any gift of $250 or more, see pg. A–4	15			
If you made a gift and got a benefit for it, see page A–4.	16	Other than by cash or check. If any gift of $250 or more, see page A–4. You **must** attach Form 8283 if over $500	16			
	17	Carryover from prior year	17			
	18	Add lines 15 through 17			18	0
Casualty and Theft Losses	19	Casualty or theft loss(es). Attach Form 4684. (See page A–5.)			19	0
Job Expenses and Most Other Miscellaneous Deductions	20	Unreimbursed employee expenses – job travel, union dues, job education, etc. You **must** attach Form 2106 or 2106-EZ if required. (See page A–5.) ▶	20			
	21	Tax preparation fees	21			
(See page A–5 for expenses to deduct here.)	22	Other expenses – investment, safe deposit box, etc. List type and amount ▶ Depreciation 5,000; Investment Expenses 89,942	22	94,942		
	23	Add lines 20 through 22	23	94,942		
	24	Enter amount from Form 1040, line 34 … 24 701,519				
	25	Multiply line 24 above by 2% (.02)	25	14,030		
	26	Subtract line 25 from line 23. If line 25 is more than line 23, enter -0-			26	80,912
Other Miscellaneous Deductions	27	Other – from list on page A–6. List type and amount ▶			27	0
Total Itemized Deductions	28	Is Form 1040, line 34, over $128,950 (over $64,475 if married filing separately)? ☐ **No.** Your deduction is not limited. Add the amounts in the far right column for lines 4 through 27. Also, enter this amount on Form 1040, line 36. ☒ **Yes.** Your deduction may be limited. See page A–6 for the amount to enter.		Reduction -17,177	28	115,092

KFA **For Paperwork Reduction Act Notice, see Form 1040 Instructions.** IF0US2 11/03/00 **Schedule A (Form 1040) 2000**

SCHEDULE D (Form 1040)
Department of the Treasury
Internal Revenue Service (99)

Capital Gains and Losses

▶ Attach to Form 1040. ▶ See Instructions for Schedule D (Form 1040).
▶ Use Schedule D-1 for more space to list transactions for lines 1 and 8.

OMB No. 1545-0074
2000
Attachment Sequence No. 12

Name(s) shown on Form 1040: N. VESTOR-PROFIT — Your social security number: 123-45-6789

Part I Short-Term Capital Gains and Losses – Assets Held One Year or Less

1 (a) Description of property (Example, 100 sh. XYZ Co.)	(b) Date acquired (Mo., day, yr.)	(c) Date sold (Mo., day, yr.)	(d) Sales price (see page D-6)	(e) Cost or other basis (see page D-6)	(f) Gain or (loss) Subtract (e) from (d)
VARIOUS	Various	Various	301,519	0	301,519

2 Enter your short-term totals, if any, from Schedule D-1, line 2	2	
3 **Total short-term sales price amounts.** Add column (d) of lines 1 and 2	3	301,519
4 Short-term gain from Form 6252 and short-term gain or (loss) from Forms 4684, 6781, and 8824	4	
5 Net short-term gain or (loss) from partnerships, S corporations, estates, and trusts from Schedule(s) K-1	5	
6 Short-term capital loss carryover. Enter the amount, if any, from line 8 of your 1999 Capital Loss Carryover Worksheet	6	( )
7 **Net short-term capital gain or (loss).** Combine column (f) of lines 1 through 6 ▶	7	301,519

Part II Long-Term Capital Gains and Losses – Assets Held More Than One Year

8 (a) Description of property (Example, 100 sh. XYZ Co.)	(b) Date acquired (Mo., day, yr.)	(c) Date sold (Mo., day, yr.)	(d) Sales price (see page D-6)	(e) Cost or other basis (see page D-6)	(f) Gain or (loss) Subtract (e) from (d)	(g) 28% rate gain or (loss) *(see instr. below)

		(d)	(f)	(g)
9 Enter your long-term totals, if any, from Schedule D-1, line 9	9			
10 **Total long-term sales price amounts.** Add column (d) of lines 8 and 9	10			
11 Gain from Form 4797, Part I; long-term gain from Forms 2439 and 6252; and long-term gain or (loss) from Forms 4684, 6781, and 8824	11			
12 Net long-term gain or (loss) from partnerships, S corporations, estates, and trusts from Schedule(s) K-1	12			
13 Capital gain distributions. See page D-1	13			
14 Long-term capital loss carryover. Enter in both columns (f) and (g) the amount, if any, from line 13 of your 1999 Capital Loss Carryover Worksheet	14		( )	( )
15 Combine column (g) of lines 8 through 14	15			
16 **Net long-term capital gain or (loss).** Combine column (f) of lines 8 through 14 ▶ **Next:** Go to Part III on the back.	16			

* **28% rate gain or loss** includes **all** "collectibles gains and losses" (as defined on page D-6) and up to 50% of the eligible gain on qualified small business stock (see page D-4).

For Paperwork Reduction Act Notice, see Form 1040 instructions. **Schedule D (Form 1040) 2000**

KFA IFOUS5 12/07/00

Schedule D (Form 1040) 2000 N. VESTOR-PROFIT 123-45-6789 Page **2**

Part III **Summary of Parts I and II**

17	Combine lines 7 and 16. If a loss, go to line 18. If a gain, enter the gain on Form 1040, line 13	17	301,519
	Next: Complete Form 1040 through line 39. Then, go to **Part IV** to figure your tax if: ● Both lines 16 and 17 are gains **and** ● Form 1040, line 39, is more than zero. Otherwise, **stop here.**		
18	If line 17 is a loss, enter here and as a (loss) on Form 1040, line 13, the **smaller** of these losses: ● The loss on line 17 **or** ● ($3,000) or, if married filing separately, ($1,500)	18	( )
	Next: Skip **Part IV** below. Instead, complete Form 1040 through line 37. Then, complete the **Capital Loss Carryover Worksheet** on page D–6 if: ● The loss on line 17 exceeds the loss on line 18 **or** ● Form 1040, line 37, is a loss.		

Part IV **Tax Computation Using Maximum Capital Gains Rates**

19	Enter your taxable income from Form 1040, line 39			19	
20	Enter the **smaller** of line 16 or line 17 of Schedule D	20			
21	If you are filing Form 4952, enter the amount from Form 4952, line 4e	21			
22	Subtract line 21 from line 20. If zero or less, enter -0-	22			
23	Combine lines 7 and 15. If zero or less, enter -0-	23			
24	Enter the **smaller** of line 15 or line 23, but not less than zero	24			
25	Enter your unrecaptured section 1250 gain, if any, from line 17 of the worksheet on page D-8	25			
26	Add lines 24 and 25	26			
27	Subtract line 26 from line 22. If zero or less, enter -0-			27	
28	Subtract line 27 from line 19. If zero or less, enter -0-			28	
29	Enter the **smaller** of: ● The amount on line 19 **or** ● $26,250 if single; $43,850 if married filing jointly or qualifying widow(er); $21,925 if married filing separately; or $35,150 if head of household			29	
30	Enter the **smaller** of line 28 or line 29	30			
31	Subtract line 22 from line 19. If zero or less, enter -0-	31			
32	Enter the **larger** of line 30 or line 31 ▶	32			
33	Figure the tax on the amount on line 32. Use the Tax Table or Tax Rate Schedules, whichever applies			33	
	Note: If the amounts on lines 29 and 30 are the same, skip lines 34 through 37 and go to line 38.				
34	Enter the amount from line 29	34			
35	Enter the amount from line 30	35			
36	Subtract line 35 from line 34 ▶	36			
37	Multiply line 36 by 10% (.10)			37	
	Note: If the amounts on lines 19 and 29 are the same, skip lines 38 through 51 and go to line 52.				
38	Enter the **smaller** of line 19 or line 27	38			
39	Enter the amount from line 36	39			
40	Subtract line 39 from line 38 ▶	40			
41	Multiply line 40 by 20% (.20)			41	
	Note: If line 26 is zero or blank, skip lines 42 through 51 and go to line 52.				
42	Enter the **smaller** of line 22 or line 25	42			
43	Add lines 22 and 32	43			
44	Enter the amount from line 19	44			
45	Subtract line 44 from line 43. If zero or less, enter -0-	45			
46	Subtract line 45 from line 42. If zero or less, enter -0- ▶	46			
47	Multiply line 46 by 25% (.25)			47	
	Note: If line 24 is zero or blank, skip lines 48 through 51 and go to line 52.				
48	Enter the amount from line 19	48			
49	Add lines 32, 36, 40, and 46	49			
50	Subtract line 49 from line 48	50			
51	Multiply line 50 by 28% (.28)			51	
52	Add lines 33, 37, 41, 47, and 51			52	
53	Figure the tax on the amount on line 19. Use the Tax Table or Tax Rate Schedules, whichever applies			53	
54	**Tax on all taxable income (including capital gains).** Enter the **smaller** of line 52 or line 53 here and on Form 1040, line 40			54	

IFOUS5A 10/24/00 **Schedule D (Form 1040) 2000**

Schedule E (Form 1040) 2000 Attachment Sequence No. **13** Page **2**

Name(s) shown on return. Do not enter name and social security number if shown on other side. | Your social security number

N. VESTOR-PROFIT | 123-45-6789

Note: If you report amounts from farming or fishing on Schedule E, you must enter your gross income from those activities on line 41 below. Real estate professionals must complete line 42 below.

Part II Income or Loss From Partnerships and S Corporations If you report a loss from an at-risk activity, you **must** check either column **(e)** or **(f)** on line 27 to describe your investment in the activity. See page E-5. If you check column **(f)**, you must attach **Form 6198.**

27	(a) Name	(b) Enter P for partnership; S for S corp.	(c) Check if foreign partnership	(d) Employer identification number	Invest. At Risk? (e) All is at risk	(f) Some is not at risk
A	1	P				
B						
C						
D						
E						

	Passive Income and Loss		Nonpassive Income and Loss		
	(g) Passive loss allowed (attach Form 8582 if required)	(h) Passive income from Schedule K-1	(i) Nonpassive loss from Schedule K-1	(j) Section 179 expense deduction from Form 4562	(k) Nonpassive income from Schedule K-1
A		200,000			
B					
C					
D					
E					
28a Totals		200,000			
b Totals					

29	Add columns (h) and (k) of line 28a	29	200,000
30	Add columns (g), (i), and (j) of line 28b	30	( )
31	Total partnership and S corporation income or (loss). Combine lines 29 and 30. Enter the result here and include in the total on line 40 below	31	200,000

Part III Income or Loss From Estates and Trusts

32	(a) Name	(b) Employer ID number
A		
B		
C		
D		

	Passive Income and Loss		Nonpassive Income and Loss	
	(c) Passive deduction or loss allowed (attach Form 8582 if required)	(d) Passive income from Schedule K-1	(e) Deduction or loss from Schedule K-1	(f) Other income from Schedule K-1
A				
B				
C				
D				
33a Totals				
b Totals				

34	Add columns (d) and (f) of line 33a	34	
35	Add columns (c) and (e) of line 33b	35	( )
36	Total estate and trust income or (loss). Combine lines 34 and 35. Enter the result here and include in the total on line 40 below	36	

Part IV Income or Loss From Real Estate Mortgage Investment Conduits (REMICs) – Residual Holder

37 (a) Name	(b) Employer identification number	(c) Excess inclusion from Schedules Q, line 2c (see page E-6)	(d) Taxable income (net loss) from Schedules Q, line 1b	(e) Income from Schedules Q, line 3b

38	Combine columns (d) and (e) only. Enter the result here and include in the total on line 40 below	38	

Part V Summary

39	Net farm rental income or (loss) from **Form 4835.** Also, complete line 41 below	39	
40	**Total** income or (loss). Combine lines 26, 31, 36, 38, and 39. Enter the result here and on Form 1040, line 17 ▶	40	200,000
41	**Reconciliation of Farming and Fishing Income:** Enter your **gross** farming and fishing income reported on Form 4835, line 7; Schedule K-1 (Form 1065), line 15b; Schedule K-1 (Form 1120S), line 23; and Schedule K-1 (Form 1041), line 14 (see page E-6) 41		
42	**Reconciliation for Real Estate Professionals.** If you were real estate professional (see pg. E-4), enter net income or (loss) you reported anywhere on Form 1040 from all rental real estate activities in which you materially participated under passive activity loss rules. 42		

IF0US7A 10/19/00 Schedule E (Form 1040) 2000

Form **4562** — **Depreciation and Amortization (Including Information on Listed Property)** — OMB No. 1545-0172 — **2000**

Department of the Treasury Internal Revenue Service (99) ▶ See separate instructions. ▶ Attach this form to your return. Attachment Sequence No. 67

Name(s) shown on return: N. VESTOR-PROFIT — Identifying number: 123-45-6789

Business or activity to which this form relates

Part I Election To Expense Certain Tangible Property (Section 179) Note: If you have any "listed property," complete Part V before you complete Part I.

1	Maximum dollar limitation. If an enterprise zone business, see page 2 of the instructions	1	$20,000
2	Total cost of section 179 property placed in service. See page 2 of the instructions	2	
3	Threshold cost of section 179 property before reduction in limitation	3	$200,000
4	Reduction in limitation. Subtract line 3 from line 2. If zero or less, enter -0-	4	
5	Dollar limitation for tax year. Subtract line 4 from line 1. If zero or less, enter -0-. If married filing separately, see page 2 of the instructions	5	

6 (a) Description of property	(b) Cost (business use only)	(c) Elected cost

7	Listed property. Enter amount from line 27	7	
8	Total elected cost of section 179 property. Add amounts in column (c), lines 6 and 7	8	
9	Tentative deduction. Enter the smaller of line 5 or line 8	9	
10	Carryover of disallowed deduction from 1999. See page 3 of the instructions	10	
11	Business income limitation. Enter the smaller of business income (not less than zero) or line 5 (see instructions)	11	
12	Section 179 expense deduction. Add lines 9 and 10, but do not enter more than line 11	12	
13	Carryover of disallowed deduction to 2001. Add lines 9 and 10, less line 12 ▶	13	

Note: Do not use Part II or Part III below for listed property (automobiles, certain other vehicles, cellular telephones, certain computers, or property used for entertainment, recreation, or amusement). Instead, use Part V for listed property.

Part II MACRS Depreciation for Assets Placed in Service Only During Your 2000 Tax Year (Do not include listed property.)

Section A - General Asset Account Election

14 If you are making the election under section 168(i)(4) to group any assets placed in service during the tax year into one or more general asset accounts, check this box. See page 3 of the instructions ▶ ☐

Section B - General Depreciation System (GDS) (See page 3 of the instructions.)

(a) Classification of property	(b) Month and year placed in service	(c) Basis for depreciation (business/investment use only - see instructions)	(d) Recovery period	(e) Convention	(f) Method	(g) Depreciation deduction
15a 3-year property						
b 5-year property						
c 7-year property						
d 10-year property						
e 15-year property						
f 20-year property						
g 25-year property			25 yrs		S/L	
h Residential rental property			27.5 yrs	MM	S/L	
			27.5 yrs	MM	S/L	
i Nonresidential real property			39 yrs	MM	S/L	
				MM	S/L	

Section C - Alternative Depreciation System (ADS): (See page 5 of the instructions.)

16a Class life					S/L	
b 12-year			12 yrs		S/L	
c 40-year			40 yrs	MM	S/L	

Part III Other Depreciation (Do not include listed property.) (See page 5 of the instructions.)

17	GDS and ADS deductions for assets placed in service in tax years beginning before 2000	17	
18	Property subject to section 168(f)(1) election	18	
19	ACRS and other depreciation	19	5,000

Part IV Summary (See page 6 of the instructions.)

20	Listed property. Enter amount from line 26	20	
21	**Total.** Add deductions from line 12, lines 15 and 16 in column (g), and lines 17 through 20. Enter here and on the appropriate lines of your return. Partnerships and S corporations - see instructions	21	5,000
22	For assets shown above and placed in service during the current year, enter the portion of the basis attributable to section 263A costs	22	

KFA **For Paperwork Reduction Act Notice, see page 9 of the instructions.** GF0US7 10/26/00 Form **4562** (2000)

Form **4952**
Department of the Treasury
Internal Revenue Service (99)

Investment Interest Expense Deduction

▶ **Attach to your tax return.**

OMB No. 1545-0191
2000
Attachment Sequence No. **72**

Name(s) shown on return	Identifying number
N. VESTOR-PROFIT	123-45-6789

Part I — Total Investment Interest Expense

1	Investment interest expense paid or accrued in 2000. See instructions	1	51,357
2	Disallowed investment interest expense from 1999 Form 4952, line 7	2	
3	**Total investment interest expense.** Add lines 1 and 2	3	51,357

Part II — Net Investment Income

4a	Gross income from property held for investment (excluding any net gain from the disposition of property held for investment)			4a	
b	Net gain from the disposition of property held for investment	4b	301,519		
c	Net capital gain from the disposition of property held for investment	4c			
d	Subtract line 4c from line 4b. If zero or less, enter -0-			4d	301,519
e	Enter all or part of the amount on line 4c, if any, that you elect to include in investment income. Do not enter more than the amount on line 4b. See instructions ▶			4e	
f	Investment income. Add lines 4a, 4d, and 4e. See instructions			4f	301,519
5	Investment expenses. See instructions			5	
6	**Net investment income.** Subtract line 5 from line 4f. If zero or less, enter -0-			6	301,519

Part III — Investment Interest Expense Deduction

7	Disallowed investment interest expense to be carried forward to 2001. Subtract line 6 from line 3. If zero or less, enter -0-	7	0
8	**Investment interest expense deduction.** Enter the **smaller** of line 3 or 6. See instructions	8	51,357

For Paperwork Reduction Act Notice, see back. Form **4952** (2000)

KFA IFOUS29 10/24/00

Example 1 *(Continued)*

Form **6251**	**Alternative Minimum Tax – Individuals**	OMB No. 1545-0227
	▶ **See separate instructions.**	**2000**
Department of the Treasury Internal Revenue Service	▶ **Attach to Form 1040 or Form 1040NR.**	Attachment Sequence No. **32**

Name(s) shown on Form 1040	Your social security number
N. VESTOR-PROFIT	123-45-6789

Part I — Adjustments and Preferences

1	If you itemized deductions on Schedule A (Form 1040), go to line 2. Otherwise, enter your standard deduction from Form 1040, line 36, here and go to line 6	**1**	
2	Medical and dental. Enter the smaller of Schedule A (Form 1040), line 4 **or** 2 1/2% of Form 1040, line 34.	**2**	
3	Taxes. Enter the amount from Schedule A (Form 1040), line 9.	**3**	
4	Certain interest on a home mortgage **not** used to buy, build, or improve your home	**4**	
5	Miscellaneous itemized deductions. Enter the amount from Schedule A (Form 1040), line 26	**5**	80,912
6	Refund of taxes. Enter any tax refund from Form 1040, line 10 or line 21.	**6**	()
7	Investment interest. Enter difference between regular tax and AMT deduction	**7**	
8	Post-1986 depreciation. Enter difference between regular tax and AMT depreciation	**8**	
9	Adjusted gain or loss. Enter difference between AMT and regular tax gain or loss.	**9**	
10	Incentive stock options. Enter excess of AMT income over regular tax income.	**10**	
11	Passive activities. Enter difference between AMT and regular tax income or loss.	**11**	
12	Beneficiaries of estates and trusts. Enter the amount from Schedule K-1 (Form 1041), line 9	**12**	
13	Tax-exempt interest from private activity bonds issued after 8/7/86.	**13**	

14 Other. Enter the amount, if any, for each item below and enter the total on line 14.

a Circulation expenditures.		h Loss limitations	
b Depletion		i Mining costs	
c Depreciation (pre-1987).		j Patron's adjustment	
d Installment sales.		k Pollution control facilities	
e Intangible drilling costs.		l Research & experimental.	
f Large partnerships		m Section 1202 exclusion	
g Long-term contracts		n Tax shelter farm activities.	
		o Related adjustments	

		14	
15	**Total Adjustments and Preferences.** Combine lines 1 through 14. ▶	**15**	80,912

Part II — Alternative Minimum Taxable Income

16	Enter the amount from **Form 1040, line 37.** If less than zero, enter as a (loss). ▶	**16**	586,427
17	Net operating loss deduction, if any, from Form 1040, line 21. Enter as a positive amount.	**17**	
18	If Form 1040, line 34, is over $128,950 (over $64,475 if married filing separately), and you itemized deductions, enter the amount, if any, from line 9 of the worksheet for Schedule A (Form 1040), line 28	**18**	(17,177)
19	Combine lines 15 through 18. ▶	**19**	650,162
20	Alternative tax net operating loss deduction. See page 6 of the instructions.	**20**	
21	**Alternative Minimum Taxable Income.** Subtract line 20 from line 19. (If married filing separately and line 21 is more than $165,000, see page 7 of the instructions.) ▶	**21**	650,162

Part III — Exemption Amount and Alternative Minimum Tax

22 **Exemption Amount.** (If this form is for a child under age 14, see page 7 of the instructions.)

IF your filing status is:	AND line 21 is not over ...	THEN enter on line 22 ...		
Single or head of household.	$112,500	$33,750		
Married filing jointly or qualifying widow(er)	150,000	45,000	}	
Married filing separately	75,000	22,500		**22**

If line 21 is **over** the amount shown above for your filing status, see page 7 of the instructions.

23	Subtract line 22 from line 21. If zero or less, enter -0- here and on lines 26 and 28 and stop here. ▶	**23**	650,162
24	If you reported capital gain distributions directly on Form 1040, line 13, **or** you completed Schedule D (Form 1040) and have an amount on line 25 or line 27 (or would have had an amount on either line if you had completed Part IV) (as refigured for the AMT, if necessary), go to Part IV of Form 6251 to figure line 24. **All others:** If line 23 is $175,000 or less ($87,500 or less if married filing separately), multiply line 23 by 26% (.26). Otherwise, multiply line 23 by 28% (.28) and subtract $3,500 ($1,750 if married filing separately) from the result ▶	**24**	178,545
25	Alternative minimum tax foreign tax credit. See page 7 of the instructions.	**25**	
26	Tentative minimum tax. Subtract line 25 from line 24. ▶	**26**	178,545
27	Enter your tax from Form 1040, line 40 (minus any tax from Form 4972 and any foreign tax credit from Form 1040, line 43).	**27**	209,895
28	**Alternative Minimum Tax.** Subtract line 27 from line 26. If zero or less, enter -0-. Enter here and on Form 1040, line 41. ▶	**28**	0

For Paperwork Reduction Act Notice, see page 8 of the instructions. Form **6251** (2000)

KFA IF0US33 10/23/00

Example 2

FORM 1040 Department of the Treasury – Internal Revenue Service
U.S. Individual Income Tax Return 2000 (99) IRS Use Only – Do not write or staple in this space.

For the year Jan. 1 – Dec. 31, 2000, or other tax year beginning , 2000, ending , 20 OMB No. 1545-0074

Label (See instructions on page 19.) Use the IRS label. Otherwise, please print or type.

LABEL HERE

Your first name and initial / Last name: A. TRADER PROFIT-NO 475
Your social security number: 123-45-6789
If a joint return, spouse's first name and initial / Last name
Spouse's social security number
Home address (number and street). If you have a P.O. box, see page 19. Apt. no.: C/O TED TESSER-6274 LINTON BLVD. #102
City, town or post office, state, and ZIP code. If you have a foreign address, see page 19.: DELRAY BEACH, FL 33484

▲ **IMPORTANT!** ▲ You **must** enter your SSN(s) above.

Presidential Election Campaign (See page 19.) **Note.** Checking "Yes" will not change your tax or reduce your refund.
Do you, or your spouse if filing a joint return, want $3 to go to this fund? ▶ You: ☐ Yes ☒ No Spouse: ☐ Yes ☐ No

Filing Status (Check only one box.)

1 [X] Single
2 [ ] Married filing joint return (even if only one had income)
3 [ ] Married filing separate return. Enter spouse's soc. sec. no. above & full name here ▶
4 [ ] Head of household (with qualifying person). (See page 19.) If the qualifying person is a child but not your dependent, enter this child's name here ▶
5 [ ] Qualifying widow(er) with dependent child (year spouse died ▶). (See page 19.)

Exemptions

6a ☒ **Yourself.** If your parent (or someone else) can claim you as a dependent on his or her tax return, **do not** check box 6a.
b ☐ **Spouse**
No. of boxes checked on 6a and 6b: 1

c **Dependents:**

(1) First Name Last name	(2) Dependent's social security number	(3) Dependent's relationship to you	(4) Chk if qualifying child for child tax credit (see page 20)

If more than six dependents, see page 20.

No. of your children on 6c who:
● lived with you
● did not live with you due to divorce or separation (see page 20)
Dependents on 6c not entered above

d Total number of exemptions claimed — Add numbers entered on lines above ▶ 1

Income

Attach Forms W-2 and W-2G here. Also attach Form 1099-R if tax was withheld.
If you did not get a W-2, see page 21.
Enclose, but do not attach any payment. Also, please use Form 1040-V.

7	Wages, salaries, tips, etc. Attach Form(s) W-2	7	200,000
8a	**Taxable** interest. Attach Schedule B if required	8a	
b	**Tax-exempt** interest. **Do not** include on line 8a — 8b		
9	Ordinary dividends. Attach Schedule B if required	9	
10	Taxable refunds, credits, or offsets of state and local income taxes (see page 22)	10	
11	Alimony received	11	
12	Business income or (loss). Attach Schedule C or C-EZ	12	-200,678
13	Capital gain or (loss). Attach Schedule D if required. If not required, check here ▶ ☐	13	301,519
14	Other gains or (losses). Attach Form 4797	14	
15a	Total IRA distributions 15a — b Taxable amount (see pg. 23)	15b	
16a	Total pensions and annuities 16a — b Taxable amount (see pg. 23)	16b	
17	Rental real estate, royalties, partnerships, S corporations, trusts, etc. Attach Schedule E	17	200,000
18	Farm income or (loss). Attach Schedule F	18	
19	Unemployment compensation	19	
20a	Social security benefits 20a — b Taxable amount (see pg. 25)	20b	
21	Other income.	21	
22	Add the amounts in the far right column for lines 7 through 21. This is your **total income** ▶	22	500,841

Adjusted Gross Income

23	IRA deduction (see page 27)	23			
24	Student loan interest deduction (see page 27)	24			
25	Medical savings account deduction. Attach Form 8853	25			
26	Moving expenses. Attach Form 3903	26			
27	One-half of self-employment tax. Attach Schedule SE	27			
28	Self-employed health insurance deduction (see page 29)	28			
29	Self-employed SEP, SIMPLE, and qualified plans	29			
30	Penalty on early withdrawal of savings	30			
31a	Alimony paid. b Recipient's SSN ▶	31a			
32	Add lines 23 through 31a			32	0
33	Subtract line 32 from line 22. This is your **adjusted gross income** ▶			33	500,841

KFA **For Disclosure, Privacy Act, and Paperwork Reduction Act Notice, see page 56.** IFOUS1 11/07/00 Form **1040** (2000)

Form 1040 (2000) A. TRADER PROFIT-NO 475 — 123-45-6789 — Page 2

Tax and Credits

34	Amount from line 33 (adjusted gross income)	34	500,841
35a	Check if: ☐ You were 65 or older, ☐ Blind; ☐ Spouse was 65 or older, ☐ Blind. Add the number of boxes checked above and enter the total here ▶ 35a		
b	If you are married filing separately and your spouse itemizes deductions, or you were a dual-status alien, see page 31 and check here ▶ 35b ☐		
36	Enter your **itemized deductions** from Schedule A, line 28, **or standard deduction** shown on the left. **But** see page 31 to find your standard deduction if you checked any box on line 35a or 35b **or** if someone can claim you as a dependent	36	4,400
37	Subtract line 36 from line 34	37	496,441
38	If line 34 is $96,700 or less, multiply $2,800 by the total number of exemptions claimed on line 6d. If line 34 is over $96,700, see the worksheet on page 32 for the amount to enter	38	0
39	**Taxable income.** Subtract line 38 from line 37. If line 38 is more than line 37, enter -0-	39	496,441
40	**Tax** (see page 32). Check if any tax is from a ☐ Form(s) 8814 b ☐ Form 4972	40	174,261
41	Alternative minimum tax. Attach Form 6251	41	
42	Add lines 40 and 41 ▶	42	174,261
43	Foreign tax credit. Attach Form 1116 if required — 43		
44	Credit for child and dependent care expenses. Att. Form 2441 — 44		
45	Credit for the elderly or the disabled. Attach Schedule R — 45		
46	Education credits. Attach Form 8863 — 46		
47	Child tax credit (see page 36) — 47		
48	Adoption credit. Attach Form 8839 — 48		
49	Other. Check if from a ☐ Form 3800 b ☐ Form 8396 c ☐ Form 8801 d ☐ Form (specify) — 49		
50	Add lines 43 through 49. These are your **total credits**	50	
51	Subtract line 50 from line 42. If line 50 is more than line 42, enter -0- ▶	51	174,261

Standard Deduction for Most People — Single: $4,400; Head of household: $6,450; Married filing jointly or Qualifying widow(er): $7,350; Married filing separately $3,675.

Other Taxes

52	Self-employment tax. Att. Sch. SE	52	
53	Social security and Medicare tax on tip income not reported to employer. Attach Form 4137	53	
54	Tax on IRAs, other retirement plans, and MSAs. Attach Form 5329 if required	54	
55	Advance earned income credit payments from Form(s) W-2	55	
56	Household employment taxes. Attach Schedule H	56	
57	Add lines 51 through 56. This is your **total tax** ▶	57	174,261

Payments

58	Federal income tax withheld from Forms W-2 and 1099	58	60,000		
59	2000 estimated tax payments and amount applied from 1999 return	59	50,000		
60a	**Earned income credit (EIC)**	60a			
b	**Nontaxable earned income: amt.** ▶ and type ▶ No				
61	Excess social security and RRTA tax withheld (see page 50)	61			
62	**Additional child tax credit. Attach Form 8812**	62			
63	**Amount paid with request for extension to file** (see page 50)	63			
64	Other payments. Check if from a ☐ Form 2439 b ☐ Form 4136	64			
65	Add lines 58, 59, 60a, and 61 through 64. These are your **total payments** ▶			65	110,000

If you have a qualifying child, attach Schedule EIC.

Refund

Have it directly deposited! See page 50 and fill in 67b, 67c, and 67d.

66	If line 65 is more than line 57, subtract line 57 from line 65. This is the amount you **overpaid**	66	
67a	Amount of line 66 you want **refunded to you** ▶	67a	
b	Routing number ▶ c Type: ☐ Checking ☐ Savings		
d	Account number		
68	Amount of line 66 you want **applied to your 2001 estimated tax** ▶ 68		

Amount You Owe

69	If line 57 is more than line 65, subtract line 65 from line 57. This is the **amount you owe.** For details on how to pay, see page 51 ▶	69	64,261
70	Estimated tax penalty. Also include on line 69 — 70		

Sign Here

Under penalties of perjury, I declare that I have examined this return and accompanying schedules and statements, and to the best of my knowledge and belief, they are true, correct, and complete. Declaration of preparer (other than taxpayer) is based on all information of which preparer has any knowledge.

Joint return? See page 19. Keep a copy for your records.

Your signature	Date	Your occupation	Daytime phone number 561-865-0071
Spouse's signature. If a joint return, **both** must sign.	Date	Spouse's occupation	May the IRS discuss this return with the preparer shown below? (see page 52)? ☒ Yes ☐ No

Paid Preparer's Use Only

Preparer's signature	Date	Check if self-employed ☐	Preparer's SSN or PTIN
Firm's name (or yours if self-employed), address, and ZIP code	Waterside Financial Serv., Inc 6274 Linton Blvd., Suite #102 Boca Raton, FL 33484	EIN 65-0664126	Phone no. (561) 865-0071

IFOUS1A 11/22/00 — Form **1040** (2000)

SCHEDULE C (Form 1040)
Department of the Treasury Internal Revenue Service (99)

Profit or Loss From Business
(Sole Proprietorship)
▶ Partnerships, joint ventures, etc., must file Form 1065 or Form 1065-B.
▶ Attach to Form 1040 or Form 1041. ▶ See Instructions for Schedule C (Form 1040).

OMB No. 1545-0074
2000
Attachment Sequence No. 09

Name of proprietor: A. TRADER PROFIT-NO 475
Social security number (SSN): 123-45-6789

A Principal business or profession, including product or service (see page C-1 of the instructions): TRADER
B Enter code from pages C-7 & 8: ▶ 523900
C Business name. If no separate business name, leave blank.
D Employer ID number (EIN), if any

E Business address (including suite or room no.) ▶
City, town or post office, state, and ZIP code

F Accounting method: (1) ☒ Cash (2) ☐ Accrual (3) ☐ Other (specify) ▶
G Did you "materially participate" in the operation of this business during 2000? If "No," see page C-2 for limit on losses ☒ Yes ☐ No
H If you started or acquired this business during 2000, check here ▶ ☐

Part I Income

1 Gross receipts or sales. **Caution:** If this income was reported to you on Form W-2 and the "Statutory employee" box on that form was checked, see page C-2 and check here ▶ ☐	1	
2 Returns and allowances	2	
3 Subtract line 2 from line 1	3	
4 Cost of goods sold (from line 42 on page 2)	4	
5 **Gross profit.** Subtract line 4 from line 3	5	
6 Other income, including Federal and state gasoline or fuel tax credit or refund (see page C-2)	6	
7 **Gross income.** Add lines 5 and 6 ▶	7	

Part II Expenses. Enter expenses for business use of your home **only** on line 30.

8 Advertising	8		19 Pension and profit-sharing plans	19	
9 Bad debts from sales or services (see page C-3)	9		20 Rent or lease (see page C-4):		
			a Vehicles, machinery & equipment	20a	5,050
10 Car and truck expenses (see page C-3)	10	3,115	b Other business property	20b	
			21 Repairs and maintenance	21	3,166
11 Commissions and fees	11		22 Supplies (not included in Part III)	22	5,069
12 Depletion	12		23 Taxes and licenses	23	
13 Depreciation and section 179 expense deduction (not included in Part III) (see page C-3)	13	23,150	24 Travel, meals, and entertainment:		
			a Travel	24a	6,511
			b Meals and entertainment 8,711		
14 Employee benefit programs (other than on line 19)	14		c Enter nondeductible amount included on line 24b (see page C-5) 4,356		
15 Insurance (other than health)	15				
16 Interest:			d Subtract line 24c from line 24b	24d	4,355
a Mortgage (paid to banks, etc.)	16a		25 Utilities	25	2,611
b Other	16b	51,357	26 Wages (less employment credits)	26	
17 Legal and professional services	17	2,250	27 Other expenses (from line 48 on page 2)	27	83,233
18 Office expense	18	4,561			

28 **Total expenses** before expenses for business use of home. Add lines 8 through 27 in columns ▶	28	194,428
29 Tentative profit (loss). Subtract line 28 from line 7	29	-194,428
30 Expenses for business use of your home. Attach **Form 8829**	30	6,250
31 **Net profit or (loss).** Subtract line 30 from line 29. • If a profit, enter on **Form 1040, line 12,** and **also** on **Schedule SE, line 2** (statutory employees, see page C-5). Estates and trusts, enter on Form 1041, line 3. • If a loss, you **must** go to line 32.	31	-200,678

32 If you have a loss, check the box that describes your investment in this activity (see page C-5).
- If you checked 32a, enter the loss on **Form 1040, line 12,** and **also** on **Schedule SE, line 2** (statutory employees, see page C-5). Estates and trusts, enter on Form 1041, line 3.
- If you checked 32b, you **must** attach **Form 6198.**

32a ☒ All investment is at risk.
32b ☐ Some investment is not at risk.

For Paperwork Reduction Act Notice, see Form 1040 instructions. **Schedule C (Form 1040) 2000**

KFA IF0US4 11/08/00

Schedule C (Form 1040) 2000 A. TRADER-PROFIT-NO 475 123-45-6789 Page **2**

Part III **Cost of Goods Sold** (see page C-6)

33 Method(s) used to value closing inventory: **a** ☐ Cost **b** ☐ Lower of cost or market **c** ☐ Other (attach explanation)

34 Was there any change in determining quantities, costs, or valuations between opening and closing inventory? If "Yes," attach explanation ☐ Yes ☐ No

35 Inventory at beginning of year. If different from last year's closing inventory, attach explanation	35	
36 Purchases less cost of items withdrawn for personal use	36	
37 Cost of labor. Do not include any amounts paid to yourself	37	
38 Materials and supplies	38	
39 Other costs	39	
40 Add lines 35 through 39	40	
41 Inventory at end of year	41	
42 **Cost of goods sold.** Subtract line 41 from line 40. Enter the result here and on page 1, line 4	42	

Part IV **Information on Your Vehicle.** Complete this part **only** if you are claiming car or truck expenses on line 10 and are not required to file Form 4562 for this business. See the instructions for line 13 on page C-3 to find out if you must file.

43 When did you place your vehicle in service for business purposes? (month, day, year) ▶ ______________

44 Of the total number of miles you drove your vehicle during 2000, enter the number of miles you used your vehicle for:

a Business ______________ **b** Commuting ______________ **c** Other ______________

45 Do you (or your spouse) have another vehicle available for personal use? ☐ Yes ☐ No

46 Was your vehicle available for use during off-duty hours? ☐ Yes ☐ No

47a Do you have evidence to support your deduction? ☐ Yes ☐ No

b If "Yes," is the evidence written? ☐ Yes ☐ No

Part V **Other Expenses.** List below business expenses not included on lines 8–26 or line 30.

COMPUTER EXPENSE		2,955
HISTORICAL DATA SERVICES		3,061
INTERNET SERVICES		2,050
ONLINE TRADING DATA		7,010
OTHER TRADING EXPENSES		4,116
PROFESSIONAL PUBLICATIONS		3,116
TRADING ADVISORY SERVICES		35,179
TRADING PERIODICALS		6,633
TRADING SEMINARS		19,113
48 **Total other expenses.** Enter here and on page 1, line 27	48	83,233

IFOUS4A 11/09/00 Schedule C (Form 1040) 2000

SCHEDULE D (Form 1040)
Department of the Treasury Internal Revenue Service (99)

Capital Gains and Losses

▶ Attach to Form 1040. ▶ See Instructions for Schedule D (Form 1040).
▶ Use Schedule D-1 for more space to list transactions for lines 1 and 8.

OMB No. 1545-0074
2000
Attachment Sequence No. **12**

Name(s) shown on Form 1040: A. TRADER PROFIT-NO 475
Your social security number: 123-45-6789

Part I Short-Term Capital Gains and Losses – Assets Held One Year or Less

1 (a) Description of property (Example, 100 sh. XYZ Co.)	(b) Date acquired (Mo., day, yr.)	(c) Date sold (Mo., day, yr.)	(d) Sales price (see page D-6)	(e) Cost or other basis (see page D-6)	(f) Gain or (loss) Subtract (e) from (d)
1	Various	Various	301,519	0	301,519

2 Enter your short-term totals, if any, from Schedule D-1, line 2	2	
3 **Total short-term sales price amounts.** Add column (d) of lines 1 and 2	3	301,519
4 Short-term gain from Form 6252 and short-term gain or (loss) from Forms 4684, 6781, and 8824	4	
5 Net short-term gain or (loss) from partnerships, S corporations, estates, and trusts from Schedule(s) K-1	5	
6 Short-term capital loss carryover. Enter the amount, if any, from line 8 of your 1999 Capital Loss Carryover Worksheet	6	( )
7 **Net short-term capital gain or (loss).** Combine column (f) of lines 1 through 6 ▶	7	301,519

Part II Long-Term Capital Gains and Losses – Assets Held More Than One Year

8 (a) Description of property (Example, 100 sh. XYZ Co.)	(b) Date acquired (Mo., day, yr.)	(c) Date sold (Mo., day, yr.)	(d) Sales price (see page D-6)	(e) Cost or other basis (see page D-6)	(f) Gain or (loss) Subtract (e) from (d)	(g) 28% rate gain or (loss) *(see instr. below)

		(f)	(g)
9 Enter your long-term totals, if any, from Schedule D-1, line 9	9		
10 **Total long-term sales price amounts.** Add column (d) of lines 8 and 9	10		
11 Gain from Form 4797, Part I; long-term gain from Forms 2439 and 6252; and long-term gain or (loss) from Forms 4684, 6781, and 8824	11		
12 Net long-term gain or (loss) from partnerships, S corporations, estates, and trusts from Schedule(s) K-1	12		
13 Capital gain distributions. See page D-1	13		
14 Long-term capital loss carryover. Enter in both columns (f) and (g) the amount, if any, from line 13 of your 1999 Capital Loss Carryover Worksheet	14	( )	( )
15 Combine column (g) of lines 8 through 14	15		
16 **Net long-term capital gain or (loss).** Combine column (f) of lines 8 through 14 ▶ **Next:** Go to Part III on the back.	16		

* **28% rate gain or loss** includes **all** "collectibles gains and losses" (as defined on page D-6) and up to 50% of the eligible gain on qualified small business stock (see page D-4).

For Paperwork Reduction Act Notice, see Form 1040 instructions. **Schedule D (Form 1040) 2000**

KFA IFOUS5 12/07/00

Schedule D (Form 1040) 2000 A. TRADER-PROFIT-NO 475 123-45-6789 Page **2**

Part III **Summary of Parts I and II**

17 Combine lines 7 and 16. If a loss, go to line 18. If a gain, enter the gain on Form 1040, line 13	17	301,519
Next: Complete Form 1040 through line 39. Then, go to **Part IV** to figure your tax if: • Both lines 16 and 17 are gains **and** • Form 1040, line 39, is more than zero. Otherwise, **stop here.**		
18 If line 17 is a loss, enter here and as a (loss) on Form 1040, line 13, the **smaller** of these losses: • The loss on line 17 **or** • ($3,000) or, if married filing separately, ($1,500)	18	( )
Next: Skip **Part IV** below. Instead, complete Form 1040 through line 37. Then, complete the **Capital Loss Carryover Worksheet** on page D-6 if: • The loss on line 17 exceeds the loss on line 18 **or** • Form 1040, line 37, is a loss.		

Part IV **Tax Computation Using Maximum Capital Gains Rates**

19 Enter your taxable income from Form 1040, line 39					19	
20 Enter the **smaller** of line 16 or line 17 of Schedule D			20			
21 If you are filing Form 4952, enter the amount from Form 4952, line 4e			21			
22 Subtract line 21 from line 20. If zero or less, enter -0-			22			
23 Combine lines 7 and 15. If zero or less, enter -0-			23			
24 Enter the **smaller** of line 15 or line 23, but not less than zero			24			
25 Enter your unrecaptured section 1250 gain, if any, from line 17 of the worksheet on page D-8			25			
26 Add lines 24 and 25			26			
27 Subtract line 26 from line 22. If zero or less, enter -0-					27	
28 Subtract line 27 from line 19. If zero or less, enter -0-					28	
29 Enter the **smaller** of: • The amount on line 19 **or** • $26,250 if single; $43,850 if married filing jointly or qualifying widow(er); $21,925 if married filing separately; or $35,150 if head of household					29	
30 Enter the **smaller** of line 28 or line 29			30			
31 Subtract line 22 from line 19. If zero or less, enter -0-			31			
32 Enter the **larger** of line 30 or line 31 ▶			32			
33 Figure the tax on the amount on line 32. Use the Tax Table or Tax Rate Schedules, whichever applies					33	
Note: If the amounts on lines 29 and 30 are the same, skip lines 34 through 37 and go to line 38.						
34 Enter the amount from line 29			34			
35 Enter the amount from line 30			35			
36 Subtract line 35 from line 34 ▶			36			
37 Multiply line 36 by 10% (.10)					37	
Note: If the amounts on lines 19 and 29 are the same, skip lines 38 through 51 and go to line 52.						
38 Enter the **smaller** of line 19 or line 27			38			
39 Enter the amount from line 36			39			
40 Subtract line 39 from line 38 ▶			40			
41 Multiply line 40 by 20% (.20)					41	
Note: If line 26 is zero or blank, skip lines 42 through 51 and go to line 52.						
42 Enter the **smaller** of line 22 or line 25			42			
43 Add lines 22 and 32	43					
44 Enter the amount from line 19	44					
45 Subtract line 44 from line 43. If zero or less, enter -0-			45			
46 Subtract line 45 from line 42. If zero or less, enter -0- ▶			46			
47 Multiply line 46 by 25% (.25)					47	
Note: If line 24 is zero or blank, skip lines 48 through 51 and go to line 52.						
48 Enter the amount from line 19			48			
49 Add lines 32, 36, 40, and 46			49			
50 Subtract line 49 from line 48			50			
51 Multiply line 50 by 28% (.28)					51	
52 Add lines 33, 37, 41, 47, and 51					52	
53 Figure the tax on the amount on line 19. Use the Tax Table or Tax Rate Schedules, whichever applies					53	
54 **Tax on all taxable income (including capital gains).** Enter the **smaller** of line 52 or line 53 here and on Form 1040, line 40					54	

IFOUS5A 10/24/00 **Schedule D (Form 1040) 2000**

Schedule E (Form 1040) 2000 Attachment Sequence No. **13** Page **2**

Name(s) shown on return. Do not enter name and social security number if shown on other side. A. TRADER-PROFIT-NO 475

Your social security number 123-45-6789

Note: If you report amounts from farming or fishing on Schedule E, you must enter your gross income from those activities on line 41 below. Real estate professionals must complete line 42 below.

Part II Income or Loss From Partnerships and S Corporations

If you report a loss from an at-risk activity, you **must** check either column **(e)** or **(f)** on line 27 to describe your investment in the activity. See page E-5. If you check column **(f)**, you must attach **Form 6198.**

27	(a) Name	(b) Enter P for partnership; S for S corp.	(c) Check if foreign partnership	(d) Employer identification number	Invest. At Risk? (e) All is at risk	(f) Some is not at risk
A	1	P				
B						
C						
D						
E						

	Passive Income and Loss		Nonpassive Income and Loss		
	(g) Passive loss allowed (attach Form 8582 if required)	(h) Passive income from Schedule K-1	(i) Nonpassive loss from Schedule K-1	(j) Section 179 expense deduction from Form 4562	(k) Nonpassive income from Schedule K-1
A		200,000			
B					
C					
D					
E					
28a Totals		200,000			
b Totals					

Line	Description	Amount
29	Add columns (h) and (k) of line 28a	200,000
30	Add columns (g), (i), and (j) of line 28b	( )
31	Total partnership and S corporation income or (loss). Combine lines 29 and 30. Enter the result here and include in the total on line 40 below	200,000

Part III Income or Loss From Estates and Trusts

32	(a) Name	(b) Employer ID number
A		
B		
C		
D		

	Passive Income and Loss		Nonpassive Income and Loss	
	(c) Passive deduction or loss allowed (attach Form 8582 if required)	(d) Passive income from Schedule K-1	(e) Deduction or loss from Schedule K-1	(f) Other income from Schedule K-1
A				
B				
C				
D				
33a Totals				
b Totals				

Line	Description	Amount
34	Add columns (d) and (f) of line 33a	
35	Add columns (c) and (e) of line 33b	( )
36	Total estate and trust income or (loss). Combine lines 34 and 35. Enter the result here and include in the total on line 40 below	

Part IV Income or Loss From Real Estate Mortgage Investment Conduits (REMICs) – Residual Holder

37	(a) Name	(b) Employer identification number	(c) Excess inclusion from Schedules Q, line 2c (see page E-6)	(d) Taxable income (net loss) from Schedules Q, line 1b	(e) Income from Schedules Q, line 3b

Line	Description	Amount
38	Combine columns (d) and (e) only. Enter the result here and include in the total on line 40 below	

Part V Summary

Line	Description	Amount
39	Net farm rental income or (loss) from **Form 4835.** Also, complete line 41 below	
40	**Total** income or (loss). Combine lines 26, 31, 36, 38, and 39. Enter the result here and on Form 1040, line 17 ▶	200,000
41	**Reconciliation of Farming and Fishing Income:** Enter your **gross** farming and fishing income reported on Form 4835, line 7; Schedule K-1 (Form 1065), line 15b; Schedule K-1 (Form 1120S), line 23; and Schedule K-1 (Form 1041), line 14 (see page E-6)	
42	**Reconciliation for Real Estate Professionals.** If you were real estate professional (see pg. E-4), enter net income or (loss) you reported anywhere on Form 1040 from all rental real estate activities in which you materially participated under passive activity loss rules.	

IFOUS7A 10/19/00 Schedule E (Form 1040) 2000

Form **4562** | **Depreciation and Amortization (Including Information on Listed Property)** | OMB No. 1545-0172 **2000**

Department of the Treasury Internal Revenue Service (99) ▶ See separate instructions. ▶ Attach this form to your return. Attachment Sequence No. **67**

Name(s) shown on return: A. TRADER PROFIT-NO 475 — Identifying number: 123-45-6789

Business or activity to which this form relates

Part I Election To Expense Certain Tangible Property (Section 179) Note: If you have any "listed property," complete Part V before you complete Part I.

1	Maximum dollar limitation. If an enterprise zone business, see page 2 of the instructions	1	$20,000
2	Total cost of section 179 property placed in service. See page 2 of the instructions	2	
3	Threshold cost of section 179 property before reduction in limitation	3	$200,000
4	Reduction in limitation. Subtract line 3 from line 2. If zero or less, enter -0-	4	
5	Dollar limitation for tax year. Subtract line 4 from line 1. If zero or less, enter -0-. If married filing separately, see page 2 of the instructions	5	20,000

6 (a) Description of property	(b) Cost (business use only)	(c) Elected cost
5-YR TRADING EQUIPMENT	50,000	20,000

7	Listed property. Enter amount from line 27	7	
8	Total elected cost of section 179 property. Add amounts in column (c), lines 6 and 7	8	20,000
9	Tentative deduction. Enter the smaller of line 5 or line 8	9	20,000
10	Carryover of disallowed deduction from 1999. See page 3 of the instructions	10	0
11	Business income limitation. Enter the smaller of business income (not less than zero) or line 5 (see instructions)	11	20,000
12	Section 179 expense deduction. Add lines 9 and 10, but do not enter more than line 11	12	20,000
13	Carryover of disallowed deduction to 2001. Add lines 9 and 10, less line 12 ▶	13	

Note: Do not use Part II or Part III below for listed property (automobiles, certain other vehicles, cellular telephones, certain computers, or property used for entertainment, recreation, or amusement). Instead, use Part V for listed property.

Part II MACRS Depreciation for Assets Placed in Service Only During Your 2000 Tax Year (Do not include listed property.)

Section A - General Asset Account Election

14 If you are making the election under section 168(i)(4) to group any assets placed in service during the tax year into one or more general asset accounts, check this box. See page 3 of the instructions ▶ ☐

Section B - General Depreciation System (GDS) (See page 3 of the instructions.)

(a) Classification of property	(b) Month and year placed in service	(c) Basis for depreciation (business/investment use only - see instructions)	(d) Recovery period	(e) Convention	(f) Method	(g) Depreciation deduction
15a 3-year property						
b 5-year property						
c 7-year property						
d 10-year property						
e 15-year property						
f 20-year property						
g 25-year property			25 yrs		S/L	
h Residential rental property			27.5 yrs	MM	S/L	
			27.5 yrs	MM	S/L	
i Nonresidential real property			39 yrs	MM	S/L	
				MM	S/L	

Section C - Alternative Depreciation System (ADS): (See page 5 of the instructions.)

16a Class life					S/L	
b 12-year			12 yrs		S/L	
c 40-year			40 yrs	MM	S/L	

Part III Other Depreciation (Do not include listed property.) (See page 5 of the instructions.)

17	GDS and ADS deductions for assets placed in service in tax years beginning before 2000	17	
18	Property subject to section 168(f)(1) election	18	
19	ACRS and other depreciation	19	3,150

Part IV Summary (See page 6 of the instructions.)

20	Listed property. Enter amount from line 26	20	
21	**Total.** Add deductions from line 12, lines 15 and 16 in column (g), and lines 17 through 20. Enter here and on the appropriate lines of your return. Partnerships and S corporations - see instructions	21	23,150
22	For assets shown above and placed in service during the current year, enter the portion of the basis attributable to section 263A costs	22	

KFA **For Paperwork Reduction Act Notice, see page 9 of the instructions.** GF0US7 10/26/00 Form **4562** (2000)

Example 2 *(Continued)*

Form **6251** Department of the Treasury Internal Revenue Service	**Alternative Minimum Tax – Individuals** ▶ **See separate instructions.** ▶ **Attach to Form 1040 or Form 1040NR.**	OMB No. 1545-0227 **2000** Attachment Sequence No. **32**
Name(s) shown on Form 1040: A. TRADER PROFIT-NO 475		Your social security number: 123-45-6789

Part I Adjustments and Preferences

1	If you itemized deductions on Schedule A (Form 1040), go to line 2. Otherwise, enter your standard deduction from Form 1040, line 36, here and go to line 6	1	4,400
2	Medical and dental. Enter the smaller of Schedule A (Form 1040), line 4 **or** 2 1/2% of Form 1040, line 34	2	
3	Taxes. Enter the amount from Schedule A (Form 1040), line 9	3	
4	Certain interest on a home mortgage **not** used to buy, build, or improve your home	4	
5	Miscellaneous itemized deductions. Enter the amount from Schedule A (Form 1040), line 26	5	
6	Refund of taxes. Enter any tax refund from Form 1040, line 10 or line 21	6	( )
7	Investment interest. Enter difference between regular tax and AMT deduction	7	
8	Post-1986 depreciation. Enter difference between regular tax and AMT depreciation	8	
9	Adjusted gain or loss. Enter difference between AMT and regular tax gain or loss	9	
10	Incentive stock options. Enter excess of AMT income over regular tax income	10	
11	Passive activities. Enter difference between AMT and regular tax income or loss	11	
12	Beneficiaries of estates and trusts. Enter the amount from Schedule K-1 (Form 1041), line 9	12	
13	Tax-exempt interest from private activity bonds issued after 8/7/86	13	
14	Other. Enter the amount, if any, for each item below and enter the total on line 14.	14	

a Circulation expenditures		h Loss limitations	
b Depletion		i Mining costs	
c Depreciation (pre-1987)		j Patron's adjustment	
d Installment sales		k Pollution control facilities	
e Intangible drilling costs		l Research & experimental	
f Large partnerships		m Section 1202 exclusion	
g Long-term contracts		n Tax shelter farm activities	
		o Related adjustments	

15	**Total Adjustments and Preferences.** Combine lines 1 through 14 ▶	15	4,400

Part II Alternative Minimum Taxable Income

16	Enter the amount from **Form 1040, line 37.** If less than zero, enter as a (loss) ▶	16	496,441
17	Net operating loss deduction, if any, from Form 1040, line 21. Enter as a positive amount	17	
18	If Form 1040, line 34, is over $128,950 (over $64,475 if married filing separately), and you itemized deductions, enter the amount, if any, from line 9 of the worksheet for Schedule A (Form 1040), line 28	18	( )
19	Combine lines 15 through 18 ▶	19	500,841
20	Alternative tax net operating loss deduction. See page 6 of the instructions	20	
21	**Alternative Minimum Taxable Income.** Subtract line 20 from line 19. (If married filing separately and line 21 is more than $165,000, see page 7 of the instructions.) ▶	21	500,841

Part III Exemption Amount and Alternative Minimum Tax

22 **Exemption Amount.** (If this form is for a child under age 14, see page 7 of the instructions.)

IF your filing status is:	**AND line 21 is not over . . .**	**THEN enter on line 22 . . .**
Single or head of household	$112,500	$33,750
Married filing jointly or qualifying widow(er)	150,000	45,000
Married filing separately	75,000	22,500

If line 21 is **over** the amount shown above for your filing status, see page 7 of the instructions. } 22

23	Subtract line 22 from line 21. If zero or less, enter -0- here and on lines 26 and 28 and stop here ▶	23	500,841
24	If you reported capital gain distributions directly on Form 1040, line 13, **or** you completed Schedule D (Form 1040) and have an amount on line 25 or line 27 (or would have had an amount on either line if you had completed Part IV) (as refigured for the AMT, if necessary), go to Part IV of Form 6251 to figure line 24. **All others:** If line 23 is $175,000 or less ($87,500 or less if married filing separately), multiply line 23 by 26% (.26). Otherwise, multiply line 23 by 28% (.28) and subtract $3,500 ($1,750 if married filing separately) from the result ▶	24	136,735
25	Alternative minimum tax foreign tax credit. See page 7 of the instructions	25	
26	Tentative minimum tax. Subtract line 25 from line 24 ▶	26	136,735
27	Enter your tax from Form 1040, line 40 (minus any tax from Form 4972 and any foreign tax credit from Form 1040, line 43)	27	174,261
28	**Alternative Minimum Tax.** Subtract line 27 from line 26. If zero or less, enter -0-. Enter here and on Form 1040, line 41 ▶	28	0

For Paperwork Reduction Act Notice, see page 8 of the instructions. Form **6251** (2000)

KFA IFOUS33 10/23/00

Example 3

FORM 1040 Department of the Treasury – Internal Revenue Service
U.S. Individual Income Tax Return 2000 (99) IRS Use Only – Do not write or staple in this space.

For the year Jan. 1 – Dec. 31, 2000, or other tax year beginning , 2000, ending , 20 | OMB No. 1545-0074

Label (See instructions on page 19.) Use the IRS label. Otherwise, please print or type. LABEL HERE

Your first name and initial / Last name: A. TRADER-PROFIT-SEC475	Your social security number: 123-45-6789
If a joint return, spouse's first name and initial / Last name	Spouse's social security number
Home address (number and street). If you have a P.O. box, see page 19. Apt. no.: C/O TED TESSER-6274 LINTON BLVD. #102	▲ **IMPORTANT!** ▲ You **must** enter your SSN(s) above.
City, town or post office, state, and ZIP code. If you have a foreign address, see page 19.: DELRAY BEACH, FL 33484	

Presidential Election Campaign (See page 19.) **Note.** Checking "Yes" will not change your tax or reduce your refund. Do you, or your spouse if filing a joint return, want $3 to go to this fund? ▶ You: ☐ Yes ☒ No — Spouse: ☐ Yes ☐ No

Filing Status (Check only one box.)

1. [X] Single
2. [ ] Married filing joint return (even if only one had income)
3. [ ] Married filing separate return. Enter spouse's soc. sec. no. above & full name here ▶
4. [ ] Head of household (with qualifying person). (See page 19.) If the qualifying person is a child but not your dependent, enter this child's name here ▶
5. [ ] Qualifying widow(er) with dependent child (year spouse died ▶). (See page 19.)

Exemptions

6a ☒ **Yourself.** If your parent (or someone else) can claim you as a dependent on his or her tax return, **do not** check box 6a.
b ☐ **Spouse** — No. of boxes checked on 6a and 6b: 1

c **Dependents:**

(1) First Name / Last name	(2) Dependent's social security number	(3) Dependent's relationship to you	(4) Chk if qualifying child for child tax credit (see page 20)

If more than six dependents, see page 20.

No. of your children on 6c who: ● lived with you ___ ● did not live with you due to divorce or separation (see page 20) ___ Dependents on 6c not entered above ___

d Total number of exemptions claimed — Add numbers entered on lines above ▶ 1

Income

Attach Forms W-2 and W-2G here. Also attach Form 1099-R if tax was withheld.

If you did not get a W-2, see page 21.

Enclose, but do not attach any payment. Also, please use Form 1040-V.

Line	Description		Amount
7	Wages, salaries, tips, etc. Attach Form(s) W-2	7	200,000
8a	**Taxable** interest. Attach Schedule B if required	8a	
b	**Tax-exempt** interest. **Do not** include on line 8a — 8b		
9	Ordinary dividends. Attach Schedule B if required	9	
10	Taxable refunds, credits, or offsets of state and local income taxes (see page 22)	10	
11	Alimony received	11	
12	Business income or (loss). Attach Schedule C or C-EZ	12	-200,678
13	Capital gain or (loss). Attach Schedule D if required. If not required, check here ▶ ☐	13	
14	Other gains or (losses). Attach Form 4797	14	301,519
15a	Total IRA distributions — 15a; b Taxable amount (see pg. 23)	15b	
16a	Total pensions and annuities — 16a; b Taxable amount (see pg. 23)	16b	
17	Rental real estate, royalties, partnerships, S corporations, trusts, etc. Attach Schedule E	17	200,000
18	Farm income or (loss). Attach Schedule F	18	
19	Unemployment compensation	19	
20a	Social security benefits — 20a; b Taxable amount (see pg. 25)	20b	
21	Other income.	21	
22	Add the amounts in the far right column for lines 7 through 21. This is your **total income** ▶	22	500,841

Adjusted Gross Income

Line	Description		Amount		Amount
23	IRA deduction (see page 27)	23			
24	Student loan interest deduction (see page 27)	24			
25	Medical savings account deduction. Attach Form 8853	25			
26	Moving expenses. Attach Form 3903	26			
27	One-half of self-employment tax. Attach Schedule SE	27			
28	Self-employed health insurance deduction (see page 29)	28			
29	Self-employed SEP, SIMPLE, and qualified plans	29			
30	Penalty on early withdrawal of savings	30			
31a	Alimony paid. b Recipient's SSN ▶	31a			
32	Add lines 23 through 31a			32	0
33	Subtract line 32 from line 22. This is your **adjusted gross income** ▶			33	500,841

KFA **For Disclosure, Privacy Act, and Paperwork Reduction Act Notice, see page 56.** IF0US1 11/07/00 Form **1040** (2000)

Example 3 *(Continued)*

Form 1040 (2000) A. TRADER-PROFIT-SEC475 — 123-45-6789 — Page **2**

Tax and Credits	34 Amount from line 33 (adjusted gross income)	34	500,841
	35a Check if: ☐ **You** were 65 or older, ☐ Blind; ☐ **Spouse** was 65 or older, ☐ Blind. Add the number of boxes checked above and enter the total here ▶ 35a		
Standard Deduction for Most People — Single: $4,400; Head of household: $6,450; Married filing jointly or Qualifying widow(er): $7,350; Married filing separately $3,675.	b If you are married filing separately and your spouse itemizes deductions, or you were a dual-status alien, see page 31 and check here ▶ 35b ☐		
	36 Enter your **itemized deductions** from Schedule A, line 28, **or standard deduction** shown on the left. **But** see page 31 to find your standard deduction if you checked any box on line 35a or 35b **or** if someone can claim you as a dependent	36	4,400
	37 Subtract line 36 from line 34	37	496,441
	38 If line 34 is $96,700 or less, multiply $2,800 by the total number of exemptions claimed on line 6d. If line 34 is over $96,700, see the worksheet on page 32 for the amount to enter	38	0
	39 **Taxable income.** Subtract line 38 from line 37. If line 38 is more than line 37, enter -0-	39	496,441
	40 **Tax** (see page 32). Check if any tax is from a ☐ Form(s) 8814 b ☐ Form 4972	40	174,261
	41 Alternative minimum tax. Attach Form 6251	41	
	42 Add lines 40 and 41 ▶	42	174,261
	43 Foreign tax credit. Attach Form 1116 if required — 43		
	44 Credit for child and dependent care expenses. Att. Form 2441 — 44		
	45 Credit for the elderly or the disabled. Attach Schedule R — 45		
	46 Education credits. Attach Form 8863 — 46		
	47 Child tax credit (see page 36) — 47		
	48 Adoption credit. Attach Form 8839 — 48		
	49 Other. Check if from a ☐ Form 3800 b ☐ Form 8396 c ☐ Form 8801 d ☐ Form (specify) — 49		
	50 Add lines 43 through 49. These are your **total credits**	50	
	51 Subtract line 50 from line 42. If line 50 is more than line 42, enter -0- ▶	51	174,261
Other Taxes	52 Self-employment tax. Att. Sch. SE	52	
	53 Social security and Medicare tax on tip income not reported to employer. Attach Form 4137	53	
	54 Tax on IRAs, other retirement plans, and MSAs. Attach Form 5329 if required	54	
	55 Advance earned income credit payments from Form(s) W-2	55	
	56 Household employment taxes. Attach Schedule H	56	
	57 Add lines 51 through 56. This is your **total tax** ▶	57	174,261
Payments	58 Federal income tax withheld from Forms W-2 and 1099 — 58 — 60,000		
If you have a qualifying child, attach Schedule EIC.	59 2000 estimated tax payments and amount applied from 1999 return — 59 — 50,000		
	60a **Earned income credit (EIC)** — 60a		
	b **Nontaxable earned income: amt.** ▶ and type ▶ No		
	61 Excess social security and RRTA tax withheld (see page 50) — 61		
	62 **Additional child tax credit. Attach Form 8812** — 62		
	63 **Amount paid with request for extension to file** (see page 50) — 63		
	64 Other payments. Check if from a ☐ Form 2439 b ☐ Form 4136 — 64		
	65 Add lines 58, 59, 60a, and 61 through 64. These are your **total payments** ▶	65	110,000
Refund Have it directly deposited! See page 50 and fill in 67b, 67c, and 67d.	66 If line 65 is more than line 57, subtract line 57 from line 65. This is the amount you **overpaid**	66	
	67a Amount of line 66 you want **refunded to you** ▶	67a	
	b Routing number ▶ c Type: ☐ Checking ☐ Savings		
	d Account number		
	68 Amount of line 66 you want **applied to your 2001 estimated tax** ▶ 68		
Amount You Owe	69 If line 57 is more than line 65, subtract line 65 from line 57. This is the **amount you owe.** For details on how to pay, see page 51 ▶	69	64,261
	70 Estimated tax penalty. Also include on line 69 — 70		

Sign Here — Joint return? See page 19. Keep a copy for your records.

Under penalties of perjury, I declare that I have examined this return and accompanying schedules and statements, and to the best of my knowledge and belief, they are true, correct, and complete. Declaration of preparer (other than taxpayer) is based on all information of which preparer has any knowledge.

Your signature	Date	Your occupation	Daytime phone number: 561-865-0071
Spouse's signature. If a joint return, **both** must sign.	Date	Spouse's occupation	May the IRS discuss this return with the preparer shown below? (see page 52)? ☒ Yes ☐ No

Paid Preparer's Use Only

Preparer's signature	Date	Check if self-employed ☐	Preparer's SSN or PTIN
Firm's name (or yours if self-employed), address, and ZIP code	Waterside Financial Serv., Inc	EIN	65-0664126
	6274 Linton Blvd., Suite #102		
	Boca Raton, FL 33484	Phone no.	(561) 865-0071

IFOUS1A 11/22/00 — Form **1040** (2000)

SCHEDULE C (Form 1040)	Profit or Loss From Business (Sole Proprietorship)	OMB No. 1545-0074
Department of the Treasury Internal Revenue Service (99)	▶ Partnerships, joint ventures, etc., must file Form 1065 or Form 1065-B. ▶ Attach to Form 1040 or Form 1041. ▶ See Instructions for Schedule C (Form 1040).	**2000** Attachment Sequence No. 09

Name of proprietor: A. TRADER-PROFIT-SEC475	Social security number (SSN): 123-45-6789
A Principal business or profession, including product or service (see page C-1 of the instructions): TRADER	**B** Enter code from pages C-7 & 8: ▶ 523900
C Business name. If no separate business name, leave blank.	**D** Employer ID number (EIN), if any

E Business address (including suite or room no.) ▶
City, town or post office, state, and ZIP code

F Accounting method: (1) ☒ Cash (2) ☐ Accrual (3) ☐ Other (specify) ▶

G Did you "materially participate" in the operation of this business during 2000? If "No," see page C-2 for limit on losses ☒ Yes ☐ No

H If you started or acquired this business during 2000, check here ▶ ☐

Part I Income

1 Gross receipts or sales. **Caution:** If this income was reported to you on Form W-2 and the "Statutory employee" box on that form was checked, see page C-2 and check here ▶ ☐	1	
2 Returns and allowances	2	
3 Subtract line 2 from line 1	3	
4 Cost of goods sold (from line 42 on page 2)	4	
5 **Gross profit.** Subtract line 4 from line 3	5	
6 Other income, including Federal and state gasoline or fuel tax credit or refund (see page C-2)	6	
7 **Gross income.** Add lines 5 and 6 ▶	7	

Part II Expenses. Enter expenses for business use of your home **only** on line 30.

8 Advertising	8		19 Pension and profit-sharing plans	19	
9 Bad debts from sales or services (see page C-3)	9		20 Rent or lease (see page C-4): a Vehicles, machinery & equipment	20a	5,050
10 Car and truck expenses (see page C-3)	10	3,115	b Other business property	20b	
11 Commissions and fees	11		21 Repairs and maintenance	21	3,166
12 Depletion	12		22 Supplies (not included in Part III)	22	5,069
13 Depreciation and section 179 expense deduction (not included in Part III) (see page C-3)	13	23,150	23 Taxes and licenses	23	
14 Employee benefit programs (other than on line 19)	14		24 Travel, meals, and entertainment: a Travel	24a	6,511
15 Insurance (other than health)	15		b Meals and entertainment 8,711		
16 Interest: a Mortgage (paid to banks, etc.)	16a		c Enter nondeductible amount included on line 24b (see page C-5) 4,356		
b Other	16b	51,357	d Subtract line 24c from line 24b	24d	4,355
17 Legal and professional services	17	2,250	25 Utilities	25	2,611
18 Office expense	18	4,561	26 Wages (less employment credits)	26	
			27 Other expenses (from line 48 on page 2)	27	83,233

28 **Total expenses** before expenses for business use of home. Add lines 8 through 27 in columns ▶	28	194,428
29 Tentative profit (loss). Subtract line 28 from line 7	29	-194,428
30 Expenses for business use of your home. Attach **Form 8829**	30	6,250
31 **Net profit or (loss).** Subtract line 30 from line 29. • If a profit, enter on **Form 1040, line 12,** and **also** on **Schedule SE, line 2** (statutory employees, see page C-5). Estates and trusts, enter on Form 1041, line 3. • If a loss, you **must** go to line 32.	31	-200,678

32 If you have a loss, check the box that describes your investment in this activity (see page C-5).
- If you checked 32a, enter the loss on **Form 1040, line 12,** and **also** on **Schedule SE, line 2** (statutory employees, see page C-5). Estates and trusts, enter on Form 1041, line 3.
- If you checked 32b, you **must** attach **Form 6198.**

32a ☒ All investment is at risk.
32b ☐ Some investment is not at risk.

For Paperwork Reduction Act Notice, see Form 1040 instructions. **Schedule C (Form 1040) 2000**

KFA IFOUS4 11/08/00

Schedule C (Form 1040) 2000 A. TRADER-PROFIT-SEC475 123-45-6789 Page 2

Part III Cost of Goods Sold (see page C-6)

33 Method(s) used to value closing inventory: a ☐ Cost b ☐ Lower of cost or market c ☐ Other (attach explanation)

34 Was there any change in determining quantities, costs, or valuations between opening and closing inventory? If "Yes," attach explanation ☐ Yes ☐ No

35 Inventory at beginning of year. If different from last year's closing inventory, attach explanation	35	
36 Purchases less cost of items withdrawn for personal use	36	
37 Cost of labor. Do not include any amounts paid to yourself	37	
38 Materials and supplies	38	
39 Other costs	39	
40 Add lines 35 through 39	40	
41 Inventory at end of year	41	
42 **Cost of goods sold.** Subtract line 41 from line 40. Enter the result here and on page 1, line 4	42	

Part IV Information on Your Vehicle. Complete this part **only** if you are claiming car or truck expenses on line 10 and are not required to file Form 4562 for this business. See the instructions for line 13 on page C-3 to find out if you must file.

43 When did you place your vehicle in service for business purposes? (month, day, year) ▶ ______________

44 Of the total number of miles you drove your vehicle during 2000, enter the number of miles you used your vehicle for:

a Business ______________ b Commuting ______________ c Other ______________

45 Do you (or your spouse) have another vehicle available for personal use? ☐ Yes ☐ No

46 Was your vehicle available for use during off-duty hours? ☐ Yes ☐ No

47a Do you have evidence to support your deduction? ☐ Yes ☐ No

b If "Yes," is the evidence written? ☐ Yes ☐ No

Part V Other Expenses. List below business expenses not included on lines 8–26 or line 30.

COMPUTER EXPENSE		2,955
HISTORICAL DATA SERVICES		3,061
INTERNET SERVICES		2,050
ONLINE TRADING DATA		7,010
OTHER TRADING EXPENSES		4,116
PROFESSIONAL PUBLICATIONS		3,116
TRADING ADVISORY SERVICES		35,179
TRADING PERIODICALS		6,633
TRADING SEMINARS		19,113
48 **Total other expenses.** Enter here and on page 1, line 27	48	83,233

IFOUS4A 11/09/00 Schedule C (Form 1040) 2000

Schedule E (Form 1040) 2000 Attachment Sequence No. **13** Page **2**

Name(s) shown on return. Do not enter name and social security number if shown on other side. A. TRADER-PROFIT-SEC475

Your social security number 123-45-6789

Note: If you report amounts from farming or fishing on Schedule E, you must enter your gross income from those activities on line 41 below. Real estate professionals must complete line 42 below.

Part II Income or Loss From Partnerships and S Corporations If you report a loss from an at-risk activity, you **must** check either column **(e)** or **(f)** on line 27 to describe your investment in the activity. See page E-5. If you check column **(f)**, you must attach **Form 6198.**

27	(a) Name	(b) Enter P for partnership; S for S corp.	(c) Check if foreign partnership	(d) Employer identification number	Invest. At Risk? (e) All is at risk	(f) Some is not at risk
A	1	P				
B						
C						
D						
E						

	Passive Income and Loss		Nonpassive Income and Loss		
	(g) Passive loss allowed (attach Form 8582 if required)	(h) Passive income from Schedule K-1	(i) Nonpassive loss from Schedule K-1	(j) Section 179 expense deduction from Form 4562	(k) Nonpassive income from Schedule K-1
A		200,000			
B					
C					
D					
E					
28a Totals		200,000			
b Totals					

29 Add columns (h) and (k) of line 28a	29	200,000
30 Add columns (g), (i), and (j) of line 28b	30	( )
31 Total partnership and S corporation income or (loss). Combine lines 29 and 30. Enter the result here and include in the total on line 40 below	31	200,000

Part III Income or Loss From Estates and Trusts

32	(a) Name	(b) Employer ID number
A		
B		
C		
D		

	Passive Income and Loss		Nonpassive Income and Loss	
	(c) Passive deduction or loss allowed (attach Form 8582 if required)	(d) Passive income from Schedule K-1	(e) Deduction or loss from Schedule K-1	(f) Other income from Schedule K-1
A				
B				
C				
D				
33a Totals				
b Totals				

34 Add columns (d) and (f) of line 33a	34	
35 Add columns (c) and (e) of line 33b	35	( )
36 Total estate and trust income or (loss). Combine lines 34 and 35. Enter the result here and include in the total on line 40 below	36	

Part IV Income or Loss From Real Estate Mortgage Investment Conduits (REMICs) – Residual Holder

37 (a) Name	(b) Employer identification number	(c) Excess inclusion from Schedules Q, line 2c (see page E-6)	(d) Taxable income (net loss) from Schedules Q, line 1b	(e) Income from Schedules Q, line 3b

38 Combine columns (d) and (e) only. Enter the result here and include in the total on line 40 below	38	

Part V Summary

39 Net farm rental income or (loss) from **Form 4835.** Also, complete line 41 below	39	
40 **Total** income or (loss). Combine lines 26, 31, 36, 38, and 39. Enter the result here and on Form 1040, line 17 ▶	40	200,000
41 **Reconciliation of Farming and Fishing Income:** Enter your **gross** farming and fishing income reported on Form 4835, line 7; Schedule K-1 (Form 1065), line 15b; Schedule K-1 (Form 1120S), line 23; and Schedule K-1 (Form 1041), line 14 (see page E-6)	41	
42 **Reconciliation for Real Estate Professionals.** If you were real estate professional (see pg. E-4), enter net income or (loss) you reported anywhere on Form 1040 from all rental real estate activities in which you materially participated under passive activity loss rules.	42	

IFOUS7A 10/19/00 Schedule E (Form 1040) 2000

Form **4562** Department of the Treasury Internal Revenue Service (99)

Depreciation and Amortization
(Including Information on Listed Property)

▶ See separate instructions. ▶ Attach this form to your return.

OMB No. 1545-0172 **2000** Attachment Sequence No. **67**

Name(s) shown on return: A. TRADER-PROFIT-SEC475 | Identifying number: 123-45-6789

Business or activity to which this form relates

Part I Election To Expense Certain Tangible Property (Section 179) Note: If you have any "listed property," complete Part V before you complete Part I.

1	Maximum dollar limitation. If an enterprise zone business, see page 2 of the instructions	1	$20,000
2	Total cost of section 179 property placed in service. See page 2 of the instructions	2	
3	Threshold cost of section 179 property before reduction in limitation	3	$200,000
4	Reduction in limitation. Subtract line 3 from line 2. If zero or less, enter -0-	4	
5	Dollar limitation for tax year. Subtract line 4 from line 1. If zero or less, enter -0-. If married filing separately, see page 2 of the instructions	5	20,000

6 (a) Description of property	(b) Cost (business use only)	(c) Elected cost
5-YR TRADING EQUIPMENT	50,000	20,000

7	Listed property. Enter amount from line 27	7	
8	Total elected cost of section 179 property. Add amounts in column (c), lines 6 and 7	8	20,000
9	Tentative deduction. Enter the smaller of line 5 or line 8	9	20,000
10	Carryover of disallowed deduction from 1999. See page 3 of the instructions	10	0
11	Business income limitation. Enter the smaller of business income (not less than zero) or line 5 (see instructions)	11	20,000
12	Section 179 expense deduction. Add lines 9 and 10, but do not enter more than line 11	12	20,000
13	Carryover of disallowed deduction to 2001. Add lines 9 and 10, less line 12 ▶	13	

Note: Do not use Part II or Part III below for listed property (automobiles, certain other vehicles, cellular telephones, certain computers, or property used for entertainment, recreation, or amusement). Instead, use Part V for listed property.

Part II MACRS Depreciation for Assets Placed in Service Only During Your 2000 Tax Year (Do not include listed property.)

Section A - General Asset Account Election

14 If you are making the election under section 168(i)(4) to group any assets placed in service during the tax year into one or more general asset accounts, check this box. See page 3 of the instructions ▶ ☐

Section B - General Depreciation System (GDS) (See page 3 of the instructions.)

(a) Classification of property	(b) Month and year placed in service	(c) Basis for depreciation (business/investment use only - see instructions)	(d) Recovery period	(e) Convention	(f) Method	(g) Depreciation deduction
15a 3-year property						
b 5-year property						
c 7-year property						
d 10-year property						
e 15-year property						
f 20-year property						
g 25-year property			25 yrs		S/L	
h Residential rental property			27.5 yrs	MM	S/L	
			27.5 yrs	MM	S/L	
i Nonresidential real property			39 yrs	MM	S/L	
				MM	S/L	

Section C - Alternative Depreciation System (ADS): (See page 5 of the instructions.)

(a)	(b)	(c)	(d)	(e)	(f)	(g)
16a Class life					S/L	
b 12-year			12 yrs		S/L	
c 40-year			40 yrs	MM	S/L	

Part III Other Depreciation (Do not include listed property.) (See page 5 of the instructions.)

17	GDS and ADS deductions for assets placed in service in tax years beginning before 2000	17	
18	Property subject to section 168(f)(1) election	18	
19	ACRS and other depreciation	19	3,150

Part IV Summary (See page 6 of the instructions.)

20	Listed property. Enter amount from line 26	20	
21	**Total.** Add deductions from line 12, lines 15 and 16 in column (g), and lines 17 through 20. Enter here and on the appropriate lines of your return. Partnerships and S corporations - see instructions	21	23,150
22	For assets shown above and placed in service during the current year, enter the portion of the basis attributable to section 263A costs	22	

KFA **For Paperwork Reduction Act Notice, see page 9 of the instructions.** GFOUS7 10/26/00 Form **4562** (2000)

Form **4797** | Department of the Treasury Internal Revenue Service (99)

Sales of Business Property

(Also Involuntary Conversions and Recapture Amounts Under Sections 179 and 280F(b)(2))

▶ Attach to your tax return. ▶ See separate instructions.

OMB No. 1545-0184 | **2000** | Attachment Sequence No. **27**

Name(s) shown on return: A. TRADER-PROFIT-SEC475 | Identifying number: 123-45-6789

1 Enter the gross proceeds from sales or exchanges reported to you for 2000 on Form(s) 1099-B or 1099-S (or substitute statement) that you are including on line 2, 10, or 20 (see instructions) 1

Part I Sales or Exchanges of Property Used in a Trade or Business and Involuntary Conversions From Other Than Casualty or Theft – Most Property Held More Than 1 Year (See instructions.)

2 (a) Description of property	(b) Date acquired (mo., day, yr.)	(c) Date sold (mo., day, yr.)	(d) Gross sales price	(e) Depreciation allowed or allowable since acquisition	(f) Cost or other basis, plus improvements and expense of sale	(g) Gain or (loss) Subtract (f) from the sum of (d) and (e)

3 Gain, if any, from Form 4684, line 39 3

4 Section 1231 gain from installment sales from Form 6252, line 26 or 37 4

5 Section 1231 gain or (loss) from like-kind exchanges from Form 8824 5

6 Gain, if any, from line 32, from other than casualty or theft 6

7 Combine lines 2 through 6. Enter the gain or (loss) here and on the appropriate line as follows: 7

Partnerships (except electing large partnerships). Report the gain or (loss) following the instructions for Form 1065, Schedule K, line 6. Skip lines 8, 9, 11, and 12 below.

S corporations. Report the gain or (loss) following the instructions for Form 1120S, Schedule K, lines 5 and 6. Skip lines 8, 9, 11, and 12 below, unless line 7 is a gain and the S corporation is subject to capital gains tax.

All others. If line 7 is zero or a loss, enter the amount from line 7 on line 11 below and skip lines 8 and 9. If line 7 is a gain and you did not have any prior year section 1231 losses, or they were recaptured in an earlier year, enter the gain from line 7 as a long-term capital gain on Schedule D and skip lines 8, 9, and 12 below.

8 Nonrecaptured net section 1231 losses from prior years (see instructions) 8

9 Subtract line 8 from line 7. If zero or less, enter -0-. Also enter on the appropriate line as follows (see instructions): 9

S corporations. Enter any gain from line 9 on Schedule D (Form 1120S), line 15, and skip lines 11 and 12 below.

All others. If line 9 is zero, enter the gain from line 7 on line 12 below. If line 9 is more than zero, enter the amount from line 8 on line 12 below, and enter the gain from line 9 as a long-term capital gain on Schedule D.

Part II Ordinary Gains and Losses

10 Ordinary gains and losses not included on lines 11 through 17 (include property held 1 year or less):

475 TRADING	INCOME			301,519		301,519

Line	Description		Amount
11	Loss, if any, from line 7	11	
12	Gain, if any, from line 7 or amount from line 8, if applicable	12	
13	Gain, if any, from line 31	13	
14	Net gain or (loss) from Form 4684, lines 31 and 38a	14	
15	Ordinary gain from installment sales from Form 6252, line 25 or 36	15	
16	Ordinary gain or (loss) from like-kind exchanges from Form 8824	16	
17	Recapture of section 179 expense deduction for partners and S corporation shareholders from property dispositions by partnerships and S corporations (see instructions)	17	
18	Combine lines 10 through 17. Enter the gain or (loss) here and on the appropriate line as follows:	18	301,519

a For all except individual returns: Enter the gain or (loss) from line 18 on the return being filed.

b For individual returns:

(1) If the loss on line 11 includes a loss from Form 4684, line 35, column (b)(ii), enter that part of the loss here. Enter the part of the loss from income-producing property on Schedule A (Form 1040), line 27, and the part of the loss from property used as an employee on Schedule A (Form 1040), line 22. Identify as from "Form 4797, line 18b(1)." See instructions .... 18b(1)

(2) Redetermine the gain or (loss) on line 18 excluding the loss, if any, on line 18b(1). Enter here and on Form 1040, line 14. .... 18b(2) 301,519

KFA **For Paperwork Reduction Act Notice, see page 7 of the instructions.** GF0US51 12/22/00 Form **4797** (2000)

Example 4

Form 1040 Department of the Treasury – Internal Revenue Service
U.S. Individual Income Tax Return 2000 (99) IRS Use Only – Do not write or staple in this space.

For the year Jan. 1 – Dec. 31, 2000, or other tax year beginning , 2000, ending , 20 OMB No. 1545-0074

Label (See instructions on page 19.) Use the IRS label. Otherwise, please print or type. LABEL HERE	Your first name and initial / Last name: N. VEST-LOSS — Your social security number: 123-45-6789
	If a joint return, spouse's first name and initial / Last name — Spouse's social security number
	Home address (number and street). If you have a P.O. box, see page 19. Apt. no.: C/O TED TESSER-6274 LINTON BLVD. #102 — ▲ IMPORTANT! ▲ You **must** enter your SSN(s) above.
	City, town or post office, state, and ZIP code. If you have a foreign address, see page 19.: DELRAY BEACH, FL 33484

Presidential Election Campaign (See page 19.) **Note.** Checking "Yes" will not change your tax or reduce your refund. Do you, or your spouse if filing a joint return, want $3 to go to this fund? ▶ You: ☐ Yes ☒ No — Spouse: ☐ Yes ☐ No

Filing Status (Check only one box.)

1. [X] Single
2. [ ] Married filing joint return (even if only one had income)
3. [ ] Married filing separate return. Enter spouse's soc. sec. no. above & full name here ▶
4. [ ] Head of household (with qualifying person). (See page 19.) If the qualifying person is a child but not your dependent, enter this child's name here ▶
5. [ ] Qualifying widow(er) with dependent child (year spouse died ▶). (See page 19.)

Exemptions

6a ☒ **Yourself.** If your parent (or someone else) can claim you as a dependent on his or her tax return, **do not** check box 6a.

b ☐ **Spouse** — No. of boxes checked on 6a and 6b: 1

c **Dependents:**

(1) First Name Last name	(2) Dependent's social security number	(3) Dependent's relationship to you	(4) Chk if qualifying child for child tax credit (see page 20)

If more than six dependents, see page 20.

No. of your children on 6c who: ● lived with you ___ ● did not live with you due to divorce or separation (see page 20) ___ Dependents on 6c not entered above ___

d Total number of exemptions claimed — Add numbers entered on lines above ▶ 1

Income

Attach Forms W-2 and W-2G here. Also attach Form 1099-R if tax was withheld.

If you did not get a W-2, see page 21.

Enclose, but do not attach any payment. Also, please use Form 1040-V.

Line	Description	Box	Amount
7	Wages, salaries, tips, etc. Attach Form(s) W-2	7	200,000
8a	**Taxable** interest. Attach Schedule B if required	8a	
b	**Tax-exempt** interest. **Do not** include on line 8a — 8b		
9	Ordinary dividends. Attach Schedule B if required	9	
10	Taxable refunds, credits, or offsets of state and local income taxes (see page 22)	10	
11	Alimony received	11	
12	Business income or (loss). Attach Schedule C or C-EZ	12	
13	Capital gain or (loss). Attach Schedule D if required. If not required, check here ▶ ☐	13	-3,000
14	Other gains or (losses). Attach Form 4797	14	
15a	Total IRA distributions — 15a — b Taxable amount (see pg. 23)	15b	
16a	Total pensions and annuities — 16a — b Taxable amount (see pg. 23)	16b	
17	Rental real estate, royalties, partnerships, S corporations, trusts, etc. Attach Schedule E	17	200,000
18	Farm income or (loss). Attach Schedule F	18	
19	Unemployment compensation	19	
20a	Social security benefits — 20a — b Taxable amount (see pg. 25)	20b	
21	Other income.	21	
22	Add the amounts in the far right column for lines 7 through 21. This is your **total income** ▶	22	397,000

Adjusted Gross Income

Line	Description	Box	Amount
23	IRA deduction (see page 27)	23	
24	Student loan interest deduction (see page 27)	24	
25	Medical savings account deduction. Attach Form 8853	25	
26	Moving expenses. Attach Form 3903	26	
27	One-half of self-employment tax. Attach Schedule SE	27	
28	Self-employed health insurance deduction (see page 29)	28	
29	Self-employed SEP, SIMPLE, and qualified plans	29	
30	Penalty on early withdrawal of savings	30	
31a	Alimony paid. b Recipient's SSN ▶	31a	
32	Add lines 23 through 31a	32	0
33	Subtract line 32 from line 22. This is your **adjusted gross income** ▶	33	397,000

KFA **For Disclosure, Privacy Act, and Paperwork Reduction Act Notice, see page 56.** IFOUS1 11/07/00 Form **1040** (2000)

Form 1040 (2000) N. VEST-LOSS 123-45-6789 Page **2**

Tax and Credits	34 Amount from line 33 (adjusted gross income)	34	397,000
	35a Check if: ☐ **You** were 65 or older, ☐ Blind; ☐ **Spouse** was 65 or older, ☐ Blind. Add the number of boxes checked above and enter the total here ▶ 35a		
	b If you are married filing separately and your spouse itemizes deductions, or you were a dual-status alien, see page 31 and check here ▶ 35b ☐		
Standard Deduction for Most People Single: $4,400; Head of household: $6,450; Married filing jointly or Qualifying widow(er): $7,350; Married filing separately $3,675.	36 Enter your **itemized deductions** from Schedule A, line 28, **or standard deduction** shown on the left. **But** see page 31 to find your standard deduction if you checked any box on line 35a or 35b **or** if someone can claim you as a dependent	36	78,960
	37 Subtract line 36 from line 34	37	318,040
	38 If line 34 is $96,700 or less, multiply $2,800 by the total number of exemptions claimed on line 6d. If line 34 is over $96,700, see the worksheet on page 32 for the amount to enter	38	0
	39 **Taxable income.** Subtract line 38 from line 37. If line 38 is more than line 37, enter -0-	39	318,040
	40 **Tax** (see page 32). Check if any tax is from a ☐ Form(s) 8814 b ☐ Form 4972	40	103,614
	41 Alternative minimum tax. Attach Form 6251	41	4,046
	42 Add lines 40 and 41 ▶	42	107,660
	43 Foreign tax credit. Attach Form 1116 if required — 43		
	44 Credit for child and dependent care expenses. Att. Form 2441 — 44		
	45 Credit for the elderly or the disabled. Attach Schedule R — 45		
	46 Education credits. Attach Form 8863 — 46		
	47 Child tax credit (see page 36) — 47		
	48 Adoption credit. Attach Form 8839 — 48		
	49 Other. Check if from a ☐ Form 3800 b ☐ Form 8396 c ☐ Form 8801 d ☐ Form (specify) — 49		
	50 Add lines 43 through 49. These are your **total credits**	50	
	51 Subtract line 50 from line 42. If line 50 is more than line 42, enter -0- ▶	51	107,660
Other Taxes	52 Self-employment tax. Att. Sch. SE	52	
	53 Social security and Medicare tax on tip income not reported to employer. Attach Form 4137	53	
	54 Tax on IRAs, other retirement plans, and MSAs. Attach Form 5329 if required	54	
	55 Advance earned income credit payments from Form(s) W-2	55	
	56 Household employment taxes. Attach Schedule H	56	
	57 Add lines 51 through 56. This is your **total tax** ▶	57	107,660
Payments	58 Federal income tax withheld from Forms W-2 and 1099 — 58 — 60,000		
If you have a qualifying child, attach Schedule EIC.	59 2000 estimated tax payments and amount applied from 1999 return — 59 — 50,000		
	60a **Earned income credit (EIC)** — 60a		
	b **Nontaxable earned income: amt.** ▶ **and type** ▶ No		
	61 Excess social security and RRTA tax withheld (see page 50) — 61		
	62 **Additional child tax credit. Attach Form 8812** — 62		
	63 **Amount paid with request for extension to file** (see page 50) — 63		
	64 Other payments. Check if from a ☐ Form 2439 b ☐ Form 4136 — 64		
	65 Add lines 58, 59, 60a, and 61 through 64. These are your **total payments** ▶	65	110,000
Refund Have it directly deposited! See page 50 and fill in 67b, 67c, and 67d.	66 If line 65 is more than line 57, subtract line 57 from line 65. This is the amount you **overpaid**	66	2,340
	67a Amount of line 66 you want **refunded to you** ▶	67a	2,340
	b Routing number ▶ c Type: ☐ Checking ☐ Savings		
	d Account number		
	68 Amount of line 66 you want **applied to your 2001 estimated tax** ▶ 68		
Amount You Owe	69 If line 57 is more than line 65, subtract line 65 from line 57. This is the **amount you owe.** For details on how to pay, see page 51 ▶	69	
	70 Estimated tax penalty. Also include on line 69 — 70		

Sign Here

Joint return? See page 19. Keep a copy for your records.

Under penalties of perjury, I declare that I have examined this return and accompanying schedules and statements, and to the best of my knowledge and belief, they are true, correct, and complete. Declaration of preparer (other than taxpayer) is based on all information of which preparer has any knowledge.

Your signature	Date	Your occupation	Daytime phone number
Spouse's signature. If a joint return, **both** must sign.	Date	Spouse's occupation	May the IRS discuss this return with the preparer shown below? (see page 52)? ☒ Yes ☐ No

Paid Preparer's Use Only

Preparer's signature	Date	Check if self-employed ☐	Preparer's SSN or PTIN
Firm's name (or yours if self-employed), address, and ZIP code	Waterside Financial Services 6274 Linton Blvd., Suite #102 Delray Beach, FL 33484	EIN	Phone no. (561) 865-0071

IF0US1A 11/22/00 Form **1040** (2000)

SCHEDULES A&B (Form 1040)		Schedule A – Itemized Deductions		OMB No. 1545-0074

2000

Department of the Treasury
Internal Revenue Service (99) ▶ **Attach to Form 1040.** ▶ **See Instructions for Schedules A and B (Form 1040).**

Attachment Sequence No. **07**

Name(s) shown on Form 1040

N. VEST-LOSS

Your social security number 123-45-6789

Medical and Dental Expenses		**Caution.** Do not include expenses reimbursed or paid by others.			
	1	Medical and dental expenses (see page A-2)	1		
	2	Enter amount from Form 1040, line 34 **2**			
	3	Multiply line 2 above by 7.5% (.075)	3		
	4	Subtract line 3 from line 1. If line 3 is more than line 1, enter –0–		4	0
Taxes You Paid	5	State and local income taxes	5		
	6	Real estate taxes (see page A-2)	6		
	7	Personal property taxes	7		
(See page A-2.)	8	Other taxes. List type and amount ▶ _	8		
	9	Add lines 5 through 8.		9	0
Interest You Paid (See page A-3.)	10	Home mortgage interest and points reported on Form 1098	10		
	11	Home mortgage interest not reported to you on Form 1098. If paid to the person from whom you bought the home, see page A-3 & show that person's name, ID no. & address ▶ _	11		
Note. Personal interest is not deductible.	12	Points not reported to you on Form 1098. See pg. A-3	12		
	13	Investment interest. Attach Form 4952, if required. (See page A-3.)	13		
	14	Add lines 10 through 13.		14	0
Gifts to Charity	15	Gifts by cash or check. If any gift of $250 or more, see pg. A-4	15		
If you made a gift and got a benefit for it, see page A-4.	16	Other than by cash or check. If any gift of $250 or more, see page A-4. You **must** attach Form 8283 if over $500	16		
	17	Carryover from prior year	17		
	18	Add lines 15 through 17.		18	0
Casualty and Theft Losses	19	Casualty or theft loss(es). Attach Form 4684. (See page A-5.)		19	0
Job Expenses and Most Other Miscellaneous Deductions	20	Unreimbursed employee expenses – job travel, union dues, job education, etc. You **must** attach Form 2106 or 2106-EZ if required. (See page A-5.) ▶ _	20		
	21	Tax preparation fees	21		
	22	Other expenses – investment, safe deposit box, etc. List type and amount ▶ Depreciation _ _ _ _ _ _ _ _ 5,000 Investment Expenses _ _ _ _ 89,942 _	22	94,942	
(See page A-5 for expenses to deduct here.)	23	Add lines 20 through 22	23	94,942	
	24	Enter amount from Form 1040, line 34 **24**	397,000		
	25	Multiply line 24 above by 2% (.02)	25	7,940	
	26	Subtract line 25 from line 23. If line 25 is more than line 23, enter –0–		26	87,002
Other Miscellaneous Deductions	27	Other – from list on page A-6. List type and amount ▶ _		27	0
Total Itemized Deductions	28	Is Form 1040, line 34, over $128,950 (over $64,475 if married filing separately)? Reduction –8,042 ☐ **No.** Your deduction is not limited. Add the amounts in the far right column for lines 4 through 27. Also, enter this amount on Form 1040, line 36. } ▶ ☒ **Yes.** Your deduction may be limited. See page A-6 for the amount to enter.		28	78,960

KFA **For Paperwork Reduction Act Notice, see Form 1040 Instructions.** IF0US2 11/03/00 Schedule A (Form 1040) 2000

SCHEDULE C (Form 1040)

Department of the Treasury
Internal Revenue Service (99)

Profit or Loss From Business

(Sole Proprietorship)

▶ Partnerships, joint ventures, etc., must file Form 1065 or Form 1065-B.

▶ Attach to Form 1040 or Form 1041. ▶ See Instructions for Schedule C (Form 1040).

OMB No. 1545-0074

2000

Attachment Sequence No. **09**

Name of proprietor: N. VEST-LOSS

Social security number (SSN): 123-45-6789

A Principal business or profession, including product or service (see page C-1 of the instructions)

B Enter code from pages C-7 & 8 ▶

C Business name. If no separate business name, leave blank.

D Employer ID number (EIN), if any

E Business address (including suite or room no.) ▶

City, town or post office, state, and ZIP code

F Accounting method: (1) ☒ Cash (2) ☐ Accrual (3) ☐ Other (specify) ▶

G Did you "materially participate" in the operation of this business during 2000? If "No," see page C-2 for limit on losses ☒ Yes ☐ No

H If you started or acquired this business during 2000, check here ▶ ☐

Part I Income

1 Gross receipts or sales. **Caution:** If this income was reported to you on Form W-2 and the "Statutory employee" box on that form was checked, see page C-2 and check here ▶ ☐	1	
2 Returns and allowances	2	
3 Subtract line 2 from line 1	3	
4 Cost of goods sold (from line 42 on page 2)	4	
5 **Gross profit.** Subtract line 4 from line 3	5	
6 Other income, including Federal and state gasoline or fuel tax credit or refund (see page C-2)	6	
7 **Gross income.** Add lines 5 and 6 ▶	7	

Part II Expenses. Enter expenses for business use of your home **only** on line 30.

8 Advertising	8		19 Pension and profit-sharing plans	19	
9 Bad debts from sales or services (see page C-3)	9		20 Rent or lease (see page C-4):		
10 Car and truck expenses (see page C-3)	10		a Vehicles, machinery & equipment	20a	
			b Other business property	20b	
			21 Repairs and maintenance	21	
11 Commissions and fees	11		22 Supplies (not included in Part III)	22	
12 Depletion	12		23 Taxes and licenses	23	
13 Depreciation and section 179 expense deduction (not included in Part III) (see page C-3)	13		24 Travel, meals, and entertainment:		
			a Travel	24a	
			b Meals and entertainment		
14 Employee benefit programs (other than on line 19)	14		c Enter nondeductible amount included on line 24b (see page C-5)		
15 Insurance (other than health)	15				
16 Interest:			d Subtract line 24c from line 24b	24d	
a Mortgage (paid to banks, etc.)	16a		25 Utilities	25	
b Other	16b		26 Wages (less employment credits)	26	
17 Legal and professional services	17		27 Other expenses		
18 Office expense	18		(from line 48 on page 2)	27	

28 **Total expenses** before expenses for business use of home. Add lines 8 through 27 in columns ▶	28	
29 Tentative profit (loss). Subtract line 28 from line 7	29	
30 Expenses for business use of your home. Attach **Form 8829**	30	
31 **Net profit or (loss).** Subtract line 30 from line 29. • If a profit, enter on **Form 1040, line 12,** and **also** on **Schedule SE, line 2** (statutory employees, see page C-5). Estates and trusts, enter on Form 1041, line 3. • If a loss, you **must** go to line 32.	31	0

32 If you have a loss, check the box that describes your investment in this activity (see page C-5).

- If you checked 32a, enter the loss on **Form 1040, line 12,** and **also** on **Schedule SE, line 2** (statutory employees, see page C-5). Estates and trusts, enter on Form 1041, line 3.
- If you checked 32b, you **must** attach **Form 6198.**

32a ☐ All investment is at risk.
32b ☐ Some investment is not at risk.

For Paperwork Reduction Act Notice, see Form 1040 instructions. **Schedule C (Form 1040) 2000**

KFA IF0US4 11/08/00

SCHEDULE D (Form 1040)	**Capital Gains and Losses**					OMB No. 1545-0074
Department of the Treasury Internal Revenue Service (99)	▶ Attach to Form 1040. ▶ See Instructions for Schedule D (Form 1040). ▶ Use Schedule D–1 for more space to list transactions for lines 1 and 8.					**2000** Attachment Sequence No. **12**

Name(s) shown on Form 1040	Your social security number
N. VEST-LOSS	123-45-6789

Part I Short–Term Capital Gains and Losses – Assets Held One Year or Less

1 (a) Description of property (Example, 100 sh. XYZ Co.)	(b) Date acquired (Mo., day, yr.)	(c) Date sold (Mo., day, yr.)	(d) Sales price (see page D–6)	(e) Cost or other basis (see page D–6)	(f) Gain or (loss) Subtract (e) from (d)	
VARIOUS	Various	Various	-100,000	0	-100,000	

2 Enter your short–term totals, if any, from Schedule D–1, line 2 .	**2**			
3 Total short–term sales price amounts. Add column (d) of lines 1 and 2	**3**	-100,000		
4 Short–term gain from Form 6252 and short–term gain or (loss) from Forms 4684, 6781, and 8824 .			**4**	
5 Net short–term gain or (loss) from partnerships, S corporations, estates, and trusts from Schedule(s) K–1			**5**	
6 Short–term capital loss carryover. Enter the amount, if any, from line 8 of your 1999 Capital Loss Carryover Worksheet .			**6**	()
7 Net short–term capital gain or (loss). Combine column (f) of lines 1 through 6 ▶			**7**	-100,000

Part II Long–Term Capital Gains and Losses – Assets Held More Than One Year

8 (a) Description of property (Example, 100 sh. XYZ Co.)	(b) Date acquired (Mo., day, yr.)	(c) Date sold (Mo., day, yr.)	(d) Sales price (see page D–6)	(e) Cost or other basis (see page D–6)	(f) Gain or (loss) Subtract (e) from (d)	(g) 28% rate gain or (loss) * (see instr. below)

9 Enter your long–term totals, if any, from Schedule D–1, line 9 .	**9**			
10 Total long–term sales price amounts. Add column (d) of lines 8 and 9	**10**			
11 Gain from Form 4797, Part I; long–term gain from Forms 2439 and 6252; and long–term gain or (loss) from Forms 4684, 6781, and 8824 .		**11**		
12 Net long–term gain or (loss) from partnerships, S corporations, estates, and trusts from Schedule(s) K–1 .		**12**		
13 Capital gain distributions. See page D–1 .		**13**		
14 Long–term capital loss carryover. Enter in both columns (f) and (g) the amount, if any, from line 13 of your 1999 Capital Loss Carryover Worksheet .		**14**	()()
15 Combine column (g) of lines 8 through 14 .		**15**		
16 Net long–term capital gain or (loss). Combine column (f) of lines 8 through 14 ▶		**16**		
Next: Go to Part III on the back.				

* **28% rate gain or loss** includes all "collectibles gains and losses" (as defined on page D–6) and up to 50% of the eligible gain on qualified small business stock (see page D–4).

For Paperwork Reduction Act Notice, see Form 1040 instructions. Schedule D (Form 1040) 2000

KFA IFOUS5 12/07/00

Schedule D (Form 1040) 2000 N. VEST-LOSS 123-45-6789 Page **2**

Part III Summary of Parts I and II

17 Combine lines 7 and 16. If a loss, go to line 18. If a gain, enter the gain on Form 1040, line 13	17	-100,000
Next: Complete Form 1040 through line 39. Then, go to **Part IV** to figure your tax if: • Both lines 16 and 17 are gains **and** • Form 1040, line 39, is more than zero. Otherwise, **stop here.**		
18 If line 17 is a loss, enter here and as a (loss) on Form 1040, line 13, the **smaller** of these losses: • The loss on line 17 **or** • ($3,000) or, if married filing separately, ($1,500)	18	(3,000)
Next: Skip **Part IV** below. Instead, complete Form 1040 through line 37. Then, complete the **Capital Loss Carryover Worksheet** on page D-6 if: • The loss on line 17 exceeds the loss on line 18 **or** • Form 1040, line 37, is a loss.		

Part IV Tax Computation Using Maximum Capital Gains Rates

19 Enter your taxable income from Form 1040, line 39					19	
20 Enter the **smaller** of line 16 or line 17 of Schedule D			20			
21 If you are filing Form 4952, enter the amount from Form 4952, line 4e			21			
22 Subtract line 21 from line 20. If zero or less, enter -0-			22			
23 Combine lines 7 and 15. If zero or less, enter -0-			23			
24 Enter the **smaller** of line 15 or line 23, but not less than zero			24			
25 Enter your unrecaptured section 1250 gain, if any, from line 17 of the worksheet on page D-8			25			
26 Add lines 24 and 25			26			
27 Subtract line 26 from line 22. If zero or less, enter -0-					27	
28 Subtract line 27 from line 19. If zero or less, enter -0-					28	
29 Enter the **smaller** of: • The amount on line 19 **or** • $26,250 if single; $43,850 if married filing jointly or qualifying widow(er); $21,925 if married filing separately; or $35,150 if head of household					29	
30 Enter the **smaller** of line 28 or line 29			30			
31 Subtract line 22 from line 19. If zero or less, enter -0-			31			
32 Enter the **larger** of line 30 or line 31 ▶			32			
33 Figure the tax on the amount on line 32. Use the Tax Table or Tax Rate Schedules, whichever applies					33	
Note: If the amounts on lines 29 and 30 are the same, skip lines 34 through 37 and go to line 38.						
34 Enter the amount from line 29			34			
35 Enter the amount from line 30			35			
36 Subtract line 35 from line 34 ▶			36			
37 Multiply line 36 by 10% (.10)					37	
Note: If the amounts on lines 19 and 29 are the same, skip lines 38 through 51 and go to line 52.						
38 Enter the **smaller** of line 19 or line 27			38			
39 Enter the amount from line 36			39			
40 Subtract line 39 from line 38 ▶			40			
41 Multiply line 40 by 20% (.20)					41	
Note: If line 26 is zero or blank, skip lines 42 through 51 and go to line 52.						
42 Enter the **smaller** of line 22 or line 25			42			
43 Add lines 22 and 32	43					
44 Enter the amount from line 19	44					
45 Subtract line 44 from line 43. If zero or less, enter -0-			45			
46 Subtract line 45 from line 42. If zero or less, enter -0- ▶			46			
47 Multiply line 46 by 25% (.25)					47	
Note: If line 24 is zero or blank, skip lines 48 through 51 and go to line 52.						
48 Enter the amount from line 19			48			
49 Add lines 32, 36, 40, and 46			49			
50 Subtract line 49 from line 48			50			
51 Multiply line 50 by 28% (.28)					51	
52 Add lines 33, 37, 41, 47, and 51					52	
53 Figure the tax on the amount on line 19. Use the Tax Table or Tax Rate Schedules, whichever applies					53	
54 **Tax on all taxable income (including capital gains).** Enter the **smaller** of line 52 or line 53 here and on Form 1040, line 40					54	

IFOUS5A 10/24/00 **Schedule D (Form 1040) 2000**

Schedule E (Form 1040) 2000 Attachment Sequence No. **13** Page **2**

Name(s) shown on return. Do not enter name and social security number if shown on other side. N. VEST-LOSS

Your social security number 123-45-6789

Note: If you report amounts from farming or fishing on Schedule E, you must enter your gross income from those activities on line 41 below. Real estate professionals must complete line 42 below.

Part II Income or Loss From Partnerships and S Corporations

If you report a loss from an at-risk activity, you **must** check either column **(e)** or **(f)** on line 27 to describe your investment in the activity. See page E-5. If you check column **(f)**, you must attach **Form 6198.**

27	(a) Name	(b) Enter P for partnership; S for S corp.	(c) Check if foreign partnership	(d) Employer identification number	Invest. At Risk? (e) All is at risk	(f) Some is not at risk
A	1	P				
B						
C						
D						
E						

	Passive Income and Loss		Nonpassive Income and Loss		
	(g) Passive loss allowed (attach Form 8582 if required)	(h) Passive income from Schedule K-1	(i) Nonpassive loss from Schedule K-1	(j) Section 179 expense deduction from Form 4562	(k) Nonpassive income from Schedule K-1
A		200,000			
B					
C					
D					
E					
28a Totals		200,000			
b Totals					

29	Add columns (h) and (k) of line 28a	29	200,000
30	Add columns (g), (i), and (j) of line 28b	30	( )
31	Total partnership and S corporation income or (loss). Combine lines 29 and 30. Enter the result here and include in the total on line 40 below	31	200,000

Part III Income or Loss From Estates and Trusts

32	(a) Name	(b) Employer ID number
A		
B		
C		
D		

	Passive Income and Loss		Nonpassive Income and Loss	
	(c) Passive deduction or loss allowed (attach Form 8582 if required)	(d) Passive income from Schedule K-1	(e) Deduction or loss from Schedule K-1	(f) Other income from Schedule K-1
A				
B				
C				
D				
33a Totals				
b Totals				

34	Add columns (d) and (f) of line 33a	34	
35	Add columns (c) and (e) of line 33b	35	( )
36	Total estate and trust income or (loss). Combine lines 34 and 35. Enter the result here and include in the total on line 40 below	36	

Part IV Income or Loss From Real Estate Mortgage Investment Conduits (REMICs) – Residual Holder

37 (a) Name	(b) Employer identification number	(c) Excess inclusion from Schedules Q, line 2c (see page E-6)	(d) Taxable income (net loss) from Schedules Q, line 1b	(e) Income from Schedules Q, line 3b

38	Combine columns (d) and (e) only. Enter the result here and include in the total on line 40 below	38	

Part V Summary

39	Net farm rental income or (loss) from **Form 4835.** Also, complete line 41 below	39	
40	**Total** income or (loss). Combine lines 26, 31, 36, 38, and 39. Enter the result here and on Form 1040, line 17 ▶	40	200,000
41	**Reconciliation of Farming and Fishing Income:** Enter your **gross** farming and fishing income reported on Form 4835, line 7; Schedule K-1 (Form 1065), line 15b; Schedule K-1 (Form 1120S), line 23; and Schedule K-1 (Form 1041), line 14 (see page E-6)	41	
42	**Reconciliation for Real Estate Professionals.** If you were real estate professional (see pg. E-4), enter net income or (loss) you reported anywhere on Form 1040 from all rental real estate activities in which you materially participated under passive activity loss rules.	42	

IF0US7A 10/19/00 Schedule E (Form 1040) 2000

Example 4 *(Continued)*

Form **4562** Department of the Treasury Internal Revenue Service (99)	**Depreciation and Amortization** **(Including Information on Listed Property)** ▶ See separate instructions. ▶ Attach this form to your return.	OMB No. 1545-0172 **2000** Attachment Sequence No. **67**

Name(s) shown on return: N. VESTOR-LOSS — Identifying number: 123-45-6789

Business or activity to which this form relates

Part I — Election To Expense Certain Tangible Property (Section 179) Note: If you have any "listed property," complete Part V before you complete Part I.

1	Maximum dollar limitation. If an enterprise zone business, see page 2 of the instructions	1	$20,000
2	Total cost of section 179 property placed in service. See page 2 of the instructions	2	
3	Threshold cost of section 179 property before reduction in limitation	3	$200,000
4	Reduction in limitation. Subtract line 3 from line 2. If zero or less, enter -0-	4	
5	Dollar limitation for tax year. Subtract line 4 from line 1. If zero or less, enter -0-. If married filing separately, see page 2 of the instructions	5	

6 (a) Description of property	(b) Cost (business use only)	(c) Elected cost

7	Listed property. Enter amount from line 27	7	
8	Total elected cost of section 179 property. Add amounts in column (c), lines 6 and 7	8	
9	Tentative deduction. Enter the smaller of line 5 or line 8	9	
10	Carryover of disallowed deduction from 1999. See page 3 of the instructions	10	
11	Business income limitation. Enter the smaller of business income (not less than zero) or line 5 (see instructions)	11	
12	Section 179 expense deduction. Add lines 9 and 10, but do not enter more than line 11	12	
13	Carryover of disallowed deduction to 2001. Add lines 9 and 10, less line 12 ▶	13	

Note: Do not use Part II or Part III below for listed property (automobiles, certain other vehicles, cellular telephones, certain computers, or property used for entertainment, recreation, or amusement). Instead, use Part V for listed property.

Part II — MACRS Depreciation for Assets Placed in Service Only During Your 2000 Tax Year (**Do not** include listed property.)

Section A – General Asset Account Election

14 If you are making the election under section 168(i)(4) to group any assets placed in service during the tax year into one or more general asset accounts, check this box. See page 3 of the instructions ▶ ☐

Section B – General Depreciation System (GDS) (See page 3 of the instructions.)

(a) Classification of property	(b) Month and year placed in service	(c) Basis for depreciation (business/investment use only - see instructions)	(d) Recovery period	(e) Convention	(f) Method	(g) Depreciation deduction
15a 3-year property						
b 5-year property						
c 7-year property						
d 10-year property						
e 15-year property						
f 20-year property						
g 25-year property			25 yrs		S/L	
h Residential rental property			27.5 yrs	MM	S/L	
			27.5 yrs	MM	S/L	
i Nonresidential real property			39 yrs	MM	S/L	
				MM	S/L	

Section C – Alternative Depreciation System (ADS): (See page 5 of the instructions.)

(a) Classification of property	(b) Month and year placed in service	(c) Basis for depreciation	(d) Recovery period	(e) Convention	(f) Method	(g) Depreciation deduction
16a Class life					S/L	
b 12-year			12 yrs		S/L	
c 40-year			40 yrs	MM	S/L	

Part III — Other Depreciation (**Do not** include listed property.) (See page 5 of the instructions.)

17	GDS and ADS deductions for assets placed in service in tax years beginning before 2000	17	
18	Property subject to section 168(f)(1) election	18	
19	ACRS and other depreciation	19	5,000

Part IV — Summary (See page 6 of the instructions.)

20	Listed property. Enter amount from line 26	20	
21	**Total.** Add deductions from line 12, lines 15 and 16 in column (g), and lines 17 through 20. Enter here and on the appropriate lines of your return. Partnerships and S corporations – see instructions	21	5,000
22	For assets shown above and placed in service during the current year, enter the portion of the basis attributable to section 263A costs	22	

KFA **For Paperwork Reduction Act Notice, see page 9 of the instructions.** GF0US7 10/26/00 Form **4562** (2000)

Form **4952**

Department of the Treasury
Internal Revenue Service (99)

Investment Interest Expense Deduction

▶ **Attach to your tax return.**

OMB No. 1545-0191

2000

Attachment Sequence No. **72**

Name(s) shown on return: N. VEST-LOSS

Identifying number: 123-45-6789

Part I — Total Investment Interest Expense

1 Investment interest expense paid or accrued in 2000. See instructions	1	51,357
2 Disallowed investment interest expense from 1999 Form 4952, line 7	2	
3 **Total investment interest expense.** Add lines 1 and 2	3	51,357

Part II — Net Investment Income

4a Gross income from property held for investment (excluding any net gain from the disposition of property held for investment)			4a	
b Net gain from the disposition of property held for investment	4b			
c Net capital gain from the disposition of property held for investment	4c			
d Subtract line 4c from line 4b. If zero or less, enter -0-			4d	0
e Enter all or part of the amount on line 4c, if any, that you elect to include in investment income. Do not enter more than the amount on line 4b. See instructions ▶			4e	
f Investment income. Add lines 4a, 4d, and 4e. See instructions			4f	
5 Investment expenses. See instructions			5	
6 **Net investment income.** Subtract line 5 from line 4f. If zero or less, enter -0-			6	0

Part III — Investment Interest Expense Deduction

7 Disallowed investment interest expense to be carried forward to 2001. Subtract line 6 from line 3. If zero or less, enter -0-	7	51,357
8 **Investment interest expense deduction.** Enter the **smaller** of line 3 or 6. See instructions	8	0

For Paperwork Reduction Act Notice, see back. Form **4952** (2000)

KFA IF0US29 10/24/00

Form **6251**		Alternative Minimum Tax – Individuals	OMB No. 1545-0227	
		▶ **See separate instructions.**	**2000**	
Department of the Treasury Internal Revenue Service		▶ **Attach to Form 1040 or Form 1040NR.**	Attachment Sequence No. **32**	

Name(s) shown on Form 1040	Your social security number
N. VEST-LOSS	123-45-6789

Part I Adjustments and Preferences

1	If you itemized deductions on Schedule A (Form 1040), go to line 2. Otherwise, enter your standard deduction from Form 1040, line 36, here and go to line 6 .	1	
2	Medical and dental. Enter the smaller of Schedule A (Form 1040), line 4 **or** 2 1/2% of Form 1040, line 34	2	
3	Taxes. Enter the amount from Schedule A (Form 1040), line 9 .	3	
4	Certain interest on a home mortgage **not** used to buy, build, or improve your home .	4	
5	Miscellaneous itemized deductions. Enter the amount from Schedule A (Form 1040), line 26	5	87,002
6	Refund of taxes. Enter any tax refund from Form 1040, line 10 or line 21 .	6	()
7	Investment interest. Enter difference between regular tax and AMT deduction .	7	
8	Post-1986 depreciation. Enter difference between regular tax and AMT depreciation .	8	
9	Adjusted gain or loss. Enter difference between AMT and regular tax gain or loss .	9	
10	Incentive stock options. Enter excess of AMT income over regular tax income. .	10	
11	Passive activities. Enter difference between AMT and regular tax income or loss .	11	
12	Beneficiaries of estates and trusts. Enter the amount from Schedule K-1 (Form 1041), line 9	12	
13	Tax-exempt interest from private activity bonds issued after 8/7/86 .	13	
14	Other. Enter the amount, if any, for each item below and enter the total on line 14.		

a	Circulation expenditures.	h	Loss limitations
b	Depletion	i	Mining costs
c	Depreciation (pre-1987).	j	Patron's adjustment
d	Installment sales.	k	Pollution control facilities . .
e	Intangible drilling costs. .	l	Research & experimental.
f	Large partnerships	m	Section 1202 exclusion . .
g	Long-term contracts . . .	n	Tax shelter farm activities.
		o	Related adjustments

		14	
15	Total Adjustments and Preferences. Combine lines 1 through 14 . ▶	15	87,002

Part II Alternative Minimum Taxable Income

16	Enter the amount from **Form 1040, line 37.** If less than zero, enter as a (loss) . ▶	16	318,040
17	Net operating loss deduction, if any, from Form 1040, line 21. Enter as a positive amount	17	
18	If Form 1040, line 34, is over $128,950 (over $64,475 if married filing separately), and you itemized deductions, enter the amount, if any, from line 9 of the worksheet for Schedule A (Form 1040), line 28 ▶	18	(8,042)
19	Combine lines 15 through 18 . ▶	19	397,000
20	Alternative tax net operating loss deduction. See page 6 of the instructions. .	20	
21	**Alternative Minimum Taxable Income.** Subtract line 20 from line 19. (If married filing separately and line 21 is more than $165,000, see page 7 of the instructions.) . ▶	21	397,000

Part III Exemption Amount and Alternative Minimum Tax

22 **Exemption Amount.** (If this form is for a child under age 14, see page 7 of the instructions.)

IF your filing status is:	AND line 21 is not over . . .	THEN enter on line 22 . . .		
Single or head of household. $112,500 $33,750			
Married filing jointly or qualifying widow(er) 150,000 45,000	}	22	
Married filing separately . 75,000 22,500			

If line 21 is **over** the amount shown above for your filing status, see page 7 of the instructions.

23	Subtract line 22 from line 21. If zero or less, enter -0- here and on lines 26 and 28 and stop here. ▶	23	397,000
24	If you reported capital gain distributions directly on Form 1040, line 13, **or** you completed Schedule D (Form 1040) and have an amount on line 25 or line 27 (or would have had an amount on either line if you had completed Part IV) (as refigured for the AMT, if necessary), go to Part IV of Form 6251 to figure line 24. **All others:** If line 23 is $175,000 or less ($87,500 or less if married filing separately), multiply line 23 by 26% (.26). Otherwise, multiply line 23 by 28% (.28) and subtract $3,500 ($1,750 if married filing separately) from the result ▶	24	107,660
25	Alternative minimum tax foreign tax credit. See page 7 of the instructions. .	25	
26	Tentative minimum tax. Subtract line 25 from line 24 . ▶	26	107,660
27	Enter your tax from Form 1040, line 40 (minus any tax from Form 4972 and any foreign tax credit from Form 1040, line 43) .	27	103,614
28	**Alternative Minimum Tax.** Subtract line 27 from line 26. If zero or less, enter -0-. Enter here and on Form 1040, line 41 . ▶	28	4,046

For Paperwork Reduction Act Notice, see page 8 of the instructions. Form **6251** (2000)

KFA IF0US33 10/23/00

Example 5

FORM **1040** Department of the Treasury – Internal Revenue Service
U.S. Individual Income Tax Return **2000** (99) IRS Use Only – Do not write or staple in this space.

For the year Jan. 1 – Dec. 31, 2000, or other tax year beginning , 2000, ending , 20 — OMB No. 1545-0074

Label (See instructions on page 19.) Use the IRS label. Otherwise, please print or type. LABEL HERE

Your first name and initial: A.TRADER LOSS NO 475	Last name	Your social security number: 123-45-6789
If a joint return, spouse's first name and initial	Last name	Spouse's social security number
Home address (number and street). If you have a P.O. box, see page 19.: C/O TED TESSER-6274 LINTON BLVD. #102	Apt. no.	▲ **IMPORTANT!** ▲ You **must** enter your SSN(s) above.
City, town or post office, state, and ZIP code. If you have a foreign address, see page 19.: DELRAY BEACH, FL 33484		

Presidential Election Campaign (See page 19.) **Note.** Checking "Yes" will not change your tax or reduce your refund.
Do you, or your spouse if filing a joint return, want $3 to go to this fund? ▶ You: ☐ Yes ☒ No — Spouse: ☐ Yes ☐ No

Filing Status (Check only one box.)

1 [X] Single
2 [ ] Married filing joint return (even if only one had income)
3 [ ] Married filing separate return. Enter spouse's soc. sec. no. above & full name here ▶
4 [ ] Head of household (with qualifying person). (See page 19.) If the qualifying person is a child but not your dependent, enter this child's name here ▶
5 [ ] Qualifying widow(er) with dependent child (year spouse died ▶). (See page 19.)

Exemptions

6a ☒ **Yourself.** If your parent (or someone else) can claim you as a dependent on his or her tax return, **do not** check box 6a.
b ☐ **Spouse**
No. of boxes checked on 6a and 6b: 1

c **Dependents:**

(1) First Name Last name	(2) Dependent's social security number	(3) Dependent's relationship to you	(4) Chk if qualifying child for child tax credit (see page 20)

If more than six dependents, see page 20.

No. of your children on 6c who: ● lived with you ● did not live with you due to divorce or separation (see page 20) Dependents on 6c not entered above

d Total number of exemptions claimed — Add numbers entered on lines above ▶ 1

Income

Attach Forms W-2 and W-2G here. Also attach Form 1099-R if tax was withheld.

If you did not get a W-2, see page 21.

Enclose, but do not attach any payment. Also, please use Form 1040-V.

Line	Description		Amount
7	Wages, salaries, tips, etc. Attach Form(s) W-2	7	200,000
8a	**Taxable** interest. Attach Schedule B if required	8a	
b	**Tax-exempt** interest. **Do not** include on line 8a — 8b		
9	Ordinary dividends. Attach Schedule B if required	9	
10	Taxable refunds, credits, or offsets of state and local income taxes (see page 22)	10	
11	Alimony received	11	
12	Business income or (loss). Attach Schedule C or C-EZ	12	-182,528
13	Capital gain or (loss). Attach Schedule D if required. If not required, check here ▶ ☐	13	-3,000
14	Other gains or (losses). Attach Form 4797	14	
15a	Total IRA distributions 15a — b Taxable amount (see pg. 23)	15b	
16a	Total pensions and annuities 16a — b Taxable amount (see pg. 23)	16b	
17	Rental real estate, royalties, partnerships, S corporations, trusts, etc. Attach Schedule E	17	200,000
18	Farm income or (loss). Attach Schedule F	18	
19	Unemployment compensation	19	
20a	Social security benefits 20a — b Taxable amount (see pg. 25)	20b	
21	Other income.	21	
22	Add the amounts in the far right column for lines 7 through 21. This is your **total income** ▶	22	214,472

Adjusted Gross Income

Line	Description				Amount
23	IRA deduction (see page 27)	23			
24	Student loan interest deduction (see page 27)	24			
25	Medical savings account deduction. Attach Form 8853	25			
26	Moving expenses. Attach Form 3903	26			
27	One-half of self-employment tax. Attach Schedule SE	27			
28	Self-employed health insurance deduction (see page 29)	28			
29	Self-employed SEP, SIMPLE, and qualified plans	29			
30	Penalty on early withdrawal of savings	30			
31a	Alimony paid. b Recipient's SSN ▶	31a			
32	Add lines 23 through 31a			32	0
33	Subtract line 32 from line 22. This is your **adjusted gross income** ▶			33	214,472

KFA **For Disclosure, Privacy Act, and Paperwork Reduction Act Notice, see page 56.** IF0US1 11/07/00 Form **1040** (2000)

Example 5 *(Continued)*

Form 1040 (2000) A. TRADER LOSS NO 475 — 123-45-6789 Page **2**

Tax and Credits

Line	Description			Box	Amount
34	Amount from line 33 (adjusted gross income)			34	214,472
35a	Check if: ☐ **You** were 65 or older, ☐ Blind; ☐ **Spouse** was 65 or older, ☐ Blind. Add the number of boxes checked above and enter the total here ▶ 35a				
b	If you are married filing separately and your spouse itemizes deductions, or you were a dual-status alien, see page 31 and check here ▶ 35b ☐				
36	Enter your **itemized deductions** from Schedule A, line 28, **or standard deduction** shown on the left. **But** see page 31 to find your standard deduction if you checked any box on line 35a or 35b **or** if someone can claim you as a dependent			36	4,400
37	Subtract line 36 from line 34			37	210,072
38	If line 34 is $96,700 or less, multiply $2,800 by the total number of exemptions claimed on line 6d. If line 34 is over $96,700, see the worksheet on page 32 for the amount to enter			38	840
39	**Taxable income.** Subtract line 38 from line 37. If line 38 is more than line 37, enter -0-			39	209,232
40	**Tax** (see page 32). Check if any tax is from a ☐ Form(s) 8814 b ☐ Form 4972			40	63,375
41	Alternative minimum tax. Attach Form 6251			41	
42	Add lines 40 and 41 ▶			42	63,375
43	Foreign tax credit. Attach Form 1116 if required	43			
44	Credit for child and dependent care expenses. Att. Form 2441	44			
45	Credit for the elderly or the disabled. Attach Schedule R	45			
46	Education credits. Attach Form 8863	46			
47	Child tax credit (see page 36)	47			
48	Adoption credit. Attach Form 8839	48			
49	Other. Check if from a ☐ Form 3800 b ☐ Form 8396 c ☐ Form 8801 d ☐ Form (specify)	49			
50	Add lines 43 through 49. These are your **total credits**			50	
51	Subtract line 50 from line 42. If line 50 is more than line 42, enter -0- ▶			51	63,375

Standard Deduction for Most People — Single: $4,400; Head of household: $6,450; Married filing jointly or Qualifying widow(er): $7,350; Married filing separately $3,675.

Other Taxes

Line	Description	Box	Amount
52	Self-employment tax. Att. Sch. SE	52	
53	Social security and Medicare tax on tip income not reported to employer. Attach Form 4137	53	
54	Tax on IRAs, other retirement plans, and MSAs. Attach Form 5329 if required	54	
55	Advance earned income credit payments from Form(s) W-2	55	
56	Household employment taxes. Attach Schedule H	56	
57	Add lines 51 through 56. This is your **total tax** ▶	57	63,375

Payments

If you have a qualifying child, attach Schedule EIC.

Line	Description			Box	Amount
58	Federal income tax withheld from Forms W-2 and 1099	58	60,000		
59	2000 estimated tax payments and amount applied from 1999 return	59	50,000		
60a	**Earned income credit (EIC)**	60a			
b	**Nontaxable earned income: amt.** ▶ **and type** ▶ No				
61	Excess social security and RRTA tax withheld (see page 50)	61			
62	**Additional child tax credit. Attach Form 8812**	62			
63	**Amount paid with request for extension to file** (see page 50)	63			
64	Other payments. Check if from a ☐ Form 2439 b ☐ Form 4136	64			
65	Add lines 58, 59, 60a, and 61 through 64. These are your **total payments** ▶			65	110,000

Refund

Have it directly deposited! See page 50 and fill in 67b, 67c, and 67d.

Line	Description		Box	Amount
66	If line 65 is more than line 57, subtract line 57 from line 65. This is the amount you **overpaid**		66	46,625
67a	Amount of line 66 you want **refunded to you** ▶		67a	46,625
b	Routing number ▶ c Type: ☐ Checking ☐ Savings			
d	Account number			
68	Amount of line 66 you want **applied to your 2001 estimated tax** ▶	68		

Amount You Owe

Line	Description		Box	Amount
69	If line 57 is more than line 65, subtract line 65 from line 57. This is the **amount you owe.** For details on how to pay, see page 51 ▶		69	
70	Estimated tax penalty. Also include on line 69	70		

Sign Here

Under penalties of perjury, I declare that I have examined this return and accompanying schedules and statements, and to the best of my knowledge and belief, they are true, correct, and complete. Declaration of preparer (other than taxpayer) is based on all information of which preparer has any knowledge.

Joint return? See page 19. Keep a copy for your records.

Your signature	Date	Your occupation	Daytime phone number 561-865-0071
Spouse's signature. If a joint return, **both** must sign.	Date	Spouse's occupation	May the IRS discuss this return with the preparer shown below? (see page 52)? ☒ Yes ☐ No

Paid Preparer's Use Only

Preparer's signature ▶	Date	Check if self-employed ☐	Preparer's SSN or PTIN
Firm's name (or yours if self-employed), address, and ZIP code ▶	Waterside Financial Services 6274 Linton Blvd., Suite #102 Delray Beach, FL 33484	EIN Phone no. (561) 865-0071	

IFOUS1A 11/22/00 — Form **1040** (2000)

SCHEDULE C (Form 1040)

Department of the Treasury
Internal Revenue Service (99)

Profit or Loss From Business
(Sole Proprietorship)

▶ Partnerships, joint ventures, etc., must file Form 1065 or Form 1065-B.
▶ Attach to Form 1040 or Form 1041. ▶ See Instructions for Schedule C (Form 1040).

OMB No. 1545-0074
2000
Attachment Sequence No. 09

Name of proprietor: A.TRADER LOSS NO 475	Social security number (SSN): 123-45-6789
A Principal business or profession, including product or service (see page C-1 of the instructions): TRADER	B Enter code from pages C-7 & 8: ▶ 523900
C Business name. If no separate business name, leave blank.	D Employer ID number (EIN), if any

E Business address (including suite or room no.) ▶
City, town or post office, state, and ZIP code

F Accounting method: (1) ☒ Cash (2) ☐ Accrual (3) ☐ Other (specify) ▶

G Did you "materially participate" in the operation of this business during 2000? If "No," see page C-2 for limit on losses ☒ Yes ☐ No

H If you started or acquired this business during 2000, check here ▶ ☐

Part I Income

1 Gross receipts or sales. **Caution:** If this income was reported to you on Form W-2 and the "Statutory employee" box on that form was checked, see page C-2 and check here ▶ ☐	1	
2 Returns and allowances	2	
3 Subtract line 2 from line 1	3	
4 Cost of goods sold (from line 42 on page 2)	4	
5 **Gross profit.** Subtract line 4 from line 3	5	
6 Other income, including Federal and state gasoline or fuel tax credit or refund (see page C-2)	6	
7 **Gross income.** Add lines 5 and 6 ▶	7	

Part II Expenses. Enter expenses for business use of your home **only** on line 30.

8 Advertising	8		19 Pension and profit-sharing plans	19	
9 Bad debts from sales or services (see page C-3)	9		20 Rent or lease (see page C-4): a Vehicles, machinery & equipment	20a	5,050
10 Car and truck expenses (see page C-3)	10	3,115	b Other business property	20b	
			21 Repairs and maintenance	21	3,166
11 Commissions and fees	11		22 Supplies (not included in Part III)	22	5,069
12 Depletion	12		23 Taxes and licenses	23	
13 Depreciation and section 179 expense deduction (not included in Part III) (see page C-3)	13	5,000	24 Travel, meals, and entertainment: a Travel	24a	6,511
			b Meals and entertainment: 8,711		
14 Employee benefit programs (other than on line 19)	14		c Enter nondeductible amount included on line 24b (see page C-5): 4,356		
15 Insurance (other than health)	15		d Subtract line 24c from line 24b	24d	4,355
16 Interest: a Mortgage (paid to banks, etc.)	16a		25 Utilities	25	2,611
b Other	16b	51,357	26 Wages (less employment credits)	26	
17 Legal and professional services	17	2,250	27 Other expenses (from line 48 on page 2)	27	83,233
18 Office expense	18	4,561			

28 **Total expenses** before expenses for business use of home. Add lines 8 through 27 in columns ▶	28	176,278
29 Tentative profit (loss). Subtract line 28 from line 7	29	-176,278
30 Expenses for business use of your home. Attach **Form 8829**	30	6,250
31 **Net profit or (loss).** Subtract line 30 from line 29. • If a profit, enter on **Form 1040, line 12,** and **also** on **Schedule SE, line 2** (statutory employees, see page C-5). Estates and trusts, enter on Form 1041, line 3. • If a loss, you **must** go to line 32.	31	-182,528

32 If you have a loss, check the box that describes your investment in this activity (see page C-5).

- If you checked 32a, enter the loss on **Form 1040, line 12,** and **also** on **Schedule SE, line 2** (statutory employees, see page C-5). Estates and trusts, enter on Form 1041, line 3.
- If you checked 32b, you **must** attach **Form 6198.**

32a ☒ All investment is at risk.
32b ☐ Some investment is not at risk.

For Paperwork Reduction Act Notice, see Form 1040 instructions. **Schedule C (Form 1040) 2000**

KFA IF0US4 11/08/00

Schedule C (Form 1040) 2000 A.TRADER LOSS NO 475 123-45-6789 Page 2

Part III Cost of Goods Sold (see page C-6)

33 Method(s) used to value closing inventory: a ☐ Cost b ☐ Lower of cost or market c ☐ Other (attach explanation)

34 Was there any change in determining quantities, costs, or valuations between opening and closing inventory? If "Yes," attach explanation ☐ Yes ☐ No

35 Inventory at beginning of year. If different from last year's closing inventory, attach explanation	35	
36 Purchases less cost of items withdrawn for personal use	36	
37 Cost of labor. Do not include any amounts paid to yourself	37	
38 Materials and supplies	38	
39 Other costs	39	
40 Add lines 35 through 39	40	
41 Inventory at end of year	41	
42 **Cost of goods sold.** Subtract line 41 from line 40. Enter the result here and on page 1, line 4	42	

Part IV Information on Your Vehicle. Complete this part **only** if you are claiming car or truck expenses on line 10 and are not required to file Form 4562 for this business. See the instructions for line 13 on page C-3 to find out if you must file.

43 When did you place your vehicle in service for business purposes? (month, day, year) ▶ ______________

44 Of the total number of miles you drove your vehicle during 2000, enter the number of miles you used your vehicle for:

a Business ______________ b Commuting ______________ c Other ______________

45 Do you (or your spouse) have another vehicle available for personal use? ☐ Yes ☐ No

46 Was your vehicle available for use during off-duty hours? ☐ Yes ☐ No

47a Do you have evidence to support your deduction? ☐ Yes ☐ No

b If "Yes," is the evidence written? ☐ Yes ☐ No

Part V Other Expenses. List below business expenses not included on lines 8–26 or line 30.

COMPUTER EXPENSE		2,955
HISTORICAL DATA SERVICES		3,061
INTERNET SERVICES		2,050
ONLINE TRADING DATA		7,010
OTHER TRADING EXPENSES		4,116
PROFESSIONAL PUBLICATIONS		3,116
TRADING ADVISORY SERVICES		35,179
TRADING PERIODICALS		6,633
TRADING SEMINARS		19,113
48 **Total other expenses.** Enter here and on page 1, line 27	48	83,233

IF0US4A 11/09/00 Schedule C (Form 1040) 2000

SCHEDULE D (Form 1040)
Department of the Treasury Internal Revenue Service (99)

Capital Gains and Losses

▶ Attach to Form 1040. ▶ See Instructions for Schedule D (Form 1040).
▶ Use Schedule D-1 for more space to list transactions for lines 1 and 8.

OMB No. 1545-0074
2000
Attachment Sequence No. 12

Name(s) shown on Form 1040: A.TRADER LOSS NO 475
Your social security number: 123-45-6789

Part I Short-Term Capital Gains and Losses – Assets Held One Year or Less

1 (a) Description of property (Example, 100 sh. XYZ Co.)	(b) Date acquired (Mo., day, yr.)	(c) Date sold (Mo., day, yr.)	(d) Sales price (see page D-6)	(e) Cost or other basis (see page D-6)	(f) Gain or (loss) Subtract (e) from (d)
SEE SCH ATTACHED	Various		0	100,000	-100,000

2 Enter your short-term totals, if any, from Schedule D-1, line 2	2	
3 **Total short-term sales price amounts.** Add column (d) of lines 1 and 2	3	
4 Short-term gain from Form 6252 and short-term gain or (loss) from Forms 4684, 6781, and 8824	4	
5 Net short-term gain or (loss) from partnerships, S corporations, estates, and trusts from Schedule(s) K-1	5	
6 Short-term capital loss carryover. Enter the amount, if any, from line 8 of your 1999 Capital Loss Carryover Worksheet	6	( )
7 **Net short-term capital gain or (loss).** Combine column (f) of lines 1 through 6 ▶	7	-100,000

Part II Long-Term Capital Gains and Losses – Assets Held More Than One Year

8 (a) Description of property (Example, 100 sh. XYZ Co.)	(b) Date acquired (Mo., day, yr.)	(c) Date sold (Mo., day, yr.)	(d) Sales price (see page D-6)	(e) Cost or other basis (see page D-6)	(f) Gain or (loss) Subtract (e) from (d)	(g) 28% rate gain or (loss) *(see instr. below)

9 Enter your long-term totals, if any, from Schedule D-1, line 9	9		
10 **Total long-term sales price amounts.** Add column (d) of lines 8 and 9	10		
11 Gain from Form 4797, Part I; long-term gain from Forms 2439 and 6252; and long-term gain or (loss) from Forms 4684, 6781, and 8824	11		
12 Net long-term gain or (loss) from partnerships, S corporations, estates, and trusts from Schedule(s) K-1	12		
13 Capital gain distributions. See page D-1	13		
14 Long-term capital loss carryover. Enter in both columns (f) and (g) the amount, if any, from line 13 of your 1999 Capital Loss Carryover Worksheet	14	( )	( )
15 Combine column (g) of lines 8 through 14	15		
16 **Net long-term capital gain or (loss).** Combine column (f) of lines 8 through 14 ▶ **Next:** Go to Part III on the back.	16		

* **28% rate gain or loss** includes **all** "collectibles gains and losses" (as defined on page D-6) and up to 50% of the eligible gain on qualified small business stock (see page D-4).

For Paperwork Reduction Act Notice, see Form 1040 instructions. **Schedule D (Form 1040) 2000**

KFA IFOUS5 12/07/00

Schedule D (Form 1040) 2000 A.TRADER LOSS NO 475 123-45-6789 Page **2**

Part III Summary of Parts I and II

17 Combine lines 7 and 16. If a loss, go to line 18. If a gain, enter the gain on Form 1040, line 13	17	-100,000
Next: Complete Form 1040 through line 39. Then, go to **Part IV** to figure your tax if: • Both lines 16 and 17 are gains **and** • Form 1040, line 39, is more than zero. Otherwise, **stop here.**		
18 If line 17 is a loss, enter here and as a (loss) on Form 1040, line 13, the **smaller** of these losses: • The loss on line 17 **or** • ($3,000) or, if married filing separately, ($1,500)	18	(3,000)
Next: Skip **Part IV** below. Instead, complete Form 1040 through line 37. Then, complete the **Capital Loss Carryover Worksheet** on page D-6 if: • The loss on line 17 exceeds the loss on line 18 **or** • Form 1040, line 37, is a loss.		

Part IV Tax Computation Using Maximum Capital Gains Rates

19 Enter your taxable income from Form 1040, line 39					19	
20 Enter the **smaller** of line 16 or line 17 of Schedule D			20			
21 If you are filing Form 4952, enter the amount from Form 4952, line 4e			21			
22 Subtract line 21 from line 20. If zero or less, enter -0-			22			
23 Combine lines 7 and 15. If zero or less, enter -0-			23			
24 Enter the **smaller** of line 15 or line 23, but not less than zero			24			
25 Enter your unrecaptured section 1250 gain, if any, from line 17 of the worksheet on page D-8			25			
26 Add lines 24 and 25			26			
27 Subtract line 26 from line 22. If zero or less, enter -0-					27	
28 Subtract line 27 from line 19. If zero or less, enter -0-					28	
29 Enter the **smaller** of: • The amount on line 19 **or** • $26,250 if single; $43,850 if married filing jointly or qualifying widow(er); $21,925 if married filing separately; or $35,150 if head of household					29	
30 Enter the **smaller** of line 28 or line 29			30			
31 Subtract line 22 from line 19. If zero or less, enter -0-			31			
32 Enter the **larger** of line 30 or line 31 ▶			32			
33 Figure the tax on the amount on line 32. Use the Tax Table or Tax Rate Schedules, whichever applies					33	
Note: If the amounts on lines 29 and 30 are the same, skip lines 34 through 37 and go to line 38.						
34 Enter the amount from line 29			34			
35 Enter the amount from line 30			35			
36 Subtract line 35 from line 34 ▶			36			
37 Multiply line 36 by 10% (.10)					37	
Note: If the amounts on lines 19 and 29 are the same, skip lines 38 through 51 and go to line 52.						
38 Enter the **smaller** of line 19 or line 27			38			
39 Enter the amount from line 36			39			
40 Subtract line 39 from line 38 ▶			40			
41 Multiply line 40 by 20% (.20)					41	
Note: If line 26 is zero or blank, skip lines 42 through 51 and go to line 52.						
42 Enter the **smaller** of line 22 or line 25			42			
43 Add lines 22 and 32	43					
44 Enter the amount from line 19	44					
45 Subtract line 44 from line 43. If zero or less, enter -0-			45			
46 Subtract line 45 from line 42. If zero or less, enter -0- ▶			46			
47 Multiply line 46 by 25% (.25)					47	
Note: If line 24 is zero or blank, skip lines 48 through 51 and go to line 52.						
48 Enter the amount from line 19			48			
49 Add lines 32, 36, 40, and 46			49			
50 Subtract line 49 from line 48			50			
51 Multiply line 50 by 28% (.28)					51	
52 Add lines 33, 37, 41, 47, and 51					52	
53 Figure the tax on the amount on line 19. Use the Tax Table or Tax Rate Schedules, whichever applies					53	
54 Tax on all taxable income (including capital gains). Enter the **smaller** of line 52 or line 53 here and on Form 1040, line 40					54	

IFOUS5A 10/24/00 **Schedule D (Form 1040) 2000**

Form **4562** Department of the Treasury Internal Revenue Service (99)

Depreciation and Amortization
(Including Information on Listed Property)

▶ See separate instructions. ▶ Attach this form to your return.

OMB No. 1545-0172 **2000** Attachment Sequence No. **67**

Name(s) shown on return: A. COMMODITIES TRADER LOSS NO 475 — Identifying number: 123-45-6789

Business or activity to which this form relates

Part I Election To Expense Certain Tangible Property (Section 179) Note: If you have any "listed property," complete Part V before you complete Part I.

1	Maximum dollar limitation. If an enterprise zone business, see page 2 of the instructions	1	$20,000
2	Total cost of section 179 property placed in service. See page 2 of the instructions	2	
3	Threshold cost of section 179 property before reduction in limitation	3	$200,000
4	Reduction in limitation. Subtract line 3 from line 2. If zero or less, enter -0-	4	
5	Dollar limitation for tax year. Subtract line 4 from line 1. If zero or less, enter -0-. If married filing separately, see page 2 of the instructions	5	

6 (a) Description of property	(b) Cost (business use only)	(c) Elected cost

7	Listed property. Enter amount from line 27	7	
8	Total elected cost of section 179 property. Add amounts in column (c), lines 6 and 7	8	
9	Tentative deduction. Enter the smaller of line 5 or line 8	9	
10	Carryover of disallowed deduction from 1999. See page 3 of the instructions	10	
11	Business income limitation. Enter the smaller of business income (not less than zero) or line 5 (see instructions)	11	
12	Section 179 expense deduction. Add lines 9 and 10, but do not enter more than line 11	12	
13	Carryover of disallowed deduction to 2001. Add lines 9 and 10, less line 12 ▶	13	

Note: Do not use Part II or Part III below for listed property (automobiles, certain other vehicles, cellular telephones, certain computers, or property used for entertainment, recreation, or amusement). Instead, use Part V for listed property.

Part II MACRS Depreciation for Assets Placed in Service Only During Your 2000 Tax Year (**Do not** include listed property.)

Section A - General Asset Account Election

14 If you are making the election under section 168(i)(4) to group any assets placed in service during the tax year into one or more general asset accounts, check this box. See page 3 of the instructions ▶ ☐

Section B - General Depreciation System (GDS) (See page 3 of the instructions.)

(a) Classification of property	(b) Month and year placed in service	(c) Basis for depreciation (business/investment use only - see instructions)	(d) Recovery period	(e) Convention	(f) Method	(g) Depreciation deduction
15a 3-year property						
b 5-year property						
c 7-year property						
d 10-year property						
e 15-year property						
f 20-year property						
g 25-year property			25 yrs		S/L	
h Residential rental property			27.5 yrs	MM	S/L	
			27.5 yrs	MM	S/L	
i Nonresidential real property			39 yrs	MM	S/L	
				MM	S/L	

Section C - Alternative Depreciation System (ADS): (See page 5 of the instructions.)

(a) Classification of property	(b)	(c)	(d)	(e)	(f)	(g)
16a Class life					S/L	
b 12-year			12 yrs		S/L	
c 40-year			40 yrs	MM	S/L	

Part III Other Depreciation (**Do not** include listed property.) (See page 5 of the instructions.)

17	GDS and ADS deductions for assets placed in service in tax years beginning before 2000	17	
18	Property subject to section 168(f)(1) election	18	
19	ACRS and other depreciation	19	5,000

Part IV Summary (See page 6 of the instructions.)

20	Listed property. Enter amount from line 26	20	
21	**Total.** Add deductions from line 12, lines 15 and 16 in column (g), and lines 17 through 20. Enter here and on the appropriate lines of your return. Partnerships and S corporations - see instructions	21	5,000
22	For assets shown above and placed in service during the current year, enter the portion of the basis attributable to section 263A costs	22	

KFA **For Paperwork Reduction Act Notice, see page 9 of the instructions.** GF0US7 10/26/00 Form **4562** (2000)

Form **6251**

Department of the Treasury
Internal Revenue Service

Alternative Minimum Tax - Individuals

▶ See separate instructions.
▶ Attach to Form 1040 or Form 1040NR.

OMB No. 1545-0227
2000
Attachment Sequence No. **32**

Name(s) shown on Form 1040: A.TRADER LOSS NO 475
Your social security number: 123-45-6789

Part I Adjustments and Preferences

		Line	Amount
1	If you itemized deductions on Schedule A (Form 1040), go to line 2. Otherwise, enter your standard deduction from Form 1040, line 36, here and go to line 6	1	4,400
2	Medical and dental. Enter the smaller of Schedule A (Form 1040), line 4 **or** 2 1/2% of Form 1040, line 34	2	
3	Taxes. Enter the amount from Schedule A (Form 1040), line 9	3	
4	Certain interest on a home mortgage **not** used to buy, build, or improve your home	4	
5	Miscellaneous itemized deductions. Enter the amount from Schedule A (Form 1040), line 26	5	
6	Refund of taxes. Enter any tax refund from Form 1040, line 10 or line 21	6	( )
7	Investment interest. Enter difference between regular tax and AMT deduction	7	
8	Post-1986 depreciation. Enter difference between regular tax and AMT depreciation	8	
9	Adjusted gain or loss. Enter difference between AMT and regular tax gain or loss	9	
10	Incentive stock options. Enter excess of AMT income over regular tax income	10	
11	Passive activities. Enter difference between AMT and regular tax income or loss	11	
12	Beneficiaries of estates and trusts. Enter the amount from Schedule K-1 (Form 1041), line 9	12	
13	Tax-exempt interest from private activity bonds issued after 8/7/86	13	
14	Other. Enter the amount, if any, for each item below and enter the total on line 14.		

a Circulation expenditures		h Loss limitations	
b Depletion		i Mining costs	
c Depreciation (pre-1987)		j Patron's adjustment	
d Installment sales		k Pollution control facilities	
e Intangible drilling costs		l Research & experimental	
f Large partnerships		m Section 1202 exclusion	
g Long-term contracts		n Tax shelter farm activities	
		o Related adjustments	

		Line	Amount
		14	
15	**Total Adjustments and Preferences.** Combine lines 1 through 14 ▶	15	4,400

Part II Alternative Minimum Taxable Income

		Line	Amount
16	Enter the amount from **Form 1040, line 37.** If less than zero, enter as a (loss) ▶	16	210,072
17	Net operating loss deduction, if any, from Form 1040, line 21. Enter as a positive amount	17	
18	If Form 1040, line 34, is over $128,950 (over $64,475 if married filing separately), and you itemized deductions, enter the amount, if any, from line 9 of the worksheet for Schedule A (Form 1040), line 28	18	( )
19	Combine lines 15 through 18 ▶	19	214,472
20	Alternative tax net operating loss deduction. See page 6 of the instructions	20	
21	**Alternative Minimum Taxable Income.** Subtract line 20 from line 19. (If married filing separately and line 21 is more than $165,000, see page 7 of the instructions.) ▶	21	214,472

Part III Exemption Amount and Alternative Minimum Tax

22 **Exemption Amount.** (If this form is for a child under age 14, see page 7 of the instructions.)

IF your filing status is:	**AND line 21 is not over . . .**	**THEN enter on line 22 . . .**
Single or head of household	$112,500	$33,750
Married filing jointly or qualifying widow(er)	150,000	45,000
Married filing separately	75,000	22,500

If line 21 is **over** the amount shown above for your filing status, see page 7 of the instructions.

		Line	Amount
22	Exemption Amount	22	8,257
23	Subtract line 22 from line 21. If zero or less, enter -0- here and on lines 26 and 28 and stop here ▶	23	206,215
24	If you reported capital gain distributions directly on Form 1040, line 13, **or** you completed Schedule D (Form 1040) and have an amount on line 25 or line 27 (or would have had an amount on either line if you had completed Part IV) (as refigured for the AMT, if necessary), go to Part IV of Form 6251 to figure line 24. **All others:** If line 23 is $175,000 or less ($87,500 or less if married filing separately), multiply line 23 by 26% (.26). Otherwise, multiply line 23 by 28% (.28) and subtract $3,500 ($1,750 if married filing separately) from the result ▶	24	54,240
25	Alternative minimum tax foreign tax credit. See page 7 of the instructions	25	
26	Tentative minimum tax. Subtract line 25 from line 24 ▶	26	54,240
27	Enter your tax from Form 1040, line 40 (minus any tax from Form 4972 and any foreign tax credit from Form 1040, line 43)	27	63,375
28	**Alternative Minimum Tax.** Subtract line 27 from line 26. If zero or less, enter -0-. Enter here and on Form 1040, line 41 ▶	28	0

For Paperwork Reduction Act Notice, see page 8 of the instructions. Form **6251** (2000)

KFA IFOUS33 10/23/00

Example 6

FORM 1040 Department of the Treasury – Internal Revenue Service
U.S. Individual Income Tax Return **2000** (99) IRS Use Only – Do not write or staple in this space.

For the year Jan. 1 – Dec. 31, 2000, or other tax year beginning , 2000, ending , 20 OMB No. 1545-0074

Label (See instructions on page 19.) Use the IRS label. Otherwise, please print or type. LABEL HERE

Your first name and initial / Last name: A. TRADER LOSS SECT.475	Your social security number: 123-45-6789
If a joint return, spouse's first name and initial / Last name	Spouse's social security number
Home address (number and street). If you have a P.O. box, see page 19. Apt. no.: C/O TED TESSER-6274 LINTON BLVD. #102	▲ **IMPORTANT!** ▲ You **must** enter your SSN(s) above.
City, town or post office, state, and ZIP code. If you have a foreign address, see page 19.: DELRAY BEACH, FL 33484	

Presidential Election Campaign (See page 19.) **Note.** Checking "Yes" will not change your tax or reduce your refund.
Do you, or your spouse if filing a joint return, want $3 to go to this fund? ▶ You: ☐ Yes ☒ No Spouse: ☐ Yes ☐ No

Filing Status (Check only one box.)

1 [X] Single
2 [ ] Married filing joint return (even if only one had income)
3 [ ] Married filing separate return. Enter spouse's soc. sec. no. above & full name here ▶
4 [ ] Head of household (with qualifying person). (See page 19.) If the qualifying person is a child but not your dependent, enter this child's name here ▶
5 [ ] Qualifying widow(er) with dependent child (year spouse died ▶). (See page 19.)

Exemptions

6a ☒ **Yourself.** If your parent (or someone else) can claim you as a dependent on his or her tax return, **do not** check box 6a.
b ☐ **Spouse**
No. of boxes checked on 6a and 6b: 1

c **Dependents:**

(1) First Name Last name	(2) Dependent's social security number	(3) Dependent's relationship to you	(4) Chk if qualifying child for child tax credit (see page 20)

If more than six dependents, see page 20.

No. of your children on 6c who: ● lived with you ____ ● did not live with you due to divorce or separation (see page 20) ____ Dependents on 6c not entered above ____

d Total number of exemptions claimed — Add numbers entered on lines above ▶ 1

Income

Attach Forms W-2 and W-2G here. Also attach Form 1099-R if tax was withheld.
If you did not get a W-2, see page 21.
Enclose, but do not attach any payment. Also, please use Form 1040-V.

Line	Description		Amount
7	Wages, salaries, tips, etc. Attach Form(s) W-2	7	200,000
8a	**Taxable** interest. Attach Schedule B if required	8a	
b	**Tax-exempt** interest. **Do not** include on line 8a — 8b		
9	Ordinary dividends. Attach Schedule B if required	9	
10	Taxable refunds, credits, or offsets of state and local income taxes (see page 22)	10	
11	Alimony received	11	
12	Business income or (loss). Attach Schedule C or C-EZ	12	-182,528
13	Capital gain or (loss). Attach Schedule D if required. If not required, check here ▶ ☐	13	
14	Other gains or (losses). Attach Form 4797	14	-100,000
15a	Total IRA distributions — 15a; b Taxable amount (see pg. 23)	15b	
16a	Total pensions and annuities — 16a; b Taxable amount (see pg. 23)	16b	
17	Rental real estate, royalties, partnerships, S corporations, trusts, etc. Attach Schedule E	17	200,000
18	Farm income or (loss). Attach Schedule F	18	
19	Unemployment compensation	19	
20a	Social security benefits — 20a; b Taxable amount (see pg. 25)	20b	
21	Other income.	21	
22	Add the amounts in the far right column for lines 7 through 21. This is your **total income** ▶	22	117,472

Adjusted Gross Income

Line	Description		Amount		
23	IRA deduction (see page 27)	23			
24	Student loan interest deduction (see page 27)	24			
25	Medical savings account deduction. Attach Form 8853	25			
26	Moving expenses. Attach Form 3903	26			
27	One-half of self-employment tax. Attach Schedule SE	27			
28	Self-employed health insurance deduction (see page 29)	28			
29	Self-employed SEP, SIMPLE, and qualified plans	29			
30	Penalty on early withdrawal of savings	30			
31a	Alimony paid. b Recipient's SSN ▶	31a			
32	Add lines 23 through 31a			32	0
33	Subtract line 32 from line 22. This is your **adjusted gross income** ▶			33	117,472

KFA **For Disclosure, Privacy Act, and Paperwork Reduction Act Notice, see page 56.** IF0US1 11/07/00 Form **1040** (2000)

Form 1040 (2000) A. TRADER LOSS SECT.475 — 123-45-6789 Page **2**

Tax and Credits	34 Amount from line 33 (adjusted gross income)			34	117,472
	35a Check if: ☐ You were 65 or older, ☐ Blind; ☐ Spouse was 65 or older, ☐ Blind. Add the number of boxes checked above and enter the total here ▶ 35a				
	b If you are married filing separately and your spouse itemizes deductions, or you were a dual-status alien, see page 31 and check here ▶ 35b ☐				
Standard Deduction for Most People Single: $4,400 Head of household: $6,450 Married filing jointly or Qualifying widow(er): $7,350 Married filing separately $3,675.	36 Enter your **itemized deductions** from Schedule A, line 28, **or standard deduction** shown on the left. **But** see page 31 to find your standard deduction if you checked any box on line 35a or 35b **or** if someone can claim you as a dependent			36	4,400
	37 Subtract line 36 from line 34			37	113,072
	38 If line 34 is $96,700 or less, multiply $2,800 by the total number of exemptions claimed on line 6d. If line 34 is over $96,700, see the worksheet on page 32 for the amount to enter			38	2,800
	39 **Taxable income.** Subtract line 38 from line 37. If line 38 is more than line 37, enter -0-			39	110,272
	40 **Tax** (see page 32). Check if any tax is from a ☐ Form(s) 8814 b ☐ Form 4972			40	28,865
	41 Alternative minimum tax. Attach Form 6251			41	
	42 Add lines 40 and 41 ▶			42	28,865
	43 Foreign tax credit. Attach Form 1116 if required	43			
	44 Credit for child and dependent care expenses. Att. Form 2441	44			
	45 Credit for the elderly or the disabled. Attach Schedule R	45			
	46 Education credits. Attach Form 8863	46			
	47 Child tax credit (see page 36)	47			
	48 Adoption credit. Attach Form 8839	48			
	49 Other. Check if from a ☐ Form 3800 b ☐ Form 8396 c ☐ Form 8801 d ☐ Form (specify)	49			
	50 Add lines 43 through 49. These are your **total credits**			50	
	51 Subtract line 50 from line 42. If line 50 is more than line 42, enter -0- ▶			51	28,865
Other Taxes	52 Self-employment tax. Att. Sch. SE			52	
	53 Social security and Medicare tax on tip income not reported to employer. Attach Form 4137			53	
	54 Tax on IRAs, other retirement plans, and MSAs. Attach Form 5329 if required			54	
	55 Advance earned income credit payments from Form(s) W-2			55	
	56 Household employment taxes. Attach Schedule H			56	
	57 Add lines 51 through 56. This is your **total tax** ▶			57	28,865
Payments	58 Federal income tax withheld from Forms W-2 and 1099	58	60,000		
If you have a qualifying child, attach Schedule EIC.	59 2000 estimated tax payments and amount applied from 1999 return	59	50,000		
	60a **Earned income credit (EIC)**	60a			
	b **Nontaxable earned income: amt.** ▶ and type ▶ No				
	61 Excess social security and RRTA tax withheld (see page 50)	61			
	62 **Additional child tax credit. Attach Form 8812**	62			
	63 **Amount paid with request for extension to file** (see page 50)	63			
	64 Other payments. Check if from a ☐ Form 2439 b ☐ Form 4136	64			
	65 Add lines 58, 59, 60a, and 61 through 64. These are your **total payments** ▶			65	110,000
Refund	66 If line 65 is more than line 57, subtract line 57 from line 65. This is the amount you **overpaid**			66	81,135
Have it directly deposited! See page 50 and fill in 67b, 67c, and 67d.	67a Amount of line 66 you want **refunded to you** ▶			67a	81,135
	b Routing number ▶ c Type: ☐ Checking ☐ Savings				
	d Account number				
	68 Amount of line 66 you want **applied to your 2001 estimated tax** ▶	68			
Amount You Owe	69 If line 57 is more than line 65, subtract line 65 from line 57. This is the **amount you owe.** For details on how to pay, see page 51 ▶			69	
	70 Estimated tax penalty. Also include on line 69	70			

Sign Here — Joint return? See page 19. Keep a copy for your records.

Under penalties of perjury, I declare that I have examined this return and accompanying schedules and statements, and to the best of my knowledge and belief, they are true, correct, and complete. Declaration of preparer (other than taxpayer) is based on all information of which preparer has any knowledge.

▶ Your signature	Date	Your occupation	Daytime phone number 561-865-0071
▶ Spouse's signature. If a joint return, **both** must sign.	Date	Spouse's occupation	May the IRS discuss this return with the preparer shown below? (see page 52)? ☒ Yes ☐ No

Paid Preparer's Use Only

Preparer's signature ▶	Date	Check if self-employed ☐	Preparer's SSN or PTIN
Firm's name (or yours if self-employed), address, and ZIP code ▶ Waterside Financial Serv., Inc 6274 Linton Blvd., Suite #102 Boca Raton, FL 33484		EIN 65-0664126	Phone no. (561) 865-0071

IFOUS1A 11/22/00 Form **1040** (2000)

Example 6 *(Continued)*

SCHEDULE C (Form 1040) — **Profit or Loss From Business (Sole Proprietorship)** — OMB No. 1545-0074 — **2000**

Department of the Treasury Internal Revenue Service (99)

▶ Partnerships, joint ventures, etc., must file Form 1065 or Form 1065-B.
▶ Attach to Form 1040 or Form 1041. ▶ See Instructions for Schedule C (Form 1040).

Attachment Sequence No. 09

Name of proprietor: A. TRADER LOSS SECT.475 — Social security number (SSN): 123-45-6789

A Principal business or profession, including product or service (see page C-1 of the instructions): TRADER — B Enter code from pages C-7 & 8: ▶ 523900

C Business name. If no separate business name, leave blank. — D Employer ID number (EIN), if any

E Business address (including suite or room no.) ▶
City, town or post office, state, and ZIP code

F Accounting method: (1) ☒ Cash (2) ☐ Accrual (3) ☐ Other (specify) ▶

G Did you "materially participate" in the operation of this business during 2000? If "No," see page C-2 for limit on losses ☒ Yes ☐ No

H If you started or acquired this business during 2000, check here ▶ ☐

Part I Income

	Line	Amount
1 Gross receipts or sales. **Caution:** If this income was reported to you on Form W-2 and the "Statutory employee" box on that form was checked, see page C-2 and check here ▶ ☐	1	
2 Returns and allowances	2	
3 Subtract line 2 from line 1	3	
4 Cost of goods sold (from line 42 on page 2)	4	
5 **Gross profit.** Subtract line 4 from line 3	5	
6 Other income, including Federal and state gasoline or fuel tax credit or refund (see page C-2)	6	
7 **Gross income.** Add lines 5 and 6 ▶	7	

Part II Expenses. Enter expenses for business use of your home **only** on line 30.

	Line	Amount		Line	Amount
8 Advertising	8		19 Pension and profit-sharing plans	19	
9 Bad debts from sales or services (see page C-3)	9		20 Rent or lease (see page C-4): a Vehicles, machinery & equipment	20a	5,050
10 Car and truck expenses (see page C-3)	10	3,115	b Other business property	20b	
11 Commissions and fees	11		21 Repairs and maintenance	21	3,166
12 Depletion	12		22 Supplies (not included in Part III)	22	5,069
13 Depreciation and section 179 expense deduction (not included in Part III) (see page C-3)	13	5,000	23 Taxes and licenses	23	
14 Employee benefit programs (other than on line 19)	14		24 Travel, meals, and entertainment: a Travel	24a	6,511
15 Insurance (other than health)	15		b Meals and entertainment: 8,711		
16 Interest:			c Enter nondeductible amount included on line 24b (see page C-5): 4,356		
a Mortgage (paid to banks, etc.)	16a		d Subtract line 24c from line 24b	24d	4,355
b Other	16b	51,357	25 Utilities	25	2,611
17 Legal and professional services	17	2,250	26 Wages (less employment credits)	26	
18 Office expense	18	4,561	27 Other expenses (from line 48 on page 2)	27	83,233

	Line	Amount
28 **Total expenses** before expenses for business use of home. Add lines 8 through 27 in columns ▶	28	176,278
29 Tentative profit (loss). Subtract line 28 from line 7	29	-176,278
30 Expenses for business use of your home. Attach **Form 8829**	30	6,250
31 **Net profit or (loss).** Subtract line 30 from line 29. • If a profit, enter on **Form 1040, line 12,** and **also** on **Schedule SE, line 2** (statutory employees, see page C-5). Estates and trusts, enter on Form 1041, line 3. • If a loss, you **must** go to line 32.	31	-182,528

32 If you have a loss, check the box that describes your investment in this activity (see page C-5).
- If you checked 32a, enter the loss on **Form 1040, line 12,** and **also** on **Schedule SE, line 2** (statutory employees, see page C-5). Estates and trusts, enter on Form 1041, line 3.
- If you checked 32b, you **must** attach **Form 6198.**

32a ☒ All investment is at risk.
32b ☐ Some investment is not at risk.

For Paperwork Reduction Act Notice, see Form 1040 instructions. **Schedule C (Form 1040) 2000**

KFA IF0US4 11/08/00

Example 6 *(Continued)*

Schedule C (Form 1040) 2000 A. TRADER LOSS SECT. 475 — 123-45-6789 Page 2

Part III — Cost of Goods Sold (see page C-6)

33 Method(s) used to value closing inventory: a ☐ Cost b ☐ Lower of cost or market c ☐ Other (attach explanation)

34 Was there any change in determining quantities, costs, or valuations between opening and closing inventory? If "Yes," attach explanation ☐ Yes ☐ No

35 Inventory at beginning of year. If different from last year's closing inventory, attach explanation	35	
36 Purchases less cost of items withdrawn for personal use	36	
37 Cost of labor. Do not include any amounts paid to yourself	37	
38 Materials and supplies	38	
39 Other costs	39	
40 Add lines 35 through 39	40	
41 Inventory at end of year	41	
42 **Cost of goods sold.** Subtract line 41 from line 40. Enter the result here and on page 1, line 4	42	

Part IV — Information on Your Vehicle. Complete this part **only** if you are claiming car or truck expenses on line 10 and are not required to file Form 4562 for this business. See the instructions for line 13 on page C-3 to find out if you must file.

43 When did you place your vehicle in service for business purposes? (month, day, year) ▶ ________________

44 Of the total number of miles you drove your vehicle during 2000, enter the number of miles you used your vehicle for:

a Business ________________ b Commuting ________________ c Other ________________

45 Do you (or your spouse) have another vehicle available for personal use? ☐ Yes ☐ No

46 Was your vehicle available for use during off-duty hours? ☐ Yes ☐ No

47a Do you have evidence to support your deduction? ☐ Yes ☐ No

b If "Yes," is the evidence written? ☐ Yes ☐ No

Part V — Other Expenses. List below business expenses not included on lines 8–26 or line 30.

COMPUTER EXPENSE		2,955
HISTORICAL DATA SERVICES		3,061
INTERNET SERVICES		2,050
ONLINE TRADING DATA		7,010
OTHER TRADING EXPENSES		4,116
PROFESSIONAL PUBLICATIONS		3,116
TRADING ADVISORY SERVICES		35,179
TRADING PERIODICALS		6,633
TRADING SEMINARS		19,113
48 **Total other expenses.** Enter here and on page 1, line 27	48	83,233

IFOUS4A 11/09/00 — Schedule C (Form 1040) 2000

Form **4797** Department of the Treasury Internal Revenue Service (99)

Sales of Business Property

(Also Involuntary Conversions and Recapture Amounts Under Sections 179 and 280F(b)(2))

▶ Attach to your tax return. ▶ See separate instructions.

OMB No. 1545-0184 **2000** Attachment Sequence No. **27**

Name(s) shown on return: A. TRADER LOSS SECT.475 | Identifying number: 123-45-6789

1 Enter the gross proceeds from sales or exchanges reported to you for 2000 on Form(s) 1099-B or 1099-S (or substitute statement) that you are including on line 2, 10, or 20 (see instructions) . . . 1

Part I **Sales or Exchanges of Property Used in a Trade or Business and Involuntary Conversions From Other Than Casualty or Theft – Most Property Held More Than 1 Year** (See instructions.)

2 (a) Description of property	(b) Date acquired (mo., day, yr.)	(c) Date sold (mo., day, yr.)	(d) Gross sales price	(e) Depreciation allowed or allowable since acquisition	(f) Cost or other basis, plus improvements and expense of sale	(g) Gain or (loss) Subtract (f) from the sum of (d) and (e)

3 Gain, if any, from Form 4684, line 39 . . . 3

4 Section 1231 gain from installment sales from Form 6252, line 26 or 37 . . . 4

5 Section 1231 gain or (loss) from like-kind exchanges from Form 8824 . . . 5

6 Gain, if any, from line 32, from other than casualty or theft . . . 6

7 Combine lines 2 through 6. Enter the gain or (loss) here and on the appropriate line as follows: 7

Partnerships (except electing large partnerships). Report the gain or (loss) following the instructions for Form 1065, Schedule K, line 6. Skip lines 8, 9, 11, and 12 below.

S corporations. Report the gain or (loss) following the instructions for Form 1120S, Schedule K, lines 5 and 6. Skip lines 8, 9, 11, and 12 below, unless line 7 is a gain and the S corporation is subject to capital gains tax.

All others. If line 7 is zero or a loss, enter the amount from line 7 on line 11 below and skip lines 8 and 9. If line 7 is a gain and you did not have any prior year section 1231 losses, or they were recaptured in an earlier year, enter the gain from line 7 as a long-term capital gain on Schedule D and skip lines 8, 9, and 12 below.

8 Nonrecaptured net section 1231 losses from prior years (see instructions) . . . 8

9 Subtract line 8 from line 7. If zero or less, enter -0-. Also enter on the appropriate line as follows (see instructions): . . . 9

S corporations. Enter any gain from line 9 on Schedule D (Form 1120S), line 15, and skip lines 11 and 12 below.

All others. If line 9 is zero, enter the gain from line 7 on line 12 below. If line 9 is more than zero, enter the amount from line 8 on line 12 below, and enter the gain from line 9 as a long-term capital gain on Schedule D.

Part II **Ordinary Gains and Losses**

10 Ordinary gains and losses not included on lines 11 through 17 (include property held 1 year or less):

475 TRADING	LOSS			-100,000		-100,000

11	Loss, if any, from line 7 . . .	11	
12	Gain, if any, from line 7 or amount from line 8, if applicable . . .	12	
13	Gain, if any, from line 31 . . .	13	
14	Net gain or (loss) from Form 4684, lines 31 and 38a . . .	14	
15	Ordinary gain from installment sales from Form 6252, line 25 or 36 . . .	15	
16	Ordinary gain or (loss) from like-kind exchanges from Form 8824 . . .	16	
17	Recapture of section 179 expense deduction for partners and S corporation shareholders from property dispositions by partnerships and S corporations (see instructions) . . .	17	
18	Combine lines 10 through 17. Enter the gain or (loss) here and on the appropriate line as follows: . . .	18	-100,000
a	For all except individual returns: Enter the gain or (loss) from line 18 on the return being filed.		
b	For individual returns:		
	(1) If the loss on line 11 includes a loss from Form 4684, line 35, column (b)(ii), enter that part of the loss here. Enter the part of the loss from income-producing property on Schedule A (Form 1040), line 27, and the part of the loss from property used as an employee on Schedule A (Form 1040), line 22. Identify as from "Form 4797, line 18b(1)." See instructions . . .	18b(1)	
	(2) Redetermine the gain or (loss) on line 18 excluding the loss, if any, on line 18b(1). Enter here and on Form 1040, line 14 . . .	18b(2)	-100,000

KFA **For Paperwork Reduction Act Notice, see page 7 of the instructions.** GF0US51 12/22/00 Form **4797** (2000)

Example 6 *(Continued)*

Form **6251**

Department of the Treasury
Internal Revenue Service

Alternative Minimum Tax – Individuals

▶ **See separate instructions.**
▶ **Attach to Form 1040 or Form 1040NR.**

OMB No. 1545-0227

2000

Attachment Sequence No. **32**

Name(s) shown on Form 1040	Your social security number
A. TRADER LOSS SECT.475	123-45-6789

Part I — Adjustments and Preferences

1	If you itemized deductions on Schedule A (Form 1040), go to line 2. Otherwise, enter your standard deduction from Form 1040, line 36, here and go to line 6	1	4,400
2	Medical and dental. Enter the smaller of Schedule A (Form 1040), line 4 **or** 2 1/2% of Form 1040, line 34	2	
3	Taxes. Enter the amount from Schedule A (Form 1040), line 9	3	
4	Certain interest on a home mortgage **not** used to buy, build, or improve your home	4	
5	Miscellaneous itemized deductions. Enter the amount from Schedule A (Form 1040), line 26	5	
6	Refund of taxes. Enter any tax refund from Form 1040, line 10 or line 21	6	( )
7	Investment interest. Enter difference between regular tax and AMT deduction	7	
8	Post-1986 depreciation. Enter difference between regular tax and AMT depreciation	8	
9	Adjusted gain or loss. Enter difference between AMT and regular tax gain or loss	9	
10	Incentive stock options. Enter excess of AMT income over regular tax income	10	
11	Passive activities. Enter difference between AMT and regular tax income or loss	11	
12	Beneficiaries of estates and trusts. Enter the amount from Schedule K-1 (Form 1041), line 9	12	
13	Tax-exempt interest from private activity bonds issued after 8/7/86	13	
14	Other. Enter the amount, if any, for each item below and enter the total on line 14.		

a Circulation expenditures		h Loss limitations	
b Depletion		i Mining costs	
c Depreciation (pre-1987)		j Patron's adjustment	
d Installment sales		k Pollution control facilities	
e Intangible drilling costs		l Research & experimental	
f Large partnerships		m Section 1202 exclusion	
g Long-term contracts		n Tax shelter farm activities	
		o Related adjustments	

		14	
15	**Total Adjustments and Preferences.** Combine lines 1 through 14 ▶	15	4,400

Part II — Alternative Minimum Taxable Income

16	Enter the amount from **Form 1040, line 37.** If less than zero, enter as a (loss) ▶	16	113,072
17	Net operating loss deduction, if any, from Form 1040, line 21. Enter as a positive amount	17	
18	If Form 1040, line 34, is over $128,950 (over $64,475 if married filing separately), and you itemized deductions, enter the amount, if any, from line 9 of the worksheet for Schedule A (Form 1040), line 28	18	( )
19	Combine lines 15 through 18 ▶	19	117,472
20	Alternative tax net operating loss deduction. See page 6 of the instructions	20	
21	**Alternative Minimum Taxable Income.** Subtract line 20 from line 19. (If married filing separately and line 21 is more than $165,000, see page 7 of the instructions.) ▶	21	117,472

Part III — Exemption Amount and Alternative Minimum Tax

22 **Exemption Amount.** (If this form is for a child under age 14, see page 7 of the instructions.)

IF your filing status is:	**AND line 21 is not over . . .**	**THEN enter on line 22 . . .**
Single or head of household	$112,500	$33,750
Married filing jointly or qualifying widow(er)	150,000	45,000
Married filing separately	75,000	22,500

If line 21 is **over** the amount shown above for your filing status, see page 7 of the instructions.

22	Exemption Amount	22	32,507
23	Subtract line 22 from line 21. If zero or less, enter -0- here and on lines 26 and 28 and stop here ▶	23	84,965
24	If you reported capital gain distributions directly on Form 1040, line 13, **or** you completed Schedule D (Form 1040) and have an amount on line 25 or line 27 (or would have had an amount on either line if you had completed Part IV) (as refigured for the AMT, if necessary), go to Part IV of Form 6251 to figure line 24. **All others:** If line 23 is $175,000 or less ($87,500 or less if married filing separately), multiply line 23 by 26% (.26). Otherwise, multiply line 23 by 28% (.28) and subtract $3,500 ($1,750 if married filing separately) from the result ▶	24	22,091
25	Alternative minimum tax foreign tax credit. See page 7 of the instructions	25	
26	Tentative minimum tax. Subtract line 25 from line 24 ▶	26	22,091
27	Enter your tax from Form 1040, line 40 (minus any tax from Form 4972 and any foreign tax credit from Form 1040, line 43)	27	28,865
28	**Alternative Minimum Tax.** Subtract line 27 from line 26. If zero or less, enter -0-. Enter here and on Form 1040, line 41 ▶	28	0

For Paperwork Reduction Act Notice, see page 8 of the instructions. Form **6251** (2000)

KFA IFOUS33 10/23/00

Example 7

FORM 1040 Department of the Treasury – Internal Revenue Service
U.S. Individual Income Tax Return 2000 (99) IRS Use Only – Do not write or staple in this space.

For the year Jan. 1 – Dec. 31, 2000, or other tax year beginning , 2000, ending , 20 OMB No. 1545-0074

Label (See instructions on page 19.) Use the IRS label. Otherwise, please print or type.

LABEL HERE	
Your first name and initial / Last name	Your social security number
COMMODITIES N. VESTOR-PROFIT	123-45-6789
If a joint return, spouse's first name and initial / Last name	Spouse's social security number
Home address (number and street). If you have a P.O. box, see page 19. Apt. no.	▲ **IMPORTANT!** ▲ You **must** enter your SSN(s) above.
C/O TED TESSER-6274 LINTON BLVD. #102	
City, town or post office, state, and ZIP code. If you have a foreign address, see page 19.	
DELRAY BEACH, FL 33484	

Presidential Election Campaign (See page 19.) **Note.** Checking "Yes" will not change your tax or reduce your refund. Do you, or your spouse if filing a joint return, want $3 to go to this fund? You: ☐ Yes ☒ No Spouse: ☐ Yes ☐ No

Filing Status (Check only one box.)

1 [X] Single
2 [ ] Married filing joint return (even if only one had income)
3 [ ] Married filing separate return. Enter spouse's soc. sec. no. above & full name here ▶
4 [ ] Head of household (with qualifying person). (See page 19.) If the qualifying person is a child but not your dependent, enter this child's name here ▶
5 [ ] Qualifying widow(er) with dependent child (year spouse died ▶). (See page 19.)

Exemptions

6a ☒ **Yourself.** If your parent (or someone else) can claim you as a dependent on his or her tax return, **do not** check box 6a.
b ☐ **Spouse** — No. of boxes checked on 6a and 6b: 1
c **Dependents:**

(1) First Name Last name	(2) Dependent's social security number	(3) Dependent's relationship to you	(4) Chk if qualifying child for child tax credit (see page 20)

If more than six dependents, see page 20.

No. of your children on 6c who: ● lived with you ● did not live with you due to divorce or separation (see page 20) — Dependents on 6c not entered above

d Total number of exemptions claimed — Add numbers entered on lines above ▶ 1

Income (Attach Forms W-2 and W-2G here. Also attach Form 1099-R if tax was withheld. If you did not get a W-2, see page 21. Enclose, but do not attach any payment. Also, please use Form 1040-V.)

Line	Description		Amount
7	Wages, salaries, tips, etc. Attach Form(s) W-2	7	200,000
8a	**Taxable** interest. Attach Schedule B if required	8a	
b	**Tax-exempt** interest. **Do not** include on line 8a — 8b		
9	Ordinary dividends. Attach Schedule B if required	9	
10	Taxable refunds, credits, or offsets of state and local income taxes (see page 22)	10	
11	Alimony received	11	
12	Business income or (loss). Attach Schedule C or C-EZ	12	
13	Capital gain or (loss). Attach Schedule D if required. If not required, check here ▶ ☐	13	301,519
14	Other gains or (losses). Attach Form 4797	14	
15a	Total IRA distributions 15a — b Taxable amount (see pg. 23)	15b	
16a	Total pensions and annuities 16a — b Taxable amount (see pg. 23)	16b	
17	Rental real estate, royalties, partnerships, S corporations, trusts, etc. Attach Schedule E	17	200,000
18	Farm income or (loss). Attach Schedule F	18	
19	Unemployment compensation	19	
20a	Social security benefits 20a — b Taxable amount (see pg. 25)	20b	
21	Other income.	21	
22	Add the amounts in the far right column for lines 7 through 21. This is your **total income** ▶	22	701,519

Adjusted Gross Income

Line	Description		Amount
23	IRA deduction (see page 27) — 23		
24	Student loan interest deduction (see page 27) — 24		
25	Medical savings account deduction. Attach Form 8853 — 25		
26	Moving expenses. Attach Form 3903 — 26		
27	One-half of self-employment tax. Attach Schedule SE — 27		
28	Self-employed health insurance deduction (see page 29) — 28		
29	Self-employed SEP, SIMPLE, and qualified plans — 29		
30	Penalty on early withdrawal of savings — 30		
31a	Alimony paid. **b** Recipient's SSN ▶ — 31a		
32	Add lines 23 through 31a	32	0
33	Subtract line 32 from line 22. This is your **adjusted gross income** ▶	33	701,519

KFA **For Disclosure, Privacy Act, and Paperwork Reduction Act Notice, see page 56.** IF0US1 11/07/00 Form **1040** (2000)

Form 1040 (2000) COMMODITIES N. VESTOR-PROFIT 123-45-6789 Page **2**

Tax and Credits

Line	Description			Amount
34	Amount from line 33 (adjusted gross income)		34	701,519
35a	Check if: ☐ **You** were 65 or older, ☐ Blind; ☐ **Spouse** was 65 or older, ☐ Blind. Add the number of boxes checked above and enter the total here ▶ 35a			
b	If you are married filing separately and your spouse itemizes deductions, or you were a dual-status alien, see page 31 and check here ▶ 35b ☐			
36	Enter your **itemized deductions** from Schedule A, line 28, **or standard deduction** shown on the left. **But** see page 31 to find your standard deduction if you checked any box on line 35a or 35b **or** if someone can claim you as a dependent		36	115,092
37	Subtract line 36 from line 34		37	586,427
38	If line 34 is $96,700 or less, multiply $2,800 by the total number of exemptions claimed on line 6d. If line 34 is over $96,700, see the worksheet on page 32 for the amount to enter		38	0
39	**Taxable income.** Subtract line 38 from line 37. If line 38 is more than line 37, enter -0-		39	586,427
40	**Tax** (see page 32). Check if any tax is from **a** ☐ Form(s) 8814 **b** ☐ Form 4972		40	174,437
41	Alternative minimum tax. Attach Form 6251		41	
42	Add lines 40 and 41 ▶		42	174,437
43	Foreign tax credit. Attach Form 1116 if required	43		
44	Credit for child and dependent care expenses. Att. Form 2441	44		
45	Credit for the elderly or the disabled. Attach Schedule R	45		
46	Education credits. Attach Form 8863	46		
47	Child tax credit (see page 36)	47		
48	Adoption credit. Attach Form 8839	48		
49	Other. Check if from **a** ☐ Form 3800 **b** ☐ Form 8396 **c** ☐ Form 8801 **d** ☐ Form (specify)	49		
50	Add lines 43 through 49. These are your **total credits**		50	
51	Subtract line 50 from line 42. If line 50 is more than line 42, enter -0- ▶		51	174,437

Standard Deduction for Most People
Single: $4,400
Head of household: $6,450
Married filing jointly or Qualifying widow(er): $7,350
Married filing separately $3,675.

Other Taxes

Line	Description			Amount
52	Self-employment tax. Att. Sch. SE		52	
53	Social security and Medicare tax on tip income not reported to employer. Attach Form 4137		53	
54	Tax on IRAs, other retirement plans, and MSAs. Attach Form 5329 if required		54	
55	Advance earned income credit payments from Form(s) W-2		55	
56	Household employment taxes. Attach Schedule H		56	
57	Add lines 51 through 56. This is your **total tax** ▶		57	174,437

Payments

If you have a qualifying child, attach Schedule EIC.

Line	Description			Amount
58	Federal income tax withheld from Forms W-2 and 1099	58	60,000	
59	2000 estimated tax payments and amount applied from 1999 return	59	50,000	
60a	**Earned income credit (EIC)**	60a		
b	**Nontaxable earned income: amt.** ▶ **and type** ▶ No			
61	Excess social security and RRTA tax withheld (see page 50)	61		
62	**Additional child tax credit. Attach Form 8812**	62		
63	**Amount paid with request for extension to file** (see page 50)	63		
64	Other payments. Check if from **a** ☐ Form 2439 **b** ☐ Form 4136	64		
65	Add lines 58, 59, 60a, and 61 through 64. These are your **total payments** ▶		65	110,000

Refund

Have it directly deposited! See page 50 and fill in 67b, 67c, and 67d.

Line	Description			Amount
66	If line 65 is more than line 57, subtract line 57 from line 65. This is the amount you **overpaid**		66	
67a	Amount of line 66 you want **refunded to you** ▶		67a	
b	Routing number ▶ **c** Type: ☐ Checking ☐ Savings			
d	Account number			
68	Amount of line 66 you want **applied to your 2001 estimated tax** ▶	68		

Amount You Owe

Line	Description			Amount
69	If line 57 is more than line 65, subtract line 65 from line 57. This is the **amount you owe.** For details on how to pay, see page 51 ▶		69	64,437
70	Estimated tax penalty. Also include on line 69	70		

Sign Here

Under penalties of perjury, I declare that I have examined this return and accompanying schedules and statements, and to the best of my knowledge and belief, they are true, correct, and complete. Declaration of preparer (other than taxpayer) is based on all information of which preparer has any knowledge.

Joint return? See page 19. Keep a copy for your records.

Your signature	Date	Your occupation	Daytime phone number
Spouse's signature. If a joint return, **both** must sign.	Date	Spouse's occupation	May the IRS discuss this return with the preparer shown below? (see page 52)? ☒ Yes ☐ No

Paid Preparer's Use Only

Preparer's signature	Date	Check if self-employed ☐	Preparer's SSN or PTIN
Firm's name (or yours if self-employed), address, and ZIP code	Waterside Financial Services 6274 Linton Blvd., Suite #102 Delray Beach, FL 33484	EIN	Phone no. (561) 865-0071

IFOUS1A 11/22/00 Form **1040** (2000)

SCHEDULES A&B (Form 1040)	Schedule A – Itemized Deductions		OMB No. 1545-0074
Department of the Treasury Internal Revenue Service (99)	▶ Attach to Form 1040. ▶ See Instructions for Schedules A and B (Form 1040).		**2000** Attachment **07** Sequence No.

Name(s) shown on Form 1040

COMMODITIES N. VESTOR-PROFIT

Your social security number

123-45-6789

Medical and Dental Expenses		**Caution.** Do not include expenses reimbursed or paid by others.					
	1	Medical and dental expenses (see page A-2) .	1				
	2	Enter amount from Form 1040, line 34	2				
	3	Multiply line 2 above by 7.5% (.075) .	3				
	4	Subtract line 3 from line 1. If line 3 is more than line 1, enter –0– .		4	0		
Taxes You Paid (See page A-2.)	5	State and local income taxes .	5				
	6	Real estate taxes (see page A-2) .	6				
	7	Personal property taxes .	7				
	8	Other taxes. List type and amount ▶ _	8				
	9	Add lines 5 through 8. .		9	0		
Interest You Paid (See page A-3.) **Note.** Personal interest is not deductible.	10	Home mortgage interest and points reported on Form 1098	10				
	11	Home mortgage interest not reported to you on Form 1098. If paid to the person from whom you bought the home, see page A-3 & show that person's name, ID no. & address ▶ _	11				
	12	Points not reported to you on Form 1098. See pg. A-3	12				
	13	Investment interest. Attach Form 4952, if required. (See page A-3.) .	13	51,357			
	14	Add lines 10 through 13. .		14	51,357		
Gifts to Charity If you made a gift and got a benefit for it, see page A-4.	15	Gifts by cash or check. If any gift of $250 or more, see pg. A-4	15				
	16	Other than by cash or check. If any gift of $250 or more, see page A-4. You **must** attach Form 8283 if over $500 .	16				
	17	Carryover from prior year .	17				
	18	Add lines 15 through 17. .		18	0		
Casualty and Theft Losses	19	Casualty or theft loss(es). Attach Form 4684. (See page A-5.) .		19	0		
Job Expenses and Most Other Miscellaneous Deductions (See page A-5 for expenses to deduct here.)	20	Unreimbursed employee expenses – job travel, union dues, job education, etc. You **must** attach Form 2106 or 2106–EZ if required. (See page A-5.) ▶ _	20				
	21	Tax preparation fees. .	21				
	22	Other expenses – investment, safe deposit box, etc. List type and amount ▶ Depreciation_ _ _ _ _ _ _ _ _ _ 5,000 Investment_Expenses_ _ _ _ _ 89,942 _	22	94,942			
	23	Add lines 20 through 22. .	23	94,942			
	24	Enter amount from Form 1040, line 34	24	701,519			
	25	Multiply line 24 above by 2% (.02) .	25	14,030			
	26	Subtract line 25 from line 23. If line 25 is more than line 23, enter –0–. .		26	80,912		
Other Miscellaneous Deductions	27	Other – from list on page A-6. List type and amount ▶ _		27	0		
Total Itemized Deductions	28	Is Form 1040, line 34, over $128,950? (over $64,475 if married filing separately)? ☐ **No.** Your deduction is not limited. Add the amounts in the far right column for lines 4 through 27. Also, enter this amount on Form 1040, line 36. ⎫ ▶ ☒ **Yes.** Your deduction may be limited. See page A-6 for the amount to enter. ⎭	Reduction -17,177	28	115,092		

KFA **For Paperwork Reduction Act Notice, see Form 1040 instructions.** IF0US2 11/03/00 Schedule A (Form 1040) 2000

SCHEDULE D (Form 1040)

Department of the Treasury Internal Revenue Service (99)

Capital Gains and Losses

▶ Attach to Form 1040. ▶ See Instructions for Schedule D (Form 1040).
▶ Use Schedule D-1 for more space to list transactions for lines 1 and 8.

OMB No. 1545-0074
2000
Attachment Sequence No. 12

Name(s) shown on Form 1040: COMMODITIES N. VESTOR-PROFIT
Your social security number: 123-45-6789

Part I Short-Term Capital Gains and Losses – Assets Held One Year or Less

1 (a) Description of property (Example, 100 sh. XYZ Co.)	(b) Date acquired (Mo., day, yr.)	(c) Date sold (Mo., day, yr.)	(d) Sales price (see page D-6)	(e) Cost or other basis (see page D-6)	(f) Gain or (loss) Subtract (e) from (d)

Line	Description	No.	Amount
2	Enter your short-term totals, if any, from Schedule D-1, line 2	2	
3	**Total short-term sales price amounts.** Add column (d) of lines 1 and 2	3	
4	Short-term gain from Form 6252 and short-term gain or (loss) from Forms 4684, 6781, and 8824	4	120,608
5	Net short-term gain or (loss) from partnerships, S corporations, estates, and trusts from Schedule(s) K-1	5	
6	Short-term capital loss carryover. Enter the amount, if any, from line 8 of your 1999 Capital Loss Carryover Worksheet	6	( )
7	**Net short-term capital gain or (loss).** Combine column (f) of lines 1 through 6 ▶	7	120,608

Part II Long-Term Capital Gains and Losses – Assets Held More Than One Year

8 (a) Description of property (Example, 100 sh. XYZ Co.)	(b) Date acquired (Mo., day, yr.)	(c) Date sold (Mo., day, yr.)	(d) Sales price (see page D-6)	(e) Cost or other basis (see page D-6)	(f) Gain or (loss) Subtract (e) from (d)	(g) 28% rate gain or (loss) * (see instr. below)

Line	Description	No.	(f)	(g)
9	Enter your long-term totals, if any, from Schedule D-1, line 9	9		
10	**Total long-term sales price amounts.** Add column (d) of lines 8 and 9	10		
11	Gain from Form 4797, Part I; long-term gain from Forms 2439 and 6252; and long-term gain or (loss) from Forms 4684, 6781, and 8824	11	180,911	
12	Net long-term gain or (loss) from partnerships, S corporations, estates, and trusts from Schedule(s) K-1	12		
13	Capital gain distributions. See page D-1	13		
14	Long-term capital loss carryover. Enter in both columns (f) and (g) the amount, if any, from line 13 of your 1999 Capital Loss Carryover Worksheet	14	( )	( )
15	Combine column (g) of lines 8 through 14	15		
16	**Net long-term capital gain or (loss).** Combine column (f) of lines 8 through 14 ▶ **Next:** Go to Part III on the back.	16	180,911	

* **28% rate gain or loss** includes **all** "collectibles gains and losses" (as defined on page D-6) and up to 50% of the eligible gain on qualified small business stock (see page D-4).

For Paperwork Reduction Act Notice, see Form 1040 instructions. **Schedule D (Form 1040) 2000**

KFA IFOUS5 12/07/00

Schedule D (Form 1040) 2000 COMMODITIES N. VESTOR-PROFIT 123-45-6789 Page **2**

Part III Summary of Parts I and II

17 Combine lines 7 and 16. If a loss, go to line 18. If a gain, enter the gain on Form 1040, line 13	17	301,519
Next: Complete Form 1040 through line 39. Then, go to **Part IV** to figure your tax if: • Both lines 16 and 17 are gains **and** • Form 1040, line 39, is more than zero. Otherwise, **stop here.**		
18 If line 17 is a loss, enter here and as a (loss) on Form 1040, line 13, the **smaller** of these losses: • The loss on line 17 **or** • ($3,000) or, if married filing separately, ($1,500)	18	( )
Next: Skip **Part IV** below. Instead, complete Form 1040 through line 37. Then, complete the **Capital Loss Carryover Worksheet** on page D–6 if: • The loss on line 17 exceeds the loss on line 18 **or** • Form 1040, line 37, is a loss.		

Part IV Tax Computation Using Maximum Capital Gains Rates

19 Enter your taxable income from Form 1040, line 39			19	586,427
20 Enter the **smaller** of line 16 or line 17 of Schedule D	20	180,911		
21 If you are filing Form 4952, enter the amount from Form 4952, line 4e	21			
22 Subtract line 21 from line 20. If zero or less, enter -0-	22	180,911		
23 Combine lines 7 and 15. If zero or less, enter -0-	23	120,608		
24 Enter the **smaller** of line 15 or line 23, but not less than zero	24			
25 Enter your unrecaptured section 1250 gain, if any, from line 17 of the worksheet on page D-8	25			
26 Add lines 24 and 25	26			
27 Subtract line 26 from line 22. If zero or less, enter -0-			27	180,911
28 Subtract line 27 from line 19. If zero or less, enter -0-			28	405,516
29 Enter the **smaller** of: • The amount on line 19 **or** • $26,250 if single; $43,850 if married filing jointly or qualifying widow(er); $21,925 if married filing separately; or $35,150 if head of household			29	26,250
30 Enter the **smaller** of line 28 or line 29	30	26,250		
31 Subtract line 22 from line 19. If zero or less, enter -0-	31	405,516		
32 Enter the **larger** of line 30 or line 31	▶ 32	405,516		
33 Figure the tax on the amount on line 32. Use the Tax Table or Tax Rate Schedules, whichever applies			33	138,255
Note: If the amounts on lines 29 and 30 are the same, skip lines 34 through 37 and go to line 38.				
34 Enter the amount from line 29	34			
35 Enter the amount from line 30	35			
36 Subtract line 35 from line 34	▶ 36			
37 Multiply line 36 by 10% (.10)			37	
Note: If the amounts on lines 19 and 29 are the same, skip lines 38 through 51 and go to line 52.				
38 Enter the **smaller** of line 19 or line 27	38	180,911		
39 Enter the amount from line 36	39			
40 Subtract line 39 from line 38	▶ 40	180,911		
41 Multiply line 40 by 20% (.20)			41	36,182
Note: If line 26 is zero or blank, skip lines 42 through 51 and go to line 52.				
42 Enter the **smaller** of line 22 or line 25	42			
43 Add lines 22 and 32 — 43				
44 Enter the amount from line 19 — 44				
45 Subtract line 44 from line 43. If zero or less, enter -0-	45			
46 Subtract line 45 from line 42. If zero or less, enter -0-	▶ 46			
47 Multiply line 46 by 25% (.25)			47	
Note: If line 24 is zero or blank, skip lines 48 through 51 and go to line 52.				
48 Enter the amount from line 19	48			
49 Add lines 32, 36, 40, and 46	49			
50 Subtract line 49 from line 48	50			
51 Multiply line 50 by 28% (.28)			51	
52 Add lines 33, 37, 41, 47, and 51			52	174,437
53 Figure the tax on the amount on line 19. Use the Tax Table or Tax Rate Schedules, whichever applies			53	209,895
54 **Tax on all taxable income (including capital gains).** Enter the **smaller** of line 52 or line 53 here and on Form 1040, line 40			54	174,437

IFOUS5A 10/24/00 **Schedule D (Form 1040) 2000**

Schedule E (Form 1040) 2000 Attachment Sequence No. **13** Page **2**

Name(s) shown on return. Do not enter name and social security number if shown on other side. COMMODITIES N. VESTOR-PROFIT

Your social security number 123-45-6789

Note: If you report amounts from farming or fishing on Schedule E, you must enter your gross income from those activities on line 41 below. Real estate professionals must complete line 42 below.

Part II Income or Loss From Partnerships and S Corporations If you report a loss from an at-risk activity, you **must** check either column **(e)** or **(f)** on line 27 to describe your investment in the activity. See page E-5. If you check column **(f)**, you must attach **Form 6198.**

27	(a) Name	(b) Enter P for partnership; S for S corp.	(c) Check if foreign partnership	(d) Employer identification number	Invest. At Risk? (e) All is at risk	(f) Some is not at risk
A	1	P				
B						
C						
D						
E						

	Passive Income and Loss: (g) Passive loss allowed (attach Form 8582 if required)	Passive Income and Loss: (h) Passive income from Schedule K-1	Nonpassive Income and Loss: (i) Nonpassive loss from Schedule K-1	Nonpassive Income and Loss: (j) Section 179 expense deduction from Form 4562	Nonpassive Income and Loss: (k) Nonpassive income from Schedule K-1
A		200,000			
B					
C					
D					
E					
28a Totals		200,000			
b Totals					

29	Add columns (h) and (k) of line 28a	29 200,000
30	Add columns (g), (i), and (j) of line 28b	30 ( )
31	Total partnership and S corporation income or (loss). Combine lines 29 and 30. Enter the result here and include in the total on line 40 below	31 200,000

Part III Income or Loss From Estates and Trusts

32	(a) Name	(b) Employer ID number
A		
B		
C		
D		

	Passive Income and Loss: (c) Passive deduction or loss allowed (attach Form 8582 if required)	Passive Income and Loss: (d) Passive income from Schedule K-1	Nonpassive Income and Loss: (e) Deduction or loss from Schedule K-1	Nonpassive Income and Loss: (f) Other income from Schedule K-1
A				
B				
C				
D				
33a Totals				
b Totals				

34	Add columns (d) and (f) of line 33a	34
35	Add columns (c) and (e) of line 33b	35 ( )
36	Total estate and trust income or (loss). Combine lines 34 and 35. Enter the result here and include in the total on line 40 below	36

Part IV Income or Loss From Real Estate Mortgage Investment Conduits (REMICs) – Residual Holder

37	(a) Name	(b) Employer identification number	(c) Excess inclusion from Schedules Q, line 2c (see page E-6)	(d) Taxable income (net loss) from Schedules Q, line 1b	(e) Income from Schedules Q, line 3b

38	Combine columns (d) and (e) only. Enter the result here and include in the total on line 40 below	38

Part V Summary

39	Net farm rental income or (loss) from **Form 4835.** Also, complete line 41 below	39
40	**Total** income or (loss). Combine lines 26, 31, 36, 38, and 39. Enter the result here and on Form 1040, line 17 ▶	40 200,000
41	**Reconciliation of Farming and Fishing Income:** Enter your **gross** farming and fishing income reported on Form 4835, line 7; Schedule K-1 (Form 1065), line 15b; Schedule K-1 (Form 1120S), line 23; and Schedule K-1 (Form 1041), line 14 (see page E-6)	41
42	**Reconciliation for Real Estate Professionals.** If you were real estate professional (see pg. E-4), enter net income or (loss) you reported anywhere on Form 1040 from all rental real estate activities in which you materially participated under passive activity loss rules.	42

IF0US7A 10/19/00 Schedule E (Form 1040) 2000

Form **4562** Department of the Treasury Internal Revenue Service (99)

Depreciation and Amortization
(Including Information on Listed Property)

▶ See separate instructions. ▶ Attach this form to your return.

OMB No. 1545-0172 **2000** Attachment Sequence No. **67**

Name(s) shown on return: COMMODITIES N. VESTOR-PROFIT — Identifying number: 123-45-6789

Business or activity to which this form relates

Part I — Election To Expense Certain Tangible Property (Section 179) Note: If you have any "listed property," complete Part V before you complete Part I.

1	Maximum dollar limitation. If an enterprise zone business, see page 2 of the instructions	1	$20,000
2	Total cost of section 179 property placed in service. See page 2 of the instructions	2	
3	Threshold cost of section 179 property before reduction in limitation	3	$200,000
4	Reduction in limitation. Subtract line 3 from line 2. If zero or less, enter -0-	4	
5	Dollar limitation for tax year. Subtract line 4 from line 1. If zero or less, enter -0-. If married filing separately, see page 2 of the instructions	5	

6 (a) Description of property	(b) Cost (business use only)	(c) Elected cost

7	Listed property. Enter amount from line 27	7	
8	Total elected cost of section 179 property. Add amounts in column (c), lines 6 and 7	8	
9	Tentative deduction. Enter the smaller of line 5 or line 8	9	
10	Carryover of disallowed deduction from 1999. See page 3 of the instructions	10	
11	Business income limitation. Enter the smaller of business income (not less than zero) or line 5 (see instructions)	11	
12	Section 179 expense deduction. Add lines 9 and 10, but do not enter more than line 11	12	
13	Carryover of disallowed deduction to 2001. Add lines 9 and 10, less line 12 ▶	13	

Note: Do not use Part II or Part III below for listed property (automobiles, certain other vehicles, cellular telephones, certain computers, or property used for entertainment, recreation, or amusement). Instead, use Part V for listed property.

Part II — MACRS Depreciation for Assets Placed in Service Only During Your 2000 Tax Year (**Do not** include listed property.)

Section A – General Asset Account Election

14 If you are making the election under section 168(i)(4) to group any assets placed in service during the tax year into one or more general asset accounts, check this box. See page 3 of the instructions ▶ ☐

Section B – General Depreciation System (GDS) (See page 3 of the instructions.)

(a) Classification of property	(b) Month and year placed in service	(c) Basis for depreciation (business/investment use only – see instructions)	(d) Recovery period	(e) Convention	(f) Method	(g) Depreciation deduction
15a 3-year property						
b 5-year property						
c 7-year property						
d 10-year property						
e 15-year property						
f 20-year property						
g 25-year property			25 yrs		S/L	
h Residential rental property			27.5 yrs	MM	S/L	
			27.5 yrs	MM	S/L	
i Nonresidential real property			39 yrs	MM	S/L	
				MM	S/L	

Section C – Alternative Depreciation System (ADS): (See page 5 of the instructions.)

16a Class life					S/L	
b 12-year			12 yrs		S/L	
c 40-year			40 yrs	MM	S/L	

Part III — Other Depreciation (**Do not** include listed property.) (See page 5 of the instructions.)

17	GDS and ADS deductions for assets placed in service in tax years beginning before 2000	17	
18	Property subject to section 168(f)(1) election	18	
19	ACRS and other depreciation	19	5,000

Part IV — Summary (See page 6 of the instructions.)

20	Listed property. Enter amount from line 26	20	
21	**Total.** Add deductions from line 12, lines 15 and 16 in column (g), and lines 17 through 20. Enter here and on the appropriate lines of your return. Partnerships and S corporations – see instructions	21	5,000
22	For assets shown above and placed in service during the current year, enter the portion of the basis attributable to section 263A costs	22	

KFA **For Paperwork Reduction Act Notice, see page 9 of the instructions.** GF0US7 10/26/00 Form **4562** (2000)

Example 7 *(Continued)*

Form **4952** Department of the Treasury Internal Revenue Service (99)	**Investment Interest Expense Deduction** ▶ **Attach to your tax return.**	OMB No. 1545-0191 **2000** Attachment Sequence No. **72**
Name(s) shown on return COMMODITIES N. VESTOR-PROFIT		Identifying number 123-45-6789

Part I — Total Investment Interest Expense

1 Investment interest expense paid or accrued in 2000. See instructions			1	51,357
2 Disallowed investment interest expense from 1999 Form 4952, line 7			2	
3 **Total investment interest expense.** Add lines 1 and 2			3	51,357

Part II — Net Investment Income

4a Gross income from property held for investment (excluding any net gain from the disposition of property held for investment)			4a	
b Net gain from the disposition of property held for investment	4b	301,519		
c Net capital gain from the disposition of property held for investment	4c	180,911		
d Subtract line 4c from line 4b. If zero or less, enter -0-			4d	120,608
e Enter all or part of the amount on line 4c, if any, that you elect to include in investment income. Do not enter more than the amount on line 4b. See instructions ▶			4e	
f Investment income. Add lines 4a, 4d, and 4e. See instructions			4f	120,608
5 Investment expenses. See instructions			5	
6 **Net investment income.** Subtract line 5 from line 4f. If zero or less, enter -0-			6	120,608

Part III — Investment Interest Expense Deduction

7 Disallowed investment interest expense to be carried forward to 2001. Subtract line 6 from line 3. If zero or less, enter -0-	7	0
8 **Investment interest expense deduction.** Enter the **smaller** of line 3 or 6. See instructions	8	51,357

For Paperwork Reduction Act Notice, see back. Form **4952** (2000)

KFA IF0US29 10/24/00

Form **6251**	**Alternative Minimum Tax – Individuals**	OMB No. 1545–0227
Department of the Treasury Internal Revenue Service	▶ See separate Instructions. ▶ Attach to Form 1040 or Form 1040NR.	**2000** Attachment Sequence No. **32**

Name(s) shown on Form 1040: COMMODITIES N. VESTOR-PROFIT
Your social security number: 123-45-6789

Part I Adjustments and Preferences

1 If you itemized deductions on Schedule A (Form 1040), go to line 2. Otherwise, enter your standard deduction from Form 1040, line 36, here and go to line 6 **1**

2 Medical and dental. Enter the smaller of Schedule A (Form 1040), line 4 or 2 1/2% of Form 1040, line 34 **2**

3 Taxes. Enter the amount from Schedule A (Form 1040), line 9 **3**

4 Certain interest on a home mortgage **not** used to buy, build, or improve your home **4**

5 Miscellaneous itemized deductions. Enter the amount from Schedule A (Form 1040), line 26 **5** 80,912

6 Refund of taxes. Enter any tax refund from Form 1040, line 10 or line 21 **6** ()

7 Investment interest. Enter difference between regular tax and AMT deduction **7**

8 Post–1986 depreciation. Enter difference between regular tax and AMT depreciation **8**

9 Adjusted gain or loss. Enter difference between AMT and regular tax gain or loss **9**

10 Incentive stock options. Enter excess of AMT income over regular tax income **10**

11 Passive activities. Enter difference between AMT and regular tax income or loss **11**

12 Beneficiaries of estates and trusts. Enter the amount from Schedule K–1 (Form 1041), line 9 **12**

13 Tax–exempt interest from private activity bonds issued after 8/7/86 **13**

14 Other. Enter the amount, if any, for each item below and enter the total on line 14.
 a Circulation expenditures.
 b Depletion
 c Depreciation (pre–1987).
 d Installment sales.......
 e Intangible drilling costs..
 f Large partnerships
 g Long–term contracts ...
 h Loss limitations
 i Mining costs
 j Patron's adjustment.....
 k Pollution control facilities .
 l Research & experimental.
 m Section 1202 exclusion ..
 n Tax shelter farm activities.
 o Related adjustments **14**

15 **Total Adjustments and Preferences.** Combine lines 1 through 14 **15** 80,912

Part II Alternative Minimum Taxable Income

16 Enter the amount from **Form 1040, line 37.** If less than zero, enter as a (loss) **16** 586,427

17 Net operating loss deduction, if any, from Form 1040, line 21. Enter as a positive amount **17**

18 If Form 1040, line 34, is over $128,950 (over $64,475 if married filing separately), and you itemized deductions, enter the amount, if any, from line 9 of the worksheet for Schedule A (Form 1040), line 28 **18** (17,177)

19 Combine lines 15 through 18 **19** 650,162

20 Alternative tax net operating loss deduction. See page 6 of the instructions **20**

21 **Alternative Minimum Taxable Income.** Subtract line 20 from line 19. (If married filing separately and line 21 is more than $165,000, see page 7 of the instructions.) **21** 650,162

Part III Exemption Amount and Alternative Minimum Tax

22 **Exemption Amount.** (If this form is for a child under age 14, see page 7 of the instructions.)

IF your filing status is:	AND line 21 is not over ...	THEN enter on line 22 ...	
Single or head of household............	$112,500	$33,750	
Married filing jointly or qualifying widow(er)	150,000	45,000	**22**
Married filing separately	75,000	22,500	

If line 21 is **over** the amount shown above for your filing status, see page 7 of the instructions.

23 Subtract line 22 from line 21. If zero or less, enter –0– here and on lines 26 and 28 and stop here **23** 650,162

24 If you reported capital gain distributions directly on Form 1040, line 13, **or** you completed Schedule D (Form 1040) and have an amount on line 25 or line 27 (or would have had an amount on either line if you had completed Part IV) (as refigured for the AMT, if necessary), go to Part IV of Form 6251 to figure line 24. **All others:** If line 23 is $175,000 or less ($87,500 or less if married filing separately), multiply line 23 by 26% (.26). Otherwise, multiply line 23 by 28% (.28) and subtract $3,500 ($1,750 if married filing separately) from the result **24** 164,072

25 Alternative minimum tax foreign tax credit. See page 7 of the instructions **25**

26 Tentative minimum tax. Subtract line 25 from line 24 **26** 164,072

27 Enter your tax from Form 1040, line 40 (minus any tax from Form 4972 and any foreign tax credit from Form 1040, line 43) **27** 174,437

28 **Alternative Minimum Tax.** Subtract line 27 from line 26. If zero or less, enter –0–. Enter here and on Form 1040, line 41 **28** 0

For Paperwork Reduction Act Notice, see page 8 of the instructions.
Form **6251** (2000)

KFA IF0US33 10/23/00

Example 7 *(Continued)*

Form 6251 (2000) COMMODITIES N. VESTOR-PROFIT 123-45-6789 Page **2**

Part IV Line 24 Computation Using Maximum Capital Gains Rates

Caution: If you **did not** complete Part IV of Schedule D (Form 1040), see page 8 of the instructions before you complete this part.

Line	Description	Line	Amount	Line	Amount
29	Enter the amount from Form 6251, line 23			29	650,162
30	Enter the amount from Schedule D (Form 1040), line 27 (as refigured for the AMT, if necessary). See page 8 of the instructions	30	180,911		
31	Enter the amount from Schedule D (Form 1040), line 25 (as refigured for the AMT, if necessary). See page 8 of the instructions	31	0		
32	Add lines 30 and 31	32	180,911		
33	Enter the amount from Schedule D (Form 1040), line 22 (as refigured for the AMT, if necessary). See page 8 of the instructions	33	180,911		
34	Enter the **smaller** of line 32 or line 33			34	180,911
35	Subtract line 34 from line 29. If zero or less, enter -0- ▶			35	469,251
36	If line 35 is $175,000 or less ($87,500 or less if married filing separately), multiply line 35 by 26% (.26). Otherwise, multiply line 35 by 28% (.28) and subtract $3,500 ($1,750 if married filing separately) from the result			36	127,890
37	Enter the amount from Schedule D (Form 1040), line 36 (as figured for the regular tax). See page 8 of the instructions	37	0		
38	Enter the **smallest** of line 29, line 30, or line 37 ▶	38			
39	Multiply line 38 by 10% (.10)			39	
40	Enter the **smaller** of line 29 or line 30	40	180,911		
41	Enter the amount from line 38	41			
42	Subtract line 41 from line 40 ▶	42	180,911		
43	Multiply line 42 by 20% (.20)			43	36,182
	Note: If line 31 is zero or blank, skip lines 44 through 47 and go to line 48.				
44	Enter the amount from line 29	44			
45	Add lines 35, 38, and 42	45			
46	Subtract line 45 from line 44	46			
47	Multiply line 46 by 25% (.25)			47	
48	Add lines 36, 39, 43, and 47			48	164,072
49	If line 29 is $175,000 or less ($87,500 or less if married filing separately), multiply line 29 by 26% (.26). Otherwise, multiply line 29 by 28% (.28) and subtract $3,500 ($1,750 if married filing separately) from the result			49	178,545
50	Enter the **smaller** of line 48 or line 49 here and on line 24			50	164,072

Form **6251** (2000)

Form **6781** Department of the Treasury Internal Revenue Service

Gains and Losses From Section 1256 Contracts and Straddles

▶ Attach to your tax return.

OMB No. 1545-0644 **2000** Attachment Sequence No. **82**

Name(s) shown on tax return: COMMODITIES N. VESTOR-PROFIT

Identifying number: 123-45-6789

Check applicable box(es) (see instructions):
A ☐ Mixed straddle election
B ☐ Straddle-by-straddle identification election
C ☐ Mixed straddle account election
D ☐ Net section 1256 contracts loss election

Part I Section 1256 Contracts Marked to Market

1 (a) Identification of account	(b) (Loss)	(c) Gain
		301,519

Line	Description		Amount
2	Add amounts on line 1 in columns (b) and (c)	2 ( )	301,519
3	Net gain or (loss). Combine columns (b) and (c) of line 2	3	301,519
4	Form 1099-B adjustments. See instructions and attach schedule	4	
5	Combine lines 3 and 4	5	301,519
	Note: If line 5 shows a net gain, skip line 6 and enter the gain on line 7. Partnerships and S corporations, see instructions.		
6	If you have a net section 1256 contracts loss and checked box D, enter the amount to be carried back	6	
7	Subtract line 6 from line 5	7	301,519
8	Short-term capital gain or (loss). Multiply line 7 by 40%. Enter here and include on Schedule D. See instructions	8	120,608
9	Long-term capital gain or (loss). Multiply line 7 by 60%. Enter here and include on Schedule D. See instructions	9	180,911

Part II Gains and Losses From Straddles. Attach a separate schedule listing each straddle and its components.

Section A – Losses From Straddles

10 (a) Description of property	(b) Date entered into or acquired	(c) Date closed out or sold	(d) Gross sales price	(e) Cost or other basis plus expense of sale	(f) Loss. If column (e) is more than (d), enter difference. Otherwise, enter -0-	(g) Unrecognized gain on offsetting positions	(h) Recognized loss. If column (f) is more than (g), enter difference. Otherwise, enter -0-	*(i) 28% rate loss (see instr. below)

11a Enter short-term portion of line 10, column (h), losses here and include on Schedule D. See instructions . . . **11a** ( )

b Enter long-term portion of losses from line 10, columns (h) and (i), here and include on Schedule D. See instrs . **11b** ( ) ( )

Section B – Gains From Straddles

12 (a) Description of property	(b) Date entered into or acquired	(c) Date closed out or sold	(d) Gross sales price	(e) Cost or other basis plus expense of sale	(f) Gain. If column (d) is more than (e), enter diff. Otherwise, enter 0	*(g) 28% Rate gain (see instr. below)

13a Enter short-term portion of line 12, column (f), gains here and include on Schedule D. See instructions . . . **13a**

b Enter long-term portion of gains from line 12, columns (f) and (g), here and include on Sch D. See instrs . **13b**

Part III Unrecognized Gains From Positions Held on Last Day of Tax Year. Memo Entry Only – See instructions.

14 (a) Description of property	(b) Date acquired	(c) Fair market value on last business day of tax year	(d) Cost or other basis as adjusted	(e) Unrecognized gain. If column (c) is more than (d), enter difference. Otherwise, enter -0-

*28% Rate Gain or Loss includes all "collectibles gains and losses" and up to 50% of the eligible gain on qualified small business stock. See instructions for Schedule D (Form 1040).

For Paperwork Reduction Act Notice, see page 3. Form **6781** (2000)

KFA GF0US16 12/27/00

Example 8

Form 1040 Department of the Treasury – Internal Revenue Service
U.S. Individual Income Tax Return 2000 (99) IRS Use Only – Do not write or staple in this space.

For the year Jan. 1 – Dec. 31, 2000, or other tax year beginning , 2000, ending , 20 OMB No. 1545-0074

Label (See instructions on page 19.) Use the IRS label. Otherwise, please print or type.

Your first name and initial / Last name: A. TRADER-COMMODITY PROFIT-NO 475	Your social security number: 123-45-6789
If a joint return, spouse's first name and initial / Last name	Spouse's social security number
Home address (number and street). If you have a P.O. box, see page 19. Apt. no.: C/O TED TESSER-6274 LINTON BLVD. #102	▲ IMPORTANT! ▲ You **must** enter your SSN(s) above.
City, town or post office, state, and ZIP code. If you have a foreign address, see page 19.: DELRAY BEACH, FL 33484	

Presidential Election Campaign (See page 19.)
Note. Checking "Yes" will not change your tax or reduce your refund.
Do you, or your spouse if filing a joint return, want $3 to go to this fund? — You: ☐ Yes ☒ No — Spouse: ☐ Yes ☐ No

Filing Status (Check only one box.)

1 [X] Single
2 ☐ Married filing joint return (even if only one had income)
3 ☐ Married filing separate return. Enter spouse's soc. sec. no. above & full name here ▶
4 ☐ Head of household (with qualifying person). (See page 19.) If the qualifying person is a child but not your dependent, enter this child's name here ▶
5 ☐ Qualifying widow(er) with dependent child (year spouse died ▶). (See page 19.)

Exemptions

6a ☒ **Yourself.** If your parent (or someone else) can claim you as a dependent on his or her tax return, **do not** check box 6a. — No. of boxes checked on 6a and 6b: 1
b ☐ **Spouse**
c **Dependents:**

(1) First Name / Last name	(2) Dependent's social security number	(3) Dependent's relationship to you	(4) Chk if qualifying child for child tax credit (see page 20)

If more than six dependents, see page 20.

No. of your children on 6c who: ● lived with you ● did not live with you due to divorce or separation (see page 20) — Dependents on 6c not entered above

d Total number of exemptions claimed — Add numbers entered on lines above ▶ 1

Income

Attach Forms W-2 and W-2G here. Also attach Form 1099-R if tax was withheld.
If you did not get a W-2, see page 21.
Enclose, but do not attach any payment. Also, please use Form 1040-V.

Line	Description		Amount
7	Wages, salaries, tips, etc. Attach Form(s) W-2	7	200,000
8a	**Taxable** interest. Attach Schedule B if required	8a	
b	**Tax-exempt** interest. **Do not** include on line 8a — 8b		
9	Ordinary dividends. Attach Schedule B if required	9	
10	Taxable refunds, credits, or offsets of state and local income taxes (see page 22)	10	
11	Alimony received	11	
12	Business income or (loss). Attach Schedule C or C-EZ	12	-200,678
13	Capital gain or (loss). Attach Schedule D if required. If not required, check here ▶ ☐	13	301,519
14	Other gains or (losses). Attach Form 4797	14	
15a	Total IRA distributions — 15a — b Taxable amount (see pg. 23)	15b	
16a	Total pensions and annuities — 16a — b Taxable amount (see pg. 23)	16b	
17	Rental real estate, royalties, partnerships, S corporations, trusts, etc. Attach Schedule E	17	200,000
18	Farm income or (loss). Attach Schedule F	18	
19	Unemployment compensation	19	
20a	Social security benefits — 20a — b Taxable amount (see pg. 25)	20b	
21	Other income.	21	
22	Add the amounts in the far right column for lines 7 through 21. This is your **total income** ▶	22	500,841

Adjusted Gross Income

Line	Description		Amount
23	IRA deduction (see page 27)	23	
24	Student loan interest deduction (see page 27)	24	
25	Medical savings account deduction. Attach Form 8853	25	
26	Moving expenses. Attach Form 3903	26	
27	One-half of self-employment tax. Attach Schedule SE	27	
28	Self-employed health insurance deduction (see page 29)	28	
29	Self-employed SEP, SIMPLE, and qualified plans	29	
30	Penalty on early withdrawal of savings	30	
31a	Alimony paid. b Recipient's SSN ▶	31a	
32	Add lines 23 through 31a	32	0
33	Subtract line 32 from line 22. This is your **adjusted gross income** ▶	33	500,841

KFA **For Disclosure, Privacy Act, and Paperwork Reduction Act Notice, see page 56.** IF0US1 11/07/00 Form **1040** (2000)

Form 1040 (2000) A. TRADER-COMMODITY PROFIT-NO 475 | 123-45-6789 | Page 2

Tax and Credits

Line	Description	Box	Amount
34	Amount from line 33 (adjusted gross income)	34	500,841
35a	Check if: ☐ You were 65 or older, ☐ Blind; ☐ Spouse was 65 or older, ☐ Blind. Add the number of boxes checked above and enter the total here ▶ 35a		
b	If you are married filing separately and your spouse itemizes deductions, or you were a dual-status alien, see page 31 and check here ▶ 35b ☐		
36	Enter your **itemized deductions** from Schedule A, line 28, **or standard deduction** shown on the left. **But** see page 31 to find your standard deduction if you checked any box on line 35a or 35b **or** if someone can claim you as a dependent	36	4,400
37	Subtract line 36 from line 34	37	496,441
38	If line 34 is $96,700 or less, multiply $2,800 by the total number of exemptions claimed on line 6d. If line 34 is over $96,700, see the worksheet on page 32 for the amount to enter	38	0
39	**Taxable income.** Subtract line 38 from line 37. If line 38 is more than line 37, enter -0-	39	496,441
40	**Tax** (see page 32). Check if any tax is from a ☐ Form(s) 8814 b ☐ Form 4972	40	138,802
41	Alternative minimum tax. Attach Form 6251	41	
42	Add lines 40 and 41 ▶	42	138,802
43	Foreign tax credit. Attach Form 1116 if required	43	
44	Credit for child and dependent care expenses. Att. Form 2441	44	
45	Credit for the elderly or the disabled. Attach Schedule R	45	
46	Education credits. Attach Form 8863	46	
47	Child tax credit (see page 36)	47	
48	Adoption credit. Attach Form 8839	48	
49	Other. Check if from a ☐ Form 3800 b ☐ Form 8396 c ☐ Form 8801 d ☐ Form (specify)	49	
50	Add lines 43 through 49. These are your **total credits**	50	
51	Subtract line 50 from line 42. If line 50 is more than line 42, enter -0- ▶	51	138,802

Standard Deduction for Most People — Single: $4,400; Head of household: $6,450; Married filing jointly or Qualifying widow(er): $7,350; Married filing separately $3,675.

Other Taxes

Line	Description	Box	Amount
52	Self-employment tax. Att. Sch. SE	52	
53	Social security and Medicare tax on tip income not reported to employer. Attach Form 4137	53	
54	Tax on IRAs, other retirement plans, and MSAs. Attach Form 5329 if required	54	
55	Advance earned income credit payments from Form(s) W-2	55	
56	Household employment taxes. Attach Schedule H	56	
57	Add lines 51 through 56. This is your **total tax** ▶	57	138,802

Payments

If you have a qualifying child, attach Schedule EIC.

Line	Description	Box	Amount	Total
58	Federal income tax withheld from Forms W-2 and 1099	58	60,000	
59	2000 estimated tax payments and amount applied from 1999 return	59	50,000	
60a	**Earned income credit (EIC)**	60a		
b	**Nontaxable earned income: amt.** ▶ and type ▶ No			
61	Excess social security and RRTA tax withheld (see page 50)	61		
62	**Additional child tax credit. Attach Form 8812**	62		
63	**Amount paid with request for extension to file** (see page 50)	63		
64	Other payments. Check if from a ☐ Form 2439 b ☐ Form 4136	64		
65	Add lines 58, 59, 60a, and 61 through 64. These are your **total payments** ▶	65		110,000

Refund

Have it directly deposited! See page 50 and fill in 67b, 67c, and 67d.

Line	Description	Box	Amount
66	If line 65 is more than line 57, subtract line 57 from line 65. This is the amount you **overpaid**	66	
67a	Amount of line 66 you want **refunded to you** ▶	67a	
b	Routing number ▶ c Type: ☐ Checking ☐ Savings		
d	Account number		
68	Amount of line 66 you want **applied to your 2001 estimated tax** ▶	68	

Amount You Owe

Line	Description	Box	Amount
69	If line 57 is more than line 65, subtract line 65 from line 57. This is the **amount you owe.** For details on how to pay, see page 51 ▶	69	28,802
70	Estimated tax penalty. Also include on line 69	70	

Sign Here

Under penalties of perjury, I declare that I have examined this return and accompanying schedules and statements, and to the best of my knowledge and belief, they are true, correct, and complete. Declaration of preparer (other than taxpayer) is based on all information of which preparer has any knowledge.

Joint return? See page 19. Keep a copy for your records.

Your signature	Date	Your occupation	Daytime phone number 561-865-0071
Spouse's signature. If a joint return, **both** must sign.	Date	Spouse's occupation	May the IRS discuss this return with the preparer shown below? (see page 52)? ☒ Yes ☐ No

Paid Preparer's Use Only

Preparer's signature	Date	Check if self-employed ☐	Preparer's SSN or PTIN
Firm's name (or yours if self-employed), address, and ZIP code	Waterside Financial Serv., Inc 6274 Linton Blvd., Suite #102 Boca Raton, FL 33484	EIN 65-0664126 Phone no. (561) 865-0071	

IFOUS1A 11/22/00 Form **1040** (2000)

Example 8 *(Continued)*

SCHEDULE C (Form 1040)
Department of the Treasury
Internal Revenue Service (99)

Profit or Loss From Business
(Sole Proprietorship)
▶ Partnerships, joint ventures, etc., must file Form 1065 or Form 1065-B.
▶ Attach to Form 1040 or Form 1041. ▶ See Instructions for Schedule C (Form 1040).

OMB No. 1545-0074
2000
Attachment Sequence No. 09

Name of proprietor: A. TRADER-COMMODITY PROFIT-NO 475
Social security number (SSN): 123-45-6789

A Principal business or profession, including product or service (see page C-1 of the instructions): TRADER
B Enter code from pages C-7 & 8 ▶ 523900
C Business name. If no separate business name, leave blank.
D Employer ID number (EIN), if any

E Business address (including suite or room no.) ▶
City, town or post office, state, and ZIP code

F Accounting method: (1) ☒ Cash (2) ☐ Accrual (3) ☐ Other (specify) ▶
G Did you "materially participate" in the operation of this business during 2000? If "No," see page C-2 for limit on losses ☒ Yes ☐ No
H If you started or acquired this business during 2000, check here ▶ ☐

Part I Income

1 Gross receipts or sales. **Caution:** If this income was reported to you on Form W-2 and the "Statutory employee" box on that form was checked, see page C-2 and check here ▶ ☐	1	
2 Returns and allowances	2	
3 Subtract line 2 from line 1	3	
4 Cost of goods sold (from line 42 on page 2)	4	
5 **Gross profit.** Subtract line 4 from line 3	5	
6 Other income, including Federal and state gasoline or fuel tax credit or refund (see page C-2)	6	
7 **Gross income.** Add lines 5 and 6 ▶	7	

Part II Expenses. Enter expenses for business use of your home **only** on line 30.

8 Advertising	8	
9 Bad debts from sales or services (see page C-3)	9	
10 Car and truck expenses (see page C-3)	10	3,115
11 Commissions and fees	11	
12 Depletion	12	
13 Depreciation and section 179 expense deduction (not included in Part III) (see page C-3)	13	23,150
14 Employee benefit programs (other than on line 19)	14	
15 Insurance (other than health)	15	
16 Interest:		
a Mortgage (paid to banks, etc.)	16a	
b Other	16b	51,357
17 Legal and professional services	17	2,250
18 Office expense	18	4,561
19 Pension and profit-sharing plans	19	
20 Rent or lease (see page C-4):		
a Vehicles, machinery & equipment	20a	5,050
b Other business property	20b	
21 Repairs and maintenance	21	3,166
22 Supplies (not included in Part III)	22	5,069
23 Taxes and licenses	23	
24 Travel, meals, and entertainment:		
a Travel	24a	6,511
b Meals and entertainment: 8,711		
c Enter nondeductible amount included on line 24b (see page C-5): 4,356		
d Subtract line 24c from line 24b	24d	4,355
25 Utilities	25	2,611
26 Wages (less employment credits)	26	
27 Other expenses (from line 48 on page 2)	27	83,233
28 **Total expenses** before expenses for business use of home. Add lines 8 through 27 in columns ▶	28	194,428
29 Tentative profit (loss). Subtract line 28 from line 7	29	-194,428
30 Expenses for business use of your home. Attach **Form 8829**	30	6,250
31 **Net profit or (loss).** Subtract line 30 from line 29. • If a profit, enter on **Form 1040, line 12,** and **also** on **Schedule SE, line 2** (statutory employees, see page C-5). Estates and trusts, enter on Form 1041, line 3. • If a loss, you **must** go to line 32.	31	-200,678

32 If you have a loss, check the box that describes your investment in this activity (see page C-5).
- If you checked 32a, enter the loss on **Form 1040, line 12,** and **also** on **Schedule SE, line 2** (statutory employees, see page C-5). Estates and trusts, enter on Form 1041, line 3.
- If you checked 32b, you **must** attach **Form 6198.**

32a ☒ All investment is at risk.
32b ☐ Some investment is not at risk.

For Paperwork Reduction Act Notice, see Form 1040 instructions. **Schedule C (Form 1040) 2000**

KFA IFOUS4 11/08/00

Schedule C (Form 1040) 2000 A. TRADER-COMMODITY PROFIT-NO 475 123-45-6789 Page **2**

Part III **Cost of Goods Sold** (see page C-6)

33 Method(s) used to value closing inventory: a ☐ Cost b ☐ Lower of cost or market c ☐ Other (attach explanation)

34 Was there any change in determining quantities, costs, or valuations between opening and closing inventory? If "Yes," attach explanation ☐ Yes ☐ No

35 Inventory at beginning of year. If different from last year's closing inventory, attach explanation	35	
36 Purchases less cost of items withdrawn for personal use	36	
37 Cost of labor. Do not include any amounts paid to yourself.	37	
38 Materials and supplies	38	
39 Other costs	39	
40 Add lines 35 through 39	40	
41 Inventory at end of year	41	
42 **Cost of goods sold.** Subtract line 41 from line 40. Enter the result here and on page 1, line 4	42	

Part IV **Information on Your Vehicle.** Complete this part **only** if you are claiming car or truck expenses on line 10 and are not required to file Form 4562 for this business. See the instructions for line 13 on page C-3 to find out if you must file.

43 When did you place your vehicle in service for business purposes? (month, day, year) ▶ _______________

44 Of the total number of miles you drove your vehicle during 2000, enter the number of miles you used your vehicle for:

a Business _______________ b Commuting _______________ c Other _______________

45 Do you (or your spouse) have another vehicle available for personal use? ☐ Yes ☐ No

46 Was your vehicle available for use during off-duty hours? ☐ Yes ☐ No

47a Do you have evidence to support your deduction? ☐ Yes ☐ No

b If "Yes," is the evidence written? ☐ Yes ☐ No

Part V **Other Expenses.** List below business expenses not included on lines 8–26 or line 30.

COMPUTER EXPENSE		2,955
HISTORICAL DATA SERVICES		3,061
INTERNET SERVICES		2,050
ONLINE TRADING DATA		7,010
OTHER TRADING EXPENSES		4,116
PROFESSIONAL PUBLICATIONS		3,116
TRADING ADVISORY SERVICES		35,179
TRADING PERIODICALS		6,633
TRADING SEMINARS		19,113
48 **Total other expenses.** Enter here and on page 1, line 27	48	83,233

IFOUS4A 11/09/00 Schedule C (Form 1040) 2000

SCHEDULE D (Form 1040)

Department of the Treasury Internal Revenue Service (99)

Capital Gains and Losses

▶ Attach to Form 1040. ▶ See Instructions for Schedule D (Form 1040).

▶ Use Schedule D-1 for more space to list transactions for lines 1 and 8.

OMB No. 1545-0074

2000

Attachment Sequence No. 12

Name(s) shown on Form 1040: A. TRADER-COMMODITY PROFIT-NO 475

Your social security number: 123-45-6789

Part I Short-Term Capital Gains and Losses - Assets Held One Year or Less

1 (a) Description of property (Example, 100 sh. XYZ Co.)	(b) Date acquired (Mo., day, yr.)	(c) Date sold (Mo., day, yr.)	(d) Sales price (see page D-6)	(e) Cost or other basis (see page D-6)	(f) Gain or (loss) Subtract (e) from (d)

2 Enter your short-term totals, if any, from Schedule D-1, line 2	2	
3 **Total short-term sales price amounts.** Add column (d) of lines 1 and 2	3	
4 Short-term gain from Form 6252 and short-term gain or (loss) from Forms 4684, 6781, and 8824	4	120,608
5 Net short-term gain or (loss) from partnerships, S corporations, estates, and trusts from Schedule(s) K-1	5	
6 Short-term capital loss carryover. Enter the amount, if any, from line 8 of your 1999 Capital Loss Carryover Worksheet	6	( )
7 **Net short-term capital gain or (loss).** Combine column (f) of lines 1 through 6 ▶	7	120,608

Part II Long-Term Capital Gains and Losses - Assets Held More Than One Year

8 (a) Description of property (Example, 100 sh. XYZ Co.)	(b) Date acquired (Mo., day, yr.)	(c) Date sold (Mo., day, yr.)	(d) Sales price (see page D-6)	(e) Cost or other basis (see page D-6)	(f) Gain or (loss) Subtract (e) from (d)	(g) 28% rate gain or (loss) *(see instr. below)

		(f)	(g)
9 Enter your long-term totals, if any, from Schedule D-1, line 9	9		
10 **Total long-term sales price amounts.** Add column (d) of lines 8 and 9	10		
11 Gain from Form 4797, Part I; long-term gain from Forms 2439 and 6252; and long-term gain or (loss) from Forms 4684, 6781, and 8824	11	180,911	
12 Net long-term gain or (loss) from partnerships, S corporations, estates, and trusts from Schedule(s) K-1	12		
13 Capital gain distributions. See page D-1	13		
14 Long-term capital loss carryover. Enter in both columns (f) and (g) the amount, if any, from line 13 of your 1999 Capital Loss Carryover Worksheet	14	( )	( )
15 Combine column (g) of lines 8 through 14	15		
16 **Net long-term capital gain or (loss).** Combine column (f) of lines 8 through 14 ▶	16	180,911	

Next: Go to Part III on the back.

* **28% rate gain or loss** includes **all** "collectibles gains and losses" (as defined on page D-6) and up to 50% of the eligible gain on qualified small business stock (see page D-4).

For Paperwork Reduction Act Notice, see Form 1040 instructions. **Schedule D (Form 1040) 2000**

KFA IFOUS5 12/07/00

Schedule D (Form 1040) 2000 A. TRADER-COMMODITY PROFIT-NO 475 123-45-6789 Page **2**

Part III Summary of Parts I and II

17 Combine lines 7 and 16. If a loss, go to line 18. If a gain, enter the gain on Form 1040, line 13			17	301,519
Next: Complete Form 1040 through line 39. Then, go to **Part IV** to figure your tax if: • Both lines 16 and 17 are gains **and** • Form 1040, line 39, is more than zero. Otherwise, **stop here.**				
18 If line 17 is a loss, enter here and as a (loss) on Form 1040, line 13, the **smaller** of these losses: • The loss on line 17 **or** • ($3,000) or, if married filing separately, ($1,500)			18	( )
Next: Skip **Part IV** below. Instead, complete Form 1040 through line 37. Then, complete the **Capital Loss Carryover Worksheet** on page D-6 if: • The loss on line 17 exceeds the loss on line 18 **or** • Form 1040, line 37, is a loss.				

Part IV Tax Computation Using Maximum Capital Gains Rates

19 Enter your taxable income from Form 1040, line 39			19	496,441
20 Enter the **smaller** of line 16 or line 17 of Schedule D	20	180,911		
21 If you are filing Form 4952, enter the amount from Form 4952, line 4e	21			
22 Subtract line 21 from line 20. If zero or less, enter -0-	22	180,911		
23 Combine lines 7 and 15. If zero or less, enter -0-	23	120,608		
24 Enter the **smaller** of line 15 or line 23, but not less than zero	24			
25 Enter your unrecaptured section 1250 gain, if any, from line 17 of the worksheet on page D-8	25			
26 Add lines 24 and 25	26			
27 Subtract line 26 from line 22. If zero or less, enter -0-			27	180,911
28 Subtract line 27 from line 19. If zero or less, enter -0-			28	315,530
29 Enter the **smaller** of: • The amount on line 19 **or** • $26,250 if single; $43,850 if married filing jointly or qualifying widow(er); $21,925 if married filing separately; or $35,150 if head of household			29	26,250
30 Enter the **smaller** of line 28 or line 29	30	26,250		
31 Subtract line 22 from line 19. If zero or less, enter -0-	31	315,530		
32 Enter the **larger** of line 30 or line 31 ▶	32	315,530		
33 Figure the tax on the amount on line 32. Use the Tax Table or Tax Rate Schedules, whichever applies			33	102,620
Note: If the amounts on lines 29 and 30 are the same, skip lines 34 through 37 and go to line 38.				
34 Enter the amount from line 29	34			
35 Enter the amount from line 30	35			
36 Subtract line 35 from line 34 ▶	36			
37 Multiply line 36 by 10% (.10)			37	
Note: If the amounts on lines 19 and 29 are the same, skip lines 38 through 51 and go to line 52.				
38 Enter the **smaller** of line 19 or line 27	38	180,911		
39 Enter the amount from line 36	39			
40 Subtract line 39 from line 38 ▶	40	180,911		
41 Multiply line 40 by 20% (.20)			41	36,182
Note: If line 26 is zero or blank, skip lines 42 through 51 and go to line 52.				
42 Enter the **smaller** of line 22 or line 25	42			
43 Add lines 22 and 32 (43)				
44 Enter the amount from line 19 (44)				
45 Subtract line 44 from line 43. If zero or less, enter -0-	45			
46 Subtract line 45 from line 42. If zero or less, enter -0- ▶	46			
47 Multiply line 46 by 25% (.25)			47	
Note: If line 24 is zero or blank, skip lines 48 through 51 and go to line 52.				
48 Enter the amount from line 19	48			
49 Add lines 32, 36, 40, and 46	49			
50 Subtract line 49 from line 48	50			
51 Multiply line 50 by 28% (.28)			51	
52 Add lines 33, 37, 41, 47, and 51			52	138,802
53 Figure the tax on the amount on line 19. Use the Tax Table or Tax Rate Schedules, whichever applies			53	174,261
54 Tax on all taxable income (including capital gains). Enter the **smaller** of line 52 or line 53 here and on Form 1040, line 40			54	138,802

IFOUS5A 10/24/00 **Schedule D (Form 1040) 2000**

Example 8 *(Continued)*

Schedule E (Form 1040) 2000 — Attachment Sequence No. **13** — Page **2**

Name(s) shown on return. Do not enter name and social security number if shown on other side.	Your social security number
A. TRADER-COMMODITY PROFIT-NO 475	123-45-6789

Note: If you report amounts from farming or fishing on Schedule E, you must enter your gross income from those activities on line 41 below. Real estate professionals must complete line 42 below.

Part II Income or Loss From Partnerships and S Corporations If you report a loss from an at-risk activity, you **must** check either column **(e)** or **(f)** on line 27 to describe your investment in the activity. See page E-5. If you check column **(f)**, you must attach **Form 6198.**

27	(a) Name	(b) Enter P for partnership; S for S corp.	(c) Check if foreign partnership	(d) Employer identification number	Invest. At Risk? (e) All is at risk	(f) Some is not at risk
A	1	P				
B						
C						
D						
E						

	Passive Income and Loss		Nonpassive Income and Loss		
	(g) Passive loss allowed (attach Form 8582 if required)	(h) Passive income from Schedule K-1	(i) Nonpassive loss from Schedule K-1	(j) Section 179 expense deduction from Form 4562	(k) Nonpassive income from Schedule K-1
A		200,000			
B					
C					
D					
E					
28a Totals		200,000			
b Totals					

29	Add columns (h) and (k) of line 28a	29	200,000
30	Add columns (g), (i), and (j) of line 28b	30	( )
31	Total partnership and S corporation income or (loss). Combine lines 29 and 30. Enter the result here and include in the total on line 40 below	31	200,000

Part III Income or Loss From Estates and Trusts

32	(a) Name	(b) Employer ID number
A		
B		
C		
D		

	Passive Income and Loss		Nonpassive Income and Loss	
	(c) Passive deduction or loss allowed (attach Form 8582 if required)	(d) Passive income from Schedule K-1	(e) Deduction or loss from Schedule K-1	(f) Other income from Schedule K-1
A				
B				
C				
D				
33a Totals				
b Totals				

34	Add columns (d) and (f) of line 33a	34	
35	Add columns (c) and (e) of line 33b	35	( )
36	Total estate and trust income or (loss). Combine lines 34 and 35. Enter the result here and include in the total on line 40 below	36	

Part IV Income or Loss From Real Estate Mortgage Investment Conduits (REMICs) – Residual Holder

37	(a) Name	(b) Employer identification number	(c) Excess inclusion from Schedules Q, line 2c (see page E-6)	(d) Taxable income (net loss) from Schedules Q, line 1b	(e) Income from Schedules Q, line 3b

38	Combine columns (d) and (e) only. Enter the result here and include in the total on line 40 below	38	

Part V Summary

39	Net farm rental income or (loss) from **Form 4835.** Also, complete line 41 below	39	
40	**Total** income or (loss). Combine lines 26, 31, 36, 38, and 39. Enter the result here and on Form 1040, line 17 ▶	40	200,000
41	**Reconciliation of Farming and Fishing Income:** Enter your **gross** farming and fishing income reported on Form 4835, line 7; Schedule K-1 (Form 1065), line 15b; Schedule K-1 (Form 1120S), line 23; and Schedule K-1 (Form 1041), line 14 (see page E-6)	41	
42	**Reconciliation for Real Estate Professionals.** If you were real estate professional (see pg. E-4), enter net income or (loss) you reported anywhere on Form 1040 from all rental real estate activities in which you materially participated under passive activity loss rules.	42	

IFOUS7A 10/19/00 — Schedule E (Form 1040) 2000

Form **4562** — **Depreciation and Amortization (Including Information on Listed Property)** — OMB No. 1545-0172 — **2000**

Department of the Treasury Internal Revenue Service (99) ▶ See separate instructions. ▶ Attach this form to your return. Attachment Sequence No. 67

Name(s) shown on return	Identifying number
A. TRADER-COMMODITY PROFIT-NO 475	123-45-6789
Business or activity to which this form relates	

Part I Election To Expense Certain Tangible Property (Section 179) Note: If you have any "listed property," complete Part V before you complete Part I.

1	Maximum dollar limitation. If an enterprise zone business, see page 2 of the instructions	1	$20,000
2	Total cost of section 179 property placed in service. See page 2 of the instructions	2	
3	Threshold cost of section 179 property before reduction in limitation	3	$200,000
4	Reduction in limitation. Subtract line 3 from line 2. If zero or less, enter -0-	4	
5	Dollar limitation for tax year. Subtract line 4 from line 1. If zero or less, enter -0-. If married filing separately, see page 2 of the instructions	5	20,000

6 (a) Description of property	(b) Cost (business use only)	(c) Elected cost
5-YR TRADING EQUIPMENT	50,000	20,000

7	Listed property. Enter amount from line 27 (7)		
8	Total elected cost of section 179 property. Add amounts in column (c), lines 6 and 7	8	20,000
9	Tentative deduction. Enter the smaller of line 5 or line 8	9	20,000
10	Carryover of disallowed deduction from 1999. See page 3 of the instructions	10	0
11	Business income limitation. Enter the smaller of business income (not less than zero) or line 5 (see instructions)	11	20,000
12	Section 179 expense deduction. Add lines 9 and 10, but do not enter more than line 11	12	20,000
13	Carryover of disallowed deduction to 2001. Add lines 9 and 10, less line 12 ▶ (13)		

Note: Do not use Part II or Part III below for listed property (automobiles, certain other vehicles, cellular telephones, certain computers, or property used for entertainment, recreation, or amusement). Instead, use Part V for listed property.

Part II MACRS Depreciation for Assets Placed in Service Only During Your 2000 Tax Year (Do not include listed property.)

Section A – General Asset Account Election

14 If you are making the election under section 168(i)(4) to group any assets placed in service during the tax year into one or more general asset accounts, check this box. See page 3 of the instructions ▶ ☐

Section B – General Depreciation System (GDS) (See page 3 of the instructions.)

(a) Classification of property	(b) Month and year placed in service	(c) Basis for depreciation (business/investment use only – see instructions)	(d) Recovery period	(e) Convention	(f) Method	(g) Depreciation deduction
15a 3-year property						
b 5-year property						
c 7-year property						
d 10-year property						
e 15-year property						
f 20-year property						
g 25-year property			25 yrs		S/L	
h Residential rental property			27.5 yrs	MM	S/L	
			27.5 yrs	MM	S/L	
i Nonresidential real property			39 yrs	MM	S/L	
				MM	S/L	

Section C – Alternative Depreciation System (ADS): (See page 5 of the instructions.)

16a Class life					S/L	
b 12-year			12 yrs		S/L	
c 40-year			40 yrs	MM	S/L	

Part III Other Depreciation (Do not include listed property.) (See page 5 of the instructions.)

17	GDS and ADS deductions for assets placed in service in tax years beginning before 2000	17	
18	Property subject to section 168(f)(1) election	18	
19	ACRS and other depreciation	19	3,150

Part IV Summary (See page 6 of the instructions.)

20	Listed property. Enter amount from line 26	20	
21	**Total.** Add deductions from line 12, lines 15 and 16 in column (g), and lines 17 through 20. Enter here and on the appropriate lines of your return. Partnerships and S corporations – see instructions	21	23,150
22	For assets shown above and placed in service during the current year, enter the portion of the basis attributable to section 263A costs (22)		

KFA **For Paperwork Reduction Act Notice, see page 9 of the instructions.** GFOUS7 10/26/00 Form **4562** (2000)

Form **6251** — Department of the Treasury, Internal Revenue Service

Alternative Minimum Tax – Individuals

▶ See separate instructions.
▶ Attach to Form 1040 or Form 1040NR.

OMB No. 1545-0227 — **2000** — Attachment Sequence No. **32**

Name(s) shown on Form 1040	Your social security number
A. TRADER-COMMODITY PROFIT-NO 475	123-45-6789

Part I — Adjustments and Preferences

1	If you itemized deductions on Schedule A (Form 1040), go to line 2. Otherwise, enter your standard deduction from Form 1040, line 36, here and go to line 6	1	4,400
2	Medical and dental. Enter the smaller of Schedule A (Form 1040), line 4 **or** 2 1/2% of Form 1040, line 34	2	
3	Taxes. Enter the amount from Schedule A (Form 1040), line 9	3	
4	Certain interest on a home mortgage **not** used to buy, build, or improve your home	4	
5	Miscellaneous itemized deductions. Enter the amount from Schedule A (Form 1040), line 26	5	
6	Refund of taxes. Enter any tax refund from Form 1040, line 10 or line 21	6	( )
7	Investment interest. Enter difference between regular tax and AMT deduction	7	
8	Post-1986 depreciation. Enter difference between regular tax and AMT depreciation	8	
9	Adjusted gain or loss. Enter difference between AMT and regular tax gain or loss	9	
10	Incentive stock options. Enter excess of AMT income over regular tax income	10	
11	Passive activities. Enter difference between AMT and regular tax income or loss	11	
12	Beneficiaries of estates and trusts. Enter the amount from Schedule K-1 (Form 1041), line 9	12	
13	Tax-exempt interest from private activity bonds issued after 8/7/86	13	
14	Other. Enter the amount, if any, for each item below and enter the total on line 14.		

a Circulation expenditures		h Loss limitations	
b Depletion		i Mining costs	
c Depreciation (pre-1987)		j Patron's adjustment	
d Installment sales		k Pollution control facilities	
e Intangible drilling costs		l Research & experimental	
f Large partnerships		m Section 1202 exclusion	
g Long-term contracts		n Tax shelter farm activities	
		o Related adjustments	

	(line 14 total)	14	
15	**Total Adjustments and Preferences.** Combine lines 1 through 14 ▶	15	4,400

Part II — Alternative Minimum Taxable Income

16	Enter the amount from **Form 1040, line 37.** If less than zero, enter as a (loss) ▶	16	496,441
17	Net operating loss deduction, if any, from Form 1040, line 21. Enter as a positive amount	17	
18	If Form 1040, line 34, is over $128,950 (over $64,475 if married filing separately), and you itemized deductions, enter the amount, if any, from line 9 of the worksheet for Schedule A (Form 1040), line 28	18	( )
19	Combine lines 15 through 18 ▶	19	500,841
20	Alternative tax net operating loss deduction. See page 6 of the instructions	20	
21	**Alternative Minimum Taxable Income.** Subtract line 20 from line 19. (If married filing separately and line 21 is more than $165,000, see page 7 of the instructions.) ▶	21	500,841

Part III — Exemption Amount and Alternative Minimum Tax

22 **Exemption Amount.** (If this form is for a child under age 14, see page 7 of the instructions.)

IF your filing status is:	AND line 21 is not over . . .	THEN enter on line 22 . . .
Single or head of household	$112,500	$33,750
Married filing jointly or qualifying widow(er)	150,000	45,000
Married filing separately	75,000	22,500

If line 21 is **over** the amount shown above for your filing status, see page 7 of the instructions.

22	Exemption Amount	22	
23	Subtract line 22 from line 21. If zero or less, enter -0- here and on lines 26 and 28 and stop here ▶	23	500,841
24	If you reported capital gain distributions directly on Form 1040, line 13, **or** you completed Schedule D (Form 1040) and have an amount on line 25 or line 27 (or would have had an amount on either line if you had completed Part IV) (as refigured for the AMT, if necessary), go to Part IV of Form 6251 to figure line 24. **All others:** If line 23 is $175,000 or less ($87,500 or less if married filing separately), multiply line 23 by 26% (.26). Otherwise, multiply line 23 by 28% (.28) and subtract $3,500 ($1,750 if married filing separately) from the result ▶	24	122,262
25	Alternative minimum tax foreign tax credit. See page 7 of the instructions	25	
26	Tentative minimum tax. Subtract line 25 from line 24 ▶	26	122,262
27	Enter your tax from Form 1040, line 40 (minus any tax from Form 4972 and any foreign tax credit from Form 1040, line 43)	27	138,802
28	**Alternative Minimum Tax.** Subtract line 27 from line 26. If zero or less, enter -0-. Enter here and on Form 1040, line 41 ▶	28	0

For Paperwork Reduction Act Notice, see page 8 of the instructions. Form **6251** (2000)

KFA IFOUS33 10/23/00

Form 6251 (2000) A. TRADER-COMMODITY PROFIT-NO 475 — 123-45-6789 Page **2**

Part IV **Line 24 Computation Using Maximum Capital Gains Rates**

Caution: If you **did not** complete Part IV of Schedule D (Form 1040), see page 8 of the instructions before you complete this part.

Line	Description	Box	Amount	Box	Amount
29	Enter the amount from Form 6251, line 23			29	500,841
30	Enter the amount from Schedule D (Form 1040), line 27 (as refigured for the AMT, if necessary). See page 8 of the instructions	30	180,911		
31	Enter the amount from Schedule D (Form 1040), line 25 (as refigured for the AMT, if necessary). See page 8 of the instructions	31	0		
32	Add lines 30 and 31	32	180,911		
33	Enter the amount from Schedule D (Form 1040), line 22 (as refigured for the AMT, if necessary). See page 8 of the instructions	33	180,911		
34	Enter the **smaller** of line 32 or line 33			34	180,911
35	Subtract line 34 from line 29. If zero or less, enter -0- ▶			35	319,930
36	If line 35 is $175,000 or less ($87,500 or less if married filing separately), multiply line 35 by 26% (.26). Otherwise, multiply line 35 by 28% (.28) and subtract $3,500 ($1,750 if married filing separately) from the result			36	86,080
37	Enter the amount from Schedule D (Form 1040), line 36 (as figured for the regular tax). See page 8 of the instructions	37	0		
38	Enter the **smallest** of line 29, line 30, or line 37 ▶	38			
39	Multiply line 38 by 10% (.10)			39	
40	Enter the **smaller** of line 29 or line 30	40	180,911		
41	Enter the amount from line 38	41			
42	Subtract line 41 from line 40 ▶	42	180,911		
43	Multiply line 42 by 20% (.20)			43	36,182
	Note: If line 31 is zero or blank, skip lines 44 through 47 and go to line 48.				
44	Enter the amount from line 29	44			
45	Add lines 35, 38, and 42	45			
46	Subtract line 45 from line 44	46			
47	Multiply line 46 by 25% (.25)			47	
48	Add lines 36, 39, 43, and 47			48	122,262
49	If line 29 is $175,000 or less ($87,500 or less if married filing separately), multiply line 29 by 26% (.26). Otherwise, multiply line 29 by 28% (.28) and subtract $3,500 ($1,750 if married filing separately) from the result			49	136,735
50	Enter the **smaller** of line 48 or line 49 here and on line 24			50	122,262

Form **6251** (2000)

IFOUS33A 10/23/00

Form **6781**

Department of the Treasury
Internal Revenue Service

Gains and Losses From Section 1256 Contracts and Straddles

▶ Attach to your tax return.

OMB No. 1545-0644

2000

Attachment Sequence No. **82**

Name(s) shown on tax return: A. TRADER-COMMODITY PROFIT-NO 475

Identifying number: 123-45-6789

Check applicable box(es) (see instructions):
A ☐ Mixed straddle election
B ☐ Straddle-by-straddle identification election
C ☐ Mixed straddle account election
D ☐ Net section 1256 contracts loss election

Part I Section 1256 Contracts Marked to Market

1 (a) Identification of account	(b) (Loss)	(c) Gain
		301,519

2	Add amounts on line 1 in columns (b) and (c)	2 ( )	301,519
3	Net gain or (loss). Combine columns (b) and (c) of line 2	3	301,519
4	Form 1099-B adjustments. See instructions and attach schedule	4	
5	Combine lines 3 and 4	5	301,519
	Note: If line 5 shows a net gain, skip line 6 and enter the gain on line 7. Partnerships and S corporations, see instructions.		
6	If you have a net section 1256 contracts loss and checked box D, enter the amount to be carried back	6	
7	Subtract line 6 from line 5	7	301,519
8	Short-term capital gain or (loss). Multiply line 7 by 40%. Enter here and include on Schedule D. See instructions	8	120,608
9	Long-term capital gain or (loss). Multiply line 7 by 60%. Enter here and include on Schedule D. See instructions	9	180,911

Part II Gains and Losses From Straddles. Attach a separate schedule listing each straddle and its components.

Section A – Losses From Straddles

10 (a) Description of property	(b) Date entered into or acquired	(c) Date closed out or sold	(d) Gross sales price	(e) Cost or other basis plus expense of sale	(f) Loss. If column (e) is more than (d), enter difference. Otherwise, enter -0-	(g) Unrecognized gain on offsetting positions	(h) Recognized loss. If column (f) is more than (g), enter difference. Otherwise, enter -0-	*(i) 28% rate loss (see instr. below)

11a Enter short-term portion of line 10, column (h), losses here and include on Schedule D. See instructions . . . . 11a ( )

b Enter long-term portion of losses from line 10, columns (h) and (i), here and include on Schedule D. See instrs . 11b ( ) ( )

Section B – Gains From Straddles

12 (a) Description of property	(b) Date entered into or acquired	(c) Date closed out or sold	(d) Gross sales price	(e) Cost or other basis plus expense of sale	(f) Gain. If column (d) is more than (e), enter diff. Otherwise, enter 0	*(g) 28% Rate gain (see instr. below)

13a Enter short-term portion of line 12, column (f), gains here and include on Schedule D. See instructions . . . 13a

b Enter long-term portion of gains from line 12, columns (f) and (g), here and include on Sch D. See instrs . 13b

Part III Unrecognized Gains From Positions Held on Last Day of Tax Year. Memo Entry Only – See instructions.

14 (a) Description of property	(b) Date acquired	(c) Fair market value on last business day of tax year	(d) Cost or other basis as adjusted	(e) Unrecognized gain. If column (c) is more than (d), enter difference. Otherwise, enter -0-

*28% Rate Gain or Loss includes all "collectibles gains and losses" and up to 50% of the eligible gain on qualified small business stock. See instructions for Schedule D (Form 1040).

For Paperwork Reduction Act Notice, see page 3.

Form **6781** (2000)

KFA GF0US16 12/27/00

Example 9

FORM 1040 Department of the Treasury – Internal Revenue Service
U.S. Individual Income Tax Return 2000 (99) IRS Use Only – Do not write or staple in this space.

For the year Jan. 1 – Dec. 31, 2000, or other tax year beginning , 2000, ending , 20 OMB No. 1545-0074

Label (See instructions on page 19.) Use the IRS label. Otherwise, please print or type. LABEL HERE

Your first name and initial / Last name: A. COMMODITIES TRADER PROFIT SEC475	Your social security number: 123-45-6789
If a joint return, spouse's first name and initial / Last name	Spouse's social security number
Home address (number and street). If you have a P.O. box, see page 19. Apt. no.: C/O TED TESSER-6274 LINTON BLVD. #102	▲ IMPORTANT! ▲ You **must** enter your SSN(s) above.
City, town or post office, state, and ZIP code. If you have a foreign address, see page 19.: DELRAY BEACH, FL 33484	

Presidential Election Campaign (See page 19.) **Note.** Checking "Yes" will not change your tax or reduce your refund. Do you, or your spouse if filing a joint return, want $3 to go to this fund? ▶ You: ☐ Yes ☒ No Spouse: ☐ Yes ☐ No

Filing Status (Check only one box.)

1 [X] Single
2 [ ] Married filing joint return (even if only one had income)
3 [ ] Married filing separate return. Enter spouse's soc. sec. no. above & full name here ▶
4 [ ] Head of household (with qualifying person). (See page 19.) If the qualifying person is a child but not your dependent, enter this child's name here ▶
5 [ ] Qualifying widow(er) with dependent child (year spouse died ▶). (See page 19.)

Exemptions

6a ☒ **Yourself.** If your parent (or someone else) can claim you as a dependent on his or her tax return, **do not** check box 6a. — No. of boxes checked on 6a and 6b: 1
b ☐ **Spouse**

c **Dependents:**

(1) First Name Last name	(2) Dependent's social security number	(3) Dependent's relationship to you	(4) Chk if qualifying child for child tax credit (see page 20)

If more than six dependents, see page 20.

No. of your children on 6c who: • lived with you ___ • did not live with you due to divorce or separation (see page 20) ___ Dependents on 6c not entered above ___

d Total number of exemptions claimed — Add numbers entered on lines above ▶ 1

Income

Attach Forms W-2 and W-2G here. Also attach Form 1099-R if tax was withheld. If you did not get a W-2, see page 21. Enclose, but do not attach any payment. Also, please use Form 1040-V.

7	Wages, salaries, tips, etc. Attach Form(s) W-2	7	200,000
8a	**Taxable** interest. Attach Schedule B if required	8a	
b	**Tax-exempt** interest. **Do not** include on line 8a — 8b		
9	Ordinary dividends. Attach Schedule B if required	9	
10	Taxable refunds, credits, or offsets of state and local income taxes (see page 22)	10	
11	Alimony received	11	
12	Business income or (loss). Attach Schedule C or C-EZ	12	-200,678
13	Capital gain or (loss). Attach Schedule D if required. If not required, check here ▶ ☐	13	301,519
14	Other gains or (losses). Attach Form 4797	14	
15a	Total IRA distributions — 15a; b Taxable amount (see pg. 23)	15b	
16a	Total pensions and annuities — 16a; b Taxable amount (see pg. 23)	16b	
17	Rental real estate, royalties, partnerships, S corporations, trusts, etc. Attach Schedule E	17	200,000
18	Farm income or (loss). Attach Schedule F	18	
19	Unemployment compensation	19	
20a	Social security benefits — 20a; b Taxable amount (see pg. 25)	20b	
21	Other income.	21	
22	Add the amounts in the far right column for lines 7 through 21. This is your **total income** ▶	22	500,841

Adjusted Gross Income

23	IRA deduction (see page 27)	23	
24	Student loan interest deduction (see page 27)	24	
25	Medical savings account deduction. Attach Form 8853	25	
26	Moving expenses. Attach Form 3903	26	
27	One-half of self-employment tax. Attach Schedule SE	27	
28	Self-employed health insurance deduction (see page 29)	28	
29	Self-employed SEP, SIMPLE, and qualified plans	29	
30	Penalty on early withdrawal of savings	30	
31a	Alimony paid. **b** Recipient's SSN ▶	31a	
32	Add lines 23 through 31a	32	0
33	Subtract line 32 from line 22. This is your **adjusted gross income** ▶	33	500,841

KFA **For Disclosure, Privacy Act, and Paperwork Reduction Act Notice, see page 56.** IF0US1 11/07/00 Form **1040** (2000)

| Form 1040 (2000) | COMMODITIES TRADER PROFIT SEC475 | | 123-45-6789 Page **2** | |

Tax and Credits

34	Amount from line 33 (adjusted gross income)	34	500,841

Standard Deduction for Most People
Single: $4,400
Head of household: $6,450
Married filing jointly or Qualifying widow(er): $7,350
Married filing separately $3,675

35a	Check if: ☐ **You** were 65 or older, ☐ Blind; ☐ **Spouse** was 65 or older, ☐ Blind.		
	Add the number of boxes checked above and enter the total here ▶ 35a		
b	If you are married filing separately and your spouse itemizes deductions, or you were a dual-status alien, see page 31 and check here ▶ 35b ☐		
36	Enter your **itemized deductions** from Schedule A, line 28, **or standard deduction** shown on the left. But see page 31 to find your standard deduction if you checked any box on line 35a or 35b or if someone can claim you as a dependent	36	4,400
37	Subtract line 36 from line 34	37	496,441
38	If line 34 is $96,700 or less, multiply $2,800 by the total number of exemptions claimed on line 6d. If line 34 is over $96,700, see the worksheet on page 32 for the amount to enter	38	0
39	**Taxable income.** Subtract line 38 from line 37. If line 38 is more than line 37, enter -0-	39	496,441
40	**Tax** (see page 32). Check if any tax is from a ☐ Form(s) 8814 b ☐ Form 4972	40	174,261
41	Alternative minimum tax. Attach Form 6251	41	
42	Add lines 40 and 41 ▶	42	174,261
43	Foreign tax credit. Attach Form 1116 if required	43	
44	Credit for child and dependent care expenses. Att. Form 2441	44	
45	Credit for the elderly or the disabled. Attach Schedule R	45	
46	Education credits. Attach Form 8863	46	
47	Child tax credit (see page 36)	47	
48	Adoption credit. Attach Form 8839	48	
49	Other. Check if from a ☐ Form 3800 b ☐ Form 8396 c ☐ Form 8801 d ☐ Form (specify)	49	
50	Add lines 43 through 49. These are your **total credits**	50	
51	Subtract line 50 from line 42. If line 50 is more than line 42, enter -0- ▶	51	174,261

Other Taxes

52	Self-employment tax. Att. Sch. SE	52	
53	Social security and Medicare tax on tip income not reported to employer. Attach Form 4137	53	
54	Tax on IRAs, other retirement plans, and MSAs. Attach Form 5329 if required	54	
55	Advance earned income credit payments from Form(s) W-2	55	
56	Household employment taxes. Attach Schedule H	56	
57	Add lines 51 through 56. This is your **total tax** ▶	57	174,261

Payments

If you have a qualifying child, attach Schedule EIC.

58	Federal income tax withheld from Forms W-2 and 1099	58	60,000		
59	2000 estimated tax payments and amount applied from 1999 return	59	50,000		
60a	**Earned income credit (EIC)**	60a			
b	Nontaxable earned income: amt. ▶ and type▶	No			
61	Excess social security and RRTA tax withheld (see page 50)	61			
62	**Additional child tax credit.** Attach Form 8812	62			
63	**Amount paid with request for extension to file** (see page 50)	63			
64	Other payments. Check if from a ☐ Form 2439 b ☐ Form 4136	64			
65	Add lines 58, 59, 60a, and 61 through 64. These are your **total payments** ▶	65	110,000		

Refund

Have it directly deposited! See page 50 and fill in 67b, 67c, and 67d.

66	If line 65 is more than line 57, subtract line 57 from line 65. This is the amount you **overpaid**	66	
67a	Amount of line 66 you want **refunded to you** ▶	67a	
b	Routing number	▶ c Type: ☐ Checking ☐ Savings	
d	Account number		
68	Amount of line 66 you want **applied to your 2001 estimated tax** ▶	68	

Amount You Owe

| 69 | If line 57 is more than line 65, subtract line 65 from line 57. This is the **amount you owe.** For details on how to pay, see page 51 ▶ | 69 | 64,261 |
| 70 | Estimated tax penalty. Also include on line 69 | 70 | |

Sign Here

Under penalties of perjury, I declare that I have examined this return and accompanying schedules and statements, and to the best of my knowledge and belief, they are true, correct, and complete. Declaration of preparer (other than taxpayer) is based on all information of which preparer has any knowledge.

Joint return? See page 19.
Keep a copy for your records.

| Your signature | Date | Your occupation | Daytime phone number 561-865-0071 |
| Spouse's signature. If a joint return, **both** must sign. | Date | Spouse's occupation | May the IRS discuss this return with the preparer shown below? (see page 52)? ☒Yes ☐No |

Paid Preparer's Use Only

| Preparer's signature ▶ | | Date | Check if self-employed ☐ | Preparer's SSN or PTIN |
| Firm's name (or yours if self-employed), address, and ZIP code | Waterside Financial Serv., Inc 6274 Linton Blvd., Suite #102 Boca Raton, FL 33484 | | EIN 65-0664126 Phone no. (561) 865-0071 | |

IF0US1A 11/22/00

Form **1040** (2000)

SCHEDULE C (Form 1040)
Department of the Treasury Internal Revenue Service (99)

Profit or Loss From Business
(Sole Proprietorship)

▶ Partnerships, joint ventures, etc., must file Form 1065 or Form 1065-B.
▶ Attach to Form 1040 or Form 1041. ▶ See Instructions for Schedule C (Form 1040).

OMB No. 1545-0074
2000
Attachment Sequence No. 09

Name of proprietor: A. COMMODITIES TRADER PROFIT SEC475
Social security number (SSN): 123-45-6789

A Principal business or profession, including product or service (see page C-1 of the instructions): TRADER
B Enter code from pages C-7 & 8: ▶ 523900

C Business name. If no separate business name, leave blank.
D Employer ID number (EIN), if any

E Business address (including suite or room no.) ▶
City, town or post office, state, and ZIP code

F Accounting method: (1) ☒ Cash (2) ☐ Accrual (3) ☐ Other (specify) ▶
G Did you "materially participate" in the operation of this business during 2000? If "No," see page C-2 for limit on losses ☒ Yes ☐ No
H If you started or acquired this business during 2000, check here ▶ ☐

Part I Income

1 Gross receipts or sales. **Caution:** If this income was reported to you on Form W-2 and the "Statutory employee" box on that form was checked, see page C-2 and check here ▶ ☐	1	
2 Returns and allowances	2	
3 Subtract line 2 from line 1	3	
4 Cost of goods sold (from line 42 on page 2)	4	
5 **Gross profit.** Subtract line 4 from line 3	5	
6 Other income, including Federal and state gasoline or fuel tax credit or refund (see page C-2)	6	
7 **Gross income.** Add lines 5 and 6 ▶	7	

Part II Expenses. Enter expenses for business use of your home **only** on line 30.

8 Advertising	8		19 Pension and profit-sharing plans	19	
9 Bad debts from sales or services (see page C-3)	9		20 Rent or lease (see page C-4): a Vehicles, machinery & equipment	20a	5,050
10 Car and truck expenses (see page C-3)	10	3,115	b Other business property	20b	
			21 Repairs and maintenance	21	3,166
11 Commissions and fees	11		22 Supplies (not included in Part III)	22	5,069
12 Depletion	12		23 Taxes and licenses	23	
13 Depreciation and section 179 expense deduction (not included in Part III) (see page C-3)	13	23,150	24 Travel, meals, and entertainment: a Travel	24a	6,511
			b Meals and entertainment 8,711		
14 Employee benefit programs (other than on line 19)	14		c Enter nondeductible amount included on line 24b (see page C-5) 4,356		
15 Insurance (other than health)	15				
16 Interest: a Mortgage (paid to banks, etc.)	16a		d Subtract line 24c from line 24b	24d	4,355
			25 Utilities	25	2,611
b Other	16b	51,357	26 Wages (less employment credits)	26	
17 Legal and professional services	17	2,250	27 Other expenses (from line 48 on page 2)	27	83,233
18 Office expense	18	4,561			

28 **Total expenses** before expenses for business use of home. Add lines 8 through 27 in columns ▶	28	194,428
29 Tentative profit (loss). Subtract line 28 from line 7	29	-194,428
30 Expenses for business use of your home. Attach **Form 8829**	30	6,250
31 **Net profit or (loss).** Subtract line 30 from line 29. • If a profit, enter on **Form 1040, line 12,** and **also** on **Schedule SE, line 2** (statutory employees, see page C-5). Estates and trusts, enter on Form 1041, line 3. • If a loss, you **must** go to line 32.	31	-200,678

32 If you have a loss, check the box that describes your investment in this activity (see page C-5).
- If you checked 32a, enter the loss on **Form 1040, line 12,** and **also** on **Schedule SE, line 2** (statutory employees, see page C-5). Estates and trusts, enter on Form 1041, line 3.
- If you checked 32b, you **must** attach **Form 6198.**

32a ☒ All investment is at risk.
32b ☐ Some investment is not at risk.

For Paperwork Reduction Act Notice, see Form 1040 instructions. **Schedule C (Form 1040) 2000**

KFA IFOUS4 11/08/00

Schedule C (Form 1040) 2000 A. COMMODITIES TRADER PROFIT SEC475 123-45-6789 Page 2

Part III Cost of Goods Sold (see page C-6)

33 Method(s) used to value closing inventory: a ☐ Cost b ☐ Lower of cost or market c ☐ Other (attach explanation)

34 Was there any change in determining quantities, costs, or valuations between opening and closing inventory? If "Yes," attach explanation ☐ Yes ☐ No

35 Inventory at beginning of year. If different from last year's closing inventory, attach explanation	35	
36 Purchases less cost of items withdrawn for personal use	36	
37 Cost of labor. Do not include any amounts paid to yourself	37	
38 Materials and supplies	38	
39 Other costs	39	
40 Add lines 35 through 39	40	
41 Inventory at end of year	41	
42 **Cost of goods sold.** Subtract line 41 from line 40. Enter the result here and on page 1, line 4	42	

Part IV Information on Your Vehicle. Complete this part **only** if you are claiming car or truck expenses on line 10 and are not required to file Form 4562 for this business. See the instructions for line 13 on page C-3 to find out if you must file.

43 When did you place your vehicle in service for business purposes? (month, day, year) ▶ ______________

44 Of the total number of miles you drove your vehicle during 2000, enter the number of miles you used your vehicle for:

a Business ______________ b Commuting ______________ c Other ______________

45 Do you (or your spouse) have another vehicle available for personal use? ☐ Yes ☐ No

46 Was your vehicle available for use during off-duty hours? ☐ Yes ☐ No

47a Do you have evidence to support your deduction? ☐ Yes ☐ No

b If "Yes," is the evidence written? ☐ Yes ☐ No

Part V Other Expenses. List below business expenses not included on lines 8–26 or line 30.

COMPUTER EXPENSE		2,955
HISTORICAL DATA SERVICES		3,061
INTERNET SERVICES		2,050
ONLINE TRADING DATA		7,010
OTHER TRADING EXPENSES		4,116
PROFESSIONAL PUBLICATIONS		3,116
TRADING ADVISORY SERVICES		35,179
TRADING PERIODICALS		6,633
TRADING SEMINARS		19,113
48 **Total other expenses.** Enter here and on page 1, line 27	48	83,233

IFOUS4A 11/09/00 Schedule C (Form 1040) 2000

Example 9 *(Continued)*

Schedule E (Form 1040) 2000 — Attachment Sequence No. **13** — Page **2**

Name(s) shown on return. Do not enter name and social security number if shown on other side. — Your social security number

A. COMMODITIES TRADER PROFIT SEC475 — 123-45-6789

Note: If you report amounts from farming or fishing on Schedule E, you must enter your gross income from those activities on line 41 below. Real estate professionals must complete line 42 below.

Part II **Income or Loss From Partnerships and S Corporations** If you report a loss from an at-risk activity, you **must** check either column **(e)** or **(f)** on line 27 to describe your investment in the activity. See page E-5. If you check column **(f)**, you must attach **Form 6198.**

27	(a) Name	(b) Enter P for partnership; S for S corp.	(c) Check if foreign partnership	(d) Employer identification number	Invest. At Risk? (e) All is at risk	(f) Some is not at risk
A	1	P				
B						
C						
D						
E						

	Passive Income and Loss		Nonpassive Income and Loss		
	(g) Passive loss allowed (attach Form 8582 if required)	(h) Passive income from Schedule K-1	(i) Nonpassive loss from Schedule K-1	(j) Section 179 expense deduction from Form 4562	(k) Nonpassive income from Schedule K-1
A		200,000			
B					
C					
D					
E					
28a Totals		200,000			
b Totals					

29	Add columns (h) and (k) of line 28a	29	200,000
30	Add columns (g), (i), and (j) of line 28b	30	( )
31	Total partnership and S corporation income or (loss). Combine lines 29 and 30. Enter the result here and include in the total on line 40 below	31	200,000

Part III **Income or Loss From Estates and Trusts**

32	(a) Name	(b) Employer ID number
A		
B		
C		
D		

	Passive Income and Loss		Nonpassive Income and Loss	
	(c) Passive deduction or loss allowed (attach Form 8582 if required)	(d) Passive income from Schedule K-1	(e) Deduction or loss from Schedule K-1	(f) Other income from Schedule K-1
A				
B				
C				
D				
33a Totals				
b Totals				

34	Add columns (d) and (f) of line 33a	34	
35	Add columns (c) and (e) of line 33b	35	( )
36	Total estate and trust income or (loss). Combine lines 34 and 35. Enter the result here and include in the total on line 40 below	36	

Part IV **Income or Loss From Real Estate Mortgage Investment Conduits (REMICs) – Residual Holder**

37	(a) Name	(b) Employer identification number	(c) Excess inclusion from Schedules Q, line 2c (see page E-6)	(d) Taxable income (net loss) from Schedules Q, line 1b	(e) Income from Schedules Q, line 3b

38	Combine columns (d) and (e) only. Enter the result here and include in the total on line 40 below	38	

Part V **Summary**

39	Net farm rental income or (loss) from **Form 4835.** Also, complete line 41 below	39	
40	**Total** income or (loss). Combine lines 26, 31, 36, 38, and 39. Enter the result here and on Form 1040, line 17 ▶	40	200,000
41	**Reconciliation of Farming and Fishing Income:** Enter your **gross** farming and fishing income reported on Form 4835, line 7; Schedule K-1 (Form 1065), line 15b; Schedule K-1 (Form 1120S), line 23; and Schedule K-1 (Form 1041), line 14 (see page E-6)	41	
42	**Reconciliation for Real Estate Professionals.** If you were real estate professional (see pg. E-4), enter net income or (loss) you reported anywhere on Form 1040 from all rental real estate activities in which you materially participated under passive activity loss rules.	42	

IFOUS7A 10/19/00 — Schedule E (Form 1040) 2000

Example 9 (Continued)

Form **4797**	**Sales of Business Property**	OMB No. 1545-0184
Department of the Treasury Internal Revenue Service (99)	(Also Involuntary Conversions and Recapture Amounts Under Sections 179 and 280F(b)(2)) ▶ Attach to your tax return. ▶ See separate instructions.	**2000** Attachment Sequence No. **27**

Name(s) shown on return	Identifying number
A. COMMODITIES TRADER PROFIT SEC475	123-45-6789

1 Enter the gross proceeds from sales or exchanges reported to you for 2000 on Form(s) 1099-B or 1099-S (or substitute statement) that you are including on line 2, 10, or 20 (see instructions) . **1**

Part I **Sales or Exchanges of Property Used in a Trade or Business and Involuntary Conversions From Other Than Casualty or Theft – Most Property Held More Than 1 Year** (See instructions.)

(a) Description of property	(b) Date acquired (mo., day, yr.)	(c) Date sold (mo., day, yr.)	(d) Gross sales price	(e) Depreciation allowed or allowable since acquisition	(f) Cost or other basis, plus improvements and expense of sale	(g) Gain or (loss) Subtract (f) from the sum of (d) and (e)
2						

3 Gain, if any, from Form 4684, line 39 .	**3**	
4 Section 1231 gain from installment sales from Form 6252, line 26 or 37. .	**4**	
5 Section 1231 gain or (loss) from like-kind exchanges from Form 8824 .	**5**	
6 Gain, if any, from line 32, from other than casualty or theft. .	**6**	
7 Combine lines 2 through 6. Enter the gain or (loss) here and on the appropriate line as follows:	**7**	

Partnerships (except electing large partnerships). Report the gain or (loss) following the instructions for Form 1065, Schedule K, line 6. Skip lines 8, 9, 11, and 12 below.

S corporations. Report the gain or (loss) following the instructions for Form 1120S, Schedule K, lines 5 and 6. Skip lines 8, 9, 11, and 12 below, unless line 7 is a gain and the S corporation is subject to capital gains tax.

All others. If line 7 is zero or a loss, enter the amount from line 7 on line 11 below and skip lines 8 and 9. If line 7 is a gain and you did not have any prior year section 1231 losses, or they were recaptured in an earlier year, enter the gain from line 7 as a long-term capital gain on Schedule D and skip lines 8, 9, and 12 below.

8 Nonrecaptured net section 1231 losses from prior years (see instructions) . **8**

9 Subtract line 8 from line 7. If zero or less, enter -0-. Also enter on the appropriate line as follows (see instructions): . **9**

S corporations. Enter any gain from line 9 on Schedule D (Form 1120S), line 15, and skip lines 11 and 12 below.

All others. If line 9 is zero, enter the gain from line 7 on line 12 below. If line 9 is more than zero, enter the amount from line 8 on line 12 below, and enter the gain from line 9 as a long-term capital gain on Schedule D.

Part II **Ordinary Gains and Losses**

10 Ordinary gains and losses not included on lines 11 through 17 (include property held 1 year or less):

475 TRADING INCOME		301,519	301,519

11 Loss, if any, from line 7. .	**11**	
12 Gain, if any, from line 7 or amount from line 8, if applicable .	**12**	
13 Gain, if any, from line 31. .	**13**	
14 Net gain or (loss) from Form 4684, lines 31 and 38a .	**14**	
15 Ordinary gain from installment sales from Form 6252, line 25 or 36 .	**15**	
16 Ordinary gain or (loss) from like-kind exchanges from Form 8824 .	**16**	
17 Recapture of section 179 expense deduction for partners and S corporation shareholders from property dispositions by partnerships and S corporations (see instructions) .	**17**	
18 Combine lines 10 through 17. Enter the gain or (loss) here and on the appropriate line as follows:	**18**	301,519

a For all except individual returns: Enter the gain or (loss) from line 18 on the return being filed.

b For individual returns:

 (1) If the loss on line 11 includes a loss from Form 4684, line 35, column (b)(ii), enter that part of the loss here. Enter the part of the loss from income-producing property on Schedule A (Form 1040), line 27, and the part of the loss from property used as an employee on Schedule A (Form 1040), line 22. Identify as from "Form 4797, line 18b(1)." See instructions . **18b(1)**

 (2) Redetermine the gain or (loss) on line 18 excluding the loss, if any, on line 18b(1). Enter here and on Form 1040, line 14. **18b(2)** | 301,519

KFA **For Paperwork Reduction Act Notice, see page 7 of the instructions.** GF0US51 12/22/00 Form **4797** (2000)

Form **6251** — **Alternative Minimum Tax – Individuals** — OMB No. 1545-0227 — **2000**

Department of the Treasury Internal Revenue Service

▶ See separate instructions.

▶ Attach to Form 1040 or Form 1040NR.

Attachment Sequence No. 32

Name(s) shown on Form 1040	Your social security number
A. COMMODITIES TRADER PROFIT SEC475	123-45-6789

Part I Adjustments and Preferences

1	If you itemized deductions on Schedule A (Form 1040), go to line 2. Otherwise, enter your standard deduction from Form 1040, line 36, here and go to line 6	1	4,400
2	Medical and dental. Enter the smaller of Schedule A (Form 1040), line 4 **or** 2 1/2% of Form 1040, line 34	2	
3	Taxes. Enter the amount from Schedule A (Form 1040), line 9	3	
4	Certain interest on a home mortgage **not** used to buy, build, or improve your home	4	
5	Miscellaneous itemized deductions. Enter the amount from Schedule A (Form 1040), line 26	5	
6	Refund of taxes. Enter any tax refund from Form 1040, line 10 or line 21	6	( )
7	Investment interest. Enter difference between regular tax and AMT deduction	7	
8	Post-1986 depreciation. Enter difference between regular tax and AMT depreciation	8	
9	Adjusted gain or loss. Enter difference between AMT and regular tax gain or loss	9	
10	Incentive stock options. Enter excess of AMT income over regular tax income	10	
11	Passive activities. Enter difference between AMT and regular tax income or loss	11	
12	Beneficiaries of estates and trusts. Enter the amount from Schedule K-1 (Form 1041), line 9	12	
13	Tax-exempt interest from private activity bonds issued after 8/7/86	13	
14	Other. Enter the amount, if any, for each item below and enter the total on line 14.		

a Circulation expenditures		h Loss limitations	
b Depletion		i Mining costs	
c Depreciation (pre-1987)		j Patron's adjustment	
d Installment sales		k Pollution control facilities	
e Intangible drilling costs		l Research & experimental	
f Large partnerships		m Section 1202 exclusion	
g Long-term contracts		n Tax shelter farm activities	
		o Related adjustments	

		14	
15	**Total Adjustments and Preferences.** Combine lines 1 through 14 ▶	15	4,400

Part II Alternative Minimum Taxable Income

16	Enter the amount from **Form 1040, line 37.** If less than zero, enter as a (loss) ▶	16	496,441
17	Net operating loss deduction, if any, from Form 1040, line 21. Enter as a positive amount	17	
18	If Form 1040, line 34, is over $128,950 (over $64,475 if married filing separately), and you itemized deductions, enter the amount, if any, from line 9 of the worksheet for Schedule A (Form 1040), line 28	18	( )
19	Combine lines 15 through 18 ▶	19	500,841
20	Alternative tax net operating loss deduction. See page 6 of the instructions	20	
21	**Alternative Minimum Taxable Income.** Subtract line 20 from line 19. (If married filing separately and line 21 is more than $165,000, see page 7 of the instructions.) ▶	21	500,841

Part III Exemption Amount and Alternative Minimum Tax

22 **Exemption Amount.** (If this form is for a child under age 14, see page 7 of the instructions.)

IF your filing status is:	**AND line 21 is not over . . .**	**THEN enter on line 22 . . .**
Single or head of household	$112,500	$33,750
Married filing jointly or qualifying widow(er)	150,000	45,000
Married filing separately	75,000	22,500

If line 21 is **over** the amount shown above for your filing status, see page 7 of the instructions. — 22

23	Subtract line 22 from line 21. If zero or less, enter -0- here and on lines 26 and 28 and stop here ▶	23	500,841
24	If you reported capital gain distributions directly on Form 1040, line 13, **or** you completed Schedule D (Form 1040) and have an amount on line 25 or line 27 (or would have had an amount on either line if you had completed Part IV) (as refigured for the AMT, if necessary), go to Part IV of Form 6251 to figure line 24. **All others:** If line 23 is $175,000 or less ($87,500 or less if married filing separately), multiply line 23 by 26% (.26). Otherwise, multiply line 23 by 28% (.28) and subtract $3,500 ($1,750 if married filing separately) from the result ▶	24	136,735
25	Alternative minimum tax foreign tax credit. See page 7 of the instructions	25	
26	Tentative minimum tax. Subtract line 25 from line 24 ▶	26	136,735
27	Enter your tax from Form 1040, line 40 (minus any tax from Form 4972 and any foreign tax credit from Form 1040, line 43)	27	174,261
28	**Alternative Minimum Tax.** Subtract line 27 from line 26. If zero or less, enter -0-. Enter here and on Form 1040, line 41 ▶	28	0

For Paperwork Reduction Act Notice, see page 8 of the instructions. Form **6251** (2000)

KFA IFOUS33 10/23/00

Example 10

FORM 1040 Department of the Treasury – Internal Revenue Service
U.S. Individual Income Tax Return **2000** (99) IRS Use Only – Do not write or staple in this space.

For the year Jan. 1 – Dec. 31, 2000, or other tax year beginning , 2000, ending , 20 OMB No. 1545-0074

Label (See instructions on page 19.) Use the IRS label. Otherwise, please print or type.

LABEL HERE

Your first name and initial / Last name: COMMODITIES N. VESTOR-LOSS	Your social security number: 123-45-6789
If a joint return, spouse's first name and initial / Last name	Spouse's social security number
Home address (number and street). If you have a P.O. box, see page 19. Apt. no.: C/O TED TESSER-6274 LINTON BLVD. #102	▲ **IMPORTANT!** ▲ You **must** enter your SSN(s) above.
City, town or post office, state, and ZIP code. If you have a foreign address, see page 19.: DELRAY BEACH, FL 33484	

Presidential Election Campaign (See page 19.) **Note.** Checking "Yes" will not change your tax or reduce your refund.
Do you, or your spouse if filing a joint return, want $3 to go to this fund? ▶ You: ☐ Yes ☒ No Spouse: ☐ Yes ☐ No

Filing Status (Check only one box.)

1 [X] Single
2 [ ] Married filing joint return (even if only one had income)
3 [ ] Married filing separate return. Enter spouse's soc. sec. no. above & full name here ▶
4 [ ] Head of household (with qualifying person). (See page 19.) If the qualifying person is a child but not your dependent, enter this child's name here ▶
5 [ ] Qualifying widow(er) with dependent child (year spouse died ▶). (See page 19.)

Exemptions

6a ☒ **Yourself.** If your parent (or someone else) can claim you as a dependent on his or her tax return, **do not** check box 6a.
b ☐ **Spouse**
No. of boxes checked on 6a and 6b: 1

c **Dependents:**

(1) First Name Last name	(2) Dependent's social security number	(3) Dependent's relationship to you	(4) Chk if qualifying child for child tax credit (see page 20)

If more than six dependents, see page 20.

No. of your children on 6c who:
● lived with you ____
● did not live with you due to divorce or separation (see page 20) ____
Dependents on 6c not entered above ____
Add numbers entered on lines above ▶ 1

d Total number of exemptions claimed

Income

Attach Forms W-2 and W-2G here. Also attach Form 1099-R if tax was withheld.

If you did not get a W-2, see page 21.

Enclose, but do not attach any payment. Also, please use Form 1040-V.

Line	Description		Amount
7	Wages, salaries, tips, etc. Attach Form(s) W-2	7	200,000
8a	**Taxable** interest. Attach Schedule B if required	8a	
b	**Tax-exempt** interest. **Do not** include on line 8a — 8b		
9	Ordinary dividends. Attach Schedule B if required	9	
10	Taxable refunds, credits, or offsets of state and local income taxes (see page 22)	10	
11	Alimony received	11	
12	Business income or (loss). Attach Schedule C or C-EZ	12	
13	Capital gain or (loss). Attach Schedule D if required. If not required, check here ▶ ☐	13	-3,000
14	Other gains or (losses). Attach Form 4797	14	
15a	Total IRA distributions — 15a — b Taxable amount (see pg. 23)	15b	
16a	Total pensions and annuities — 16a — b Taxable amount (see pg. 23)	16b	
17	Rental real estate, royalties, partnerships, S corporations, trusts, etc. Attach Schedule E	17	200,000
18	Farm income or (loss). Attach Schedule F	18	
19	Unemployment compensation	19	
20a	Social security benefits — 20a — b Taxable amount (see pg. 25)	20b	
21	Other income.	21	
22	Add the amounts in the far right column for lines 7 through 21. This is your **total income** ▶	22	397,000

Adjusted Gross Income

Line	Description		Amount		Total
23	IRA deduction (see page 27)	23			
24	Student loan interest deduction (see page 27)	24			
25	Medical savings account deduction. Attach Form 8853	25			
26	Moving expenses. Attach Form 3903	26			
27	One-half of self-employment tax. Attach Schedule SE	27			
28	Self-employed health insurance deduction (see page 29)	28			
29	Self-employed SEP, SIMPLE, and qualified plans	29			
30	Penalty on early withdrawal of savings	30			
31a	Alimony paid. b Recipient's SSN ▶	31a			
32	Add lines 23 through 31a			32	0
33	Subtract line 32 from line 22. This is your **adjusted gross income** ▶			33	397,000

KFA **For Disclosure, Privacy Act, and Paperwork Reduction Act Notice, see page 56.** IF0US1 11/07/00 Form **1040** (2000)

Example 10 *(Continued)*

Form 1040 (2000) COMMODITIES N. VESTOR-LOSS 123-45-6789 Page **2**

Tax and Credits	34 Amount from line 33 (adjusted gross income)			34	397,000
	35a Check if: ☐ **You** were 65 or older, ☐ Blind; ☐ **Spouse** was 65 or older, ☐ Blind. Add the number of boxes checked above and enter the total here ▶ 35a				
Standard Deduction for Most People — Single: $4,400; Head of household: $6,450; Married filing jointly or Qualifying widow(er): $7,350; Married filing separately $3,675.	b If you are married filing separately and your spouse itemizes deductions, or you were a dual-status alien, see page 31 and check here ▶ 35b ☐				
	36 Enter your **itemized deductions** from Schedule A, line 28, **or standard deduction** shown on the left. **But** see page 31 to find your standard deduction if you checked any box on line 35a or 35b **or** if someone can claim you as a dependent			36	78,960
	37 Subtract line 36 from line 34			37	318,040
	38 If line 34 is $96,700 or less, multiply $2,800 by the total number of exemptions claimed on line 6d. If line 34 is over $96,700, see the worksheet on page 32 for the amount to enter			38	0
	39 **Taxable income.** Subtract line 38 from line 37. If line 38 is more than line 37, enter -0-			39	318,040
	40 **Tax** (see page 32). Check if any tax is from a ☐ Form(s) 8814 b ☐ Form 4972			40	103,614
	41 Alternative minimum tax. Attach Form 6251			41	4,046
	42 Add lines 40 and 41 ▶			42	107,660
	43 Foreign tax credit. Attach Form 1116 if required	43			
	44 Credit for child and dependent care expenses. Att. Form 2441	44			
	45 Credit for the elderly or the disabled. Attach Schedule R	45			
	46 Education credits. Attach Form 8863	46			
	47 Child tax credit (see page 36)	47			
	48 Adoption credit. Attach Form 8839	48			
	49 Other. Check if from a ☐ Form 3800 b ☐ Form 8396 c ☐ Form 8801 d ☐ Form (specify)	49			
	50 Add lines 43 through 49. These are your **total credits**			50	
	51 Subtract line 50 from line 42. If line 50 is more than line 42, enter -0- ▶			51	107,660
Other Taxes	52 Self-employment tax. Att. Sch. SE			52	
	53 Social security and Medicare tax on tip income not reported to employer. Attach Form 4137			53	
	54 Tax on IRAs, other retirement plans, and MSAs. Attach Form 5329 if required			54	
	55 Advance earned income credit payments from Form(s) W-2			55	
	56 Household employment taxes. Attach Schedule H			56	
	57 Add lines 51 through 56. This is your **total tax** ▶			57	107,660
Payments	58 Federal income tax withheld from Forms W-2 and 1099	58	60,000		
If you have a qualifying child, attach Schedule EIC.	59 2000 estimated tax payments and amount applied from 1999 return	59	50,000		
	60a **Earned income credit (EIC)**	60a			
	b **Nontaxable earned income: amt.** ▶ and type ▶ No				
	61 Excess social security and RRTA tax withheld (see page 50)	61			
	62 **Additional child tax credit. Attach Form 8812**	62			
	63 **Amount paid with request for extension to file** (see page 50)	63			
	64 Other payments. Check if from a ☐ Form 2439 b ☐ Form 4136	64			
	65 Add lines 58, 59, 60a, and 61 through 64. These are your **total payments** ▶			65	110,000
Refund	66 If line 65 is more than line 57, subtract line 57 from line 65. This is the amount you **overpaid**			66	2,340
Have it directly deposited! See page 50 and fill in 67b, 67c, and 67d.	67a Amount of line 66 you want **refunded to you** ▶			67a	2,340
	b Routing number ▶ c Type: ☐ Checking ☐ Savings				
	d Account number				
	68 Amount of line 66 you want **applied to your 2001 estimated tax** ▶	68			
Amount You Owe	69 If line 57 is more than line 65, subtract line 65 from line 57. This is the **amount you owe.** For details on how to pay, see page 51 ▶			69	
	70 Estimated tax penalty. Also include on line 69	70			

Sign Here

Joint return? See page 19. Keep a copy for your records.

Under penalties of perjury, I declare that I have examined this return and accompanying schedules and statements, and to the best of my knowledge and belief, they are true, correct, and complete. Declaration of preparer (other than taxpayer) is based on all information of which preparer has any knowledge.

Your signature	Date	Your occupation	Daytime phone number
Spouse's signature. If a joint return, **both** must sign.	Date	Spouse's occupation	May the IRS discuss this return with the preparer shown below? (see page 52)? ☒ Yes ☐ No

Paid Preparer's Use Only

Preparer's signature	Date	Check if self-employed ☐	Preparer's SSN or PTIN
Firm's name (or yours if self-employed), address, and ZIP code	Waterside Financial Serv., Inc 6274 Linton Blvd., Suite #102 Boca Raton, FL 33484	EIN 65-0664126	Phone no. (561) 865-0071

IFOUS1A 11/22/00 Form **1040** (2000)

Example 10 *(Continued)*

SCHEDULES A&B (Form 1040)
Department of the Treasury Internal Revenue Service (99)

Schedule A – Itemized Deductions

▶ Attach to Form 1040. ▶ See Instructions for Schedules A and B (Form 1040).

OMB No. 1545-0074
2000
Attachment Sequence No. 07

Name(s) shown on Form 1040: COMMODITIES N. VESTOR-LOSS
Your social security number: 123-45-6789

Section	Line	Description	Line	Amount	Line	Total
Medical and Dental Expenses		**Caution.** Do not include expenses reimbursed or paid by others.				
	1	Medical and dental expenses (see page A-2)	1			
	2	Enter amount from Form 1040, line 34 ... [2]				
	3	Multiply line 2 above by 7.5% (.075)	3			
	4	Subtract line 3 from line 1. If line 3 is more than line 1, enter -0-			4	0
Taxes You Paid	5	State and local income taxes	5			
	6	Real estate taxes (see page A-2)	6			
	7	Personal property taxes	7			
(See page A-2.)	8	Other taxes. List type and amount ▶	8			
	9	Add lines 5 through 8			9	0
Interest You Paid	10	Home mortgage interest and points reported on Form 1098	10			
(See page A-3.)	11	Home mortgage interest not reported to you on Form 1098. If paid to the person from whom you bought the home, see page A-3 & show that person's name, ID no. & address ▶	11			
Note. Personal interest is not deductible.	12	Points not reported to you on Form 1098. See pg. A-3	12			
	13	Investment interest. Attach Form 4952, if required. (See page A-3.)	13			
	14	Add lines 10 through 13			14	0
Gifts to Charity	15	Gifts by cash or check. If any gift of $250 or more, see pg. A-4	15			
If you made a gift and got a benefit for it, see page A-4.	16	Other than by cash or check. If any gift of $250 or more, see page A-4. You **must** attach Form 8283 if over $500	16			
	17	Carryover from prior year	17			
	18	Add lines 15 through 17			18	0
Casualty and Theft Losses	19	Casualty or theft loss(es). Attach Form 4684. (See page A-5.)			19	0
Job Expenses and Most Other Miscellaneous Deductions	20	Unreimbursed employee expenses – job travel, union dues, job education, etc. You **must** attach Form 2106 or 2106-EZ if required. (See page A-5.) ▶	20			
	21	Tax preparation fees	21			
(See page A-5 for expenses to deduct here.)	22	Other expenses – investment, safe deposit box, etc. List type and amount ▶ Depreciation 5,000; Investment Expenses 89,942	22	94,942		
	23	Add lines 20 through 22	23	94,942		
	24	Enter amount from Form 1040, line 34 ... [24] 397,000				
	25	Multiply line 24 above by 2% (.02)	25	7,940		
	26	Subtract line 25 from line 23. If line 25 is more than line 23, enter -0-			26	87,002
Other Miscellaneous Deductions	27	Other – from list on page A-6. List type and amount ▶			27	0
Total Itemized Deductions	28	Is Form 1040, line 34, over $128,950 (over $64,475 if married filing separately)? ☐ **No.** Your deduction is not limited. Add the amounts in the far right column for lines 4 through 27. Also, enter this amount on Form 1040, line 36. ☒ **Yes.** Your deduction may be limited. See page A-6 for the amount to enter. Reduction -8,042 ▶			28	78,960

KFA **For Paperwork Reduction Act Notice, see Form 1040 instructions.** IFOUS2 11/03/00 **Schedule A (Form 1040) 2000**

SCHEDULE D (Form 1040)

Department of the Treasury Internal Revenue Service (99)

Capital Gains and Losses

▶ Attach to Form 1040. ▶ See Instructions for Schedule D (Form 1040).
▶ Use Schedule D-1 for more space to list transactions for lines 1 and 8.

OMB No. 1545-0074
2000
Attachment Sequence No. **12**

Name(s) shown on Form 1040: COMMODITIES N. VESTOR-LOSS

Your social security number: 123-45-6789

Part I Short-Term Capital Gains and Losses - Assets Held One Year or Less

1 (a) Description of property (Example, 100 sh. XYZ Co.)	(b) Date acquired (Mo., day, yr.)	(c) Date sold (Mo., day, yr.)	(d) Sales price (see page D-6)	(e) Cost or other basis (see page D-6)	(f) Gain or (loss) Subtract (e) from (d)

2 Enter your short-term totals, if any, from Schedule D-1, line 2	2	
3 **Total short-term sales price amounts.** Add column (d) of lines 1 and 2	3	
4 Short-term gain from Form 6252 and short-term gain or (loss) from Forms 4684, 6781, and 8824	4	-40,000
5 Net short-term gain or (loss) from partnerships, S corporations, estates, and trusts from Schedule(s) K-1	5	
6 Short-term capital loss carryover. Enter the amount, if any, from line 8 of your 1999 Capital Loss Carryover Worksheet	6	( )
7 **Net short-term capital gain or (loss).** Combine column (f) of lines 1 through 6 ▶	7	-40,000

Part II Long-Term Capital Gains and Losses - Assets Held More Than One Year

8 (a) Description of property (Example, 100 sh. XYZ Co.)	(b) Date acquired (Mo., day, yr.)	(c) Date sold (Mo., day, yr.)	(d) Sales price (see page D-6)	(e) Cost or other basis (see page D-6)	(f) Gain or (loss) Subtract (e) from (d)	(g) 28% rate gain or (loss) *(see instr. below)

	Line	(f)	(g)
9 Enter your long-term totals, if any, from Schedule D-1, line 9	9		
10 **Total long-term sales price amounts.** Add column (d) of lines 8 and 9	10		
11 Gain from Form 4797, Part I; long-term gain from Forms 2439 and 6252; and long-term gain or (loss) from Forms 4684, 6781, and 8824	11	-60,000	
12 Net long-term gain or (loss) from partnerships, S corporations, estates, and trusts from Schedule(s) K-1	12		
13 Capital gain distributions. See page D-1	13		
14 Long-term capital loss carryover. Enter in both columns (f) and (g) the amount, if any, from line 13 of your 1999 Capital Loss Carryover Worksheet	14	( )	( )
15 Combine column (g) of lines 8 through 14	15		
16 **Net long-term capital gain or (loss).** Combine column (f) of lines 8 through 14 ▶	16	-60,000	

Next: Go to Part III on the back.

* **28% rate gain or loss** includes **all** "collectibles gains and losses" (as defined on page D-6) and up to 50% of the eligible gain on qualified small business stock (see page D-4).

For Paperwork Reduction Act Notice, see Form 1040 instructions. **Schedule D (Form 1040) 2000**

KFA IFOUS5 12/07/00

Schedule D (Form 1040) 2000 COMMODITIES N. VESTOR-LOSS | 123-45-6789 Page 2

Part III Summary of Parts I and II

17 Combine lines 7 and 16. If a loss, go to line 18. If a gain, enter the gain on Form 1040, line 13	17	-100,000
Next: Complete Form 1040 through line 39. Then, go to **Part IV** to figure your tax if: • Both lines 16 and 17 are gains **and** • Form 1040, line 39, is more than zero. Otherwise, **stop here.**		
18 If line 17 is a loss, enter here and as a (loss) on Form 1040, line 13, the **smaller** of these losses: • The loss on line 17 **or** • ($3,000) or, if married filing separately, ($1,500)	18	(3,000)
Next: Skip **Part IV** below. Instead, complete Form 1040 through line 37. Then, complete the **Capital Loss Carryover Worksheet** on page D-6 if: • The loss on line 17 exceeds the loss on line 18 **or** • Form 1040, line 37, is a loss.		

Part IV Tax Computation Using Maximum Capital Gains Rates

19 Enter your taxable income from Form 1040, line 39			19	
20 Enter the **smaller** of line 16 or line 17 of Schedule D	20			
21 If you are filing Form 4952, enter the amount from Form 4952, line 4e	21			
22 Subtract line 21 from line 20. If zero or less, enter -0-	22			
23 Combine lines 7 and 15. If zero or less, enter -0-	23			
24 Enter the **smaller** of line 15 or line 23, but not less than zero	24			
25 Enter your unrecaptured section 1250 gain, if any, from line 17 of the worksheet on page D-8	25			
26 Add lines 24 and 25	26			
27 Subtract line 26 from line 22. If zero or less, enter -0-			27	
28 Subtract line 27 from line 19. If zero or less, enter -0-			28	
29 Enter the **smaller** of: • The amount on line 19 **or** • $26,250 if single; $43,850 if married filing jointly or qualifying widow(er); $21,925 if married filing separately; or $35,150 if head of household			29	
30 Enter the **smaller** of line 28 or line 29	30			
31 Subtract line 22 from line 19. If zero or less, enter -0-	31			
32 Enter the **larger** of line 30 or line 31	▶ 32			
33 Figure the tax on the amount on line 32. Use the Tax Table or Tax Rate Schedules, whichever applies			33	
Note: If the amounts on lines 29 and 30 are the same, skip lines 34 through 37 and go to line 38.				
34 Enter the amount from line 29	34			
35 Enter the amount from line 30	35			
36 Subtract line 35 from line 34	▶ 36			
37 Multiply line 36 by 10% (.10)			37	
Note: If the amounts on lines 19 and 29 are the same, skip lines 38 through 51 and go to line 52.				
38 Enter the **smaller** of line 19 or line 27	38			
39 Enter the amount from line 36	39			
40 Subtract line 39 from line 38	▶ 40			
41 Multiply line 40 by 20% (.20)			41	
Note: If line 26 is zero or blank, skip lines 42 through 51 and go to line 52.				
42 Enter the **smaller** of line 22 or line 25	42			
43 Add lines 22 and 32	43			
44 Enter the amount from line 19	44			
45 Subtract line 44 from line 43. If zero or less, enter -0-	45			
46 Subtract line 45 from line 42. If zero or less, enter -0-	▶ 46			
47 Multiply line 46 by 25% (.25)			47	
Note: If line 24 is zero or blank, skip lines 48 through 51 and go to line 52.				
48 Enter the amount from line 19	48			
49 Add lines 32, 36, 40, and 46	49			
50 Subtract line 49 from line 48	50			
51 Multiply line 50 by 28% (.28)			51	
52 Add lines 33, 37, 41, 47, and 51			52	
53 Figure the tax on the amount on line 19. Use the Tax Table or Tax Rate Schedules, whichever applies			53	
54 **Tax on all taxable income (including capital gains).** Enter the **smaller** of line 52 or line 53 here and on Form 1040, line 40			54	

IFOUS5A 10/24/00 **Schedule D (Form 1040) 2000**

Schedule E (Form 1040) 2000 — Attachment Sequence No. 13 — Page 2

Name(s) shown on return. Do not enter name and social security number if shown on other side.

COMMODITIES N. VESTOR-LOSS

Your social security number: 123-45-6789

Note: If you report amounts from farming or fishing on Schedule E, you must enter your gross income from those activities on line 41 below. Real estate professionals must complete line 42 below.

Part II — Income or Loss From Partnerships and S Corporations If you report a loss from an at-risk activity, you **must** check either column **(e)** or **(f)** on line 27 to describe your investment in the activity. See page E-5. If you check column **(f)**, you must attach **Form 6198.**

27	(a) Name	(b) Enter P for partnership; S for S corp.	(c) Check if foreign partnership	(d) Employer identification number	Invest. At Risk? (e) All is at risk	(f) Some is not at risk
A	1	P				
B						
C						
D						
E						

	Passive Income and Loss: (g) Passive loss allowed (attach Form 8582 if required)	(h) Passive income from Schedule K-1	Nonpassive Income and Loss: (i) Nonpassive loss from Schedule K-1	(j) Section 179 expense deduction from Form 4562	(k) Nonpassive income from Schedule K-1
A		200,000			
B					
C					
D					
E					
28a Totals		200,000			
b Totals					

29	Add columns (h) and (k) of line 28a	29 200,000
30	Add columns (g), (i), and (j) of line 28b	30 ( )
31	Total partnership and S corporation income or (loss). Combine lines 29 and 30. Enter the result here and include in the total on line 40 below	31 200,000

Part III — Income or Loss From Estates and Trusts

32	(a) Name	(b) Employer ID number
A		
B		
C		
D		

	Passive Income and Loss: (c) Passive deduction or loss allowed (attach Form 8582 if required)	(d) Passive income from Schedule K-1	Nonpassive Income and Loss: (e) Deduction or loss from Schedule K-1	(f) Other income from Schedule K-1
A				
B				
C				
D				
33a Totals				
b Totals				

34	Add columns (d) and (f) of line 33a	34
35	Add columns (c) and (e) of line 33b	35 ( )
36	Total estate and trust income or (loss). Combine lines 34 and 35. Enter the result here and include in the total on line 40 below	36

Part IV — Income or Loss From Real Estate Mortgage Investment Conduits (REMICs) – Residual Holder

37	(a) Name	(b) Employer identification number	(c) Excess inclusion from Schedules Q, line 2c (see page E-6)	(d) Taxable income (net loss) from Schedules Q, line 1b	(e) Income from Schedules Q, line 3b

38 Combine columns (d) and (e) only. Enter the result here and include in the total on line 40 below — 38

Part V — Summary

39	Net farm rental income or (loss) from **Form 4835.** Also, complete line 41 below	39
40	**Total** income or (loss). Combine lines 26, 31, 36, 38, and 39. Enter the result here and on Form 1040, line 17 ▶	40 200,000
41	**Reconciliation of Farming and Fishing Income:** Enter your **gross** farming and fishing income reported on Form 4835, line 7; Schedule K-1 (Form 1065), line 15b; Schedule K-1 (Form 1120S), line 23; and Schedule K-1 (Form 1041), line 14 (see page E-6)	41
42	**Reconciliation for Real Estate Professionals.** If you were real estate professional (see pg. E-4), enter net income or (loss) you reported anywhere on Form 1040 from all rental real estate activities in which you materially participated under passive activity loss rules.	42

IF0US7A 10/19/00 — Schedule E (Form 1040) 2000

Form **4562** — Department of the Treasury, Internal Revenue Service (99)

Depreciation and Amortization
(Including Information on Listed Property)

▶ See separate instructions. ▶ Attach this form to your return.

OMB No. 1545-0172 — **2000** — Attachment Sequence No. **67**

Name(s) shown on return: COMMODITIES N. VESTOR-LOSS — Identifying number: 123-45-6789

Business or activity to which this form relates

Part I Election To Expense Certain Tangible Property (Section 179) Note: If you have any "listed property," complete Part V before you complete Part I.

1	Maximum dollar limitation. If an enterprise zone business, see page 2 of the instructions	1	$20,000
2	Total cost of section 179 property placed in service. See page 2 of the instructions	2	
3	Threshold cost of section 179 property before reduction in limitation	3	$200,000
4	Reduction in limitation. Subtract line 3 from line 2. If zero or less, enter -0-	4	
5	Dollar limitation for tax year. Subtract line 4 from line 1. If zero or less, enter -0-. If married filing separately, see page 2 of the instructions	5	

6 (a) Description of property	(b) Cost (business use only)	(c) Elected cost

7	Listed property. Enter amount from line 27	7	
8	Total elected cost of section 179 property. Add amounts in column (c), lines 6 and 7	8	
9	Tentative deduction. Enter the smaller of line 5 or line 8	9	
10	Carryover of disallowed deduction from 1999. See page 3 of the instructions	10	
11	Business income limitation. Enter the smaller of business income (not less than zero) or line 5 (see instructions)	11	
12	Section 179 expense deduction. Add lines 9 and 10, but do not enter more than line 11	12	
13	Carryover of disallowed deduction to 2001. Add lines 9 and 10, less line 12 ▶	13	

Note: Do not use Part II or Part III below for listed property (automobiles, certain other vehicles, cellular telephones, certain computers, or property used for entertainment, recreation, or amusement). Instead, use Part V for listed property.

Part II MACRS Depreciation for Assets Placed in Service Only During Your 2000 Tax Year (**Do not** include listed property.)

Section A - General Asset Account Election

14 If you are making the election under section 168(i)(4) to group any assets placed in service during the tax year into one or more general asset accounts, check this box. See page 3 of the instructions ▶ ☐

Section B - General Depreciation System (GDS) (See page 3 of the instructions.)

(a) Classification of property	(b) Month and year placed in service	(c) Basis for depreciation (business/investment use only - see instructions)	(d) Recovery period	(e) Convention	(f) Method	(g) Depreciation deduction
15a 3-year property						
b 5-year property						
c 7-year property						
d 10-year property						
e 15-year property						
f 20-year property						
g 25-year property			25 yrs		S/L	
h Residential rental property			27.5 yrs	MM	S/L	
			27.5 yrs	MM	S/L	
i Nonresidential real property			39 yrs	MM	S/L	
				MM	S/L	

Section C - Alternative Depreciation System (ADS): (See page 5 of the instructions.)

(a) Classification of property	(b) Month and year placed in service	(c) Basis for depreciation	(d) Recovery period	(e) Convention	(f) Method	(g) Depreciation deduction
16a Class life					S/L	
b 12-year			12 yrs		S/L	
c 40-year			40 yrs	MM	S/L	

Part III Other Depreciation (**Do not** include listed property.) (See page 5 of the instructions.)

17	GDS and ADS deductions for assets placed in service in tax years beginning before 2000	17	
18	Property subject to section 168(f)(1) election	18	
19	ACRS and other depreciation	19	5,000

Part IV Summary (See page 6 of the instructions.)

20	Listed property. Enter amount from line 26	20	
21	**Total.** Add deductions from line 12, lines 15 and 16 in column (g), and lines 17 through 20. Enter here and on the appropriate lines of your return. Partnerships and S corporations - see instructions	21	5,000
22	For assets shown above and placed in service during the current year, enter the portion of the basis attributable to section 263A costs	22	

KFA **For Paperwork Reduction Act Notice, see page 9 of the instructions.** GF0US7 10/26/00 Form **4562** (2000)

Example 10 *(Continued)*

Form **4952** Department of the Treasury Internal Revenue Service (99)

Investment Interest Expense Deduction

▶ Attach to your tax return.

OMB No. 1545-0191 **2000** Attachment Sequence No. **72**

Name(s) shown on return	Identifying number
COMMODITIES N. VESTOR-LOSS	123-45-6789

Part I Total Investment Interest Expense

1	Investment interest expense paid or accrued in 2000. See instructions	1	51,357
2	Disallowed investment interest expense from 1999 Form 4952, line 7	2	
3	**Total investment interest expense.** Add lines 1 and 2	3	51,357

Part II Net Investment Income

4a	Gross income from property held for investment (excluding any net gain from the disposition of property held for investment)			4a	
b	Net gain from the disposition of property held for investment	4b			
c	Net capital gain from the disposition of property held for investment	4c			
d	Subtract line 4c from line 4b. If zero or less, enter -0-			4d	0
e	Enter all or part of the amount on line 4c, if any, that you elect to include in investment income. Do not enter more than the amount on line 4b. See instructions ▶			4e	
f	Investment income. Add lines 4a, 4d, and 4e. See instructions			4f	
5	Investment expenses. See instructions			5	
6	**Net investment income.** Subtract line 5 from line 4f. If zero or less, enter -0-			6	0

Part III Investment Interest Expense Deduction

7	Disallowed investment interest expense to be carried forward to 2001. Subtract line 6 from line 3. If zero or less, enter -0-	7	51,357
8	**Investment interest expense deduction.** Enter the **smaller** of line 3 or 6. See instructions	8	0

For Paperwork Reduction Act Notice, see back. Form **4952** (2000)

KFA IFOUS29 10/24/00

Example 10 *(Continued)*

Form **6251** — Department of the Treasury, Internal Revenue Service

Alternative Minimum Tax - Individuals

▶ See separate instructions.
▶ Attach to Form 1040 or Form 1040NR.

OMB No. 1545-0227 — **2000** — Attachment Sequence No. **32**

Name(s) shown on Form 1040: COMMODITIES N. VESTOR-LOSS — Your social security number: 123-45-6789

Part I Adjustments and Preferences

1 If you itemized deductions on Schedule A (Form 1040), go to line 2. Otherwise, enter your standard deduction from Form 1040, line 36, here and go to line 6	1	
2 Medical and dental. Enter the smaller of Schedule A (Form 1040), line 4 **or** 2 1/2% of Form 1040, line 34	2	
3 Taxes. Enter the amount from Schedule A (Form 1040), line 9	3	
4 Certain interest on a home mortgage **not** used to buy, build, or improve your home	4	
5 Miscellaneous itemized deductions. Enter the amount from Schedule A (Form 1040), line 26	5	87,002
6 Refund of taxes. Enter any tax refund from Form 1040, line 10 or line 21	6	( )
7 Investment interest. Enter difference between regular tax and AMT deduction	7	
8 Post-1986 depreciation. Enter difference between regular tax and AMT depreciation	8	
9 Adjusted gain or loss. Enter difference between AMT and regular tax gain or loss	9	
10 Incentive stock options. Enter excess of AMT income over regular tax income	10	
11 Passive activities. Enter difference between AMT and regular tax income or loss	11	
12 Beneficiaries of estates and trusts. Enter the amount from Schedule K-1 (Form 1041), line 9	12	
13 Tax-exempt interest from private activity bonds issued after 8/7/86	13	
14 Other. Enter the amount, if any, for each item below and enter the total on line 14.		

a Circulation expenditures		h Loss limitations	
b Depletion		i Mining costs	
c Depreciation (pre-1987)		j Patron's adjustment	
d Installment sales		k Pollution control facilities	
e Intangible drilling costs		l Research & experimental	
f Large partnerships		m Section 1202 exclusion	
g Long-term contracts		n Tax shelter farm activities	
		o Related adjustments	

14	14	
15 **Total Adjustments and Preferences.** Combine lines 1 through 14 ▶	15	87,002

Part II Alternative Minimum Taxable Income

16 Enter the amount from **Form 1040, line 37.** If less than zero, enter as a (loss) ▶	16	318,040
17 Net operating loss deduction, if any, from Form 1040, line 21. Enter as a positive amount	17	
18 If Form 1040, line 34, is over $128,950 (over $64,475 if married filing separately), and you itemized deductions, enter the amount, if any, from line 9 of the worksheet for Schedule A (Form 1040), line 28	18	(8,042)
19 Combine lines 15 through 18 ▶	19	397,000
20 Alternative tax net operating loss deduction. See page 6 of the instructions	20	
21 **Alternative Minimum Taxable Income.** Subtract line 20 from line 19. (If married filing separately and line 21 is more than $165,000, see page 7 of the instructions.) ▶	21	397,000

Part III Exemption Amount and Alternative Minimum Tax

22 **Exemption Amount.** (If this form is for a child under age 14, see page 7 of the instructions.)

IF your filing status is:	**AND line 21 is not over . . .**	**THEN enter on line 22 . . .**
Single or head of household	$112,500	$33,750
Married filing jointly or qualifying widow(er)	150,000	45,000
Married filing separately	75,000	22,500

If line 21 is **over** the amount shown above for your filing status, see page 7 of the instructions.

22	22	
23 Subtract line 22 from line 21. If zero or less, enter -0- here and on lines 26 and 28 and stop here ▶	23	397,000
24 If you reported capital gain distributions directly on Form 1040, line 13, **or** you completed Schedule D (Form 1040) and have an amount on line 25 or line 27 (or would have had an amount on either line if you had completed Part IV) (as refigured for the AMT, if necessary), go to Part IV of Form 6251 to figure line 24. **All others:** If line 23 is $175,000 or less ($87,500 or less if married filing separately), multiply line 23 by 26% (.26). Otherwise, multiply line 23 by 28% (.28) and subtract $3,500 ($1,750 if married filing separately) from the result ▶	24	107,660
25 Alternative minimum tax foreign tax credit. See page 7 of the instructions	25	
26 Tentative minimum tax. Subtract line 25 from line 24 ▶	26	107,660
27 Enter your tax from Form 1040, line 40 (minus any tax from Form 4972 and any foreign tax credit from Form 1040, line 43)	27	103,614
28 **Alternative Minimum Tax.** Subtract line 27 from line 26. If zero or less, enter -0-. Enter here and on Form 1040, line 41 ▶	28	4,046

For Paperwork Reduction Act Notice, see page 8 of the instructions. Form **6251** (2000)

KFA IFOUS33 10/23/00

Example 10 *(Continued)*

Form **6781**

Department of the Treasury
Internal Revenue Service

Gains and Losses From Section 1256 Contracts and Straddles

▶ **Attach to your tax return.**

OMB No. 1545-0644

2000

Attachment Sequence No. **82**

Name(s) shown on tax return: COMMODITIES N. VESTOR-LOSS

Identifying number: 123-45-6789

Check applicable box(es) (see instructions):
A ☐ Mixed straddle election
B ☐ Straddle-by-straddle identification election
C ☐ Mixed straddle account election
D ☐ Net section 1256 contracts loss election

Part I — Section 1256 Contracts Marked to Market

1 (a) Identification of account	(b) (Loss)	(c) Gain
	100,000	

Line	Description	Box	Amount
2	Add amounts on line 1 in columns (b) and (c).	2	(100,000)
3	Net gain or (loss). Combine columns (b) and (c) of line 2	3	-100,000
4	Form 1099-B adjustments. See instructions and attach schedule	4	
5	Combine lines 3 and 4	5	-100,000
	Note: If line 5 shows a net gain, skip line 6 and enter the gain on line 7. Partnerships and S corporations, see instructions.		
6	If you have a net section 1256 contracts loss and checked box D, enter the amount to be carried back	6	
7	Subtract line 6 from line 5	7	-100,000
8	Short-term capital gain or (loss). Multiply line 7 by 40%. Enter here and include on Schedule D. See instructions	8	-40,000
9	Long-term capital gain or (loss). Multiply line 7 by 60%. Enter here and include on Schedule D. See instructions	9	-60,000

Part II — Gains and Losses From Straddles. Attach a separate schedule listing each straddle and its components.

Section A – Losses From Straddles

10 (a) Description of property	(b) Date entered into or acquired	(c) Date closed out or sold	(d) Gross sales price	(e) Cost or other basis plus expense of sale	(f) Loss. If column (e) is more than (d), enter difference. Otherwise, enter -0-	(g) Unrecognized gain on offsetting positions	(h) Recognized loss. If column (f) is more than (g), enter difference. Otherwise, enter -0-	*(i) 28% rate loss (see instr. below)

11a Enter short-term portion of line 10, column (h), losses here and include on Schedule D. See instructions. . . . . . 11a ( )

b Enter long-term portion of losses from line 10, columns (h) and (i), here and include on Schedule D. See instrs . 11b ( ) ( )

Section B – Gains From Straddles

12 (a) Description of property	(b) Date entered into or acquired	(c) Date closed out or sold	(d) Gross sales price	(e) Cost or other basis plus expense of sale	(f) Gain. If column (d) is more than (e), enter diff. Otherwise, enter 0	*(g) 28% Rate gain (see instr. below)

13a Enter short-term portion of line 12, column (f), gains here and include on Schedule D. See instructions . . . 13a

b Enter long-term portion of gains from line 12, columns (f) and (g), here and include on Sch D. See instrs . 13b

Part III — Unrecognized Gains From Positions Held on Last Day of Tax Year. Memo Entry Only – See instructions.

14 (a) Description of property	(b) Date acquired	(c) Fair market value on last business day of tax year	(d) Cost or other basis as adjusted	(e) Unrecognized gain. If column (c) is more than (d), enter difference. Otherwise, enter -0-

*28% Rate Gain or Loss includes all "collectibles gains and losses" and up to 50% of the eligible gain on qualified small business stock. See instructions for Schedule D (Form 1040).

For Paperwork Reduction Act Notice, see page 3.
KFA
GF0US16 12/27/00
Form **6781** (2000)

Example 11

FORM 1040 Department of the Treasury – Internal Revenue Service
U.S. Individual Income Tax Return 2000 (99) IRS Use Only – Do not write or staple in this space.

For the year Jan. 1 – Dec. 31, 2000, or other tax year beginning , 2000, ending , 20 OMB No. 1545-0074

Label (See instructions on page 19.) Use the IRS label. Otherwise, please print or type. LABEL HERE

Your first name and initial / Last name: A. COMMODITIES TRADER LOSS NO 475

Your social security number: 123-45-6789

If a joint return, spouse's first name and initial / Last name

Spouse's social security number

Home address (number and street). If you have a P.O. box, see page 19. Apt. no.: C/O TED TESSER-6274 LINTON BLVD. #102

City, town or post office, state, and ZIP code. If you have a foreign address, see page 19.: DELRAY BEACH, FL 33484

▲ **IMPORTANT!** ▲ You **must** enter your SSN(s) above.

Presidential Election Campaign (See page 19.) **Note.** Checking "Yes" will not change your tax or reduce your refund.
Do you, or your spouse if filing a joint return, want $3 to go to this fund? ▶ You: ☐ Yes ☒ No   Spouse: ☐ Yes ☐ No

Filing Status (Check only one box.)

1 [X] Single
2 [ ] Married filing joint return (even if only one had income)
3 [ ] Married filing separate return. Enter spouse's soc. sec. no. above & full name here ▶
4 [ ] Head of household (with qualifying person). (See page 19.) If the qualifying person is a child but not your dependent, enter this child's name here ▶
5 [ ] Qualifying widow(er) with dependent child (year spouse died ▶). (See page 19.)

Exemptions

6a ☒ **Yourself.** If your parent (or someone else) can claim you as a dependent on his or her tax return, **do not** check box 6a.
b ☐ **Spouse**

No. of boxes checked on 6a and 6b: 1

c **Dependents:**

(1) First Name Last name	(2) Dependent's social security number	(3) Dependent's relationship to you	(4) Chk if qualifying child for child tax credit (see page 20)

If more than six dependents, see page 20.

No. of your children on 6c who:
● lived with you
● did not live with you due to divorce or separation (see page 20)
Dependents on 6c not entered above
Add numbers entered on lines above ▶ 1

d Total number of exemptions claimed

Income

Attach Forms W-2 and W-2G here. Also attach Form 1099-R if tax was withheld.

If you did not get a W-2, see page 21.

Enclose, but do not attach any payment. Also, please use Form 1040-V.

7	Wages, salaries, tips, etc. Attach Form(s) W-2	7	200,000
8a	**Taxable** interest. Attach Schedule B if required	8a	
b	**Tax-exempt** interest. **Do not** include on line 8a ... 8b		
9	Ordinary dividends. Attach Schedule B if required	9	
10	Taxable refunds, credits, or offsets of state and local income taxes (see page 22)	10	
11	Alimony received	11	
12	Business income or (loss). Attach Schedule C or C-EZ	12	-182,528
13	Capital gain or (loss). Attach Schedule D if required. If not required, check here ▶ ☐	13	-3,000
14	Other gains or (losses). Attach Form 4797	14	
15a	Total IRA distributions ... 15a ... b Taxable amount (see pg. 23)	15b	
16a	Total pensions and annuities ... 16a ... b Taxable amount (see pg. 23)	16b	
17	Rental real estate, royalties, partnerships, S corporations, trusts, etc. Attach Schedule E	17	200,000
18	Farm income or (loss). Attach Schedule F	18	
19	Unemployment compensation	19	
20a	Social security benefits ... 20a ... b Taxable amount (see pg. 25)	20b	
21	Other income.	21	
22	Add the amounts in the far right column for lines 7 through 21. This is your **total income** ▶	22	214,472

Adjusted Gross Income

23	IRA deduction (see page 27)	23			
24	Student loan interest deduction (see page 27)	24			
25	Medical savings account deduction. Attach Form 8853	25			
26	Moving expenses. Attach Form 3903	26			
27	One-half of self-employment tax. Attach Schedule SE	27			
28	Self-employed health insurance deduction (see page 29)	28			
29	Self-employed SEP, SIMPLE, and qualified plans	29			
30	Penalty on early withdrawal of savings	30			
31a	Alimony paid. b Recipient's SSN ▶	31a			
32	Add lines 23 through 31a			32	0
33	Subtract line 32 from line 22. This is your **adjusted gross income** ▶			33	214,472

KFA **For Disclosure, Privacy Act, and Paperwork Reduction Act Notice, see page 56.** IFOUS1 11/07/00 Form **1040** (2000)

Example 11 *(Continued)*

Form 1040 (2000) A. COMMODITIES TRADER LOSS NO 475 — 123-45-6789 Page **2**

Tax and Credits

Line	Description		Amount
34	Amount from line 33 (adjusted gross income)		214,472
35a	Check if: ☐ **You** were 65 or older, ☐ Blind; ☐ **Spouse** was 65 or older, ☐ Blind. Add the number of boxes checked above and enter the total here ▶ 35a		
b	If you are married filing separately and your spouse itemizes deductions, or you were a dual-status alien, see page 31 and check here ▶ 35b ☐		
36	Enter your **itemized deductions** from Schedule A, line 28, **or standard deduction** shown on the left. **But** see page 31 to find your standard deduction if you checked any box on line 35a or 35b **or** if someone can claim you as a dependent		4,400
37	Subtract line 36 from line 34		210,072
38	If line 34 is $96,700 or less, multiply $2,800 by the total number of exemptions claimed on line 6d. If line 34 is over $96,700, see the worksheet on page 32 for the amount to enter		840
39	**Taxable income.** Subtract line 38 from line 37. If line 38 is more than line 37, enter -0-		209,232
40	**Tax** (see page 32). Check if any tax is from **a** ☐ Form(s) 8814 **b** ☐ Form 4972		63,375
41	Alternative minimum tax. Attach Form 6251		
42	Add lines 40 and 41 ▶		63,375
43	Foreign tax credit. Attach Form 1116 if required		
44	Credit for child and dependent care expenses. Att. Form 2441		
45	Credit for the elderly or the disabled. Attach Schedule R		
46	Education credits. Attach Form 8863		
47	Child tax credit (see page 36)		
48	Adoption credit. Attach Form 8839		
49	Other. Check if from **a** ☐ Form 3800 **b** ☐ Form 8396 **c** ☐ Form 8801 **d** ☐ Form (specify)		
50	Add lines 43 through 49. These are your **total credits**		
51	Subtract line 50 from line 42. If line 50 is more than line 42, enter -0- ▶		63,375

Standard Deduction for Most People
Single: $4,400
Head of household: $6,450
Married filing jointly or Qualifying widow(er): $7,350
Married filing separately $3,675.

Other Taxes

Line	Description		Amount
52	Self-employment tax. Att. Sch. SE		
53	Social security and Medicare tax on tip income not reported to employer. Attach Form 4137		
54	Tax on IRAs, other retirement plans, and MSAs. Attach Form 5329 if required		
55	Advance earned income credit payments from Form(s) W-2		
56	Household employment taxes. Attach Schedule H		
57	Add lines 51 through 56. This is your **total tax** ▶		63,375

Payments

If you have a qualifying child, attach Schedule EIC.

Line	Description		Amount
58	Federal income tax withheld from Forms W-2 and 1099	60,000	
59	2000 estimated tax payments and amount applied from 1999 return	50,000	
60a	**Earned income credit (EIC)**		
b	**Nontaxable earned income: amt.** ▶ **and type** ▶ No		
61	Excess social security and RRTA tax withheld (see page 50)		
62	**Additional child tax credit. Attach Form 8812**		
63	**Amount paid with request for extension to file** (see page 50)		
64	Other payments. Check if from **a** ☐ Form 2439 **b** ☐ Form 4136		
65	Add lines 58, 59, 60a, and 61 through 64. These are your **total payments** ▶		110,000

Refund

Have it directly deposited! See page 50 and fill in 67b, 67c, and 67d.

Line	Description		Amount
66	If line 65 is more than line 57, subtract line 57 from line 65. This is the amount you **overpaid**		46,625
67a	Amount of line 66 you want **refunded to you** ▶		46,625
b	Routing number ▶ **c** Type: ☐ Checking ☐ Savings		
d	Account number		
68	Amount of line 66 you want **applied to your 2001 estimated tax** ▶		

Amount You Owe

Line	Description		Amount
69	If line 57 is more than line 65, subtract line 65 from line 57. This is the **amount you owe.** For details on how to pay, see page 51 ▶		
70	Estimated tax penalty. Also include on line 69		

Sign Here

Joint return? See page 19. Keep a copy for your records.

Under penalties of perjury, I declare that I have examined this return and accompanying schedules and statements, and to the best of my knowledge and belief, they are true, correct, and complete. Declaration of preparer (other than taxpayer) is based on all information of which preparer has any knowledge.

Your signature	Date	Your occupation	Daytime phone number
			561-865-0071
Spouse's signature. If a joint return, **both** must sign.	Date	Spouse's occupation	May the IRS discuss this return with the preparer shown below? (see page 52)? ☒ Yes ☐ No

Paid Preparer's Use Only

Preparer's signature ▶	Date	Check if self-employed ☐	Preparer's SSN or PTIN
Firm's name (or yours if self-employed), address, and ZIP code ▶	Waterside Financial Services 6274 Linton Blvd., Suite #102 Delray Beach, FL 33484	EIN	Phone no. (561) 865-0071

IFOUS1A 11/22/00 — Form **1040** (2000)

SCHEDULE C (Form 1040)
Department of the Treasury Internal Revenue Service (99)

Profit or Loss From Business
(Sole Proprietorship)

▶ Partnerships, joint ventures, etc., must file Form 1065 or Form 1065-B.
▶ Attach to Form 1040 or Form 1041. ▶ See Instructions for Schedule C (Form 1040).

OMB No. 1545-0074
2000
Attachment Sequence No. **09**

Name of proprietor: A. COMMODITIES TRADER LOSS NO 475
Social security number (SSN): 123-45-6789

A Principal business or profession, including product or service (see page C-1 of the instructions): TRADER
B Enter code from pages C-7 & 8: ▶ 523900
C Business name. If no separate business name, leave blank.
D Employer ID number (EIN), if any
E Business address (including suite or room no.) ▶
City, town or post office, state, and ZIP code
F Accounting method: (1) ☒ Cash (2) ☐ Accrual (3) ☐ Other (specify) ▶
G Did you "materially participate" in the operation of this business during 2000? If "No," see page C-2 for limit on losses ☒ Yes ☐ No
H If you started or acquired this business during 2000, check here ▶ ☐

Part I Income

Line	Description	Amount
1	Gross receipts or sales. **Caution:** If this income was reported to you on Form W-2 and the "Statutory employee" box on that form was checked, see page C-2 and check here ▶ ☐	
2	Returns and allowances	
3	Subtract line 2 from line 1	
4	Cost of goods sold (from line 42 on page 2)	
5	**Gross profit.** Subtract line 4 from line 3	
6	Other income, including Federal and state gasoline or fuel tax credit or refund (see page C-2)	
7	**Gross income.** Add lines 5 and 6 ▶	

Part II Expenses. Enter expenses for business use of your home **only** on line 30.

Line	Description	Amount	Line	Description	Amount
8	Advertising		19	Pension and profit-sharing plans	
9	Bad debts from sales or services (see page C-3)		20	Rent or lease (see page C-4):	
			20a	Vehicles, machinery & equipment	5,050
			20b	Other business property	
10	Car and truck expenses (see page C-3)	3,115	21	Repairs and maintenance	3,166
11	Commissions and fees		22	Supplies (not included in Part III)	5,069
12	Depletion		23	Taxes and licenses	
13	Depreciation and section 179 expense deduction (not included in Part III) (see page C-3)	5,000	24	Travel, meals, and entertainment:	
			24a	Travel	6,511
			b	Meals and entertainment	8,711
14	Employee benefit programs (other than on line 19)		c	Enter nondeductible amount included on line 24b (see page C-5)	4,356
15	Insurance (other than health)		24d	Subtract line 24c from line 24b	4,355
16	Interest:		25	Utilities	2,611
16a	Mortgage (paid to banks, etc.)		26	Wages (less employment credits)	
16b	Other	51,357			
17	Legal and professional services	2,250	27	Other expenses (from line 48 on page 2)	83,233
18	Office expense	4,561			

Line	Description	Amount
28	**Total expenses** before expenses for business use of home. Add lines 8 through 27 in columns ▶	176,278
29	Tentative profit (loss). Subtract line 28 from line 7	-176,278
30	Expenses for business use of your home. Attach **Form 8829**	6,250
31	**Net profit or (loss).** Subtract line 30 from line 29. • If a profit, enter on **Form 1040, line 12,** and **also** on **Schedule SE, line 2** (statutory employees, see page C-5). Estates and trusts, enter on Form 1041, line 3. • If a loss, you **must** go to line 32.	-182,528

32 If you have a loss, check the box that describes your investment in this activity (see page C-5).
- If you checked 32a, enter the loss on **Form 1040, line 12,** and **also** on **Schedule SE, line 2** (statutory employees, see page C-5). Estates and trusts, enter on Form 1041, line 3.
- If you checked 32b, you **must** attach **Form 6198.**

32a ☒ All investment is at risk.
32b ☐ Some investment is not at risk.

For Paperwork Reduction Act Notice, see Form 1040 instructions. **Schedule C (Form 1040) 2000**

KFA IFOUS4 11/08/00

Schedule C (Form 1040) 2000 A. COMMODITIES TRADER LOSS NO 475 123-45-6789 Page **2**

Part III Cost of Goods Sold (see page C-6)

33 Method(s) used to value closing inventory: a ☐ Cost b ☐ Lower of cost or market c ☐ Other (attach explanation)

34 Was there any change in determining quantities, costs, or valuations between opening and closing inventory? If "Yes," attach explanation ☐ Yes ☐ No

35 Inventory at beginning of year. If different from last year's closing inventory, attach explanation	35	
36 Purchases less cost of items withdrawn for personal use	36	
37 Cost of labor. Do not include any amounts paid to yourself	37	
38 Materials and supplies	38	
39 Other costs	39	
40 Add lines 35 through 39	40	
41 Inventory at end of year	41	
42 **Cost of goods sold.** Subtract line 41 from line 40. Enter the result here and on page 1, line 4	42	

Part IV Information on Your Vehicle. Complete this part **only** if you are claiming car or truck expenses on line 10 and are not required to file Form 4562 for this business. See the instructions for line 13 on page C-3 to find out if you must file.

43 When did you place your vehicle in service for business purposes? (month, day, year) ▶ ________

44 Of the total number of miles you drove your vehicle during 2000, enter the number of miles you used your vehicle for:

a Business ________ b Commuting ________ c Other ________

45 Do you (or your spouse) have another vehicle available for personal use? ☐ Yes ☐ No

46 Was your vehicle available for use during off-duty hours? ☐ Yes ☐ No

47a Do you have evidence to support your deduction? ☐ Yes ☐ No

b If "Yes," is the evidence written? ☐ Yes ☐ No

Part V Other Expenses. List below business expenses not included on lines 8-26 or line 30.

COMPUTER EXPENSE		2,955
HISTORICAL DATA SERVICES		3,061
INTERNET SERVICES		2,050
ONLINE TRADING DATA		7,010
OTHER TRADING EXPENSES		4,116
PROFESSIONAL PUBLICATIONS		3,116
TRADING ADVISORY SERVICES		35,179
TRADING PERIODICALS		6,633
TRADING SEMINARS		19,113
48 **Total other expenses.** Enter here and on page 1, line 27	48	83,233

IFOUS4A 11/09/00 Schedule C (Form 1040) 2000

SCHEDULE D (Form 1040)

Department of the Treasury Internal Revenue Service (99)

Capital Gains and Losses

▶ Attach to Form 1040. ▶ See Instructions for Schedule D (Form 1040).
▶ Use Schedule D-1 for more space to list transactions for lines 1 and 8.

OMB No. 1545-0074

2000

Attachment Sequence No. **12**

Name(s) shown on Form 1040: A. COMMODITIES TRADER LOSS NO 475

Your social security number: 123-45-6789

Part I Short-Term Capital Gains and Losses – Assets Held One Year or Less

1 (a) Description of property (Example, 100 sh. XYZ Co.)	(b) Date acquired (Mo., day, yr.)	(c) Date sold (Mo., day, yr.)	(d) Sales price (see page D-6)	(e) Cost or other basis (see page D-6)	(f) Gain or (loss) Subtract (e) from (d)

Line	Description		Amount
2	Enter your short-term totals, if any, from Schedule D-1, line 2	2	
3	**Total short-term sales price amounts.** Add column (d) of lines 1 and 2	3	
4	Short-term gain from Form 6252 and short-term gain or (loss) from Forms 4684, 6781, and 8824	4	-40,000
5	Net short-term gain or (loss) from partnerships, S corporations, estates, and trusts from Schedule(s) K-1	5	
6	Short-term capital loss carryover. Enter the amount, if any, from line 8 of your 1999 Capital Loss Carryover Worksheet	6	( )
7	**Net short-term capital gain or (loss).** Combine column (f) of lines 1 through 6 ▶	7	-40,000

Part II Long-Term Capital Gains and Losses – Assets Held More Than One Year

8 (a) Description of property (Example, 100 sh. XYZ Co.)	(b) Date acquired (Mo., day, yr.)	(c) Date sold (Mo., day, yr.)	(d) Sales price (see page D-6)	(e) Cost or other basis (see page D-6)	(f) Gain or (loss) Subtract (e) from (d)	(g) 28% rate gain or (loss) *(see instr. below)

Line	Description		(f)	(g)
9	Enter your long-term totals, if any, from Schedule D-1, line 9	9		
10	**Total long-term sales price amounts.** Add column (d) of lines 8 and 9	10		
11	Gain from Form 4797, Part I; long-term gain from Forms 2439 and 6252; and long-term gain or (loss) from Forms 4684, 6781, and 8824	11	-60,000	
12	Net long-term gain or (loss) from partnerships, S corporations, estates, and trusts from Schedule(s) K-1	12		
13	Capital gain distributions. See page D-1	13		
14	Long-term capital loss carryover. Enter in both columns (f) and (g) the amount, if any, from line 13 of your 1999 Capital Loss Carryover Worksheet	14	( )	( )
15	Combine column (g) of lines 8 through 14	15		
16	**Net long-term capital gain or (loss).** Combine column (f) of lines 8 through 14 ▶ **Next:** Go to Part III on the back.	16	-60,000	

* **28% rate gain or loss** includes **all** "collectibles gains and losses" (as defined on page D-6) and up to 50% of the eligible gain on qualified small business stock (see page D-4).

For Paperwork Reduction Act Notice, see Form 1040 instructions. **Schedule D (Form 1040) 2000**

KFA IFOUS5 12/07/00

Schedule D (Form 1040) 2000 A. COMMODITIES TRADER LOSS NO 475 123-45-6789 Page **2**

Part III Summary of Parts I and II

17	Combine lines 7 and 16. If a loss, go to line 18. If a gain, enter the gain on Form 1040, line 13 **Next:** Complete Form 1040 through line 39. Then, go to **Part IV** to figure your tax if: • Both lines 16 and 17 are gains **and** • Form 1040, line 39, is more than zero. Otherwise, **stop here.**	17	-100,000
18	If line 17 is a loss, enter here and as a (loss) on Form 1040, line 13, the **smaller** of these losses: • The loss on line 17 **or** • ($3,000) or, if married filing separately, ($1,500)	18	(3,000)
	Next: Skip **Part IV** below. Instead, complete Form 1040 through line 37. Then, complete the **Capital Loss Carryover Worksheet** on page D-6 if: • The loss on line 17 exceeds the loss on line 18 **or** • Form 1040, line 37, is a loss.		

Part IV Tax Computation Using Maximum Capital Gains Rates

19	Enter your taxable income from Form 1040, line 39			19	
20	Enter the **smaller** of line 16 or line 17 of Schedule D	20			
21	If you are filing Form 4952, enter the amount from Form 4952, line 4e	21			
22	Subtract line 21 from line 20. If zero or less, enter -0-	22			
23	Combine lines 7 and 15. If zero or less, enter -0-	23			
24	Enter the **smaller** of line 15 or line 23, but not less than zero	24			
25	Enter your unrecaptured section 1250 gain, if any, from line 17 of the worksheet on page D-8	25			
26	Add lines 24 and 25	26			
27	Subtract line 26 from line 22. If zero or less, enter -0-			27	
28	Subtract line 27 from line 19. If zero or less, enter -0-			28	
29	Enter the **smaller** of: • The amount on line 19 **or** • $26,250 if single; $43,850 if married filing jointly or qualifying widow(er); $21,925 if married filing separately; or $35,150 if head of household			29	
30	Enter the **smaller** of line 28 or line 29	30			
31	Subtract line 22 from line 19. If zero or less, enter -0-	31			
32	Enter the **larger** of line 30 or line 31 ▶	32			
33	Figure the tax on the amount on line 32. Use the Tax Table or Tax Rate Schedules, whichever applies			33	
	Note: If the amounts on lines 29 and 30 are the same, skip lines 34 through 37 and go to line 38.				
34	Enter the amount from line 29	34			
35	Enter the amount from line 30	35			
36	Subtract line 35 from line 34 ▶	36			
37	Multiply line 36 by 10% (.10)			37	
	Note: If the amounts on lines 19 and 29 are the same, skip lines 38 through 51 and go to line 52.				
38	Enter the **smaller** of line 19 or line 27	38			
39	Enter the amount from line 36	39			
40	Subtract line 39 from line 38 ▶	40			
41	Multiply line 40 by 20% (.20)			41	
	Note: If line 26 is zero or blank, skip lines 42 through 51 and go to line 52.				
42	Enter the **smaller** of line 22 or line 25	42			
43	Add lines 22 and 32 — 43				
44	Enter the amount from line 19 — 44				
45	Subtract line 44 from line 43. If zero or less, enter -0-	45			
46	Subtract line 45 from line 42. If zero or less, enter -0- ▶	46			
47	Multiply line 46 by 25% (.25)			47	
	Note: If line 24 is zero or blank, skip lines 48 through 51 and go to line 52.				
48	Enter the amount from line 19	48			
49	Add lines 32, 36, 40, and 46	49			
50	Subtract line 49 from line 48	50			
51	Multiply line 50 by 28% (.28)			51	
52	Add lines 33, 37, 41, 47, and 51			52	
53	Figure the tax on the amount on line 19. Use the Tax Table or Tax Rate Schedules, whichever applies			53	
54	**Tax on all taxable income (including capital gains).** Enter the **smaller** of line 52 or line 53 here and on Form 1040, line 40			54	

IFOUS5A 10/24/00 **Schedule D (Form 1040) 2000**

Example 11 *(Continued)*

Schedule E (Form 1040) 2000 | Attachment Sequence No. **13** | Page **2**

Name(s) shown on return. Do not enter name and social security number if shown on other side. — A. COMMODITIES TRADER LOSS NO 475

Your social security number — 123-45-6789

Note: If you report amounts from farming or fishing on Schedule E, you must enter your gross income from those activities on line 41 below. Real estate professionals must complete line 42 below.

Part II **Income or Loss From Partnerships and S Corporations** If you report a loss from an at-risk activity, you **must** check either column **(e)** or **(f)** on line 27 to describe your investment in the activity. See page E-5. If you check column **(f)**, you must attach **Form 6198.**

27	(a) Name	(b) Enter P for partnership; S for S corp.	(c) Check if foreign partnership	(d) Employer identification number	Invest. At Risk? (e) All is at risk	(f) Some is not at risk
A	1	P				
B						
C						
D						
E						

	Passive Income and Loss		Nonpassive Income and Loss		
	(g) Passive loss allowed (attach Form 8582 if required)	(h) Passive income from Schedule K-1	(i) Nonpassive loss from Schedule K-1	(j) Section 179 expense deduction from Form 4562	(k) Nonpassive income from Schedule K-1
A		200,000			
B					
C					
D					
E					
28a Totals		200,000			
b Totals					

29	Add columns (h) and (k) of line 28a	29	200,000
30	Add columns (g), (i), and (j) of line 28b	30	( )
31	Total partnership and S corporation income or (loss). Combine lines 29 and 30. Enter the result here and include in the total on line 40 below	31	200,000

Part III **Income or Loss From Estates and Trusts**

32	(a) Name	(b) Employer ID number
A		
B		
C		
D		

	Passive Income and Loss		Nonpassive Income and Loss	
	(c) Passive deduction or loss allowed (attach Form 8582 if required)	(d) Passive income from Schedule K-1	(e) Deduction or loss from Schedule K-1	(f) Other income from Schedule K-1
A				
B				
C				
D				
33a Totals				
b Totals				

34	Add columns (d) and (f) of line 33a	34	
35	Add columns (c) and (e) of line 33b	35	( )
36	Total estate and trust income or (loss). Combine lines 34 and 35. Enter the result here and include in the total on line 40 below	36	

Part IV **Income or Loss From Real Estate Mortgage Investment Conduits (REMICs) – Residual Holder**

37	(a) Name	(b) Employer identification number	(c) Excess inclusion from Schedules Q, line 2c (see page E-6)	(d) Taxable income (net loss) from Schedules Q, line 1b	(e) Income from Schedules Q, line 3b

38	Combine columns (d) and (e) only. Enter the result here and include in the total on line 40 below	38	

Part V **Summary**

39	Net farm rental income or (loss) from **Form 4835.** Also, complete line 41 below	39	
40	**Total** income or (loss). Combine lines 26, 31, 36, 38, and 39. Enter the result here and on Form 1040, line 17 ▶	40	200,000
41	**Reconciliation of Farming and Fishing Income:** Enter your **gross** farming and fishing income reported on Form 4835, line 7; Schedule K-1 (Form 1065), line 15b; Schedule K-1 (Form 1120S), line 23; and Schedule K-1 (Form 1041), line 14 (see page E-6)	41	
42	**Reconciliation for Real Estate Professionals.** If you were real estate professional (see pg. E-4), enter net income or (loss) you reported anywhere on Form 1040 from all rental real estate activities in which you materially participated under passive activity loss rules.	42	

IFOUS7A 10/19/00 — Schedule E (Form 1040) 2000

Form **4562** | **Depreciation and Amortization (Including Information on Listed Property)** | OMB No. 1545-0172 **2000**

Department of the Treasury Internal Revenue Service (99) ▶ See separate instructions. ▶ Attach this form to your return. Attachment Sequence No. 67

Name(s) shown on return: A. COMMODITIES TRADER LOSS NO 475 — Identifying number: 123-45-6789

Business or activity to which this form relates

Part I Election To Expense Certain Tangible Property (Section 179) Note: If you have any "listed property," complete Part V before you complete Part I.

1	Maximum dollar limitation. If an enterprise zone business, see page 2 of the instructions	1	$20,000
2	Total cost of section 179 property placed in service. See page 2 of the instructions	2	
3	Threshold cost of section 179 property before reduction in limitation	3	$200,000
4	Reduction in limitation. Subtract line 3 from line 2. If zero or less, enter -0-	4	
5	Dollar limitation for tax year. Subtract line 4 from line 1. If zero or less, enter -0-. If married filing separately, see page 2 of the instructions	5	

6 (a) Description of property	(b) Cost (business use only)	(c) Elected cost

7	Listed property. Enter amount from line 27	7	
8	Total elected cost of section 179 property. Add amounts in column (c), lines 6 and 7	8	
9	Tentative deduction. Enter the smaller of line 5 or line 8	9	
10	Carryover of disallowed deduction from 1999. See page 3 of the instructions	10	
11	Business income limitation. Enter the smaller of business income (not less than zero) or line 5 (see instructions)	11	
12	Section 179 expense deduction. Add lines 9 and 10, but do not enter more than line 11	12	
13	Carryover of disallowed deduction to 2001. Add lines 9 and 10, less line 12 ▶	13	

Note: Do not use Part II or Part III below for listed property (automobiles, certain other vehicles, cellular telephones, certain computers, or property used for entertainment, recreation, or amusement). Instead, use Part V for listed property.

Part II MACRS Depreciation for Assets Placed in Service Only During Your 2000 Tax Year (**Do not** include listed property.)

Section A – General Asset Account Election

14 If you are making the election under section 168(i)(4) to group any assets placed in service during the tax year into one or more general asset accounts, check this box. See page 3 of the instructions ▶ ☐

Section B – General Depreciation System (GDS) (See page 3 of the instructions.)

(a) Classification of property	(b) Month and year placed in service	(c) Basis for depreciation (business/investment use only – see instructions)	(d) Recovery period	(e) Convention	(f) Method	(g) Depreciation deduction
15a 3-year property						
b 5-year property						
c 7-year property						
d 10-year property						
e 15-year property						
f 20-year property						
g 25-year property			25 yrs		S/L	
h Residential rental property			27.5 yrs	MM	S/L	
			27.5 yrs	MM	S/L	
i Nonresidential real property			39 yrs	MM	S/L	
				MM	S/L	

Section C – Alternative Depreciation System (ADS): (See page 5 of the instructions.)

16a Class life					S/L	
b 12-year			12 yrs		S/L	
c 40-year			40 yrs	MM	S/L	

Part III Other Depreciation (**Do not** include listed property.) (See page 5 of the instructions.)

17	GDS and ADS deductions for assets placed in service in tax years beginning before 2000	17	
18	Property subject to section 168(f)(1) election	18	
19	ACRS and other depreciation	19	5,000

Part IV Summary (See page 6 of the instructions.)

20	Listed property. Enter amount from line 26	20	
21	**Total.** Add deductions from line 12, lines 15 and 16 in column (g), and lines 17 through 20. Enter here and on the appropriate lines of your return. Partnerships and S corporations – see instructions	21	5,000
22	For assets shown above and placed in service during the current year, enter the portion of the basis attributable to section 263A costs	22	

KFA **For Paperwork Reduction Act Notice, see page 9 of the instructions.** GF0US7 10/26/00 Form **4562** (2000)

Example 11 *(Continued)*

Form **6251** Department of the Treasury Internal Revenue Service	**Alternative Minimum Tax – Individuals** ▶ **See separate instructions.** ▶ **Attach to Form 1040 or Form 1040NR.**	OMB No. 1545-0227 **2000** Attachment Sequence No. **32**
Name(s) shown on Form 1040 A. COMMODITIES TRADER LOSS NO 475		Your social security number 123-45-6789

Part I Adjustments and Preferences

1	If you itemized deductions on Schedule A (Form 1040), go to line 2. Otherwise, enter your standard deduction from Form 1040, line 36, here and go to line 6	1	4,400
2	Medical and dental. Enter the smaller of Schedule A (Form 1040), line 4 **or** 2 1/2% of Form 1040, line 34	2	
3	Taxes. Enter the amount from Schedule A (Form 1040), line 9	3	
4	Certain interest on a home mortgage **not** used to buy, build, or improve your home	4	
5	Miscellaneous itemized deductions. Enter the amount from Schedule A (Form 1040), line 26	5	
6	Refund of taxes. Enter any tax refund from Form 1040, line 10 or line 21	6	( )
7	Investment interest. Enter difference between regular tax and AMT deduction	7	
8	Post-1986 depreciation. Enter difference between regular tax and AMT depreciation	8	
9	Adjusted gain or loss. Enter difference between AMT and regular tax gain or loss	9	
10	Incentive stock options. Enter excess of AMT income over regular tax income	10	
11	Passive activities. Enter difference between AMT and regular tax income or loss	11	
12	Beneficiaries of estates and trusts. Enter the amount from Schedule K-1 (Form 1041), line 9	12	
13	Tax-exempt interest from private activity bonds issued after 8/7/86	13	
14	Other. Enter the amount, if any, for each item below and enter the total on line 14.		
	a Circulation expenditures. / **h** Loss limitations		
	b Depletion / **i** Mining costs		
	c Depreciation (pre-1987). / **j** Patron's adjustment		
	d Installment sales / **k** Pollution control facilities		
	e Intangible drilling costs. / **l** Research & experimental.		
	f Large partnerships / **m** Section 1202 exclusion		
	g Long-term contracts / **n** Tax shelter farm activities.		
	o Related adjustments	14	
15	**Total Adjustments and Preferences.** Combine lines 1 through 14 ▶	15	4,400

Part II Alternative Minimum Taxable Income

16	Enter the amount from **Form 1040, line 37.** If less than zero, enter as a (loss) ▶	16	210,072
17	Net operating loss deduction, if any, from Form 1040, line 21. Enter as a positive amount	17	
18	If Form 1040, line 34, is over $128,950 (over $64,475 if married filing separately), and you itemized deductions, enter the amount, if any, from line 9 of the worksheet for Schedule A (Form 1040), line 28	18	( )
19	Combine lines 15 through 18 ▶	19	214,472
20	Alternative tax net operating loss deduction. See page 6 of the instructions	20	
21	**Alternative Minimum Taxable Income.** Subtract line 20 from line 19. (If married filing separately and line 21 is more than $165,000, see page 7 of the instructions.) ▶	21	214,472

Part III Exemption Amount and Alternative Minimum Tax

22 Exemption Amount. (If this form is for a child under age 14, see page 7 of the instructions.)

IF your filing status is:	**AND line 21 is not over . . .**	**THEN enter on line 22 . . .**
Single or head of household	$112,500	$33,750
Married filing jointly or qualifying widow(er)	150,000	45,000
Married filing separately	75,000	22,500

If line 21 is **over** the amount shown above for your filing status, see page 7 of the instructions.

22	Exemption Amount	22	8,257
23	Subtract line 22 from line 21. If zero or less, enter -0- here and on lines 26 and 28 and stop here ▶	23	206,215
24	If you reported capital gain distributions directly on Form 1040, line 13, **or** you completed Schedule D (Form 1040) and have an amount on line 25 or line 27 (or would have had an amount on either line if you had completed Part IV) (as refigured for the AMT, if necessary), go to Part IV of Form 6251 to figure line 24. **All others:** If line 23 is $175,000 or less ($87,500 or less if married filing separately), multiply line 23 by 26% (.26). Otherwise, multiply line 23 by 28% (.28) and subtract $3,500 ($1,750 if married filing separately) from the result ▶	24	54,240
25	Alternative minimum tax foreign tax credit. See page 7 of the instructions	25	
26	Tentative minimum tax. Subtract line 25 from line 24 ▶	26	54,240
27	Enter your tax from Form 1040, line 40 (minus any tax from Form 4972 and any foreign tax credit from Form 1040, line 43)	27	63,375
28	**Alternative Minimum Tax.** Subtract line 27 from line 26. If zero or less, enter -0-. Enter here and on Form 1040, line 41 ▶	28	0

For Paperwork Reduction Act Notice, see page 8 of the instructions. Form **6251** (2000)

KFA IFOUS33 10/23/00

Form **6781**
Department of the Treasury
Internal Revenue Service

Gains and Losses From Section 1256 Contracts and Straddles

▶ Attach to your tax return.

OMB No. 1545-0644
2000
Attachment Sequence No. **82**

Name(s) shown on tax return: A. COMMODITIES TRADER LOSS NO 475
Identifying number: 123-45-6789

Check applicable box(es) (see instructions):
A ☐ Mixed straddle election
B ☐ Straddle-by-straddle identification election
C ☐ Mixed straddle account election
D ☐ Net section 1256 contracts loss election

Part I — Section 1256 Contracts Marked to Market

1 (a) Identification of account	(b) (Loss)	(c) Gain
	100,000	

Line	Description	Box	Amount
2	Add amounts on line 1 in columns (b) and (c)	2	(100,000)
3	Net gain or (loss). Combine columns (b) and (c) of line 2	3	-100,000
4	Form 1099-B adjustments. See instructions and attach schedule	4	
5	Combine lines 3 and 4	5	-100,000
	Note: If line 5 shows a net gain, skip line 6 and enter the gain on line 7. Partnerships and S corporations, see instructions.		
6	If you have a net section 1256 contracts loss and checked box D, enter the amount to be carried back	6	
7	Subtract line 6 from line 5	7	-100,000
8	Short-term capital gain or (loss). Multiply line 7 by 40%. Enter here and include on Schedule D. See instructions	8	-40,000
9	Long-term capital gain or (loss). Multiply line 7 by 60%. Enter here and include on Schedule D. See instructions	9	-60,000

Part II — Gains and Losses From Straddles. Attach a separate schedule listing each straddle and its components.

Section A – Losses From Straddles

10 (a) Description of property	(b) Date entered into or acquired	(c) Date closed out or sold	(d) Gross sales price	(e) Cost or other basis plus expense of sale	(f) Loss. If column (e) is more than (d), enter difference. Otherwise, enter -0-	(g) Unrecognized gain on offsetting positions	(h) Recognized loss. If column (f) is more than (g), enter difference. Otherwise, enter -0-	*(i) 28% rate loss (see instr. below)

11a Enter short-term portion of line 10, column (h), losses here and include on Schedule D. See instructions . . . 11a ( )

b Enter long-term portion of losses from line 10, columns (h) and (i), here and include on Schedule D. See instrs . 11b ( ) ( )

Section B – Gains From Straddles

12 (a) Description of property	(b) Date entered into or acquired	(c) Date closed out or sold	(d) Gross sales price	(e) Cost or other basis plus expense of sale	(f) Gain. If column (d) is more than (e), enter diff. Otherwise, enter 0	*(g) 28% Rate gain (see instr. below)

13a Enter short-term portion of line 12, column (f), gains here and include on Schedule D. See instructions . . . 13a

b Enter long-term portion of gains from line 12, columns (f) and (g), here and include on Sch D. See instrs . 13b

Part III — Unrecognized Gains From Positions Held on Last Day of Tax Year. Memo Entry Only – See instructions.

14 (a) Description of property	(b) Date acquired	(c) Fair market value on last business day of tax year	(d) Cost or other basis as adjusted	(e) Unrecognized gain. If column (c) is more than (d), enter difference. Otherwise, enter -0-

*28% Rate Gain or Loss includes all "collectibles gains and losses" and up to 50% of the eligible gain on qualified small business stock. See instructions for Schedule D (Form 1040).

For Paperwork Reduction Act Notice, see page 3. Form **6781** (2000)

KFA GF0US16 12/27/00

Example 12

Form 1040 Department of the Treasury – Internal Revenue Service
U.S. Individual Income Tax Return 2000 (99) IRS Use Only – Do not write or staple in this space.

For the year Jan. 1 – Dec. 31, 2000, or other tax year beginning , 2000, ending , 20 OMB No. 1545-0074

Label (See instructions on page 19.) Use the IRS label. Otherwise, please print or type. LABEL HERE

Your first name and initial / Last name: A. COMMODITIES TRADER LOSS SECT.475
Your social security number: 123-45-6789
If a joint return, spouse's first name and initial / Last name
Spouse's social security number
Home address (number and street). If you have a P.O. box, see page 19. Apt. no.: C/O TED TESSER-6274 LINTON BLVD. #102
City, town or post office, state, and ZIP code. If you have a foreign address, see page 19.: DELRAY BEACH, FL 33484

▲ **IMPORTANT!** ▲ You **must** enter your SSN(s) above.

Presidential Election Campaign (See page 19.) **Note.** Checking "Yes" will not change your tax or reduce your refund.
Do you, or your spouse if filing a joint return, want $3 to go to this fund? ▶ You: ☐ Yes ☒ No Spouse: ☐ Yes ☐ No

Filing Status (Check only one box.)

1 [X] Single
2 [ ] Married filing joint return (even if only one had income)
3 [ ] Married filing separate return. Enter spouse's soc. sec. no. above & full name here ▶
4 [ ] Head of household (with qualifying person). (See page 19.) If the qualifying person is a child but not your dependent, enter this child's name here ▶
5 [ ] Qualifying widow(er) with dependent child (year spouse died ▶). (See page 19.)

Exemptions

6a ☒ **Yourself.** If your parent (or someone else) can claim you as a dependent on his or her tax return, **do not** check box 6a.
b ☐ **Spouse**
No. of boxes checked on 6a and 6b: 1

c **Dependents:**

(1) First Name Last name	(2) Dependent's social security number	(3) Dependent's relationship to you	(4) Chk if qualifying child for child tax credit (see page 20)

No. of your children on 6c who: ● lived with you ● did not live with you due to divorce or separation (see page 20)
Dependents on 6c not entered above
If more than six dependents, see page 20.

d Total number of exemptions claimed — Add numbers entered on lines above ▶ 1

Income

Attach Forms W-2 and W-2G here. Also attach Form 1099-R if tax was withheld.
If you did not get a W-2, see page 21.
Enclose, but do not attach any payment. Also, please use Form 1040-V.

Line	Description		Amount
7	Wages, salaries, tips, etc. Attach Form(s) W-2	7	200,000
8a	**Taxable** interest. Attach Schedule B if required	8a	
b	**Tax-exempt** interest. **Do not** include on line 8a — 8b		
9	Ordinary dividends. Attach Schedule B if required	9	
10	Taxable refunds, credits, or offsets of state and local income taxes (see page 22)	10	
11	Alimony received	11	
12	Business income or (loss). Attach Schedule C or C-EZ	12	-182,528
13	Capital gain or (loss). Attach Schedule D if required. If not required, check here ▶ ☐	13	
14	Other gains or (losses). Attach Form 4797	14	-100,000
15a	Total IRA distributions — 15a — b Taxable amount (see pg. 23)	15b	
16a	Total pensions and annuities — 16a — b Taxable amount (see pg. 23)	16b	
17	Rental real estate, royalties, partnerships, S corporations, trusts, etc. Attach Schedule E	17	200,000
18	Farm income or (loss). Attach Schedule F	18	
19	Unemployment compensation	19	
20a	Social security benefits — 20a — b Taxable amount (see pg. 25)	20b	
21	Other income.	21	
22	Add the amounts in the far right column for lines 7 through 21. This is your **total income** ▶	22	117,472

Adjusted Gross Income

23	IRA deduction (see page 27)	23			
24	Student loan interest deduction (see page 27)	24			
25	Medical savings account deduction. Attach Form 8853	25			
26	Moving expenses. Attach Form 3903	26			
27	One-half of self-employment tax. Attach Schedule SE	27			
28	Self-employed health insurance deduction (see page 29)	28			
29	Self-employed SEP, SIMPLE, and qualified plans	29			
30	Penalty on early withdrawal of savings	30			
31a	Alimony paid. b Recipient's SSN ▶	31a			
32	Add lines 23 through 31a			32	0
33	Subtract line 32 from line 22. This is your **adjusted gross income** ▶			33	117,472

KFA **For Disclosure, Privacy Act, and Paperwork Reduction Act Notice, see page 56.** IF0US1 11/07/00 Form **1040** (2000)

Form 1040 (2000) A. COMMODITIES TRADER LOSS SECT.475 123-45-6789 Page **2**

Tax and Credits	**34** Amount from line 33 (adjusted gross income) .		**34**	117,472

35a Check if: ☐ **You** were 65 or older, ☐ Blind; ☐ **Spouse** was 65 or older, ☐ Blind.
Add the number of boxes checked above and enter the total here ▶ **35a** ☐

Standard Deduction for Most People
Single:
$4,400
Head of household:
$6,450
Married filing jointly or Qualifying widow(er):
$7,350
Married filing separately:
$3,675.

b If you are married filing separately and your spouse itemizes deductions, or you were
a dual-status alien, see page 31 and check here . ▶ **35b** ☐

36 Enter your **itemized deductions** from Schedule A, line 28, **or standard deduction** shown on the left. But see page 31 to find your standard deduction if you checked any box on line 35a or 35b or if someone can claim you as a dependent .	**36**	4,400
37 Subtract line 36 from line 34 .	**37**	113,072
38 If line 34 is $96,700 or less, multiply $2,800 by the total number of exemptions claimed on line 6d. If line 34 is over $96,700, see the worksheet on page 32 for the amount to enter	**38**	2,800
39 **Taxable income.** Subtract line 38 from line 37. If line 38 is more than line 37, enter -0-	**39**	110,272
40 **Tax** (see page 32). Check if any tax is from **a** ☐ Form(s) 8814 **b** ☐ Form 4972	**40**	28,865
41 Alternative minimum tax. Attach Form 6251 .	**41**	
42 Add lines 40 and 41 . ▶	**42**	28,865

43 Foreign tax credit. Attach Form 1116 if required	**43**		
44 Credit for child and dependent care expenses. Att. Form 2441	**44**		
45 Credit for the elderly or the disabled. Attach Schedule R	**45**		
46 Education credits. Attach Form 8863	**46**		
47 Child tax credit (see page 36) .	**47**		
48 Adoption credit. Attach Form 8839	**48**		
49 Other. Check if from **a** ☐ Form 3800 **b** ☐ Form 8396 **c** ☐ Form 8801 **d** ☐ Form (specify)	**49**		

50 Add lines 43 through 49. These are your **total credits**		**50**	
51 Subtract line 50 from line 42. If line 50 is more than line 42, enter -0- ▶		**51**	28,865

Other Taxes	**52** Self-employment tax. Att. Sch. SE .		**52**	
	53 Social security and Medicare tax on tip income not reported to employer. Attach Form 4137		**53**	
	54 Tax on IRAs, other retirement plans, and MSAs. Attach Form 5329 if required		**54**	
	55 Advance earned income credit payments from Form(s) W-2 .		**55**	
	56 Household employment taxes. Attach Schedule H .		**56**	
	57 Add lines 51 through 56. This is your **total tax** . ▶		**57**	28,865

Payments	**58** Federal income tax withheld from Forms W-2 and 1099	**58**	60,000	
If you have a qualifying child, attach Schedule EIC.	**59** 2000 estimated tax payments and amount applied from 1999 return .	**59**	50,000	
	60a Earned income credit (EIC) .	**60a**		
	b Nontaxable earned income: amt. ▶ and type▶		No	
	61 Excess social security and RRTA tax withheld (see page 50)	**61**		
	62 **Additional child tax credit. Attach Form 8812**	**62**		
	63 **Amount paid with request for extension to file** (see page 50)	**63**		
	64 Other payments. Check if from **a** ☐ Form 2439 **b** ☐ Form 4136 . .	**64**		
	65 Add lines 58, 59, 60a, and 61 through 64. These are your **total payments** ▶		**65**	110,000

Refund Have it directly deposited! See page 50 and fill in 67b, 67c, and 67d.	**66** If line 65 is more than line 57, subtract line 57 from line 65. This is the amount you **overpaid**		**66**	81,135
	67a Amount of line 66 you want **refunded to you** . ▶		**67a**	81,135

b Routing number [] ▶ **c** Type: ☐ Checking ☐ Savings
d Account number []

68 Amount of line 66 you want **applied to your 2001 estimated tax** ▶	**68**	

Amount You Owe	**69** If line 57 is more than line 65, subtract line 65 from line 57. This is the **amount you owe.** For details on how to pay, see page 51 . ▶	**69**		
	70 Estimated tax penalty. Also include on line 69	**70**		

Sign Here
Joint return?
See page 19.
Keep a copy for your records.

Under penalties of perjury, I declare that I have examined this return and accompanying schedules and statements, and to the best of my knowledge and belief, they are true, correct, and complete. Declaration of preparer (other than taxpayer) is based on all information of which preparer has any knowledge.

Your signature	Date	Your occupation	Daytime phone number 561-865-0071
Spouse's signature. If a joint return, **both** must sign.	Date	Spouse's occupation	May the IRS discuss this return with the preparer shown below? (see page 52)? ☒ Yes ☐ No

Paid Preparer's Use Only

Preparer's signature ▶		Date	Check if self-employed ☐	Preparer's SSN or PTIN
Firm's name (or yours if self-employed), address, and ZIP code	▶ Waterside Financial Serv., Inc 6274 Linton Blvd., Suite #102 Boca Raton, FL 33484		EIN 65-0664126 Phone no. (561) 865-0071	

IF0US1A 11/22/00 Form **1040** (2000)

SCHEDULE C (Form 1040) — Department of the Treasury, Internal Revenue Service (99)

Profit or Loss From Business
(Sole Proprietorship)

▶ Partnerships, joint ventures, etc., must file Form 1065 or Form 1065-B.
▶ Attach to Form 1040 or Form 1041. ▶ See Instructions for Schedule C (Form 1040).

OMB No. 1545-0074 — **2000** — Attachment Sequence No. 09

Name of proprietor: A. COMMODITIES TRADER LOSS SECT.475	Social security number (SSN): 123-45-6789
A Principal business or profession, including product or service (see page C-1 of the instructions): TRADER	B Enter code from pages C-7 & 8: ▶ 523900
C Business name. If no separate business name, leave blank.	D Employer ID number (EIN), if any

E Business address (including suite or room no.) ▶
City, town or post office, state, and ZIP code

F Accounting method: (1) ☒ Cash (2) ☐ Accrual (3) ☐ Other (specify) ▶

G Did you "materially participate" in the operation of this business during 2000? If "No," see page C-2 for limit on losses ☒ Yes ☐ No

H If you started or acquired this business during 2000, check here ▶ ☐

Part I Income

	Line	Amount
1 Gross receipts or sales. **Caution:** If this income was reported to you on Form W-2 and the "Statutory employee" box on that form was checked, see page C-2 and check here ▶ ☐	1	
2 Returns and allowances	2	
3 Subtract line 2 from line 1	3	
4 Cost of goods sold (from line 42 on page 2)	4	
5 **Gross profit.** Subtract line 4 from line 3	5	
6 Other income, including Federal and state gasoline or fuel tax credit or refund (see page C-2)	6	
7 **Gross income.** Add lines 5 and 6 ▶	7	

Part II Expenses. Enter expenses for business use of your home **only** on line 30.

	Line	Amount		Line	Amount
8 Advertising	8		19 Pension and profit-sharing plans	19	
9 Bad debts from sales or services (see page C-3)	9		20 Rent or lease (see page C-4):		
			a Vehicles, machinery & equipment	20a	5,050
			b Other business property	20b	
10 Car and truck expenses (see page C-3)	10	3,115	21 Repairs and maintenance	21	3,166
11 Commissions and fees	11		22 Supplies (not included in Part III)	22	5,069
12 Depletion	12		23 Taxes and licenses	23	
			24 Travel, meals, and entertainment:		
13 Depreciation and section 179 expense deduction (not included in Part III) (see page C-3)	13	5,000	a Travel	24a	6,511
			b Meals and entertainment — 8,711		
14 Employee benefit programs (other than on line 19)	14		c Enter nondeductible amount included on line 24b (see page C-5) — 4,356		
15 Insurance (other than health)	15				
16 Interest:			d Subtract line 24c from line 24b	24d	4,355
a Mortgage (paid to banks, etc.)	16a		25 Utilities	25	2,611
b Other	16b	51,357	26 Wages (less employment credits)	26	
17 Legal and professional services	17	2,250	27 Other expenses (from line 48 on page 2)	27	83,233
18 Office expense	18	4,561			

	Line	Amount
28 **Total expenses** before expenses for business use of home. Add lines 8 through 27 in columns ▶	28	176,278
29 Tentative profit (loss). Subtract line 28 from line 7	29	-176,278
30 Expenses for business use of your home. Attach **Form 8829**	30	6,250
31 **Net profit or (loss).** Subtract line 30 from line 29. • If a profit, enter on **Form 1040, line 12,** and **also** on **Schedule SE, line 2** (statutory employees, see page C-5). Estates and trusts, enter on Form 1041, line 3. • If a loss, you **must** go to line 32.	31	-182,528

32 If you have a loss, check the box that describes your investment in this activity (see page C-5).
- If you checked 32a, enter the loss on **Form 1040, line 12,** and **also** on **Schedule SE, line 2** (statutory employees, see page C-5). Estates and trusts, enter on Form 1041, line 3.
- If you checked 32b, you **must** attach **Form 6198.**

32a ☒ All investment is at risk.
32b ☐ Some investment is not at risk.

For Paperwork Reduction Act Notice, see Form 1040 instructions. **Schedule C (Form 1040) 2000**

KFA IF0US4 11/08/00

Example 12 *(Continued)*

Schedule C (Form 1040) 2000 A. COMMODITIES TRADER LOSS SECT.475 123-45-6789 Page 2

Part III Cost of Goods Sold (see page C-6)

33 Method(s) used to value closing inventory: a ☐ Cost b ☐ Lower of cost or market c ☐ Other (attach explanation)

34 Was there any change in determining quantities, costs, or valuations between opening and closing inventory? If "Yes," attach explanation ☐ Yes ☐ No

35 Inventory at beginning of year. If different from last year's closing inventory, attach explanation	35	
36 Purchases less cost of items withdrawn for personal use	36	
37 Cost of labor. Do not include any amounts paid to yourself	37	
38 Materials and supplies	38	
39 Other costs	39	
40 Add lines 35 through 39	40	
41 Inventory at end of year	41	
42 **Cost of goods sold.** Subtract line 41 from line 40. Enter the result here and on page 1, line 4	42	

Part IV Information on Your Vehicle. Complete this part **only** if you are claiming car or truck expenses on line 10 and are not required to file Form 4562 for this business. See the instructions for line 13 on page C-3 to find out if you must file.

43 When did you place your vehicle in service for business purposes? (month, day, year) ▶ _______________

44 Of the total number of miles you drove your vehicle during 2000, enter the number of miles you used your vehicle for:

a Business _______________ b Commuting _______________ c Other _______________

45 Do you (or your spouse) have another vehicle available for personal use? ☐ Yes ☐ No

46 Was your vehicle available for use during off-duty hours? ☐ Yes ☐ No

47a Do you have evidence to support your deduction? ☐ Yes ☐ No

b If "Yes," is the evidence written? ☐ Yes ☐ No

Part V Other Expenses. List below business expenses not included on lines 8-26 or line 30.

COMPUTER EXPENSE		2,955
HISTORICAL DATA SERVICES		3,061
INTERNET SERVICES		2,050
ONLINE TRADING DATA		7,010
OTHER TRADING EXPENSES		4,116
PROFESSIONAL PUBLICATIONS		3,116
TRADING ADVISORY SERVICES		35,179
TRADING PERIODICALS		6,633
TRADING SEMINARS		19,113
48 **Total other expenses.** Enter here and on page 1, line 27	48	83,233

IFOUS4A 11/09/00 Schedule C (Form 1040) 2000

Example 12 *(Continued)*

Schedule E (Form 1040) 2000 — Attachment Sequence No. **13** — Page **2**

Name(s) shown on return. Do not enter name and social security number if shown on other side. | Your social security number

A. COMMODITIES TRADER LOSS SECT.475 | 123-45-6789

Note: If you report amounts from farming or fishing on Schedule E, you must enter your gross income from those activities on line 41 below. Real estate professionals must complete line 42 below.

Part II Income or Loss From Partnerships and S Corporations If you report a loss from an at-risk activity, you **must** check either column **(e)** or **(f)** on line 27 to describe your investment in the activity. See page E-5. If you check column **(f)**, you must attach **Form 6198.**

27	**(a)** Name	**(b)** Enter P for partnership; S for S corp.	**(c)** Check if foreign partnership	**(d)** Employer identification number	Invest. At Risk? **(e)** All is at risk	**(f)** Some is not at risk
A	1	P				
B						
C						
D						
E						

	Passive Income and Loss		Nonpassive Income and Loss		
	(g) Passive loss allowed (attach **Form 8582** if required)	**(h)** Passive income from **Schedule K-1**	**(i)** Nonpassive loss from **Schedule K-1**	**(j)** Section 179 expense deduction from **Form 4562**	**(k)** Nonpassive income from **Schedule K-1**
A		200,000			
B					
C					
D					
E					
28a Totals		200,000			
b Totals					

29	Add columns (h) and (k) of line 28a	29	200,000
30	Add columns (g), (i), and (j) of line 28b	30	( )
31	Total partnership and S corporation income or (loss). Combine lines 29 and 30. Enter the result here and include in the total on line 40 below	31	200,000

Part III Income or Loss From Estates and Trusts

32	**(a)** Name	**(b)** Employer ID number
A		
B		
C		
D		

	Passive Income and Loss		Nonpassive Income and Loss	
	(c) Passive deduction or loss allowed (attach **Form 8582** if required)	**(d)** Passive income from **Schedule K-1**	**(e)** Deduction or loss from **Schedule K-1**	**(f)** Other income from **Schedule K-1**
A				
B				
C				
D				
33a Totals				
b Totals				

34	Add columns (d) and (f) of line 33a	34	
35	Add columns (c) and (e) of line 33b	35	( )
36	Total estate and trust income or (loss). Combine lines 34 and 35. Enter the result here and include in the total on line 40 below	36	

Part IV Income or Loss From Real Estate Mortgage Investment Conduits (REMICs) – Residual Holder

37	**(a)** Name	**(b)** Employer identification number	**(c)** Excess inclusion from **Schedules Q**, line 2c (see page E-6)	**(d)** Taxable income (net loss) from **Schedules Q**, line 1b	**(e)** Income from **Schedules Q**, line 3b

38	Combine columns (d) and (e) only. Enter the result here and include in the total on line 40 below	38	

Part V Summary

39	Net farm rental income or (loss) from **Form 4835.** Also, complete line 41 below	39	
40	**Total** income or (loss). Combine lines 26, 31, 36, 38, and 39. Enter the result here and on Form 1040, line 17 ▶	40	200,000
41	**Reconciliation of Farming and Fishing Income:** Enter your **gross** farming and fishing income reported on Form 4835, line 7; Schedule K-1 (Form 1065), line 15b; Schedule K-1 (Form 1120S), line 23; and Schedule K-1 (Form 1041), line 14 (see page E-6)	41	
42	**Reconciliation for Real Estate Professionals.** If you were real estate professional (see pg. E-4), enter net income or (loss) you reported anywhere on Form 1040 from all rental real estate activities in which you materially participated under passive activity loss rules.	42	

IE0US7A 10/19/00 — Schedule E (Form 1040) 2000

Form **4797** — Department of the Treasury, Internal Revenue Service (99)

Sales of Business Property

(Also Involuntary Conversions and Recapture Amounts Under Sections 179 and 280F(b)(2))

▶ Attach to your tax return. ▶ See separate instructions.

OMB No. 1545-0184 — **2000** — Attachment Sequence No. **27**

Name(s) shown on return	Identifying number
A. COMMODITIES TRADER LOSS SECT.475	123-45-6789

1 Enter the gross proceeds from sales or exchanges reported to you for 2000 on Form(s) 1099-B or 1099-S (or substitute statement) that you are including on line 2, 10, or 20 (see instructions) 1

Part I — Sales or Exchanges of Property Used in a Trade or Business and Involuntary Conversions From Other Than Casualty or Theft – Most Property Held More Than 1 Year (See instructions.)

2 (a) Description of property	(b) Date acquired (mo., day, yr.)	(c) Date sold (mo., day, yr.)	(d) Gross sales price	(e) Depreciation allowed or allowable since acquisition	(f) Cost or other basis, plus improvements and expense of sale	(g) Gain or (loss) Subtract (f) from the sum of (d) and (e)

3 Gain, if any, from Form 4684, line 39 3

4 Section 1231 gain from installment sales from Form 6252, line 26 or 37 4

5 Section 1231 gain or (loss) from like-kind exchanges from Form 8824 5

6 Gain, if any, from line 32, from other than casualty or theft 6

7 Combine lines 2 through 6. Enter the gain or (loss) here and on the appropriate line as follows: 7

Partnerships (except electing large partnerships). Report the gain or (loss) following the instructions for Form 1065, Schedule K, line 6. Skip lines 8, 9, 11, and 12 below.

S corporations. Report the gain or (loss) following the instructions for Form 1120S, Schedule K, lines 5 and 6. Skip lines 8, 9, 11, and 12 below, unless line 7 is a gain and the S corporation is subject to capital gains tax.

All others. If line 7 is zero or a loss, enter the amount from line 7 on line 11 below and skip lines 8 and 9. If line 7 is a gain and you did not have any prior year section 1231 losses, or they were recaptured in an earlier year, enter the gain from line 7 as a long-term capital gain on Schedule D and skip lines 8, 9, and 12 below.

8 Nonrecaptured net section 1231 losses from prior years (see instructions) 8

9 Subtract line 8 from line 7. If zero or less, enter -0-. Also enter on the appropriate line as follows (see instructions): 9

S corporations. Enter any gain from line 9 on Schedule D (Form 1120S), line 15, and skip lines 11 and 12 below.

All others. If line 9 is zero, enter the gain from line 7 on line 12 below. If line 9 is more than zero, enter the amount from line 8 on line 12 below, and enter the gain from line 9 as a long-term capital gain on Schedule D.

Part II — Ordinary Gains and Losses

10 Ordinary gains and losses not included on lines 11 through 17 (include property held 1 year or less):

475 TRADING	LOSS			-100,000		-100,000

11 Loss, if any, from line 7 11

12 Gain, if any, from line 7 or amount from line 8, if applicable 12

13 Gain, if any, from line 31 13

14 Net gain or (loss) from Form 4684, lines 31 and 38a 14

15 Ordinary gain from installment sales from Form 6252, line 25 or 36 15

16 Ordinary gain or (loss) from like-kind exchanges from Form 8824 16

17 Recapture of section 179 expense deduction for partners and S corporation shareholders from property dispositions by partnerships and S corporations (see instructions) 17

18 Combine lines 10 through 17. Enter the gain or (loss) here and on the appropriate line as follows: . . . . . 18 -100,000

a For all except individual returns: Enter the gain or (loss) from line 18 on the return being filed.

b For individual returns:

(1) If the loss on line 11 includes a loss from Form 4684, line 35, column (b)(ii), enter that part of the loss here. Enter the part of the loss from income-producing property on Schedule A (Form 1040), line 27, and the part of the loss from property used as an employee on Schedule A (Form 1040), line 22. Identify as from "Form 4797, line 18b(1)." See instructions . . . . . 18b(1)

(2) Redetermine the gain or (loss) on line 18 excluding the loss, if any, on line 18b(1). Enter here and on Form 1040, line 14 . . . . . 18b(2) -100,000

KFA **For Paperwork Reduction Act Notice, see page 7 of the instructions.** GF0US51 12/22/00 Form **4797** (2000)

Form **6251** — Department of the Treasury, Internal Revenue Service

Alternative Minimum Tax - Individuals

▶ See separate instructions.
▶ Attach to Form 1040 or Form 1040NR.

OMB No. 1545-0227 | **2000** | Attachment Sequence No. **32**

Name(s) shown on Form 1040: A. COMMODITIES TRADER LOSS SECT.475 | Your social security number: 123-45-6789

Part I Adjustments and Preferences

1	If you itemized deductions on Schedule A (Form 1040), go to line 2. Otherwise, enter your standard deduction from Form 1040, line 36, here and go to line 6	1	4,400
2	Medical and dental. Enter the smaller of Schedule A (Form 1040), line 4 **or** 2 1/2% of Form 1040, line 34	2	
3	Taxes. Enter the amount from Schedule A (Form 1040), line 9	3	
4	Certain interest on a home mortgage **not** used to buy, build, or improve your home	4	
5	Miscellaneous itemized deductions. Enter the amount from Schedule A (Form 1040), line 26	5	
6	Refund of taxes. Enter any tax refund from Form 1040, line 10 or line 21	6	( )
7	Investment interest. Enter difference between regular tax and AMT deduction	7	
8	Post-1986 depreciation. Enter difference between regular tax and AMT depreciation	8	
9	Adjusted gain or loss. Enter difference between AMT and regular tax gain or loss	9	
10	Incentive stock options. Enter excess of AMT income over regular tax income	10	
11	Passive activities. Enter difference between AMT and regular tax income or loss	11	
12	Beneficiaries of estates and trusts. Enter the amount from Schedule K-1 (Form 1041), line 9	12	
13	Tax-exempt interest from private activity bonds issued after 8/7/86	13	
14	Other. Enter the amount, if any, for each item below and enter the total on line 14.		
	a Circulation expenditures. ___ h Loss limitations ___		
	b Depletion ___ i Mining costs ___		
	c Depreciation (pre-1987). ___ j Patron's adjustment ___		
	d Installment sales ___ k Pollution control facilities ___		
	e Intangible drilling costs ___ l Research & experimental ___		
	f Large partnerships ___ m Section 1202 exclusion ___		
	g Long-term contracts ___ n Tax shelter farm activities ___		
	o Related adjustments ___	14	
15	**Total Adjustments and Preferences.** Combine lines 1 through 14 ▶	15	4,400

Part II Alternative Minimum Taxable Income

16	Enter the amount from **Form 1040, line 37.** If less than zero, enter as a (loss) ▶	16	113,072
17	Net operating loss deduction, if any, from Form 1040, line 21. Enter as a positive amount	17	
18	If Form 1040, line 34, is over $128,950 (over $64,475 if married filing separately), and you itemized deductions, enter the amount, if any, from line 9 of the worksheet for Schedule A (Form 1040), line 28	18	( )
19	Combine lines 15 through 18 ▶	19	117,472
20	Alternative tax net operating loss deduction. See page 6 of the instructions	20	
21	**Alternative Minimum Taxable Income.** Subtract line 20 from line 19. (If married filing separately and line 21 is more than $165,000, see page 7 of the instructions.) ▶	21	117,472

Part III Exemption Amount and Alternative Minimum Tax

22 **Exemption Amount.** (If this form is for a child under age 14, see page 7 of the instructions.)

IF your filing status is:	AND line 21 is not over . . .	THEN enter on line 22 . . .
Single or head of household	$112,500	$33,750
Married filing jointly or qualifying widow(er)	150,000	45,000
Married filing separately	75,000	22,500

If line 21 is **over** the amount shown above for your filing status, see page 7 of the instructions.

22	Exemption Amount	22	32,507
23	Subtract line 22 from line 21. If zero or less, enter -0- here and on lines 26 and 28 and stop here ▶	23	84,965
24	If you reported capital gain distributions directly on Form 1040, line 13, **or** you completed Schedule D (Form 1040) and have an amount on line 25 or line 27 (or would have had an amount on either line if you had completed Part IV) (as refigured for the AMT, if necessary), go to Part IV of Form 6251 to figure line 24. **All others:** If line 23 is $175,000 or less ($87,500 or less if married filing separately), multiply line 23 by 26% (.26). Otherwise, multiply line 23 by 28% (.28) and subtract $3,500 ($1,750 if married filing separately) from the result ▶	24	22,091
25	Alternative minimum tax foreign tax credit. See page 7 of the instructions	25	
26	Tentative minimum tax. Subtract line 25 from line 24 ▶	26	22,091
27	Enter your tax from Form 1040, line 40 (minus any tax from Form 4972 and any foreign tax credit from Form 1040, line 43)	27	28,865
28	**Alternative Minimum Tax.** Subtract line 27 from line 26. If zero or less, enter -0-. Enter here and on Form 1040, line 41 ▶	28	0

For Paperwork Reduction Act Notice, see page 8 of the instructions. Form **6251** (2000)

KFA IF0US33 10/23/00

Example 13 Summary Comparison

	Investor	Trader—No 475	Trader—475
Profitable—Stocks			
	Example 1	*Example 2*	*Example 3*
Expense deductions	$115,092	$200,678	$200,678
Loss deductions	NA	NA	NA
Exemptions	0	0	0
Standard deduction	0	4,400	4,400
Alternative minimum tax	0	0	0
Total tax due/(refund*)	$99,895	$ 64,261	$ 64,261
Nonprofitable—Stocks			
	Example 4	*Example 5*	*Example 6*
Expense deductions	$78,960	$182,528	$182,528
Loss deductions	3,000	3,000	100,000
Exemptions	0	840	2,800
Standard deduction	0	4,400	4,400
Alternative minimum tax	4,046	0	0
Total tax due/(refund*)	$(2,340)*	$(46,625)*	$(81,135)*
Profitable—Commodities			
	Example 7	*Example 8*	*Example 9*
Expense deductions	$115,092	$200,678	$200,678
Loss deductions	NA	NA	NA
Exemptions	0	0	0
Standard deduction	0	4,400	4,400
Alternative minimum tax	0	0	0
Total tax due/(refund*)	$ 64,437	$ 8,802	$ 64,261
Nonprofitable—Commodities			
	Example 10	*Example 11*	*Example 12*
Expense deductions	$78,960	$182,528	$182,528
Loss deductions	3,000	3,000	100,000
Exemptions	0	840	2,800
Standard deduction	0	4,400	4,400
Alternative minimum tax	4,046	0	0
Total tax due/(refund*)	$(2,340)*	$(46,625)*	$(81,135)*

Example 14

Form **3115** (Rev. May 1999)
Department of the Treasury
Internal Revenue Service

Application for Change in Accounting Method

OMB No. 1545-0152

► See page 1 of the instructions for the Automatic Change Procedures.

Name of applicant (If a joint return is filed, also give spouse's name.) A. TRADER	Identification number (See page 3 of the instructions.) 123-45-6789
Number, street, and room or suite no. (If a P.O. box, see page 3 of the instructions.) C/O WATERSIDE FINANCIAL SVCES-7400 N. FEDRL HWY	Tax year of change begins (mo., day, yr.) and ends (mo., day, yr.) 1/1/99 – 12/31/99
City or town, state, and ZIP code BOCA RATON, FL 33434	District director's office having jurisdiction SEE INSTRUCTIONS
Name of person to contact (If not the applicant, a power of attorney must be submitted.) A. TRADER	Contact person's telephone number/Fax number (800) 556-9829 / ( )

Check the appropriate box to indicate who is filing this form.

- ☒ Individual
- ☐ Corporation
- ☐ Cooperative (Sec. 1381)
- ☐ Qualified Personal Service Corporation (Sec. 448(d)(2))
- ☐ Exempt organization. Enter code section ►
- ☐ Partnership
- ☐ S Corporation
- ☐ Insurance Co. (Sec. 816(a))
- ☐ Insurance Co. (Sec. 831)
- ☐ Other (specify) ►

Check the appropriate box to indicate the type of accounting method change being requested. (See page 3 of the instructions.)

- ☐ Depreciation or Amortization
- ☐ Financial Products and/or Financial Activities of Financial Institutions SECTION 475
- ☒ Other (specify) ► MARK TO MARKET

Part I Eligibility To Request Change (All applicants complete Parts I through IV.) (See page 2 of the instructions.)

		Yes	No
1	Is the applicant changing its method of accounting under a revenue procedure or other published guidance that provides for an automatic change? (See page 1 of the instructions.)	X	
	If "Yes," enter the citation of the revenue procedure or other published guidance ► REV PROC 99-17		
2	Is the applicant changing its method of accounting under sections 263A, 447, 448, 460, or 585(c) for the first tax year the applicant is required to change?		X
	If "Yes," the applicant is required to make the change in accounting method under the automatic change procedures set forth in the applicable regulations.		
3a	Does the applicant have any Federal income tax returns under examination by the IRS? See section 3.07 of Rev. Proc. 97-27, 1997-1 C.B. 680 (MANDATORY RESPONSE)		X
	If "Yes," complete line 3b.		
b	Is the method of accounting the applicant is requesting to change: (i) an issue under consideration or (ii) an issue placed in suspense by the examining agent(s)? See sections 3.08(1) and 6.01 of Rev. Proc. 97-27.		
	If "Yes," the applicant is not eligible to request the change in accounting method. If "No," complete lines 3c through 3e.		
c	Indicate the "window period" the applicant is filing under or state if the change is being requested with the consent of the district director. ► ______ See section 6.01 of Rev. Proc. 97-27.		
d	Has a copy of this Form 3115 been provided to the examining agent(s) for all examinations that are in process? See section 6.01 of Rev. Proc. 97-27.		
e	Enter the name(s) and telephone number(s) of the examining agent(s). ► ______ See section 6.01 of Rev. Proc. 97-27.		
4a	Is the applicant before an appeals office with respect to any Federal income tax return issue?		X
	If "Yes," complete line 4b. (MANDATORY RESPONSE)		
b	Is the method of accounting the applicant is requesting to change an issue under consideration by the appeals office? See sections 3.08(2) and 6.02 of Rev. Proc. 97-27		
	If "Yes," the applicant is not eligible to request the change in accounting method. If "No," complete lines 4c and 4d.		
c	Has a copy of this Form 3115 been provided to the appeals officer? See section 6.02 of Rev. Proc. 97-27		
d	Enter the name and telephone number of the appeals officer. ► ______ See section 6.02 of Rev. Proc. 97-27.		

Signature—All Applicants *(See page 3 of the instructions.)*

Under penalties of perjury, I declare that I have examined this application, including accompanying documents, and, to the best of my knowledge and belief, the application contains all the relevant facts relating to the application, and such facts are true, correct, and complete. Declaration of preparer (other than applicant) is based on all information of which preparer has any knowledge.

Applicant	Parent corporation (if applicable)
Officer's signature and date	Parent officer's signature and date
A. TRADER Name and title (print or type)	Name and title (print or type)
Signature(s) of individual or firm preparing the application and date	WATERSIDE FINANCIAL SVCES, INC. Name of firm preparing the application

For Privacy Act and Paperwork Reduction Act Notice, see page 1 of the instructions. Cat. No. 19280E Form **3115** (Rev. 5-99)

Form 3115 (Rev. 5-99) Page **2**

Part I **Eligibility To Request Change** (continued)

		Yes	No
5a	Is the applicant before a Federal court with respect to any Federal income tax issue? If "Yes," complete line 5b.		X
b	Is the method of accounting the applicant is requesting to change an issue under consideration by the Federal court? See sections 3.08(3) and 6.03 of Rev. Proc. 97-27. If "Yes," the applicant is not eligible to request the change in accounting method. If "No," complete lines 5c and 5d.		
c	Has a copy of this Form 3115 been provided to the counsel for the government? See section 6.03 of Rev. Proc. 97-27.		
d	Enter the name and telephone number of the counsel for the government. ▶ ______ See section 6.03 of Rev. Proc. 97-27.		
6a	Is the applicant a member of an affiliated group filing a consolidated return for the year of change?		X
b	If "Yes," attach a statement listing the parent corporation's (1) name, (2) identification number, (3) address, and (4) tax year.		
c	Has the applicant ever been a member of a consolidated group other than the current group? If "Yes," complete line 6b for each group of which the applicant was formerly a member.		
d	If the applicant is (or was formerly) a member of a consolidated group, is any consolidated group under examination, before an appeals office, or before a Federal court for a tax year(s) that the applicant was a member of the group? See sections 3.07(1) and 4.02(5) of Rev. Proc. 97-27. If "Yes," complete lines 3b through 3e, 4b through 4d, or 5b through 5d (whichever are applicable).		
7	If the applicant is an entity (including a limited liability company) treated as a partnership or an S corporation for Federal income tax purposes, is the method of accounting the applicant is requesting to change an issue under consideration in an examination of a partner, member, or shareholder's Federal income tax return or an issue under consideration by an appeals office or by a Federal court with respect to a partner, member, or shareholder's Federal income tax return? See sections 3.08 and 4.02(6) of Rev. Proc. 97-27. If "Yes," the applicant is not eligible to request the change in accounting method.		X

Part II **Description of Change**

		Yes	No
8	Is the applicant requesting to change its **overall** method of accounting? INVENTORY: MARK TO MARKET OF TRADING VEHICLES If "Yes," check the appropriate boxes below to indicate the applicant's present and proposed methods of accounting. Also complete Schedule A on page 4 of the form. **Present method:** ☐ Cash ☐ Accrual ☐ Hybrid (attach description) **Proposed method:** ☐ Cash ☐ Accrual ☐ Hybrid (attach description)		X
9	If the applicant is **not** changing its overall method of accounting, attach a description of each of the following:		
a	The item being changed.		
b	The applicant's present method for the item being changed.		
c	The applicant's proposed method for the item being changed.		
d	The applicant's present overall method of accounting (cash, accrual, or hybrid).		
10	Attach an explanation of the legal basis supporting the proposed method for the item being changed. Include all authority (statutes, regulations, published rulings, court cases, etc.) supporting the proposed method. The applicant is encouraged to include a discussion of any authorities that may be contrary to the proposed method.		
11	Attach a description of the applicant's trade or business, including the goods and services it provides and any other types of activities it engages in that generate gross income.		
12	Attach a copy of all documents directly related to the proposed change. (See page 3 of the instructions.)		
13	Attach a statement of the applicant's reasons for the proposed change.		
14a	Attach an explanation of whether the proposed method of accounting will be used for the taxpayer's books and records and financial statements. (Insurance companies, see page 3 of the instructions.)		
b	Attach an explanation of whether the proposed method of accounting conforms to generally accepted accounting principles (GAAP) and to the best accounting practice in the applicant's trade or business.		
15a	Does the applicant have more than one trade or business as defined in Regulations section 1.446-1(d)?		X
b	If "Yes," is each trade or business accounted for separately? If "Yes," for each trade or business, attach a description of the type of business, the overall method of accounting, whether the business has changed any accounting method in the past 4 years, and whether the business is changing any accounting method as part of this application or as a separate application.		
16	If the applicant is a member of an affiliated group filing a consolidated return for the year of change, do all other members of the consolidated group use the proposed method of accounting for the item being changed? If "No," attach an explanation.		X
17	If the applicant is changing to the cash method, or to the inventory price index computation (IPIC) method under Regulations section 1.472-8(e)(3), or is changing its method of accounting under sections 263A, 448, or 460, enter the gross receipts for the 4 tax years preceding the year of change. (See page 3 of the instructions.)		

1st preceding year ended: mo. yr.	2nd preceding year ended: mo. yr.	3rd preceding year ended: mo. yr.	4th preceding year ended: mo. yr.
$	$	$	$

Form 3115 (Rev. 5-99) Page **3**

Part II **Description of Change** (continued)

18 Attach a statement addressing whether the applicant has entered (or is considering entering) into a transaction to which section 381(c)(4) or (c)(5) applies (e.g., a reorganization or merger) during the tax year of change determined without regard to any (potential) closing of the year under section 381(b)(1). Also include in the statement an explanation of any changes in method of accounting that resulted (or will result) from the transaction(s).

Part III **Section 481(a) Adjustment**

		Yes	No
19	Enter the net section 481(a) adjustment for the year of change. Indicate whether the adjustment is an increase (+) or a decrease (-) in income. ▶ $ ________ (IF APPLICABLE)		
20	Has the section 481(a) adjustment been reduced by a pre-1954 amount?		X
21a	If the section 481(a) adjustment is less than $25,000 (positive or negative), does the applicant elect to take the entire amount of the adjustment into account in the year of change? (IF APPLICABLE)	X	
b	If "No," (or if the applicant declines to elect to take the entire amount of the adjustment into account in the year of change), enter the applicable period over which the applicant proposes to take the adjustment into account. ▶ 4 YEARS		
22	Is any part of the section 481(a) adjustment attributable to transactions between members of an affiliated group, a controlled group, or other related parties? If "Yes," attach an explanation.		X

Part IV **Additional Information**

		Yes	No
23	Has the applicant, its predecessor, or a related party requested or made (under either an automatic change procedure or a procedure requiring advance consent) a change in accounting method or accounting period in the past 4 years? If "Yes," attach a description of each change and the year of change. If the application was withdrawn, not perfected, or denied, or if a Consent Agreement was sent to the taxpayer but was not signed and returned to the IRS, or if the change was not made, include an explanation.		X
24	Does the applicant, its predecessor, or a related party currently have pending any request for a private letter ruling, a request for change in accounting method or accounting period, or a request for technical advice? If "Yes," for each request, indicate the name(s) of the taxpayer, the type of request (private letter ruling, request for change in accounting method or accounting period, or request for technical advice), and the specific issue in the request.		X
25	Has the applicant attached **Form 2848,** Power of Attorney and Declaration of Representative? (See the instructions for line 25 and "Person To Contact" on page 3 of the instructions.)		X
26	Does the applicant request a **conference of right** at the IRS National Office if the IRS proposes an adverse response?		X
27	Enter the amount of **user fee** attached to this application. ▶ $ NONE DUE (See page 2 of the instructions.) DUE TO AUTOMATIC CHANGE		
28	If the applicant qualifies for a reduced user fee for identical accounting method changes, has the information required by section 15.07 of Rev. Proc. 99-1, 1999-1 I.R.B. 6, been attached?		

Form 3115 (Rev. 5-99) Page 4

Schedule A—Change in Overall Method of Accounting (If Schedule A applies, Part I below must be completed.)

Attach copies of the profit and loss statement (Schedule F (Form 1040) for farmers) and the balance sheet, if applicable, as of the close of the tax year preceding the year of change. On a separate sheet, state the accounting method used when preparing the balance sheet. If books of account are not kept, attach a copy of the business schedules submitted with the Federal income tax return or other return (e.g., tax-exempt organization returns) for that period. If the amounts in Part I, lines 1a through 1g, do not agree with those shown on both the profit and loss statement and the balance sheet, explain the differences on a separate sheet.

Part I Change in Overall Method (See page 3 of the instructions.)

1 Enter the following amounts as of the close of the tax year preceding the year of change. If none, state "None." Also attach a statement providing a breakdown of the amounts entered on lines 1a through 1g.

		Amount
a	Income accrued but not received	$ NONE
b	Income received or reported before it was earned. Attach a description of the income and the legal basis for the proposed method. (See page 3 of the instructions.)	NONE
c	Expenses accrued but not paid.	NONE
d	Prepaid expense previously deducted.	NONE
e	Supplies on hand previously deducted	NONE
f	Inventory on hand previously deducted. Complete Schedule C, Part II	NONE
g	Other amounts (specify) ▶	NONE
h	**Net section 481(a) adjustment** (Add lines 1a–1g.) (See page 3 of the instructions.)	$SEE SCHEDULE ATTACHED

2 Is the applicant also requesting the recurring item exception (section 461(h))? (See page 4 of the instructions.) ☐ Yes ☒ No

Part II Change to the Cash Method (See page 4 of the instructions.)

Applicants requesting a change to the cash method must attach the following information.

1 A description of the applicant's investment in capital items and leased equipment used in the trade or business, and the relationship between these items and the services performed by the business.

2 A description of inventory items (items that produce income when sold) and materials and supplies used in carrying out the business.

3 The number of employees, shareholders, partners, associates, etc., and a description of their duties in carrying out the applicant's business.

4 A schedule showing the age of receivables for each of the 4 tax years preceding the year of change.

5 A schedule showing the applicant's taxable income (loss) for each of the 4 tax years preceding the year of change.

6 A profit and loss statement showing the taxable income (loss) based on the cash method for each of the 4 tax years preceding the year of change.

Explanations of Form 3115
Application for Change in Accounting Method
Tax Year: ______

Explanation: A taxpayer is filing this Form 3115 "change of accounting method" in connection with his Trading in Securities/Commodities business reported on Schedule C.

The following notes refer to lines 9 to 14 of Part II on page 2 of Form 3115.

Line 9:

- **a.** The *item being changed* by the taxpayer's change in accounting method is the mark-to-market election to recognize realized and unrealized gains or losses from the sale of securities sold and security positions held open at the end of the year as ordinary income.
- **b.** The *present method* used is to recognize capital gain or loss as short-term or long-term on Schedule D.
- **c.** *Proposed mark-to-market method* is in accordance with Section 475 and Revenue Procedure 99-17 and delineated on the following note referenced to Line 10.
- **d.** The taxpayer's *present overall method* of accounting is the cash method.

Line 10 (Explanation of the legal basis supporting proposed method):

IRS Revenue Procedure 99-17 (1999-7 IRB 1, IRC Sec(s). 47). "Mark to market accounting method for dealers in securities—election for traders and dealers" provides for this change of accounting method. This revenue procedure provides the exclusive procedure for traders in securities and/or commodities to make an election to use the mark-to-market method of accounting under Section 475(f) of the Internal Revenue Code.

Effect of Election—An election under Section 475(f) determines the method of accounting that an electing taxpayer is required to use for federal income tax purposes for securities or commodities subject to the election. Thus, beginning with the first year for which the election is effective (this year) and continuing for all subsequent taxable years, a method of accounting for securities or commodities subject to the election is permissible for an electing taxpayer in accordance with Section 475 and the regulations thereunder. If a taxpayer described in Section 3 of this revenue procedure makes an election under Section 5 of this revenue procedure and if the taxpayer's method of accounting for its taxable year immediately preceding the election year is inconsistent with

Section 475, the taxpayer is required to change its method of accounting to comply with its election. Section 6 of this revenue procedure contains procedures for effecting this change. A taxpayer that makes a Section 475(f) election but fails to change its method of accounting to comply with that election is using an impermissible method.

For a taxpayer to make a Section 475(f) election that is effective for a taxable year that begins before January 1, 1999, and for which the original federal income tax return is filed on or after March 18, 1999, the taxpayer must make the election by attaching a statement that satisfies the requirements in Section 5.04 of this revenue procedure to an original federal income tax return for the election year that is timely filed (including extensions).

A change in a taxpayer's method of accounting to mark-to-market accounting is a change in method of accounting to which the provisions of Sections 446 and 481 and the regulations thereunder apply. The Commissioner hereby grants consent for a taxpayer to change its method of accounting for securities or commodities, as appropriate, if the following conditions are satisfied:

1. The taxpayer is described in Section 3 of this revenue procedure.
2. The taxpayer complies with the election requirements set forth in Section 5 of this revenue procedure.
3. The method of accounting to which the taxpayer is changing is in accordance with its election under Section 475.
4. The year of change is the election year.
5. The taxpayer complies with the applicable requirements of this Section 6.

A. Trader meets all five conditions just listed.

Line 11 (Description of the applicant's trade or business):

Taxpayer qualifies as a *"Trader in Securities/Commodities"* in accordance with the below listed IRS revenue procedures and recent Tax Acts of 1997 and 1998.

- IRS Revenue Procedure 99-17, 1999-7 IRB 1, IRC Sec(s). 475 "Mark to market accounting method for dealers in securities—election for traders and dealers."
- "Trader in Securities" tax legislation passed by Congress in the 1997 and 1998 Tax Acts.

Taxpayer's intent and actual transactions for 1998 indicate that he purchased and sold securities and commodities on a frequent, regular, and continuous basis and had a substantial number of trades in an effort to catch changes in daily market and individual instrument movements and to profit on a short-term basis. There was no intent to hold securities for long-term price appreciation, dividend payments, or stock splits or spin-offs. Purchases and sales are conducted continuously and frequently. The trading business is set up for short-term trading, and income is derived from the sale of securities. Taxpayer managed his own investments, made his own decisions, and used his own research on a continuous daily basis. Activities were substantial, extensive, varied, continuous, and regular. Taxpayer is not a dealer and trades for his own account not for the general public.

Line 12 (Documents related to the proposed change):

All the appropriate IRS cites are specified above.

Line 13 (Reason for the proposed change):

Taxpayer is an active Trader in Securities/Commodities, and the mark-to-market treatment better reflects taxpayer's economic reality, as intended by Congress.

Line 14: Taxpayer will use the mark-to-market accounting method for his Trader in Securities/Commodities transactions (buying and selling of securities and commodities), and this method is in accordance with GAAP (generally accepted accounting principles).

Taxpayer agrees to all the terms and conditions in Revenue Procedure 99-17. There is no Section 481(a) adjustment for this Form 3115 and Form 1040. The taxpayer's only open positions at year-end 1997 were Section 1256 Contracts Property. Section 1256 Contracts Property is by legal definition already marked to market at year-end. Therefore no Section 481(a) adjustment is required for 1998.

Appendix H
Logs and Journals

A SIMPLE SYSTEM

This next section will give the reader, first, a step-by-step system for keeping track of and for documenting expenses, insulating himself or herself from audit changes, and, second, a method for transforming his or her records into courtroom evidence.

The first section to follow is a simple system for keeping track of and for documenting expenses as they occur. It consists of two sets of envelopes, to be prepared by the reader using the templates in this book.

Step 1. Make a list of and number the most common expenses used in the business. It might look something like this:

KEY to Business Expenses

1. Business periodicals and newspapers
2. Business meals
3. Transportation
4. Travel receipts (seminars)
5. Entertainment
6. Supplies
7. Computer related expenses
8. Repairs
9. Data
10. Trading systems
11. Auto repairs
12. Auto gasoline
13. Office expense
14. Misc. ____________
15. Misc. ____________

Step 2. Take a small pocket-sized envelope (one that you can carry around in your breast pocket) and copy this key onto the back of it for *daily* use. You then carry it around with you in your wallet or pocket so that when you get a receipt, you can number it and file it in the envelope as it comes to you.

Step 3. Create 12 larger envelopes, one for each month, with a *monthly* summary of each type of expense on the outside. Every day, after taking the numbered receipts out of your small envelope, you place them into the larger monthly envelope.

Step 4. Once a month, you take an hour or two to add up the various categories of expense, staple them together, and put the monthly total on the top receipt. You also transfer that total to the front of the monthly envelope and the monthly log.

Step 5. You then enter them into the journals to follow and file them away into a summary monthly envelope that you have created as a file for all receipts received in January, February, March, and so forth. Following are examples of the small expense envelopes and the larger monthly envelopes. The format can be photocopied directly from here, but you should tailor this to meet your own needs—this is just an example.

The log that you set up can also be photocopied from these next few pages. It will contain a summary of the individual expenses on a monthly basis, taken from three sources: cash receipts, credit card chits, and checks.

Step 6. The credit card receipts and checks can be put together in a separate envelope and summarized in the same manner as the cash receipts. The monthly totals are recorded in the following log books. This will give you an ongoing account of your business income and expenses. You don't need Quick Books or some other exotic computer program, just a pencil and paper.

You will also use the log to keep track of your income, and it will follow the same format as the preceding simple example.

It is my contention that most people put their time into the wrong areas in order to accumulate wealth. They worry about squeezing the last point out of a trade. They take on second jobs and try to make more money. They worry about the cost of their children's college education or their mortgage payments.

If people would put just a fraction of that time into structuring their lives properly from a tax-wise perspective—such as by making use of these logs and this system—they would be infinitely better off. In fact, by putting just a few minutes a day into this system plus an hour or two at the end of each month, you can reduce your taxes substantially. You can, in fact, increase your wealth significantly over the course of your lifetime. It may be worth millions of dollars to you, as I have shown in the first section of this book, and the cost can be as little as an hour or two a month!

CONTEMPORANEOUS LOGS AND JOURNALS

The next section involves the documenting of contemporaneous logs and journals. This is done to keep track of the time spent using business assets and your time spent conducting other business activities.

As traders, this is extremely important because the primary focus of the IRS has been to take the position that traders are not in business. By using this system, you can provide evidence to the contrary. In fact, you will have much more evidence that you did what you stated you did than the IRS will have that you did not. After all, they did not keep logs or journals of your activities to prove that you did not engage in them.

Furthermore, by putting a statement on the bottom of your logs (as illustrated in the following examples), dating and signing it on a monthly or even quarterly basis, and then having it notarized, you will have created courtroom evidence of valid business deductions. This will prove to the IRS unequivocally that you did not sit up the night before the audit with 10 different colored pens creating these logs. This will be more than enough proof to become victorious in audit. I have used it for years and seen it work.

Monthly Envelope

Month ________

Expense Type	**Total for Month**
1. ______________________	__________
2. ______________________	__________
3. ______________________	__________
4. ______________________	__________
5. ______________________	__________
6. ______________________	__________
7. ______________________	__________
8. ______________________	__________
9. ______________________	__________
10. ______________________	__________
11. ______________________	__________
12. ______________________	__________
13. ______________________	__________
14. ______________________	__________
15. ______________________	__________
16. ______________________	__________
17. ______________________	__________

BUSINESS INCOME SUMMARIES

Month: January ______________ **Year:** ______________

Investment Account Income:

Shares of Stock, Commodity Contracts, Bond, Options, etc.	Date Acquired	Cost Basis	Date Sold	Amount Received	Gain/ Loss

(Use attached schedule for additional trades)

Salary Income:

Date	Payee	Gross	Fed WHT	FICA	State WHT	Other

Other Income:

Date	Payee	Gross	Fed WHT

BUSINESS EXPENSE SUMMARIES

Month: January________ **Year:** ____________

Expenses	**Cash This Month**	**Check This Month**	**Credit Card This Month**	**Total This Month**	**Total Yr to Date**
1. Periodicals	______	______	______	______	______
2. Meals	______	______	______	______	______
3. Transportation	______	______	______	______	______
4. Travel	______	______	______	______	______
5. Entertainment	______	______	______	______	______
6. Supplies	______	______	______	______	______
7. Computer	______	______	______	______	______
8. Repairs	______	______	______	______	______
9. Data	______	______	______	______	______
10. Systems	______	______	______	______	______
11. Auto	______	______	______	______	______
12. Gas	______	______	______	______	______
13. Office	______	______	______	______	______
14. Misc. ______	______	______	______	______	______
15. Misc. ______	______	______	______	______	______
16. Misc. ______	______	______	______	______	______

Time Sheet for Children:

		Activity	**Hours Worked**
Name	____________________	________________	______
Name	____________________	________________	______
Name	____________________	________________	______
Name	____________________	________________	______
Name	____________________	________________	______

BUSINESS INCOME SUMMARIES

Month: February **Year:** ____________

Investment Account Income:

Shares of Stock, Commodity Contracts, Bond, Options, etc.	Date Acquired	Cost Basis	Date Sold	Amount Received	Gain/ Loss

(Use attached schedule for additional trades)

Salary Income:

Date	Payee	Gross	Fed WHT	FICA	State WHT	Other

Other Income:

Date	Payee	Gross	Fed WHT

BUSINESS EXPENSE SUMMARIES

Month: February ____________ **Year:** ____________

Expenses	Cash This Month	Check This Month	Credit Card This Month	Total This Month	Total Yr to Date
1. Periodicals					
2. Meals					
3. Transportation					
4. Travel					
5. Entertainment					
6. Supplies					
7. Computer					
8. Repairs					
9. Data					
10. Systems					
11. Auto					
12. Gas					
13. Office					
14. Misc. ________					
15. Misc. ________					
16. Misc. ________					

Time Sheet for Children:

	Activity	Hours Worked
Name		
Name		
Name		
Name		
Name		

BUSINESS INCOME SUMMARIES

Month: March **Year:** ____________

Investment Account Income:

Shares of Stock, Commodity Contracts, Bond, Options, etc.	Date Acquired	Cost Basis	Date Sold	Amount Received	Gain/ Loss

(Use attached schedule for additional trades)

Salary Income:

Date	Payee	Gross	Fed WHT	FICA	State WHT	Other

Other Income:

Date	Payee	Gross	Fed WHT

BUSINESS EXPENSE SUMMARIES

Month: March ________ Year: ________

Expenses	Cash This Month	Check This Month	Credit Card This Month	Total This Month	Total Yr to Date
1. Periodicals					
2. Meals					
3. Transportation					
4. Travel					
5. Entertainment					
6. Supplies					
7. Computer					
8. Repairs					
9. Data					
10. Systems					
11. Auto					
12. Gas					
13. Office					
14. Misc. ________					
15. Misc. ________					
16. Misc. ________					

Time Sheet for Children:

		Activity	Hours Worked
Name			
Name			
Name			
Name			
Name			

BUSINESS INCOME SUMMARIES

Month: April __________ **Year:** ________________

Investment Account Income:

Shares of Stock, Commodity Contracts, Bond, Options, etc.	Date Acquired	Cost Basis	Date Sold	Amount Received	Gain/ Loss

(Use attached schedule for additional trades)

Salary Income:

Date	Payee	Gross	Fed WHT	FICA	State WHT	Other

Other Income:

Date	Payee	Gross	Fed WHT

BUSINESS EXPENSE SUMMARIES

Month: April **Year:** ______

Expenses	Cash This Month	Check This Month	Credit Card This Month	Total This Month	Total Yr to Date
1. Periodicals					
2. Meals					
3. Transportation					
4. Travel					
5. Entertainment					
6. Supplies					
7. Computer					
8. Repairs					
9. Data					
10. Systems					
11. Auto					
12. Gas					
13. Office					
14. Misc. ______					
15. Misc. ______					
16. Misc. ______					

Time Sheet for Children:

		Activity	Hours Worked
Name			
Name			
Name			
Name			
Name			

BUSINESS INCOME SUMMARIES

Month: May **Year:** ______

Investment Account Income:

Shares of Stock, Commodity Contracts, Bond, Options, etc.	Date Acquired	Cost Basis	Date Sold	Amount Received	Gain/ Loss

(Use attached schedule for additional trades)

Salary Income:

Date	Payee	Gross	Fed WHT	FICA	State WHT	Other

Other Income:

Date	Payee	Gross	Fed WHT

BUSINESS EXPENSE SUMMARIES

Month: May________ **Year:** ________

Expenses	**Cash This Month**	**Check This Month**	**Credit Card This Month**	**Total This Month**	**Total Yr to Date**
1. Periodicals	____	____	____	____	____
2. Meals	____	____	____	____	____
3. Transportation	____	____	____	____	____
4. Travel	____	____	____	____	____
5. Entertainment	____	____	____	____	____
6. Supplies	____	____	____	____	____
7. Computer	____	____	____	____	____
8. Repairs	____	____	____	____	____
9. Data	____	____	____	____	____
10. Systems	____	____	____	____	____
11. Auto	____	____	____	____	____
12. Gas	____	____	____	____	____
13. Office	____	____	____	____	____
14. Misc. ____	____	____	____	____	____
15. Misc. ____	____	____	____	____	____
16. Misc. ____	____	____	____	____	____

Time Sheet for Children:

		Activity	**Hours Worked**
Name	________	________	____
Name	________	________	____
Name	________	________	____
Name	________	________	____
Name	________	________	____

BUSINESS INCOME SUMMARIES

Month: June __________ Year: __________

Investment Account Income:

Shares of Stock, Commodity Contracts, Bond, Options, etc.	Date Acquired	Cost Basis	Date Sold	Amount Received	Gain/ Loss

(Use attached schedule for additional trades)

Salary Income:

Date	Payee	Gross	Fed WHT	FICA	State WHT	Other

Other Income:

Date	Payee	Gross	Fed WHT

BUSINESS EXPENSE SUMMARIES

Month: June ______________ **Year:** ______________

Expenses	Cash This Month	Check This Month	Credit Card This Month	Total This Month	Total Yr to Date
1. Periodicals	________	________	________	________	________
2. Meals	________	________	________	________	________
3. Transportation	________	________	________	________	________
4. Travel	________	________	________	________	________
5. Entertainment	________	________	________	________	________
6. Supplies	________	________	________	________	________
7. Computer	________	________	________	________	________
8. Repairs	________	________	________	________	________
9. Data	________	________	________	________	________
10. Systems	________	________	________	________	________
11. Auto	________	________	________	________	________
12. Gas	________	________	________	________	________
13. Office	________	________	________	________	________
14. Misc. ________	________	________	________	________	________
15. Misc. ________	________	________	________	________	________
16. Misc. ________	________	________	________	________	________

Time Sheet for Children:

		Activity	Hours Worked
Name	____________________	____________________	________
Name	____________________	____________________	________
Name	____________________	____________________	________
Name	____________________	____________________	________
Name	____________________	____________________	________

BUSINESS INCOME SUMMARIES

Month: July ______________ **Year:** ______________

Investment Account Income:

Shares of Stock, Commodity Contracts, Bond, Options, etc.	Date Acquired	Cost Basis	Date Sold	Amount Received	Gain/ Loss

(Use attached schedule for additional trades)

Salary Income:

Date	Payee	Gross	Fed WHT	FICA	State WHT	Other

Other Income:

Date	Payee	Gross	Fed WHT

BUSINESS EXPENSE SUMMARIES

Month: July ____________ **Year:** ______________

Expenses	Cash This Month	Check This Month	Credit Card This Month	Total This Month	Total Yr to Date
1. Periodicals					
2. Meals					
3. Transportation					
4. Travel					
5. Entertainment					
6. Supplies					
7. Computer					
8. Repairs					
9. Data					
10. Systems					
11. Auto					
12. Gas					
13. Office					
14. Misc. ________					
15. Misc. ________					
16. Misc. ________					

Time Sheet for Children:

	Activity	Hours Worked
Name		
Name		
Name		
Name		
Name		

BUSINESS INCOME SUMMARIES

Month: August **Year:** ____________

Investment Account Income:

Shares of Stock, Commodity Contracts, Bond, Options, etc.	Date Acquired	Cost Basis	Date Sold	Amount Received	Gain/ Loss

(Use attached schedule for additional trades)

Salary Income:

Date	Payee	Gross	Fed WHT	FICA	State WHT	Other

Other Income:

Date	Payee	Gross	Fed WHT

BUSINESS EXPENSE SUMMARIES

Month: August **Year:** ________

Expenses	**Cash This Month**	**Check This Month**	**Credit Card This Month**	**Total This Month**	**Total Yr to Date**
1. Periodicals					
2. Meals					
3. Transportation					
4. Travel					
5. Entertainment					
6. Supplies					
7. Computer					
8. Repairs					
9. Data					
10. Systems					
11. Auto					
12. Gas					
13. Office					
14. Misc. ________					
15. Misc. ________					
16. Misc. ________					

Time Sheet for Children:

	Activity	**Hours Worked**
Name		
Name		
Name		
Name		
Name		

BUSINESS INCOME SUMMARIES

Month: September ____________ Year: ____________

Investment Account Income:

Shares of Stock, Commodity Contracts, Bond, Options, etc.	Date Acquired	Cost Basis	Date Sold	Amount Received	Gain/ Loss

(Use attached schedule for additional trades)

Salary Income:

Date	Payee	Gross	Fed WHT	FICA	State WHT	Other

Other Income:

Date	Payee	Gross	Fed WHT

BUSINESS EXPENSE SUMMARIES

Month: September________ **Year:** ______________

Expenses	Cash This Month	Check This Month	Credit Card This Month	Total This Month	Total Yr to Date
1. Periodicals					
2. Meals					
3. Transportation					
4. Travel					
5. Entertainment					
6. Supplies					
7. Computer					
8. Repairs					
9. Data					
10. Systems					
11. Auto					
12. Gas					
13. Office					
14. Misc. ________					
15. Misc. ________					
16. Misc. ________					

Time Sheet for Children:

	Activity	Hours Worked
Name		
Name		
Name		
Name		
Name		

BUSINESS INCOME SUMMARIES

Month: October **Year:** ______________

Investment Account Income:

Shares of Stock, Commodity Contracts, Bond, Options, etc.	Date Acquired	Cost Basis	Date Sold	Amount Received	Gain/ Loss

(Use attached schedule for additional trades)

Salary Income:

Date	Payee	Gross	Fed WHT	FICA	State WHT	Other

Other Income:

Date	Payee	Gross	Fed WHT

BUSINESS EXPENSE SUMMARIES

Month: October ____________ **Year:** ____________

Expenses	Cash This Month	Check This Month	Credit Card This Month	Total This Month	Total Yr to Date
1. Periodicals	______	______	______	______	______
2. Meals	______	______	______	______	______
3. Transportation	______	______	______	______	______
4. Travel	______	______	______	______	______
5. Entertainment	______	______	______	______	______
6. Supplies	______	______	______	______	______
7. Computer	______	______	______	______	______
8. Repairs	______	______	______	______	______
9. Data	______	______	______	______	______
10. Systems	______	______	______	______	______
11. Auto	______	______	______	______	______
12. Gas	______	______	______	______	______
13. Office	______	______	______	______	______
14. Misc. ______	______	______	______	______	______
15. Misc. ______	______	______	______	______	______
16. Misc. ______	______	______	______	______	______

Time Sheet for Children:

		Activity	Hours Worked
Name	____________	____________	______
Name	____________	____________	______
Name	____________	____________	______
Name	____________	____________	______
Name	____________	____________	______

BUSINESS INCOME SUMMARIES

Month: November Year: ____________

Investment Account Income:

Shares of Stock, Commodity Contracts, Bond, Options, etc.	Date Acquired	Cost Basis	Date Sold	Amount Received	Gain/ Loss

(Use attached schedule for additional trades)

Salary Income:

Date	Payee	Gross	Fed WHT	FICA	State WHT	Other

Other Income:

Date	Payee	Gross	Fed WHT

BUSINESS EXPENSE SUMMARIES

Month: November ______________ **Year:** ______________

Expenses	**Cash This Month**	**Check This Month**	**Credit Card This Month**	**Total This Month**	**Total Yr to Date**
1. Periodicals					
2. Meals					
3. Transportation					
4. Travel					
5. Entertainment					
6. Supplies					
7. Computer					
8. Repairs					
9. Data					
10. Systems					
11. Auto					
12. Gas					
13. Office					
14. Misc. ________					
15. Misc. ________					
16. Misc. ________					

Time Sheet for Children:

	Activity	**Hours Worked**
Name		
Name		
Name		
Name		
Name		

BUSINESS INCOME SUMMARIES

Month: December **Year:** ____________

Investment Account Income:

Shares of Stock, Commodity Contracts, Bond, Options, etc.	Date Acquired	Cost Basis	Date Sold	Amount Received	Gain/ Loss

(Use attached schedule for additional trades)

Salary Income:

Date	Payee	Gross	Fed WHT	FICA	State WHT	Other

Other Income:

Date	Payee	Gross	Fed WHT

BUSINESS EXPENSE SUMMARIES

Month: December ________ **Year:** ____________

Expenses	**Cash This Month**	**Check This Month**	**Credit Card This Month**	**Total This Month**	**Total Yr to Date**
1. Periodicals	______	______	______	______	______
2. Meals	______	______	______	______	______
3. Transportation	______	______	______	______	______
4. Travel	______	______	______	______	______
5. Entertainment	______	______	______	______	______
6. Supplies	______	______	______	______	______
7. Computer	______	______	______	______	______
8. Repairs	______	______	______	______	______
9. Data	______	______	______	______	______
10. Systems	______	______	______	______	______
11. Auto	______	______	______	______	______
12. Gas	______	______	______	______	______
13. Office	______	______	______	______	______
14. Misc. ______	______	______	______	______	______
15. Misc. ______	______	______	______	______	______
16. Misc. ______	______	______	______	______	______

Time Sheet for Children:

	Activity	**Hours Worked**
Name ____________________	____________________	______
Name ____________________	____________________	______
Name ____________________	____________________	______
Name ____________________	____________________	______
Name ____________________	____________________	______

Equipment on Hand

(Equipment, furniture, tools, etc., that you had PRIOR to starting your business but that are now used for business.)

Item	Date Placed in Service	Cost	Bus.%	Date Sold	Amt. Rec'd	Comments

Floor Plan and Business Area of Your Home (Adapt to your home, and shade only areas that apply to your business.)

Home Office Log ________________________________

Date	Task Performed	Time In	Time Out	Total

Equipment Office Log

Date	Task Performed	Time In	Time Out	Total

Stock Transactions

Month ______________ Year __________

Buy Date	Sell Date	Stock	No. of Shares	Price Per Share	Total Purchase	Gain (Loss)	______

Asset Purchases Log

Month ______________ Year __________

Date	Check No.	Asset Purchased	From Whom Purchased	New/Used	Cost

Business Mileage Log

Month ______________ Year __________

Date	Mileage Start	Mileage Stop	Business Miles	Business Purpose	Gas/Oil Repairs	Tolls	Parking

Income Log No. 1

Monthly Income Log

_________ Income

Month _______________ Year ____________

Date	Employer or Payer	Withholding/Estimated Payments Gross	FWT	FICA	State	Local
	Totals					

MEMOS	VERIFICATION
____________________	The entries in this log were made contemporaneously during the month of __________, 20_____, and reflect all of the income earned by me (or by __________________ business) from the source indicated above.
____________________	Signature ____________________
____________________	Signature/Seal of Notary ____________
____________________	Date by Notary ____________________
____________________	
____________________	
____________________	

The use of this statement at the end of your log will turn it into courtroom evidence. Have it notarized monthly, and it will prove that it was done on a contemporaneous basis.

Income Log No. 2

Stock Transactions Log

Month ________________ Year ____________

Buy Date	Sell Date	Stock	No. of Shares	Price Per Share	Total Purchase	Gain (Loss)	______
				Totals			

Expense Log No. 1

General: ______________________________ Expense Log

Month ______________ Year ___________

	Totals							

Memos

Expense Log No. 2

Residential Improvements Log

Month ________________ Year ____________

Date	Check No.	Type of Improvement	To Whom Paid	Amount
			Total	

MEMOS	VERIFICATION
________________________________	The entries in this log were made contemporaneously during the month of _________, 20___, and reflect ordinary and necessary expenses of the kind described. Each and every entry is true, correct, and complete in all respects and is an accurate reflection of expenses incurred by me (or by____________ business) and paid in cash or by check on the date and for the purpose indicated
________________________________	Signature ________________________
________________________________	Signature/Seal of Notary ______________
________________________________	Date by Notary ____________________
________________________________	
________________________________	
________________________________	

Expense Log No. 3

Travel–Meals–Entertainment Log

Month ______________ Year ___________

Date	Purpose of Travel/ Cities Visited	Fares	Lodging	Meals	Entertainment	Purpose, Persons Entertained, Bus. Discussions
	Totals					

MEMOS	VERIFICATION
______________________	The entries in this log were made contemporaneously during the month of _________, 20___, and reflect ordinary and necessary expenses of the kind described. Each and every entry is true, correct, and complete in all respects and is an accurate reflection of expenses incurred by me (or by___________ business) and paid in cash or by check on the date and for the purpose indicated
______________________	Signature ______________________
______________________	Signature/Seal of Notary ______________
______________________	Date by Notary ____________________
______________________	
______________________	
______________________	

Expense Log No. 4

Business Mileage Log

Month ______________ Year ___________

Date	Mileage Start	Mileage Stop	Business Miles	Business Purpose	Gas/Oil Repairs	Tolls	Parking

MEMOS	VERIFICATION
________________________________ ________________________________ ________________________________ ________________________________ ________________________________ ________________________________ ________________________________	The entries in this log were made contemporaneously during the month of _________, 20___, and reflect ordinary and necessary expenses of the kind described. Each and every entry is true, correct, and complete in all respects and is an accurate reflection of expenses incurred by me (or by____________ business) and paid in cash or by check on the date and for the purpose indicated Signature ________________________ Signature/Seal of Notary ______________ Date by Notary ____________________

Expense Log No. 5

Alimony or Support Payments Log

Month ________________ Year ____________

Date	Check No.	Payee	Type of Payment	Amount

MEMOS	VERIFICATION
____________________ ____________________ ____________________ ____________________ ____________________ ____________________ ____________________	The entries in this log were made contemporaneously during the month of _________, 20___, and reflect ordinary and necessary expenses of the kind described. Each and every entry is true, correct, and complete in all respects and is an accurate reflection of expenses incurred by me (or by____________ business) and paid in cash or by check on the date and for the purpose indicated Signature ____________________ Signature/Seal of Notary ______________ Date by Notary __________________

Specialty Log No. 1

IRA and Keogh Plan Contributions
Month ________________ Year ____________

Date	Check No.	Payee	Plan Type	Nature of Investment	Amount

MEMOS

____

____

____

____

____

____

____

VERIFICATION

The entries in this log were made contemporaneously during the month of ________, 20___, and reflect ordinary and necessary expenses of the kind described. Each and every entry is true, correct, and complete in all respects and is an accurate reflection of expenses incurred by me (or by____________ business) and paid in cash or by check on the date and for the purpose indicated

Signature ____________________________

Signature/Seal of Notary ______________

Date by Notary _______________________

Specialty Log No. 2

Home Office Log

Date	Task Performed	Time In	Time Out	Total

Specialty Log No. 3

Equipment Usage Log

Date	Bus.	Pers.	Task Performed	Time In	Time Out	Total

Specialty Log No. 4

Entertaining-at-Home Guest Log

Date ________________

Name of Person Title/Company	Business Relationship Occupation	Nature of Discussion

Specialty Log No. 5

Entertaining-at-Home Expense Log

Month ______________ Year ___________

Date	Check No.	Payee	Food	Beverages	Catering	Supplies	Other

Specialty Log No. 6

Trading Log Diary

Month ______________ Year ___________

Date Time	Market	Evaluation	Description of Trade	Amount P/L

MEMOS	VERIFICATION
______________________________	The entries in this log were made contemporaneously during the month of _________, 20___, and reflect ordinary and necessary expenses of the kind described. Each and every entry is true, correct, and complete in all respects and is an accurate reflection of expenses incurred by me (or by___________ business) and paid in cash or by check on the date and for the purpose indicated
______________________________	Signature ______________________
______________________________	Signature/Seal of Notary ______________
______________________________	Date by Notary ___________________
______________________________	
______________________________	
______________________________	

Appendix I

It's All a Matter of Time (The Reality of the Wash Sale Rule)

One of the most misunderstood and questioned areas of the code is the wash sale rule. Contrary to some people's belief, Traders not electing 475, mark-to-market, are still very much subject to the wash sale rule (A 475, mark-to-market election will preclude a Trader from being subject to the wash sale rule).

Imagine you're long a particular stock when the market takes a downturn, pulling your stock down with it. You have faith the stock will rebound in the near future, but it occurs to you that by selling the stock now, you can realize a loss (for income tax purposes) that can be offset against gains realized earlier in the year. Then another thought comes to mind. If you immediately repurchase the stock, you'll have the best of both worlds: You'll have a realized loss and you get to keep your position in the stock.

Right?

Wrong!

The scenario above may violate the wash sale rule.

The wash sale rule states that a tax loss arising from the sale of a security cannot be claimed if a "substantially identical" security is acquired within a period of 30 days before or after the sale of the security. In other words, a wash sale violation occurs if you sell securities for a loss and purchase or repurchase substantially identical securities 30 days before or after the day of sale.

How substantial is substantial? What is a "substantially identical" security? Are shares of two companies within the same sector substantially identical? Are shares of two different companies that produce substantially identical products "substantially identical" securities? The answer to both of these questions is no. A good rule of thumb is that substantially identical shares are shares of stock from the same issuer. Shares of IBM, for example, are substantially identical to shares of IBM but not Apple, even though both companies produce an identical product (computers).

In its simplest form, though, a wash sale violation would occur if you were long a stock, sold it for a loss, then repurchased the same stock within 30 days of the sale. For example, you are long Apple at 34, sell it at 32 for a 2-point loss, then buy it again 10 days later at 30. Still, there are some gray areas concerning the wash sale rule.

For example, what about selling a company's preferred stock for a loss, then buying the common stock or vice versa? Common stock and preferred stock are not essentially the same security; therefore, there would be no wash sale violation. Things get even more confusing.

Consider buying an option (or selling a put) on a stock after you've sold the stock. Although this situation is not clearly defined in the Tax Code, most professionals feel that the repurchase of an option may constitute a wash sale rule violation if it is an option on the same stock that was sold for a loss.

As far as short sales are concerned, the same is true. So, if you short a stock, buy it back at a loss, and then resell it within 30 days, you've violated the wash sale rule.

The consequences of violating the wash sale rule are threefold. First, you do not get the immediate benefit of claiming the loss on the sale of the security. This makes sense. Uncle Sam does not want you to retain a position in a stock while simultaneously getting a tax deduction. Second, the disallowed loss is added to the basis of the replacement stock. Say on June 2 you purchase 100 shares of ABC Corporation at $20. On June 9, you sell your shares at $15 for a $500 loss. On June 30, you purchase 100 shares of ABC at $10 (the replacement shares). The wash sale rule applies in this example because the purchase of replacement shares (on June 30) was within 30 days of the loss sale (June 9). Therefore, you do not get to claim the $500 loss you incurred on June 9 (consequence #1). Moreover, the basis in the replacement shares is adjusted to include the $1,000 you paid for the shares plus the $500 disallowed loss. Therefore, for tax purposes, you bought ABC at $15 per share (consequence #2). The third consequence of the wash sale rule is the holding period of the replacement stock includes the holding period of the stock you sold. In the previous example, your holding period for ABC (for tax purposes) would begin on June 2, even though you have sold all the shares you purchased for that day. This rule can prevent a long-term loss from becoming short-term.

Long-term investors have a much easier time avoiding the wash sale rule than short-term traders. If you are a short-term trader, you will most likely have a large number of wash sale violations each tax year. The record keeping necessary to ensure wash sale rule compliance would be extremely burdensome for an individual making thousand of trades every year. How does a short-term trader avoid, or at least minimize, the effect of the wash sale rule?

One option is to refrain from repurchasing shares of the same stock for at least 31 days after selling for a loss. This, however, is easier said than done for the typical short-term trader. Another option is to elect Section 475 (Mark-to-Market "Trader Status").

A trader who makes the mark-to-market election is free from the confines of the wash sale rule. When you make this election, all your positions are marked to market at the end of the year. Therefore, all your gains and losses for the year are taxed, even if you hold open positions. In this case, there is no need for the wash sale rule.

However, there are serious consequences to electing Section 475, not the least of which is that it can stay with you for life. There are also strict deadlines as to when you can elect mark-to-market. Consult your tax advisor to discuss how this election applies to your particular situation. You can also avoid the wash sale rule by selling shares for a loss, then contributing the cash from the sale to your retirement plan (if you are eligible for a retirement plan). If you then repurchase the shares within your retirement plan, the purchase of shares by your retirement plan is considered a new purchase by a different entity; therefore, the wash sale rule does not apply.

The wash sale rule does not apply to futures transactions, as they have no holding period—they are marked to market every day. This includes futures contracts, options on futures, and certain index options.

Two final points. Remember, the wash sale rule does not apply to gains. The government will allow you to buy and sell a stock for a gain ad infinitum—and recognize the gain. And, a point that most traders forget—the wash sale rule is, after all, just a matter of timing. The loss that you may not be able to recognize this year is not permanently lost. Rather, it is deferred. That is, it can be recognized at some future point—when 31 days have passed between transactions. It can eventually be deducted on your tax return. It is just a matter of time!

Notes

Chapter 1 The Basics of Accumulating Wealth and Keeping It

1. Janet Novack and Laura Saunders, "Tax Shelter Hustlers," *Forbes.*

Chapter 2 The Trader's Tax Solution

1. *U.S. Master Tax Guide,* CCH, Inc., 1992, pp. 27–28, paragraph 42.
2. *U.S. Master Tax Guide,* CCH, Inc., 1992, p. 445, paragraph 1903.
3. Ibid., p. 218.
4. Ibid., p. 219, p. 426, paragraph 1760.
5. Scott P. Murphy, "You May Have a Trader in Your Midst," *The Tax Advisor* (August 1992) pp. 517–518.
6. U.S. Court of Appeals, 2nd Circuit: 89-4045, 89-4059, 11/7/89. Affirming in part, reversing and remanding in part a Tax Court decision, 55 TCM 1101, Dec. 44,843(M), T.C. Memo. 1988-264.
7. *U.S. Tax Cases,* 1989, CCH, paragraph 9633.
8. Ibid., p. 225.
9. Ibid., p. 226.
10. Ibid.
11. *New York Times,* March 1995, p. 1.

Chapter 6 Providing for a Wealthy Retirement

1. These figures are based on a study done by the *New York Times*/CBS News Poll performed March 9–March 12, 1995. It included 1,156 adults throughout the United States, excluding Alaska and Hawaii. The sample of telephone exchanges that were called were selected from a computer-generated list of all exchanges in the country. Exchanges were chosen in such a manner to give representation of each region in the country proportional to its population.

For each exchange, the telephone numbers dialed were put together with random digits, thereby permitting access to both listed and unlisted telephone numbers. Within each household, one adult was designated as being the respondent to the survey. The results were then weighted to take into account the size of the household.

The percentage of respondents who answered "I don't know" or had no answer are not shown and were not considered as part of the survey.

2. It is worth mentioning that a study conducted at Yale University showed that individuals with a written financial plan had a much higher success rate than those who did not have one. A survey of the graduating class of Yale University in 1957 determined that only 3 percent of the graduating seniors had a written plan for their financial future. Twenty-five years later in 1982, they examined the financial status of the same graduating class. The results were startling: the 3 percent of the class with a written financial plan had accumulated more wealth than the entire 97 percent who did not.

Chapter 8 Income and Expenses: A Review

1. Very briefly, a *cash-basis* taxpayer is one who declares income and deductions, "as the cash flows," either in or out (i.e., when salary is received, rather than earned). This is the opposite of an *accrual-basis* taxpayer who recognizes income and expense as they are incurred. A *calendar-year* taxpayer recognizes the tax year as being from January 1 to December 31, as opposed to any other 12-month period.

2. *U.S. Master Tax Guide,* CCH, Inc., 1992, p. 184, paragraph 710.

3. *U.S. Master Tax Guide,* CCH, Inc., 1992, p. 234, paragraph 902.

4. Ending principal minus the $10,000 originally invested ($25,937 – $10,000 and $21,588 – $10,000, respectively).

5. $145,937 – $9,690 actual return on investment using the 5.87 percent *true yield* ($17,690 – $10,000 original investment).

6. $8,247 overstatement/$7,690 true return on investment.

7. $7,690 return/$10,000 investment.

Chapter 10 New World Estate Planning

1. Charles J. Givens, *More Wealth without Risk* (New York: Simon & Schuster, 1991), p. 251.

2. Robert C. Carlson, *Tax Liberty* (Baltimore, MD: Agora Publishing, 1991), p. 93.

Chapter 15 Knowing Your Limits: How Far Can You Go?

1. Randy B. Blaustein, *IRS Confidential Report,* Boardroom Reports, Inc., 1987, 1988, p. 59. Reprinted with permission of: Boardroom Classics, 330 West 42nd St., New York, NY 10036.

2. "Your Rights as a Taxpayer," Publication No. 1 (6-89), Department of the Treasury, Internal Revenue Service.

3. "Information About Your Notice, Penalty and Interest," Notice No. 746 (Revised 10/89), Department of the Treasury, Internal Revenue Service.

4. "File Two Years Late and Not Pay a Penalty?" *Tax Avoidance Digest* (March 1992), 2, no. 3.

5. Ibid., p. 140.

6. Ibid.

7. Robert C. Carlson, *Tax Liberty* (Baltimore, MD: Agora Publishing, 1991).

8. Charles J. Givens, *More Wealth without Risk* (New York: Simon & Schuster, 1991), p. 175.

9. Ibid., p. 186.

10. Ibid., p. 190.

11. Ralph J. Pribble, "The IRS Hit List," *IRS Confidential Report,* Boardroom Reports, Inc. 1987, 1988, p. 55. Reprinted with permission of: Boardroom Classics, 330 West 42nd St., New York, NY 10036.

12. Ibid., p. 153.

13. *Tax Avoidance Digest* (February 1992), 2, no. 2.

14. Ibid., p. 162.

15. Ms. X, *How to Beat the IRS* (Millburn, NJ: Boardroom Books, 1988). Reprinted with permission of: Boardroom Classics, 330 West 42nd St., New York, NY 10036.

16. Philip P. Storrer, *The 1981 Tax Fighter's Guide* (New York: Harbor Publishing Co., 1981).

17. *IRS Confidential Report,* Boardroom Books., Inc. 1987, 1988, p. 58. Reprinted with permission of: Boardroom Classics, 330 West 42nd St., New York, NY 10036.

18. Randy Bruce Blaustein, *How to Do Business with the IRS* (New York: Prentice-Hall, 1982/1990).

19. *IRS Manual Transmittal,* 4200-471.

Disclaimer

Because of the continual shifting of legal and regulatory precedents, taxpayers should seek competent professional advice regarding investment, trading, and transactions on an on-going basis. This book is by no means an exhaustive work on the tax consequences of futures and futures options transactions. It should not be used in lieu of competent legal and/or accounting advice, but I hope it provides some insight into the tax issues and complications involved in the investment and trading industry.

About the Author

Ted Tesser is a Certified Public Accountant, a member of the New York State Society of Certified Public Accountants, and president of Waterside Financial Services, Inc., with offices in Boca Raton and Delray Beach, Florida, and New York City, New York. He has a master's degree in accounting from New York University, with a specialty in investment-related taxation, and is an active investor and trader, as well as a CPA. Ted has been involved in the financial markets for the past 25 years and counsels traders and investors on issues regarding tax, retirement, estate, and financial planning.

His professional experience began in 1972 on the staff of Price Waterhouse & Company, where he serviced such Fortune 500 clients as Coca-Cola, IBM, Exxon, International Nickel Company (INCO), Chemical Bank, and Chase Manhattan Bank. His professional career led him to develop a specialty in investments and the effect of taxation on the total return of high-net-worth investors. He served as manager of the tax department for Charles Pratt & Company, a Wall Street accounting firm that had a high-net-worth-client base including fourth- and fifth-generation descendants of the founder of Exxon Oil, Charles Pratt. Ted Tesser's clients have included many prominent investors and several members of the U.S. government, including an ex-Secretary of State, an ex-Secretary of the Treasury, and several other members of Congress.

Ted Tesser started Waterside Financial Services, Inc., in 1986 as a company that specializes in *integrated financial planning.* His belief that the concepts of tax planning, financial planning, retirement planning, and estate planning are inseparable and that each could not be achieved alone was, and still is, at the center of his organization's structure. As such, Mr. Tesser has obtained licenses and degrees in the various areas that comprise these fields.

He is the author of the *Serious Investor's Tax Survival Guide* (Trader's Library, 1993), *The Trader's Tax Survival Guide (Original and Revised Editions)* (John Wiley & Sons, 1995, 1997), *The NEW Trader's Tax Solution* (John Wiley & Sons, 2002). He has recorded four video tapes on investment taxation: *The Ultimate Tax Shelter* (Futures Learning Center, 1995), *Tax Strategies for Traders* (Futures Learning Center, 1997), *Million Dollar Tax Tips* (Futures Learning Center, 1998), *Traders—Cut Your Taxes in Half Now: A Dozen Legal Ways to Eliminate Your Tax Debt This Year!* (Futures Learning Center, 1999). Ted Tesser has developed and his firm currently markets *The Trader's Tax Kit*, which includes several videos, manuals, and a specific blueprint for attaining tax freedom. It assists investors in bulletproofing their case for Trader Status and for maximizing their tax benefits as traders or investors under the current law!

Ted Tesser is a featured speaker at the semiannual Futures International Conference, the Dow Jones/Telerate Seminars, the Reuters International Conferences, the Market Analysts of Southern California, the Market Technicians Association of New York and California, Futures Truth Annual Conference, and The Samurai Traders Group, and he has been a frequent guest on CNBC, NBC Portland (AM Northwest), and KWHY TV-Los Angeles. He is also a frequent guest on TheStreet.com internet site and a host of their Yahoo! chatroom, addressing such technical questions as the tax aspects of investing and qualifying for Trader Status.

His popular seminar series entitled "Stock Market and Mutual Fund Investors: Cut Your Taxes in Half!" has been attended by many prominent and successful investors who wish to gain insight into the areas of retirement planning and income and estate-tax planning. Mr. Tesser's work has been reviewed in such prominent publications as the *Wall Street Journal, Technical Analysis of Stocks and Commodities, Trader's World,* and *Futures Magazine.* He has written articles for and has been interviewed in many other widely respected publications in the investment field including *Futures Magazine, Investment Advisor Magazine, Bottom Line, The Tax Hotline, The Journal of Medical Economics, Trader's World Magazine, The SOHO Journal,* the *Watersider,* and *AIQ's Opening Bell.*

Waterside Financial Services, Inc., of Boca Raton, Florida, specializes in counseling investors and traders on tax-reduction strategies and retirement-, estate-, and financial-planning issues. It assists traders and investors in creating and managing more profitable investing and trading businesses through the implementation of sound business and tax-management structures and strategies.

Waterside Financial Services, Inc.
P.O. Box 812006
Boca Raton, FL 33481-2006
Toll Free: 1-800-556-9829
Fax: 1-877-456-9829
Web site: www.taxtrader.com Email: tbtesser@aol.com

Index